Sadlier

God's Law Guides Us

School Edition Teacher Guide

Grade Four

Sadlier
A Division of William H. Sadlier, Inc.

This advance publication copy of the Sadlier *We Believe* Grade 4 Teacher Guide has been printed prior to final publication and pending ecclesiastical approval.

The Ad Hoc Committee to Oversee the Use of the Catechism, United States Conference of Catholic Bishops, has found the doctrinal content of this teacher manual, copyright 2004, to be in conformity with the *Catechism of the Catholic Church*.

Printed in the United States of America.

S® is a registered trademark of William H. Sadlier, Inc.
We Believe™ is a registered trademark of William H. Sadlier, Inc.

William H. Sadlier, Inc.
9 Pine Street
New York, NY 10005-1002

ISBN: 0-8215-5414-X
123456789/07 06 05 04 03

Sadlier

We Believe Drawn from the wisdom of the community, this program was developed by nationally recognized experts in catechesis, curriculum, and child development. These teachers of the faith and practitioners helped to frame these age-appropriate and appealing lessons. In addition, a team including respected catechetical, liturgical, pastoral, and theological experts shared their insights and inspired the development of the program.

Contributors to the inspiration and development of the program are:

Gerard F. Baumbach, Ed.D.
Executive Vice President and Publisher

Carole M. Eipers, D.Min.
Director of Catechetics

Catechetical and Liturgical Consultants

Reverend Monsignor John F. Barry
Pastor, American Martyrs Parish
Manhattan Beach, CA

Sister Linda Gaupin, CDP, Ph.D.
Director of Religious Education
Diocese of Orlando

Sister Maureen Shaughnessy, SC
Assistant Secretary for Catechesis
and Leadership Formation,
USCCB, Department of Education

Mary Jo Tully
Chancellor, Archdiocese of Portland

Reverend Monsignor John M. Unger
Assoc. Superintendent for Religious Education
Archdiocese of St. Louis

Curriculum and Child Development Consultants

Brother Robert R. Bimonte, FSC
Former Superintendent of Catholic Education
Diocese of Buffalo

Gini Shimabukuro, Ed.D.
Associate Director/Associate Professor
Institute for Catholic Educational Leadership
School of Education, University of San Francisco

Catholic Social Teaching Consultants

John Carr
Secretary, Department of Social Development
and World Peace, USCCB

Joan Rosenhauer
Coordinator, Special Projects
Department of Social Development and
World Peace, USCCB

Inculturation Consultants

Reverend Allan Figueroa Deck, SJ, Ph.D.
Executive Director, Loyola Institute for
Spirituality, Orange, CA

Kirk Gaddy
Principal, St. Katharine School
Baltimore, MD

Reverend Nguyễn Việt Hưng
Vietnamese Catechetical Committee

Dulce M. Jiménez-Abreu
Director of Spanish Programs
William H. Sadlier, Inc.

Scriptural Consultant

Reverend Donald Senior, CP, Ph.D., S.T.D.
Member, Pontifical Biblical Commission
President, The Catholic Theological Union
Chicago, IL

Theological Consultants

Most Reverend Edward K. Braxton, Ph.D., S.T.D.
Official Theological Consultant
Bishop of Lake Charles

Norman F. Josaitis, S.T.D.
Staff Theologian, William H. Sadlier, Inc.

Reverend Joseph A. Komonchak, Ph.D.
Professor, School of Religious Studies
The Catholic University of America

Most Reverend Richard J. Malone, Th.D.
Auxiliary Bishop, Archdiocese of Boston

Sister Maureen Sullivan, OP, Ph.D.
Assistant Professor of Theology
St. Anselm College, Manchester, NH

Mariology Consultant

Sister M. Jean Frisk, ISSM, S.T.L.
International Marian Research Institute
Dayton, OH

Media/Technology Consultants

Sister Caroline Cerveny, SSJ, D.Min.
Director of Educational Learning Technology
William H. Sadlier, Inc.

Sister Judith Dieterle, SSL
Past President, National Association of
Catechetical Media Professionals

Sister Jane Keegan, RDC
Editor in Chief, CyberFaith.com
William H. Sadlier, Inc.

Educational Advisors

Grade K Noelle Deinken, Thousand Oaks, CA
Bernadette Miller, Wantagh, NY

Grade 1 Gerry Mayes, Vero Beach, FL
Nancy McGuirk, Staten Island, NY

Grade 2 Joan Fraher, Altamonte Springs, FL
Dr. Jeannette Holmes, Stockton, CA

Grade 3 Robin Keough, Boston, MA
Mary Olson, Buffalo Grove, IL

Grade 4 Michaele Durant, San Diego, CA
Sarah Pollard, Covington, KY

Grade 5 Rose Heinrichs, Grosse Pointe, MI
Anne Kreitsch, Howard Beach, NY

Grade 6 Barbara Connors, Seekonk, MA
Sue MacPherson, Ballwin, MO

Contents

Scope & Sequence, Grades 3, 4, and 5 . . . . .T8
Program Overview T14
Outline of the Catechist Development Topics T21
Catechist Development Topic:
Understanding the Child 10A

Introductory Chapter 10

UNIT 1 Growing in Jesus Christ 17

1 Jesus—the Way, the Truth, and the Life
Plan and Prepare 19A
Catechist Development Topic: *Catechesis Today and the Catechist* 19E
Reproducible Master 1 . . . . .19G
Lesson Plan 19
• God sent his only Son to us. • Jesus shows us how to live. • Jesus Christ is our Savior. • The disciples spread the good news of Jesus Christ.
John 1:29; 6:35; 8:12; 10:11; 11:25; 14:6–7
As Catholics . . . The Name Jesus Christ
Our Catholic Life: Dorothy Day
Sharing Faith with My Family

2 Jesus Leads Us to Happiness
Plan and Prepare 31A
Catechist Development Topic: *Connecting to the Family* 31E
Reproducible Master 2 . . . . .31G
Lesson Plan 31
• Jesus trusted God his Father. • Jesus taught the Beatitudes. • Jesus taught about the Kingdom of God. • Jesus' disciples share his mission.
Matthew 4:10; 5:1–10, 12; John 11:41–42; Luke 17:20–21; 22:42
As Catholics . . . Social Justice
Our Catholic Life: Archbishop Oscar Romero
Sharing Faith with My Family

3 Sin in Our World
Plan and Prepare 43A
Catechist Development Topic: *Creating an Environment for Catechesis* 43E
Reproducible Master 3 . . . . .43G
Lesson Plan 43
• God gives us the freedom to choose. • Sin leads us away from God. • Sin can be things people do or fail to do. • We are called to value and respect all people.
Luke 10:30–34; Galatians 3:26–28
As Catholics . . . Immaculate Conception
Our Catholic Life: Saint John Vianney
Sharing Faith with My Family

4 Our Conscience, Our Guide
Plan and Prepare 55A
Catechist Development Topic: *Using Storytelling with Children* 55E
Reproducible Master 4 . . . . .55G
Lesson Plan 55
• God calls us to be close to him. • God gives us the gift of conscience. • We form our conscience. • We examine our conscience.
Psalm 139:1–3; Luke 15:11–12, 14, 17–20; 1 Timothy 1:5
As Catholics . . . The Teaching Church
Our Catholic Life: Saint Thomas More
Sharing Faith with My Family

5 Celebrating Penance and Reconciliation
Plan and Prepare 67A
Catechist Development Topic: *Nurturing Prayer in Children* .67E
Reproducible Master 5 . . . . .67G
Lesson Plan 67
• Jesus tells us about God's forgiveness and love. • We receive God's forgiveness in the sacrament of Reconciliation. • We celebrate the sacrament of Reconciliation. • Reconciliation brings peace and unity.
Psalm 51:3, 4, 8, 12; Luke 15:4–7; Matthew 9:12; John 20:21–23; 2 Corinthians 13:11; Rite of Penance
As Catholics . . . Seal of Confession
Our Catholic Life: Ministering to the Sick
Sharing Faith with My Family

6 The Liturgical Year
Plan and Prepare 79A
Lesson Plan 79
• Throughout the liturgical year we remember and celebrate Jesus Christ.
Psalm 113:3; Revelation 22:20; The Roman Missal
Sharing Faith with My Family
Reproducible Master 6/Projects 84A/B

7 Ordinary Time
Plan and Prepare 85A
Lesson Plan 85
• During the season of Ordinary Time, we celebrate the life and teachings of Jesus Christ.
Psalm 25:4; Matthew 7:12; Mark 6:50; Luke 6:36; John 15:12; Galatians 6:14, 16, 18
Sharing Faith with My Family
Reproducible Master 7/Projects 90A/B

Unit 1 Assessment 91
Unit 1 Alternative Assessment 321

UNIT 2 The Commandments Help Us to Love God 93

UNIT 4 We Are Called to Holiness

GRADE 3 Scope & Sequence

	Unit 1 Jesus Gives Us the Church	Unit 2 We Are Members of the Church
FAITH STATEMENTS FOR EACH CHAPTER	1 God the Son became one of us. • Jesus grew up in Nazareth. • Jesus begins his work. • Jesus shows us how to live as his followers. 2 Jesus tells us how much God loves us. • Jesus teaches about the Kingdom of God. • Jesus teaches about the gift of faith. • Jesus dies and rises to save us. 3 Jesus has power over life and death. • Jesus will come again. • When Jesus Christ comes again, he will judge all people. • Jesus teaches us to love others. 4 Jesus promises to send the Holy Spirit. • The Holy Spirit comes to the disciples. • The Church begins on Pentecost. • The early Church grows. 5 The apostles led the Church. • The disciples of Jesus share the good news. • The followers of Jesus stood up for their faith. • Many of our ancestors in faith are examples of holiness. 6 The Church Year celebrates Jesus. 7 In Ordinary Time, we celebrate the life and teachings of Jesus Christ.	8 Jesus chose the apostles to lead the Church. • The pope and bishops are the successors of the apostles. • The Church is one and holy. • The Church is catholic and apostolic. 9 The Church is the Body of Christ and the people of God. • We profess our faith through the Apostles' Creed. • The Holy Spirit guides the Church. • The Church continues to teach the true message of Jesus. 10 Jesus teaches his followers how to pray. • We can pray with others or by ourselves. • There are different kinds of prayer. • The Church prays at all times. 11 We belong to a parish. • Many people serve our parish. • Our parish worships together. • Our parish cares for others. 12 God calls each of us. • God calls everyone to be holy. • God calls some men to be priests. • God calls some people to religious life. 13 The season of Advent helps us prepare for the coming of the Son of God. 14 The Christmas season is a special time to celebrate that God is with us.
CATECHISM OF THE CATHOLIC CHURCH	Paragraphs: 460, 533, 517, 561, 104–108, 541, 153, 638, 547–549, 671, 678, 1970, 729, 731, 732, 849, 551, 763–765, 769, 2030, 1168, 1163	Paragraphs: 765, 880, 811, 823, 830, 857, 782, 789, 194, 798, 771, 2759, 2655, 2626–2643, 2691, 2697, 2179, 1348, 2182, 2186, 1213, 825, 1719, 1565, 915, 524, 526
SCRIPTURE AND THE RITES OF THE CHURCH	Luke 1:26–35; 2:41–51; 4:14–15; 1:38; 17:5–6; 23:33–34; 24:1–12 Matthew 3:2,17; 13:55; 6:26–33; 24:42; 25:31–43; 28:16–20; 28:19; 28:20 1 Corinthians 12:3 Romans 10:13 Psalm 118:1 Mark 4:35–41; 10:45; 12:28–32; 11:9 John 11:1–3, 17–44; 16:22; 15:12 Acts of the Apostles 2:1–4, 32, 36, 38, 41, 42; 9:3–5; 2:42, 45 2 Corinthians 13:13	John 6:35; 8:12; 11:25; 14:26; 15:15; 13:34 1 John 4:11,12 Matthew 16:18; 18:20; 25:40 1 Corinthians 12:14–21 1 Peter 2:10 Psalms 113:3; 141:2a Luke 11:1, 9; 3:4; 2:1–12 1 Samuel 3:10 Isaiah 43:1 Philippians 4:4–5
SAINTS AND CATHOLIC PROFILES; FEASTS AND DEVOTIONS	Saint Peter Claver Mary, An Example of Faith Saint Paul Saint Perpetua Saint Felicity Saint Augustine The Bible The Feast of All Saints The Feast of the Holy Cross The Church Year Ordinary Time	Saint Teresa of Avila Saint Martin de Porres Blessed Pope John XXIII Saint Francis of Assisi Saint Clare of Assisi Saint Nicholas Saint Lucy Saint Stephen Saint John Holy Innocents The Apostles' Creed The Lord's Prayer Prayer Posture Forms of Prayer The Liturgy of the Hours Pilgrimages Advent Christmas

Unit 3 The Church Leads Us in Worship

15 The Church celebrates the sacraments. • Baptism, Confirmation, and Eucharist are the sacraments of Christian initiation. • Reconciliation and Anointing of the Sick are sacraments of healing. • Holy Orders and Matrimony are sacraments of service to others.

16 Jesus celebrated Passover and the Last Supper. • The Mass is a sacrifice and a meal. • We take part in the Mass. • We celebrate Mass each week.

17 We gather to praise God. • We listen to God's word. • We receive Jesus Christ. • We go out to love and serve the Lord.

18 We make the choice to love God. • God is our forgiving Father. • The sacrament of Reconciliation has several parts. • The Church celebrates the sacrament of Reconciliation.

19 Jesus cared for and healed the sick. • The Church heals us in Jesus' name. • We believe in eternal life with God. • The Church celebrates eternal life with God.

20 The season of Lent is a time of preparation for Easter.

21 The Three Days celebrate that Jesus passed from death to new life.

Paragraphs: 1113, 1212, 1421, 1534, 1340, 1323, 1348, 1343, 1359, 1349, 1355, 1694, 1428, 1439, 1450–1460, 1469, 1503, 1511, 1681, 1684, 540, 647

John 3:16–17
Luke 5:17–25; 22:19; 15:11–32;
Psalms 106:1; 118:28
Matthew 26:26–28; 28:1; 14:35,36
The Roman Missal
Rite of Penance
Rite of Anointing of the Sick
Isaiah 55:3
Rite of Baptism
Mark 10:46–52

Saint Katharine Drexel
Our Lady of Guadalupe
Pope John Paul II
Martyrs of El Salvador: Srs. I. Ford, M. Clarke, and D. Kazel; Jean Donovan
Saint Isaac Jogues
Saint Joan of Arc

Blessed Sacrament
Sacramentals
Ash Wednesday
Holy Days of Obligation
Celebration of the Mass
Mass Cards
Lent
The Three Days

Unit 4 We Are Called to Discipleship

22 Jesus brings God's life and love to all people.• Jesus shares his mission with his disciples. • The Church works for justice and peace. • We live out the good news of Jesus Christ.

23 People around the world have different beliefs about God. • The Jewish faith is important to Christians. • Christ calls his followers to be united. • The Church works for Christian unity.

24 The Catholic Church is all over the world. • Catholics share the same faith. • Catholics celebrate their faith in different ways. • We are the light of the world.

25 We belong to the communion of saints. • Mary is the greatest of all the saints. • The Church remembers and honors Mary. • God calls us to be saints.

26 Jesus used parables to teach about the Kingdom of God. • Jesus taught that the Kingdom of God will grow. • Jesus' miracles were signs of the Kingdom of God. • The Kingdom of God grows.

27 In the Easter season, we celebrate the Resurrection of Jesus.

Paragraphs: 543, 551, 2419, 2449, 843, 839, 838, 855, 835, 1203, 1204, 2105, 957, 972, 971, 2013, 546, 541, 548, 2818, 644

John 20:19,21; 17:20–21; 20:19–29
Luke 4:16–19; 4:42–43; 1:38; 11:1; 13:18–19; 2:10
Deuteronomy 6:4
Matthew 5:14,16; 13:3–8, 18–23; 14:22–33
Psalm 86:10–13
Romans 8:14

Saint John the Baptist
Mary, greatest of all the saints
Saint Elizabeth of Hungary
Saint Louise de Marillac
Saint Charles Lwanga
Saint Joan of Arc
Saint Andrew Nam-Thuong
Saint Dominic Savio
Being canonized a saint

All Souls' Day
The Mysteries of the Rosary
Hail Mary
Litany
The Easter Season

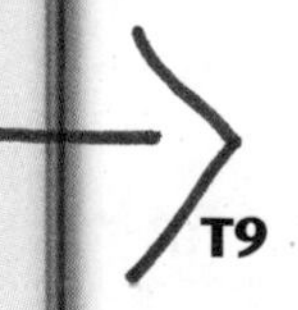

GRADE 4 Scope & Sequence

	Unit 1 Growing in Jesus Christ	Unit 2 The Commandments Help Us to Love God
FAITH STATEMENTS FOR EACH CHAPTER	1 God sent his only Son to us. • Jesus shows us how to live. • Jesus Christ is our Savior. • The disciples spread the good news of Jesus Christ. 2 Jesus trusted God his Father. • Jesus taught the Beatitudes. • Jesus taught about the Kingdom of God. • Jesus' disciples share his mission. 3 God gives us the freedom to choose. • Sin leads us away from God. • Sin can be things people do or fail to do. • We are called to value and respect all people. 4 God calls us to be close to him • God gives us the gift of conscience. • We form our conscience. • We examine our conscience. 5 Jesus tells us about God's forgiveness and love. • We receive God's forgiveness in the sacrament of Reconciliation. • We celebrate the sacrament of Reconciliation. • Reconciliation brings peace and unity. 6 Throughout the liturgical year we remember and celebrate Jesus Christ. 7 During the season of Ordinary Time, we celebrate the life and teachings of Jesus Christ.	8 God calls his people. • The Ten Commandments are God's laws for his people. • Jesus teaches us about God's law. • Jesus teaches us to love one another. 9 We believe in the one true God. • We honor the one true God. • We love God above all things. • We place our hope and trust in God. 10 God's name is holy. • We respect God's name. • We call upon God's name. • We respect and honor sacred places. 11 God gave us a special day to rest and to worship him. • We keep the Lord's Day holy by participating in Sunday Mass. • The Lord's Day is a day for rest and relaxation. • We keep the Lord's Day holy by caring for the needs of others. 12 The Introductory Rites unite us and prepare us for worship. • During the Liturgy of the Word, we hear the word of God. • During the Liturgy of the Eucharist, we offer gifts of bread and wine and receive the Body and Blood of Jesus Christ. • In the Concluding Rite we are sent to live as disciples of Jesus. 13 In Advent we prepare for the coming of the Lord. 14 During the Christmas season we celebrate the Son of God coming into the world.
CATECHISM OF THE CATHOLIC CHURCH	Paragraphs: 422, 544, 430, 767, 609, 1716, 543, 764, 387, 1850, 1853, 1878, 1776, 1777, 1785, 1454, 1423–1424, 1441, 1448, 1468–1469, 1168, 1163	Paragraphs: 2057, 2060, 2052–2053, 2055, 2085, 2096, 2093, 2098, 2143, 2144, 2153, 1186, 2172, 2177, 2185, 2186, 1348, 1349, 1355, 1397, 524, 528
SCRIPTURE AND THE RITES OF THE CHURCH	John 1:29; 6:35; 8:12; 10:11; 11:25; 14:6–7; 11:41–42; 20:21–23; 15:12 Matthew 4:10; 5:1–10, 12; 9:12; 7:12 Luke 17:20–21; 22:42; 10:30–34; 15:11–12, 14, 17–20; 15:4–7; 6:36 Galatians 3:26–28; 6:14, 16, 18 Psalms 139:1–3; 51:3, 4, 8, 12; 113:3; 25:4 1 Timothy 1:5 2 Corinthians 13:11 Rite of Penance Revelation 22:20 The Roman Missal Mark 6:50	Psalms 119:33–35; 86:10–12; 105:3; 113:3 Exodus 3:6–10; 13:21–22; 20:2–5; 3:14; 20:8 Isaiah 9:5; 60:1–4 Matthew 22:36–37, 39; 5:8; 6:21, 25–26; 21:12, 13; 5:7; 18:20; 2:1–12 John 13:34–35 Deuteronomy 6:4–5 Luke 1:30, 38; 4:1–8; 11:2; 22:19; 1:46–49 1 Corinthians 3:21–23; 11:23–26 Acts of the Apostles 2:42; 9:4 The Roman Missal Revelation 21:4
SAINTS AND CATHOLIC PROFILES; FEASTS AND DEVOTIONS	Saint Rose Philippine Duchesne Saints Matthew, apostle and evangelist Saint Mark, evangelist Saint Luke, evangelist Saint John, apostle and evangelist Saint Francis of Assisi Saint John Vianney Saint Thomas More Dorothy Day Oscar Romero Feast of the Immaculate Conception Act of Contrition The Liturgical Year Ordinary Time	Saint Paul Saint Brigid Our Lady of Guadalupe Saint Juan Diego The prophet Isaiah Adoration of the Blessed Sacrament The Jesus Prayer Veneration of the Saints Feast of Our Lady of Guadalupe Holy Days of Obligation Corporal Works of Mercy Spiritual Works of Mercy The Mass: Liturgy of the Word Liturgy of the Eucharist Advent Christmas The Feast of the Epiphany

Unit 3 The Commandments Help Us to Love Others

15 God wants us to love and respect others. • In our families we learn to love God and others. • In our families we have the responsibility to love and respect one another. • Citizens and leaders work together for peace.

16 Human life is sacred. • The right to life is the most basic human right. • We respect the gift of life. • Promoting peace is a way to respect life.

17 God creates each person with the ability to show and share love. • We are called to chastity. • Friendships are one way we grow in love. • The love between a husband and wife is very special.

18 We are called to act with justice. • We respect the property of others. • God's creation is meant for all people. • We are called to help all people meet their basic needs.

19 God teaches us what it means to be true. • We are called to witness to the truth of our faith. • We have a responsibility to tell the truth. • We have a responsibility to respect the truth.

20 Lent is the season of preparation for Easter.

21 The Easter Triduum celebrates the joy of the cross.

Paragraphs: 2199, 2207, 2206, 2238, 2258, 2270, 2288, 2304, 2331, 2348, 2347, 2361, 2401, 2412, 2415, 2446, 2465, 2472, 2483, 2469, 540, 617

Luke 2:46–52; 3:11; 19:8
Matthew 8:4; 22:37, 39; 5:4, 21–22, 43–45; 6:11; 5:6; 5:10, 37; 7:12; 19:30; 1:18–21, 24
Exodus 20:12; 20:13; 20:14; 20:15; 20:16
Jeremiah 1:5
Psalms 139:14; 33:4; 119:89, 90, 142, 145
Deuteronomy 5:17
Genesis 1:27–28; 30–31
Isaiah 58:5–7; 43:20; 53:1, 10
James 2:15–17
John 18:37; 13:4–5
Acts of the Apostles 1:8
Sirach 19:6
The Roman Missal

Saint Edith Stein
Saint Vincent de Paul
Saint Louise de Marillac
Saint Charles Lwanaga and the Uganda Martyrs
Saint Joseph
Saint John the Baptist
Frederic Ozanam

Feast of the Holy Family
Saint Joseph's Day practices
Respect Life Sunday
National Prayer Vigil for Life
Prayer of Saint Francis
Lent
The Easter Triduum
The Veneration of the Cross

Unit 4 We Are Called to Holiness

22 Feelings are a gift from God. • God created us to share love. • God calls us to be pure of heart. • The virtue of modesty helps us to be pure of heart.

23 We are called to have generous hearts. • Jesus taught us to trust in God above all things. • Depending upon God brings happiness. • Jesus teaches us that God's law is love.

24 Jesus is our model of holiness. • We open our hearts and minds in prayer. • The sacraments draw us closer to God. • The Holy Spirit shares special gifts with us.

25 The Church is a worldwide community. • We have responsibilities as members of the Church. • We celebrate the sacraments. • We have an active role in the Church community.

26 The virtues of faith, hope, and love bring us closer to God. • Mary is our model for virtue and discipleship. • The cardinal virtues guide us. • We are called to live a life of love.

27 During the season of Easter, we celebrate the Resurrection of Jesus.

Paragraphs: 2516, 2520, 2519, 2524, 2538, 2544, 2547, 1970, 1698, 2766, 1123, 1831, 814, 2041, 2042, 2043, 1813, 967, 1805, 1825, 645

Ezekiel 36:26–28
Matthew 3:16; 5:8; 9:25; 5:3, 17; 11:25; 18:20; 5:9, 16; 10:32–33; 22:39
Mark 11:15
Luke 1:38; 12:15, 22–24; 22:42; 23:34; 10:16; 2:51
John 11:35; 11:41–42; 14:26; 16:13; 13:6–17; 21:1–14
Exodus 20:17
Romans 13:10; 5:5
Acts of the Apostles 20:33–35; 1:3–12; 2:1–4
Galatians 5:22–23
1 Corinthians 11:24; 13:13
Psalms 103:1–5; 119:33
1 Thessalonians 5:18

Saint Katharine Drexel
Saint Thérèse of Lisieux
Blessed Pope John XXIII
Saint Teresa de los Andes
Saint Josephine Bakhita
Saints Isidore and Maria
Saint Monica
Saint Augustine
Mary, our model
Pope John Paul II
Saint Francis of Assisi

Sacramentals
Liturgy of the Hours
The Feast of the Ascension
The Feast of Pentecost

GRADE 5 Scope & Sequence

	Unit 1 Jesus Christ Shares His Life with Us	Unit 2 Confirmation and Eucharist Complete Our Initiation
FAITH STATEMENTS FOR EACH CHAPTER	1 Jesus is the Son of God. • Jesus shows us God's love. • Jesus invites people to follow him. • Jesus' disciples continue his work. 2 We are joined to Jesus Christ and to one another. • We proclaim the good news of Christ by what we say and do. • In the liturgy we celebrate Christ's Paschal Mystery. • When we serve others we give witness to Christ. 3 Jesus gave the Church seven sacraments. • The sacraments of Christian initiation are Baptism, Confirmation, and Eucharist. • The sacraments of healing are Reconciliation and Anointing of the Sick. • Holy Orders and Matrimony are sacraments of service to others. 4 Baptism is the foundation of Christian life. • In Baptism we are freed from sin and become children of God. • We are a priestly, prophetic, and royal people. • Because of our Baptism, we have hope of eternal life. 5 The Church welcomes all to be baptized. • The parish community participates in the celebration of Baptism. • Water is an important sign of Baptism. • The baptized begin their new life as children of God. 6 Throughout the liturgical year we remember and celebrate the life of Christ. 7 Ordinary Time is a special season to learn about the life of Christ and to grow as his followers.	8 On Pentecost the Holy Spirit came upon the first disciples. • Laying on of hands and anointing are signs of the Holy Spirit's presence. • In Confirmation we become more like Christ and are strengthened to be his witnesses. • Preparation is an important part of Confirmation. 9 Confirmation leads us from Baptism to the Eucharist. • In the sacrament of Confirmation, we are sealed with the Gift of the Holy Spirit. • The gifts of the Holy Spirit help those who are confirmed. • Confirmation calls those anointed to live out their Baptism as witnesses of Jesus Christ. 10 In the Eucharist we celebrate and receive Jesus Christ. • The Eucharist is a memorial, a meal, and a sacrifice. • We recognize Jesus in the breaking of the bread. • Jesus is the Bread of Life. 11 The Introductory Rites bring us together as a community. • During the Liturgy of the Word, we listen and respond to the word of God. • During the Liturgy of the Eucharist, we pray the great prayer of thanksgiving and receive the Body and Blood of Christ. • The Concluding Rite sends us out to be the Body of Christ to others. 12 Jesus teaches us to pray. • We are called to pray daily. • Sacramentals are a part of the Church's prayer life. • Catholics have a rich tradition of special practices and popular devotions. 13 Advent is a season of joyful expectation and preparation for the coming of the Son of God. 14 The season of Christmas is a time to rejoice in the Incarnation.
CATECHISM OF THE CATHOLIC CHURCH	Paragraphs: 535, 543, 546, 737, 787, 863, 1067, 2449, 1210, 1212, 1421, 1534, 1213, 1265, 783, 1274, 1226, 1248, 1217–1222, 1254, 1163, 1168	Paragraphs: 1287, 1288–1289, 1303, 1309, 1298, 1300, 1299, 1305, 1324, 1328–1330, 1329, 1338, 1348, 1349, 1352, 1355, 1396, 2765, 1174, 1670, 1674 , 524, 457
SCRIPTURE AND THE RITES OF THE CHURCH	Matthew 3:11, 14, 17; 7:1–2; 9:35, 36; 10:2–4; 11:28; 13:32; 28: 18:20; 25:31–40; 28:19–20; Mark 1:15; 8:2; 1:11; Luke 4:16–22; 18:35–43; John 15:4–5, 9; 15:9–12; 11:25–26; Romans 12:5; Colossians 1:18 Isaiah 44:1, 3 Acts of the Apostles 2:38; 16:19–33 Rite of Baptism; Psalms 90:1–2; 145:2	Ezekiel 37:14; Acts of the Apostles 1:8; 2:1–47; 2:42 John 14:26; 16:12–13; 6:1–14, 27, 35, 51, 55, 56; 11:41; 4:25, 26; 1:14; Galatians 5:22–23; Rite of Confirmation; Luke 22:19–20; 24:13–35; 22:15–20; 18:13; 23:34; 2:1–14 The Roman Missal; Psalms 121:1–6; 146:2 2 Corinthians 13:13; Philippians 1:9 1 Thessalonians 5:17; Ephesians 6:18; Isaiah 61:10
SAINTS AND CATHOLIC PROFILES: FEASTS AND DEVOTIONS	Saint Elizabeth Ann Seton Saint Anthony Claret Patron Saints Saint Barbara Pope Gregory XIII Blessings with Sign of the Cross Feast of All Saints Feast of All Souls Solemnities Ash Wednesday Liturgy of the Hours Corporal Works of Mercy Spiritual Works of Mercy The Liturgical Year Ordinary Time	Saint John Bosco Blessed Kateri Tekakwitha Our Lady of Guadalupe Feast of Pentecost The Feast of the Body and Blood of Christ—Corpus Christi Our Lady of Guadalupe Chrismation Forms of prayer Sacramentals The Mass Adoration of Blessed Sacrament Holy Days of Obligation Popular devotions: novenas, stations of the cross, and pilgrimages Las Posadas Advent Christmas

Unit 3 The Sacraments of Healing Restore Us

15 Jesus calls us to conversion. • Jesus forgives as only God can do. • Jesus continues to forgive us through the Church. • We are reconciled with God and the Church.

16 The sacrament of Reconciliation strengthens our relationship with God and others. • In the sacrament of Reconciliation, the Church celebrates God's forgiveness. • In the sacrament of Reconciliation we trust in God's mercy. • Together we turn our hearts and minds to God.

17 Jesus heals those who are sick. • Jesus' apostles preach and heal in his name. • The Church continues Jesus' healing ministry. • We are called to care for those who are sick.

18 Jesus is with us when we are suffering. • The Anointing of the Sick continues Jesus' saving work of healing. • The Church celebrates the Anointing of the Sick. • Jesus is with those who hope for eternal life.

19 Mary is Jesus' first disciple. • Mary is most blessed among women. • Mary is the greatest of all the saints. • The Church remembers and honors Mary.

20 Lent is the season of preparation for the great celebration of Easter.

21 The Easter Triduum is our greatest celebration of the Paschal Mystery.

Paragraphs: 1427, 1441, 1442, 1445, 1468–1469, 1484, 1470, 1474, 1503, 1506, 1509, 2288, 1521, 1520, 1522, 1517, 494, 492, 963, 971, 559, 654

Matthew 18:21, 22; 9:35–36; 14:13–14; 25:40;
1:20–21; 21:1–11; Mark 1:15; 2:1–12; 6:13; 16:18;
10:13–14, 16; Luke 15:11–24; 15:1–7; 1:26–45;
John 20:21–23; 4:46–53; 6:54; 19:26, 27; 13:1;
Colossians 3:12–13; Rite of Penance
Acts of the Apostles 3:1–10; 1 Corinthians 12:25–26;
1:25; James 5:13–15; Pastoral Care of the Sick
Joel 2:12–13; 1 John 4:7, 9, 11; The Roman Missal

Saint Dominic
Saint Joseph
Saint Alexius
Blessed Pope Pius IX
Blessing of oils
The Hail Mary
The Rosary
Feast Days of Mary
O Antiphons
The Confiteor
Act of Contrition
National Shrine of the Immaculate Conception
Retreat Days
Lent
Ash Wednesday
Passion (Palm) Sunday
Easter Triduum

Unit 4 We Love and Serve as Jesus Did

22 We believe in God and all that the Church teaches. • We trust in God and are confident in his love and care for us.• We are able to love God and one another. • The saints are models for living the life of virtue.

23 Jesus calls the baptized to serve him in the priesthood of the faithful. • The laity share in the mission to bring the good news of Christ to the world. • Women and men in religious life serve Christ, their communities, and the whole Church. • Friendships prepare us for future vocation.

24 Marriage was part of God's plan from the very beginning. • The marriage covenant is built on Christ's love for the Church. • In the sacrament of Matrimony, a man and woman promise to always love and be true to each other. • Families are very important communities.

25 Jesus shares his ministry in a special way with the apostles. • Holy Orders is the sacrament through which the Church continues the apostles' mission. • Bishops, priests, and deacons serve the Church in different ways. • The laying on of hands and prayer of consecration are the main parts of the sacrament of Holy Orders.

26 The Church is one and holy. • The Church is catholic and apostolic. • The Church respects all people. • The Church works for justice and peace.

27 The Easter season is a special time to rejoice over the new life we have in Christ.

Paragraphs: 1814, 1817, 1822, 828, 1546, 900, 917, 959, 1605, 1616, 1644, 1657, 551, 1562, 1554, 1573, 813, 823, 830–831, 857, 855, 2442, 655

Matthew 5:3–10; 22:37–39; 19:6; 4:18–20; 9:9;
28:19; Luke 17:5; 6:13; 10:2; 22:27; 4:18–19;
1:41–43; John 13:34–35; 14:12–13; 13:20; 20:21–22;
21:15, 16, 17; 17:20–21; 15:5
1 Corinthians 13:2–4, 13; 12:13, 26
Deuteronomy 6:4–7; Genesis 1:28; 2:24
Rite of Marriage; Mark 6:7; 16:1–10
Rites of Ordination; Ephesians 2:19, 20; 4:4, 5–6
1 Peter 5:4; James 1:12; The Roman Missal
Galatians 5:13

Saint Andrew Kim Taegon
Saint Josephine Bakhita
Martyrs of Vietnam
Saint Margaret of Scotland
The Canonization process—Saint Padre Pio
The Easter Season
The Easter Octave
Mary and May Crowning

Welcome !

Sadlier WE BELIEVE Program Overview

Across the ages, Jesus calls to each student we teach: *"Follow me"* (Luke 9:23). Each student looks to the Church for help in answering "yes" to Jesus.

Your vocation to teach young people about Jesus is an awesome one. The *We Believe* program is designed for you.

We Believe consistently integrates:

Content that is faithful to the teachings of the Catholic Church and that holistically embraces the four pillars of the *Catechism of the Catholic Church*: Creed, Liturgy and Sacraments, Moral Life, Prayer

Reliance on Scripture, Catholic social teaching, vocation awareness, and mission

Music and prayer that echo and anticipate liturgical celebrations

Reflection and activities that integrate catechesis, liturgy and life

Media and technology used in service to faith and in the context of family

Methodologies that engage the experience of the student, modeled on Jesus' "pedagogy of faith" (cf. *General Directory for Catechesis,* 137, 140)

Review and assessment that reinforce the essential content of the lesson

Activities and reflections that involve the students and their families in catechesis, prayer, and living their faith

The Theological and Catechetical Foundations

Jesus sent the apostles to "Go . . . make disciples of all nations" (Matthew 28:19).

The Church in every age has embraced this mission of evangelization and proclaimed the gospel of Jesus through its catechetical ministry.

As you carry on Jesus' mission, you can rely on *We Believe* because it is:

- **Rooted in Scripture**
- **Faithful to the Tradition of the Catholic Church**
- **Spirited by the *General Directory for Catechesis***
  - **Christocentric**, centering on the Person of Jesus Christ
  - **Trinitarian**, inviting relationship with God the Father, God the Son, and God the Holy Spirit
  - **Ecclesial**, supporting faith that is lived in the domestic church and the universal Church.

The Student's Pages

Sadlier WE BELIEVE Program Overview

Together in the footsteps of Jesus

To help you, the catechist, to nurture each student's relationship with Jesus and to facilitate each student's faith response, this program employs an easy-to-use catechetical process for each lesson: *We Gather, We Believe, We Respond.* This three-part process echoes the "pedagogy of the faith" which Jesus himself modeled.

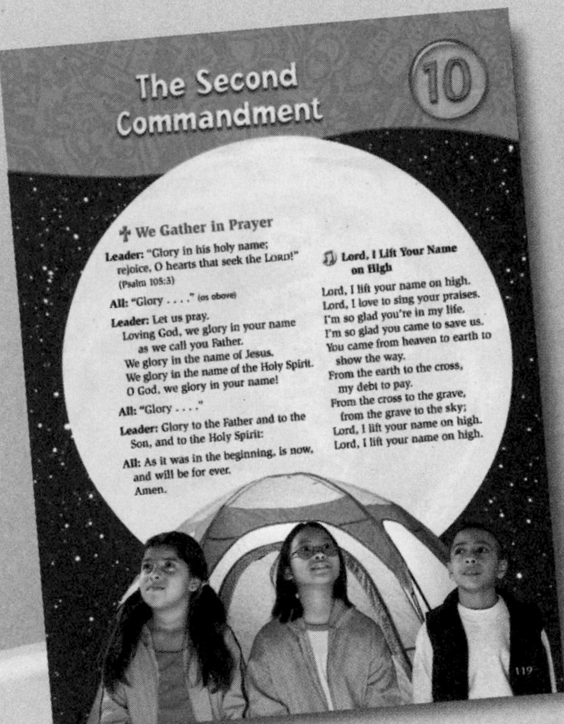

The Second Commandment

10

We Gather in Prayer

Leader: "Glory in his holy name; rejoice, O hearts that seek the LORD!" (Psalm 105:3)

All: "Glory . . . ." (as above)

Leader: Let us pray.
Loving God, we glory in your name
as we call you Father.
We glory in the name of Jesus.
We glory in the name of the Holy Spirit.
O God, we glory in your name!

All: "Glory . . . ."

Leader: Glory to the Father and to the Son, and to the Holy Spirit:

All: As it was in the beginning, is now, and will be for ever.
Amen.

Lord, I Lift Your Name on High

Lord, I lift your name on high.
Lord, I love to sing your praises.
I'm so glad you're in my life.
I'm so glad you came to save us.
You came from heaven to earth to
show the way.
From the earth to the cross,
my debt to pay.
From the cross to the grave,
from the grave to the sky;
Lord, I lift your name on high.
Lord, I lift your name on high.

119

WE GATHER

Students gather in prayer at the beginning of every chapter. They gather to pray and focus on their life as they begin each day's lesson. They respond to God's call and his grace through prayer and reflection on their experience. They pray, sing, and explore the ways the faith speaks to their lives.

WE BELIEVE

Each chapter presents the truths of the Catholic faith found in Sacred Scripture and Tradition, and in accordance with the Magisterium of the Church. One of the four main faith statements of the chapter is highlighted on each of days 1 through 4. The content of faith is presented in ways that are age-appropriate, culturally sensitive, and varied.

We are called to help all people meet their basic needs.

WE GATHER

God, your mercy endures forever!

What are the basic things that people need to live? Does everyone have these things? Discuss your answers.

WE BELIEVE

In the Beatitudes Jesus calls us to "hunger and thirst for righteousness" (Matthew 5:6). *Righteousness* is another word for justice. We work for justice when we imitate Jesus. As disciples of Jesus we share Jesus' concern for others. We help the people whose basic needs are not being met.

Jesus expects his disciples to share and to be generous toward others, especially the poor. Jesus showed care and love for those who were suffering. He showed mercy to people, especially those who were poor and powerless. We are asked to do more than pray for the poor. We must respond to their needs.

Saint James made this point very clear in his letter to some of the first disciples of Jesus. He said, "If a brother or sister has nothing to wear and has no food for the day, and one of you says to them, 'Go in peace, keep warm, and eat well,' but you do not give them the necessities of the body, what good is it? So also faith of itself, if it does not have works, is dead" (James 2:15–17).

Every person is created in God's image. This makes all people equal, sharing the same human dignity. We need to respect the human rights of all people. We need to stand up for those who do not have the things that are basic to life.

214

YOU SHALL NOT STEAL.

The Church calls us to work together so that all people are treated justly. By performing the Works of Mercy, we care for the needs of others. The Works of Mercy are things that we do to care for the physical and spiritual needs of others. Our acts of love may help people meet their basic needs.

Design a mural that illustrates the Works of Mercy.

Take a few moments to think quietly and prayerfully about ways you follow the seventh commandment. These questions may help you.

Have I cared for the gifts of creation?

Have I taken care of my belongings?

Have I taken things that do not belong to me?

Have I respected the property of others?

Have I been honest in taking tests and playing games?

Have I shared what I have with those who are in need?

Have I worked with my family, parish, or school to care for those who are poor or to make their lives better?

Have I performed Works of Mercy?

Blessed are they...

Saint Vincent de Paul and Saint Louise de Marillac

To "hunger and thirst" for something means to want something very badly. Vincent de Paul knew what it was to want justice since he had once been forced into slavery by pirates. When he escaped, he began to care for those who were poor and in need. He asked Louise de Marillac to help him, and together they founded the Daughters of Charity. The sisters of this community still serve the poor today. The sisters work in schools and hospitals, in services to children and the elderly, and in parishes. Saint Louise is the patroness of social workers.

Vincent also founded the Congregation of the Mission. This is a community of priests and brothers who preach, give retreats, work in parishes, and teach in schools. Saint Vincent's feast day is September 27. Saint Louise's feast day is March 15

"Blessed are they who hunger and thirst for righteousness, for they will be satisfied." (Matthew 5:6)

WE RESPOND

New Heart and New Spirit

Refrain:
New heart and new spirit
give us, O God,
New heart and new spirit,
to live in love.

Your word gives us hope
that there is a way to live
in your justice and peace each day.
(Refrain)

215

WE RESPOND

Throughout each chapter students are encouraged to respond in prayer, faith, and life. Each day they are invited to respond to the message of the lesson. Through prayer, song, and actions that express their beliefs, students are called to live out their discipleship among their peers, their families, and their school and parish communities.

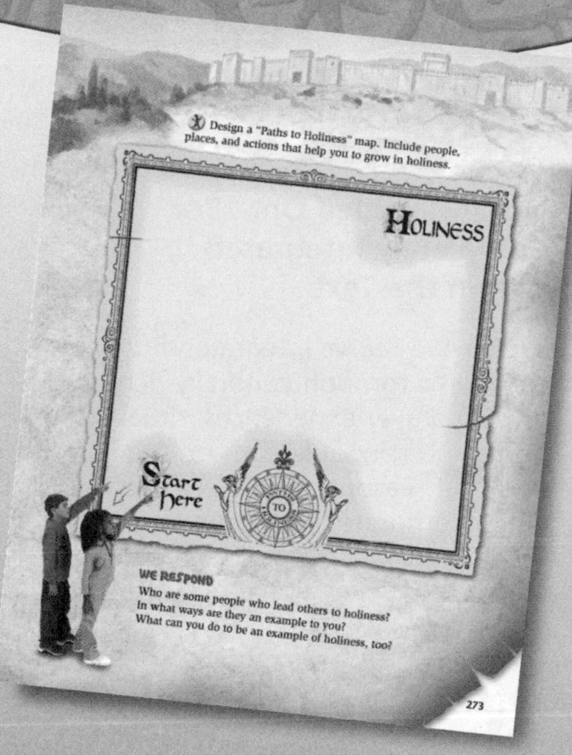

Design a "Paths to Holiness" map. Include people, places, and actions that help you to grow in holiness.

Holiness

Start here

WE RESPOND

Who are some people who lead others to holiness? In what ways are they an example to you? What can you do to be an example of holiness, too?

273

Plus . . .

The chapter concludes with a *Review* page that offers standard and alternative assessments. These provide opportunities for students to demonstrate learning and express faith. In addition, the *We Respond in Faith* page invites the students to take time to reflect and pray. They remember the four main doctrinal statements and Key Words as well as gain inspiration from a true story of Catholics living out their faith in the world.

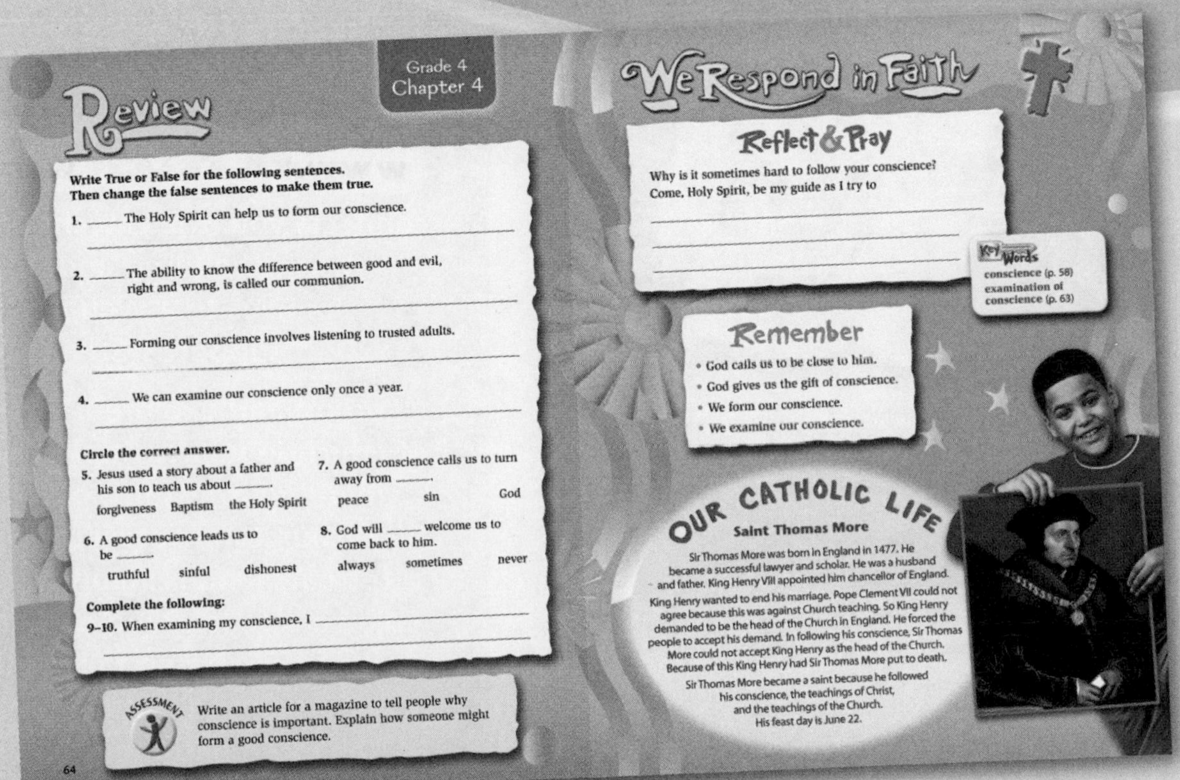

Grade 4 Chapter 4

Review

Write True or False for the following sentences. Then change the false sentences to make them true.

1. _____ The Holy Spirit can help us to form our conscience.
2. _____ The ability to know the difference between good and evil, right and wrong, is called our communion.
3. _____ Forming our conscience involves listening to trusted adults.
4. _____ We can examine our conscience only once a year.

Circle the correct answer.

5. Jesus used a story about a father and his son to teach us about _____.
   forgiveness   Baptism   the Holy Spirit
6. A good conscience leads us to be _____.
   truthful   sinful   dishonest
7. A good conscience calls us to turn away from _____.
   peace   sin   God
8. God will _____ welcome us to come back to him.
   always   sometimes   never

Complete the following:

9–10. When examining my conscience, I _____

ASSESSMENT: Write an article for a magazine to tell people why conscience is important. Explain how someone might form a good conscience.

64

We Respond in Faith

Reflect & Pray

Why is it sometimes hard to follow your conscience? Come, Holy Spirit, be my guide as I try to

Key Words
conscience (p. 58)
examination of conscience (p. 63)

Remember

- God calls us to be close to him.
- God gives us the gift of conscience.
- We form our conscience.
- We examine our conscience.

OUR CATHOLIC LIFE

Saint Thomas More

Sir Thomas More was born in England in 1477. He became a successful lawyer and scholar. He was a husband and father. King Henry VIII appointed him chancellor of England. King Henry wanted to end his marriage. Pope Clement VII could not agree because this was against Church teaching. So King Henry demanded to be the head of the Church in England. He forced the people to accept his demand. In following his conscience, Sir Thomas More could not accept King Henry as the head of the Church. Because of this King Henry had Sir Thomas More put to death.

Sir Thomas More became a saint because he followed his conscience, the teachings of Christ, and the teachings of the Church. His feast day is June 22.

The Seasonal Chapters and the Web site for We Believe

Not Just Added On...But Completely Integrated Within the Text.

Sadlier *We Believe* integrates liturgy and catechesis through culturally-rich and diverse prayer experiences, ritual celebrations, and special lessons on the liturgical year and seasons. *We Believe* Music CDs also incorporate liturgical music to foster the student's participation in parish worship and devotional practices.

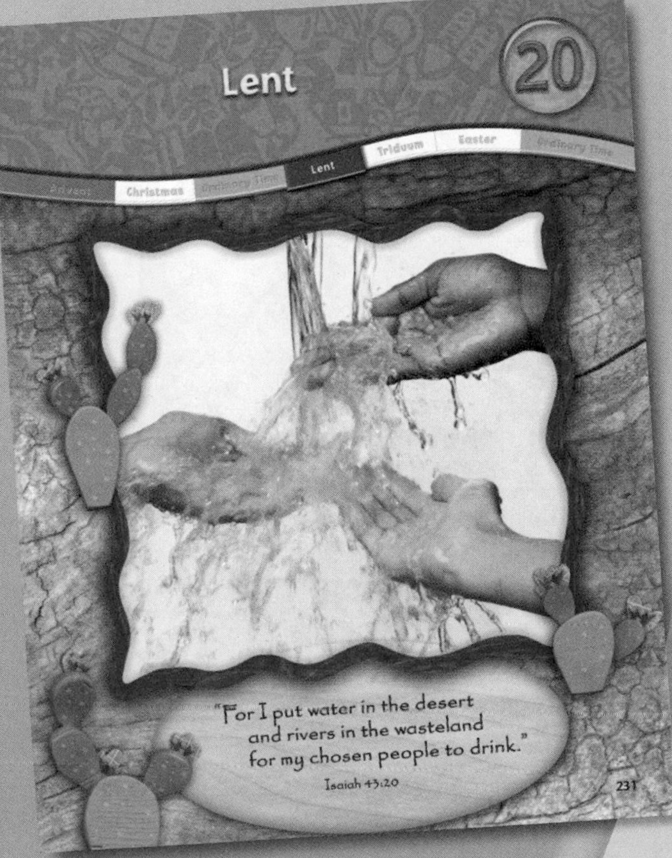

Colorful photos and illustrations set the tone for successful learning experiences.

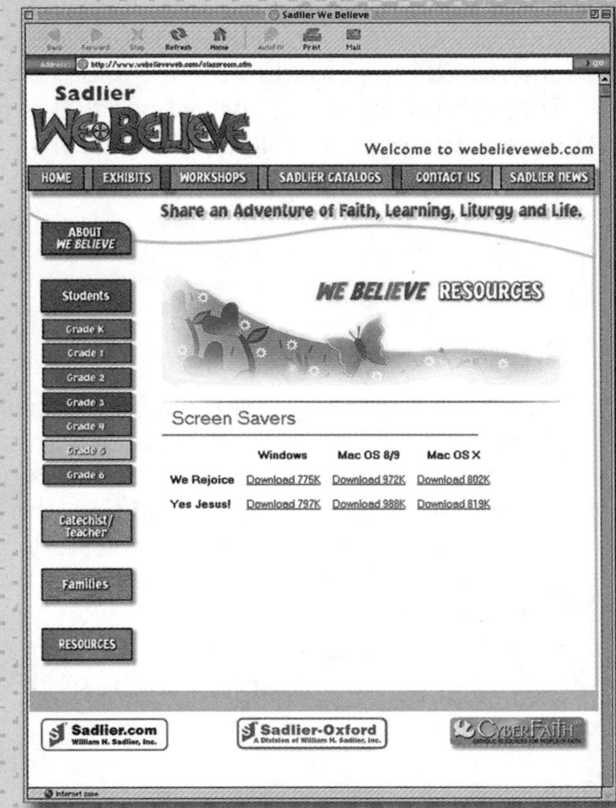

www.WeBelieveweb.com connects you, the catechist, as well as the children and their families to a Web-based support system.

Log on and explore a rich array of educational activities to complement your lessons, plus great resources for prayer, liturgy, retreats, and religion projects. Enjoy a safe learning environment with family-based faith activities that are motivating and fun for children and their families.

The Family Pages

No other catechetical program has so much for the family.

Three special family components are integrated into the pupil text and, when utilized together throughout the program, complete the circle of catechesis.

Sharing Faith as a Family

These four unit openers provide an overview of the doctrine, additional resources and faith formation for parents, and applications to family life. The activities and discussion on these pages are directed by a family member.

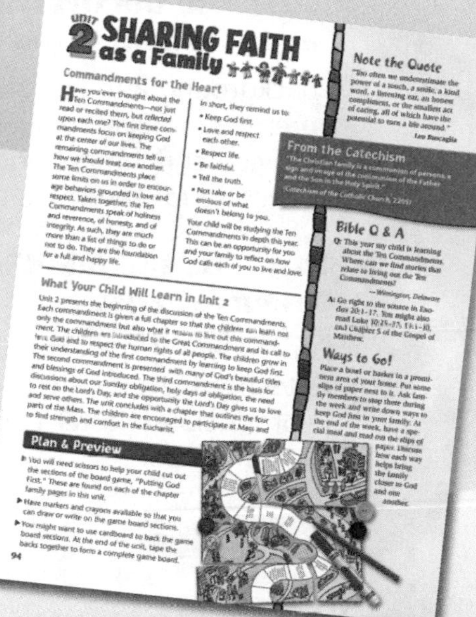

UNIT 2 SHARING FAITH as a Family

Commandments for the Heart

Have you ever thought about the Ten Commandments—not just read or recited them, but reflected upon each one? The first three commandments focus on keeping God at the center of our lives. The remaining commandments tell us how we should treat one another. The Ten Commandments place some limits on us in order to encourage behaviors grounded in love and respect. Taken together, the Ten Commandments speak of holiness and reverence, of honesty, and of integrity. As such, they are much more than a list of things to do or not to do. They are the foundation for a full and happy life.

In short, they remind us to:

- Keep God first.
- Love and respect each other.
- Respect life.
- Be faithful.
- Tell the truth.
- Not take or be envious of what doesn't belong to you.

Your child will be studying the Ten Commandments in depth this year. This can be an opportunity for you and your family to reflect on how God calls each of you to live and love.

What Your Child Will Learn in Unit 2

Unit 2 presents the beginning of the discussion of the Ten Commandments. Each commandment is given a full chapter so that the children can learn not only the commandment but also what it means to live out this commandment. The children are introduced to the Great Commandment and its call to [illegible] God and to respect the human rights of all people. The children grow in their understanding of the first commandment by learning to keep God first. The second commandment is presented with many of God's beautiful titles and blessings of God introduced. The third commandment is the basis for discussions about our Sunday obligation, holy days of obligation, the need to rest on the Lord's Day, and the opportunity the Lord's Day gives us to love and serve others. The unit concludes with a chapter that outlines the four parts of the Mass. The children are encouraged to participate at Mass and to find strength and comfort in the Eucharist.

Plan & Preview

- You will need scissors to help your child cut out the sections of the board game, "Putting God First." These are found on each of the chapter family pages in this unit.
- Have markers and crayons available so that you can draw or write on the game board sections.
- You might want to use cardboard to back the game board sections. At the end of the unit, tape the backs together to form a complete game board.

94

Note the Quote

"Too often we underestimate the power of a touch, a smile, a kind word, a listening ear, an honest compliment, or the smallest act of caring, all of which have the potential to turn a life around."

Leo Buscaglia

From the Catechism

"The Christian family is a communion of persons, a sign and image of the communion of the Father and the Son in the Holy Spirit."

(Catechism of the Catholic Church, 2205)

Bible Q & A

Q: This year my child is learning about the Ten Commandments. Where can we find stories that relate to living out the Ten Commandments?

—Wilmington, Delaware

A: Go right to the source in Exodus 20:1–17. You might also read Luke 10:25–37, 19:1–10, and Chapter 5 of the Gospel of Matthew.

Ways to Go!

Place a bowl or basket in a prominent area of your home. Put some slips of paper next to it. Ask family members to stop there during the week and write down ways to keep God first in your family. At the end of the week, have a special meal and read out the slips of paper. Discuss how each way helps bring the family closer to God and one another.

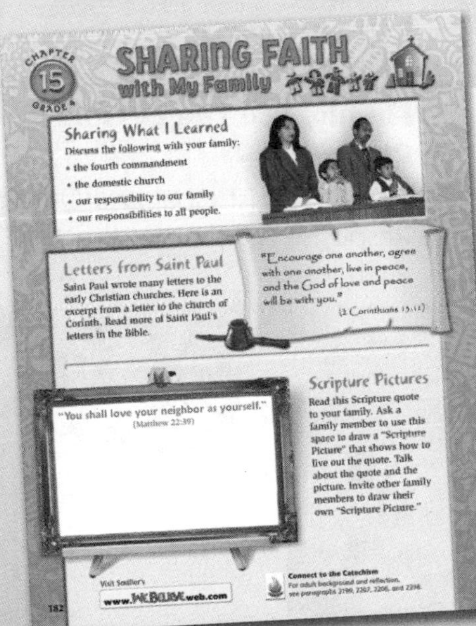

CHAPTER 15 GRADE 4 SHARING FAITH with My Family

Sharing What I Learned

Discuss the following with your family:

- the fourth commandment
- the domestic church
- our responsibility to our family
- our responsibilities to all people.

Letters from Saint Paul

Saint Paul wrote many letters to the early Christian churches. Here is an excerpt from a letter to the church of Corinth. Read more of Saint Paul's letters in the Bible.

"Encourage one another, agree with one another, live in peace, and the God of love and peace will be with you."

(2 Corinthians 13:11)

"You shall love your neighbor as yourself."
(Matthew 22:39)

Scripture Pictures

Read this Scripture quote to your family. Ask a family member to use this space to draw a "Scripture Picture" that shows how to live out the quote. Talk about the quote and the picture. Invite other family members to draw their own "Scripture Picture."

Visit Sadlier's www.WEBELIEVEweb.com

Connect to the Catechism

For adult background and reflection, see paragraphs 2190, 2207, 2206, and 2208.

182

Sharing Faith with My Family

These 27 family pages invite participation in each chapter through prayer, activities, information, and review. Activities and discussions on these pages are student-initiated, inviting the student to be the evangelizer.

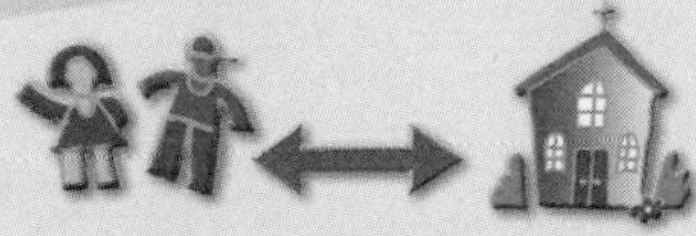

Sharing Faith in Class and at Home

This unique chapter in each book integrates the grade level material and utilizes a combination of stories, discussion questions, and activities that further the connections among catechists, students, and families. Suggested ways to utilize this chapter can be found in the Chapter 28 Planning Guide.

SHARING FAITH In Class and at Home 28

Why Do We Need Laws?

Laws or rules are everywhere. Sensible laws remind us to behave in ways that will not put others or ourselves in danger. Some laws may seem silly to us. They might need to be changed in order to keep up with the times or with the way a person grows. The best laws help us to become loving and kind.

Because We Believe

Laws are really agreements that we live out each day. When we obey a law, we agree to act and think in a certain way.

"LORD, teach me the way of your laws." Psalm 119:33

In the Bible we read that God made a special agreement with Moses and his people. God promised to be their God if they would be his people. This special agreement is called a *covenant*. God gave Moses and his people the law that he wanted them to follow. The Ten Commandments are God's laws. God's people promised to keep the Ten Commandments as part of their covenant with God.

The Ten Commandments are God's laws for us, too. They help us to put God first in our lives. The Ten Commandments help people and communities treat one another with respect.

How do we show that we believe this?

313

Don't Forget...

Families will also have access to the program Web site, finding safe web activities for their children and family-based faith activities to share.

www.WEBELIEVEweb.com

The Catechist's Pages

Sadlier **We Believe** Program Overview

Your Guide—Clear, Concise, Complete !

First, Use the Overview and Planning Pages.

Background and Lesson preparation Planning Guide provide enrichment and structure for the catechist.

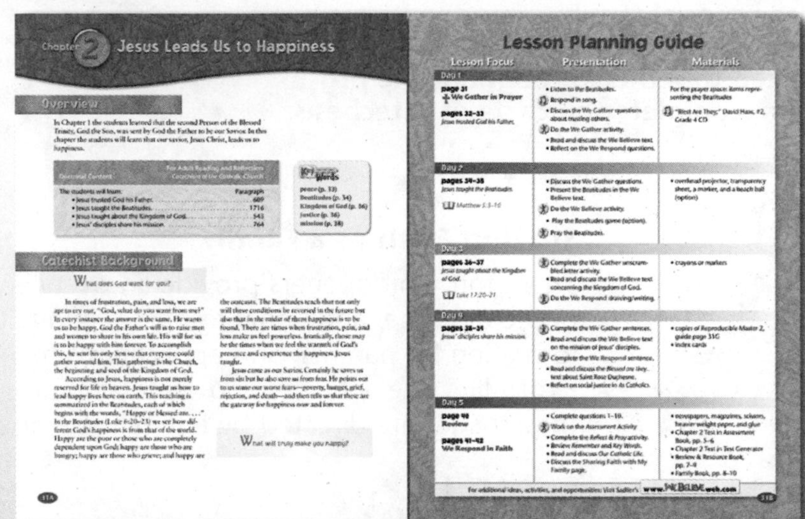
Chapter 2 Jesus Leads Us to Happiness

Overview

Catechist Background

What does God want for you?

Lesson Planning Guide

Lesson Focus	Presentation	Materials

Then, Use the Additional Resource Pages.

Enrichment, Connections, Catechist Development, and Reproducible Master pages are all in your Guide.

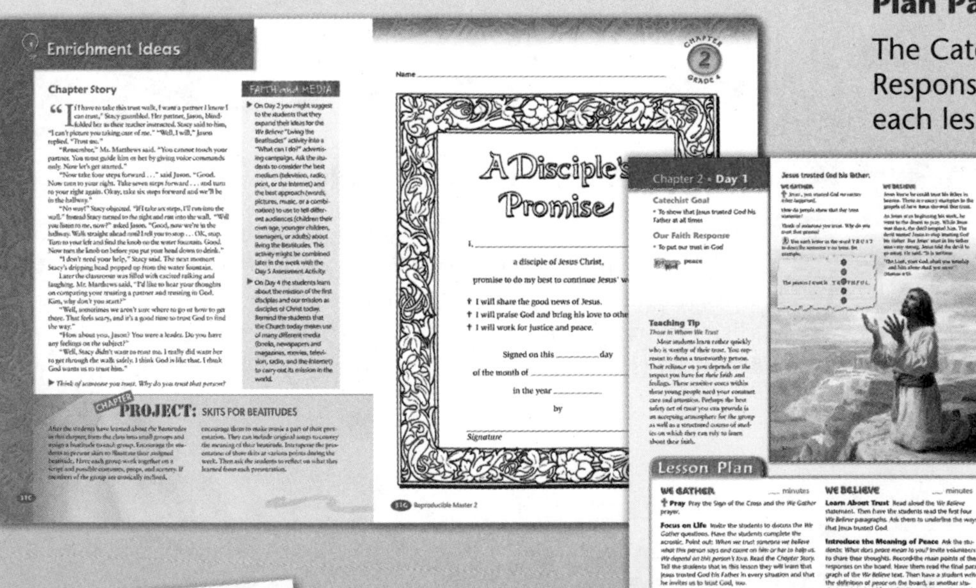
Enrichment Ideas

Chapter Story

Faith and Media

Chapter Project: Skits for Beatitudes

A Disciple's Promise

I will share the good news of Jesus.

I will praise God and bring his love to others.

I will work for justice and peace.

116 Reproducible Master 2

Finally, Use the Lesson Plan Pages.

The Catechist Goal and Our Faith Response reflect the direction of each lesson.

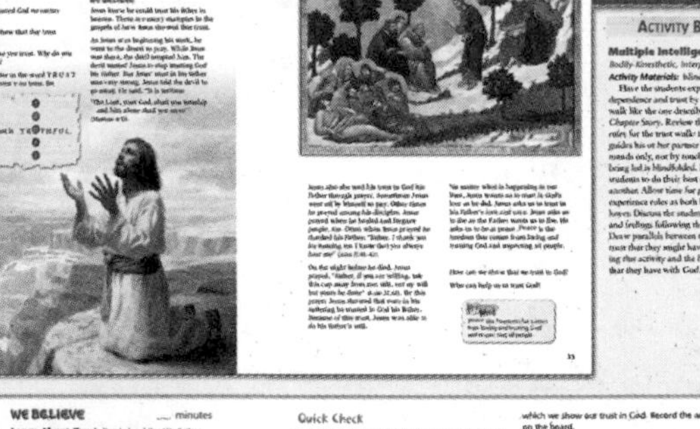
Chapter 2 • Day 1

Catechist Goal

Our Faith Response

Teaching Tip

Lesson Plan

We Gather

We Believe

Quick Check

Activity Bank

Plan Ahead for Day 2

All you need to get started is

1. your grade level Sadlier *We Believe* text for each student in your class
2. your grade level *We Believe* guide
3. your grade level *We Believe* Music CD.

Catechist Development

Sadlier is committed to supporting you, the catechist, in your faith and in your ministry. The Sadlier *We Believe* program includes twenty-one Catechist Development articles. Each article provides you with on-going development and helps you to become more aware of the elements of effective catechesis. The opening article precedes the Introductory Chapter and the other articles precede the five core chapters in each unit— Chapters 1–5, 8–12, 15–19, and 22–26.

Each article addresses a specific topic and is written by a nationally recognized expert in that field. The *Resources* section follows each article and offers print and video suggestions to enable you to delve further into the topic. The *Ways to Implement* offers some practical ideas to bring the topic to life in your class. Finally, the *Catechist Corner* features an idea from a catechist and the successful implementation of that idea.

Here are the twenty-one topics, their authors, and the pages on which you can find the articles in your Sadlier *We Believe* Teacher Guide:

Topics and Authors

For additional ideas, activities, and opportunities: Visit Sadlier's **www.WEBELIEVEweb.com**

Catechist Development

Understanding the Child

by Gini Shimabukuro, Ed.D.

Dr. Gini Shimabukuro is a Professor and Associate Director of the Institute for Catholic Educational Leadership at the University of San Francisco. She is rooted in Catholic education, with teaching experience at the elementary level.

Essential to the building of a gospel-based learning community is the sincere, ongoing effort to understand each child. This understanding permits the educator to fulfill the Christian call to formation and transformation of learners.

Since the Second Vatican Council in the 1960s, Church documentation related to education offers insight into this concept through the "integral formation" of the child. "Integral formation" refers to teaching that fosters the unification of the many aspects of the child—spiritual, moral, religious, intellectual, developmental, social, emotional, physical—and to learning that enables the child to make necessary connections among these interior dimensions.

Effective formation, then, precludes an awareness of these many human dimensions as active in the learning process and of their relationship to each other: emotional with religious, intellectual with physical, moral with developmental, and so on.

In order to achieve this holistic goal of learning that is integrated and formative, it is necessary to understand that teaching is more than mere transmission of knowledge. We need to design content-based processes that will empower the child to interiorize his or her learning.

Catechist Development Topics (Topic and Guide Page)

Resources

Groome, Thomas. *Educating for Life.* Allen, Texas: Thomas More Publishing Co. 1998.

The Congregation for Catholic Education, The Religious Dimension of Education in a Catholic School, Boston: Daughters of St. Paul, 1988.

Ways to Implement Understanding the Child

- Explore the preferred learning style of each child in your class or group. Discuss the different ways that people learn, sharing your own preferred style. Design lessons that embrace a variety of learning styles.

- When building a classroom or group community, introduce activities that encourage all members to know each other better, such as, exercises that prompt students to share their ethnic backgrounds, childhood experiences, feelings, hopes for the future, and so on. Appropriate sharing in these areas provides the "glue" for a tightly knit learning community.

- Investigate the emerging research on the brain and learning in order to incorporate the best classroom practices in the design and delivery of instruction.

- Be available to the children by modeling active listening skills. Encourage their social, moral and emotional development.

With thanks to:
Catherine Foley
Grade 3 Catechist
St. Anthony of Padua Church
Red Bank, New Jersey

Catherine designs a bulletin board that contains a church on one side and types of homes on the other. A footbridge connects the two sides of the display. On the "church side," Catherine displays pictures of people and events from the parish. She asks the children to contribute pictures of themselves with their families and pictures of themselves during a church celebration (Baptism, first Eucharist, a wedding). The pictures of the children and their families are placed on the "home side" of the display. The pictures of the children celebrating special church events are placed on the footbridge. The bulletin board is a great conversation piece that helps Catherine get to know the children and their families.

Notes

We Believe

The *We Believe* program will help us to

learn

celebrate

share

and

live our Catholic faith.

Throughout the year we will hear about many saints and holy people.

Saint Augustine
Saint Brigid
Saint Charles Lwanga and the Martyrs of Uganda
Dorothy Day
Saint Edith Stein
Saint Francis of Assisi
Frederic Ozanam
Isaiah the Prophet
Saint Isidore
Saint John, apostle and evangelist
Saint John the Baptist
Blessed John XXIII
Pope John Paul II
Saint John Vianney
Saint Joseph
Saint Josephine Bakhita
Saint Juan Diego
Saint Katharine Drexel
Saint Louise de Marillac
Saint Luke, evangelist
Saint Maria
Saint Mark, evangelist
Saint Matthew, apostle and evangelist
Saint Monica
Oscar Romero
Our Lady of Guadalupe
Saint Paul
Saint Rose Philippine Duchesne
Saint Teresa de los Andes
Saint Thérèse of Lisieux
Saint Thomas More
Saint Vincent de Paul

Together, let us grow as a community of faith.

Welcome!

We Gather in Prayer

Leader: Welcome, everyone, to Grade 4 *We Believe*. As we begin each chapter, we gather in prayer. We pray to God together. Sometimes, we will read from Scripture, other times we will say the prayers of the Church or sing a song of thanks and praise to God.

Today, let us sing the *We Believe* song!

We Believe, We Believe in God

Refrain:

We believe in God;
We believe, we believe in Jesus;
We believe in the Spirit who gives us life.
We believe, we believe in God.

We believe in the Holy Spirit,
Who renews the face of the earth.
We believe we are part of a living Church,
And forever we will live with God.

(Refrain)

Each day we learn more about God.

We Gather, we begin by
taking a moment

WE GATHER

✝ *Thank you, God, for all our classmates.*

Then we

think about
talk about
act out
draw about
write about

Life

at school
at home
in our parish
in our world
in our neighborhood

Talk about your life right now. What groups, teams, or clubs do you belong to?

Why do you like being a part of these groups?

What does belonging to these groups tell other people about you?

When we see **We Believe**
we learn more about our
Catholic faith.

WE BELIEVE

We learn about:

- the Blessed Trinity—God the Father, God the Son, and God the Holy Spirit
- Jesus, the Son of God, who became one of us
- the Church and its history and teachings
- the Mass and the sacraments
- our call to be a disciple of Jesus.

Growing in Jesus Christ
Jesus said, "I am the way and the truth and the life." (John 14:6)

The Commandments Help Us to Love God
"LORD, teach me the way of your laws;
I shall observe them with care." (Psalm 119:33)

The Commandments Help Us to Love Others
"You shall love your neighbor as yourself." (Matthew 22:39)

We Are Called to Holiness
"Do this in remembrance of me." (1 Corinthians 11:24)

A major theme in your ***We Believe*** textbook this year is learning more about the Ten Commandments. Your book is divided into four units.

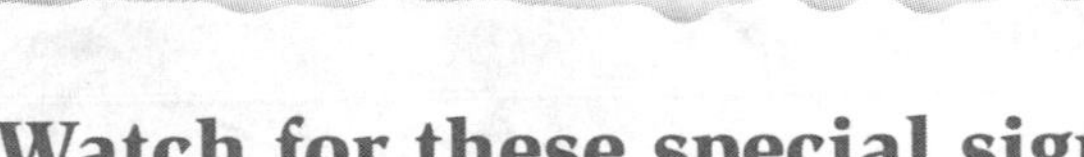

Watch for these special signs:

Whenever we see ✝ we make the sign of the cross. We pray and begin our day's lesson.

📖 is an open Bible. When we see it, or a reference like this (John 13:34), we hear the word of God. We hear about God and his people. We hear about Jesus and the Holy Spirit.

When we see 🏃 we do an activity.

We might:

- talk together
- write a story
- draw a picture
- act out a story or situation
- imagine ourselves doing something
- sing a song together, or make up one
- work together on a special project.

There are all kinds of activities! We might see 🏃 in any part of our day's lesson. Be on the lookout!

Can you guess what ♫ means? That's right, it means it is time to sing, or listen to music! We sing songs we know, make up our own, and sing along with those in our *We Believe* music program.

When we see Key Words we review the meanings of important words we have learned in the day's lesson.

As Catholics...

Here we discover something special about our faith. We reflect on what we have discovered and try to make it a part of our life. Don't forget to read it!

WE RESPOND

We can respond by:

- thinking about ways our faith affects the things we say and do
- sharing our thoughts and feelings
- praying to God.

Then in our home, neighborhood, school, parish, and world, we say and do the things that show love for God and others.

When we see **We Respond** we reflect and act on what we have learned about God and our Catholic faith.

Draw yourself doing something that shows you are a disciple of Jesus Christ.

We are so happy you are with us!

Here we check to see what we have learned in this chapter.

Reflect & Pray

We take a few moments to think about our faith and to pray.

We review the meanings of important words from the chapter.

Grade 4
Chapter 1

Review

Circle the correct answer.

1. The truth that the Son of God became man is the _____.
   Blessed Trinity   Incarnation   Pentecost
2. Because Jesus died and rose to save us from sin, he is our _____.
   disciple   Blessed Trinity   Savior
3. The _____ is the three Persons in one God.
   Blessed Trinity   Holy Spirit   Incarnation
4. The gift of God's life in us is _____.
   grace   Savior   sin

Complete the following:

5. The community of people who are baptized and follow Jesus Christ is the _____________________
6. The people who said yes to Jesus' call and followed him were his _____________________
7. The first human beings turned away from God and committed _____________________
8. Stories about Jesus' life are in the books of the New Testament called the _____________________

Write a sentence to answer the question.

9–10. What is the Church? _____________________

Make a drawing or a clay sculpture or write a short story that shows people who are trying to live as Jesus taught us.

28

We Respond in Faith

Reflect & Pray

Holy Spirit, make me a stronger disciple of Jesus. Help me to _____________________

Key Words

Incarnation (p. 20)
disciples (p. 23)
Blessed Trinity (p. 23)
original sin (p. 24)
Savior (p. 24)
Church (p. 27)
grace (p. 27)

Remember

- God sent his only Son to us.
- Jesus shows us how to live.
- Jesus Christ is our Savior.
- The disciples spread the good news of Jesus Christ.

OUR CATHOLIC LIFE

Dorothy Day

Dorothy Day wanted to help people who were homeless or hungry. She stood up for peace and against injustice. She started a soup kitchen to feed the poor in New York City. Following her example, people in other cities started soup kitchens to help the poor, too. Under her leadership, the Catholic Worker Movement grew. This group of people joins together to feed hungry people, to work for greater justice, and to continue the work of Jesus in the world.

ASSESSMENT

We do a chapter activity in which we show that we have discovered more about our Catholic faith.

OUR CATHOLIC LIFE

Here we read an interesting story about the ways people make the world better by living out their Catholic faith.

Remember

We recall the four main faith statements of the chapter.

SHARING FAITH with My Family

At the end of each chapter, you will bring a page like this home to your family. It will offer fun activities that the whole family can enjoy!

Sharing What I Learned

Discuss the following with your family.

WE GATHER

WE BELIEVE

WE RESPOND

WE BELIEVE Family Contract

As a **We Believe** family, this year we promise to

____

____

Names

____

____

____

A Family Prayer

Lead your family in prayer.

People who love us make love grow. Thank you, God, for our family.

People who love us make love grow. Thank you, God, for all the friends of our family.

Most of all, thank you, God, for loving us!

Look here for connections to the Web and to the Catechism.

Visit Sadlier's

www.WEBELIEVEweb.com

Connect to the Catechism of the Catholic Church

For adult background and reflection, Catechism paragraph references are given here.

Growing in Jesus Christ

UNIT 1

UNIT 1 SHARING FAITH as a Family

The Benefits of Gratitude

Children are often taught early in life to say "thank you." This makes sense. It's good to be grateful, isn't it? According to recent research, the answer to this question is an unqualified yes! Psychologists have found that appreciative people are less likely to be negative or overly materialistic. They resist destructive impulses of greed and envy and are more likely to experience higher levels of positive emotions, such as happiness, vitality, optimism, and hope. Positive emotions help people heal more quickly after surgery and may even prolong people's life span. Gratitude can be good for you—physically, emotionally, and spiritually!

This is old news for the Church. Attitudes of gratitude have permeated worship for centuries, and prayers of thanksgiving are as old as the Bible. Giving thanks is considered one of the basic forms of Christian prayer.

What Your Child Will Learn in Unit 1

The first unit of Grade 4 invites the children to focus on the life and ministry of Jesus Christ, who is the center of our faith. The children come to understand that Jesus is both human and divine, the second Person of the Blessed Trinity who became one of us. They comprehend the need for Jesus as our Savior and become more aware of their life of grace begun at Baptism and strengthened by the Holy Spirit. All this leads to a presentation of becoming a disciple of Jesus.

The children are helped to understand the true meaning of the Beatitudes. Next, the reality of sin is presented. This is followed by a thorough discussion of our conscience, our guide in making decisions that keep us close to Christ. As the unit ends, the children learn the need for reconciliation as celebrated in the sacrament of Penance and Reconciliation.

Plan & Preview

- Scissors will be needed for the chapter family pages (*Sharing Faith with My Family*) in this unit.
- Have markers and crayons available so that you can draw or write on the puzzle pieces. Use a glue stick and pieces of stiff paper or cardboard to create a sturdy backing for the puzzle.

Note the Quote

"He is happiest, be he king or peasant, who finds peace in his home."

Johann von Goethe
(German poet, playwright, novelist, and scientist)

From the Catechism

"Parents have the first responsibility for the education of their children."

(Catechism of the Catholic Church, 2223)

Peaceful Prayer

Schedule some quiet time to be by yourself. Sit or lie down in a quiet room. Put on some soothing music, and relax. Breathe very deeply, in and out. With each exhaled breath, push away any negative thoughts and anxieties. Breathe in comforting thoughts.

Then quietly pray these words,

Glory to God in the highest, *pause*
Peace to his people on earth, *pause*
We worship you, *pause*
We give you thanks, *pause*
We praise you for your glory.

Listen to the words as you say them quietly to yourself. What is God saying to you? What are you saying to God?

Did You Know?

Here are some Internet statistics concerning the family:

34% of parents say the Internet has helped them plan weekend outings

27% of parents say the Internet has helped them shop for birthday and holiday gifts for family members

26% of parents say it has improved the way they spend time with their children

19% of parents say it has improved the way they care for their children's health.

(from Pew Internet and American Life Project. *Internet Influence*. June 20, 2001)

Class Connection

Point out the unit title to the students. Ask them what they think they will be learning more about in this unit. Have a class discussion, preparing the students for this unit.

Home Connection

Sharing Faith as a Family

Sadlier *We Believe* calls on families to become involved in:

- learning the faith
- prayer and worship
- living their faith.

Highlighting of these unit family pages and the opportunities they offer will strengthen the partnership of the Church and the home.

For additional information and activities, encourage families to visit Sadlier's

www.WEBELIEVEweb.com

Chapter 1 Jesus—the Way, the Truth, and the Life

Overview

In this chapter the students will continue to learn more about Jesus, who shows us the way God the Father wants us to live. They will begin to understand that Jesus is the way, the truth, and the life. By following Jesus, we grow closer to God the Father, Son, and Holy Spirit.

Doctrinal Content	For Adult Reading and Reflection *Catechism of the Catholic Church*
The students will learn:	Paragraph
• God sent his only Son to us.	422
• Jesus shows us how to live.	544
• Jesus Christ is our Savior.	430
• The disciples spread the good news of Jesus Christ.	767

Key Words

Incarnation (p. 20)
disciples (p. 23)
Blessed Trinity (p. 23)
original sin (p. 24)
Savior (p. 24)
Church (p. 27)
grace (p. 27)

Catechist Background

How does being a Christian make a difference in your life?

The Son of God became man in the mystery of the Incarnation. Saint Paul used an early Christian hymn to describe this mystery.

Who, though he was in the form of God,
did not regard equality with God something
to be grasped.
Rather, he emptied himself,
taking the form of a slave,
coming in human likeness;
and found human in appearance,
he humbled himself,
becoming obedient to death,
even death on a cross (Philippians 2:5–8).

The human Jesus was born into a Jewish family in ancient Israel. Mary and Joseph raised him and taught him the prayers and traditions of the Jewish faith. After his Baptism by John, Jesus became a preacher, wandering throughout the country talking to the people and teaching them about God.

Throughout his ministry, Jesus' teaching and his miracles astonished his followers. After Jesus' Resurrection, his followers used the Greek title *Christos*, the anointed one, to proclaim his divinity.

Jesus' disciples were the men and women who traveled with him, learned from him, and went out to teach others about him. Today we are Jesus' disciples. It is now our task to carry the message of Jesus to the people of our time.

As you begin this year what do you ask of Jesus in prayer?

Lesson Planning Guide

Lesson Focus	Presentation	Materials
Day 1		
page 19 **We Gather in Prayer** **pages 20–21** *God sent his only Son to us.* *John 14:6-7*	• Listen to Scripture. • Respond in prayer. • Discuss the **We Gather** question. • Read and discuss the **We Believe** text about Jesus and the Incarnation. Make a mobile for the **We Respond** activity.	For the prayer space: white tablecloth, two large cardboard hearts, a loaf of bread, a stick fashioned to look like a shepherd's staff, a battery-powered candle, and a Bible • strips of paper and yarn, markers, index cards, plastic clothes hangers
Day 2		
pages 22–23 *Jesus shows us how to live.*	 Do the **We Gather** activity. • Read and discuss the **We Believe** text. Complete the **We Respond** activity.	• chart paper and colorful markers • copies of Reproducible Master 1, guide page 19G
Day 3		
pages 24–25 *Jesus Christ is our Savior.* *John 1:29*	• Discuss the **We Gather** questions. • Read and discuss the **We Believe** text. • Share why Jesus is important. 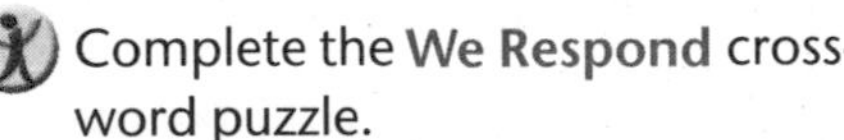 Complete the **We Respond** crossword puzzle. • Read and talk about the name of Jesus in the *As Catholics* text.	
Day 4		
pages 26–27 *The disciples spread the good news of Jesus Christ.*	 Do the **We Gather** activity about ways students have grown and changed. • Read and discuss the **We Believe** text. • Describe ways the disciples spread the good news. Complete the **We Respond** statements and answer the question.	• large strips of poster board and markers
Day 5		
page 28 **Review** **pages 29–30** **We Respond in Faith**	• Complete questions 1–10. Work on the *Assessment Activity*. • Complete the *Reflect & Pray* activity. • Review *Remember* and *Key Words*. • Read and discuss *Our Catholic Life*. • Discuss the **Sharing Faith with My Family** page.	• clay or papier-mâché • Chapter 1 Test in Assessment Book, pp. 3–4 • Chapter 1 Test in Test Generator • Review & Resource Book, pp. 4–6 • Family Book, pp. 5–7

For additional ideas, activities, and opportunities: Visit Sadlier's **www.WEBELIEVEweb.com**

Chapter Story

It was time to get on the bus, but Sara Klein was busy talking to the rabbi. "Lizzie, why don't you get on the bus with us and save a seat for Sarah?" Mrs. Klein asked. Lizzie was glad she agreed because now she had a great seat in the front of the bus and was waiting for Sarah.

The Klein's synagogue had planned this trip to hear a Klezmer group play lively Jewish folk music. Sarah's parents knew Lizzie would enjoy it and invited her to join them. Lizzie was the only person on the bus who did not worship at the synagogue, but that was okay because the Kleins were like her second family.

Lizzie remembered the first day that she met Sarah at preschool. Lizzie was always kind of shy but not Sarah! Sarah came right over to Lizzie, took her by the hand, and asked her if she wanted to play. Sarah and Lizzie became best friends.

Even though they go to different schools now, Sarah and Lizzie still eat at each other's homes. They love it when they can have a sleep over. That's how Lizzie came to know Klezmer music. The Klein home always had music playing, and Lizzie liked the Jewish folk music best of all. She couldn't understand the words, but the beat was great.

"Thanks, for the seat," Sarah said as she got onto the bus. Her cheerful voice brought Lizzie back to the present. "The rabbi said that he heard this group once before and we will really like them."

▶ *How did Lizzie and her friend Sarah get to know each other?*

FAITH and MEDIA

▶ As you talk about the importance of growing in faith, remind the students that they can also learn more about Jesus, about ways to live their faith, and about God's law through media. As they watch television, go to the movies, listen to music, read newspapers and magazines, and use the Internet in the coming weeks, have them be attentive to ways the media can be used to help people grow in faith. Ask the students to imagine what kinds of influence they would have as writers, reporters, newscasters, actors, artists, musicians, Webmasters, or media workers. Have them name ways they would promote the message of Jesus Christ through media. Invite them to do the optional Day 1 "Video Profile of Jesus" activity (Activity Bank) as a starting point.

CHAPTER PROJECT: DISCIPLESHIP POSTERS

Invite the students to make posters that call people's attention to discipleship. Provide poster paper, magazines, markers, and/or crayons. Have the students work with a partner to design posters that remind everyone that disciples of Jesus spread the good news of Jesus Christ. The students can include what they learn in this chapter about Jesus. Display these posters in some prominent place. Then arrange a time for the students to explain their posters to the younger students. The project might also be used as a home assignment during the coming week.

Connections

To Liturgy

Explain to the students that at each Sunday Mass the gospel reading offers us another invitation to learn how to follow Christ's way. Suggest that, when they return home from Mass, they read the day's gospel again. Getting into this habit will help them to become familiar with the four gospels.

To Catholic Social Teaching

Option for the Poor and Vulnerable
Explain to the students that during his public ministry, Jesus reached out to those who were poor, lonely, and in need. He associated with people that others ignored or excluded, such as lepers and tax collectors. Encourage the students to follow Jesus' example of caring for others. Invite them to pray for those in need and look for opportunities to connect the mission of Jesus with the Church's work to help people in desperate need throughout the world.

To Stewardship

Remind the students that Jesus' life on earth was humble. He had few material possessions. Sometimes we have many possessions. Ask the students to consider donating a game or some clothing to a local drive for those in need.

Meeting Individual Needs

Challenging Students to Do Their Best

Students need to be challenged in ways that stimulate their creativity and talents. This does not mean continually asking them to help others or giving them extra work. Rather, try to offer various outlets for them to grow and learn. For example, have the students teach part of a lesson, work with a partner who has special needs, or develop a project on their own. These avenues of enrichment should be based on their own interests and selected by the young people themselves.

ADDITIONAL RESOURCES

Book *115 Saintly Fun Facts,* Bernadette McCarver Snyder, Liguori Publications, 1993. Find out interesting facts about how common people followed the way of Jesus and became saints in the process.

Video *Saul of Tarsus,* Nest Publications, 1990. Saul is changed forever when Jesus appears to him on the road to Damascus. He becomes one of the greatest missionaries in the Church. (30 minutes)

To find more ideas for books, videos, and other learning material, visit Sadlier's

www.WEBELIEVEweb.com

Chapter 1 • Day 1

Catechist Goal

- To teach that God the Father sent his only Son to us

Our Faith Response

- To recognize that Jesus leads us to God the Father

 **Incarnation**

Lesson Materials

- strips of paper and yarn
- markers
- index cards
- plastic clothes hanger for each student

Teaching Note

Transition

Fourth grade is a bridge or transition stage for children. Fourth grade students are starting to grasp more complex ideas, work more independently, and take more notes. Encourage the students to ask questions and build on prior knowledge.

God sent his only Son to us.

WE GATHER

✝ *Jesus, help me to know you.*

Think of someone you know well. How did you get to know that person?

Share your answers.

WE BELIEVE

Who is Jesus? How can we learn about him? One way we can find out about Jesus is by reading the Bible.

In the New Testament we learn that God the Father sent his Son into the world to become one of us. The **Incarnation** is the truth that the Son of God became human.

Jesus is the Son of God. He is both divine and human. We can read about Jesus' life in the four books of the New Testament called the *gospels.* We learn that Jesus grew up in Nazareth with his mother Mary and his foster father Joseph. Jesus loved them and all his family. He learned about his Jewish faith and prayed to God.

As Jesus grew older, he talked to people in many towns. He taught them about God. Jesus talked about God in a way that no one ever had before. Jesus called God "Abba." The word *abba* means "father."

As we get to know more about Jesus, we learn more about the Father. In the gospel of Saint John, we read that Jesus said, "I am the way and the truth and the life. No one comes to the Father except through me. If you know me, then you will also know my Father" (John 14:6–7).

Through his life and teaching, Jesus leads us to God the Father. Jesus tells us about God. Jesus shows us the life that God wants us to share.

Key Word
Incarnation the truth that the Son of God became man

20

Lesson Plan

WE GATHER ___ minutes

Time Allotment

✝ **Pray** Pray the Sign of the Cross and the *We Gather* prayer.

Focus on Life Share the *Chapter Story* on guide page 19C. Then have them read and think about the *We Gather* question. Invite volunteers to share their answers. You may initiate the discussion by offering some brief anecdotes that illustrate how you got to know one of your friends. Tell the students that in this lesson they will learn how they can get to know God the Father through Jesus, his only Son.

WE BELIEVE ___ minutes

Read the Text Have volunteers read aloud the *We Believe* statement and section. Discuss the illustration. Stress that Jesus is both fully human and fully divine. Have them highlight the definition of the word *Incarnation.*

Explore the Word *Abba* Write the word *Father* on the board. Ask: *What name did Jesus use for God?* Write the word *Abba* on the board. Explain to them that by using this name, Jesus, God the Son, was describing his unique relationship with God the Father.

Build on the Ideas To help students understand who Jesus is, make a graphic organizer. Make two columns on the board. Label the first *Divine* and the

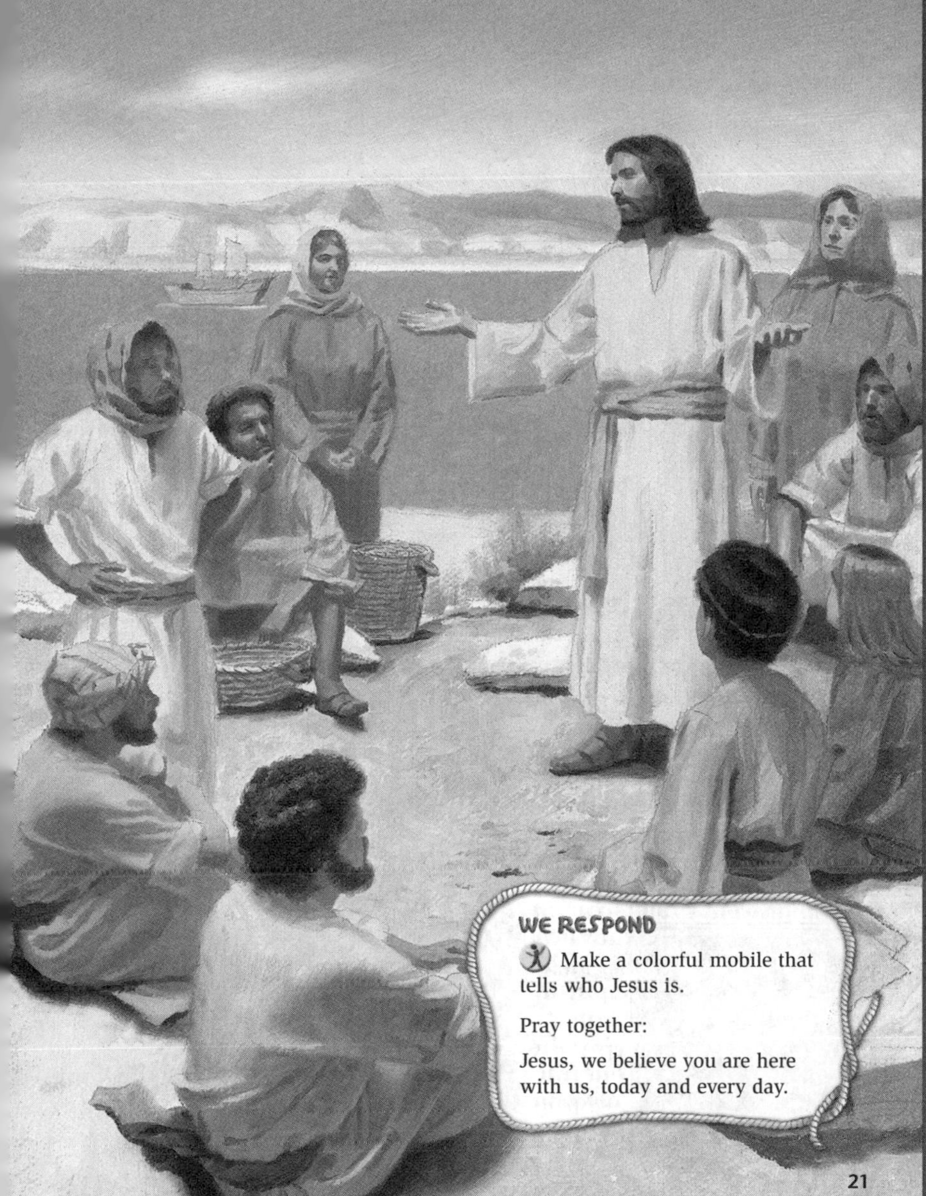

WE RESPOND
Make a colorful mobile that tells who Jesus is.
Pray together:
Jesus, we believe you are here with us, today and every day.
21

Activity Bank

Faith and Media

Video Profile of Jesus

Activity Materials: Bible, simple costumes

Form small groups and ask each group to select an event from the life of Jesus to dramatize. Encourage the groups to think about their favorite stories from the life of Jesus. Be available to help them locate these stories in the Bible. Have them use the Bible as a resource for making up dialogue and plots for their dramatizations. You might have each group choose a story that illustrates the divinity of Jesus and something that expresses his humanity. If possible, videotape the dramatizations to make a student-made profile of Jesus.

second *Human*. Encourage them to remember what they have learned about Jesus from their families, at Mass, and in their third grade class. Then invite them to list ways that Jesus showed both his divinity, such as performing miracles, rising from the dead, forgiving sins and so on; and his humanity, such as obeying his earthly parents, befriending the poor and outcasts, and so on.

Quick Check

✔ *What do we call the truth that the Son of God became human?* (We call this truth the Incarnation.)

✔ *Jesus is the Son of God who became one of us. What does Jesus teach us?* (Jesus teaches us about God the Father.)

We Respond

___ minutes

Connect to Life Invite the students to describe who Jesus is. Have them make a mobile using 3″ × 5″ index cards, yarn, markers, and a clothes hanger. Remind them that in coming to know Jesus, they will also come to know his heavenly Father. Encourage them to think of Jesus as the way, the truth, and the life. Jesus leads them to the Father in heaven.

Pray Conclude the lesson with the *We Respond* prayer.

Plan Ahead for Day 2

Catechist Goal: To present the truth that Jesus shows us how to live

Preparation: Have available chart paper and colorful markers. Make copies of Reproducible Master 1 (option).

Catechist Goal

- To present the truth that Jesus shows us how to live

Our Faith Response

- To identify what it means to live as Christ did

 **disciples**
Blessed Trinity

Lesson Materials

- copies of Reproducible Master 1 (option)
- chart paper
- colorful markers

Teaching Note

What Is a Disciple?

In the New Testament, the word *disciple* is frequently used to describe the apostles. However, the word *disciple* has a broader meaning. It refers to someone who believes and follows another. In the Acts of the Apostles, the term *disciple* is used to refer to converts and believers, both men and women.

Jesus shows us how to live.

WE GATHER

✝ *Jesus, we praise you.*

Have you ever done something good because you saw someone else do it? What did you do?

____

____

____

____

____

____

____

WE BELIEVE

Jesus wanted all people to know about God's love for them. He was just and fair to those he met. He reached out to help those who were poor, unwanted, or sinners. He cared for those who were sick or lonely.

Many people saw the good things Jesus did. Some were so impressed by Jesus' words and actions that they wanted to find out more about him. Jesus asked them to come and learn from him. Those who said yes to Jesus' call and followed him were his **disciples**.

Jesus spent about three years with his disciples. Jesus asked them to live as he did. He asked them to spread his message of God's love. Jesus tried to prepare the disciples for the time when he would no longer be with them. He knew that they needed help to continue his work.

When Jesus' life on earth was coming to an end, he made a promise. Jesus promised that the Father would send the Holy Spirit. The Holy Spirit would help the disciples to remember and to believe all that Jesus had told them.

The Holy Spirit is the third Person of the Blessed Trinity. The **Blessed Trinity** is the three Persons in one God: God the Father, God the Son, and God the Holy Spirit.

Holy Trinity, Playfair Book of Hours, late 15th century. Victoria & Albert Museum, London, Great Britain. This illuminated manuscript page is a drawing of and a prayer to the Blessed Trinity.

Lesson Plan

WE GATHER ___ minutes

✝ **Pray** Pray the Sign of the Cross and the *We Gather* prayer.

Focus on Life Share a personal experience of how you followed another person's good example. Have a volunteer read aloud the *We Gather* questions. Encourage students to share answers. Tell the students that in this lesson they will be learning how people witnessed Jesus' good works and became his disciples.

WE BELIEVE ___ minutes

Read the Text Invite a student to read aloud the *We Believe* statement. Have several volunteers read aloud the *We Believe* paragraphs. Emphasize the following:

- In his public ministry, Jesus reached out to people who needed his love and care, especially those who were poor, sick, and unwanted.
- Many people who witnessed the good works of Jesus were drawn to him and wanted to become his disciples.
- Jesus promised the disciples that he would send the Holy Spirit to help and strengthen them.

Make an Acrostic Invite the students to consider the meaning of the word *disciple*. Write this word vertically on chart paper, using a different colored marker for each letter. Encourage the students to brainstorm adjectives that describe a disciple of Jesus. For example, they could say *D* is for *devoted* or *daring*; *I* is for *inviting* or *involved*; *S* is for *strong* or *spiritual*, and so on.

The Last Supper scene from the motion picture King of Kings (1961).

Key Words

disciples those who said yes to Jesus' call to follow him

Blessed Trinity the three Persons in one God: God the Father, God the Son, and God the Holy Spirit

WE RESPOND

Jesus asked his disciples to live as he did. What did that mean?

Think of a television show, movie, or book that you like. Name some characters in it that you think are following Jesus' example. Tell how they are doing this.

____

____

____

____

____

ACTIVITY BANK

Curriculum Connection

The Arts

Activity Materials: Optional videotaping equipment, props

Ask the students to work in pairs to make commercials that promote the way Jesus wants us to live. Have them show the way Jesus lived his own life and ways we can imitate him. Encourage the students to make use of music, dance, and art. If possible, videotape the commercials to share with others.

Use the Reproducible Master At this point you may want to distribute copies of Reproducible Master 1. Read the directions aloud and have the students either complete the activity in class or at home.

Quick Check

✔ *What do we call those who said yes to Jesus' call to follow him?* (We call them disciples.)

✔ *Who are the three Persons of the Blessed Trinity?* (The three Persons of the Blessed Trinity are God the Father, God the Son, and God the Holy Spirit.)

WE RESPOND

___ minutes

Connect to Life Ask the students: *What are ways that you can live as Jesus wants us to live?* Encourage them to be aware of the good people around them who strive to follow Jesus. Read the directions for the *We Respond* activity. Provide quiet time for the students to reflect and write. Invite students to share their responses to the *We Respond* activity.

Pray Invite the students to join you in praying,
Jesus Christ, we are your disciples all,
Jesus Lord, help us to say yes when you call.
Amen.

Plan Ahead for Day 3

Catechist Goal: To emphasize that Jesus Christ is our Savior

Preparation: Think of examples that show how hurt feelings affect relationships.

Catechist Goal

- To emphasize that Jesus Christ is our Savior

Our Faith Response

- To accept and believe in Jesus as our Savior

original sin
Savior

As Catholics...

The Name Jesus Christ

After presenting the lesson, have volunteers, read aloud the *As Catholics* paragraphs. Invite the students to think about the meaning of the name of Jesus. Remind them that the name of Jesus reveals his important mission. Explain that many people bow their heads whenever they say the name of Jesus. Suggest that the students always use the name of Jesus with respect and love.

Jesus Christ is our Savior.

WE GATHER

✝ *God, we believe in you, Father, Son, and Holy Spirit.*

Think about one of your friends. Have you ever done something that hurt his or her feelings?

Did it change your friendship? How?

WE BELIEVE

God created people to share in his love and to live in his friendship. He created them to be close to him. However, the first human beings turned away from God's love and disobeyed him. They committed the first sin, which is called **original sin.** Everyone is born with original sin. Original sin makes it harder for us to love and obey God.

Even though they had sinned, God did not turn away from his people. God promised to save them from sin. He sent his only Son to save all people. Jesus is the Son of God who came to take away the sin of the world. John the Baptist said of Jesus, "Behold, the Lamb of God, who takes away the sin of the world" (John 1:29).

By his dying on the cross and rising to new life, Jesus saves all people from sin. This is why we call Jesus the *Savior*. **Savior** is a title given to Jesus because he died and rose to save us from sin.

At the celebration of the Mass, we remember that Jesus Christ is our Savior. We pray:

"Lord, by your cross and resurrection
you have set us free.
You are the Savior of the world."

Jesus lived among us to show us God's love. Because of Jesus we can live in God's love forever.

original sin the first sin committed by the first human beings

Savior a title given to Jesus because he died and rose to save us from sin

24

Lesson Plan

WE GATHER ___ minutes

✝ **Pray** Invite the students to profess their faith in the Blessed Trinity by praying the Sign of the Cross and the *We Gather* prayer.

Focus on Life Have the students answer the *We Gather* questions. Invite them to share responses. For an objective discussion, tell the students about an actual event, a television show, or novel that shows how hurt feelings can affect a friendship. Tell the students that in this lesson they will be learning about Jesus as our Savior.

WE BELIEVE ___ minutes

Read the Text Read aloud the *We Believe* statement. Write the word *Savior* on the board. Beneath it, write the word *save.* Ask volunteers to read aloud the *We Believe* paragraphs. Emphasize the following:

- When the first humans disobeyed God, they committed the first sin, original sin.
- All humans are born with original sin.
- God sent his only Son to save us from sin.
- Jesus' death on the cross saved us from sin and enabled us to live in God's love forever.

Think About Jesus Ask the students: *What are some ways you have learned about Jesus?* Have each one of them name something about Jesus that is of personal importance. Invite them to share their responses.

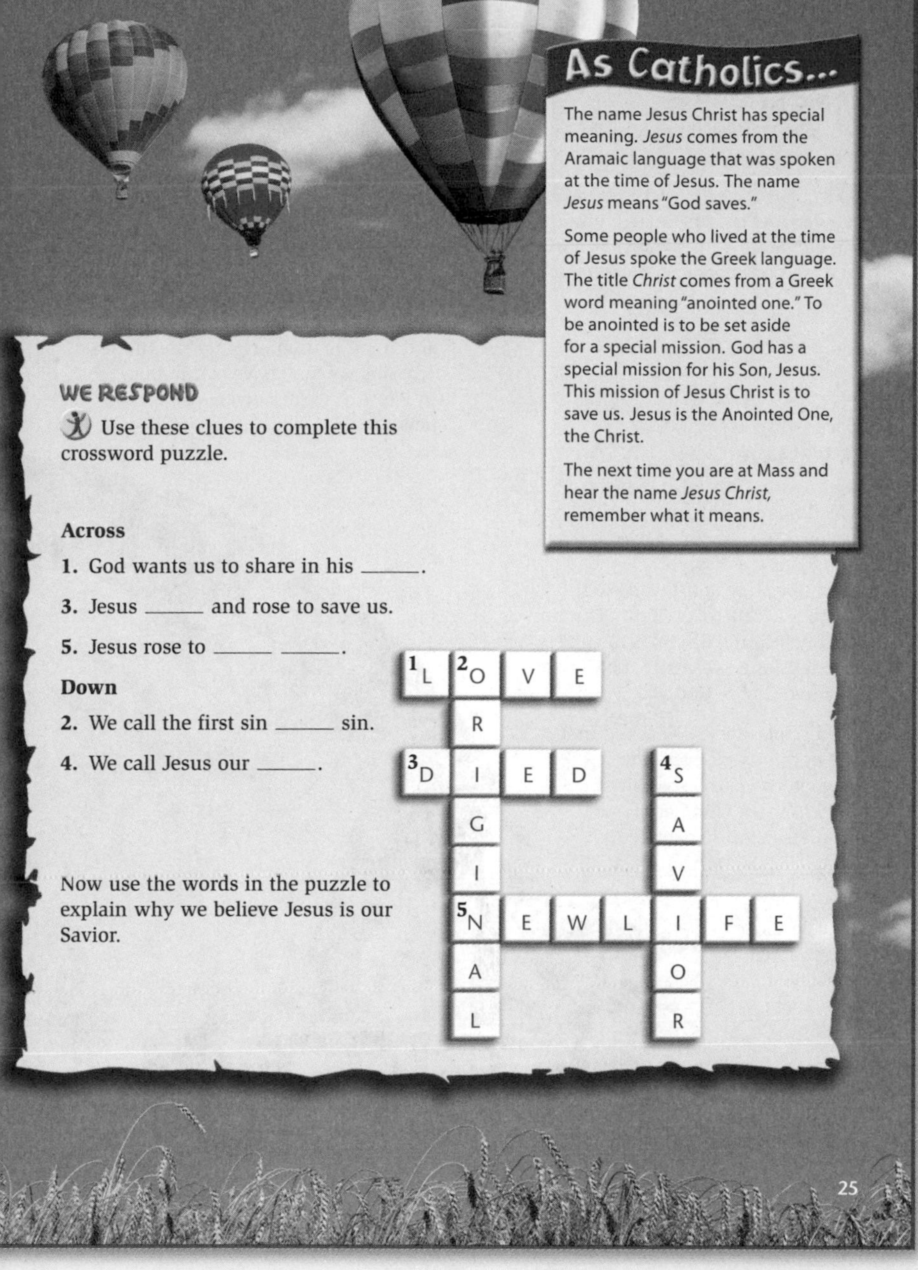

As Catholics...

The name Jesus Christ has special meaning. *Jesus* comes from the Aramaic language that was spoken at the time of Jesus. The name *Jesus* means "God saves."

Some people who lived at the time of Jesus spoke the Greek language. The title *Christ* comes from a Greek word meaning "anointed one." To be anointed is to be set aside for a special mission. God has a special mission for his Son, Jesus. This mission of Jesus Christ is to save us. Jesus is the Anointed One, the Christ.

The next time you are at Mass and hear the name *Jesus Christ,* remember what it means.

WE RESPOND

Use these clues to complete this crossword puzzle.

Across

1. God wants us to share in his _____.

3. Jesus _____ and rose to save us.

5. Jesus rose to _____ _____.

Down

2. We call the first sin _____ sin.

4. We call Jesus our _____.

Now use the words in the puzzle to explain why we believe Jesus is our Savior.

Activity Bank

Liturgy

Celebrate Jesus our Savior.

Activity Materials: Bible, hymnals, banner-making materials

Involve the fourth graders in preparing a school Mass. Invite them to work on committees: selecting hymns, choosing readings, making banners, decorating the church, and compiling a list of general intercession prayers. Be sure to review their contributions with the priest who will preside.

Multicultural Connection

Jesus Saves Us All

Activity Materials: felt or burlap to make a banner, glue, scissors, foreign language dictionaries or Internet Web sites that offer translation

Ask a librarian, parents with foreign language backgrounds, or search the Internet to help students find out how to write the word *Savior* in different languages. Teach them how people say the word *Savior* in their native languages. Invite the students to make a banner that proclaims the word *Savior* in these languages. Display the banner in your classroom or parish hall.

Quick Check

✔ *What did Jesus' dying on the cross do for us?* (His dying saved us from sin.)

✔ *What does original sin make it difficult for us to do?* (Original sin makes it difficult for us to love and obey God.)

WE RESPOND

___ minutes

Connect to Life Have the students complete the crossword. Invite volunteers to explain why Jesus is our Savior.

Revisit the Prayer Space Gather around the prayer table. Say the titles *Lamb of God, Bread of Life,* and *Light of the World.* Ask the students to hold up objects associated with these titles. Then invite the students to pray silently in gratitude to Jesus.

Plan Ahead for Day 4

Catechist Goal: To highlight that the disciples spread the good news of Jesus Christ

Preparation: Have available large strips of poster board and markers.

Chapter 1 • Day 4

Catechist Goal

• To highlight that the disciples spread the good news of Jesus Christ

Our Faith Response

• To identify ways the Church spreads the good news of Jesus Christ today

Church

grace

Lesson Materials

• large strips of poster board

• markers

Teaching Note

Disciples of Christ

In his farewell to his disciples, Jesus reminded them, "It was not you who chose me, but I who chose you" (John 15:16). That is the good news that you and your students should celebrate throughout the year. At Baptism God chose us to be his children. We not only become disciples of Christ but also brothers and sisters in Christ.

The disciples spread the good news of Jesus Christ.

WE GATHER

✝ *Loving Father, thank you for sending your Son to save us!*

During the past year you have changed and grown. Take a minute to think about this time last year. Write one way you have changed since then.

____

____

____

WE BELIEVE

Jesus kept his promise to his disciples. After Jesus ascended to his Father in heaven, the Holy Spirit was sent to strengthen the disciples. The day on which the Holy Spirit came to the disciples is called *Pentecost*. The Holy Spirit helped the disciples to believe that the risen Jesus was truly the Christ, the Anointed One of God.

The disciples were so excited that they began to tell everyone the good news of Jesus Christ. Many of those who heard this message were baptized.

The disciples went everywhere teaching about Jesus. They wanted all people to learn about Jesus.

They wanted others to come to believe in him as the Christ and to be baptized. This was the beginning of the Church. The **Church** is the community of people who are baptized and follow Jesus Christ.

When we are baptized we become members of the Church. Baptism cleanses and frees us from original sin and from any sins we may have committed. In Baptism we are given new life.

26

Lesson Plan

WE GATHER ___ minutes

✝ **Pray** Pray the Sign of the Cross and recite the *We Gather* prayer.

Focus on Life Read aloud the directions for the *We Gather* activity. Invite the students to write down one way they have changed. Ask them to share responses. Then discuss why each photo shows a change or growth. Tell the students that in this lesson they will learn that in following Jesus, the disciples' lives were changed.

WE BELIEVE ___ minutes

Read the Text Have volunteers read aloud the *We Believe* paragraphs. Emphasize these important points:

• Jesus sent the Holy Spirit to strengthen the disciples. The disciples spread the good news of Jesus. We are disciples of Jesus.

• The Church is the community of disciples who are baptized and follow Jesus. We are members of the Church.

• In Baptism we are freed from original sin. We receive grace, a share in God's own life.

Report the Work of the Disciples Give the students large strips of poster board and markers. Ask them to write newspaper headlines that describe ways the disciples spread the good news. Share the headlines with the group. You may want to display them in the hallway or in the parish hall.

The new life we receive is a share in God's own life. This gift of God's life in us is **grace**.

The gift of grace helps us to be Jesus' disciples. As disciples we remember how Jesus lived. We work together to live as he did. When we follow the example of Jesus and share his love, we help the Church to grow.

WE RESPOND

Complete these statements.

I am the community of people who are baptized and follow Jesus Christ.

I am the

C H U R C H.

I am the day that the Holy Spirit came upon the disciples.

I am

P E N T E C O S T.

I am the gift of God's life.

I am

G R A C E.

The first disciples shared all they knew about Jesus. How does the Church do this today?

____

____

____

Key Words

Church the community of people who are baptized and follow Jesus Christ

grace the gift of God's life in us

27

Activity Bank

Parish

Preparing for the Sacrament of Initiation

Activity Materials: construction paper, markers or crayons

Invite people who are participating in the RCIA (Rite of Christian Initiation of Adults) in your parish to speak to your class about their experiences in the RCIA. Encourage the students to ask appropriate questions of these visitors. Encourage the students to make and send friendship cards to people enrolled in your parish RCIA program and to pray for them as they prepare for the sacraments of Baptism, Confirmation, and the Eucharist.

Multiple Intelligences

Bodily-Kinesthetic

Activity Materials: videocassette recorder

Invite the students to work in small groups to make a cheer, rap song, or dance performance about spreading the good news. Encourage them to consult their text for ideas. Arrange for the presentation of performances.

Quick Check

✔ *Why did the disciples spread the news of Jesus?* (The apostles spread the good news because they wanted people to learn about and believe in Jesus.)

✔ *What gift do we receive in Baptism that helps us to be Jesus' disciples?* (We receive the gift of grace in Baptism.)

WE RESPOND

___ minutes

Connect to Life Have the students complete the statements in the *We Respond* activity. Explain: *The missing words are from the We Believe section of the day's lesson.* Help the students see the connection between the disciples' work and the Church's work of today.

Pray Invite the students to pray silently.

Plan Ahead for Day 5

Catechist Goal: To review chapter ideas and their relationship to our faith life

Preparation: Make copies of Chapter 1 Test in the Grade 4 Assessment Book (option)

Enrichment Ideas

Chapter Story

"If I have to take this trust walk, I want a partner I know I can trust," Stacy grumbled. Her partner, Jason, blindfolded her as their teacher instructed. Stacy said to him, "I can't picture you taking care of me." "Well, I will," Jason replied. "Trust me."

"Remember," Mr. Matthews said. "You cannot touch your partner. You must guide him or her by giving voice commands only. Now let's get started."

"Now take four steps forward . . ." said Jason. "Good. Now turn to your right. Take seven steps forward . . . and turn to your right again. Okay, take six steps forward and we'll be in the hallway."

"No way!" Stacy objected. "If I take six steps, I'll run into the wall." Instead Stacy turned to the right and ran into the wall. "Will you listen to me, now?" asked Jason. "Good, now we're in the hallway. Walk straight ahead until I tell you to stop . . . OK, stop. Turn to your left and find the knob on the water fountain. Good. Now turn the knob on before you put your head down to drink."

"I don't need your help," Stacy said. The next moment Stacy's dripping head popped up from the water fountain.

Later the classroom was filled with excited talking and laughing. Mr. Matthews said, "I'd like to hear your thoughts on comparing your trusting a partner and trusting in God. Kim, why don't you start?"

"Well, sometimes we aren't sure where to go or how to get there. That feels scary, and it's a good time to trust God to find the way."

"How about you, Jason? You were a leader. Do you have any feelings on the subject?"

"Well, Stacy didn't want to trust me. I really did want her to get through the walk safely. I think God is like that. I think God wants us to trust him."

▶ *Think of someone you trust. Why do you trust that person?*

FAITH and MEDIA

▶ On Day 2 you might suggest to the students that they expand their ideas for the *We Believe* "Living the Beatitudes" activity into a "What can I do?" advertising campaign. Ask the students to consider the best medium (television, radio, print, or the Internet) and the best approach (words, pictures, music, or a combination) to use to tell different audiences (children their own age, younger children, teenagers, or adults) about living the Beatitudes. This activity might be combined later in the week with the Day 5 Assessment Activity.

▶ On Day 4 the students learn about the mission of the first disciples and our mission as disciples of Christ today. Remind the students that the Church today makes use of many different media (books, newspapers and magazines, movies, television, radio, and the Internet) to carry out its mission in the world.

CHAPTER PROJECT: SKITS FOR BEATITUDES

After the students have learned about the Beatitudes in this chapter, form the class into small groups and assign a beatitude to each group. Encourage the students to present skits to illustrate their assigned beatitude. Have each group work together on a script and possible costumes, props, and scenery. If members of the group are musically inclined, encourage them to make music a part of their presentation. They can include original songs to convey the meaning of their beatitude. Intersperse the presentation of these skits at various points during the week. Then ask the students to reflect on what they learned from each presentation.

Connections

To Liturgy

After the Last Supper Jesus prayed that the cup of suffering might be taken away. Yet he chose not his will but his Father's will to be done. Even in his suffering on the cross Jesus trusted in God his Father. When we pray the Our Father at each celebration of the Eucharist, we are reminded of Jesus' trust in God. We say "Thy will be done on earth as it is in heaven." Only in perfect trust could Jesus do his Father's will and endure the pain of the cross to save all people.

To Catholic Social Teaching

Life and Dignity of the Human Person
Emphasize that the Beatitudes of Jesus are a strong defense of the human dignity of all people. Jesus' words remind us that all people are valuable in God's eyes. Those who are the poor will inherit the Kingdom of God. Those who suffer from hunger will be satisfied. As Jesus' followers, we can help God's kingdom grow by helping to feed the poor, by standing up for the most vulnerable in our society—the unborn and the elderly.

To Vocations

Discuss with the students the importance of responding to God's love by the way they choose to live their lives. The call to serve God, whether as priest, married, religious, or single, is founded upon our baptismal vocation. That original calling is to become like Christ. Following the Beatitudes and serving one another mean trusting in God to give us the grace to do so. Use the photos on pages 38–39 to illustrate ways of serving God.

Meeting Individual Needs

Students with Auditory Needs

Allow auditory learners to read the chapter into a tape recorder. This will help them to hear the chapter as they are reading it. It will also allow them to play it back as often as they want to listen to it. You may also want to enlist the help of the students who are excellent readers to prepare audiotapes of key chapters. Prepare a listening corner in your classroom and encourage the students to use it often.

ADDITIONAL RESOURCES

Book *Prayers and Practices for Young Catholics,* William H. Sadlier, 1997. This is a good summary of basic Catholic prayers and practices. Pages 27 through 32 are good at this time.

Video *The Sermon on the Mount,* CCC of America, 1997. From the series, *A Kingdom Without Frontiers,* this video presents the Beatitudes followed by the Parable of the Rich Man and Lazarus. (30 minutes)

To find more ideas for books, videos, and other learning material, visit Sadlier's

www.WEBELIEVEweb.com

Catechist Development

Connecting to the Family

by Kathy Hendricks

Kathy Hendricks is a speaker and writer specializing in topics related to religious education, spirituality, and family life. She has over 25 years' experience as a pastoral minister, teacher, and catechetical leader. Kathy is married and has two grown children.

Faith begins in the home. The family is the first school of Christian love, the place where faith is seeded, where it grows and matures. Here are six ways this happens in the midst of everyday life.

Storytelling Families tell stories—about who they are, where they come from, and what they hold dear. These stories are about ways to live and behave towards one another, about life and death, forgiveness and healing. They are stories about love. Storytelling occurs around the dinner table and in the car, at funerals and weddings, when persons, new or familiar, come to visit or stay. Family stories are essentially connected to the larger story of faith.

Celebration Welcoming new family members, sharing meals, forgiving one another are all ways in which families celebrate the presence of God in their lives. Cherished rituals and symbols express love, care, and healing in ways that go beyond what words can convey.

Prayer As they gather around a table or prepare to go to bed at night, families share and teach prayer within the framework of daily life. The rhythmic nature of prayer is woven into the fabric of each day and throughout the seasons of the year.

Morality When families set rules and provide guidelines for behavior, they promote an understanding of Christian morality as a code of conduct that puts family members in strong relationship with God and with one another.

Catechist Development Topics (Topic and Guide Page)

Community Taking one's place in the family provides the first experience of what it means to belong to something bigger than oneself. It means belonging to a community of people who love and care for one another.

Outreach Families' love often spills beyond itself and into the larger community through acts of charity and justice. Whether hosting a foreign exchange student or fixing a Thanksgiving basket for someone in need, families can demonstrate the Church's mission of bringing the good news of Jesus Christ to others.

Resources

A Family Perspective in Church and Society—Tenth Anniversary Edition. Washington, D.C.: United States Catholic Conference, Inc., 1998.

Curran, Dolores. *Traits of a Healthy Family.* New York: Ballantine Books, 1983.

Ways to Implement Connecting to the Family

- Invite the children to draw a picture and tell a story about a favorite family celebration. What did they do (ritual)? What special food or treasured family artifacts (symbol) did they use?
- Send home simple prayer ideas that families can use together. These might come from *We Believe*, other resources, or from the children themselves. Younger children can write simple prayers and take them home. Older children might compose a class prayer for use as grace before or after meals or at another family gathering.
- Create a class mural about families. Have each child color a part of the mural, including a picture of who lives in his or her family and what is special or unique about the household.
- Emphasize images of God who loves us the way loving parents and guardians care for their children.
- Compile a list of rules that the children might want to live by when they are at home. Compare the rules to the ways that we are asked to behave as Christians.
- Be sensitive to various family situations. Use language that keeps in mind children who come from single-parent homes, from blended families, or from homes where a guardian is the primary caregiver.

For additional ideas, activities, and opportunities, visit Sadlier's

www.WEBELIEVEweb.com

With thanks to:

Debby Welch
St. Margaret of Scotland Parish
Green Tree, PA

Debby uses a fun game that involves the children and their family with the parish. Each week, the children are encouraged to lead their families as disciples of Jesus Christ. At the end of the week, Debby invites each child to stand up and tell what his or her family has done to help someone in need. The name of the child and the family's good deed is written on the chalkboard. All the children and their families are congratulated. Then Debby asks her group to decide on the family who will receive a torch. This unlit torch is made by the children from construction paper, plastic cups and dial rods. The "Good News" torch is sent home with the child to the family with a thank-you card signed by the entire class. Debby makes sure that all families get a chance to "win." The children love the game, and families have offered positive feedback.

Notes

Name ____________________

A Disciple's Promise

I, ________________________________,

a disciple of Jesus Christ,

promise to do my best to continue Jesus' work.

- ✝ I will share the good news of Jesus.
- ✝ I will praise God and bring his love to others.
- ✝ I will work for justice and peace.

Signed on this __________ day

of the month of ____________________

in the year __________

by

____

Signature

Jesus Leads Us to Happiness

✝ We Gather in Prayer

Leader: Let us listen to what Jesus promises to those who trust in his ways.

Reader: "When he saw the crowds, he went up the mountain, and after he had sat down, his disciples came to him. He began to teach them, saying:

'Blessed are the poor in spirit,
for theirs is the kingdom of heaven.
Blessed are they who mourn,
for they will be comforted.'"
(Matthew 5:1–4)

Blest Are They

Refrain:
Rejoice and be glad!
Blessed are you, holy are you!
Rejoice and be glad!
Yours is the kingdom of God!

Reader: "Blessed are the meek,
for they will inherit the land.
Blessed are they who hunger
and thirst for righteousness,
for they will be satisfied."
(Matthew 5:5–6)

(Refrain)

Reader: "Blessed are the merciful,
for they will be shown mercy.
Blessed are the clean of heart,
for they will see God."
(Matthew 5:7–8)

(Refrain)

Reader: "Blessed are the peacemakers,
for they will be called children of God.
Blessed are they who are persecuted for the sake of righteousness,
for theirs is the kingdom of heaven."
(Matthew 5:9–10)

(Refrain)

31

Preparing to Pray

In this prayer the students will reflect on Jesus' teaching of the Beatitudes and rejoice in the happiness that comes from trusting in God.

- Practice singing.
- Assign the parts of leader, readers, and those who will place the items on the prayer table. Allow the students who will read time to practice.

For words and music to all the songs on the Grade 4 CD, see Sadlier's *We Believe* Program Songbook.

The Prayer Space

Gather the following items. They represent each beatitude (in the order presented in the *We Gather* prayer). Obtain pictures of: Mary, someone who is sad or crying, an individual helping another person, and a court room; a crucifix; a heart made from white paper; an image of two people shaking hands; a book on the lives of the saints.

This Week's Liturgy

Visit **www.webelieveweb.com** for this week's liturgical readings and other seasonal material.

Lesson Plan

We Gather in Prayer ___ minutes

✝ Pray

- Invite the students to gather together with the words *We gather in prayer.*
- Ask the students to open their books to page 31, and read the title of the chapter together.
- Pray the Sign of the Cross with the students and signal the leader to begin.
- As the readers read each Beatitude, the designated students should display the item and then place it on the prayer table.
- In conclusion invite the students to explain which beatitude is depicted in the photo. (Accept all reasonable answers.)

Home Connection Update

Review the activities on the Chapter 1 family page. Ask volunteers to give examples that show the family page helped to bring them closer to God and to their families.

Catechist Goal

- To introduce the Beatitudes taught by Jesus

Our Faith Response

- To identify ways to live out the Beatitudes as a disciple of Jesus

Beatitudes

Lesson Materials

- overhead projector
- transparency sheet
- marker
- beach ball (option)

Teaching Tip

Personal Safety

Without discounting the emphasis on trust in this unit, alert the students to the fact that no one—parent, teacher, priest, or any other authority figure in their lives—may abuse or betray their trust. Caution them that if they feel that someone is acting inappropriately toward them, they should get out of the situation quickly and tell someone about it.

Jesus taught the Beatitudes.

WE GATHER

✝ *God, help us to live as you want us to.*

Think about a time when you did something that was good and kind. How did you feel?

WE BELIEVE

The disciples saw how Jesus treated people. He cared about others and responded to their needs. Jesus taught his disciples to do the same.

Jesus wanted the disciples to live the way he lived. The **Beatitudes** are teachings of Jesus that describe the way to live as his disciples. We learn from the Beatitudes that God offers hope to every person. We each have a reason to trust in God's love.

In the Beatitudes the word *blessed* means "happy." Jesus explains in the Beatitudes that we will be happy when we love God and trust him as Jesus did.

In the first column on the chart is a list of the Beatitudes. In the second column is a list of ways we can live the Beatitudes. In the third column write what you can do to live each Beatitude. Share your examples.

Key Word

Beatitudes teachings of Jesus that describe the way to live as his disciples

34

Lesson Plan

WE GATHER ___ minutes

✝ **Pray** Pray the Sign of the Cross and the *We Gather* prayer.

Focus on Life Have the students share their answers to the *We Gather* question. Explain: *Doing kind deeds for others not only makes other people happy but also brings us a sense of happiness, too.* Tell the students that in this lesson they will learn about the happiness that comes from living out the Beatitudes.

WE BELIEVE ___ minutes

Identify Key Concepts Have volunteers read aloud the *We Believe* paragraphs. Ask the students to identify the main idea in each paragraph. List the main ideas on the board.

Do the Activity Explain the directions for this activity. You may want to begin by helping the students describe how to live the first Beatitude. This activity may be done individually or with a partner. Allow the students time to share their examples of living the Beatitudes.

Play a Beatitudes Game Help the students to remember the Beatitudes by playing a game. Beforehand, have the Beatitudes printed on a transparency for all to see. Gather the students in a circle and give one student a beach ball. The first student chooses a Beatitude and says the first part, *Blessed are the poor in spirit . . .* and then passes the ball to another classmate who finishes the Beatitude, *. . . for theirs is the kingdom of heaven.* That person then chooses another Beatitude and the game continues. The students can refer to the transparency if necessary.

Matthew 5:3–10

The Beatitudes	Living the Beatitudes	I can ...
"Blessed are the poor in spirit, for theirs is the kingdom of heaven.	We are "poor in spirit" when we depend on God and make God more important than anyone or anything else in our lives.	
Blessed are they who mourn, for they will be comforted.	We "mourn" when we are sad because of the selfish ways people treat one another.	
Blessed are the meek, for they will inherit the land.	We are "meek" when we are patient, kind, and respectful to all people, even those who do not respect us.	
Blessed are they who hunger and thirst for righteousness, for they will be satisfied.	We "hunger and thirst for righteousness" when we search for justice and treat everyone fairly.	
Blessed are the merciful, for they will be shown mercy.	We are "merciful" when we forgive others and do not take revenge on those who hurt us.	
Blessed are the clean of heart, for they will see God.	We are "clean of heart" when we are faithful to God's teachings and try to see God in all people and in all situations.	
Blessed are the peacemakers, for they will be called children of God.	We are "peacemakers" when we treat others with love and respect and when we help others to stop fighting and make peace.	
Blessed are they who are persecuted for the sake of righteousness, for theirs is the kingdom of heaven."	We are "persecuted for the sake of righteousness" when others disrespect us for living as disciples of Jesus and following his example.	

Jesus has a message for those who live the Beatitudes. He says, "Rejoice and be glad, for your reward will be great in heaven" (Matthew 5:12).

WE RESPOND

Pray the Beatitudes. Ask Jesus to help you to follow them and to live as his disciples.

35

ACTIVITY BANK

Faith and Media

Beatitudes Presentation

Activity Materials: overhead projector, blank transparencies, transparency markers

Form small groups and provide them with transparencies and markers. Assign each group one of the Beatitudes. Ask them to work together to draw a visual representation of the Beatitude. Ask each group to explain its drawing. Invite comments from the rest of the class. Congratulate each group for its presentation.

Multiple Intelligences

Musical-Rhythmic

Activity Materials: recordings or sheet music of songs depicting the Beatitudes

Many of the songs and hymns sung during Mass echo the words of the Beatitudes. Use songs that the students sing regularly at Mass in their parishes. One example is "Blest Are They," by David Haas, which was sung in the opening prayer of this chapter. Have the students identify the lyrics that refer to the Beatitudes.

Quick Check

✔ *What are the Beatitudes?* (The Beatitudes are teachings of Jesus that describe the way to live as his disciples.)

✔ *What role does trust play in living out the Beatitudes?* (As Jesus' disciples, we trust that the Beatitudes will lead us to happiness and greater reliance on God.)

WE RESPOND

___ minutes

Pray Read aloud the Beatitudes. Invite the students to reflect prayerfully on the Beatitude that they feel has the most meaning for their lives. Invite those who wish to share to do so now. Conclude by asking the students to pray silently to Jesus, asking for his help to live out the Beatitudes.

Plan Ahead For Day 3

Catechist Goal: To explain that Jesus taught about the Kingdom of God

Preparation: Have suggestions ready for the *We Respond* activity.

Chapter 2 • Day 3

Catechist Goal

- To explain that Jesus taught about the Kingdom of God

Our Faith Response

- To recognize ways we can help God's Kingdom grow

Kingdom of God
justice

Lesson Materials

- crayons or markers

Teaching Note

Presenting the Kingdom of God

Explain that the Kingdom of God is real. When Jesus announced that the Kingdom of God was at hand, he also proclaimed a plan of action: *live the Beatitudes*. The poor, the meek, the hungry, and the peacemakers will share in the kingdom. The Church teaches that these are people who need to be served now and as Jesus' disciples we must serve them. Take a few moments to read Matthew 25: 31–40. This passage clearly shows that the Kingdom of God is real.

Jesus taught about the Kingdom of God.

WE GATHER

✝ *Blessed and happy are they who follow God's way.*

Unscramble these letters to answer the clue.

E A B I E T D T U S

Some of Jesus' most important teachings were the

B E A T I T U D E S.

WE BELIEVE

We learn from the gospels that the Kingdom of God was an important part of Jesus' teaching. Jesus taught that the **Kingdom of God** is the power of God's love active in the world. This power is shown in Jesus' words and actions.

Jesus taught that the Kingdom of God would grow if people believed in and shared God's love. This is why the Beatitudes are so important. The Beatitudes give us a picture of the way disciples of Christ should act and think. They help us to understand how to live as Christians.

Jesus taught his disciples about God's Kingdom. He tried to explain to them that the Kingdom of God had already begun.

Luke 17:20–21

Jesus was once asked when the Kingdom of God would come. He answered, "The coming of the kingdom of God cannot be observed, and no one will announce, 'Look, here it is,' or, 'There it is.' For behold, the kingdom of God is among you" (Luke 17:20–21).

Jesus wanted his disciples to know that God's love was a powerful force among them. Jesus showed them that God's Kingdom is a kingdom of love and justice. **Justice** means respecting the rights of others and giving them what is rightfully theirs.

When we live as Jesus did, we help to bring God's love to others. When we are forgiving, merciful, just, and faithful to God, we help to build the Kingdom of God.

As more and more people receive God's love and live as Jesus did, the Kingdom of God grows. It will continue to grow until Jesus returns in glory at the end of time.

Kingdom of God the power of God's love active in the world

justice respecting the rights of others and giving them what is rightfully theirs

36

Lesson Plan

WE GATHER

___ minutes

✝ **Pray** Pray the Sign of the Cross and the *We Gather* prayer.

Focus on Life Have a volunteer read aloud the *We Gather* activity directions. Have the students work in pairs. Help the students to understand that the Beatitudes teach us how to live as God wants us to live. Tell the students that in this lesson they will learn how we are to help the Kingdom of God to grow.

WE BELIEVE

___ minutes

Read the Text Ask a volunteer to read aloud the *We Believe* statement. Then have volunteers read aloud the first three *We Believe* paragraphs. Ask them:

- *What is the Kingdom of God?* (The Kingdom of God is the power of God's love active in the world.)
- *What did Jesus say people needed to do in order for the kingdom of God to grow?* (The Kingdom of God will grow if people believe in and share God's love.)
- *What do the Beatitudes teach us?* (The Beatitudes teach us how to live as Christians in service of the kingdom.)

Discuss Scripture Have a student read aloud Luke 17:20–21. Ask: *Did Jesus' answer satisfy those who questioned him? If no, why?* Explain that Jesus' answer had two parts. One part was negative. A person cannot see the kingdom the way he or she expects to. The second part is positive. A person who believes and trusts in Jesus' words and actions knows the Kingdom of God is already here. Ask a volunteer to read aloud the rest of *We Believe*.

WE RESPOND

Through Jesus' actions and words, the Kingdom of God was made present. Draw or write about one way that Jesus did this. Write one way you can do this, too.

37

Activity Bank

Catholic Social Teaching

Call to Family, Community, and Participation

Activity Materials: drawing paper; crayons or markers

Explain that in serving others in our families and communities, we serve God and help his kingdom grow. Yet we need to know our limits, what we can do and not do, as disciples of Jesus. Encourage the students to prepare now by learning basic skills, such as planning a course of action and learning to focus on manageable tasks. Invite them to think of specific ways they can help God's Kingdom to grow in their family and community. Suggest that they form groups to design a pamphlet identifying these ways. Circulate the pamphlets among the students' families. Display a few of the pamphlets in the classroom or church's vestibule.

Imagine God's Kingdom Have the students ask themselves: *What would today's world be like if we all followed Jesus' way?* Have a volunteer list the responses on the board. These answers can help the students when they complete the *We Respond* activity.

Quick Check

✔ *How did Jesus describe the Kingdom of God?* (Jesus said that the Kingdom of God was one of love and service.)

✔ *How can we help make God's Kingdom grow?* (We can help God's Kingdom to grow by sharing God's love with others in our words and actions in Jesus' name.)

WE RESPOND

___ minutes

Connect to Life Have the students complete the *We Respond* activity. Provide time for the students to share what they wrote or drew.

Revisit the Prayer Space Gather the students in the prayer space. Invite the students to recall how the world would be today if we followed Jesus' way. Conclude the lesson with the song in the opening prayer.

Plan Ahead For Day 4

Catechist Goal: To examine how Jesus' disciples share his mission

Preparation: Make copies of Reproducible Master 2. Have index cards available.

Catechist Goal

• To examine how Jesus' disciples share his mission

Our Faith Response

• To identify ourselves with Jesus' mission

mission

Lesson Materials

- copies of Reproducible Master 2
- index cards
- colored pencils or markers

As Catholics...

Social Justice

After you have presented the day's lesson, read aloud the *As Catholics* text. Highlight ways that parishioners are involved in the work of making peace and justice a reality. Ask the students to choose one way they will help in their parish efforts.

Jesus' disciples share his mission.

WE GATHER

✝ *Jesus, teach us how to live a blessed life.*

Read the following sentences. What could you do in each situation? How could your actions show others that you are a disciple of Jesus Christ?

Someone is having trouble opening a door.

I ______________________ .

Two friends are bullying a classmate.

I ______________________ .

Two family members are having an argument.

I ______________________ .

A new family has moved into the neighborhood.

I ______________________ .

WE BELIEVE

Jesus spread the message of God's love everywhere he went. This was Jesus' work, or mission. He asked his disciples to do the same work.

After Jesus' Ascension, the disciples continued Jesus' work. Their **mission** was to share the good news of Jesus Christ and to spread the Kingdom of God. This is how they carried out their mission:

- They told others the good news that Jesus is the Son of God who died and rose to save us from sin.
- They baptized those who heard the good news and believed.
- They gathered together to praise God and break bread as Jesus did at the Last Supper.
- They showed by their words and actions that God's love was active in their lives and in the world.
- They reached out to the poor and healed the sick and suffering.

Key Word

mission the work of sharing the good news of Jesus Christ and spreading the Kingdom of God

38

Lesson Plan

WE GATHER ___ minutes

✝ **Pray** Pray the Sign of the Cross and the *We Gather* prayer.

Focus on Life Have the students work independently on the *We Gather* activity. When they have finished writing, discuss what a disciple of Jesus would do in each situation. Tell the students that in this lesson they will learn ways to carry out Christ's mission.

WE BELIEVE ___ minutes

Describe Our Mission Ask a volunteer to read the *We Believe* statement. Ask the students: *What do you think the word* mission *means?* Form small groups. Ask the groups to read the *We Believe* paragraphs. Have them develop a word web around the word *mission*. Encourage them to add words and phrases to describe the mission Jesus asks his disciples to continue. Then ask the groups to share their work with the entire class.

Declare Our Promise Distribute Reproducible Master 2. Invite the students to read, sign, and color the promise. Suggest that they keep it in a place where they will see it often and remember what they have promised.

Quick Check

✔ *What was Jesus' mission?* (Jesus' mission was to share the message of God's love and spread his Kingdom.)

✔ *Who helps us continue Christ's mission?* (Jesus present in the Eucharist, our families, the Church, and the Holy Spirit can strengthen us and help us live out our mission.)

The mission of the first disciples is the mission of the Church today. In Baptism we become Jesus' disciples. We, too, are called to continue Jesus' work.

Like the first disciples we do not do this alone. We are joined with our families and all the members of the Church. At the Eucharist we receive Christ's Body and Blood. We are strengthened and led by the Holy Spirit to carry out Christ's mission. The Holy Spirit helps us to share the good news of Jesus Christ and to spread the Kingdom of God.

Blessed are they...

Saint Rose Philippine Duchesne

Rose Philippine Duchesne was a missionary to the United States. She was born in France, and was sent to Missouri. In St. Charles, she founded the first convent of the Society of the Sacred Heart in the United States. She had a special love for native Americans, and worked among the Potawatomi tribe in Kansas.

Saint Rose always felt that she was a failure as a missionary because she could never learn the Potawatomi language. However, she was successful. She was patient and respectful to the Potawatomi people. Her heart was always with God, and she spent much time in prayer. The tribe could sense her prayers for them, and they called her "Woman Who Prays Always." Her feast day is November 18.

"Blessed are the meek, for they will inherit the land." (Matthew 5:5)

As Catholics...

Your Catholic faith is not a private matter between you and God. You have a role to play in the mission of the Church. The Church stands up for those who are unjustly treated or denied their basic needs. The Beatitudes teach all people to do this. Right now you can pray for people who need help. You can also join with other members of the Church to work for peace and justice for all people.

Find out how the members of your parish work for peace and justice.

WE RESPOND

What are some of the ways we can live our mission as disciples of Jesus?

Complete this sentence and share your ideas with the class:

I feel most like a disciple of Jesus when I

____

____

39

ACTIVITY BANK

Church

Make a Mission I.D. Card

Activity Materials: index cards

Give each student one index card. Ask them to make a "Disciples of Jesus" identification card. Have each student print his or her name on the card and a brief description of his or her mission as a disciple. Suggest that they carry their cards in their school bags or wallets.

Multicultural Connection

Needs of the World

Activity Materials: optional tape of a newscast

Encourage the students to watch the evening news with their parents. As they watch the broadcast, have them list events or places they see locally and abroad in which Jesus' disciples can help. Discuss specific actions that could be taken to help those in distress. Discuss what the students could do about helping those in need.

WE RESPOND

___ minutes

Connect to Life Encourage the students to discuss the *We Respond* question. Have them complete the activity. Share responses. Emphasize that the Church requires all of us, according to our abilities, to continue the mission of Jesus.

Blessed are they... Explain to the students: *In eight chapters of your* **We Believe** *book a different Beatitude is featured. You will read about a saint or a group of saints who trusted in God and are an example of living out that particular Beatitude.* Have two volunteers read the text on Saint Rose Philippine Duchesne. Point out: *Saint Rose was patient, humble about her accomplishments, and relied on God in prayer. She is an example of the "meek" who give their time and love without concern for reward.*

Pray Pray this prayer to conclude the lesson: *Dear Jesus, help us to continue your mission. We want to spread the Kingdom of God by sharing your love. Amen.*

Plan Ahead for Day 5

Catechist Goal: To review chapter ideas and their relationship to our faith life

Preparation: Make copies of the Chapter 2 Test found in the Grade 4 Assessment Book (option). Provide paper, magazines, newspapers, scissors, and glue for the Assessment Activity.

Chapter 2 • **Day 5**

Catechist Goal

• To review chapter ideas and their relationship to our faith life

Our Faith Response

• To apply what has been learned to our lives

CHAPTER TEST

The Chapter 2 Test is provided in the Grade 4 Assessment Book.

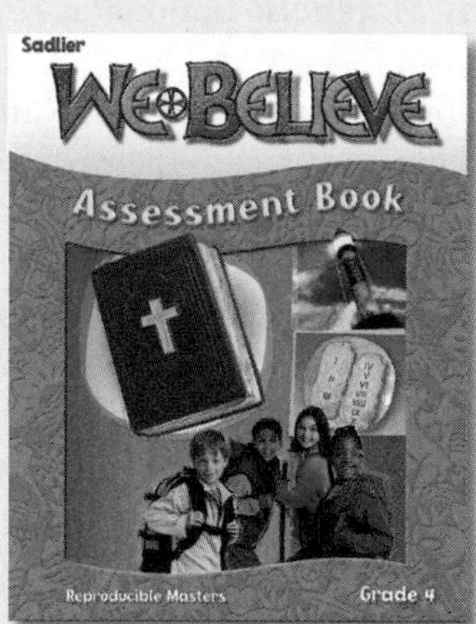

Grade 4
Chapter 2

Complete each sentence.

1. The Beatitudes are teachings of Jesus that describe the way to live as Jesus' disciples.
2. The freedom that comes from loving and trusting God and respecting all people is peace.
3. The mission of the disciples was to share the good news and to spread the Kingdom of God.
4. In the Beatitudes, the word *blessed* means "happy".

Write True or False for the following sentences. Then change the false sentences to make them true.

5. False Jesus stopped trusting God when he was tempted by the devil.
   Jesus showed his trust in God when he was tempted by the devil.
6. True We learn from the Beatitudes that God offers hope to every person.
7. True The Kingdom of God is a kingdom of love and justice.
8. False The Church today does not continue the mission of the first disciples.
   The Church today continues the mission of the first disciples.

Write a sentence to answer the question.

9–10. What did Jesus tell us about the Kingdom of God?
See pages 36–37.

Use magazines and newspapers to cut out some words and pictures that you think express the Beatitudes. Paste them on a piece of paper. Label the pictures with the Beatitudes that they describe.

40

Lesson Plan

___ minutes

Chapter Review Explain to the students that they are now going to check their understanding of the key concepts in this chapter. Have them answer questions 1–8. When finished, discuss the answers and make sure that everyone understands the chapter's content. Ask the students to complete question 9–10. Invite volunteers to share their answers. Allow pairs to use the chapter review to quiz each other.

Assessment Activity Read the activity directions to the class. Invite the students to work in pairs or in groups. Once the students have finished their collages, display them in the prayer space.

___ minutes

Reflect and Pray Discuss the students' responses to the question. Encourage them to give specific examples of what they can do. Then allow them time to write their own prayer.

Key Words Write the words on the board. Ask the students to write a sentence that illustrates the meaning without directly stating its definition. *(Example: When I pray the Beatitudes, I am encouraged to live as a disciple of Jesus.)*

Remember Have volunteers read aloud the four *We Believe* statements. Review the Beatitudes. Ask them to

We Respond in Faith

Reflect & Pray

Jesus taught us how to live as his followers when he gave us the Beatitudes. What can we do to be "poor in spirit" or "meek" or "merciful" or "peacemakers"?

Write your own prayer asking God to give you the happiness that comes from loving God and living as Jesus did.

____

____

Key Words

- **peace** (p. 33)
- **Beatitudes** (p. 34)
- **Kingdom of God** (p. 36)
- **justice** (p. 36)
- **mission** (p. 38)

Remember

- Jesus trusted God his Father.
- Jesus taught the Beatitudes.
- Jesus taught about the Kingdom of God.
- Jesus' disciples share his mission.

Our Catholic Life

Archbishop Oscar Romero

In the 1970s Oscar Romero was an archbishop in the country of El Salvador. El Salvador is in Central America. Archbishop Romero saw how the poor people were suffering and dying from hunger and war. He was dedicated to serving and defending the Church and the poor. There were some people who wanted to stop him from teaching about peace. They also did not want him speaking against injustices. Because of this he was killed one day while celebrating the Mass. Archbishop Oscar Romero's life was a living example of the Beatitudes.

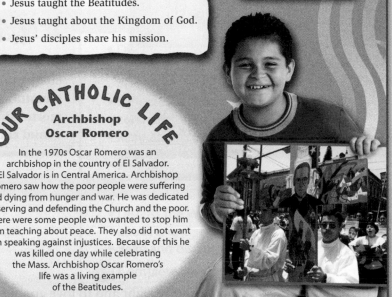

Home Connection

Sharing Faith with My Family

Make sure to send home the family page (text page 42).

Encourage the students to pray Psalm 27 with their families. Remind them to save the completed puzzle piece.

For additional information and activities, encourage families to visit Sadlier's

www.WEBELIEVEweb.com

name ways the Beatitude helps us to recognize the Kingdom of God. Explain that the Beatitudes teach us about God's Kingdom.

Our Catholic Life Read aloud the text. Ask: *Why do you think Archbishop Oscar Romero's life is called "a living example of the Beatitudes"?* Find El Salvador on the map. Encourage the students to pray for the people of El Salvador and the success of the mission of peace and justice that the archbishop started in that country. Suggest that they imitate Archbishop Oscar Romero's commitment to peace and justice. Discuss the photo and why the archbishop's image has been placed on a cross.

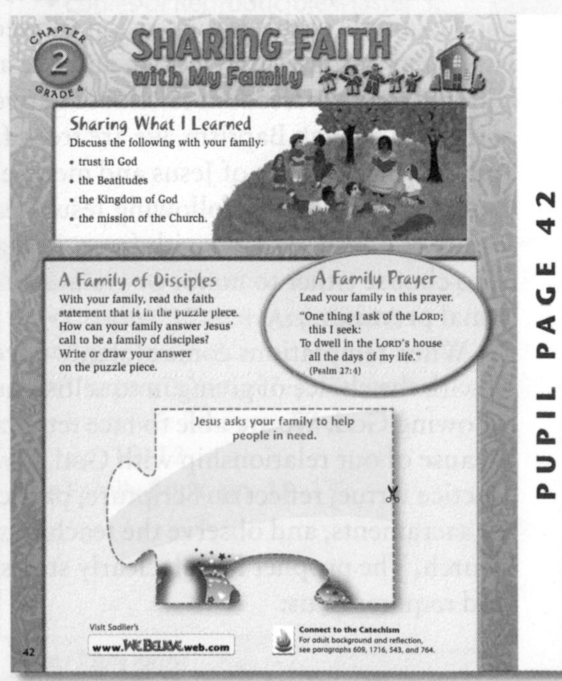

Chapter 2 Grade 4

SHARING FAITH with My Family

Sharing What I Learned

Discuss the following with your family:

- trust in God
- the Beatitudes
- the Kingdom of God
- the mission of the Church.

A Family of Disciples

With your family, read the faith statement that is in the puzzle piece. How can your family answer Jesus' call to be a family of disciples? Write or draw your answer on the puzzle piece.

A Family Prayer

Lead your family in this prayer.

"One thing I ask of the LORD; this I seek:
To dwell in the LORD's house all the days of my life."
(Psalm 27:4)

Jesus asks your family to help people in need.

Visit Sadlier's www.WEBELIEVEweb.com

Connect to the Catechism For adult background and reflection, see paragraphs 609, 1716, 543, and 764.

42

PUPIL PAGE 42

Enrichment Ideas

Chapter Story

David was usually excited about school, but lately he felt that something was wrong. This began when a new student named Devin came to school. Devin just didn't fit in with the others in the class. Their teacher had asked the class to show Devin around and be friends with him. This didn't happen. From his first day at lunch, Devin became the target of jokes and name-calling.

David listened as others made fun of Devin. David didn't join in, but he still felt bad. He wanted to tell them to leave Devin alone, but he didn't want to become another target of their jokes.

David didn't know what to do. Then Rinaldo, another boy in the class, said to David, " I noticed that you're not laughing at Devin. Let's make a pact. We'll both tell the group to stop being mean to Devin. If they laugh at us, then maybe they'll stop picking on Devin for a little while." David agreed to Rinaldo's idea. The two of them told the group to stop calling Devin names. David asked them to put themselves in Devin's place.

Some people in the group decided that Rinaldo and David were right. Some even apologized to Devin and asked him to join them during recess.

▶ *How did Rinaldo help David do the right thing?*

FAITH and MEDIA

▶ On Day 1, as the students prepare to do the *We Respond* public service announcement activity, have them recall what they have discussed in previous chapters about media as a tool for spreading God's word.

▶ On Day 3, as part of your discussion of the Good Samaritan story, ask the students to recall versions of this story or similar stories they may have seen on television, on video, in movies, or in books. This discussion also might become part of the optional activity in the Day 3 Activity Bank. Remind the students that a puppet show or dramatization of this story is another example of the many different ways we can use media to tell others the stories that Jesus told.

CHAPTER PROJECT: WORKERS FOR JUSTICE

Form small groups. Ask each group to write a modern version of the Good Samaritan story. Have each group decide which of its members will take on the roles in their modern drama. Have them practice acting out the stories they have written. Have them present their dramatizations on Day 5.

Connections

To Family

Invite the students to think of their own family members as valuable sources of advice. Allow them to reflect and share times when they faced a difficult decision and received help from their families. Help the students realize the importance of family in times of struggle.

To Catholic Social Teaching

Solidarity

As the students learn more about the effects of sin on their relationship with God and others, ask them to think of ways to counteract these effects. Point out that different groups work together for the good of others. These groups promote and advocate peace and justice in families, communities, and nations. Help the students to see that when they make an effort to serve the common good, they can make a difference in society.

To Scripture

The structures of social sin existed in Jesus' time. Find a scriptural passage that illustrates this problem, such as Jesus rejecting the disciples' desire to punish those people who did not choose to follow him (Luke 9:51–57) or Jesus' teaching about loving our enemies (Luke 6:27–36). Discuss how problems that existed in biblical times might be similar to situations that exist today (for example, oppression, slavery, economic injustices). Help the students to understand that everyone must work together to dismantle the systems and structures that support social sin.

Meeting Individual Needs

Students Who Are Visual Learners

Visual learners may have trouble if the lessons contain a great deal of discussion. Try to use visual aids along with the discussion to keep these students involved. For example, list on the board the students' responses to questions or have the students role play Scripture stories or situational activities.

ADDITIONAL RESOURCES

Videos *The Good Samaritan* Nest Entertainment, 1989. When Jesus is asked "What is the greatest commandment?" he answers with this parable. (30 minutes)

McGee and Me! Skate Expectations Tyndale Christian Video, 1990. Eleven-year-old Nicholas and friend McGee learn the value of showing love and kindness, even to those who are different from them. (30 minutes)

To find more ideas for books, videos, and other learning material, visit Sadlier's

www.WEBELIEVEweb.com

Creating an Environment for Catechesis

by Eleanor Ann Brownell, D. Min.

Eleanor Ann Brownell, D. Min. and Vice President for Religion at William H. Sadlier, Inc., has served in Catholic school and parish ministries for over forty years. She is recognized nationally and internationally for her enthusiastic seminars and workshops in Catholic education and leadership. Eleanor has a profound influence on Catholic religious education.

As a catechist, creating an environment that promotes the catechesis of your students is an important goal. A welcoming environment that promotes love and understanding is essential to enrich the children on their faith journey.

Create an environment for catechesis *within* you. The beginning to successful catechesis begins with you. The manner and spirit in which you present the stories and truths of our faith will do more to create a welcoming environment than any physical object that you place in a room.

Think for moment. How do you communicate with others? What is your personal learning style? How does this influence your teaching style? What are your strengths? What are your weaknesses? What are some ways that you can foster love and learning in your students? Solicit the opinions of your colleagues in faith. Make a plan. How would you like to guide your group on their faith journey?

Creating an environment for catechesis *around* you. There are many wonderful things you can do to physically create a welcoming environment for catechesis, such as a prayer space, learning centers, colorful posters on the walls, etc. Greeting the children personally as they enter the room, is one way to help everyone feel welcomed.

Using the *We Believe* process of "We Gather," "We Believe," and "We Respond" offers excellent opportunities of creating an environment for catechesis around you. For example, the questions found in the "We Gather" allow the children to share their life experiences. This feature is an excellent teaching tool that gives you, the catechist, an opportunity to show respect for the children's stories and opinions, while learning about their experiences.

Creating an environment for catechesis begins with you. Be open. Be honest. Be an example to the children of how a follower of Jesus listens and shares.

Catechist Development Topics (Topic and Guide Page)

Resources

Coles, Robert. *The Spiritual Life of Children.* Boston: Houghton-Mifflin, 1990.

Mongoven, Anne Marie. *The Prophetic Spirit of Catechesis.* Mahwah: Paulist Press, 2000.

Ways to Implement Creating an Environment for Catechesis

- Share your own ideas and stories with the children. As they get to know you, they will be more willing to participate in the class or group.

- Invite the children to make a group or class list of words that "help" or "heal," and encourage them to avoid using words that "hurt." Set an example by being encouraging, complimentary, and optimistic. Avoid critical or judgmental responses.

- Get to know your children. Try to have causal conversations individually and as a group, as often as possible. Meet the children's parents or guardians. Encourage interactive communication between the home and the parish or school.

- You might want to have music playing as the children settle for the "We Gather" discussion or activity. The *We Believe* CDs are excellent resources.

- Build community in your class or group by encouraging everyone to participate. Include fun activities in your lessons. Share a laugh with your class or group. Bring your children together by showing how much you enjoy being with them.

- Personalize your room however possible. Display photographs of the children, class work, artwork, etc. Children who see their names in the room get a feeling of belonging.

For additional ideas, activities, and opportunities, visit Sadlier's

www.WEBELIEVEweb.com

With thanks to:

Zee Ann Poerio
Third Grade Teacher
St. Louise de Marillac School
Pittsburgh, PA

Zee Ann Poerio asks her students, "What would Jesus want us to do?" to create an environment for catechesis. At the beginning of the year, Zee Ann has her students work together to make a list of classroom rules. She writes their rules on a large poster board. Then, she tells her students that they only need to remember one thing and tears up the rules. She writes on the board, *What would Jesus want us to do?* Zee Ann tells her children to ask themselves that question whenever they are making a choice. If ever there is a problem in the class during the year, she asks her students, "Is that something Jesus would want us to do?" This one question helps everyone learn to make the right choices.

Notes

Name ____

Work with a partner. Find the answers for 1–5. Then write the circled letters of each answer in the larger cirles below. Now unscramble them to find the word that completes the sentence at the bottom of the page.

1. Through faith we are all _____ of God in Christ Jesus.

2. Jesus went out of his way to care for the rich and _____.

3. Jesus' _____ is our example of the way to live in society.

4. We are called to value and _____ all people.

5. In Jesus' time, there was hatred between the Jews and the _____.

As _____ of Jesus, we should live a life that shows we value and respect all human beings.

Sin in Our World

3

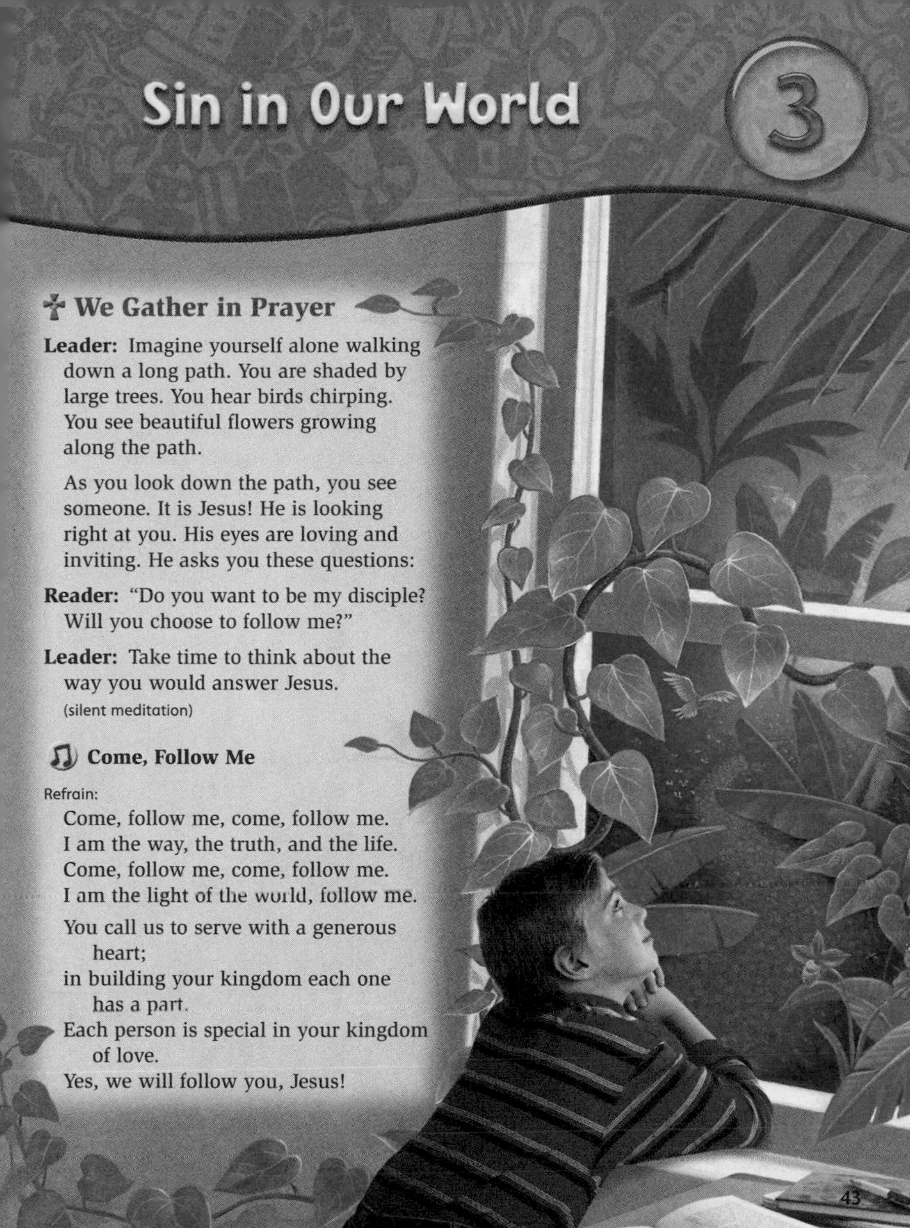

We Gather in Prayer

Leader: Imagine yourself alone walking down a long path. You are shaded by large trees. You hear birds chirping. You see beautiful flowers growing along the path.

As you look down the path, you see someone. It is Jesus! He is looking right at you. His eyes are loving and inviting. He asks you these questions:

Reader: "Do you want to be my disciple? Will you choose to follow me?"

Leader: Take time to think about the way you would answer Jesus.
(silent meditation)

Come, Follow Me

Refrain:
Come, follow me, come, follow me.
I am the way, the truth, and the life.
Come, follow me, come, follow me.
I am the light of the world, follow me.

You call us to serve with a generous heart;
in building your kingdom each one has a part.
Each person is special in your kingdom of love.
Yes, we will follow you, Jesus!

Preparing to Pray

The students will reflect on being disciples of Jesus and respond in song.

• Play "Come, Follow Me," #3, Grade 4 CD. Have the students practice singing.

• Choose a volunteer to be the reader. Give him or her the time to practice reading the questions.

The Prayer Space

• Place a small table in the prayer space. On the table place a picture or statue of Jesus (if possible, one with his arms extended) and a Bible opened to the gospels.

• Display photographs of roads or pathways. Also display photos of different sources of light.

This Week's Liturgy

Visit **www.webelieveweb.com** for this week's readings, liturgical colors, and feasts of saints.

Lesson Plan

We Gather in Prayer ___ minutes

Pray

• Use the words *We Gather in prayer* to invite the students to gather at the table.

• Explain: *For this prayer, I want you to use your imagination. Close your eyes. Listen carefully.*

• Read the leader's words. Have the reader read the question. Then provide a minute for silent meditation.

• Sing "Come, Follow Me" together.

Home Connection Update

Review the activities on the Chapter 2 family page. Call on volunteers to share ways their families help people in need. Remind the students to save the puzzle piece.

Chapter 3 • Day 1

Catechist Goal

- To present that God gives us the freedom to choose

Our Faith Response

- To make good choices at home and school

free will
sin
temptation

Lesson Materials

- puppets (store-bought or homemade)

Teaching Note

Focus on God's Love

An original meaning of the word *scruple* is a small stone. The word *scruple* is the root of the word *scrupulosity*. In approaching the topics of free will, choice, and sin, an overemphasis on human failure might plant the seeds of scrupulosity in certain young people. Instead, encourage your students by emphasizing God's great love and his willingness to forgive us.

God gives us the freedom to choose.

WE GATHER

✝ *Jesus, I choose to follow you.*

Have you ever seen a puppet show? The puppeteer controls every move of each puppet. Think about the way you would feel if someone controlled your every move.

WE BELIEVE

When God created us he gave us the gift of **free will**. Free will is the freedom to decide when and how to act. We use our free will when we think for ourselves and make decisions.

God wants us to follow his law to love him, ourselves, and others. However, God does not force us to do this.

Choices people make that help them to know, love, and serve God are good choices. Yet sometimes people choose things that lead them away from God's love.

44

Lesson Plan

WE GATHER ___ minutes

✝ **Pray** Pray the Sign of the Cross together and the *We Gather* prayer.

Focus on Life Read aloud the *We Gather* questions. Have a few volunteers use puppets to interact with the rest of the students. Have the students share the way they would feel about someone controlling everything they do. Use the *Chapter Story* to illustrate the importance of making our own choices. After discussing the story, tell the students that in this lesson they will learn that God gives us the freedom to choose to love him and follow his laws and avoid sin.

WE BELIEVE ___ minutes

Read the Text Have a volunteer read aloud the *We Believe* statement. Have volunteers read aloud the *We Believe* paragraphs. Emphasize these points:

- Free will is a gift we have been given by God. God gave us this freedom so we can choose to love him.
- Although we have the freedom to choose, God wants us to follow his law to love him and others.
- When we choose to turn away from God's love, we sin.
- Temptation is an attraction to choose sin.

Remember the Key Words Write each key word on the board. Invite the students to recall aloud the definitions.

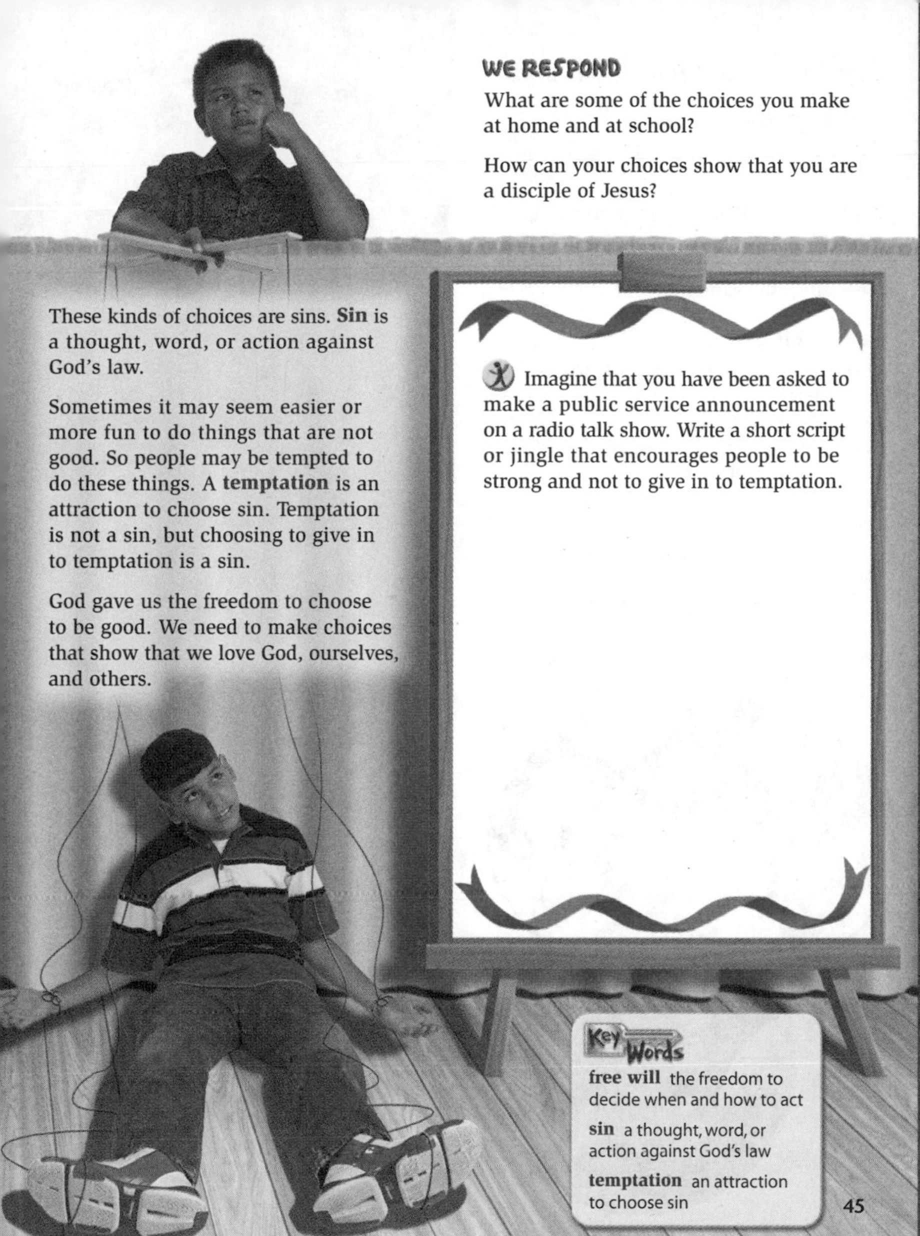

WE RESPOND

What are some of the choices you make at home and at school?

How can your choices show that you are a disciple of Jesus?

These kinds of choices are sins. **Sin** is a thought, word, or action against God's law.

Sometimes it may seem easier or more fun to do things that are not good. So people may be tempted to do these things. A **temptation** is an attraction to choose sin. Temptation is not a sin, but choosing to give in to temptation is a sin.

God gave us the freedom to choose to be good. We need to make choices that show that we love God, ourselves, and others.

Imagine that you have been asked to make a public service announcement on a radio talk show. Write a short script or jingle that encourages people to be strong and not to give in to temptation.

Key Words

free will the freedom to decide when and how to act

sin a thought, word, or action against God's law

temptation an attraction to choose sin

45

ACTIVITY BANK

Multiple Intelligences

Bodily-Kinesthetic

Form small groups. Encourage each group to write a short skit portraying temptation to sin. Each skit should have two different endings. In one ending the character will give in to temptation, while in the other he or she will follow God's laws. Have groups present their skits. Conclude by emphasizing that good choices are ones that help us to know, love, and serve God.

Quick Check

✔ *When do we use free will?* (We use our free will when we think for ourselves and make decisions.)

✔ *What is sin?* (Sin is a thought, word, or action against God's law.)

WE RESPOND ___ minutes

Connect to Life Have the students read the *We Respond* questions. Ask volunteers to share their responses. Read the directions for the *We Respond* activity. Have the students work in groups to write public service announcements. Provide time for the groups to share their work with the class.

Pray Pray the Sign of the Cross and the following prayer: *God, help us always to choose good.*

Plan Ahead for Day 2

Catechist Goal: To explain the fact that sin leads us away from God

Preparation: Be prepared to discuss archery in *Focus on Life.*

Chapter 3 • Day 2

Catechist Goal

- To explain the fact that sin leads us away from God

Our Faith Response

- To take responsibility for our own choices

mortal sin
venial sin

As Catholics...

Immaculate Conception.

After you have completed the lesson, invite a volunteer to read aloud the text. You may want to explain the day we call the feast of the Immaculate Conception is a holy day of obligation in the United States. On this feast day we gather with other Catholics for the celebration of the Mass.

Sin leads us away from God.

WE GATHER

✝ *Loving God, help us not to give in to temptation.*

In archery, athletes shoot an arrow at a target. Sometimes the arrow falls short of the center, or bull's-eye. How does that affect the game?

WE BELIEVE

Because we have free will, we are responsible for our choices. If we choose to do something that leads us away from God, we commit a personal sin. When we sin, we fall short of being the person God wants us to be. However, there are many people in our lives who can help us to make good choices. We can talk with and ask advice from our families, friends, and people in our schools and parishes. Most importantly, we can always call on God to help us to choose what is good.

Every sin weakens our friendship with God and others. Some people commit very serious sins. A very serious sin that breaks a person's friendship with God is a **mortal sin**. To commit mortal sin someone must freely choose to do something that he or she knows is seriously wrong. Those who commit mortal sin lose grace. Yet God never stops loving them.

A less serious sin that hurts a person's friendship with God is **venial sin**. Venial sins hold people back from being as good as God made them to be. However, those who commit venial sin still have God's gift of grace.

46

Lesson Plan

WE GATHER ___ minutes

✝ **Pray** Pray the Sign of the Cross. Ask the students to close their eyes and think about God's love for them. Then pray the *We Gather* prayer.

Focus on Life Direct the students' attention to the *We Gather* question. Encourage a discussion about the goal of archery. Point out that no archer always hits the target. This does not mean that the archer gives up. Help the students to see that everyone has imperfections. Tell the students that in this lesson they will learn how sin affects our relationship with God.

WE BELIEVE ___ minutes

Think About "Decision Helpers" Read aloud the *We Believe* statement and the first paragraph. Discuss what is happening in the two photos. Ask the students to think of people whom they can turn to when they need help making good choices. Have them list these people and refer to the list when they need advice.

Read the Text Have volunteers read aloud the remaining *We Believe* text. Emphasize these points:

- We are not alone in our decision-making. There are people who can help us to make good choices.
- Mortal sins break friendship with God, while venial sins hurt the friendship.
- If we sin, we must ask for God's forgiveness.

Key Words

mortal sin very serious sin that breaks a person's friendship with God

venial sin less serious sin that hurts a person's friendship with God

If our choices lead us away from God, we need to ask for his forgiveness. God's love and forgiveness are always there to heal and strengthen us, especially through the sacraments.

WE RESPOND

We are responsible for our choices. What does this mean to you?

Pray together:

Forgive me, Lord,
for the times I have not shown
love for you, myself, and others.

As Catholics...

In 1854, Blessed Pope Pius IX declared the Immaculate Conception of Mary, the mother of Jesus, an official teaching of the Catholic Church. This doctrine means that from the very first moment of her life, Mary was free from original sin. She was full of God's grace. We celebrate Mary's Immaculate Conception on December 8.

How does your parish celebrate this feast of Mary?

47

ACTIVITY BANK

Liturgy

Our Father

At Mass, we pray the Our Father to ask God for his forgiveness and express our forgiveness for those who hurt us. Have the students share their experiences of this part of the Mass. Invite volunteers to list on the board the different ways they have prayed the Our Father during Mass (for example, singing, holding hands, raising hands, gathering around the altar, and so on). Then invite them to share their experiences with the sign of peace that follows the Our Father (for example, handshaking, hugging, kissing family members, greetings, and so on). Help the students realize that the sign of peace represents their willingness to live in peace with their brothers and sisters in Christ. Ask the students to name some ways from our daily life we can show this willingness to live in peace.

Quick Check

✔ *What happens to our friendship with God when we sin?* (If it is a mortal sin, we break our friendship with God. If it is a venial sin, we hurt our friendship with God.)

✔ *What should we do if our choices lead us away from God?* (If our choices lead us away from God, we need to ask for his forgiveness.)

WE RESPOND

___ minutes

Connect to Life Direct the students' attention to the *We Respond* statement and question. Allow them a few minutes to write their thoughts and feelings. Invite discussion of what it means to be individuals responsible for our own choices.

Pray Pray together the *We Respond* prayer.

Plan Ahead for Day 3

Catechist Goal: To explain that sin can be both what people do and fail to do

Preparation: Be prepared to give examples of ways that failing to do something can lead people away from God.

Catechist Goal

- To explain that sin can be both what people do and fail to do

Our Faith Response

- To name ways we can help people who are in need

Sins can be things people do or fail to do.

WE GATHER

✝ *And lead us not into temptation, but deliver us from evil. Amen.*

Do your family and friends ever get angry with you over things that you do?

Do they get angry with you over things that you do not do?

WE BELIEVE

Every day, people try to love God and others. But sometimes people act in ways that offend God and other people. These kinds of offenses against God and others are called *sins of commission*. People actually *do* something wrong.

People can also sin by what they do *not do*. These kinds of sins are called *sins of omission*. For example, people may sin by *not* honoring God or *not* respecting others.

When we pray we can ask for God's forgiveness. When we celebrate the sacrament of Penance and Reconciliation, we ask God to forgive us for the wrongs that we do and for what we fail to do. We also ask for forgiveness at Mass when we pray: "I have sinned through my own fault in my thoughts and in my words, in what I have done and in what I have failed to do."

48

Teaching Tip

Bulletin Board

Make a bulletin board entitled *Good Samaritans*. Invite students to recognize people in the school, parish, or community who have gone out of their way to care for others. Ask them to write the names of these people on an index card and pin these cards on the board. Each day, thank God for the example of these Good Samaritans. Urge everyone to try to act like the Good Samaritan each day.

Lesson Plan

WE GATHER

___ minutes

✝ **Pray** Pray the *We Gather* prayer. Ask them whether they know the source of the words. Explain that these words are from the Our Father and that with these words we ask God to help us avoid temptation.

Focus on Life Have a volunteer read aloud the *We Gather* questions. Invite discussion. Help students to understand that people do not stop loving us when they get angry with us. If we have chosen to do something wrong, people who love us try to help us understand why what we did was hurtful. Tell the students that in this lesson they will learn that not doing something can be against God's law and can affect our friendship with God and others.

WE BELIEVE

___ minutes

Read the Text Read aloud the *We Believe* statement. Invite volunteers to read the *We Believe* paragraphs on page 48. Stress that sins of commission are any thought, word, or action that a person knows is wrong and then proceeds to do anyway. For example, taking God's name in vain is a sin of commission. Then explain that sins of omission are sins in which people do *not* do something that they are supposed to, such as respect God or others; for example, remaining silent when a sibling or friend is accused of a wrongdoing that someone else actually committed. We cannot judge whether a person's action (or lack of action) is a sin. That judgment is between God and that person. Whether we sin by commission or omission, we can ask for God's forgiveness.

In the Gospel of Luke we find the following story that Jesus told:

"A man fell victim to robbers as he went down from Jerusalem to Jericho. They stripped and beat him and went off leaving him half-dead. A priest happened to be going down that road, but when he saw him, he passed by on the opposite side. Likewise a Levite came to the place, and when he saw him, he passed by on the opposite side. But a Samaritan traveler who came upon him was moved with compassion at the sight. He approached the victim, poured oil and wine over his wounds and bandaged them. Then he lifted him up on his own animal, took him to an inn and cared for him."
(Luke 10:30–34)

The Samaritan made the choice to help the man who had been robbed. The priest and the Levite chose not to. Jesus asks us to choose to love God and one another. He teaches us how to overcome sin by turning to God the Father and following his will. He gives us the Holy Spirit to strengthen us. Jesus promises us that we can always count on God's mercy.

WE RESPOND

Describe the actions of the Samaritan.

How can we act more like the Samaritan in our lives?

Pray to God the Father, God the Son, and God the Holy Spirit for the strength to do good and to avoid sin.

49

Chapter 3 • **Day 3**

ACTIVITY BANK

Curriculum Connection

Art

Activity Materials: paper bags for puppets, markers, crayons or decorative material for puppets, copy of the story of the Good Samaritan. In advance set up a time when your students can spend fifteen minutes with a younger class.

Form the students into groups. Have them reread the story of the Good Samaritan. Invite them to make paper bag puppets to act out this story in a play or a puppet show for younger students. Encourage their creativity. When the students are ready, go to the classroom of the youngest students and have them perform their puppet shows.

Share a Bible Reading Invite volunteers to tell what they know about the Parable of the Good Samaritan. Ask a volunteer to read aloud the scriptural passage on page 49. Read aloud the final *We Believe* paragraph. Ask the students to think about the lack of action of the first two passers-by. In passing by the man, they might have committed the sin of omission.

Quick Check

✔ *What is a sin of commission?* (This is a sin committed by thought, word, or action.)

✔ *What is a sin of omission?* (This is a sin committed by not doing something that should be done.)

✔ *What can we do if we commit sins of commission or omission?* (We can ask for God's forgiveness and try to overcome sin.)

WE RESPOND ___ minutes

Connect to Life Read aloud the *We Respond* activity and question. Invite student responses. Help them see that God has called us to love one another. If we do all we can to love God and others, we will do good and avoid sin. Remind them that there are people who can help us to make good decisions.

Pray Pray together the Sign of the Cross. Read aloud the directions for prayer.

Plan Ahead for Day 4

Catechist Goal: To highlight that we are called to value and respect all people

Preparation: Make copies of Reproducible Master 3.

Chapter 3 • Day 4

Catechist Goal

- To highlight that we are called to value and respect all people

Our Faith Response

- To treat other people with respect

Lesson Materials

- copies of Reproducible Master 3

Teaching Tip

Confidentiality

Remind the students that confidentiality is important in the sharing process of learning. Each person in the class must feel confident that he or she can trust that others will respect and not talk about personal sharing that takes place during class discussions.

We are called to value and respect all people.

WE GATHER

✝ *Dear Jesus, open our eyes today to all of our chances to do good things for others.*

Think about all the people in the world. How are people the same? How are they different?

WE BELIEVE

Human beings do not live their lives alone. We live with others in a society, or community. An example of a society is the group of people in a town or state.

Jesus' life is our example of how to live in society. He valued and respected all human beings. He went out of his way to care for those who were poor, young, old, sick, sinners, and from other countries. Jesus taught us that we are all children of God. These words from Saint Paul remind us of Jesus' teachings:

"For through faith you are all children of God in Christ Jesus. For all of you who were baptized into Christ have clothed yourselves with Christ. There is neither Jew nor Greek, there is neither slave nor free person, there is not male and female; for you are all one in Christ Jesus." (Galatians 3:26–28)

As children of God it is important to remember that every person is created in God's image. Sometimes people forget this. Sometimes they lose sight of the equality of all people. They disregard the human dignity of others. They cooperate, or take part, in *social sin*.

This happens for many reasons. Here are a few:

- People are afraid to speak out against injustices.
- People only care about problems (for example, poverty) if they are affected by them.
- Their lives are better if the social sin exists. For example, people might make more money themselves by not paying their own workers a fair wage.

Social sin happened in Jesus' time, too. Jesus knew that there was hatred between Jews and Samaritans. Thus, when he told the story about the Samaritan, he was telling people to think about others. He was asking them to put aside their differences and help one another.

These kinds of differences still cause problems in our world today. Social sin should not be accepted. As disciples of Jesus we should live a life that shows that we value and respect all human beings.

WE RESPOND

Why do you think some people do not respect others?

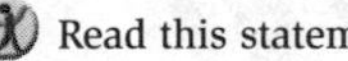

Read this statement:

Sometimes people are ignored or treated unjustly because of their skin color, nationality, gender, age, or religion.

Discuss a specific example of the statement. What can be done to correct this injustice?

50

Lesson Plan

WE GATHER ___ minutes

✝ **Pray** Pray the Sign of the Cross and the *We Gather* prayer.

Focus on Life Ask the *We Gather* questions. Emphasize that all people have similar needs and feelings, regardless of their differences in culture or ethnicity. Help the students see that appreciating and respecting these differences make our society better. Tell the students that in this lesson they will learn that God wants us to value and respect all people.

WE BELIEVE ___ minutes

Talk About Relationships Read aloud the *We Believe* statement. Invite the students to imagine living their lives without relationships to any other people. Ask them to list ways that their lives would be different. Write their ideas on the board. Remind the students that most people rely on others in their lives. For that reason, it is important for us to value and respect one another.

Read the Text Have volunteers read aloud the *We Believe* paragraphs. Then ask the students to underline key ideas. Review their ideas, making sure that they understand that we are all children of God, that we are all created in God's image, that social sin ignores human dignity, and that disciples of Jesus value and respect all human beings.

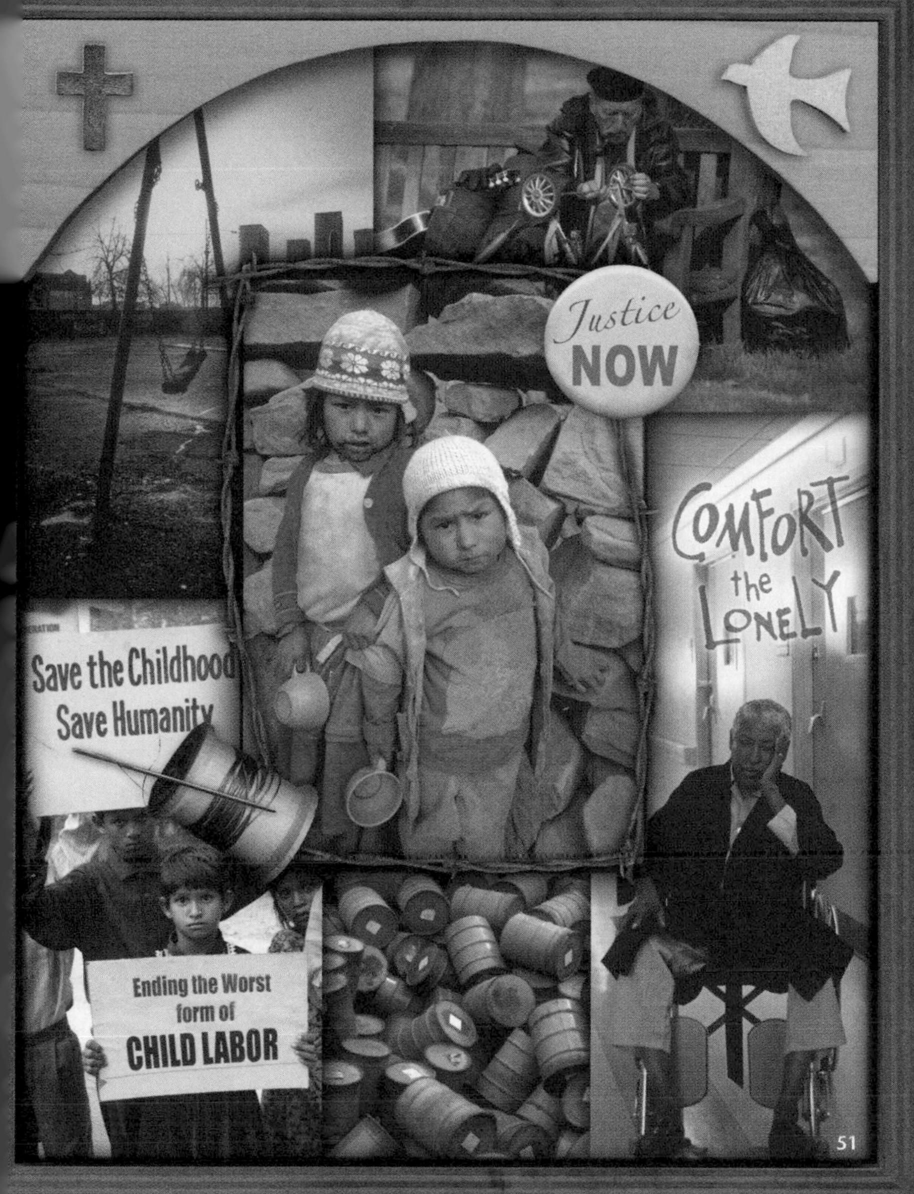

Activity Bank

Community

Problem Solvers

Activity Materials: construction paper, markers or crayons, material to decorate or illustrate brochure

Form groups and ask them to discuss one or more of the problems caused by social sin in our own society. Ask them to think of a club or group that they could form to reduce these problems. Have them decide on the name of the group and the reason for the name, who would be likely to join, the group's goals, and the action they will take to stop injustice. They should also decide when and where the group will meet, and how the group will attract new members.

When the students have answered all of these questions, have them make a brochure or flyer that can be sent out to advertise the new group. Make copies of these and distribute them. Have the class choose one practical action to follow up on.

Use the Reproducible Master Distribute copies of Reproducible Master 3, which reinforces *We Believe.* Read the directions aloud. The answers are: children (c, i, d circled), poor (p circled), life (l, i circled), respect (e, s circled), Samaritans (last s circled), and disciples.

Quick Check

✔ *What is social sin?* (Social sin occurs when people deny the value, dignity, and equality of other people.)

✔ *How did Jesus' respect for others set an example for us?* (Jesus valued and respected all people and went out of his way to care for everyone.)

WE RESPOND ___ minutes

Connect to Life Read and reflect on the *We Respond* question. Read aloud the activity directions. List specific injustices on the board. Discuss ways to correct each injustice.

Pray Pray the Sign of the Cross and this prayer: *Dear Jesus, help us to find ways to be just in our world today. Amen.*

Plan Ahead for Day 5

Catechist Goal: To review chapter ideas and their relationship to our faith life

Preparation: Make copies of Chapter 3 Test in the Grade 4 Assessment Book (option).

Chapter 3 • Day 5

Catechist Goal

- To review chapter ideas and their relationship to our faith life

Our Faith Response

- To apply what has been learned to our lives

CHAPTER TEST

The Chapter 3 Test is provided in the Grade 4 Assessment Book.

Grade 4 Chapter 3

Circle the correct answer.

1. An attraction to choose sin is a ______.
   commission   omission   (temptation)

2. Sin that hurts our friendship with God is ______.
   (venial sin)   free will   temptation

3. Serious sin that breaks our friendship with God is ______.
   venial sin   temptation   (mortal sin)

4. When we fail to do something good we may commit a sin of ______.
   (omission)   commission   temptation

Write the letter of the phrase that defines each of the following:

5. __c__ Free will
6. __d__ Sin
7. __a__ Social sin
8. __b__ Mortal sin

a. happens when we lose sight of the equality of all people and disregard their human dignity.

b. breaks friendship with God, is seriously wrong, and causes the loss of grace.

c. is the freedom to decide when and how to act.

d. is a thought, word, or action against God's law.

Write a sentence to answer the question.

9–10. Why does social sin exist?

See page 50.

Watch the evening news on television. Choose and report on one story that you think is an example of social sin.

52

Lesson Plan

___ minutes

Chapter Review Introduce the review by explaining to the students that they are now going to check their understanding of what they have learned in this chapter. Then allow time for the class to complete numbers 1–8.

When finished, use the review to help to clear up any misconceptions that might arise. Go over the correct answers.

Have the students look at question 9–10. Ask them to remember the reasons given for the existence of social sin. After the students write their answers, invite them to share them with the class. Then go a step further and discuss how social sin can be overcome. Encourage them to share ideas about how we can treat one another with respect.

Assessment Activity This activity can be done as a homework assignment. Invite the students to respond to a story on the news that they think is an example of social sin. Have them write a short report on what they have seen.

___ minutes

Reflect and Pray Allow time for the students to reflect and fill in the blank. When finished, invite volunteers to share their ideas. Then pray the prayer together.

We Respond in Faith

Reflect & Pray

Sometimes I forget to ask God and others for help. When I need help making choices I should

____

Jesus, help me to listen when people who care talk to me about my choices.

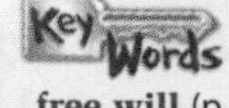

free will (p. 45)
sin (p. 45)
temptation (p. 45)
mortal sin (p. 47)
venial sin (p. 47)

Remember

- God gives us the freedom to choose.
- Sin leads us away from God.
- Sins can be things people do or fail to do.
- We are called to value and respect all people.

Our Catholic Life

Saint John Vianney

John Vianney was ordained a priest in 1815 in France. He soon became famous for his ministry to sinners. He often heard confessions for sixteen hours a day. He wanted to help people to seek God's forgiveness. He was canonized a saint in 1925. Today, he is the patron saint of parish priests. Saint John Vianney's feast day is August 4.

Home Connection

Sharing Faith with My Family

Be sure to send home the family page.

Encourage the students to continue the Family of Disciples activity begun in Chapters 1 and 2.

For additional information and activities, encourage families to visit Sadlier's

www.WEBELIEVEweb.com

Key Words Make five columns on the board. Write one of the key words (*free will, sin, temptation, mortal sin, and venial sin*) at the top of each column. Invite each student to come up to the board and write something about one of the words in the correct column. Discuss what has been written on the board. Recall the definitions of the key words.

Remember Invite the students to review the four *We Believe* statements. Have a student to read them aloud. Discuss how each statement applies to their lives. Talk about examples of problems and their possible solutions.

Our Catholic Life Have a volunteer read aloud the paragraph about Saint John Vianney. Ask the students: *Why do you think Saint John was named the patron saint of parish priests?*

CHAPTER 3 GRADE 4

SHARING FAITH with My Family

Sharing What I Learned

Discuss the following with your family:
- free will, temptation, and sin
- friendship with God
- the story of the Samaritan
- respect for all people.

A Family of Disciples

With your family, read the faith statement that is in the puzzle piece. How can your family answer Jesus' call to be a family of disciples? Write or draw your answer on the puzzle piece.

Jesus asks your family to try to avoid sin.

A Family Prayer

Lead your family in this prayer.

"Answer when I call, my saving God. In my troubles, you cleared a way; show me favor; hear my prayer." (Psalm 4:2)

Visit Sadlier's www.WEBELIEVEweb.com

Connect to the Catechism
For adult background and reflection, see paragraphs 387, 1850, 1853, and 1878.

54

PUPIL PAGE 54

Enrichment Ideas

Chapter Story

Alejandra had two best friends, Colleen and Nina. Recently, these two friends had fallen into the habit of gossiping about other students. They seldom said nice things about anyone. They even told lies to make other students look bad.

When the three girls got together, Colleen and Nina often would make jokes or unkind statements about kids in the school. They expected Alejandra to join them in gossiping about others. So far, she had remained silent or found excuses to leave when the unkind talk began. Alejandra was sure that Colleen and Nina noticed her behavior. She knew that if she didn't join her friends in their "fun," they would start talking about her. She also was afraid to lose their friendship.

Alejandra wasn't sure what to do. She thought long and hard about it and then decided to. . . .

▶ *(Have the students write an ending to this story. Share as many proposed endings as time allows.)*

FAITH and MEDIA

▶ After reading the *Our Catholic Life* text about Saint Thomas More, you might want to introduce the students to Robert Bolt. In 1960 this English playwright wrote a play about Thomas More, a man who followed his conscience. Bolt called his play "A Man for All Seasons." The play was a hit on the stage. In 1966 the play was turned into an Academy Award-winning movie. Thus, over the years, through the media of drama and film, millions of people around the world have learned about this great saint of the Catholic Church.

CHAPTER PROJECT: CONSCIENCE SKITS

Form small groups. Ask each group to think of situations that require decision making. Here are some examples. *A boy promised to visit his aunt on a Saturday but later was invited by a friend to go to the movies. A student has the chance to copy the answers from another student's test page. A person has the choice either to go to Sunday Mass or to a sporting event.* Have each group come up with a situation or choose one of these, and then work as a team to write a brief skit about it. Each skit should show a person that is in a difficult situation and needs to make a decision. In each skit one of the characters should personify the conscience. The conscience should talk about the person's choice before, during, and after the decision is made. Allow the students time to perform their skits. Ask them to discuss alternative decisions and their effects.

Connections

To Family

We learn about the difference between good and evil, right and wrong from our families, the Church, and our communities. Look for opportunities to help the students to name the ways people in their families have helped them to learn the skills involved in making good choices. Encourage them to thank their families for their guidance.

To Stewardship

The Church teaches that human beings are called to care for and protect our planet. We do this because we live our faith in relationship with all of God's creation. Explain to the students that in making decisions we need to be guided by our conscience. Encourage them to respect the environment. The ways we use our limited resources now will have a future impact. Have them seek out more information about conservation, recycling, and preservation.

To Scripture

Encourage the students to read the New Testament. Point them toward the gospels where there are many examples of Jesus calling us to seek God's forgiveness. Invite them to read one of the following passages: Jesus forgiving the paralyzed man (Mark 2:1–12); the Parable of the Pharisee and the Tax Collector (Luke 18:9–14); the Parable of the Lost Sheep (Luke 15:1–7). Remind them that Jesus continues to forgive sins in the sacrament of Reconciliation.

Meeting Individual Needs

Students Who Are Language Learners

Many of the concepts and terms in this chapter are abstract. Students who are learning English may have difficulty with some of these terms. Provide these students with index cards. They can work with a partner to write definitions for the following terms: conscience, examination of conscience, decisions, and forgiveness. It may be beneficial to pair these students with partners who are fluent in both languages. They can write the definition first in their native language and then translate into English. Encourage them to do the same for any other terms with which they might be having difficulty.

ADDITIONAL RESOURCES

Book *What's Wrong With Lying and Cheating?* James Phillips, St. Anthony Messenger Press, 2000. This book helps young people explore the consequences of lying and cheating.

Video *McGee and Me! Do the Right Thing,* Tyndale Christian Video, 1990. The focus of eleven year old Nicholas and MeGee is learning about decisions, right and wrong, and consequences. (30 minutes)

To find more ideas for books, videos, and other learning material, visit Sadlier's

www.WEBELIEVEweb.com

Catechist Development

Using Storytelling with Children

by Julie Brunet

Julie Brunet is an author and national creative consultant for William H. Sadlier, Inc. Julie received her B.A. in religious studies from Loyola University in New Orleans and a B.A. in elementary education from the University of Southwestern Louisiana in Lafayette, LA.

Jesus was a master teacher. He knew how very important the experiences of his listeners were. Jesus taught by using parables—stories that touched on the daily life experiences of his listeners—so that they could understand the meaning behind the stories.

Storytelling is an integral aspect of educating children in the truths of our faith. Used to teach values as well as to entertain, stories can be a great way for children to learn about the world around them. Not only is information communicated easily and effectively through a story, but children themselves benefit as well. They can explore their own ideas and feelings. They can express themselves so that others get to know them better even as they get to know themselves. Socialization skills are practiced, and language abilities are developed. A child's cultural heritage can be explored and shared as well.

How can stories be included effectively in the classroom? They can be used to begin, develop, reinforce, or conclude a lesson. Stories can provide information, emphasize lesson themes, and help children make connections and discover insights into what they are learning.

One of the most important aspects of storytelling is the relationship between the teller and the listener. Select stories that will be interesting for the children. The stories should be interesting and varied. Familiarize yourself with the story beforehand so that you can tell it confidently and enthusiastically.

Catechist Development Topics (Topic and Guide Page)

Develop your own storytelling style by using your voice and gestures to make the story come alive. Involve the children directly to make them partners in the experience. Adapt details to personalize the story for your listeners, and invite

(continued on next page)

Resources

Cooper, Patsy. *When Stories Come to School: Telling, Writing & Performing Stories in the Early Childhood Classroom.* New York: Teachers and Writers Collaborative, 2000.

MacDonald, Margaret Read. *The Storyteller's Start-up Book.* Little Rock, Arkansas: August House Publishers, Inc., 1993.

Storytelling, Learning and Sharing, with Sandy Jenkins, 45 minutes, Coyote Creek Productions, 1995. (VHS format)

them to repeat a response, a sound, or an action as you tell the story. Being open to the unexpected can enhance your listeners' experience of the story as well as your own.

Ways to Implement Using Storytelling with Children

- Choose stories that appeal to the group.
- Be familiar with the story.
- Establish eye contact with the listeners.
- Use music and poetry to embellish the story.
- Have the children repeat phrases or patterns from the story.
- Provide props for the children to manipulate as the story unfolds.
- Have the children represent characters in the story, acting out the story as it is told.
- Ask thought-provoking questions throughout the story to encourage the children to become active participants.
- Have the children make up the ending of the story or retell the story with a new ending.
- Have the children make up a story as a group.
- Provide puppets for the children to use to act out the story as it is told.
- Provide flannel-board characters for the children to use to retell the story.

For additional ideas, activities, and opportunities, visit Sadlier's

www.WEBELIEVEweb.com

Catechist Corner

With thanks to:
Veronica Clark
Third Grade Teacher
St. Margaret of Scotland Parish
Green Tree, PA

Veronica uses drawing as a storytelling tool with her third grade class. For example, when the children learn about a story from Scripture, they are asked to illustrate a part of the story at home or in the classroom. The next time that the children come together, Veronica asks them to retell the story using the pictures they drew. The children's pictures are compiled into one book. This book of drawings is then shared with another class.

Notes

CHAPTER
4
GRADE 4

Name ____

Think about Jesus' story of the father and the son. Write words to describe how the following people felt at these specific times:

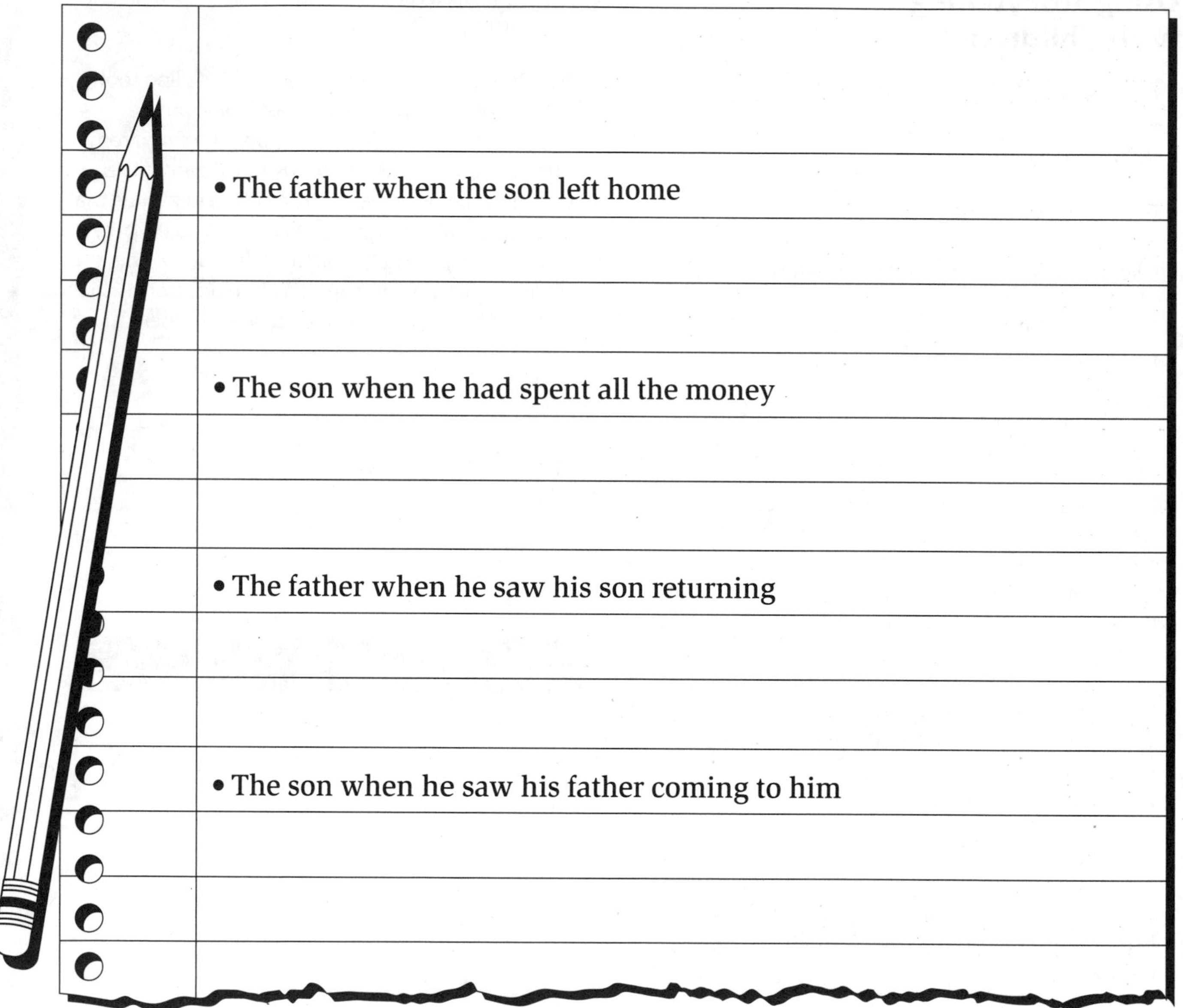
• The father when the son left home
• The son when he had spent all the money
• The father when he saw his son returning
• The son when he saw his father coming to him

Use your descriptions of their feelings to help you act out a brief skit of the story.

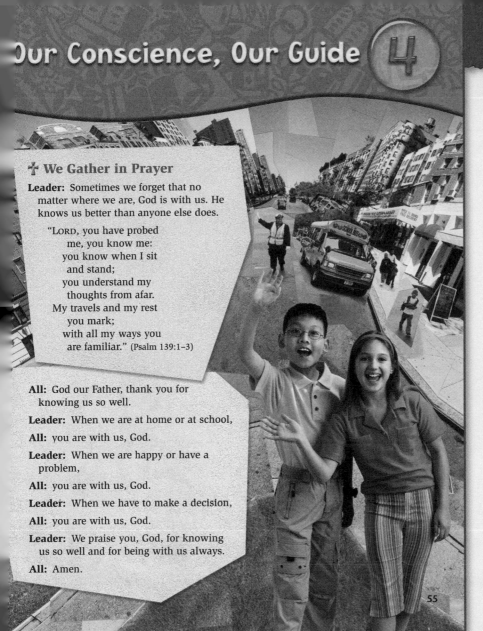

Our Conscience, Our Guide 4

✝ We Gather in Prayer

Leader: Sometimes we forget that no matter where we are, God is with us. He knows us better than anyone else does.

"LORD, you have probed
me, you know me:
you know when I sit
and stand;
you understand my
thoughts from afar.
My travels and my rest
you mark;
with all my ways you
are familiar." (Psalm 139:1–3)

All: God our Father, thank you for knowing us so well.

Leader: When we are at home or at school,

All: you are with us, God.

Leader: When we are happy or have a problem,

All: you are with us, God.

Leader: When we have to make a decision,

All: you are with us, God.

Leader: We praise you, God, for knowing us so well and for being with us always.

All: Amen.

55

PREPARING TO PRAY

In this gathering prayer students prayerfully acknowledge God's constant presence with them.

- Invite one of the students to be the prayer leader. Give the student time to read over his or her part.
- With the students, practice the response *You are with us, God.*
- Invite three volunteers to place the pictures on the prayer table at the appointed time.

The Prayer Space

- You may want to ask students to trace their shoe prints. Cut the prints out and place them in pairs in the prayer space.
- Have available photographs of places where nine- and ten-year-olds spend time.
- Display a sign that says *God is with us always.*

This Week's Liturgy

Visit **www.webelieveweb.com** for this week's liturgical readings and other seasonal material.

Lesson Plan

We Gather in Prayer ___ minutes

✝ Pray

- Invite the students to gather together in the prayer space.
- Begin by praying the Sign of the Cross.
- After the opening prayer have each volunteer display the photo of a place and then put it on the prayer table.
- Continue the prayer.

Home Connection Update

Review the activities on the Chapter 3 family page. Invite the students to share ways their families make good choices and answer Jesus' call to discipleship.

Chapter 4 • **Day 1**

Catechist Goal

• To emphasize that God calls us to be close to him

Our Faith Response

• To trust in God as our loving Father

Lesson Materials

• copies of Reproducible Master 4 (option, *Activity Bank*)

Teaching Note

Self-evaluation: How Am I Doing?

Sometimes it is a good idea to take stock of how you are doing as a catechist. Reflect on your strengths and weaknesses in and outside the classroom. Whether you are in your first year as a catechist or your tenth, it is always beneficial to ask your colleagues for help in practical management strategies or to request input from the person in charge of the catechetical program in the parish or school.

God calls us to be close to him.

WE GATHER

✝ *Loving Father, we believe in your love for us.*

Dawn woke up in a bad mood. She yelled at her brother and talked back to her mother. After breakfast she slammed the door on her way out to school.

At school Dawn remembered how she had acted that morning. She realized her words and actions did not show her love for her family. What do you think she will do now?

WE BELIEVE

Through our Baptism each of us is called to become more like Jesus. We are called to follow the example of Jesus who always remained close to God his Father.

When we think, speak, and act as Jesus did, we become more like him. Yet, sometimes we do not follow Jesus' example. Instead of moving closer to God, we move farther away from him.

In the Gospel of Saint Luke we can find this story that Jesus told about a father and a son:

"A man had two sons, and the younger son said to his father, 'Father, give me the share of your estate that should come to me.' . . . When he had freely spent everything, a severe famine struck that country, and he found himself in dire need. . . . Coming to his senses he thought, 'How many of my father's hired workers have more than enough food to eat, but here am I, dying from hunger. I shall get up and go to my father and I shall say to him, "Father, I have sinned against heaven and against you. I no longer deserve to be called your son; treat me as you would treat one of your hired workers."' So he got up and went back to his father. While he was still a long way off, his father caught sight of him, and was filled with compassion. He ran to his son, embraced him and kissed him." (Luke 15:11–12, 14, 17–20)

56

Lesson Plan

WE GATHER ___ minutes

✝ **Pray** Pray the *We Gather* prayer.

Focus on Life Invite a student to read the *We Gather* story. Have the students discuss in groups what they think Dawn will do. Tell the students that in this lesson they will learn that God calls us to follow the example of Jesus and that God always loves us.

WE BELIEVE ___ minutes

Reflect on Following Jesus Have a volunteer read aloud the *We Believe* statement. Ask: *What do you think it means to be close to God?* Then have volunteers read aloud the first two *We Believe* paragraphs. On the board, make a list of the good things Jesus did for others. Invite the students to name ways they follow Jesus' example. Help them to understand that when they follow Jesus' example, they grow closer to God.

Read and Reflect on Scripture Continue by reading the passage from Saint Luke's Gospel. Have one student be the narrator, another read the words of the son, and another the words of the father. After the students have listened to the passage from the Gospel of Luke, ask them to complete the activity. Lead a discussion about their answers. Help the students to understand that the feelings of the father in the parable are like God's when we turn away and then decide to return to him. Read aloud the last *We believe* paragraph. Encourage the students to rely on God's unconditional love for us.

Think about the father in this story. Write what his thoughts might have been:

- when his son asked for his share of the money
- while the son was away from home
- when his son returned home.

Jesus told this story to remind us that God is our loving Father. God will always welcome us back to him. When we forget his love or turn away from it, God is always ready to welcome us back as his children.

WE RESPOND

How can knowing that God is our loving Father help you when you have choices to make?

Pray together:

God, you are our loving Father. Help us to remember that you will always welcome us back. Amen.

57

ACTIVITY BANK

Curriculum Connection

Language Arts

Invite the students to dramatize the Parable of the Forgiving Father (Luke 15:11–20). Distribute Reproducible Master 4 to guide the students. Have them work independently to complete the first part and in groups to compose the dialogue between the characters. Encourage the students to be creative and make props and/or costumes from materials in the classroom. Invite groups to act out their plays.

Quick Check

✔ *How can we become more like Jesus?* (We can become more like Jesus by thinking, speaking, and acting as he did.)

✔ *What will God do for us, even when we turn away from him?* (God will always welcome us back as his children.)

WE RESPOND

___ minutes

Connect to Life Provide a few minutes for the students to reflect on the *We Respond* question. Remind students that we are called to make choices that bring us closer to God.

Pray Pray the *We Respond* prayer. Suggest that the students say this prayer daily.

Plan Ahead for Day 2

Catechist Goal: To recall that God gives us the gift of conscience

Preparation: Prepare to explain the way conscience works in each situation listed in *We Gather.*

Catechist Goal

• To recall that God gives us the gift of conscience

Our Faith Response

• To listen to our conscience in our moral decision making

 **conscience**

Teaching Tip

Class Participation

It is easy to grow accustomed to calling on the same students to answer questions. Encourage the participation of all students by telling them that all responses are valuable. Be sensitive by giving all students positive reinforcement for their responses.

God gives us the gift of conscience.

WE GATHER

✝ *Lord, be with us.*

Making decisions is part of everyone's life. Your family members have decisions to make. You have decisions to make, too. The choices that you make are up to you. What helps you to make good choices?

WE BELIEVE

God loves each of us and wants to share his life with us. He wants us to be close to him. If at times our choices lead us away from God, he calls us back to him. He calls us to turn away from sin and to live a life of goodness and love.

How do we know whether the things we do are good or sinful? To help us, God has given us a conscience. Our **conscience** is the ability to know the difference between good and evil, right and wrong. It is like an inner voice that helps us to choose good over evil.

Conscience works in three ways:

- It works *before* we make decisions. It helps us know what is good. It helps us consider the results of our choices.
- It works *while* we are making the decision. It brings about feelings of peace or discomfort depending on the choices we have made.
- It works *after* we make decisions. It enables us to judge, as good or evil, the decisions we have made.

God's gift of conscience guides us in our choices. It helps us to turn away from sin and to turn toward God.

conscience the ability to know the difference between good and evil, right and wrong

58

Lesson Plan

WE GATHER ___ minutes

✝ **Pray** Pray the Sign of the Cross and invite students to name times and places that they would like God to be with them. Then pray the *We Gather* prayer.

Focus on Life Have the students write some choices and decisions they have made so far in their lives. Give them a moment to read the *We Gather* question. Invite them to circle the good choices on their list and explain how they know the choices are good. Share the *Chapter Story* and have the students discuss possible endings to the story. Tell the students that in this lesson they will learn that God's gift of conscience helps us make good decisions.

WE BELIEVE ___ minutes

Read About Our Conscience Have a student read the *We Believe* statement. Invite volunteers to read aloud the *We Believe* paragraphs.

Then illustrate our conscience at work. Share the following situations with the students.

• You want some candy but you don't have enough money. The store owner isn't looking, so you steal the candy.

• You just got some new markers for your birthday. Your classmate doesn't have any markers, so you share yours with her.

• Your elderly neighbor hurt her back, so you help rake the leaves on her lawn.

WE RESPOND
How would our world be different if no one had a conscience?
Make a cartoon storyboard showing a person doing good and avoiding evil by following his or her conscience.
59

ACTIVITY BANK

Catholic Social Teaching

Life and Dignity of the Human Person

Activity Materials: construction paper; crayons, markers, or colored pencils

Catholic social teaching emphasizes respect for human life at all stages. Encourage the students to reflect on the way Jesus cared for others. Explain that students can show care for elderly people who are often forgotten. They can write letters and draw pictures for those who are unable to leave their homes or for residents an eldercare facility. Invite the students to talk about people they know in these situations. Then have the students write a letter or draw a picture for someone. Have a list of people available for those students who do not know of someone personally.

Have the students describe or act out how their conscience would work before, during, and after each of these situations. Emphasize that our conscience guides us in making decisions and helps us know when we have made a right or wrong choice.

Remember the Key Word Encourage the students to look at the *Key Word* box. Have volunteers use the word *conscience* in a sentence.

Quick Check

- ✔ *What does our conscience help us to know?* (Our conscience is the ability to know the difference between good and evil, right and wrong.)
- ✔ *What are the three times when conscience works?* (Conscience works before, during, and after we make decisions.)

WE RESPOND

___ minutes

Connect to Life Invite students to share their responses to the *We Respond* question. Have a student read aloud the directions for the *We Respond* activity. Give the students time to complete their storyboards. Invite students to share their cartoons.

Pray Have the student pray silently, thanking God for the gift of conscience.

Plan Ahead for Day 3

Catechist Goal: To examine how we form our conscience

Preparation: Prepare to share why conscience is a gift to us.

Catechist Goal

- To examine how we form our conscience

Our Faith Response

- To continue to form a good conscience

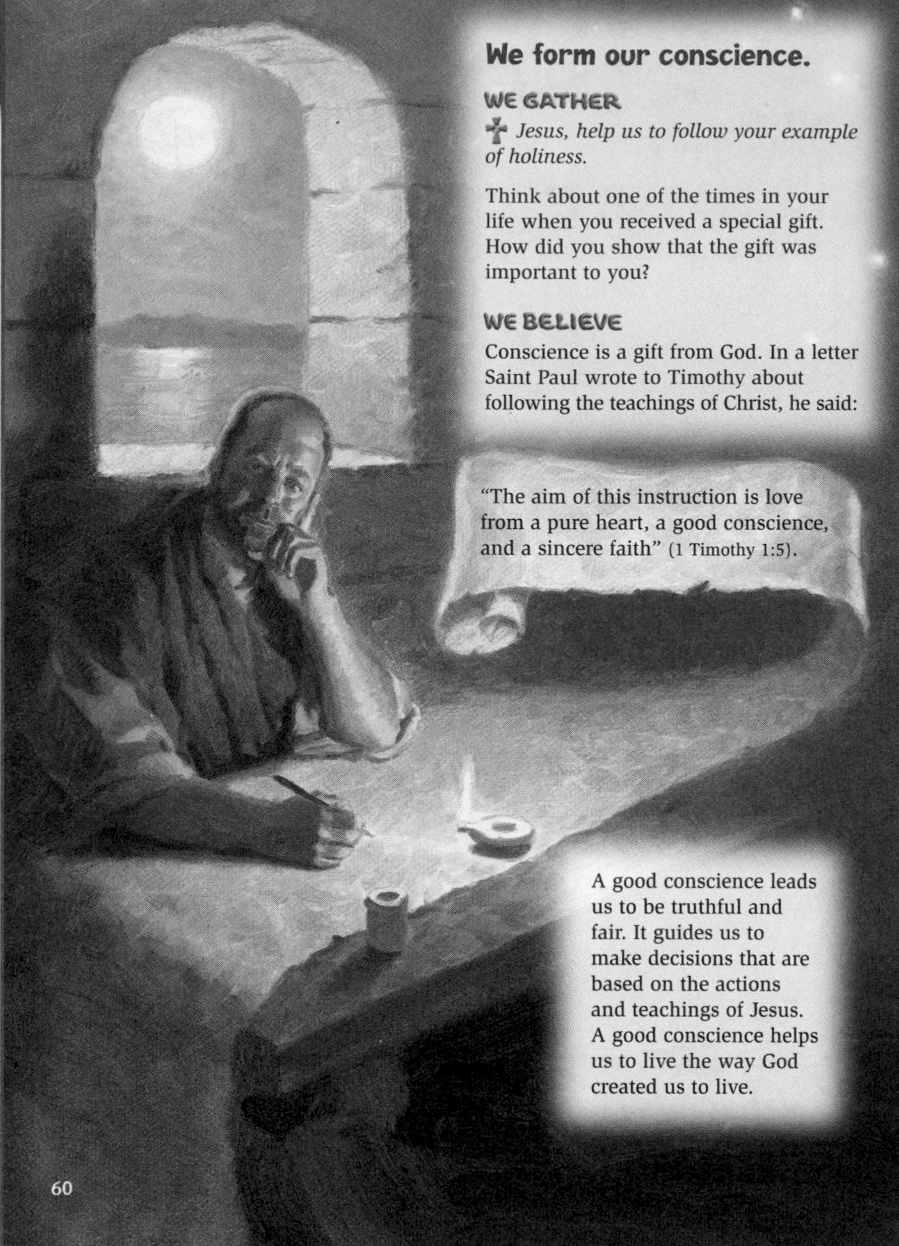

We form our conscience.
WE GATHER
✝ Jesus, help us to follow your example of holiness.
Think about one of the times in your life when you received a special gift. How did you show that the gift was important to you?
WE BELIEVE
Conscience is a gift from God. In a letter Saint Paul wrote to Timothy about following the teachings of Christ, he said:
"The aim of this instruction is love from a pure heart, a good conscience, and a sincere faith" (1 Timothy 1:5).
A good conscience leads us to be truthful and fair. It guides us to make decisions that are based on the actions and teachings of Jesus. A good conscience helps us to live the way God created us to live.
60

Teaching Note

Interior Life

To hear what someone says, we have to listen. This applies to accessing our conscience. To hear the advice of our conscience, we must listen to it. To listen and follow our conscience, we must have some form of interior life. To have an interior life, we need to take time out from the demands of the day to pray and quietly review our day and ourselves.

Lesson Plan

WE GATHER

___ minutes

✝ **Pray** Ask the students to name some of the good things Jesus did for others. After volunteers have shared some examples, pray the *We Gather* prayer.

Focus on Life Have students recall times when they have received a special gift, such as on a birthday, at Christmas, or First Communion. Ask them to share why the gift was important to them. Tell the students that in this lesson they will learn that we must form our own good conscience to grow closer to God and others.

WE BELIEVE

___ minutes

Do the Activity Have volunteers read aloud the *We Believe* statement and the *We Believe* text on page 60. Then have students work in pairs to complete the chart. Lead a general discussion about what the partners have written.

Reflect on Responsibility Write the word *responsibility* on the board. Ask the students what the word means to them. Explain: *A responsibility is something for which a person is responsible.* Under *responsibility* write *first grader, fourth grader,* and *adult* across the board. Ask the students to think of responsibilities that they might have had and might have at these different stages in life. Have the students highlight or underline the statement that follows the chart: *Forming a good conscience is our responsibility.* Ask a volunteer to read aloud the last two *We Believe* paragraphs.

Write your answers.

A good conscience is formed by . . .	One way to do this is . . .
• listening to God the Holy Spirit	
• asking your parents or guardians, priests, teachers, and catechists in the Church to help you	
• following the good example of a life of one of the saints	
• deepening your love for God	
• learning more about God through Scripture	
• learning more about God through Church teachings.	

Forming a good conscience is our responsibility. This responsibility continues throughout our lives.

A good conscience helps us to follow the teachings of Christ. By listening to a good conscience, we can grow closer to God and others.

We Respond

Think about a time when you had a difficult decision to make. How did your conscience guide you?

61

Activity Bank

Curriculum Connection

Reading and Writing

Activity Materials: resource materials to research saints

Explain to the students that one way we can form a good conscience is to follow the example of the saints. Tell the students to read about the life of a saint or research it on the Internet. They can write an essay or give a presentation describing the saint's life.

Quick Check

✔ *What does a good conscience lead us to do?* (A good conscience leads us to be truthful and fair, to live the way God wants us to, to be like Jesus, and to be closer to God and others.)

✔ *How can you form your good conscience?* (Possible answers are found in the on-page chart.)

We Respond

___ minutes

Connect to Life Provide a few minutes of quiet time for the students to reflect on the *We Respond* question. Then share with the students why conscience is a gift.

Pray Invite the students to pray for people who have helped them form a good conscience. Conclude by praying: *Thank you, God, for all the people who help us form a good conscience. May our conscience guide us every day. Amen.*

Plan Ahead for Day 4

Catechist Goal: To explore the need to examine our conscience

Preparation: Prepare possible responses to the *We Gather* activity.

Chapter 4 • Day 4

Catechist Goal

• To explore the need to examine our conscience

Our Faith Response

• To name ways we can examine our conscience

examination of conscience

As Catholics...

The Teaching Church

After the lesson is completed, invite the students to share some ways the Church teaches us. Through its teachings the Church helps us form a good conscience. *(Some examples are through religion classes, homilies at Mass, letters from the bishops, papal statements, and the good example set by parents and parish members.)* Read aloud the text. Invite volunteers to respond to the question.

We examine our conscience.

WE GATHER

✝ *Holy Spirit, open our ears, minds, and hearts to hear your voice.*

What might people think as they rate their own performances after each of the following?

• a musical recital or play

____

• a martial-arts or fitness class

____

• a sporting event

____

(Add an event and question of your own.)

• ______________________________

____

Why is it important for people to look back on what they have done?

WE BELIEVE

No matter how busy we are, it is important to think about the things we do and say every day. An **examination of conscience** is the act of determining whether the choices we have made showed love for God, ourselves, and others. Examining our conscience helps us to realize how much God loves us. He always forgives us if we are truly sorry.

Examining our conscience can help us to think about what we will say and do before we act. The more we examine our conscience the easier it is to hear and follow our conscience.

But how can we examine our conscience? First, we try to think about the ways we have loved God and others. We think about the ways we are living as disciples of Jesus and as members of the Church.

Next, we ask ourselves whether we have sinned, either by *doing* things that we know are evil, or by *not doing* the good things that we could have done. We ask the Holy Spirit to help us to judge the goodness of our thoughts, words, and actions.

As Catholics...

We do not form our conscience alone. The Church helps us in many ways. One way is through her teachings. The pope and the bishops have the authority to teach us in Jesus' name. They rely on Scripture and Tradition to help Catholics form their consciences.

What are some things that the pope and bishops teach us?

Lesson Plan

WE GATHER

___ minutes

✝ **Pray** Encourage the students to take time to listen to God. Offer them a few moments of silence for meditation. Invite the students to pray the *We Gather* prayer.

Focus on Life Have the students work in small groups to complete the *We Gather* activity. Have a representative of each group share what the group has written. Then have a general discussion about the importance of people looking back on what they have done. Help the students see that we can learn from what we have done in the past. Tell the students that in this lesson they will learn how and why we examine our conscience.

WE BELIEVE

___ minutes

Think About the Key Word Remind the students that in previous years they have learned about an examination of conscience. Ask volunteers to share what they remember. Have a volunteer read the first *We Believe* paragraph. Ask the students to name the three relationships we think about when we examine our choices *(with God, with ourselves, with others)*. Write the correct answer on the board.

Read the Text Invite volunteers to read aloud the next three paragraphs. Ask students to explain a way a person would examine his or her conscience. Have a volunteer read the fourth paragraph. Encourage them to give examples of possible answers. *(For example, not participating in the celebration of Sunday Mass is a way we fail*

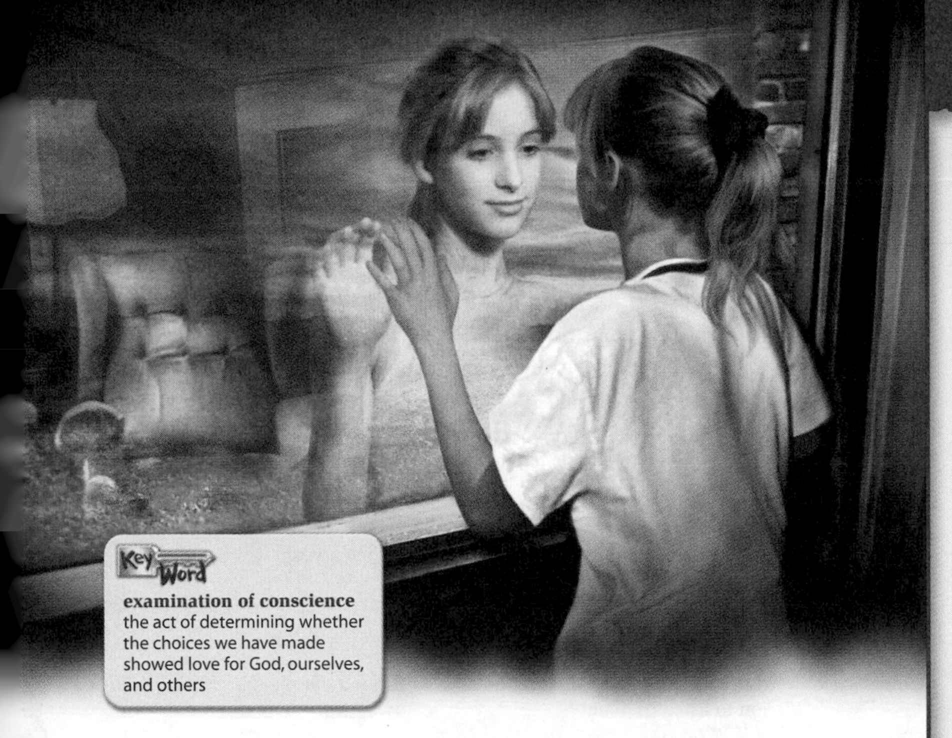

Key Word
examination of conscience
the act of determining whether the choices we have made showed love for God, ourselves, and others

When we examine our conscience we ask ourselves questions like the ones below.

- How have I shown love, or failed to show love, for God in my thoughts, words, and actions?
- How have I shown love, or failed to show love, for others in my thoughts, words, and actions?
- How have I shown love, or failed to show love, for myself as a person made in God's image?

We can examine our conscience any time. One possible time is before we fall asleep at night. Another time is when we celebrate the sacrament of Penance and Reconciliation.

When we examine our conscience we can thank God for giving us the strength to make good choices. Reflecting on the choices we have made helps us to make choices that bring us closer to God.

WE RESPOND

When are times you can examine your conscience?

Pray to the Holy Spirit for guidance in listening to your conscience.

63

Activity Bank

Meeting Individual Needs

Challenging Student Creativity

Students might need extra activities to express themselves and remain focused. Give them one of these assignments:

- Write a story that describes a character who faces a difficult choice.
- Read a book or story and give an oral report on it. The book or story should include a situation in which a character can make a right or wrong choice. The report should indicate the consequences of that choice.
- Make a cartoon strip that illustrates a person listening to his or her conscience.

to show love for God.) Invite two more volunteers to finish reading the last two *We Believe* paragraphs.

Quick Check

✔ *What kind of question can we ask ourselves when examining our conscience?* (Possible answers include questions listed on page 63.)

✔ *Why would you want to thank God after you examine your conscience?* (Possible answers include: because God still loves me even when I make a mistake; because God helps me make good choices.)

WE RESPOND

___ minutes

Connect to Life Invite students to share their answers to the *We Respond* question. Have the students name times *(at Mass, in the morning, at nighttime)* and ways *(thinking, talking with someone, writing)* to examine their conscience. Point out the photo and ask how it relates to the lesson. Help the students to understand that an examination of conscience helps us to look back at our actions.

Pray Conclude the lesson by praying to the Holy Spirit for guidance in following our conscience.

Plan Ahead for Day 5

Catechist Goal: To review chapter ideas and their relationship to our faith life

Preparation: Make copies of Chapter 4 Test in the Grade 4 Assessment Book (option).

Catechist Goal

- To review chapter ideas and their relationship to our faith life

Our Faith Response

- To apply what has been learned to our lives

CHAPTER TEST

Chapter 4 Test is provided in the Grade 4 Assessment Book.

Grade 4
Chapter 4

Write True or False for the following sentences. Then change the false sentences to make them true.

1. True The Holy Spirit can help us to form our conscience.

2. False The ability to know the difference between good and evil, right and wrong, is called our communion.

   The ability to know the difference between good and evil, right and wrong, is called our conscience.

3. True Forming our conscience involves listening to trusted adults.

4. False We can examine our conscience only once a year.

   We can examine our conscience any time.

Circle the correct answer.

5. Jesus used a story about a father and his son to teach us about ____.

   (forgiveness) Baptism the Holy Spirit

6. A good conscience leads us to be ____.

   (truthful) sinful dishonest

7. A good conscience calls us to turn away from ____.

   peace (sin) God

8. God will ____ welcome us to come back to him.

   (always) sometimes never

Complete the following:

9–10. When examining my conscience, I See pages 62–63.

Write an article for a magazine to tell people why conscience is important. Explain how someone might form a good conscience.

64

Lesson Plan

___ minutes

Chapter Review Have the students complete questions 1–8. After they have finished, have volunteers share their answers. Clear up any misconceptions that may have arisen.

Ask the students to remember how and why we examine our conscience. After the students have completed the statement in question 9–10, have volunteers share their answers.

Assessment Activity Review the activity directions with the students. When the students have completed their articles, encourage them to share their writing with classmates. You may want to collect the articles to display on a bulletin board in the classroom or parish.

___ minutes

Reflect & Pray Read the question under *Reflect & Pray* to students. Give the students time to complete the prayer.

Key Words Review these words with the students. Form pairs. Ask each pair to pretend that his or her partner has never heard the words. They should explain what the words means in their own words.

Remember Have the students number the *We Believe* statements 1–4. Give them time to list three things they learned about each statement.

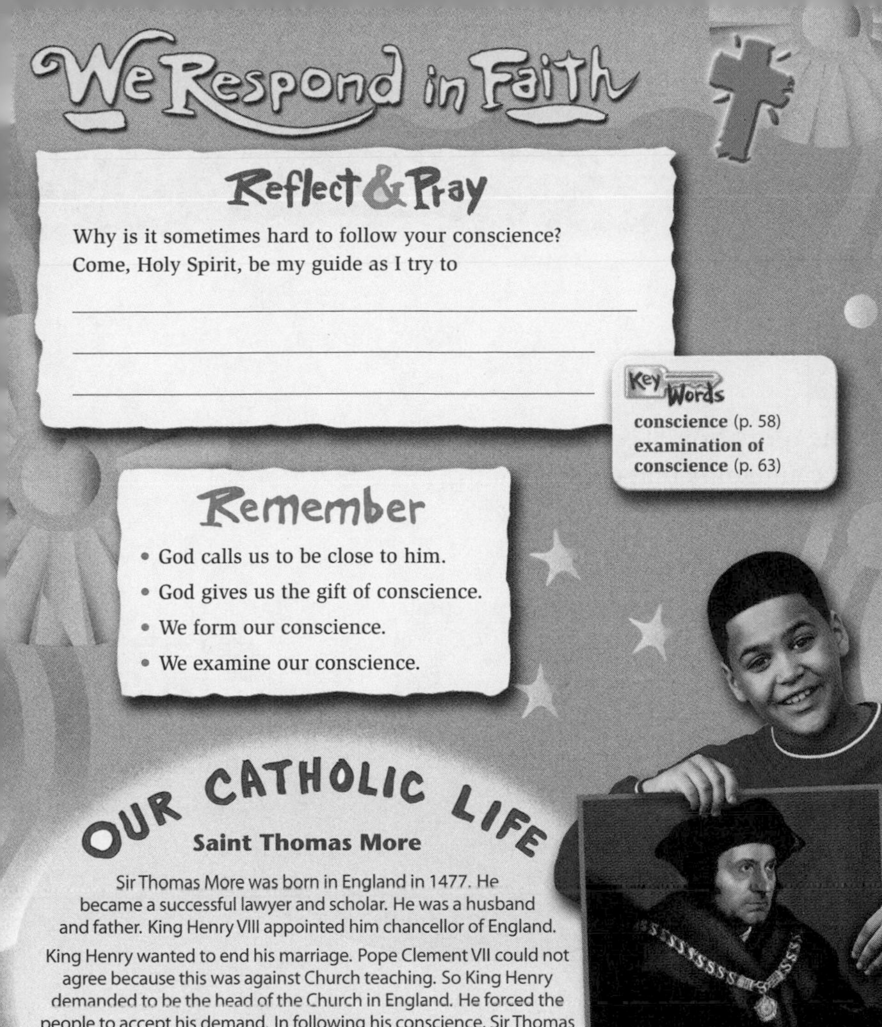

Our Catholic Life

Saint Thomas More

Sir Thomas More was born in England in 1477. He became a successful lawyer and scholar. He was a husband and father. King Henry VIII appointed him chancellor of England.

King Henry wanted to end his marriage. Pope Clement VII could not agree because this was against Church teaching. So King Henry demanded to be the head of the Church in England. He forced the people to accept his demand. In following his conscience, Sir Thomas More could not accept King Henry as the head of the Church. Because of this King Henry had Sir Thomas More put to death.

Sir Thomas More became a saint because he followed his conscience, the teachings of Christ, and the teachings of the Church. His feast day is June 22.

Home Connection

Sharing Faith with My Family

Make sure to send home the family page (text page 66).

Encourage the students to discuss Jesus' story about the father and the son with their families. Remind them to save the completed puzzle piece.

For additional information and activities, encourage families to visit Sadlier's

www.WEBELIEVEweb.com

Our Catholic Life Read aloud the text about Saint Thomas More. Ask the students to share what they most admire about the saint.

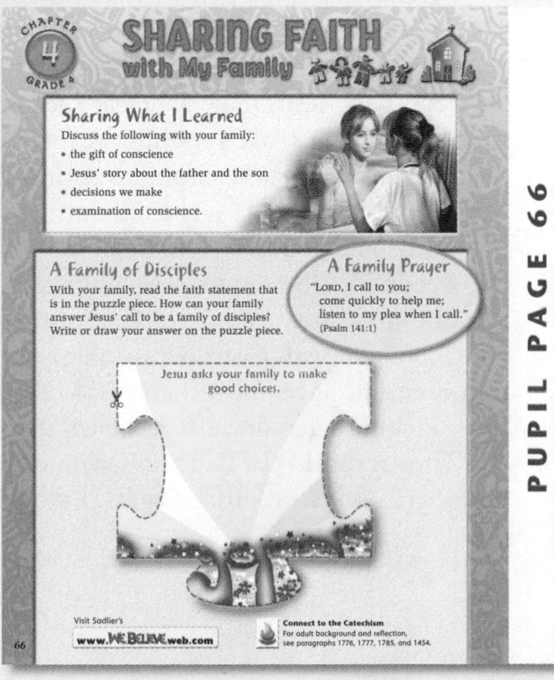

Chapter 5 Celebrating Penance and Reconciliation

Overview

In Chapter 4 the students learned about the formation of conscience. In this chapter, they will learn about the peace and unity that comes from receiving God's forgiveness and love through the sacrament of Reconciliation.

Doctrinal Content	For Adult Reading and Reflection *Catechism of the Catholic Church*
The students will learn:	Paragraph
• Jesus tells us about God's forgiveness and love.	1423–1424
• We receive God's forgiveness in the sacrament of Reconciliation.	1441
• We celebrate the sacrament of Reconciliation.	1448
• Reconciliation brings peace and unity.	1468–1469

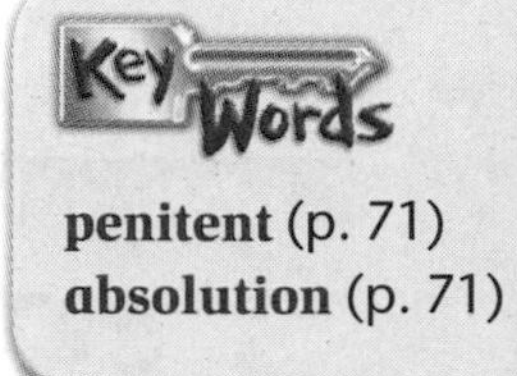

penitent (p. 71)
absolution (p. 71)

Catechist Background

Think of a time when you needed to apologize. What feelings did you experience when you apologized?

In Matthew's Gospel, we read the first message Jesus preached: "Repent, for the kingdom of God is at hand (Matthew 4:17). By beginning his ministry this way, Jesus makes it clear that repentance and reconciliation are very important. Jesus underscored their importance numerous times throughout his public ministry as he taught forgiveness by his words and actions.

Reconciliation requires repentance, a reopening of our minds and hearts to God. It also requires a continual renewal of our baptismal promises. And if our actions have hurt others, reconciliation also must include a genuine effort to heal that wrong.

The sacrament of Reconciliation offers us a chance to seek God's forgiveness. By regularly celebrating this sacrament, we can express our sorrow for sin, talk to a priest who represents both God and the community, and receive God's forgiveness through the words of absolution. To emphasize the need to change our lives, the priest usually asks us to say a prayer or perform a penitential action. The priest is bound to secrecy by the seal of confession. Thus, we can confidently use the sacrament to overcome whatever sin is keeping us from a deeper union with God.

How in your own life are you a reconciler?

Lesson Planning Guide

Lesson Focus	Presentation	Materials
Day 1		
page 67 **We Gather in Prayer** **pages 68–69** *Jesus tells us about God's forgiveness and love.* 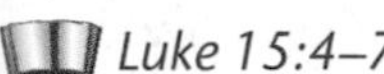 *Luke 15:4–7*	• Listen to the psalm. • Pray the responsorial prayer. Act out the **We Gather** situations. • Read and discuss the **We Believe** text about Jesus' message of forgiveness and love. • Discuss the **We Respond** questions. 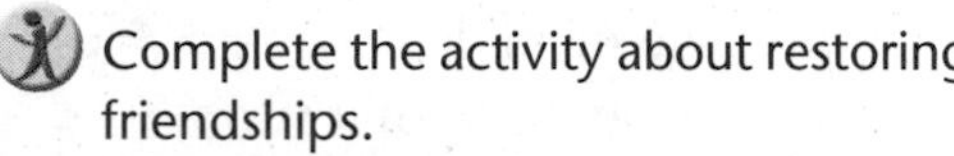 Complete the activity about restoring friendships.	For the prayer space: copy of the Act of Contrition, picture frame, candle, picture of Jesus
Day 2		
pages 70–71 *We receive God's forgiveness in the sacrament of Reconciliation.* *John 20:21–23*	• Discuss the **We Gather** questions concerning forgiveness. • Read and discuss the **We Believe** text. • Reflect on the **We Respond** question about the importance of God's forgiveness. • Read and discuss the *As Catholics* text on the seal of confession.	
Day 3		
pages 72–73 *We celebrate the sacrament of Reconciliation.*	• Discuss the **We Gather** question. • Read about and discuss the celebration of Reconciliation in the **We Believe** text. Complete the Act of Contrition activity. • Discuss the **We Respond** challenge.	• copies of Reproducible Master 5, guide page 67G • poster board
Day 4		
pages 74–75 *Reconciliation brings peace and unity.*  *2 Corinthians 13:11*	• Reflect on the **We Gather** questions. • Read and discuss the **We Believe** text on the effects of Reconciliation.  Discuss the **We Respond** question and complete the activity on peace and unity.	• slips of paper and the box labeled "Peace Begins with Us"
Day 5		
pages 76 **Review** **pages 77–78** **We Respond in Faith**	• Complete questions 1–10. Complete the *Assessment Activity.* • Complete the *Reflect and Pray* banner activity. • Review *Remember* and *Key Words.* • Read and discuss *Our Catholic Life.* • Discuss the **Sharing Faith with My Family** page	• magazines, newspapers, poster board, scissors, glue • Chapter 5 Test in Assessment Book, pp. 11–12 • Chapter 5 Test in Test Generator • Review & Resource Book, pp. 16–18 • Family Book, pp. 17–19

For additional ideas, activities, and opportunities: Visit Sadlier's **www.WEBELIEVEweb.com**

Enrichment Ideas

Chapter Story

At last, it was Friday! Kathleen had been waiting the entire week for the day of the school raffle. The school board was raffling numerous prizes including books, games, stuffed animals, and movies to help raise money for the school. Kathleen did not care one bit about any of these prizes. There was only one that she wanted with her whole heart: the Best Friend doll. She had begged and pleaded with her parents for this kind of doll for months and was always told that it was too expensive. The raffle was her only chance.

Kathleen patiently waited for the principal to announce the winner of the doll. Finally, she heard, "the winner of the Best Friend doll is Sara Kelly. Congratulations, Sara!"

Kathleen's jaw dropped in shock and disappointment. Sara Kelly was her little sister. She was only four years old! Their mother must have put Sara's name on one of the raffle tickets. Kathleen's teacher asked Kathleen to take the doll home to her sister. This gave Kathleen an idea. Since neither Sara nor her parents would even know who won it, Kathleen could claim the doll as her own. And that is what she did.

Although Kathleen convinced her family that she had won the doll, she could not let herself forget what she had done. She felt terrible whenever she looked at the doll. She didn't even want to play with it. A few days later, Kathleen told her parents what she had done. Kathleen's parents embraced her and asked what she wanted to do now. Kathleen knew right away what she wanted and needed to do.

She walked to her room, picked up the doll, and took it to Sara. "Sara," Kathleen calmly said, "this Best Friend doll is yours. You won it at the raffle, and I'm sorry I kept it from you."

▶ *If you were Kathleen, how might you feel now that you listened to your conscience and did the right thing?*

FAITH and MEDIA

▶ On Day 4, the students use the *We Respond* activity to list the things they can do to spread peace and unity. It is an opportunity to remind them of the media's power to influence people. In its 2002 document, *The Church and the Internet,* the Pontifical Council for Social Communication says, "young people need to learn how to function well in the world of cyberspace, make discerning judgments according to sound moral criteria about what they find there, and use the new technology for their integral development and the benefit of others" (number 7).

CHAPTER PROJECT: RECONCILIATION GUIDEBOOKS

This chapter project gives the students a chance to share what they will learn with others. Have them fold two pieces of any light colored construction paper in half in the same direction. Make a book by placing one folded sheet within another folded sheet. Explain that for each lesson of this chapter they will be given time to fashion a page in a Reconciliation Guidebook for next year's fourth graders. Have students design a cover for the book. Provide ten to fifteen minutes each day to work on the books. Each page will be a summary of that day's main ideas. Encourage the students to use both pictures and words to teach the lesson to others through their books.

Connections

To Liturgy

Explain that at the Penitential Rite at Mass we can examine our conscience and be assured of God's forgiveness of any venial sins. "You were sent to heal the contrite: Lord, have mercy . . . You came to call sinners: Christ, have mercy . . . You plead for us at the right hand of the Father: Lord, have mercy. May almighty God have mercy on us, forgive us our sins, and bring us to everlasting life. Amen." (*Penitential Rite*, I) Have the students work in pairs to write their own prayer based on this Penitential Rite.

To Family

Sharing stories is a way to show that different situations can be reconciled through peace and forgiveness. Have the students write a questionnaire. They could ask each family member to complete sentences, such as "I had to forgive someone when . . . " and "I was forgiven by someone when . . . " Discussing stories of forgiveness help students see examples of reconciliation in their own families.

To Parish

Reconciliation is one of the seven sacraments. It is a sacrament of healing in which, through the words and actions of the priest, we are forgiven by God. Have the students find out the schedule for the sacrament in their parish. Also give them information about special celebrations of Reconciliation during the seasons of Advent and Lent.

Meeting Individual Needs

Children with Reading Needs

Pictures can provide a great deal of valuable information for students, especially for those who struggle with reading. Emphasize the importance of pictures and how they visualize what we are learning. Encourage the students to gain new ideas and insights from the photo or artwork about the topic being studied. Help them to improve their skill of complementing the text with the pictures.

Additional Resources

Book *Reconciliation Services for Children: Eighteen Prayer Services to Celebrate God's Forgiveness*, Gwen Costello, Twenty-Third Publications, 1992. This book offers insights into celebrating Reconciliation in meaningful ways with your students.

Video *The Good Shepherd* CCC of America, 2000 From the series *A Kingdom Without Frontiers*. Jesus shows us how the Good Shepherd embraces all of us with his loving forgiveness. (30 minutes)

To find more ideas for books, videos, and other learning material, visit Sadlier's

www.WEBELIEVEweb.com

Nurturing Prayer in Children

by John Stack

The late John Stack was a vital member of the sales team at William H. Sadlier, Inc. for over nineteen years. In addition, John served as a Catholic schoolteacher and a catechist in the Diocese of Pittsburgh, PA and Wheeling-Charleston, WV for over thirty years. His talks and workshops will be remembered fondly by the thousands of people who were inspired by his unique gifts and his extraordinary witness for Christ.

The followers of Jesus made a request of him: "Lord, teach us to pray."(Luke 11:1) I firmly believe that, to this day, the greatest gift that we as catechists can share with the children is to develop a lifelong, personal relationship with God through the power of prayer.

We know that prayer is conversation with God, but sometimes we overlook the fact that this conversation is part of a *relationship* and is a *dialogue*, not a monologue. Prayer comes from who we are and is necessary to our relationship with God. Help to nurture the children's relationship with God by encouraging them to "talk" to God everyday. Let them know that they can talk to God about anything at anytime anywhere.

The Scriptures show us the way Jesus wants us to pray when he taught us the Lord's Prayer. Children learn by example. Encourage the children to pray using Jesus as a model. Jesus turned to his Father in prayer before important moments in his life. Children need to know that they can turn to God in the decisive moments of their lives. As Jesus drew apart from his followers to pray in solitude, children need to learn to set aside time regularly to be alone with God as well. Children can also learn to pray in faith as Jesus did. They can learn from his example to rely on God in everything and to ask for what they need.

Remind the children that they can pray in thanksgiving and praise, to bless, to ask for help (petition), and pray for others and themselves (intercession). Help the children to learn the cycle of the liturgical year and its great feasts. These provide the basic rhythms of the Catholic life of prayer. Invite the children to learn to focus their attention on Jesus for brief periods of time in order to lay the groundwork for meditation and contemplation later on in their lives.

Whenever possible include prayer for the children's families as part of your own personal prayer as well as classroom or group prayer. Encourage families to participate in prayer whenever possible at home, at school, and in the parish.

Catechist Development Topics (Topic and Guide Page)

Resources

Cronin, Gaynell Bordes. *Friend Jesus: Prayers for Children (Guiding Children into Daily Prayer)*. Cincinnati: St. Anthony's Messenger Press, 1999.

Gargiulo, Barbara. *How Do I Talk to God?* Allen, TX: Thomas More Publishing Co., 1998.

Ways to Implement Nurturing Prayer in Children

- At the beginning of the year gather the building blocks for your prayer space: the Bible, a crucifix, various colored cloths (green, purple, red, and white) to reflect the liturgical year, natural elements of the seasons, and pictures or statues of the saints whose feast days are celebrated in a particular month.

- Gather information to personalize the class or group prayer experience. A "Good News" center is a great way to collect information about the children's life stories. Ask for their birthdays, their baptismal dates, the names of their pets, and family members' birthdays. From this information, you can personalize the prayer space throughout the year. You will have the names of the children who are celebrating birthdays each week. For the feast of Saint Francis of Assisi on October 4, you can display the names of the children's pets. On the Baptism of the Lord, showcase the children's names and their baptismal dates.

- Develop the children's global awareness of the necessity of prayer. Using an inflatable globe and a box of adhesive bandages, encourage the children to place a bandage on the part of the world where the people who most need comfort and prayer live.

- Make a visit to the church. Stand by the ambo and pray for everyone who proclaims the word of God. Or perhaps you can walk to the rectory and pray for strong leadership to guide your parish and to pray for vocations.

- Build into each lesson a few moments for the children to meditate. Meditation engages thought, imagination, and emotion as well as strengthens the will to follow Jesus.

For additional ideas, activities, and opportunities, visit Sadlier's

www.WEBELIEVEweb.com

With thanks to:

Rosemary Hart
Teacher and Catechist
Saint Margaret Mary Church
Lomita, California

Rosemary uses a prayer collection to expand her students' knowledge, appreciation, and love of prayer. She asks each catechist in her parish to submit his or her favorite prayer and a brief explanation, describing how the prayer became known to the catechist. Then, Rosemary compiles the catechists' favorite prayers and explanations into a prayer collection for her students. During the year, she shares these prayers with the class. As the students become acquainted with the prayers, she asks everyone to share the prayers with their families. As an end-of-the-year project, Rosemary asks her students to submit their own favorite prayers for another collection of prayers. This collection is made available for each student to share with his or her family.

Notes

Name ____

Rite for Reconciliation of Several Penitents	Rite for Reconciliation of Individual Penitents
	I examine my conscience before meeting with the priest.
We sing an opening hymn and the priest greets us. The priest prays an opening prayer.	The priest greets me. I make the sign of the cross. The priest asks me to trust in God's mercy.
We listen to a reading from the Bible and a homily.	The priest or I may read something from the Bible.
We examine our conscience. We pray an act of contrition. We may say a prayer or sing a song, and then pray the Our Father.	
I meet individually with the priest. I confess my sins. The priest talks to me about loving God and others. He gives me a penance.	I meet individually with the priest. I confess my sins. The priest talks to me about loving God and others. He gives me a penance.
	I pray an act of contrition.
The priest extends his hand and gives me absolution.	The priest extends his hand and gives me absolution.
After everyone has met with the priest, we join together to conclude the celebration. The priest blesses us, and we go in the peace and joy of Christ.	Together the priest and I give thanks to God for his forgiveness.

Celebrating Penance and Reconciliation

✝ We Gather in Prayer

Leader: Let us listen to these words from the Bible.

Reader: "Have mercy on me, God,
in your goodness . . .
Wash away all my guilt;
from my sin cleanse me."

All: A clean heart create for me, O God.

Reader: "Still, you insist on
sincerity of heart;
in my inmost being teach me wisdom."

All: A clean heart create for me, O God.

Reader: "A clean heart create for me, God;
renew in me a steadfast spirit."
(Psalm 51:3, 4, 8, 12)

All: A clean heart create for me, O God.

Leader: God our Father, you sent your Son to show us how to be your loving children, but sometimes we fail to live as Jesus taught us. Show us your mercy and love in the sacrament of Penance and Reconciliation.

All: Amen.

67

Preparing to Pray

In this prayer the students will pray from the psalms and call on God to be merciful.

• Ask two students to lead the opening prayer. One will read the leader's part and the other will take the reader's part. Give them time to practice.

The Prayer Space

• Display a copy of the Act of Contrition from text page 73 of this chapter. Place the prayer in a picture frame and set it on the prayer table.

• Place a battery-operated candle on the prayer table. Set a picture of Jesus next to the candle.

This Week's Liturgy

Visit **www.webelieveweb.com** for this week's liturgical readings and other seasonal material.

Lesson Plan

We Gather in Prayer ___ minutes

✝ Pray

• Invite the students to gather together at the prayer space by saying *We gather in prayer.* Remind them about the need for quiet and stillness during today's prayer.

• Pray the Sign of the Cross. Then invite the selected volunteers to begin the opening prayer. Conclude with the Sign of the Cross.

Home Connection Update

Invite the students to talk about the Chapter 4 family page. How did their families pray together? Call on volunteers to share how their family makes good choices.

Catechist Goal

- To examine what Jesus tells us about God's forgiveness and love

Our Faith Response

- To experience what it means to repent and be reconciled to God

Teaching Tip

Peacemaking in the Classroom

Minor disputes are bound to occur in a group. At times these disputes may be difficult to resolve to everyone's satisfaction. Try to minimize these conflicts by encouraging students to make wise choices. Ask them to think before they act and decide whether their behavior reflects the teachings of Jesus. Remind students that they are in control of their actions. Urge them to seek one another's and God's forgiveness when unkind words or actions threaten to harm friendships and disrupt the group's unity.

Jesus tells us about God's forgiveness and love.

WE GATHER

✝ *God, we rejoice in your goodness.*

Think about what the friends might say to each other in each situation. With a partner, act out one of these situations.

- A friend who promises to meet you at the library never shows up.
- You borrow a friend's new CD and carelessly scratch it.
- You remain quiet while others in the class are making fun of your friend.

Discuss how the words and actions might affect the friendships.

WE BELIEVE

Jesus wanted all people to be brought back into complete friendship with God his Father. This restoring of friendship and peace is called *reconciliation*. Jesus' words and actions showed the importance of reconciliation.

In this parable Jesus taught that reconciliation is something to be celebrated:

"What man among you having a hundred sheep and losing one of them would not leave the ninety-nine in the desert and go after the lost one until he finds it? And when he does find it, he sets it on his shoulders with great joy and, upon his arrival home, he calls together his friends and neighbors and says to them, 'Rejoice with me because I have found my lost sheep.' I tell you, in just the same way there will be more joy in heaven over one sinner who repents than over ninety-nine righteous people who have no need of repentance." (Luke 15:4–7)

68

Lesson Plan

WE GATHER ___ minutes

✝ **Pray** Invite the students to pray the Sign of the Cross and the *We Gather* prayer.

Focus on Life Have a volunteer read the directions for the *We Gather* activity. Then group the students in pairs and ask them to consider these questions as they prepare their role-plays: *What do you say to your friend? What does your friend say to you?* Have them write down which situation they will act out and what they think the friends will say. After the students have a chance to practice, ask for volunteers to perform their skit in front of the class. Discuss in what ways they responded in those situations and what effect their actions might have on the friendship. Tell the students that in this lesson they will learn that God is always willing to forgive us because of his great love for us.

WE BELIEVE ___ minutes

Identify the Concept Have a volunteer read aloud the *We Believe* statement. Then have another volunteer read aloud the first *We Believe* paragraph. Explain: *Jesus' words and actions brought people peace and helped them understand that God loves them always.*

Discuss Scripture Have a volunteer read the parable about the lost sheep. Invite the students to share what this parable means to them. Then have a volunteer read the next *We Believe* paragraph that explains what Jesus was teaching about in this parable.

Talk About God's Love for All People Have the students read the final *We Believe* paragraphs silently. Emphasize that God is always willing to forgive us.

Jesus did not ignore sinners. He offered them his Father's love and forgiveness. Many times when Jesus forgave sinners he invited them to eat with him. It sometimes angered people that Jesus cared so much for sinners. But Jesus told them, "Those who are well do not need a physician, but the sick do" (Matthew 9:12).

Jesus reminded people how much God loved them. He encouraged them to ask for God's forgiveness and love. He wanted them to be reconciled with God his Father.

The word *repent* means to turn away from sin and to live the way God wants us to live. In this parable Jesus was encouraging people to repent. He taught them that if they repented God would rejoice and welcome them back.

WE RESPOND

What does it mean to repent?

What does it mean to be reconciled to God? to others?

Work with a partner. Think about a time when reconciliation was needed in your school or neighborhood. Write about the ways that the people worked to restore friendship and peace. Then share your work with the class.

69

ACTIVITY BANK

Faith and Media

Blessed Are the Peacemakers

Activity materials: heavyweight paper, glue, and newspapers.

In our world there is conflict all around us, but there are also peacemakers who work toward reconciliation. Have the students look in newspapers for headlines and pictures that show how people settle their differences. Have them construct a collage from the headlines and pictures they find. Collages can be done individually or cooperatively. Encourage the students to propose possible titles for the collage. The titles should promote the themes of peace and forgiveness.

Quick Check

✔ *What is reconciliation?* (Reconciliation is the restoration of friendship and peace with God and the Church.)

✔ *What did Jesus encourage the people to do?* (He asked them to turn to God for forgiveness and love, to repent, to turn away from sin, and to live the way God wants us to live.)

WE RESPOND ___ minutes

Connect to Life Invite the students to reflect on the *We Respond* questions. Ask a volunteer to read aloud the directions to the *We Respond* activity. Have the students work in pairs to discuss a situation in which people needed to be reconciled. Direct them to write ways that friendship and peace were restored in the situation. Have the students share their work.

Pray Invite the children to offer a prayer of thanksgiving for God's love and forgiveness.

Plan Ahead For Day 2

Catechist Goal: To show that we receive God's forgiveness in the sacrament of Reconciliation

Preparation: Be prepared to share why it is important to ask for God's forgiveness.

Chapter 5 • Day 2

Catechist Goal

- To show that we receive God's forgiveness in the sacrament of Reconciliation

Our Faith Response

- To understand the importance of asking for God's forgiveness

penitent
absolution

As Catholics...

Seal of Confession

After you have presented the lesson, call on a volunteer to read aloud *As Catholics*. Discuss the question. Stress that every priest is bound by the seal of confession. Encourage the students to speak freely to the priest who acts in the person of Jesus in the sacrament of Reconciliation.

We receive God's forgiveness in the sacrament of Reconciliation.

WE GATHER

✝ *Lord Jesus, you understand our weaknesses and show us mercy.*

How do you show that you forgive someone?

How do others show that they forgive you?

WE BELIEVE

We all need to be reconciled with God and with others. That is why forgiveness was an important part of Jesus' ministry.

Jesus wanted all people to be able to receive God's forgiveness. So Jesus gave his apostles the power to forgive sins in his name:

"'Peace be with you. As the Father has sent me, so I send you.' And when he had said this, he breathed on them and said to them, 'Receive the holy Spirit. Whose sins you forgive are forgiven them, and whose sins you retain are retained.'" (John 20:21–23)

Bishops and priests continue to forgive sins in the name of Christ and through the power of the Holy Spirit. They do this in the sacrament of Reconciliation.

If we sin, we can ask for God's forgiveness in the sacrament of Reconciliation. In this sacrament we receive God's mercy and celebrate our friendship with him. Our friendship with God and the Church is restored.

In the celebration of the sacrament of Reconciliation, the **penitent** is the person seeking God's forgiveness.

Contrition, confession, penance, and absolution are always part of the celebration of the sacrament of Reconciliation.

70

Lesson Plan

WE GATHER ___ minutes

✝ **Pray** Remind the students that the sacrament of Reconciliation is a celebration of God's forgiveness. Pray aloud the *We Gather* prayer.

Focus on Life Ask a volunteer to read the *We Gather* questions about ways people show forgiveness. Have the students reflect for a few moments, and then invite volunteers to share their responses. Tell the students that in this lesson they will learn that as members of the Church, we all need to be reconciled with God and with one another.

WE BELIEVE ___ minutes

Learn About the History Read aloud the *We Believe* statement. Invite volunteers to read aloud the *We Believe* paragraphs on page 70. Discuss with the students why Jesus passed on the power to forgive sin in his name. (He wanted all people to know and receive God's forgiveness.) Emphasize that this sacramental power has been given to priests at their ordination. Through the power of the Holy Spirit and the words of the priest, we are forgiven of sins.

Learn the Steps of Reconciliation Divide the class into four groups and assign each group one part of the sacrament (contrition, confession, penance, and absolution) as described on page 71. Have each group discuss its assigned part and then present this aspect of the sacrament to the entire class. Use the description on page 71 to correct any misunderstandings. Call on volunteers to explain what is happening in each photo on page 70.

The penitent:		The priest:	
contrition	• has a deep sorrow for sins committed • is truly sorry for sins and firmly intends not to sin again • prays an act of contrition.	***absolution***	• gives the penitent absolution. **Absolution** is God's forgiveness of sins through the words of the priest. The priest extends his hand and prays, "God, the Father of mercies, through the death and resurrection of his Son has reconciled the world to himself and sent the Holy Spirit among us for the forgiveness of sins; through the ministry of the Church may God give you pardon and peace, and I absolve you from your sins in the name of the Father, and of the Son, † and of the Holy Spirit."
confession	• tells, or confesses, his or her sins to the priest • talks with the priest about ways to love God and others.		
penance	• is asked by the priest to say a prayer or do something that shows sorrow for his or her sins. This prayer or action is called a *penance.* It can help the penitent to make up for any harm caused by sin and to grow as a disciple of Christ.		

penitent the person seeking God's forgiveness in the sacrament of Reconciliation

absolution God's forgiveness of sins through the words of the priest

As Catholics...

Celebrating the sacrament of Reconciliation strengthens our friendship with God. When we confess our sins to the priest, we tell him the thoughts, words, and actions that have led us away from God. Because we have received absolution we are able to let go of whatever might be keeping us from loving God.

It is important to remember that the priest can never, for any reason whatsoever, tell anyone what we have confessed. He is bound to secrecy by the sacrament. This secrecy is called the *seal of confession.*

Why do you think the seal of confession is important?

WE RESPOND

In Reconciliation, we ask God to forgive our sins. Why is it important to ask for God's forgiveness?

71

Chapter 5 • Day 2

ACTIVITY BANK

Multiple Intelligences

Visual-Linguistic

Activity materials: construction paper, string, colored markers

Have the students cut a large piece of construction paper into four ballooned-shaped pieces. Ask them to label each balloon with one of the parts of the sacrament of Reconciliation. Have them include either a picture or a sentence that explains what happens during that part. Have the students decorate the balloons with crayons or markers, put the string on them, and hang them around the room to show the steps in the sacramental celebration.

Curriculum Connection

Language-Vocabulary

There are many difficult vocabulary words in this section (*penitent, contrition, confession, penance,* and *absolution*). Allow the students time to understand the words' relationship to the celebration of Reconciliation. Give them the option of drawing each word's meaning, making a crossword puzzle, or writing a story that includes the five difficult words.

Quick Check

✔ *What is the sacrament of Reconciliation?* (It is the sacrament in which we receive God's forgiveness, and our friendship with God and the Church is restored.)

✔ *Name and describe each part of the celebration of the sacrament of Reconciliation.* (See chart in the book on page 71.)

WE RESPOND ___ minutes

Connect to Life Read aloud the *We Respond* section. Allow students a moment to think about the question. Ask them to imagine a world without forgiveness. Share your personal response with the students. Invite them to share their own.

Pray Conclude the lesson by thanking God for forgiveness. Pray the Our Father.

Plan Ahead For Day 3

Catechist Goal: To present the sacrament of Reconciliation as a celebration

Preparation: Have available copies of Reproducible Master 5 and a sheet of poster board.

Chapter 5 • **Day 3**

Catechist Goal

- To present the sacrament of Reconciliation as a celebration

Our Faith Response

- To identify ways to prepare for the sacrament of Reconciliation

Lesson Materials

- copies of Reproducible Master 5
- sheet of poster board

Teaching Note

Personal Testimony

As a catechist, you influence the students by teaching and by sharing your faith. Witnessing to your own belief in and experience of God's forgiveness can help the students as they prepare for Reconciliation. It is wise to plan ahead for what you will share so that your presentition is appropriate and the focus remains on God's forgiveness.

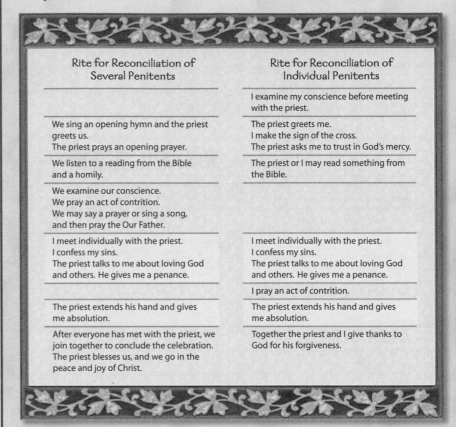

We celebrate the sacrament of Reconciliation.

WE GATHER

✝ *Lord Jesus Christ, grant us the grace to forgive one another as you have forgiven each one of us.*

Think about a time when you forgave someone. How did you reconcile with the person?

WE BELIEVE

When we are truly sorry for our sins, God forgives us. He gives us the grace to return to him and to be reconciled to him and the Church.

Here are two ways the Church celebrates the sacrament of Reconciliation.

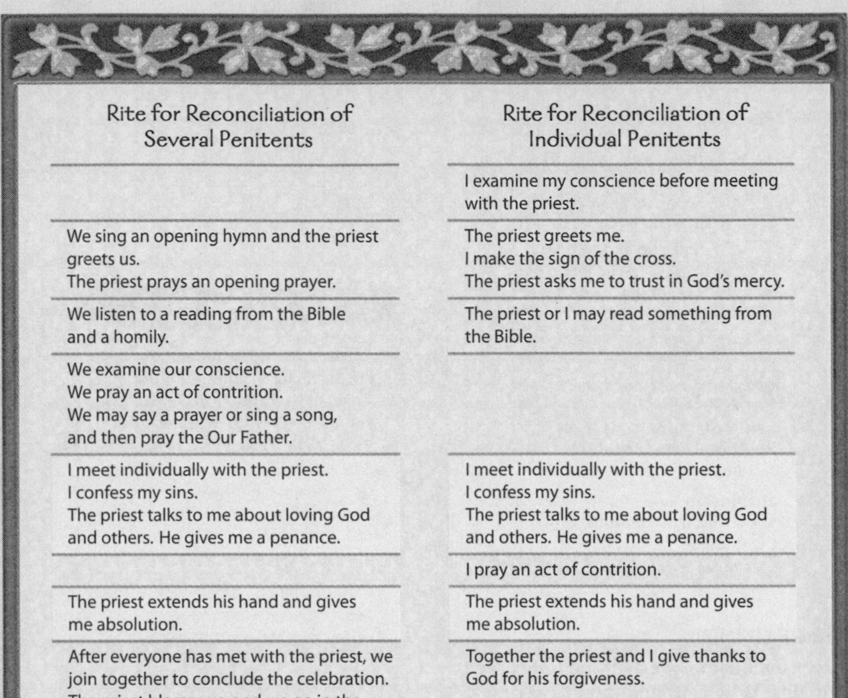

Rite for Reconciliation of Several Penitents	Rite for Reconciliation of Individual Penitents
	I examine my conscience before meeting with the priest.
We sing an opening hymn and the priest greets us. The priest prays an opening prayer.	The priest greets me. I make the sign of the cross. The priest asks me to trust in God's mercy.
We listen to a reading from the Bible and a homily.	The priest or I may read something from the Bible.
We examine our conscience. We pray an act of contrition. We may say a prayer or sing a song, and then pray the Our Father.	
I meet individually with the priest. I confess my sins. The priest talks to me about loving God and others. He gives me a penance.	I meet individually with the priest. I confess my sins. The priest talks to me about loving God and others. He gives me a penance.
	I pray an act of contrition.
The priest extends his hand and gives me absolution.	The priest extends his hand and gives me absolution.
After everyone has met with the priest, we join together to conclude the celebration. The priest blesses us, and we go in the peace and joy of Christ.	Together the priest and I give thanks to God for his forgiveness.

72

Lesson Plan

WE GATHER ___ minutes

✝ **Pray** Invite the students to think of someone who brings healing and forgiveness to others. Pray the *We Gather* prayer.

Focus on Life Read the *We Gather* question aloud. Remind the students that to reconcile with someone is to restore friendship and peace with that person. Give the students a moment to reflect. Tell the students that in this lesson they will learn about God's loving forgiveness in the sacrament of Reconciliation.

WE BELIEVE ___ minutes

Discuss What It Means to Be Sorry Have a student read aloud the *We Believe* statement. Ask the students what they mean when they say to God the words *I am sorry*. Discuss their opinions and reasons. Explain to them that when we say we are sorry, there is a real sense of trust or faith in God's mercy and forgiveness. God forgives our sins when we are truly sorry.

Describe the Celebration Ask a volunteer to read aloud the two *We Believe* paragraphs. Distribute copies of Reproducible Master 5 and have a volunteer read aloud the column titled "Rite for Reconciliation of Several Penitents." Have another volunteer read aloud the column titled "Rite for Reconciliation of Individual Penitents." Ask volunteers to give examples of celebrating each way. Tell the students to save their charts and refer to them each time they celebrate Reconciliation.

Think about this act of contrition. Write what this prayer, taken from the *Rite of Penance,* means to you.

Act of Contrition	What does this mean to you?
My God, I am sorry for my sins with all my heart.	______________________
In choosing to do wrong and failing to do good, I have sinned against you whom I should love above all things.	______________________
I firmly intend, with your help, to do penance, to sin no more, and to avoid whatever leads me to sin.	______________________
Our Savior Jesus Christ suffered and died for us. In his name, my God, have mercy.	______________________

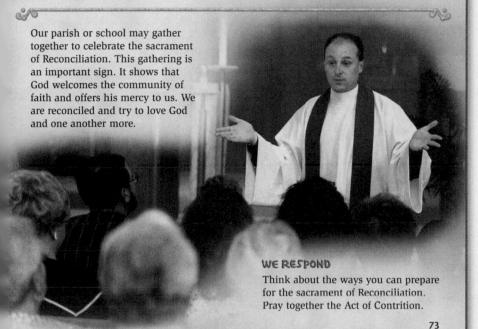

Our parish or school may gather together to celebrate the sacrament of Reconciliation. This gathering is an important sign. It shows that God welcomes the community of faith and offers his mercy to us. We are reconciled and try to love God and one another more.

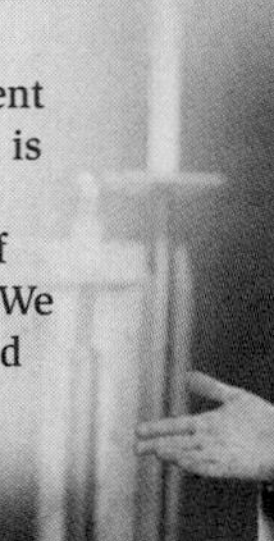

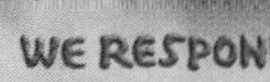

WE RESPOND

Think about the ways you can prepare for the sacrament of Reconciliation. Pray together the Act of Contrition.

73

ACTIVITY BANK

Multicultural Connection

Learning to Pray in Another Language

Activity Materials: an audio tape of a prayer in another language

Ask your school or community librarian to help you obtain an audio tape of prayers in another language. Preferably, the tape would have a recording of the Act of Contrition, the Our Father, or another prayer in which we ask God for forgiveness. Provide students with the English translation of the prayer. Encourage them to learn at least a short portion of the prayer in the other language. Talk about the emotions and ideas that the prayer expresses.

Reflect on the Act of Contrition Read aloud the Act of Contrition. Call on volunteers to explain its meaning. Ask the students to reread the prayer and write what the prayer means to them. Then invite them to read silently the last paragraph and explain how the photo relates to it.

Quick Check

✔ *Explain two of the ways the Church celebrates the sacrament of Reconciliation.* (The Church celebrates Reconciliation with several penitents and with individual penitents. In both ways, the penitents meet with the priest individually to confess sins and receive absolution.)

✔ *What does the Act of Contrition mean to you?* (Accept all reasonable answers.)

WE RESPOND ___ minutes

Connect to Life Ask the students to respond to the *We Respond* statement. List on a poster board students' ideas about preparing for the sacrament and display it.

Pray Pray aloud the Act of Contrition.

Plan Ahead For Day 4

Catechist Goal: To emphasize that reconciliation brings peace and unity

Preparation: Make a special box labeled "Peace Begins with Us" for a classroom project. Have available slips of paper.

Catechist Goal

- To emphasize that reconciliation brings peace and unity

Our Faith Response

- To share God's gift of peace and unity with other people

Lesson Materials

- box labeled "Peace Begins with Us"
- slips of paper

Teaching Tip

Wait-time

If you find that the same students continually answer the questions posed in class, then you may want to use wait-time to get other students involved. Instead of having students raise their hands to answer questions, you can have them give you a signal that indicates that they have an answer. Wait until you have received signals from at least half the class before you call on anyone. A signal can be a thumbs up, a nod, or pointing in your direction.

Reconciliation brings peace and unity.

WE GATHER

✝ *God, help us to be at peace.*

What can you do to make your home a happier place? a more peaceful place?

WE BELIEVE

When an early Christian community was having trouble with some of its members, Saint Paul wrote to them. He told them to stop arguing and to start working toward reconciliation. He said, "Mend your ways, encourage one another, agree with one another, live in peace, and the God of love and peace will be with you" (2 Corinthians 13:11).

Paul wanted the early Christians to treat one another with respect. He taught them to take care of those in the community who had needs. Today we can do the same.

- In our homes we can help our parents by doing our chores.
- In our school we can pay attention in class and treat others with respect.
- In sports and games we can include everyone. We can encourage everyone to work as a team.
- In our neighborhood we can respect the differences in the people around us. We can help those who need our help.
- In our parish we can celebrate the sacraments. We can participate in the parish activities that reach out to those in need.

These actions can help bring peace and unity to our communities. They can help to bring reconciliation where it is needed.

74

Lesson Plan

WE GATHER ___ minutes

✝ **Pray** Remind the students that listening and talking to God can help them draw closer to him. Invite the students to pray the Sign of the Cross and the *We Gather* prayer.

Focus on Life Have the students close their eyes and think quietly about their home. Have them imagine a peaceful time at home. Invite them to think about what is happening and what words are being said. Have the students read the *We Gather* questions. Invite them to share their ideas. Tell the students that in this lesson they will learn that we must act in ways that bring peace and unity to our homes, classrooms, and communities. Explain that today they will learn about a saint who tried to help a community that was not getting along.

WE BELIEVE ___ minutes

Learn About Saint Paul Have a student read aloud the *We Believe* statement. Give the students an opportunity to share their experiences of helping others to reconcile their differences. Invite volunteers to read aloud the first two *We Believe* paragraphs. Emphasize the following points.

- Saint Paul taught the people about Jesus Christ.
- Saint Paul wanted the early Christians to treat one another with respect.
- He taught that the people should take care of the needs of the people in the community.
- Today we can continue to follow Saint Paul's advice.

Make the Connections Ask a volunteer to read aloud the list of ways we can act as Saint Paul

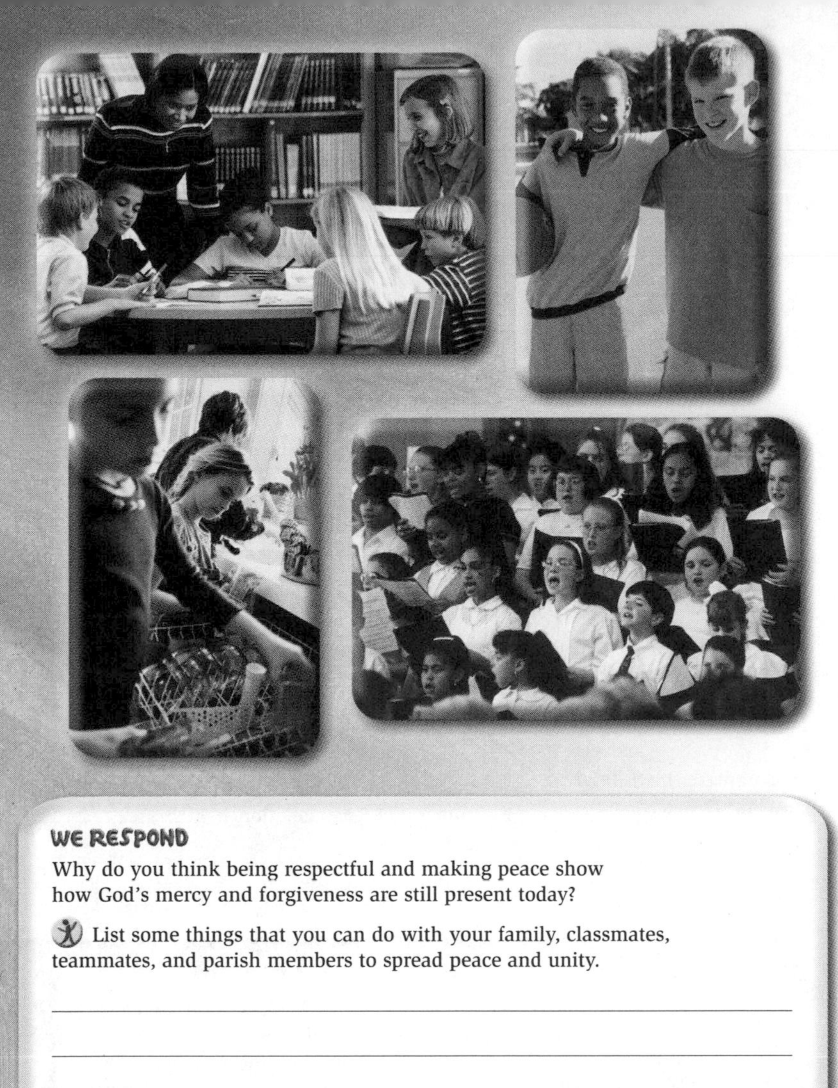

WE RESPOND

Why do you think being respectful and making peace show how God's mercy and forgiveness are still present today?

List some things that you can do with your family, classmates, teammates, and parish members to spread peace and unity.

75

ACTIVITY BANK

Catholic Social Teaching

Call to Family, Community, and Participation

Activity Materials: stationery, envelopes, stamps, and pens

Remind the students that Saint Paul took action when he saw others were not getting along. Saint Paul wrote a letter to the troubled community in the city of Corinth. He told them of the peace and love God wanted for them. Invite the students to use Saint Paul's example and think of a person in their community who needs more peace and love in his or her life. Ask them to take some quiet time to write this person a letter to offer friendship and encouragement.

suggested. Give the students an opportunity to think about their responses in the given settings. Have them think of ways they could help build a more peaceful and caring atmosphere.

Work Together as a Class Ask the students one way they could build peace. Include everyone in the peace-building effort. Place slips of paper next to a special box labeled "Peace Begins with Us." Encourage them to write what they hope to accomplish.

Quick Check

✔ *What message did Saint Paul have for an early Christian community?* (Stop arguing and start working towards reconciliation; spread the good news.)

✔ *How can we respect and care for those in the community who have needs that are not being met?* (Accept all reasonable answers.)

WE RESPOND ___ minutes

Connect to Life Have a volunteer read aloud the *We Respond* question. Discuss how each photo illustrates respect. Have the students work with a partner to complete the activity. Have the pairs share their ideas with the class.

Pray Pray aloud the Act of Contrition.

Plan Ahead For Day 5

Catechist Goal: To review chapter ideas and their relationship to our faith life

Preparation: Make copies of Chapter 5 Test in the Grade 4 Assessment Book. (option)

Chapter 5 • **Day 5**

Catechist Goal

- To review chapter ideas and their relationship to our faith life

Our Faith Response

- To apply what has been learned to our lives

CHAPTER TEST

Chapter 5 Test is provided in the Grade 4 Assessment Book.

Grade 4
Chapter 5

Write the letter of the phrase that defines each of the following:

1. d Absolution
2. c Penitent
3. a Reconciliation
4. b Repent

a. is the restoring of friendship and peace.

b. means to turn away from sin and live the way God wants us to live.

c. is the person seeking God's forgiveness in the sacrament of Reconciliation.

d. is God's forgiveness of sins through the words of the priest.

Circle the words that are part of the celebration of the sacrament of Reconciliation. Explain what the circled words mean.

(confession) baptism (penance)

beatitude (absolution) (contrition)

5. See pages 70–71. ______
7. ______
6. ______
8. ______

Complete the following:

9–10. In the celebration of the sacrament of Reconciliation See pages 72–73. ______

In a magazine, a newspaper, or on television, find a story about two groups of people who need to be reconciled. If you can, cut out the story or a photo. Write about the problem between the two groups and tell why they need reconciliation. Then report to the class on your findings.

76

Lesson Plan

___ minutes

Chapter Review Explain to the students that they are going to review what they have learned. Next, have the students complete questions 1–8. After they are finished, ask volunteers to say aloud each of the correct answers. Then have the students write their answer to question 9–10.

Assessment Activity Read the directions aloud. When the students have completed the activity, have them share the problem they found and why reconciliation is needed. As a class, discuss some possible ways to facilitate reconciliation in conflicts presented by the students.

___ minutes

Reflect & Pray Guide the students through the banner activity and create a peaceful atmosphere for the prayer. Pray together.

Key Words Write the key words on the board, leaving a large space in between. As a class, create a web around each word with lists of other related words. After the webs are made, review by recalling the definition of the word as it appears in the lesson.

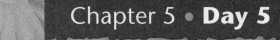

We Respond in Faith

Reflect & Pray

Write the words for a banner inviting parishioners of all ages to celebrate the sacrament of Reconciliation.

____

____

Key Words

penitent (p. 71)
absolution (p. 71)

Remember

- Jesus tells us about God's forgiveness and love.
- We receive God's forgiveness in the sacrament of Reconciliation.
- We celebrate the sacrament of Reconciliation.
- Reconciliation brings peace and unity.

Our Catholic Life

Ministering to the Sick

When Catholics are sick, at home or in the hospital, they can still receive the sacraments. A priest can visit and celebrate the sacrament of Reconciliation with them. The priest can also offer them Holy Communion. Together they will ask for God's healing and strength.

Sometimes a deacon or a special minister of the Eucharist will visit those who are sick. They will pray together and the deacon or special minister of the Eucharist will offer the sick person Holy Communion.

Home Connection

Sharing Faith with My Family

Make sure to send home the family page (text page 78).

Explain that the final piece of the discipleship puzzle is in this chapter's family page. Invite the students to put all the pieces of the puzzle together and to report the results. (It spells Disciples.)

For additional information and activities, encourage families to visit Sadlier's

www.WEBELIEVEweb.com

Remember Review the four *We Believe* statements. Divide the class into four groups and give each group a large piece of paper. Have the groups use their books to write information that supports and expands the main ideas. Have each group present the information they found to the class.

Our Catholic Life Before reading, check the students' prior knowledge by asking them ways parishes can care for people who are sick. Read aloud the *Our Catholic Life* text. After you finish reading, ask the students whether they know anyone who has received the sacraments while sick.

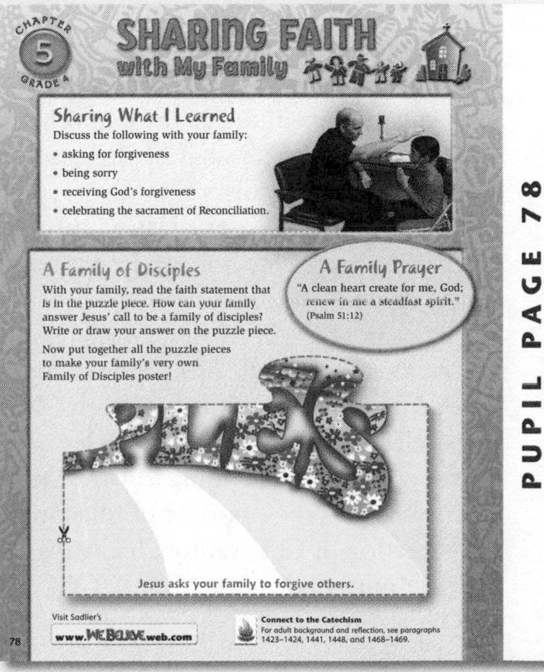
Chapter 5 Grade 4

SHARING FAITH with My Family

Sharing What I Learned

Discuss the following with your family:

- asking for forgiveness
- being sorry
- receiving God's forgiveness
- celebrating the sacrament of Reconciliation.

A Family of Disciples

With your family, read the faith statement that is in the puzzle piece. How can your family answer Jesus' call to be a family of disciples? Write or draw your answer on the puzzle piece.

Now put together all the puzzle pieces to make your family's very own Family of Disciples poster!

A Family Prayer

"A clean heart create for me, God; renew in me a steadfast spirit." (Psalm 51:12)

Jesus asks your family to forgive others.

Visit Sadlier's www.WEBELIEVEweb.com

Connect to the Catechism
For adult background and reflection, see paragraphs 1423–1424, 1441, 1448, and 1468–1469.

78

PUPIL PAGE 78

Chapter 6 The Liturgical Year

Advent | Christmas | Ordinary Time | Lent | Triduum | Easter | Ordinary Time

The Liturgical Year

By means of the yearly cycle the Church celebrates the whole mystery of Christ, from his incarnation until the day of Pentecost and the expectation of his coming again.

(Norms Governing Liturgical Calendars, 17)

Overview

In this chapter the students will learn that throughout the liturgical year we remember and celebrate Jesus Christ.

For Adult Reading and Reflection
You may want to refer to paragraphs 1168 and 1171 of the *Catechism of the Catholic Church*.

Catechist Background

Which of nature's seasons is most appealing to you? Why?

The celebration of the liturgical year exerts "a special sacramental power and influence which strengthens Christian life" [1](*Sharing the Light of Faith*, 144). Each of the passing seasons is invested with spiritual meaning as the Church remembers and celebrates the Paschal Mystery of Christ's passion, death and Resurrection. By participating mindfully in the seasons of the Church year, Christians keep time holy and "put on the Lord Jesus Christ" (Romans 13:14).

Since the time of Moses, God's people have celebrated an annual cycle of feast days commemorating the events of salvation history. Both Christians and Jews celebrate the Passover. "For Jews, it is the Passover of history, tending toward the future; for Christians, it is the Passover fulfilled in the death and Resurrection of Christ, though always in expectation of its definitive consummation" (CCC 1096).

Throughout the Church year, the liturgical celebrations of the Eucharist, the other sacraments, and the Liturgy of the Hours unfold the mystery of Christ. They also honor Mary, the Mother of God, and the birthdays (or days of death) of the saints. By their example and intercession, Mary and the saints draw us to the Father through the Son.

The Church each year not only recalls the mysteries of the redemption, but makes the "riches of her Lord's powers and merits" present to the faithful in every age" (CCC 1163). Thus, believers grow in grace and are formed in likeness to Christ.

How do you celebrate the meaning and significance of the liturgical year in your own life? in your family? with your students?

Lesson Planning Guide

Lesson Focus	Presentation	Materials
Day 1		
Guide page 79C **Text page 79** **Introduce the Season**	• Read the *Chapter Story*. • Introduce the Liturgical Year. • Proclaim the words on the banner.	
Day 2		
Guide and Text pages 80–81 **We Gather** **We Believe**	• Discuss special days and times in the **We Gather** questions. • Read and discuss the **We Believe** text about the seasons of the liturgical year.	
Day 3		
Guide page and Text page 82 **We Respond**	Complete the chart on the colors used during liturgical year. • Read and discuss the text about Mary and the saints. Fill in the calendar with events in the **We Respond** activity.	• calendars
Day 4		
Guide page and Text page 83 **We Respond in Prayer**	• Listen to scriptural verses. • Respond in prayer.	• prayer space items: a liturgical calendar
Day 5		
Guide pages 84A–84B **We Respond in Faith**	• Explain the individual The Liturgical Year project. • Explain the group The Liturgical Year project. • Discuss the **Sharing Faith with My Family** page.	• copies of Reproducible Master 6, guide page 84A

For additional ideas, activities, and opportunities: Visit Sadlier's **www.WEBELIEVEweb.com**

Chapter Story

From the moment Hilda was up in the morning to the moment she fell into bed at night, she was on the go. Usually, she ran out of the house and skipped breakfast. She had too many other more important things to do.

Even before the school day started, Hilda rushed to the gym for gymnastics practice. She worked very hard on the flying rings and the pommel horse. Then she rushed to her schoolroom just on time for the opening announcements. Hilda worked hard in all of her classes.

After school, Hilda went to soccer practice or dance lessons. Many of her friends did the same. "Sometimes I just wish I had nothing to do," Hilda told her best friend Jennifer one day after practice. Jennifer nodded and replied, "One day last week I skipped practice and just went home and read a book. It was like having a vacation."

That word "vacation" kept popping up in Hilda's head like a flashlight in a dark room. The next day, with her mother's permission, she called her dance teacher and said, "Mrs. Trimble, I can't come to practice today. I'm taking a vacation." And that's exactly what Hilda did.

She curled up with a book, but kept nodding off and on while trying to read it. She felt good just relaxing and having time to herself. Her vacation from her usual hectic routine had given her a chance to think about some important things she might be overlooking. One of the most important things she knew she was forgetting was prayer in her life. She used to begin and end the day with prayer. She remembered what her grandfather had once told her, "God is paying attention to you twenty-four hours a day, Hilda. So it couldn't hurt for you to pay attention to him a little, could it?"

▶ *Would you describe your daily schedule as busy as Hilda's? What could you do to set aside some time and pay attention to what you might be missing in your life?*

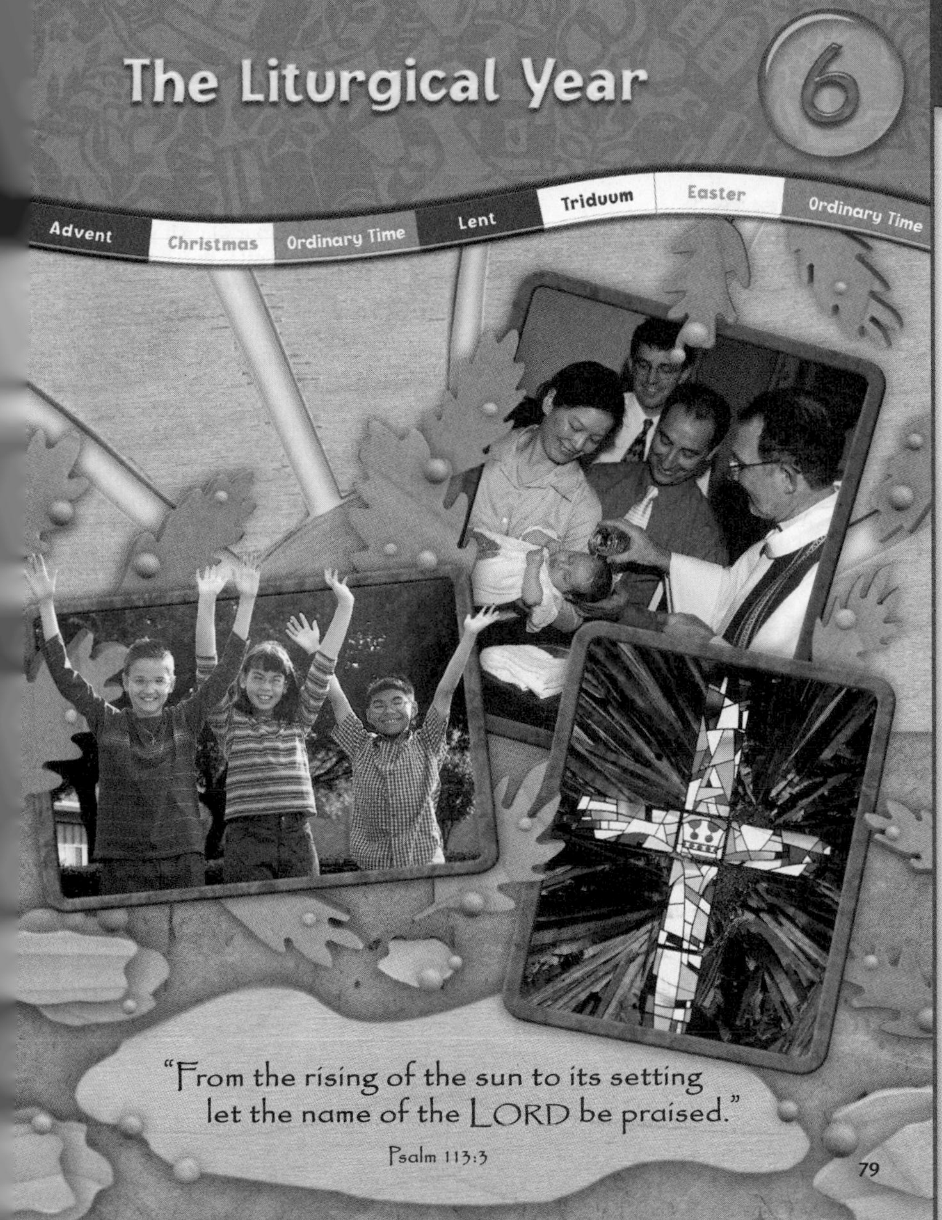

The Liturgical Year
6
Advent
Christmas
Ordinary Time
Lent
Triduum
Easter
Ordinary Time
"From the rising of the sun to its setting
let the name of the LORD be praised."
Psalm 113:3
79

Catechist Goal

- To emphasize that throughout the liturgical year we remember and celebrate Jesus Christ

Our Faith Response

- To appreciate the Church's the liturgical seasons within the regular calendar year

ADDITIONAL RESOURCES

Book *Celebrating the Liturgical Year: Special Seasons, Special Feasts,* Hi-Time Pflaum, 2000. These reproducible handouts offer activities for each liturgical season.

Video *The Angel's Church Year Lesson,* Twenty-Third Publications, 2001. Three angels take children on a journey through the Church year to show how Jesus is with us always. (11 minutes)

To find more ideas for books, videos, and other learning material, visit Sadlier's

www.WEBELIEVEweb.com

Lesson Plan

Introduce the Season ___ minutes

Pray the Sign of the Cross and the prayer "From the rising of the sun to its setting /let the name of the Lord be praised" (Psalm 113:3).

- **Read** aloud the *Chapter Story* on guide page 79C. Discuss the students' responses to the follow-up question. Help them to see that like Hilda they too need to step back and reflect on what is important in life. Encourage them to take a "vacation" as Hilda did. It might be an opportunity to get in touch with their prayer lives.

- **Have** the students open their text to page 79. Read aloud the chapter title. Explain: *The liturgical year is the term we use to describe the times and seasons of the Church year.*

- **Invite** the students to study the photos. Ask: *What do you see in these photos that tell you about celebrating the Church's liturgical seasons?* Have volunteers share what they might know about the Church's liturgical year.

- **Proclaim** together the words on the banner under the photo.

Lesson Materials
- calendars
- copies of Reproducible Master 6

Teaching Note

Autumn Blessings

In the autumn months of September and October there are special feast days that can be celebrated with blessings. Either the feast of Archangels Michael, Gabriel and Raphael (September 29) or the feast of the Guardian Angels (October 2) may be observed with a blessing of flower bulbs to be planted. The feast of Saint Francis of Assisi (October 4) is the traditional date for the blessing of animals.

Throughout the liturgical year we remember and celebrate Jesus Christ.

WE GATHER

✝ *God, we are your people throughout all time.*

How do we find out the day of the week, the month, and the year? Why is it important to know these things?

Are certain days special to you? Are certain times of the year special to you? Why?

WE BELIEVE

As members of the Church, we, too, have days and times of the year that are special. We remember these times in a very important way when we celebrate the liturgy, the official public prayer of the Church. The celebration of the Eucharist, also called the Mass, is liturgy. The liturgy also includes the celebration of the other sacraments and the Liturgy of the Hours. The Liturgy of the Hours is a special prayer of the Church that is prayed several times during the day.

The liturgy is so important to the life of the Church that our Church year is called the liturgical year. Throughout the liturgical year, we remember and celebrate everything about Jesus Christ: his birth, life, death, Resurrection, and Ascension.

When we celebrate the life of Christ, we show that we believe in God the Father, the Son, and the Holy Spirit. As we go through the year with Christ, we grow in faith, hope, and love. We discover that every day of the year is a day to live in joyful hope and praise of God.

The readings we hear, the colors we see, and the songs we sing help us to know what season we are celebrating. Do you know what season we are celebrating now? Use this diagram of the liturgical year to help you to find out.

The liturgical year begins in late November or early December with the season of Advent.

80

Lesson Plan

WE GATHER

___ minutes

Focus on Life Discuss the *We Gather* questions about special days and times of the year. Make a list of their responses on the board.

• **Have** the students open their books to text page 80. Explain: *Today you will examine why it is important to know about and participate in the seasons of the Church year.*

WE BELIEVE

___ minutes

• **Invite** a student read aloud the *We Believe* statement. Have a volunteer read aloud the first three *We Believe* paragraphs. Stress that throughout the cycle of the liturgical year we celebrate the entire life and work of Jesus Christ. Point out that each day the Church celebrates the Eucharist and also prays the Liturgy of the Hours to praise and thank God the Father, God the Son, and God the Holy Spirit.

Advent
Christmas
Ordinary Time
Lent
Three Days
Easter
Ordinary Time

Advent The season of Advent prepares us for the celebration of Jesus' first coming. Over two thousand years ago Jesus was born, the Son of God became one of us. During Advent we also celebrate that Christ is in the world today, and that Christ will come again. We watch, wait, and pray, "Come, Lord Jesus!" (Revelation 22:20).

Christmas The Christmas season begins on Christmas Day with the celebration of the birth of the Son of God. During the Christmas season we celebrate that God is with us. We rejoice because "A Son is born to us, and he is the Prince of Peace. Alleluia!"

Lent The season of Lent begins on Ash Wednesday. Lent is a special time to remember that Jesus suffered, died, and rose to new life for us. During Lent we try to become more like Jesus through prayer and acts of mercy and kindness. We pray, "Jesus, help us to follow you." In these ways we prepare for the Church's greatest celebration.

Triduum The Easter Triduum is the Church's greatest and most important celebration. The word *triduum* means "three days." During these three days, from Holy Thursday evening until Easter Sunday evening, we remember the death of Jesus and celebrate his Resurrection. We pray, "We worship you, Lord. Through the cross you brought joy to the world."

Easter The season of Easter begins on Easter Sunday evening and continues until Pentecost Sunday. We sing for joy because "Christ is risen, and makes all things new. Alleluia!"

Ordinary Time The season of Ordinary Time is celebrated in two parts: the first part is between Christmas and Lent, and the second part between Easter and Advent. During this season we celebrate the whole life of Christ. We learn more about Jesus and the Christian life. We listen to God's word and act on it. We pray, "Here am I, Lord; I come to do your will."

THE LITURGICAL YEAR

81

Activity Bank

Curriculum Connection

Language Arts-Spelling

Activity Materials: graph paper or blank paper with rulers

This chapter includes many faith words that will be repeated throughout the text's liturgical lessons. This first overview lesson provides a good opportunity to begin to introduce the students to the new words. Invite them to make word walls or checkerboard charts of the words listed below. Distribute markers or crayons and have partners quiz each other on how to spell each word on the wall. As they spell a word correctly, the students color in that square. The project may continue over several weeks until the word walls are completely colored. A list you might build upon could include the following terms: liturgical, Resurrection, Ascension, Triduum, Easter, Eucharist, celebrate, Christmas, alleluia, Advent, Ordinary, disciple, feast, saint, and season.

• **Introduce** the students to the liturgical calendar by reading aloud the fourth *We Believe* paragraph. Have the students work with partners to read and underline the important points of each of the six seasons. Have volunteers share their important points with the group. Help the students to decide which season of the Church year is being celebrated now.

Quick Check

✔ *What do we do throughout the liturgical year?* (Throughout the liturgical year we remember and celebrate the birth, life, death, Resurrection, and Ascension of Jesus Christ.)

✔ *What are the names of the liturgical seasons?* (The names of the seasons are Advent, Christmas, Lent, Easter Triduum, Easter, and Ordinary Time.)

Connection

To Family

Family Involvement in the Liturgy

The involvement of the students and their families in the celebration of the Church year is the bedrock of their faith lives. Their participation in the Church's liturgy nourishes and supports them as they journey with their brothers and sisters within the Body of Christ, the Church. Have the students identify ways that might encourage more family members to participate in their parish's liturgical celebrations throughout the year. Encourage the students to reflect on the impact the liturgy has on their own faith and lives.

Take another look at the diagram of the liturgical year. Then work with a partner and complete this chart. Remember that some colors are used in more than one season.

color	sign of	season(s)
violet	expectation, waiting, penance	Advent, Lent
white or gold	joy and light	Christmas, Triduum (Holy Thursday and Easter Vigil), Easter
green	life and hope	Ordinary Time
red	royalty, fire, death	Triduum (Good Friday)

Honoring Mary and the Saints

In every liturgical season there are feast days that honor Mary, the mother of Jesus, with special love. The Church is devoted to Mary because she is the mother of the Son of God. We believe that she is our mother and the Mother of the Church, too. She is a great example for living as a disciple of Jesus. On her feast days we remember the ways that God blessed Mary. We recall important events in her life and in the life of Jesus.

During the liturgical year we also remember the saints—women, men, and children who have lived lives of holiness on earth and now share eternal life with God in heaven.

The saints were faithful followers of Christ. They loved and cared for others as Jesus did. Some of the saints even died for their belief in Christ. We celebrate that their lives are examples of faith for us. We ask the saints to pray with us to God.

We Respond

Work with a partner. Get a twelve-month calendar and show the liturgical season you are in as you go from January 1 to December 31. Talk about where the liturgical seasons fit into the regular calendar year. What might be happening in school, at home, or in the neighborhood during each liturgical season? Brainstorm some ways that those every day activities can help us to live in joyful hope and praise.

82

Lesson Plan

We Believe (continued) ___ minutes

Read aloud the activity directions. When the students are finished, have them share answers.

• **Read** aloud the *We Believe* paragraphs about honoring Mary and the saints. Stress the special role Mary played in the life of Jesus. Also note that the saints are honored throughout the year on their feast days. Ask the students to find out the feast day of their parishes' patron saints.

We Respond ___ minutes

Connect to Life Read aloud the directions to the *We Respond* activity. Encourage the students to be creative in making their calendars. Circulate among them as they work on their calendars. Share results as a group. Remind the students to share with their families what they are learning about the liturgical year. Encourage them to connect their daily prayer with the current season.

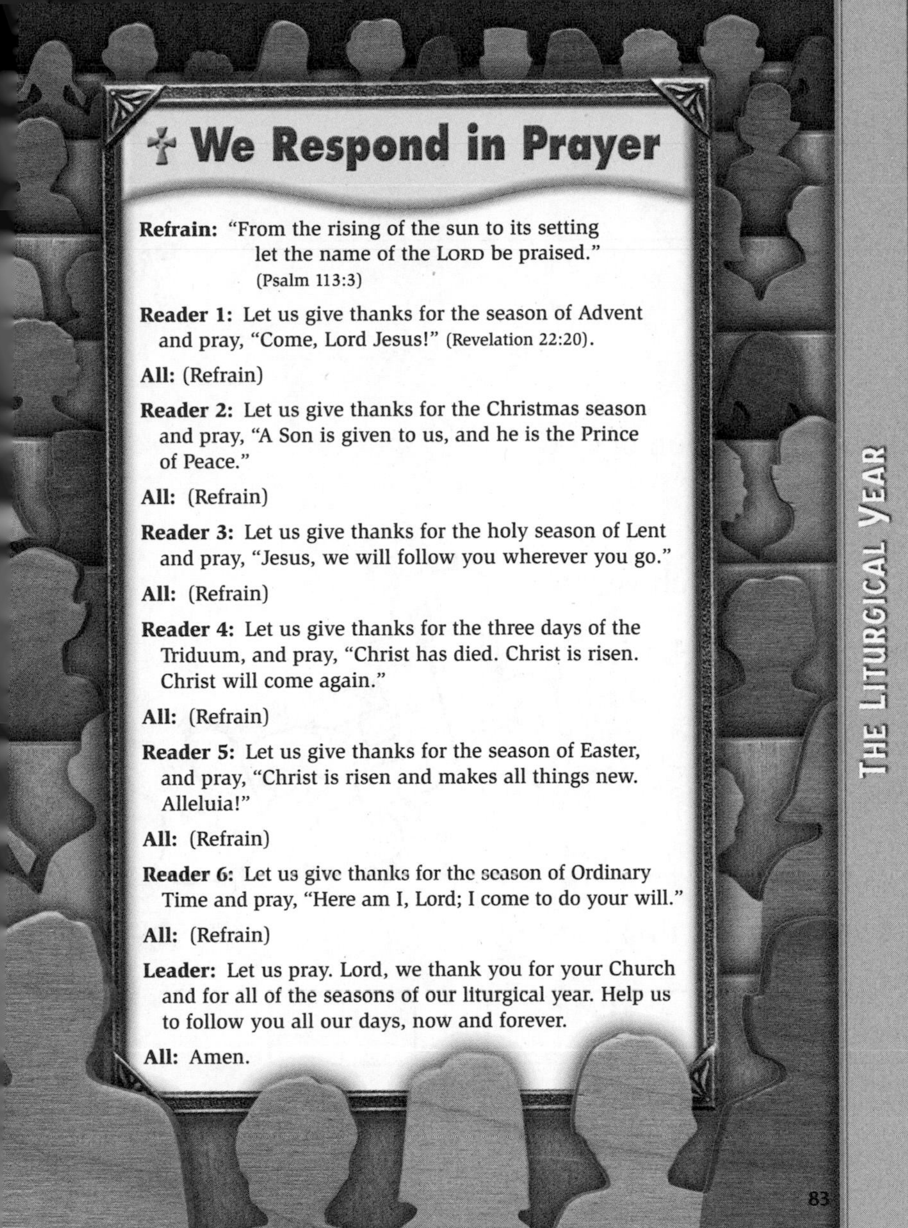

We Respond in Prayer

Refrain: "From the rising of the sun to its setting let the name of the LORD be praised." (Psalm 113:3)

Reader 1: Let us give thanks for the season of Advent and pray, "Come, Lord Jesus!" (Revelation 22:20).

All: (Refrain)

Reader 2: Let us give thanks for the Christmas season and pray, "A Son is given to us, and he is the Prince of Peace."

All: (Refrain)

Reader 3: Let us give thanks for the holy season of Lent and pray, "Jesus, we will follow you wherever you go."

All: (Refrain)

Reader 4: Let us give thanks for the three days of the Triduum, and pray, "Christ has died. Christ is risen. Christ will come again."

All: (Refrain)

Reader 5: Let us give thanks for the season of Easter, and pray, "Christ is risen and makes all things new. Alleluia!"

All: (Refrain)

Reader 6: Let us give thanks for the season of Ordinary Time and pray, "Here am I, Lord; I come to do your will."

All: (Refrain)

Leader: Let us pray. Lord, we thank you for your Church and for all of the seasons of our liturgical year. Help us to follow you all our days, now and forever.

All: Amen.

THE LITURGICAL YEAR

83

PREPARING TO PRAY

The students will respond to several scriptural readings with a refrain from Psalm 113.

- Choose six readers to proclaim the readings.
- Practice the refrain.

The Prayer Space

- Display a liturgical calendar on or near the prayer table.

This Week's Liturgy

Visit **www.webelieveweb.com** for this week's liturgical readings and other seasonal material.

We Respond in Prayer ___ minutes

- **Have** the students gather in the prayer space.
- **Pray** the Sign of the Cross.
- **Act** as leader. Signal the students when to pray the refrain and the readers when to proclaim their messages.
- **Conclude** by calling upon Mary and all the saints to pray for us now and throughout the liturgical year.

Name ____

Complete the crossword puzzle.

Across

2. Season when we celebrate the birth of the Son of God
4. Season that begins on Ash Wednesday
5. The most important celebration of the Church year
6. Another name for the celebration of the Eucharist
8. Season celebrated in two parts
9. Season when we celebrate Jesus' Resurrection

Down

1. Season when we prepare to celebrate Jesus' first coming
3. We praise God from the rising of the ______
4. The name we give to the Church year is the ______ year
6. Mother of Jesus, Mother of the Church
7. The person whose life we celebrate throughout the Church year

We Respond in Faith

Individual Project

Distribute Reproducible Master 6. Discuss the directions. Use this activity to review the important terms introduced in this chapter.

When the students have completed the puzzle, have volunteers share their responses.
(Across: 2. Christmas, 4. Lent, 5. Triduum, 6. Mass, 8. Ordinary Time, 9. Easter; Down: 1. Advent, 3. sun, 4. liturgical, 6. Mary, 7 Jesus)

Group Project

Have the students form five groups. Assign each group one decade of the rosary from the Joyful Mysteries. For example, the first group would be assigned the first Joyful Mystery the Annunciation. Have each group decide when it will pray the decade and for whom the group wishes to pray. Stress that this Marian prayer is focused on the important events of Jesus' life and Mary's participation in them.

Home Connection

Sharing Faith with My Family

Make sure to send home the family page (text page 84).

Encourage the students to share the seasonal matching exercise and talk about the family's seasonal activities.

For additional information and activities, encourage families to visit Sadlier's

www.WEBELIEVEweb.com

CHAPTER 6 GRADE 4

SHARING FAITH with My Family

Sharing What I Learned

Discuss the following with your family:

- the liturgy
- the liturgical year and seasons
- Jesus, Mary, and the saints.

Activities for Each Season

Advent Bake Christmas cookies. Give some to a family or neighbor who may not have any.

Christmas On Holy Family Sunday or Epiphany, write thank-you notes together. Pray for all those who have been good to your family.

Lent Make a Lenten prayer calendar. List the six weeks of Lent. Write a special intention that you will pray for during each week. It might be for the needs of someone, justice and peace in the world. Find a time to pray these intentions together.

Triduum Display and pray this family prayer. "Jesus, help us follow you from sorrow to joy and from death to life. Amen."

Easter Make an Easter basket for a neighbor or someone who may not receive one.

Ordinary Time As a family share your talent, time, and treasure with others during all of Ordinary Time.

Liturgical Seasons

Ask the members of your family to read these Bible verses. Then write the season that each describes.

Luke 24: 1–7 ________

John 1:19–23 ________

Matthew 1:18–21 ________

Mark 1:12–13 ________

Visit Sadlier's www.WEBELIEVEweb.com

Connect to the Catechism
For adult background and reflection see paragraph 1168.

84

PUPIL PAGE 84

Ordinary Time

Apart from those seasons having their own distinctive character, thirty-three or thirty-four weeks remain in the yearly cycle that do not celebrate a specific aspect of the mystery of Christ. Rather, especially on the Sundays, they are devoted to the mystery of Christ in all its aspects. This period is known as Ordinary Time.

(Norms Governing Liturgical Calendars, 43)

Overview

In this chapter the students will learn that during the season of Ordinary Time, we celebrate the life and teachings of Jesus Christ.

For Adult Reading and Reflection
You may want to refer to paragraphs 1163 and 1167 of the *Catechism of the Catholic Church*.

Catechist Background

How do you encounter Christ in your daily life?

Ordinary Time in the liturgical year refers to those numbered weeks that fall between the seasons of Christmas and Lent and between the seasons of Easter and Advent. This season lasts a total of thirty-three or thirty-four weeks. During these weeks the Church celebrates "no specific aspect of the mystery of Christ" but "the mystery of Christ in all its aspects" (*General Norms for the Liturgical Year and the Calendar*, 43). As on all the Sundays of the Church year, we continue to experience and appropriate Christ's dying and rising.

The Sunday cycle of gospel readings for Ordinary Time progresses through the synoptic Gospels of Matthew (Year A), Mark (Year B), and Luke (Year C). The Gospel of John is proclaimed primarily during the seasons of Christmas, Lent, and Easter. Because the stories of Jesus' life and teachings are read in sequential order during Ordinary Time, the Church is immersed in a particular evangelist's narration for an entire year. We are led by the synoptics from the beginning of Jesus' public ministry to his final journey to Jerusalem.

In this way, the good news first proclaimed and recorded by the four evangelists continues to be proclaimed by the faith community. "Moreover, the Good News of the Kingdom which is coming and which has begun is meant for all people of all times. Those who have received the Good News and who have been gathered by it into the community of salvation can and must communicate and spread it" (*On Evangelization in the Modern World*, 13).

How do I encounter Jesus and experience the good news? Consider reading reflectively the gospel being used for the liturgical year.

Lesson Planning Guide

Lesson Focus	Presentation	Materials
Day 1		
Guide page 85C **Guide and Text page 85** **Introduce the Season**	• Read the *Chapter Story*. • Introduce the season of Ordinary Time. • Proclaim the words on the banner.	
Day 2		
Guide and Text pages 86–87 **We Gather** **We Believe**	• Discuss the We Gather questions. • Read and define *Ordinary Time* and learn about the four evangelists in We Believe.	
Day 3		
Guide and Text page 88 **We Respond**	Complete the We Respond activity.	
Day 4		
Guide and Text page 89 **We Respond in Prayer**	• Listen to Scripture. Respond in song.	"Prayer of Saint Francis/Oracion de San Francisco," #4, Grade 4 CD • prayer space items: symbols of season, statue of Saint Francis of Assisi, green tablecloth
Day 5		
Guide and Text pages 90A–90B **We Respond in Faith**	• Explain the individual project for Ordinary Time. • Explain the group project for Ordinary Time. • Discuss the Sharing Faith with My Family page.	• copies of Reproducible Master 7, guide page 90A

For additional ideas, activities, and opportunities: Visit Sadlier's **www.WEBELIEVEweb.com**

Focus on Life

Chapter Story

Although George Wong's parents belonged to the Buddhist faith, they sent him to a Catholic school. George was attracted to the faith of his classmates. He prayed for guidance and then asked his parents if he could be baptized. They agreed.

As an adult, George prayed that God would help him decide what to do to live out his faith. After praying and talking with his closest friends, George decided to become a Jesuit. He was ordained in China just before that country was taken over by the Communists. The Communist regime did not believe in God or in freedom of religion. On both counts, Father George was arrested and put in prison.

While in prison, Father George did not have a calendar. He kept track of the date by reading a newspaper. The date told him what season of the Church year it was, whether it was Advent or Christmas, Lent or Easter, or Ordinary Time. Father George felt he was praying with whole Church even in prison. He knew that Christ was with him through all the seasons of his imprisonment.

When his cell mate asked to become a Catholic, Father George came up with an ingenious way to teach him the Our Father, the Hail Mary, and the Apostles' Creed. He printed out each prayer with a wet rag on the prison cell door. When the man asked to be baptized, the priest again came up with a plan. The man walked behind the priest into the outdoor showers. Father George then sprinkled water over his shoulder on the convert's head and whispered, "I baptize you in the name of the Father, and of the Son, and of the Holy Spirit."

Father George Wong was finally freed from prison in 1983. He came to the United States. He died in 2001. Throughout his imprisonment, he prayed daily with his fellow Catholics around the world whom he could not see. "I simply trusted God," he said.

▶ *How did George's faith help him to follow Christ as a young person? As a priest?*

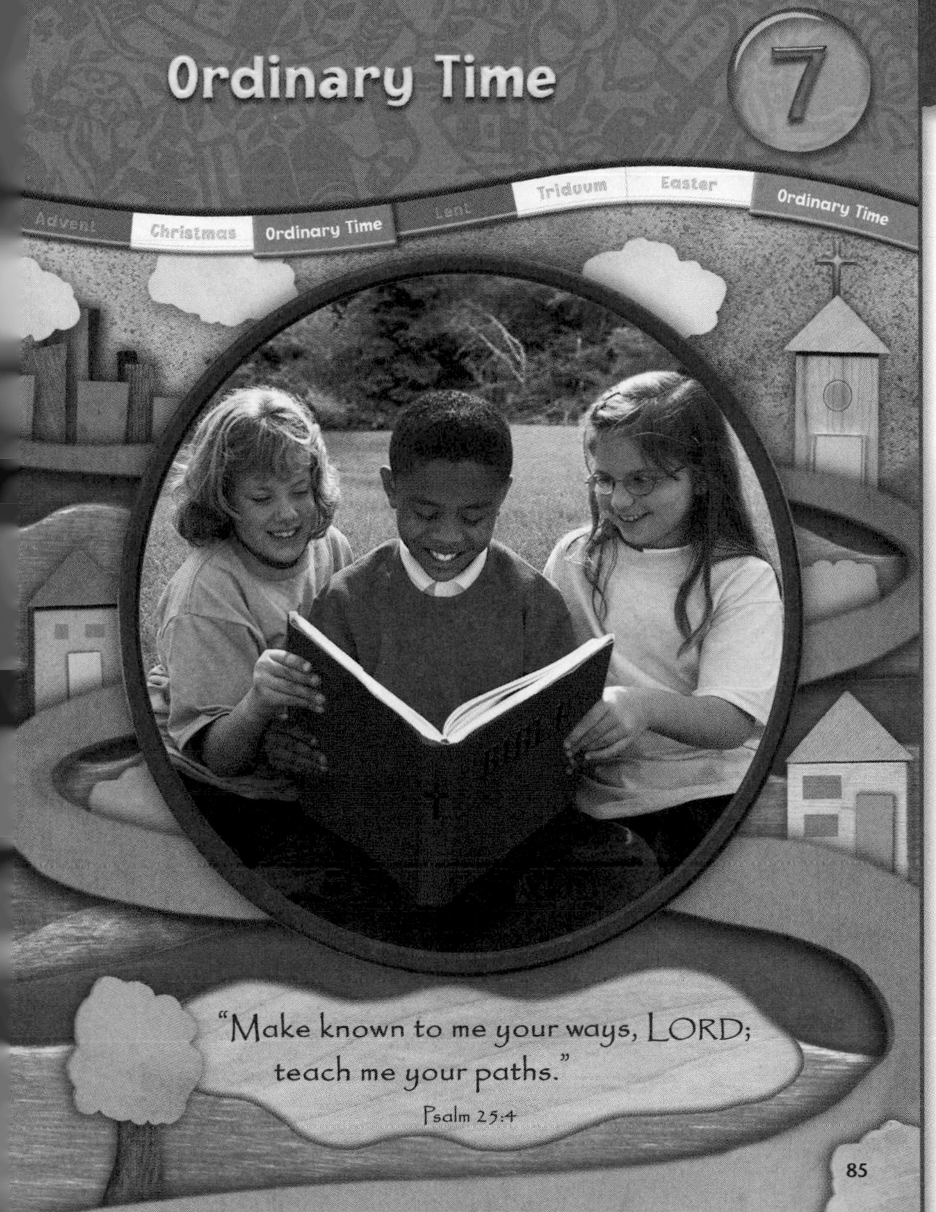

Ordinary Time
7
Advent
Christmas
Ordinary Time
Lent
Triduum
Easter
Ordinary Time
"Make known to me your ways, LORD;
teach me your paths."
Psalm 25:4
85

Catechist Goal

- To explain that during the season of Ordinary Time, we celebrate the life and teachings of Jesus Christ

Our Faith Response

- To celebrate Ordinary Time by praying, learning about Christ, and spreading the good news

ADDITIONAL RESOURCES

Videos *Following Jesus Through the Church Year: Christian Corner,* Twenty-Third Publications, 1991. Krispin travels to Damascus and hears of Paul's conversion. (10 minutes)

Following Jesus Through the Church Year: Witness Way, Twenty-Third Publications, 1991. Krispin travels with Paul and is finally baptized into the Christian community. (10 Minutes)

To find more ideas for books, videos, and other learning material, visit Sadlier's

www.WEBELIEVEweb.com

Lesson Plan

Introduce the Season ___ minutes

- **Pray** the Sign of the Cross and the psalm verse "Make known to me your ways, Lord; teach me your paths" (Psalm 25:4).
- **Read** aloud the *Chapter Story* on guide page 85C. Point out the way Father George kept track of the seasons of the Church year and knew that Jesus was with him.
- **Have** the students look at page 85. Read aloud the chapter title. Explain: *Ordinary Time is a season of the Church year. During this time we celebrate the whole life of Christ. We focus on learning his teachings and following his example.*
- **Ask** the students to discuss the on-page photos and artwork. Remind them that God guides us in all that we say and do. God's paths lead us to him.
- **Proclaim** together the words on the banner under the photo.

Lesson Materials
- Bible
- Grade 4 CD
- copies of Reproducible Master 7

Teaching Note

A Change of Pace

Whenever students need a change of pace in the classroom schedule, have them play "Hidden Identity." Attach to each person's back a name tag of a familiar biblical character. One person at a time stands back-to a small group. He or she then asks the group four questions to try to discover his or her hidden identity. The process goes on until everyone guesses correctly.

During the season of Ordinary Time, we celebrate the life and teachings of Jesus Christ.

WE GATHER

✝ *Jesus, help us live in your love every day of the year.*

What do you think of when you hear the word *ordinary*? Can you think of some other words that mean the same thing?

WE BELIEVE

During the season of Ordinary Time we celebrate the whole life of Jesus Christ. We listen to his teachings about God the Father, and about his love and forgiveness. We learn what it means to be a disciple. We celebrate everything that Jesus did for us. We celebrate his life, death, and Resurrection.

The season of Ordinary Time lasts thirty-three to thirty-four weeks. It is the longest season of the year, and is the only season that is celebrated in two parts. The first part is celebrated between the seasons of Christmas and Lent. The second part of Ordinary Time lasts many weeks and spans the time between the seasons of Easter and Advent.

Ordinary Time does not mean that every day in this season is just an ordinary day! It is called Ordinary Time because the weeks are "ordered," or named in number order. For example, the First Sunday in Ordinary Time is followed by the Second Sunday in Ordinary Time, and so on. During Ordinary Time one of the gospels is also read in number order, chapter by chapter, so that we learn about the life of Jesus.

There are four gospel writers, or *evangelists*: Matthew, Mark, Luke, and John. Each year at the Sunday and weekday Masses during Ordinary Time we hear one of the gospels of Matthew, Mark, or Luke in its entirety. So it takes three years to read all three of these gospels. Then the cycle starts over again.

The Gospel of John is not usually read at Mass during Ordinary Time. However, it is read during the other seasons of the year.

86

Lesson Plan

WE GATHER ___ minutes

Focus on Life Have the students discuss the *We Gather* questions. Stress that ordinary activities are a special part of who they are and of what keeps their relationships alive and well. Tell the students that today's lesson describes not only the season of Ordinary Time but also the sources of our stories about the life and teachings of Jesus.

WE BELIEVE ___ minutes

• **Have** a volunteer read aloud the *We Believe* statement. Invite the students to read silently the first three *We Believe* paragraphs. Ask: *Where does the name Ordinary Time come from?* (ordered or numbered) *How long does the season of Ordinary Time last?* (thirty-three or thirty-four weeks) *What do we celebrate during Ordinary Time?* (the life and teachings of Jesus)

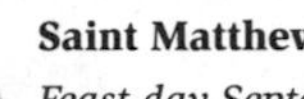

Saint Matthew

Feast day September 21

Matthew was a tax collector. He gave up everything to follow Jesus. The Gospel of Matthew focuses in a special way on Jesus being both divine and human. Over the centuries, each gospel was identified by a symbol. The symbol of Matthew's Gospel is an angelic young man. This symbol means that Jesus is both God and man.

Saint Mark

Feast day April 25

Mark's Gospel is the shortest one, and it may be the very first gospel written. The symbol of Mark's Gospel is a royal winged lion. It is a symbol of kingship. Mark's Gospel has many references to Jesus as the king who has come to bring his kingdom to us.

Saint Luke

Feast day October 18

Luke wrote both a gospel and the Acts of the Apostles. Luke's Gospel, like the Gospel of Matthew, includes the stories of Mary, Joseph, and the coming of the Son of God into the world. The symbol of Luke's Gospel is the winged ox. During the time of Jesus, an ox was an animal that was sacrificed in the Temple. In Luke's Gospel, we learn that Jesus is our new sacrifice. He offered himself to save us and because of his death and Resurrection we have new life.

Saint John

Feast day December 27

The evangelist John wrote a Gospel that is very different from the other three gospels. The symbol of John's Gospel is an eagle. An eagle can see from very far away, and it carries its young on its wings. An eagle can soar high, up to the heavens. The Gospel of John helps us to see God's plan lived out in Jesus' life, death, and Resurrection. Like an eagle, the risen Christ carries us to God.

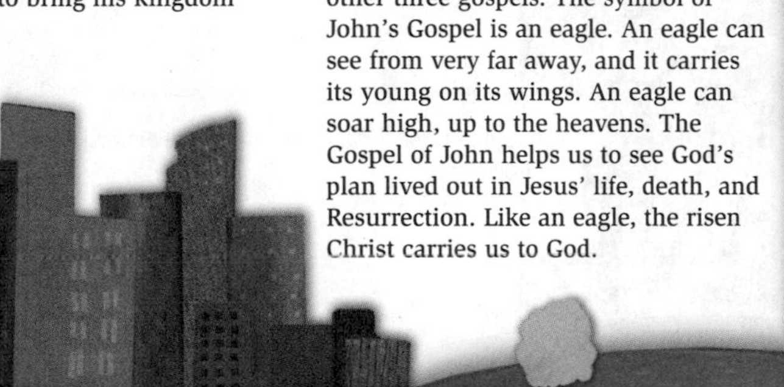

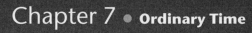

ACTIVITY BANK

Multiple Intelligences

Visual-Spatial

Form four small groups and distribute markers and newsprint or butcher paper. Display the following psalm verses on poster board or the board:

- "You show me the path to life" (16:11a).
- "My steps have kept to your paths; my feet have not faltered" (17:5).
- "You guide me along the right path for the sake of your name" (23:3).
- "Your word is a lamp for my feet, a light for my path" (119:105).

Ask each group to consider how it will either illustrate its psalm verse or communicate it through a rebus (using pictures or symbols). Have each group work on its own section of the newsprint or butcher paper. Entitle the prayer chart, *Guide us, Lord.*

- **Call** on volunteers to alternate reading aloud the remaining *We Believe* paragraphs about the evangelists on pages 86 and 87.
- **Invite** a volunteer to write the names of the four evangelists on the board as headings for four columns. (Matthew, Mark, Luke, John) Have the other students identify the symbol for each evangelist as the volunteer writes it under the correct evangelist. (Matthew: angelic young man, Mark: royal winged lion, Luke: ox, John: eagle) Next ask the students to name the gospels that are read in Ordinary Time as the volunteer places a check mark under the appropriate name. (Matthew, Mark, Luke)

Quick Check

✔ *What do we do during the season of Ordinary Time?* (We celebrate the life and teachings of Jesus Christ.)

✔ *Who are the four evangelists?* (The four evangelists are the gospel writers Matthew, Mark, Luke and John.)

CONNECTION

To Church

Evangelization

This chapter introduces the students to the four evangelists and to the primary focus of each gospel writer. Although Matthew, Mark, Luke, and John have different emphases, each wrote about the good news of Jesus Christ. By our Baptism, we share in the evangelists' mission of making the good news known throughout the world. Help the students to become more aware that the Church carries on this primary mission by using various media.

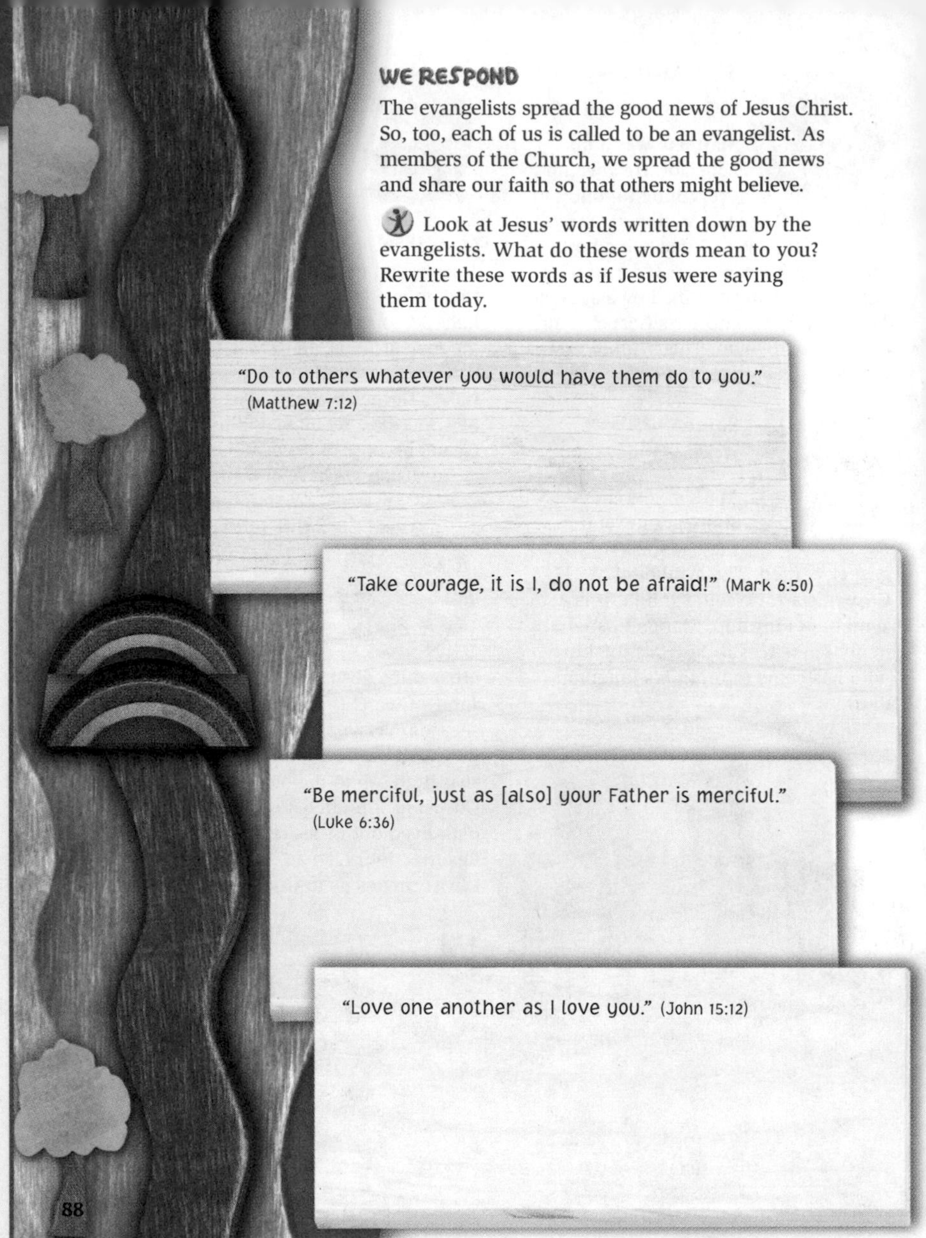

WE RESPOND

The evangelists spread the good news of Jesus Christ. So, too, each of us is called to be an evangelist. As members of the Church, we spread the good news and share our faith so that others might believe.

Look at Jesus' words written down by the evangelists. What do these words mean to you? Rewrite these words as if Jesus were saying them today.

"Do to others whatever you would have them do to you." (Matthew 7:12)

"Take courage, it is I, do not be afraid!" (Mark 6:50)

"Be merciful, just as [also] your Father is merciful." (Luke 6:36)

"Love one another as I love you." (John 15:12)

88

Lesson Plan

WE RESPOND ___ minutes

Connect to Life Read aloud the opening paragraph under the *We Respond* section. Have a student read aloud the directions to the *We Respond* activity. Share responses as a group.

• **Pray** the Sign of the Cross. Read aloud Matthew 28:16-20. After a brief silence, have all respond: *Here we are, Lord. Send us.*

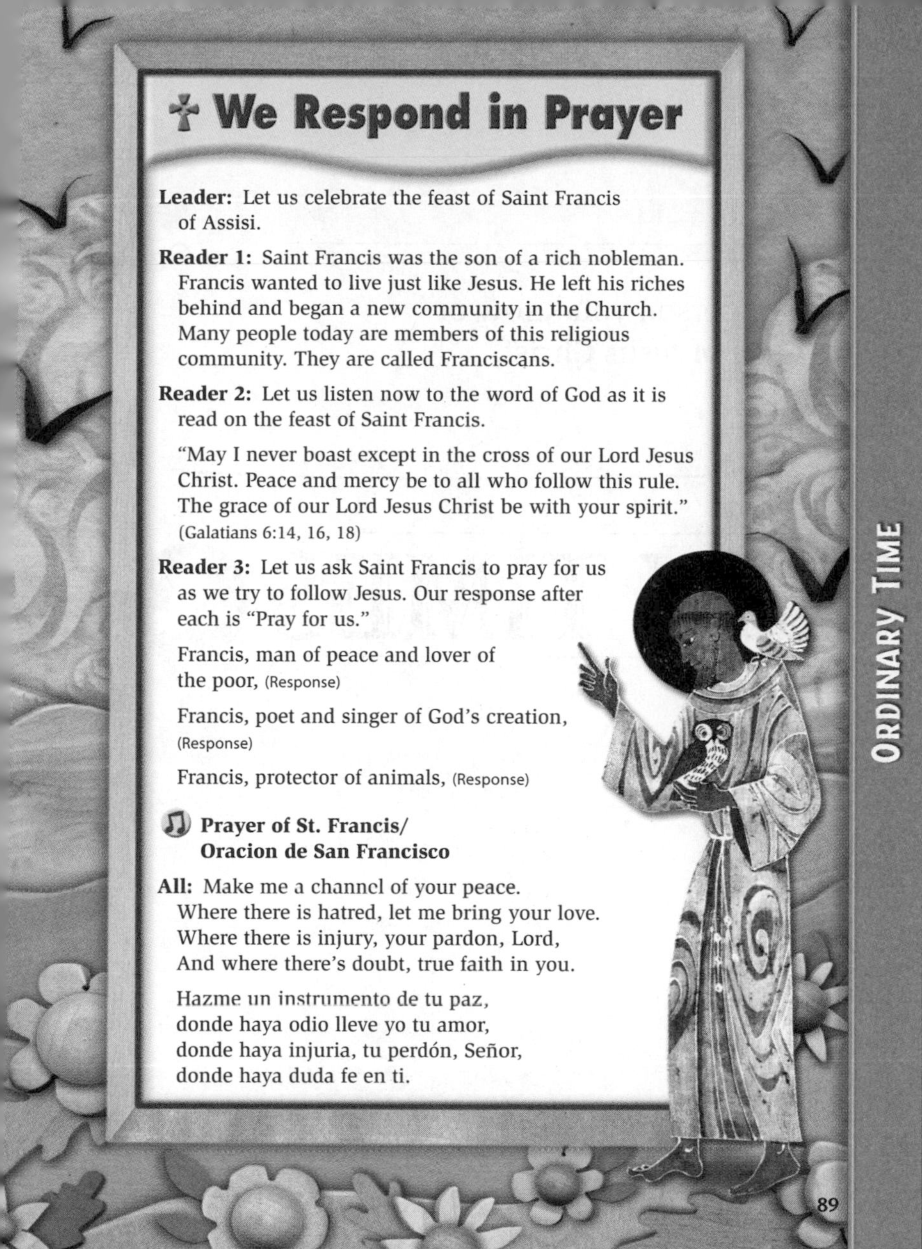

We Respond in Prayer

Leader: Let us celebrate the feast of Saint Francis of Assisi.

Reader 1: Saint Francis was the son of a rich nobleman. Francis wanted to live just like Jesus. He left his riches behind and began a new community in the Church. Many people today are members of this religious community. They are called Franciscans.

Reader 2: Let us listen now to the word of God as it is read on the feast of Saint Francis.

"May I never boast except in the cross of our Lord Jesus Christ. Peace and mercy be to all who follow this rule. The grace of our Lord Jesus Christ be with your spirit." (Galatians 6:14, 16, 18)

Reader 3: Let us ask Saint Francis to pray for us as we try to follow Jesus. Our response after each is "Pray for us."

Francis, man of peace and lover of the poor, (Response)

Francis, poet and singer of God's creation, (Response)

Francis, protector of animals, (Response)

Prayer of St. Francis/ Oracion de San Francisco

All: Make me a channel of your peace.
Where there is hatred, let me bring your love.
Where there is injury, your pardon, Lord,
And where there's doubt, true faith in you.

Hazme un instrumento de tu paz,
donde haya odio lleve yo tu amor,
donde haya injuria, tu perdón, Señor,
donde haya duda fe en ti.

ORDINARY TIME

89

Preparing to Pray

In this prayer the students will remember Saint Francis as an example of living at peace with Christ, creation, and one another.

- Tell the students you will lead the prayer.
- Select three readers and give them time to prepare.
- Practice the song.

The Prayer Space

- Display any symbols of the calendar season particular to the region; a statue of Saint Francis of Assisi; place green table cloth on the prayer table.

This Week's Liturgy

Visit **www.webelieveweb.com** for this week's liturgical readings and other seasonal material.

We Respond in Prayer ___ minutes

- **Pray** the Sign of the Cross and the opening prayer.
- **Have** the three readers read aloud their segments.
- **Conclude** by singing the song, "Prayer of Saint Francis/Oracion de San Francisco" on Grade 4 CD.

Name ____

Use words, poetry, or art to tell the story of a person you know or have heard about who spreads the good news of Jesus Christ. Be sure to include a headline for your work.

ORDINARY TIMES

We Respond in Faith

Individual Project

Distribute Reproducible Master 7. Read the directions aloud. Talk about people who spread the good news of Jesus. When the students have finished, ask volunteers to share their responses.

Group Project

The students may choose to celebrate autumn Ordinary Time by doing something out of the ordinary for a community soup kitchen or shelter. Remind them that autumn is harvest time in many regions of our country. Vegetables like potatoes, pumpkins and squash are ready to be eaten. Wheat for flour is being harvested. Enlist the students and their families in gathering or providing the vegetables, breads and autumn flowers for those in need. Have them prepare baskets or boxes of food and flowers.

Suggest that the students make gift cards with brief greetings, prayers or scriptural messages such as John 10:10b or Matthew 6:26.

Home Connection

Sharing Faith with My Family

Make sure to send home the family page (text page 90).

Encourage the students to set up an icon corner with their families.

For additional information and activities, encourage families to visit Sadlier's

www.WEBELIEVEweb.com

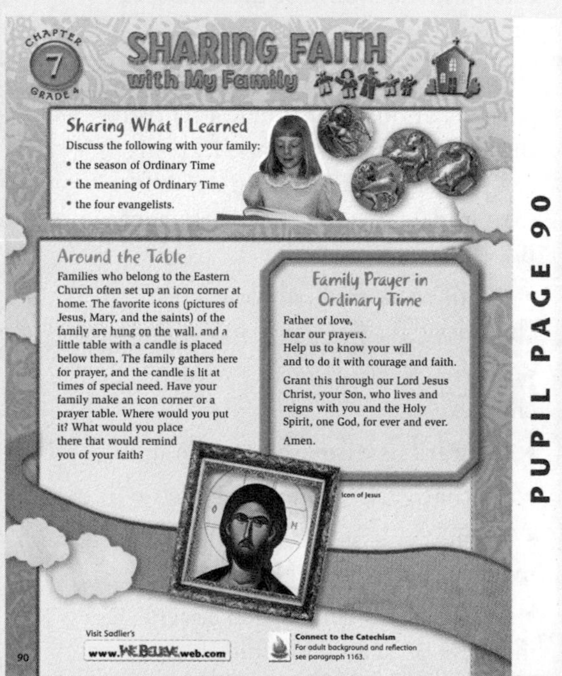

Chapter 7 Grade 4

SHARING FAITH with My Family

Sharing What I Learned

Discuss the following with your family:

- the season of Ordinary Time
- the meaning of Ordinary Time
- the four evangelists.

Around the Table

Families who belong to the Eastern Church often set up an icon corner at home. The favorite icons (pictures of Jesus, Mary, and the saints) of the family are hung on the wall, and a little table with a candle is placed below them. The family gathers here for prayer, and the candle is lit at times of special need. Have your family make an icon corner or a prayer table. Where would you put it? What would you place there that would remind you of your faith?

Family Prayer in Ordinary Time

Father of love,
hear our prayers.
Help us to know your will
and to do it with courage and faith.

Grant this through our Lord Jesus Christ, your Son, who lives and reigns with you and the Holy Spirit, one God, for ever and ever.

Amen.

Icon of Jesus

Visit Sadlier's www.WEBELIEVEweb.com

Connect to the Catechism
For adult background and reflection see paragraph 1163.

90

PUPIL PAGE 90

ASSESSMENT

In the *We Believe* program each core chapter ends with a review of the content presented, and with activities that encourage the students to reflect and act on their faith. The review is presented in two formats, standard and alternative.

Each unit is also followed by both standard and alternative assessment. The standard test measures basic knowledge and vocabulary assimilation. The alternative assessment allows the students another option—often utilizing another learning style—to express their understanding of the concepts presented.

Using both forms of assessment, perhaps at different times, attends to the various ways students' learning can be measured. You can also see the Grade 4 *We Believe* Assessment Book for:

- standard assessment for each chapter
- alternative assessment for each chapter
- standard assessment for each unit
- alternative assessment for each unit
- a semester assessment which covers material presented in Units 1 and 2
- a final assessment which covers material presented in Units 1, 2, 3, and 4.

For answers to Assessment questions: 17–18, see Chapter 4, page 61; 19–20, see Chapter 2, page 36.

Grade 4
Unit 1

Fill in the circle beside the correct answer.

1. Jesus called God *Abba*, a word that means ______.
   ● Father ○ Savior ○ Anointed One
2. In Baptism we are given ______, the gift of God's life in us.
   ○ Incarnation ● grace ○ Pentecost
3. In the Beatitudes, Jesus explains that we will be happy when we love God and ______ him as Jesus did.
   ○ fear ● trust ○ tempt
4. Respecting the rights of others and giving them what is rightfully theirs is ______.
   ○ peace ○ mercy ● justice
5. Because we have ______, we are responsible for the choices we make.
   ○ original sin ○ social sin ● free will
6. God gave us the gift of ______ to help us know the difference between good and evil, right and wrong.
   ● conscience ○ reconciliation ○ forgiveness
7. During the celebration of the sacrament of Reconciliation, we pray an act of ______.
   ○ commission ○ absolution ● contrition
8. In the sacrament of Reconciliation we receive God's ______.
   ● forgiveness ○ repentance ○ confession

91

Write True or False for the following sentences. Then change the false sentences to make them true.

9. True The truth that the Son of God became man is the Incarnation.
10. False *Savior* is a title given to Jesus Christ because he called disciples to follow him.
    Savior is a title given to Jesus Christ because he died and rose to save us from sin.
11. False In the Beatitudes the word *blessed* means "clean of heart."
    In the Beatitudes the word *blessed* means "happy."
12. True In Baptism we are given new life and become members of the Church.
13. False A temptation is a thought, word, or action against God's law.
    A sin is a thought, word, or action against God's law.
14. True A sin that we commit by *not* doing something is called a sin of omission.
15. True A good conscience works in three ways: before, while, and after we make a decision.
16. False In the sacrament of Reconciliation, the priest gives the penitent contrition in the name of the Father, the Son, and the Holy Spirit.
    The priest gives the penitent absolution in the name of the Father, the Son and the Holy Spirit.

Answer the questions.

17–18. A good conscience helps us to live the way God created us to live. What can each of us do to form a good conscience?

19–20. Jesus taught his disciples that God's Kingdom is a kingdom of justice and peace. What are some things Jesus taught his disciples about justice and peace?

92

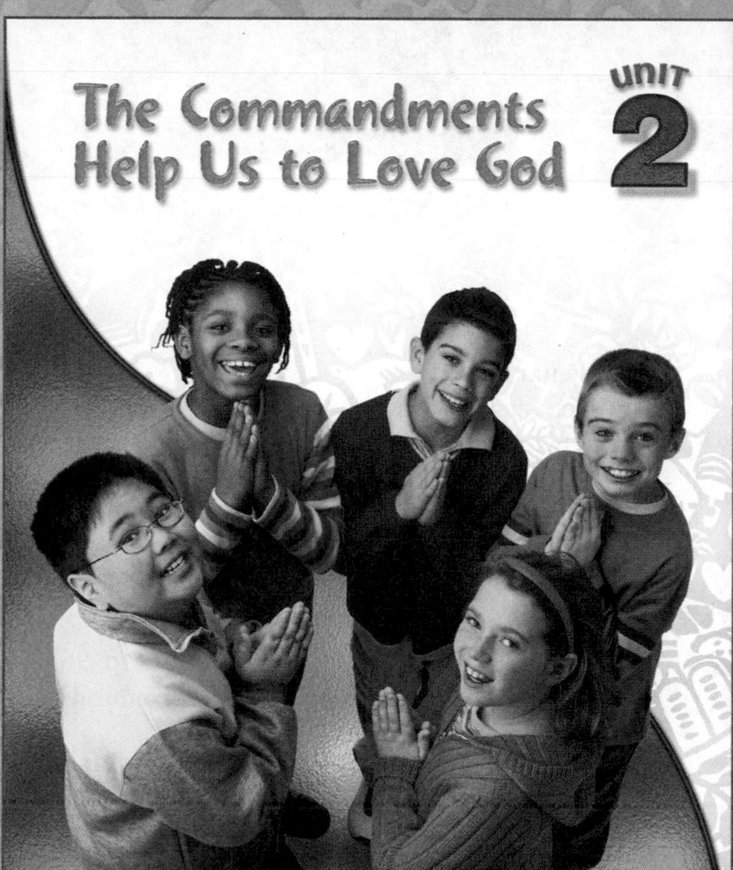

The Commandments Help Us to Love God
UNIT 2
93

UNIT 2 SHARING FAITH as a Family

Commandments for the Heart

Have you ever thought about the Ten Commandments—not just read or recited them, but *reflected* upon each one? The first three commandments focus on keeping God at the center of our lives. The remaining commandments tell us how we should treat one another. The Ten Commandments place some limits on us in order to encourage behaviors grounded in love and respect. Taken together, the Ten Commandments speak of holiness and reverence, of honesty, and of integrity. As such, they are much more than a list of things to do or not to do. They are the foundation for a full and happy life.

In short, they remind us to:

- Keep God first.
- Love and respect each other.
- Respect life.
- Be faithful.
- Tell the truth.
- Not take or be envious of what doesn't belong to you.

Your child will be studying the Ten Commandments in depth this year. This can be an opportunity for you and your family to reflect on how God calls each of you to live and love.

What Your Child Will Learn in Unit 2

Unit 2 presents the beginning of the discussion of the Ten Commandments. Each commandment is given a full chapter so that the children can learn not only the commandment but also what it means to live out this commandment. The children are introduced to the Great Commandment and its call to love God and to respect the human rights of all people. The children grow in their understanding of the first commandment by learning to keep God first. The second commandment is presented with many of God's beautiful titles and blessings of God introduced. The third commandment is the basis for discussions about our Sunday obligation, holy days of obligation, the need to rest on the Lord's Day, and the opportunity the Lord's Day gives us to love and serve others. The unit concludes with a chapter that outlines the four parts of the Mass. The children are encouraged to participate at Mass and to find strength and comfort in the Eucharist.

Plan & Preview

- ▶ You will need scissors to help your child cut out the sections of the board game, "Putting God First." These are found on each of the chapter family pages in this unit.
- ▶ Have markers and crayons available so that you can draw or write on the game board sections.
- ▶ You might want to use cardboard to back the game board sections. At the end of the unit, tape the backs together to form a complete game board.

94

Note the Quote

"Too often we underestimate the power of a touch, a smile, a kind word, a listening ear, an honest compliment, or the smallest act of caring, all of which have the potential to turn a life around."

Leo Buscaglia

From the Catechism

"The Christian family is a communion of persons, a sign and image of the communion of the Father and the Son in the Holy Spirit."

(Catechism of the Catholic Church, 2205)

Bible Q & A

Q: This year my child is learning about the Ten Commandments. Where can we find stories that relate to living out the Ten Commandments?

—Wilmington, Delaware

A: Go right to the source in Exodus 20:1–17. You might also read Luke 10:25–37, 19:1–10, and Chapter 5 of the Gospel of Matthew.

Ways to Go!

Place a bowl or basket in a prominent area of your home. Put some slips of paper next to it. Ask family members to stop there during the week and write down ways to keep God first in your family. At the end of the week, have a special meal and read out the slips of paper. Discuss how each way helps bring the family closer to God and one another.

CLASS CONNECTION

Point out the unit title to the students. Ask them what they think they will be learning more about in this unit. Have a class discussion, preparing the students for this unit.

HOME CONNECTION

Sharing Faith as a Family

Sadlier *We Believe* calls on families to become involved in:

- learning the faith
- prayer and worship
- living their faith.

Highlighting of these unit family pages and the opportunities they offer will strengthen the partnership of the Church and the home.

For additional information and activities, encourage families to visit Sadlier's

www.WEBELIEVEweb.com

Chapter 8 Learning About God's Law

Overview

In Chapter 5 the students learned about the sacrament of Penance and Reconciliation. In this chapter they will learn about God's covenant with Moses and the Israelites, the promise God kept by sending his Son, and Jesus' teaching about God's law.

Doctrinal Content	For Adult Reading and Reflection *Catechism of the Catholic Church*
The students will learn:	Paragraph
• God calls his people.	2057
• The Ten Commandments are God's laws for his people.	2060
• Jesus teaches us about God's law.	2052–2053
• Jesus teaches us to love one another.	2055

covenant (p. 98)
Ten Commandments (p. 98)
human rights (p. 102)

Catechist Background

Think of an agreement you have made with another person. What did each of you promise to do?

"After the patriarchs, God formed Israel as his people by freeing them from slavery in Egypt. He established with them the covenant of Mount Sinai and, through Moses, gave them his law so that they would recognize him and serve him as the one living and true God, the provident Father and just judge, and so that they would look for the promised Savior" (CCC 62).

Later, through his prophets, God promised to establish a new and everlasting covenant, one that was intended for all people. God, the provident Father, kept his promise and sent his only Son to be our Savior.

Jesus was the Father's last word. In the Letter to the Hebrews we read: "In times past, God spoke in partial and various ways to our ancestors through the prophets; in these last days, he spoke to us through a son, whom he made heir of all things and through whom he created the universe" (Hebrews 1:1–2). Through his death and Resurrection, Jesus established a new and eternal covenant.

In Jesus, the Father has said everything. God needs to tell us no more. Everything we need to know about God can be found in Jesus. We need not look for any further revelation from God, although we will continue to come to a deeper understanding and appreciation for this revelation. Until Jesus returns in glory, the Father's new covenant established through his Son will not pass away and it will not be surpassed.

What are some practical ways that you can respond to God's covenant of fidelity and love?

Lesson Planning Guide

Lesson Focus	Presentation	Materials
Day 1		
page 95 **We Gather in Prayer** **pages 96–97** *God calls his people.* *Exodus 3:6–10*	• Listen to Scripture. • Respond in prayer. • Discuss the **We Gather** question. • Read and discuss the **We Believe** text. • Read Scripture about the call of Moses. Illustrate ways God acted on behalf of his people. • Discuss the **We Respond** question. • Pray together.	For the prayer space: image of Jesus, a Bible • crayons or markers
Day 2		
pages 98–99 *The Ten Commandments are God's laws for his people.*	• Discuss the **We Gather** questions. • Discuss the covenant and Ten Commandments in the **We Believe** text. Sing Psalm 100 in **We Respond**.	"Psalm 100: We Are His People," Mark Friedman, #6 and #7 Grade 4 CD
Day 3		
pages 100–101 *Jesus teaches us about God's law.*	• Discuss keeping agreements in the **We Gather** questions. • Read and discuss God sending the prophets and his Son in **We Believe**. Complete the **We Respond** activity. • Read and discuss the *As Catholics* text. • Pray together.	
Day 4		
pages 102–103 *Jesus teaches us to love one another.*	• Discuss setting good example in the **We Gather** questions. • Read and discuss the **We Believe** text. Complete the **We Respond** activity. • Pray the Our Father.	• copies of Reproducible Master 8, guide page 95G (option)
Day 5		
page 104 **Review** **pages 105–106** **We Respond in Faith**	• Complete questions 1–10. Work on *Assessment Activity*. • Complete the *Reflect & Pray* activity. • Review *Remember* and *Key Words*. • Read and discuss in *Our Catholic Life*. • Discuss the **Sharing Faith with My Family** page.	• magazines and newspapers to clip for the activity • Chapter 8 Test in Assessment Book, pp. 15–16 • Chapter 8 Test in Test Generator • Review & Resource Book, pp. 19–21 • Family Book, pp. 24–26

For additional ideas, activities, and opportunities: Visit Sadlier's **www.WEBELIEVEweb.com**

Enrichment Ideas

Chapter Story

It was September, and the new school year was beginning for the children of Holy Cross Primary School in Belfast, Northern Ireland. The school was located in an area where Catholics were a minority, but most of the time Catholics and non-Catholics managed to get along with one another. But as the students walked to school with their parents on this day, angry protesters shouted at them, called them names, and made fun of them. The police had to be called to protect the children. This ugly incident made the news all around the world. Many non-Catholics in Belfast were ashamed of those who had acted so violently.

A few days later a reporter noticed a sign inside the front door of Holy Cross School. It read, "If we had been born and taught where they were born and taught, we would believe what they believe." The parents, priests, and teachers wanted the children to forgive those who had attacked them. They did not want the children to return hatred for hatred. Instead, the children needed to be told that the intolerant attackers had not been taught to respect the human dignity of their Catholic neighbors. In the end, the children at Holy Cross School learned to respect others even when they did not act respectfully. As one ten-year-old girl named Nicole said, "There's a little bad and a lot of good in everybody."

▶ *What have the students and staff of Holy Cross School taught by their example?*

FAITH and MEDIA

▶ On Day 3, as part of your discussion of the *As Catholics* text about the prophet Isaiah, point out that, in a way, Isaiah and the other prophets of the Old Testament were acting as "press secretaries." They brought God's message to his people much as a press secretary for the pope, the president of the United States, or another prominent person today conveys messages to representatives of the media or directly to the people at press briefings, at news conferences, and via the Internet.

▶ On Day 3, if the students are going to do the Storytelling Bible search in the Activity Bank, you might show them how to search the Bible online at the Web site of the United States Conference of Catholic Bishops.

CHAPTER PROJECT: LEADER OF THE DAY

Discuss good leadership skills. Point out that good Christian leaders love and respect God, themselves, and others. Invite the students to suggest words to describe good leaders. List the words on chart paper or poster paper. Each day have the students review the words on the list before choosing a "leader of the day." Invite the students to make nominations, explaining why they think these people are good leaders. Then vote by a show of hands for the day's leader. These leaders can be people the students have learned about or people in the parish or the local community.

Connections

To Family

As the students learn how God wants us to love and treat one another, remind them that such love should begin where we spend most of our time—at home. Talk with the students about the challenges they sometimes face in loving their siblings, parents, and guardians. Encourage the students to surprise a family member with an unusual act of love, such as doing chores without being asked. Share the result of their actions with the class.

To Catholic Social Teaching

Rights and Responsibilities of the Human Person
Jesus connected loving God and following his law with love of neighbor. Jesus showed his disciples that all people are created in God's image and deserve to be treated equally and with respect. Remind the students that because of this equality all people share certain rights, among them being the fundamental right to life and a right to those things necessary for a decent life. We also have the responsibility to protect those rights and to make sure people have the things they need to live.

To Mission

The Church lives out its mission to share the gospel message in many ways. One way the Church does this is by sending missionaries throughout the world to spread the good news to all peoples. Explain to the students that missionaries show respect for the local cultures in the countries they serve and present the gospel to the people in their own languages. Share with the students mission magazines (such as *Maryknoll* magazine) and encourage the students to find out about missionary work in their diocese.

Meeting Individual Needs

Students with Language Needs

Students with language needs may be helped with one or more of the following skills: using words in correct context, using correct grammar, understanding vocabulary, or expressing ideas. When possible, consider asking seventh or eighth-grade students to mentor fourth graders who have language impairments to help the younger students practice these skills.

ADDITIONAL RESOURCES

Book *Can You Find Bible Heroes? Introducing Your Child to the Old Testament,* Phillip D. Gallery, St. Anthony Messenger Press, 1998. Learn about God's movement in the lives Old Testament heroes.

Video *The Ten Commandments,* CCC of America, 1995. From the series, In the Beginning, this fully animated video tells the story of Moses and the Ten Commandments. (30 minutes)

To find more ideas for books, videos, and other learning material, visit Sadlier's

www.WEBELIEVEweb.com

Teaching to Multiple Intelligences

by Brother Robert R. Bimonte, FSC

Brother Robert is currently the Executive Director of the NCEA Elementary Department. He holds graduate degrees in education, psychology, and theology, and conducts workshops for schools, dioceses, and religious communities throughout the country.

Catechist Development Topics (Topic and Guide Page)

The Theory of Multiple Intelligences was developed in 1983 by Dr. Howard Gardner, a professor of education at Harvard University. The theory confirms what teachers have always known—all children learn differently. Through Gardner's research, multiple-intelligence theory has expanded our understanding of intelligence. It has helped us to see that children can be "smart" in a variety of ways.

Dr. Gardner proposed that there are eight types of intelligence or learning styles. They are:

- Musical intelligence (music "smart")
- Linguistic intelligence (word "smart")
- Logical-Mathematical intelligence (reasoning/number "smart")
- Spatial intelligence (picture "smart")
- Bodily-Kinesthetic intelligence (physically "smart")
- Naturalist intelligence (nature "smart")
- Interpersonal intelligence (people "smart")
- Intrapersonal intelligence (self "smart")

Dr. Gardner emphasizes that everyone possesses all eight intelligences to one degree or another. Among the first six, we each have a dominant one, but usually have a repertoire of two or more in which we are comfortable. Between Interpersonal intelligence and Intrapersonal intelligence, Dr. Gardner indicates that individuals have a preference.

Lessons that incorporate multiple intelligences must become a regular part of our teaching methodology. Giving children the option of drawing a picture, making a chart, or acting out a skit taps into several intelligences. Simultaneously, using the multiple-intelligence theory in the classroom or parish setting allows children to express themselves in the way that is most natural for them as well as the manner in which they learn best. There is no question that the best learning takes place when children are actively involved and emotionally engaged in the learning process.

Resources

Armstrong, Thomas. *Multiple Intelligences in the Classroom*. Virginia: ASCD, 1994.

Gardner, Howard. *Intelligence Reframed: Multiple Intelligences for the 21st Century*. New York: Basic Books, 2000.

Ways to Implement Teaching to Multiple Intelligences

- For children with Musical intelligence, include hymns that are connected to the main theological point of the lessons. Encourage them to use music and song to respond to material.
- For children with Linguistic intelligence, include dramatic readings of Scripture, poems and prayers written by saints, and creative writing to connect to the lessons.
- For children with Logical-Mathematical intelligence, include problem-solving activities, timelines, and graphs that relate to the lesson. Introduce the children to ancient units of measure, such as the ephah and the omer.
- For children with Spatial intelligence, include maps of the Bible and other holy places that relate to the lesson. Use art to teach concepts.
- For children with Bodily-Kinesthetic intelligence, include gestures and movements when praying and singing. Engage the children in social service activities that involve physical activity such as walkathons, painting, sorting food/clothes, etc.
- For children with Naturalist intelligence, include information about plants and animals in biblical times that relate to the lessons. Encourage them to care for the environment by planting or tending to a class/parish garden.
- For children with Interpersonal intelligence, include group activities and discussions that relate to the lesson.
- For children with Intrapersonal intelligence, include opportunities for them to spend time working on their own. Encourage the children to keep a journal with reflections on the material.

For additional ideas, activities, and opportunities, visit Sadlier's

www.WEBELIEVEweb.com

With thanks to:
Regina Doherty, CRE
Catechist (2nd grade)
Immaculate Conception Parish
Stony Point, New York

Regina incorporates multiple intelligences to help her students prepare for first Reconciliation and Eucharist. She does this by her development of a mini-retreat format that is based on Reconciliation and Eucharist. The children "visit" different learning stations that are based on multiple intelligences to learn about Reconciliation and Eucharist. For example, there is a meditation station, a story-telling station, a food station (for a Reconciliation meal such as Zacchaeus might have served and Jesus tasted), an activity station (for Eucharist a study of the chalice is offered), and a craft station (for Reconciliation the children make a crucifix).

Notes

Name ______________________________

Think about someone in your life who gives you good example and shows you how to follow Jesus. Write a thank-you note to this person explaining ways he or she has helped you. Draw an interesting border on your note.

Learning About God's Law

✝ We Gather in Prayer

Leader: Let us listen to a reading from the Book of Psalms.

Reader: "LORD, teach me the way
of your laws;
I shall observe them
with care.
Give me insight to
observe your teaching,
to keep it with all my heart.
Lead me in the path of
your commands,
for that is my delight."
(Psalm 119:33–35)

All: "LORD, teach me the way
of your laws." (Psalm 119:33)

Leader: Let us pray.
Father, we want to respect your laws. Help us to love you and our neighbors. We ask this in the name of Jesus our Lord.

All: Amen.

95

PREPARING TO PRAY

In this gathering prayer, the students will pray Psalm 119 to ask God for help and guidance in following his Law.

• Choose a prayer leader and a reader. Allow them time to practice what they will read and pray.

The Prayer Space

• On the prayer table place an image of Jesus and a Bible opened to Matthew 22.

This Week's Liturgy

Visit **www.webelieveweb.com** for this week's liturgical readings and other seasonal material.

Lesson Plan

We Gather in Prayer ___ minutes

✝ Pray

• Gather the students in the prayer space with the words *We gather in prayer.*

• Pray the Sign of the Cross and, if necessary, prompt the leader to begin.

Home Connection Update

Ask the students what they found when they put the puzzle pieces from unit 1 together. Talk about ways their families are disciples of Jesus.

Chapter 8 • Day 1

Catechist Goal

- To explore the relationship between God and the Israelites

Our Faith Response

- To follow God's laws with his help

Lesson Materials

- crayons or markers

Teaching Tip

Giving Good Example

A catechist or teacher thrives on caring for students. You do it willingly, and you freely choose to go the extra mile for any child who wants to learn. As you teach young people to value and respect one another, remember that you are a prime example to them. Showing respect for yourself, taking care of yourself, and not running on empty will send students the message that respect for others begins with self-respect.

God calls his people.

WE GATHER

✝ *Father, help me to hear your call.*

Think of a time when you were chosen to do something. What was it?

WE BELIEVE

In the Old Testament we learn about the relationship between God and his people. We read the history of God's people in the time before the birth of Jesus.

God called Abraham to be the father of his people. Abraham and his wife, Sarah, had no children. So God promised that they would have a child and many grandchildren. Abraham and Sarah did have a child, Isaac, and many grandchildren.

Jacob was one of Abraham and Sarah's many descendants. God chose Jacob as he had chosen Abraham. God changed Jacob's name to Israel. From then on, these people whom God chose as his own were called the Israelites.

God showed his great love for the Israelites, and they showed their love for God. They called on God for help and guidance. They gave praise to God's name. God remembered his people and heard them. He cared for and protected them.

God's people were living in the area of the Middle East that is now the country called Israel. However, in the time of the Old Testament, this land was called Canaan. Once a great famine forced God's people to leave their homes in Canaan. They went to Egypt to find food. They stayed in Egypt, but they later lost their freedom there. God's people became slaves. They were forced to work for the pharaoh, the ruler of Egypt.

God wanted his people to be free to love and worship him. So God chose Moses to lead the people out of Egypt to freedom.

Exodus 3:6–10

God said to Moses, "'I am the God of your father,' he continued, 'the God of Abraham, the God of Isaac, the God of Jacob.'"

God told Moses that he had seen the way his people were suffering in Egypt. God said, "Therefore I have come down to rescue them from the hands of the Egyptians and lead them out of that land into a good and spacious land, a land flowing with milk and honey."

96

Lesson Plan

WE GATHER ___ minutes

✝ **Pray** Pray together the Sign of the Cross and the *We Gather* prayer.

Focus on Life Have a volunteer read aloud the *We Gather* question. Encourage them to recall how it felt to be chosen to do something. Ask: *How do you feel when you are asked to do something good for someone else?* Invite the students to share their own experiences. Tell the students that in this lesson they will learn that God chose leaders for his people.

WE BELIEVE ___ minutes

Learn About God's People Ask volunteers to read aloud the *We Believe* paragraphs up to the passage from Exodus. Discuss how God showed his love for his people and how they showed their love for God.

Explain: *The Israelites were farmers or sheep herders. But there was a long period of time when it did not rain. The crops did not grow and so there was little or no food.* Explain: *The Israelites went to Egypt to find food. After a while the Israelites became the slaves of the Egyptians. But God wanted his people to be free. He chose Moses to lead the people back to their own land.*

Read Scripture Have the students read along quietly as you read aloud the remaining *We Believe* text. Then ask: *What did God ask Moses to do?* (God asked Moses to lead the Israelites out of Egypt to a life of freedom in their own land.) Talk with the students about the illustrations.

Illustrate some of the ways God acted in the lives of his people.

Then God said to Moses, "Come, now! I will send you to Pharaoh to lead my people, the Israelites, out of Egypt" (Exodus 3:6, 8, 10).

With Moses to lead them and God guiding their way, the people left Egypt. They were heading for Canaan, the land God had promised them.

WE RESPOND

Moses answered God's call to lead the people to freedom. God guided Moses and his people. How does God guide us today?

97

ACTIVITY BANK

Multiple Intelligences

Interpersonal, Bodily-Kinesthetic
Activity Materials: Bibles

Invite the students to learn more about Moses. Read aloud Exodus 3:1–15. Form groups to act out this story for the class. Have each group state what it learned about Moses and about God from this story.

Do the Activity Ask a volunteer to read aloud the activity directions. Explain to the students that they may illustrate by writing or drawing. Let the students share and compare their completed work.

Quick Check

✔ *How did God help the Israelites when they were slaves in Egypt?* (God chose Moses to lead the Israelites out of Egypt.)

✔ *In what part of the Bible do we read the stories of God's relationship with his people before the birth of Jesus?* (We read it in the Old Testament.)

WE RESPOND ___ minutes

Connect to Life Ask a volunteer to read aloud the *We Respond* section. Discuss the question and write the students' responses on the board. (Possible responses: through his word in the Bible; through prayer; through the guidance of our family and the Church.)

Pray Pray together: *God, thank you for guiding us.*

Plan Ahead for Day 2

Catechist Goal: To teach that the Ten Commandments are God's laws for his people

Preparation: Have available the Grade 4 CD.

Catechist Goal

- To teach that the Ten Commandments are God's laws for his people

Our Faith Response

- To express joy that we are called to be God's people

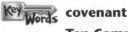

covenant
Ten Commandments

Lesson Materials

- Grade 4 CD

Teaching Tip

The Need for Rules and Laws

A helpful preface to your presentation of the Ten Commandments is to ask the students about laws that affect their lives. Discuss laws that govern society such as those that concern driving, crime, equality, and so on. Have them talk about rules that they observe at home and rules that exist at school.

Guido Reni (1575–1642), Moses with the Tablets of the Law

The Ten Commandments are God's laws for his people.

WE GATHER

✝ *God, your laws show us how to live a life of love.*

Did you ever make an agreement with a teacher, a coach, or a parent? If you did, what did you agree to do? What did the other person agree to do? Why are agreements important?

WE BELIEVE

As Moses and God's people escaped Egypt, "The LORD preceded them, in the daytime by means of a column of cloud to show them the way, and at night by means of a column of fire to give them light. Thus they could travel both day and night. Neither the column of cloud by day nor the column of fire by night ever left its place in front of the people" (Exodus 13:21–22).

In the desert between Egypt and Canaan, the Israelites came to a mountain called Mount Sinai. God asked Moses to climb the mountain. There on the mountain God made a special agreement with Moses and the people. God promised to be their God if they would be his people. This special agreement between God and his people is called a **covenant**.

The covenant describes the relationship between God and his people. In this covenant God promised to protect his people and to help them live in freedom. In return the Israelites promised to live as God wanted them to live. They promised to worship him, the one true God.

On Mount Sinai God gave Moses and his people the law that he wanted them to follow. He gave them the Ten Commandments. God's people promised to keep the Ten Commandments as their part of the covenant.

The **Ten Commandments** are the laws of God's covenant given to Moses on Mount Sinai. The Israelites, who later became known as the Jewish people, followed these laws. The Ten Commandments are God's laws for us, too.

We find the Ten Commandments in the Old Testament. They are listed in the books of Exodus and Deuteronomy.

covenant a special agreement between God and his people

Ten Commandments the laws of God's covenant given to Moses on Mount Sinai

Lesson Plan

WE GATHER ___ minutes

✝ **Pray** Provide a few moments of silence for the students to thank God for guiding us. Then pray together the Sign of the Cross and the *We Believe* prayer.

Focus on Life Discuss the *We Gather* question. Then ask the students to agree to do something this week. One possibility would be to keep their desks and classroom neat and clean. Tell the students that in this lesson they will learn about a special agreement between God and his people.

WE BELIEVE ___ minutes

Continue the Exodus Story Have a volunteer read the *We Believe* statement. Explain to the students that the Israelites traveled by walking. They kept moving because they did not want the Egyptians to capture them. Have a volunteer read aloud the passage from Exodus.

Discuss the Covenant Write the word *covenant* on the board. Pronounce it and explain that it is an agreement between God and his people. On the board make a chart with two columns. At the top of the left-hand column write *God promises*; at the top of the right-hand column, *God's people promise*. Ask four students to read aloud the next four *We Believe* paragraphs. As they read, have volunteers fill in the columns on the board. Review the work that the volunteers wrote on the board. Stress that the covenant is a relationship between God and his people.

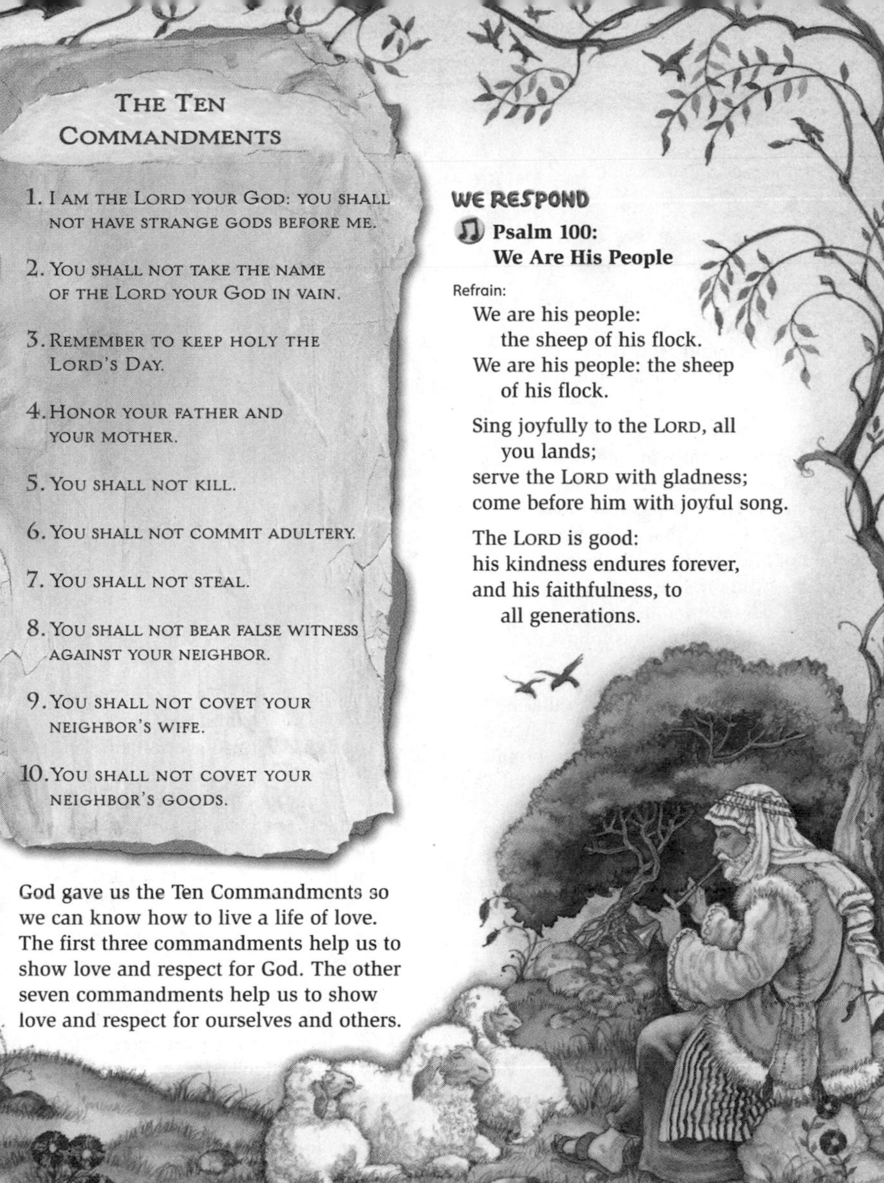

The Ten Commandments

1. I am the Lord your God: you shall not have strange gods before me.
2. You shall not take the name of the Lord your God in vain.
3. Remember to keep holy the Lord's Day.
4. Honor your father and your mother.
5. You shall not kill.
6. You shall not commit adultery.
7. You shall not steal.
8. You shall not bear false witness against your neighbor.
9. You shall not covet your neighbor's wife.
10. You shall not covet your neighbor's goods.

WE RESPOND

Psalm 100: We Are His People

Refrain:

We are his people:
the sheep of his flock.
We are his people: the sheep
of his flock.

Sing joyfully to the LORD, all
you lands;
serve the LORD with gladness;
come before him with joyful song.

The LORD is good:
his kindness endures forever,
and his faithfulness, to
all generations.

God gave us the Ten Commandments so we can know how to live a life of love. The first three commandments help us to show love and respect for God. The other seven commandments help us to show love and respect for ourselves and others.

Activity Bank

Curriculum Connection

Geography

Activity Materials: maps

Encourage small groups of students to find the places referred to so far in this chapter (Egypt, Israel, the desert region between Egypt and Israel, and Mount Sinai) on a map. Suggest that the students trace outline maps of the area and label the places on the maps. Encourage the students to add drawings to their maps to illustrate such key parts of the Israelites' story as their escape from slavery in Egypt, their wandering in the desert, God calling Moses to lead them out of Egypt, and Moses receiving the Ten Commandments from God. Display the maps in the classroom.

Present the Ten Commandments Emphasize that the Ten Commandments are God's laws for us, too. Form the class into two groups. Have one group read aloud the first three commandments. Explain: *These laws help us show love and respect for God.* Have the second group read aloud the fourth through the tenth commandments. Explain: *These seven laws help us show love and respect for ourselves and others.*

Quick Check

✔ *What is a covenant?* (A covenant is an agreement between God and his people.)

✔ *What are the laws God gave to Moses called?* (God's laws to Moses are known as the Ten Commandments.)

WE RESPOND

___ minutes

Connect to Life Invite the students to reflect on the ways God has helped people throughout history to lead lives of love. Explain that being "the sheep of his flock" means that we follow God and that God protects us.

Pray Prayerfully sing or pray aloud "Psalm 100: We Are His People," from the Grade 4 CD. Play #6 and #7.

Plan Ahead for Day 3

Catechist Goal: To explain that Jesus teaches us about God's law

Preparation: Bookmark Deuteronomy 6:5 and Leviticus 19:18 in a Bible.

Catechist Goal

• To explain that Jesus teaches us about God's law

Our Faith Response

• To live as Jesus' followers, as sons and daughters of God

As Catholics...

The Prophet Isaiah

After you have presented the day's lesson, have the students break into groups. Have them read and discuss the *As Catholics* text. Have the students talk about why they think Isaiah's message is so important.

Jesus teaches us about God's law.

WE GATHER

✝ *Jesus, you show us how to live God's law.*

Think again of an agreement you have had with a teacher, a coach, or a parent.

How did you keep your part of the agreement? How did they keep their part of the agreement?

WE BELIEVE

Throughout history people have loved God and have wanted to live by his law. Yet when we read the Bible, we see that God's people did not always live up to their part of the covenant. Even though they loved God and tried to be faithful to him, they did not always follow the Ten Commandments.

God loved his people so much that he never turned away from them. When he saw his people failing, God sent prophets to remind them to keep the covenant. The prophets told the people about God's love for them. By their words and actions, the prophets encouraged the people to trust in God and have faith in him. The prophets reminded the people that God had promised to save them from sin.

God kept his promise. He sent his own Son into the world to save all people from sin. Jesus is the Son of God.

When Jesus was growing up in Nazareth, he studied the teachings of the Old Testament. He learned about the covenant God made with his people. He studied the Ten Commandments. He lived his life according to the covenant. People saw that Jesus lived his life in love for God his Father and in service to others.

One day someone asked Jesus, "Teacher, which commandment in the law is the greatest?" We call Jesus' answer the Great Commandment. Jesus said to the man, "You shall love the Lord, your God, with all your heart, with all your soul, and with all your mind" (Matthew 22:36–37). This is the first part of the Great Commandment. It sums up the first three of the Ten Commandments.

100

Lesson Plan

WE GATHER ___ minutes

✝ **Pray** Have the students think about the many good things Jesus did for others. Then invite them to pray aloud the *We Gather* prayer.

Focus on Life Have the students reflect on the *We Gather* questions. Invite volunteers to share their responses. Ask: *Is it hard, sometimes, to keep your agreements? Who can help you?* Tell the students that in this lesson they will learn what Jesus teaches about God's law.

WE BELIEVE ___ minutes

Read About the Prophets Read together the *We Believe* statement. Emphasize that Jesus lived according to the covenant and helped others to do the same.

Explain: *God's people did not always keep their part of the covenant. God sent prophets to help them.* Have volunteers read aloud the first two *We Believe* paragraphs.

Learn About the Great Commandment The students learned about the Great Commandment in previous grades. Ask: *What do you remember about the Great Commandment Jesus taught us?* After the students have responded, ask volunteers to read aloud the remaining *We Believe* text.

Cite the Old Testament You may wish to share with the students some verses in the Old Testament that relate to the Great Commandment. Remind the students that Jesus would have studied these verses as a boy:

Jesus also told the man, "You shall love your neighbor as yourself" (Matthew 22:39). This part of the Great Commandment sums up the fourth through tenth commandments.

Jesus himself lived out the Great Commandment. He showed us that keeping the Ten Commandments means loving God above all else and loving others as ourselves.

WE RESPOND

With a partner, talk about ways that Jesus may have showed his love for God and others. Then in the space below, make a Word Find using those things. Exchange your puzzle with another group and have them find and circle the words.

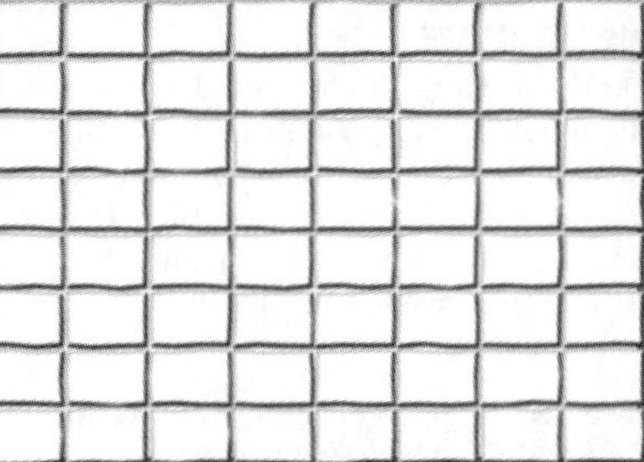

Discuss the ways you can live as Jesus did.

As Catholics...

God sent many prophets to his people. The greatest of these was Isaiah. Isaiah told the people that God would never abandon them, that God would send them a Savior. Christians believe that Jesus is the Savior Isaiah told the people about.

Every year during Advent and Christmas, we hear the words of Isaiah: "For a child is born to us, a son is given us" (Isaiah 9:5). Jesus is the Son of God and our Savior.

101

ACTIVITY BANK

Curriculum Connection

Storytelling

Activity Materials: Bibles

Invite the students to do a "Jesus in action" Bible search. Working in pairs, they can look up one of the following references to see that Jesus lived the Great Commandment. Have them prepare to tell or act out their stories to the class and suggest one way fourth graders might follow Jesus' example in their own lives. (Gospel references to be researched are Matthew 9:1–8; Mark 8:1–10; Luke 4:1–13; John 13:1–15.)

- "Therefore, you shall love the Lord, your God, with all your heart, with all your soul, and with all your strength" (Deuteronomy 6:5).
- "You shall love your neighbor as yourself" (Leviticus 19:18).

Quick Check

✔ *Whom did God send to help his people keep the covenant?* (God sent the prophets to remind the people of the covenant. Then he sent his only Son, Jesus, to fulfill the law and covenant.)

✔ *What are the two parts of the Great Commandment?* ("You shall love the Lord, your God, with all your heart, with all your soul, and with all your mind." "You shall love your neighbor as yourself.")

WE RESPOND ___ minutes

Connect to Life Invite the students to read the *We Respond* activity directions. Clarify any misunderstandings. Give the students time to make and exchange their puzzles.

Pray Invite the students to gather in the prayer space. Pray together: *God of love, guide us by your Great Commandment. Amen.*

Plan Ahead for Day 4

Catechist Goal: To emphasize that Jesus taught us about loving one another

Preparation: Decide on examples for each human right; make copies of Reproducible Master 8 (option).

Chapter 8 • Day 4

Catechist Goal

- To emphasize that Jesus taught us about loving one another

Our Faith Response

- To identify ways we can show love for others by our actions

human rights

Lesson Materials

- copies of Reproducible Master 8 (option)

Teaching Note

The Law and the Prophets

The law and the prophets are like inseparable twins. Without the zeal and courage of the prophets, the law seems abstract and cold. Without the law, the prophets' words sound empty and without purpose. As you teach about Jesus' love of his Father's commands, show Jesus as *the* prophet and the *new* Moses. Jesus fulfills the law and the prophets in his coming to show us the way to the Father.

Jesus teaches us to love one another.

WE GATHER

✝ *Jesus, teach me to love others as you did.*

Discuss someone who is a good example to you. What does this person do? How does the person act? What makes you want to do or say the same kinds of things?

WE BELIEVE

On the night before he died, Jesus told his disciples, "I give you a new commandment: love one another. As I have loved you, so you also should love one another. This is how all will know that you are my disciples, if you have love for one another" (John 13:34–35).

Jesus was a perfect example of love for God and neighbor. He lived by the Ten Commandments. When we love as Jesus did, we also show love for God and others. Loving one another as Jesus did helps us to follow the Ten Commandments.

Jesus showed his love in many ways. He listened to those who were lonely. He went out of his way to help people in need. He spoke out for the freedom of all people and for those who were treated unjustly. Jesus protected people who could not protect themselves. He treated all people equally and respected the dignity of each person.

All people are created by God to share in his life and love. We are called to respect the human dignity of all people. Each and every person has the same basic rights. We call the basic rights that all people have **human rights**.

These rights include the

- right to life. This the most basic of all human rights.
- right to faith and family
- right to education and work
- right to equal treatment and safety
- right to housing and health care.

Talk about what these human rights mean to you.

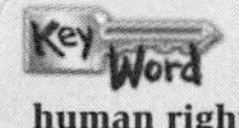

human rights the basic rights that all people have

102

Lesson Plan

WE GATHER ___ minutes

✝ **Pray** Have the students pray the *We Gather* prayer reverently and quietly to themselves.

Focus on Life Discuss the *We Gather* questions. Read the *Chapter Story*. Tell the students that in this lesson they will learn what Jesus taught us about loving our neighbor.

WE BELIEVE ___ minutes

Recall Jesus' Teaching Help the students to recall what Jesus taught us about neighbors. Ask: *How are we to treat our neighbors?* (as ourselves) *How are we to know how to treat others?* (by thinking of how we want to be treated) Have a volunteer read aloud the *We Believe* statement.

Identify the Main Points Have the students work in pairs. Let the pairs read the first three *We Believe* paragraphs together. Encourage them to list three of the main points from their reading. Then let the pairs share their ideas with the class. Write the ideas on the board or on a chart as the students present them. Continue until all the students are satisfied that their ideas are represented in the list. Discuss what people might have thought and learned when they saw the way Jesus treated others. Distribute Reproducible Master 8 for the students to complete in class or at home.

Discuss Human Rights Read aloud the last *We Believe* paragraph. Then have a different student read aloud each human right listed. Discuss the meaning of each of the basic human rights.

WE RESPOND

Write or tell how you would use Jesus' "new commandment" to show love for the person in each of the following situations.

1. A tornado destroyed the home of a family in your town.

____

____

____

2. Your friend tells you that she is embarrassed to read aloud in class because she in not a good reader. She is afraid that the other students will laugh at her.

____

____

____

3. A new student is in your class. You notice that, during recess, he is standing by himself, not talking or playing games.

____

____

____

103

Activity Bank

Community

Human Rights

Activity Materials: poster board, drawing paper, markers

Give the students a choice of designing a Web page or making a poster on the theme of human rights. Have the students review the rights listed on page 102. Ask each student to choose one human right about which he or she is most concerned. Then have them decide how best to persuade others in the local community to uphold or defend that right. Share and display the completed works.

Quick Check

✔ *What new commandment did Jesus give his disciples?* (to love one another as he has loved them)

✔ *What are human rights?* (the basic rights that all people have)

WE RESPOND

___ minutes

Connect to Life Encourage the students to think about what Jesus' new commandment teaches us. Then have the students complete the *We Respond* activity. Invite volunteers to share their responses.

Pray Pray the Our Father together.

Plan Ahead for Day 5

Catechist Goal: To review chapter ideas and their relationship to our faith life

Preparation: Make copies of Chapter 8 Test in the Grade 4 Assessment Book (option).

Catechist Goal

- To review chapter ideas and their relationship to our faith life

Our Faith Response

- To apply what has been learned to our lives

Chapter Test

The Chapter 8 Test is provided in the Grade 4 Assessment Book.

Review

Circle the correct answer.

1. In the Old Testament we learn about the relationship between God and ______.
   the apostles — Jesus — (the Israelites)
2. A covenant is a special ______ between God and his people.
   prayer — (agreement) — vision
3. Jesus taught us to love God above all else and to ______ our neighbors as ourselves.
   fear — (love) — trust
4. The most basic of all human rights is the right to ______.
   faith — equal treatment — (life)

Write True or False next to the following sentences. Then change the false sentences to make them true.

5. True The Ten Commandments help us to live a life of love.
6. True The Great Commandment sums up the Ten Commandments.
7. False Following the first three commandments helps us to love and respect our neighbors.
   Following the first three commandments helps us to love and respect God. (or, Following the last seven ... neighbors.)
8. False God gave the Ten Commandments to Jesus on Mount Sinai.
   God gave the Ten Commandments to Moses on Mount Sinai.

Complete the following:

9–10. We believe the Ten Commandments See pages 98–99.

Make a "bulletin board of respect." Cut out pictures and phrases from magazines and newspapers that show examples of the following: respect for God, respect for self, and respect for others.

104

Lesson Plan

___ minutes

Chapter Review Introduce the *Review* section by explaining to the students that they are going to check their understanding of what they have learned. Then ask them to answer questions 1–10. After they have completed the questions, ask the students to say aloud each of their answers. Clear up any misconceptions. Then ask them to look again at question 5. Remind them that the Ten Commandments are important because they tell us how to love God and others.

Assessment Activity Invite a volunteer to read aloud the directions. Provide the students with newspapers and magazines and form the class into small groups to look through the materials. Encourage each group to find articles, pictures, and phrases to place on the bulletin board. Continue adding to this bulletin board as the class reads the chapters about individual commandments.

___ minutes

Reflect & Pray Remind the students that the Holy Spirit is always here to help and guide us. Read the first sentence under *Reflect & Pray*. Provide time for the students to complete the prayer.

Key Words To review the *Key Words*, play three games of "Guess the Letters" using the words *covenant, Ten Commandments,* and *human rights.* For each game, write on the board as many dashes as

We Respond in Faith

Reflect & Pray

Holy Spirit, help me to live by the Ten Commandments.

Help me ______________________________

____

____

covenant (p. 98)
Ten Commandments (p. 98)
human rights (p. 102)

Remember

- God calls his people.
- The Ten Commandments are God's laws for his people.
- Jesus teaches us about God's law.
- Jesus teaches us to love one another.

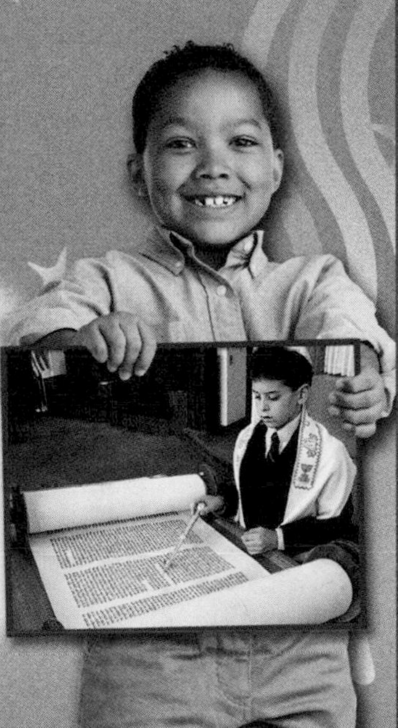

Our Catholic Life

The Covenant Today

The covenant that God made with Moses is still honored and lived today by the Jewish people. The Ten Commandments are part of what is called "The Torah," which in Hebrew means, "The Law." The scrolls on which the Law is written have a place of honor in every synagogue.

When Jesus gave us his Body and Blood, he said, "This cup is the new covenant in my blood, which will be shed for you" (Luke 22:20). When we receive the Eucharist, we say yes to the new covenant with God in Jesus. This is the covenant that Catholics honor and live today.

Home Connection

Sharing Faith with My Family

Make sure to ask the students to take home the family page (text page 106).

Read the directions for the "Putting God First" game which will be on the family pages for Chapters 8-12. Encourage the students to have their families play this game and pray the family prayer.

For additional information and activities, encourage families to visit Sadlier's

www.WEBELIEVEweb.com

there are letters in a word. Students guess the missing letters. After the class correctly guesses each word, ask the students to define the term in their own words.

Remember Review the important ideas of the chapter by discussing the four *We Believe* statements. Help the students recall the Great Commandment and Jesus' new commandment.

Our Catholic Life Invite a student to read aloud *Our Catholic Life*. Help the students to understand that we celebrate our covenant with God when we celebrate the Eucharist. Ask the students to explain what the boy in the photo is doing. (He is reading from scrolls on which Scripture has been written in Hebrew.)

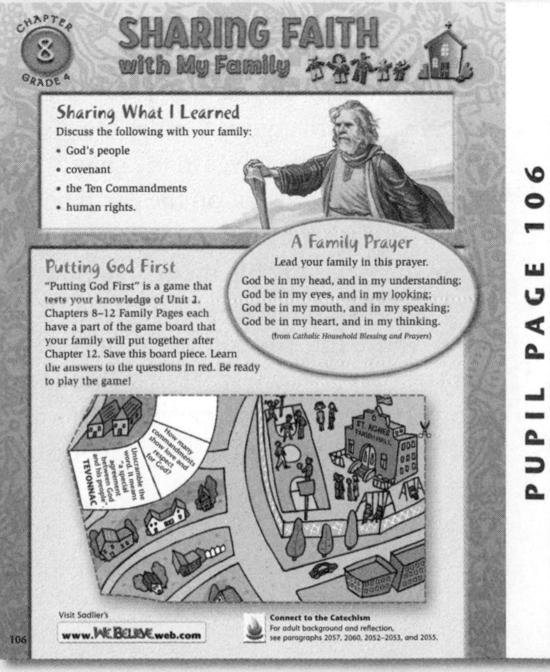

CHAPTER 8 GRADE 4

SHARING FAITH with My Family

Sharing What I Learned

Discuss the following with your family:

- God's people
- covenant
- the Ten Commandments
- human rights.

A Family Prayer

Lead your family in this prayer.

God be in my head, and in my understanding;
God be in my eyes, and in my looking;
God be in my mouth, and in my speaking;
God be in my heart, and in my thinking.

(from *Catholic Household Blessing and Prayers*)

Putting God First

"Putting God First" is a game that tests your knowledge of Unit 2. Chapters 8–12 Family Pages each have a part of the game board that your family will put together after Chapter 12. Save this board piece. Learn the answers to the questions in red. Be ready to play the game!

Visit Sadlier's www.WEBELIEVEweb.com

Connect to the Catechism
For adult background and reflection, see paragraphs 2057, 2060, 2052–2053, and 2055.

106

PUPIL PAGE 106

Chapter 9 The First Commandment

Overview

In Chapter 8 the students learned about God's covenant and the Ten Commandments. They also learned about Jesus' teaching of the Great Commandment. This chapter will present the first commandment, which teaches us that there is but one true God.

Doctrinal Content	For Adult Reading and Reflection *Catechism of the Catholic Church*
The students will learn:	Paragraph
• We believe in the one true God.	2085
• We honor the one true God.	2096
• We love God above all things.	2093
• We place our hope and trust in God.	2098

prayer (p. 110)
worship (p. 110)
idolatry (p. 112)

Catechist Background

How do you spend your time and energy?

We are accustomed to reading the first commandment in its shortened form: "I am the Lord your God: you shall not have strange gods before me." However, a more complete version from the Book of Exodus delivers additional insight into the commandment: "I, the Lord, am your God, who brought you out of the land of Egypt, that place of slavery. You shall have no other gods besides me. You shall not carve idols for yourselves in the shape of anything from the skies above or on the earth below or in the waters beneath the earth; you shall not bow down before them or worship them" (Exodus 20:2–5).

The fuller version speaks of slavery and carving idols. And while the commandment does not connect the two directly, it takes a small leap of the imagination to see that carving idols and worshiping them leads to a slave-like devotion to these false gods.

Most people these days do not carve idols and then bow down before them. Instead some people pay homage to things such as wealth, power, and status. These become gods that substitute for the one true God. And devoting most of their time and energy to acquiring these things becomes another form of idol worship. As Jesus said, "No one can serve two masters. He will either hate one and love the other, or be devoted to one and despise the other. You cannot serve God and mammon" (Matthew 6:24).

How can you make God a greater priority in your life this week?

Lesson Planning Guide

Lesson Focus	Presentation	Materials
Day 1		
page 107 **We Gather in Prayer** **pages 108–109** *We believe in the one true God.*	• Pray Psalm 86:10–12. • Discuss belief in others in the **We Gather** questions. • Read and discuss the **We Believe** text about the first commandment.  Sing in **We Respond**.	For the prayer space: Bible, sign with words of first commandment "Glory and Praise to Our God," Dan Schutte, #8 Grade 4 CD
Day 2		
pages 110–111 *We honor the one true God.*	• Discuss the word *honor* in the **We Gather** questions. • Discuss honoring God in the **We Believe** text. Compose a poem honoring God in the **We Respond** activity. • Read and discuss the veneration of saints in the *As Catholics* text.	• chart paper
Day 3		
pages 112–113 *We love God above all things.* *Luke 4:1–8*	• Discuss the **We Gather** directive. • Read and discuss loving God above all things in the **We Believe** text. Answer the **We Respond** questions. • Read about and discuss Saint Paul.	• copies of Reproducible Master 9, guide page 107G
Day 4		
pages 114–115 *We place our hope and trust in God.*	• Discuss trusting someone in the **We Gather** questions. • Read and discuss the **We Believe** text about Mary's trusting and hoping in God. • Reflect on the first commandment.  Complete the **We Respond** activity.	
Day 5		
page 116 **Review** **pages 117–118** **We Respond in Faith**	• Complete questions 1–10. Work on the *Assessment Activity.* • Discuss the *Reflect & Pray* question. • Review *Remember* and *Key Words.* • Discuss the monastic life in *Our Catholic Life.* • Discuss the **Sharing Faith with My Family** page.	• Chapter 9 Test in Assessment Book, pp. 17–18 • Chapter 9 Test in Test Generator • Review & Resource Book, pp. 22–24 • Family Book, pp. 27–29

For additional ideas, activities, and opportunities: Visit Sadlier's **www.WEBELIEVEweb.com**

Enrichment Ideas

Chapter Story

Many exciting things were happening in Alex's family. His mother had just gotten a new job. His father was helping to coach Alex's soccer team, and the team was doing well.

Alex really liked school this year, and he was getting along with all his friends. Alex's older sister passed her driving test and got her license.

For all these reasons Alex was surprised when his father said before dinner, "I really think we need to pray more as a family."

Alex said, "Why, Dad? Is something wrong? I thought great things were happening for us."

Alex's father said, "You're right, Alex. That is why it is important for us to stop and pray. We should thank God for these happy times. We need to ask God to be with us always."

▶ *Why is it important to pray in good times as well as in bad times?*

FAITH and MEDIA

Recognizing Idols

▶ Organize several small groups of students to work together on media searches for possible idols in our culture. Suggest that the students scan magazines and newspapers, search the Internet, and check TV programs and video games. The goal is to recognize and list anything that is being honored as a false god (examples: money, possessions, people). Then have each group choose one of these idols to portray in silhouette (a symbolic shape cut from black construction paper and mounted on white poster board). Display the silhouettes on a bulletin board under the heading, Beware of Idols!

CHAPTER PROJECT: TAKE TIME FOR GOD

Have the students work in small groups to write a service message about the importance of taking time for prayer and worship. Explain that the message should be two or three minutes long as it would be if it were on television.

Tell the students to work on the project during the week. Allow time for each group to give its presentation at the end of the week. If possible, videotape the presentations to show to other groups in the school or parish.

Connections

To Stewardship

As the students learn that they are to believe in and honor God, remind them that they can do so both by praying to and worshiping God and by providing help to others. Jesus is an example of this: He helped others because it was what God his Father called him to do. Invite the students to suggest ways that they can help or serve others, such as by helping tutor a younger student. Help them to see that doing God's will in this way shows honor and love for God.

To Prayer

Prayer is a central to living out the first commandment. By his words and actions, Jesus showed his followers the importance of prayer. Jesus prayed to his Father often, asking him to have mercy on others, thanking him, or calling upon his presence. Jesus prayed alone and among his disciples. He prayed with his family and the community gathered at the Temple. We can follow Jesus' example of prayer. We can call on God in many different ways, privately, with our family and parish, and among our friends.

To Mary

The Church honors Mary as the greatest of saints. She is a model for living by God's law and trusting in his ways. Mary put God first in her life, and she believed in his love for her. We can ask Mary to pray for us so that we, too, can trust in God and place our hope in him. The Litany of the Blessed Virgin Mary is one prayer that we can use to ask Mary to intercede for us. Explain to the students that a litany is a form of prayer that includes titles and phrases that are meant to be repeated.

Meeting Individual Needs

Students with Attention Deficit Disorder

Students with Attention Deficit Disorder (ADD) often have difficulty completing tasks in a timely manner. They need habitual guidance in starting and completing various activities. Whenever you plan group activities make sure your ADD students are with others who will encourage them to stay on course.

ADDITIONAL RESOURCES

Book *Here I Am, Lord,* Lonni Collins Pratt, Our Sunday Visitor, 1998. This innovative book allows children to keep a record of their prayers honoring God.

Video *Temptations in the Desert,* CCC of America, 1997. From the series, *A Kingdom Without Frontiers,* here the devil tempts Jesus' faith with promises of fame and fortune. (30 minutes)

To find more ideas for books, videos, and other learning material, visit Sadlier's

www.WEBELIEVEweb.com

Meeting Individual Needs

by Kirk Gaddy

Kirk Gaddy is principal of St. Katharine School in Baltimore, Maryland. A past president of the Elementary School Principals Association as well as a professionally certified catechist, Mr. Gaddy has served the Archdiocese of Baltimore on the Collaborative Council of the Division of Catholic Schools and on the Board of Directors of the Office of African American Catholic Ministries.

The purpose of catechesis is to form disciples of Jesus Christ. This formation is a process "undertaken to reach the maturity of the faith 'given as Christ allotted it' (*Eph* 4:7) and according to the possibilities and the needs of everyone." (*GDC* 143)

Each student we catechize has unique possibilities and needs. To be an effective catechist, one must get to know each student in order to recognize his/her individual strengths and weaknesses. By being aware of the individual student's developmental stage, reasoning abilities, comprehension level, and social skills, the catechist can effectively build on the student's existing strengths and help with weaknesses.

Catechists need to observe students to determine how well each student is learning. Regular assessments can enable the catechist to identify teaching strategies that prove effective for each learner. Assessment can also help the catechist to note the faith concepts that an individual student may need reinforced. No matter what his or her abilities are catechists should have positive expectations for each student.

If catechists teach as Jesus did, students will know they are understood, accepted, and supported. They will feel welcomed and included in each lesson, as well as called to learn and grow in their knowledge and practice of the faith.

Each student, made in the image and likeness of God, is an equally important member of the school or parish community. It is the catechist who takes the lead in ensuring an atmosphere of acceptance toward each student. Through this modeling behavior, students, too develop an attitude of acceptance of all, thus helping to build the kingdom of God on earth.

Catechist Development Topics (Topic and Guide Page)

Resources

Levine, Mel D. *A Mind at a Time: America's Top Learning Expert Shows How Every Child Can Succeed.* New York: Simon & Schuster, 2002.

Vail, Priscilla L. *Smart Kids with School Problems: Things to Know & Ways to Help.* New York: Penguin, 1988.

Ways to Implement Meeting Individual Needs

Catechists can effectively meet the various learning needs of each student by doing the following:

- Meet basic needs for physical comfort with appropriate furniture and equipment, ventilation, and opportunities for movement.
- Know and review regularly the developmental stages of the children to target their specific needs.
- Identify the strengths of the students and invite them to use their unique gifts.
- Use cooperative learning with partners or groups selected to balance needs and talents.
- Offer opportunities for success in a safe and caring atmosphere that fosters self-esteem.
- Provide clear expectations, concise directions, and explicit time frames for assignments and activities.
- Be flexible with class or group procedures to accommodate particular student needs or situations.
- Employ a variety of teaching techniques and learning experiences. Use visual, auditory, and tactile aids when teaching abstract concepts of faith.
- Send "good news" notes home affirming not only the students' performance but their qualities and behaviors that are consistent with our faith.
- Review important material with the students before introducing new information.
- Relate the content of the lesson to the students' life experiences.

For additional ideas, activities, and opportunities, visit Sadlier's

www.WEBELIEVEweb.com

With thanks to:
Trace Woodson
St. Katharine School
Baltimore, Maryland

Trace incorporates cooperative group activities as a means of assisting those of her students with special needs. Trace has found that cooperative group activities that engage each child provide opportunities for children with special needs to receive support from their peers, practice the skills of teamwork, and build self-confidence. In her favorite activity (called "Surprise!), the class is divided into smaller groups. Every group is given a brown paper bag to decorate. Each child writes an affirmation for each member of his or her group. (For example, *John is a good listener.*) The affirmations are then placed in the individual group's bag. The "Surprise!" bags are placed on a table near the prayer corner. Then all the children come together in prayer to share the "surprises" in each group's bag, to give praise to Jesus, and to give thanks for the special gifts of each person.

Notes

Name ______________________________

Write an **N** next to the things that you think you need to survive.
Write a **W** next to the things that you want but do not need to survive.
Then answer the question at the bottom of the page.

_____ food

_____ television

_____ money

_____ air conditioning

_____ a swimming pool

_____ clothing

_____ toothpaste

_____ ice cream

_____ CDs

_____ video games

_____ friends

_____ a pet dog

_____ a bicycle

_____ water

_____ candy

_____ posters

_____ a scooter

_____ family

The first commandment has a very important message for us about all the things we need or want. What is the message?

____

____

____

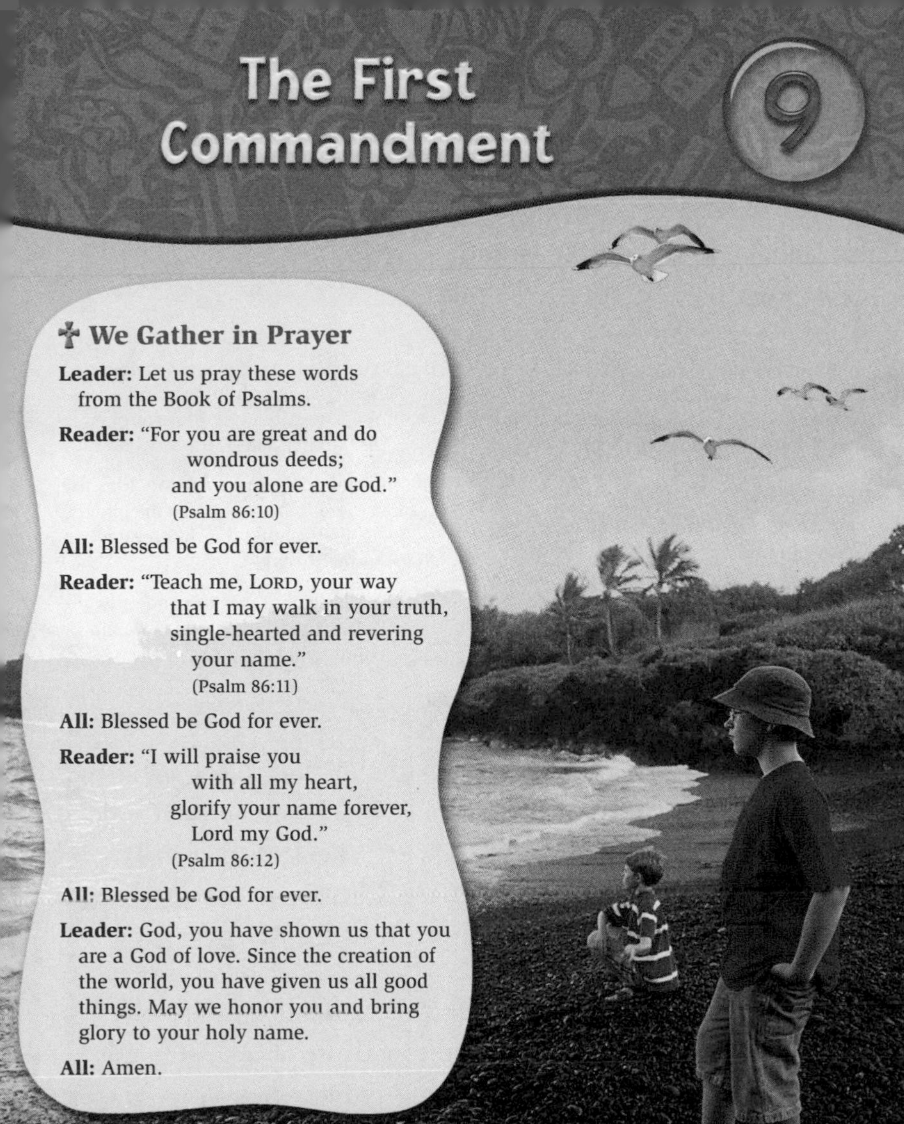

The First Commandment

9

✝ We Gather in Prayer

Leader: Let us pray these words from the Book of Psalms.

Reader: "For you are great and do wondrous deeds;
and you alone are God."
(Psalm 86:10)

All: Blessed be God for ever.

Reader: "Teach me, LORD, your way
that I may walk in your truth,
single-hearted and revering
your name."
(Psalm 86:11)

All: Blessed be God for ever.

Reader: "I will praise you
with all my heart,
glorify your name forever,
Lord my God."
(Psalm 86:12)

All: Blessed be God for ever.

Leader: God, you have shown us that you are a God of love. Since the creation of the world, you have given us all good things. May we honor you and bring glory to your holy name.

All: Amen.

107

PREPARING TO PRAY

In this prayer the students honor God for his many works and praise God as the one true God.

• Play the chorus of the song "Glory and Praise to Our God," Dan Schutte, #8 Grade 4 CD.

• Choose volunteers to be the leader and the reader and allow them time to prepare.

• Explain that *single-hearted* means dedicated, and that *revering* is another word for honoring.

• Instruct the students to raise their arms high in the air during the All responses of "Blessed be God for ever."

The Prayer Space

• Place the Bible on the prayer table and open the book to Exodus, chapter 20.

• Make a sign showing the words of the first commandment. Stand the sign on prayer table.

This Week's Liturgy

Visit **www.webelieveweb.com** for this week's liturgical readings and other seasonal material.

Lesson Plan

We Gather in Prayer ___ minutes

✝ Pray

• Invite the students to gather near the prayer table. Ask them to sing the chorus of "Glory and Praise to Our God" (words on text page 109) as they gather.

• Pray the Sign of the Cross together and then begin the prayer.

• At the "All" responses lift your arms high in the air to cue the students to do the same.

Home Connection Update

Invite the students to share their families' experiences with the "Putting God First" game and the family prayer suggested on the Chapter 8 family page.

Chapter 9 • Day 1

Catechist Goal

- To present that we believe in the one true God

Our Faith Response

- To give thanks and praise to God

Lesson Materials

- Grade 4 CD

Teaching Tip

Working in Small Groups

Students who have an interpersonal style of learning enjoy working with others. Those who have an intrapersonal style prefer working alone. Many students will have a preference for one, or may be more comfortable with the other. However, these styles are not mutually exclusive, and it is helpful to encourage the students to work in both situations. When deciding on assigning students to small groups, make sure you include both types in each group. This will ensure a balanced discussion.

I AM THE LORD YOUR GOD: YOU SHALL NOT HAVE STRANGE GODS BEFORE ME.

We believe in the one true God.

WE GATHER

✝ *God, you alone are holy.*

Think of people you are close to or look up to. How do you show them you believe in them? Why is it important that they know you believe in them?

WE BELIEVE

In the first commandment God tells us to believe in him alone. Out of his great love, God created us. In return he asks us to believe in him, to love him, and to honor him above all else. The first commandment states that, "I am the LORD your God. You shall not have strange gods before me."

In the Old Testament we read that not everyone believed in the one true God as the Israelites did. There were people who believed in many gods—gods of the sun, moon, water, and earth. These people imagined how their gods would look. They carved images of them from wood and stone.

The Israelites lived among people who worshiped these gods. So God said to his people:

"I, the LORD, am your God, who brought you out of the land of Egypt, that place of slavery. You shall not have other gods besides me. You shall not carve idols for yourselves in the shape of anything in the sky above or on the earth below or in the waters beneath the earth; you shall not bow down before them or worship them" (Exodus 20:2–5).

God wanted his people to know him. He wanted them to honor him as the one true God. He also wanted them to remember to love him always.

Here is a special prayer the Israelites prayed. It is called the Shema. *Shĕmá* is the Hebrew word meaning "hear."

"Hear, O Israel!
The LORD is our God,
the LORD alone!
Therefore, you shall love
the LORD, your God,
with all your heart,
and with all your soul,
and with all your strength."
(Deuteronomy 6:4–5)

108

Lesson Plan

WE GATHER ___ minutes

✝ **Pray** Pray together the *We Gather* prayer.

Focus on Life Discuss the *We Gather* questions. Remind the students: *We often look up to people who set good examples for us and help us.* Invite volunteers to act out or explain some ways we can show people that we believe in them. Tell the students that in today's lesson they will learn that we believe in, love, and honor God.

WE BELIEVE ___ minutes

Read About the One True God Read together the *We Believe* statement. Invite volunteers to read aloud the first two *We Believe* paragraphs. Emphasize the following points:

- God loves us completely, and he asks us to believe in him, honor him, and love him in return.
- Not everyone believed in the one true God.
- God wanted to be known and honored as the one true God.

Then have a volunteer read aloud the Scripture passage and the following *We Believe* paragraph. Have the students highlight the last two sentences of this paragraph.

Learn About the Shema Read aloud the next paragraph. Invite all to read aloud the Shema. Ask: *What do the words remind you of?* (the first part of the Great Commandment) Explain that Jesus used this prayer when he was teaching about loving God. Finish reading the *We Believe* text. Then have the students read aloud the First Commandment.

Jesus grew up in a Jewish family and learned the Shema. He used this prayer in some of his teachings. This prayer reminds us to love the one true God who made us.

Today, Jews all around the world still pray the Shema every day.

WE RESPOND

♫ **Glory and Praise to Our God**

Refrain:

Glory and praise to our God,
who alone gives light to our days.
Many are the blessings he bears
to those who trust in his ways.

We, the daughters and sons of him
who built the valleys and plains,
praise the wonders our God has
done
in ev'ry heart that sings. (Refrain)

109

Chapter 9 • Day 1

ACTIVITY BANK

Music

Liturgical Music

Activity Materials: parish songbooks

As the students study the first commandment, they may begin to understand better the songs they sing at Mass. If possible, allow the students to look through the parish songbooks for references to the ideas discussed in this chapter. Because many songs refer to our giving honor and glory to God, the students should be successful in their search. Discuss any lyrics they do not understand, and help them make a list of songs that relate to this chapter.

Quick Check

✔ *What does God ask of us?* (God asks us to believe in him, to love him, and to honor him above all else.)

✔ *What is the name of the prayer that the Jews still pray today to proclaim their love for the one true God?* (The ancient Israelites prayed, and Jews today still pray, the Shema.)

WE RESPOND ___ minutes

Connect to Life Have the students work in small groups. Ask the groups to read the words to "Glory and Praise to our God." Then have the groups name some of the blessings and wonders God has done for us. Ask someone in each group to record the members' responses.

Pray Invite the students to close their eyes and visualize some of God's blessings and wonders. Remind the students that we can pray to God by singing. Play or sing "Glory and Praise to Our God," from the Grade 4 CD.

Plan Ahead for Day 2

Catechist Goal: To explore ways we can worship and honor the one true God

Preparation: Have chart paper available.

Catechist Goal

- To explore ways we can worship and honor the one true God

Our Faith Response

- To give praise and honor to God

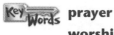

prayer
worship

Lesson Materials

- chart paper

As Catholics...

Veneration of the Saints

After the lesson has been presented, have a volunteer read the *As Catholics* text. Explain that saints were people who often faced many challenges and obstacles in worshiping the one true God. They were human like we are, but they persevered and kept their faith. This is why we honor them.

We honor the one true God.

WE GATHER

✢ *God, we adore you.*

What do you think of when you hear the word *honor?* What are some different ways people use this word?

WE BELIEVE

When we live out the first commandment, we honor God. We honor God by believing in him, praying to him, and worshiping him. We also honor God by loving others.

Prayer is listening and talking to God with our minds and hearts. We thank and bless him. We ask him for forgiveness and help. We remember those who need his love and care. Through prayer we can grow closer to God.

Worship is giving God thanks and praise. We praise him for his goodness. We give glory to him as our creator and savior. We adore God and admit that everything is a gift from him. We offer, or give, our love to God.

Our greatest act of love and worship is the celebration of the Mass. At Mass we are united to Jesus, who offered himself on the cross to save us.

Jesus, God's Son, always praised his Father for his many blessings. After he healed the sick or performed miracles, Jesus thanked God his Father. Those who saw Jesus' great deeds praised and honored God, too.

Key Words

prayer listening and talking to God with our minds and hearts

worship giving God thanks and praise

110

Lesson Plan

WE GATHER ___ minutes

✢ **Pray** Ask the students to recall that in the first commandment God tells us to believe in him, to love him, and to honor him. Then pray the Sign of the Cross and the *We Gather* prayer.

Focus on Life Have the students work in small groups. Ask each group to make a word web for the word *honor*. After a few minutes ask the groups to share their word webs with the class. Tell the students that in today's lesson they will learn more about the ways we honor God.

WE BELIEVE ___ minutes

Discuss Ways to Honor God Have a volunteer read the *We Believe* statement. Ask: *What are some ways we honor God?* Have the students list some ways. Then have them read the first two *We Believe* paragraphs. Emphasize:

- We honor God when we pray to and worship him. We also honor God when we obey him and love others.
- We grow closer to God through prayer, which is talking and listening to God.
- When we offer our love and praise to God and thank him for all his gifts, we are worshiping him.
- Invite the students to share some ways that they pray and worship.

Have volunteers read aloud the last two *We Believe* paragraphs. Then discuss how Jesus is an example for praising and honoring God his Father. Recap the reasons the Mass is the greatest act of love and worship of God (We are united to Jesus who offered himself to save us.)

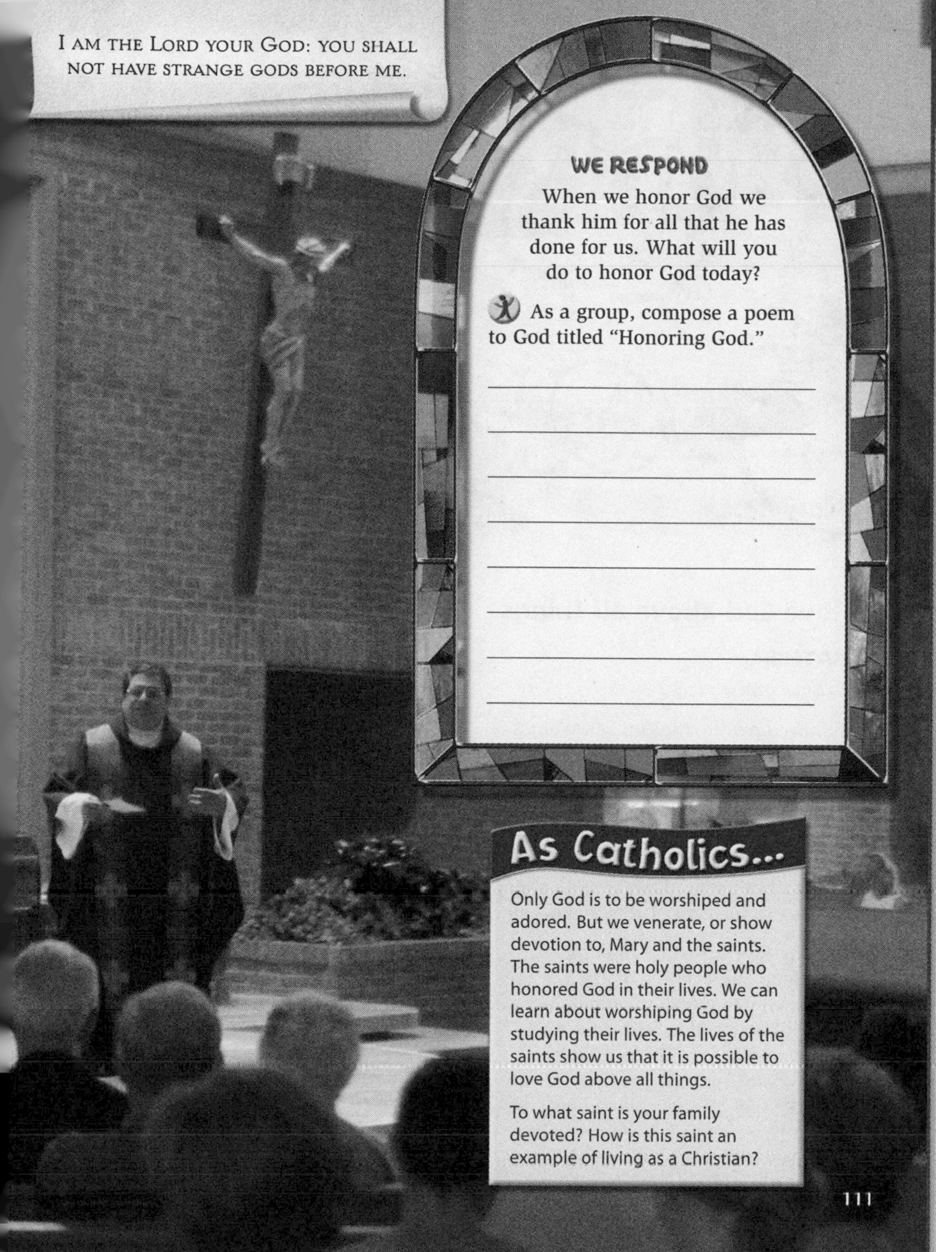

I AM THE LORD YOUR GOD: YOU SHALL NOT HAVE STRANGE GODS BEFORE ME.

WE RESPOND

When we honor God we thank him for all that he has done for us. What will you do to honor God today?

As a group, compose a poem to God titled "Honoring God."

As Catholics...

Only God is to be worshiped and adored. But we venerate, or show devotion to, Mary and the saints. The saints were holy people who honored God in their lives. We can learn about worshiping God by studying their lives. The lives of the saints show us that it is possible to love God above all things.

To what saint is your family devoted? How is this saint an example of living as a Christian?

111

ACTIVITY BANK

Church

Saints

Activity Materials: "Lives of the Saints" books

Have the students work in groups. Ask each group to research a particular saint's story. The saint should be someone who showed us that it is possible to love God above all things. Suggestions might include Saint Thomas More, Saint Therese of Liseiux, Saint Francis of Assisi, Blessed Pierre Toussaint, and Blessed Kateri Tekakwitha. Invite each group to act out a particular event in the life of the saint it selected.

Quick Check

✔ *How can we honor God?* (We can honor God by believing in him, praying to him, worshiping him, and loving others.)

✔ *What is our greatest act of love and worship?* (The celebration of the Mass is our greatest act of love and worship.)

WE RESPOND

___ minutes

Connect to Life Read the *We Respond* question. Invite the students to list and share ways that they can honor God.

Then as a group compose a poem honoring God. When the poem has been written and agreed upon, make a copy on chart paper and have the students copy it into their own books.

Pray Allow a few minutes of quiet time during which the students can decide what they will do to honor God today. Then invite the students to pray these words: *God, we want to grow closer to you by praying to you. Amen.*

Plan Ahead for Day 3

Catechist Goal: To emphasize that we must put God first in our lives

Preparation: Make copies of Reproducible Master 9; have highlighters or markers available.

Chapter 9 • Day 3

Catechist Goal

• To emphasize that we must put God first in our lives

Our Faith Response

• To show that we love God above all other things

 **idolatry**

Lesson Materials

• copies of Reproducible Master 9

Blessed are they...

Saint Paul

After you have completed the lesson, invite volunteers to read aloud about Saint Paul. Explain: Saint Paul wrote letters to early Christian communities. Saint Paul's words help all of us understand what it means to live by the Beatitudes.

We love God above all things.

WE GATHER

✝ *God, we praise you.*

We all have favorite things that we enjoy doing. Think about some things that you always find time to do.

WE BELIEVE

God wants us to be happy. He wants us to have the things we need. He wants us to help others to have what they need, too.

Many things are necessary to our lives. We need food and clothing, a place to live, and a way to travel from one place to another. We need to enjoy time with our family and friends. We need the chance to make a living. But God asks us not to make these things more important to us than he is. He wants us to remember that we need him more than anything.

The first commandment reminds us that we must put God first in our lives. Everything we do and say should show how important God is to us.

Sometimes we put someone or something before God. If we honor or worship a person or a thing instead of God, we are setting up a false god. Giving worship to a creature or thing instead of God is **idolatry**.

idolatry giving worship to a creature or thing instead of God

112

Lesson Plan

WE GATHER ___ minutes

✝ **Pray** Invite the students to think quietly of all of the things that God has given us and done for us. Then have them pray together the *We Gather* prayer.

Focus on Life Read aloud the *We Gather* paragraph. Share something that you enjoy and do on a regular basis, such as reading or exercising. Ask the students to share things that they always find time to do. Tell students that in today's lesson they will learn that God should come before all things.

WE BELIEVE ___ minutes

Read the Text Have the students read the *We Believe* statement. Ask a volunteer to read aloud the first three paragraphs. Stress: *God wants us to have the things we need, but he does not want these things to be more important to us than he is.*

Think About Needs and Wants Distribute Reproducible Master 9 and read the directions aloud. Have the students to complete the survey independently. Invite volunteers to share their responses. (The commandment reminds us to put God first in our lives.)

Learn About Idolatry Write the word *idolatry* on the board. Explain the definition as given in the fourth paragraph. Circle the word *idol*. Explain that *idol* is another word for false god.

Read About Jesus' Example Read aloud the Scripture passage about Jesus in the desert. Ask a volunteer to read aloud the last *We Believe* paragraph.

I AM THE LORD YOUR GOD: YOU SHALL NOT HAVE STRANGE GODS BEFORE ME.

By his life and words, Jesus kept God first in his life.

Luke 4:1–8

Before Jesus began his work among the people, he went to the desert to pray. There the devil offered Jesus all the lands of the world. He would give Jesus all their riches and power. He said to Jesus, "All this will be yours, if you worship me" (Luke 4:7).

Jesus refused the devil, saying,

"You shall worship the Lord, your God,
and him alone shall you serve"
(Luke 4:8).

Riches and power were not important to Jesus. Nothing was more important to Jesus than serving God his Father. He loved his Father above all things. Jesus wanted his followers to love and serve the Father as he did. Jesus wants us to love God above all things and to serve him throughout our lives.

WE RESPOND

Think about the way people live today. Are there things that people love and honor more than God? If so, what are some of these things?

____

____

____

____

How can we remember to love God above all things?

Blessed are they...

Saint Paul

Saint Paul's original name was Saul, and he persecuted the followers of Christ. Jesus himself appeared to Saul and asked, "Why are you persecuting me?" (Acts of the Apostles 9:4). Then Saul realized that when he persecuted Christians he was persecuting Christ himself.

The enemy of Christians, Saul, became the great apostle of Jesus, Paul. He traveled from city to city, country to country, to tell the good news of Jesus Christ. He wrote to the early followers of Jesus, "Everything belongs to you . . . and you to Christ" (1 Corinthians 3:21–23). The feast of the Conversion of Saint Paul is January 25.

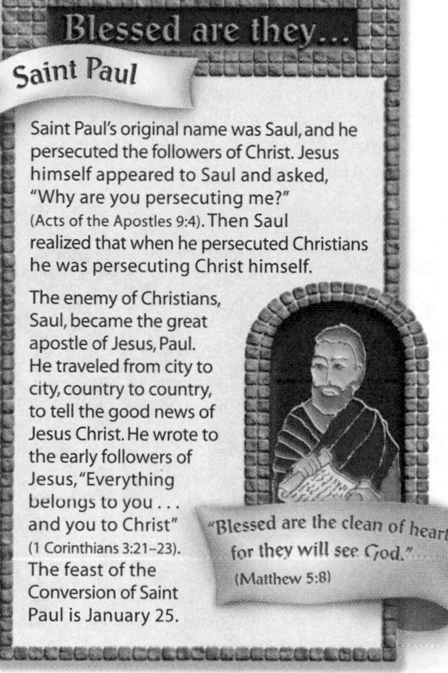

"Blessed are the clean of heart, for they will see God." (Matthew 5:8)

113

Chapter 9 • Day 3

ACTIVITY BANK

Curriculum Connection

Literature

Activity Materials: books such as *King Midas and the Golden Touch* and *The Emperor's New Clothes.*

Ask the students to retell familiar stories about people who had problems because they put importance on having riches or power. Provide a few suggestions of classic tales such as *King Midas and the Golden Touch* and *The Emperor's New Clothes.* Discuss the characters' problems and the consequences of their actions. Then ask the students to retell the stories having the characters make unselfish rather than selfish choices.

Have the students highlight or underline the last two sentences.

Quick Check

✔ *What does God want for us?* (God wants us to have what we need, to be happy, to help others have what they need, and to always put him first in our lives.)

✔ *What is idolatry?* (Idolatry is giving worship to a creature or thing instead of God.)

WE RESPOND

___ minutes

Connect to Life Have the students work with a partner to complete the *We Respond* activity. Invite the students to share their responses with the class.

Pray Invite the students to say a silent prayer to God. In this prayer they should thank God for giving them the many blessings that are theirs and tell God how much they love him. They should also reflect on ways to remember to love God above all things.

Plan Ahead for Day 4

Catechist Goal: To examine why we should place our hope and trust in God

Preparation: Plan how and where the students can reflect quietly.

Catechist Goal

- To examine why we should place our hope and trust in God

Our Faith Response

- To place our hope and trust in God

Teaching Tip

Time and Space for Reflection

Today's lesson involves letting the students take time for personal reflection. Arrange the seats in the classroom to provide more space between individuals and ask the students to show respect by not distracting others.

We place our hope and trust in God.

WE GATHER

✠ *God, we place our trust in you.*

What does it mean to trust someone? How do you show that you trust someone?

WE BELIEVE

Jesus wanted his followers to believe in God's love and care. Jesus taught people to trust and hope in God. Jesus said: "Therefore I tell you, do not worry about your life, what you will eat [or drink], or about your body, what you will wear. Is not life more than food and the body more than clothing? Look at the birds in the sky; they do not sow or reap, they gather nothing into barns, yet your heavenly Father feeds them. Are not you more important than they?" (Matthew 6:25–26).

When we trust and hope in God, we will be happy. Trusting and hoping in God is part of living out the first commandment. God the Holy Spirit helps us to trust and hope. Trusting God means believing in his love for us. Putting our hope in God means we are confident in God's blessings in our lives.

The Blessed Virgin Mary, the mother of Jesus, is a great example of hope and trust. When she was a young girl, an angel of the Lord came to her. The angel told her, "Do not be afraid, Mary, for you have found favor with God" (Luke 1:30). Mary then learned that God had chosen her to be the mother of his Son. She must have been both amazed and confused. But Mary believed in God's love for her. So she said, "Behold, I am the handmaid of the Lord. May it be done to me according to your word" (Luke 1:38).

Mary was blessed by God. She put her hope in him and in his Son. Mary was confident of God's care for her, and was willing to do what God asked of her. In all that she did, Mary trusted God completely.

The Annunciation, Fra Angelico, c.1450

114

Lesson Plan

WE GATHER ___ minutes

✠ **Pray** Ask the students to think about the people whom they trust. Then pray together the Sign of the Cross and the *We Gather* prayer.

Focus on Life Discuss the *We Gather* questions. Have volunteers act out situations in which people show their trust in each other. At this time you may want to share the *Chapter Story*. Tell the students that in this lesson they will learn about hoping and trusting in God.

WE BELIEVE ___ minutes

Discuss Trust and Hope Read the *We Believe* statement together. Form two groups. Have one group read and discuss the first *We Believe* paragraph and the other read and discuss the second *We Believe* paragraph. Ask representatives from each group to explain in their own words the main ideas of their respective paragraphs. Stress: *Jesus taught us to place our trust in God.*

Read About Mary Ask: *What do you know about Mary?* After a brief discussion, have volunteers read aloud the next two *We Believe* paragraphs. Point out: *Mary is a model of discipleship. She was confident in God's love for her, and she placed her hope in him.*

Consider Challenges to Trust Have the students follow along as you read aloud the three bulleted situations in the fourth *We Believe* paragraph. Encourage the students to consider how they would feel at these times. Invite volunteers to name other times when it might be difficult to place hope and trust in God. Then

I AM THE LORD YOUR GOD: YOU SHALL NOT HAVE STRANGE GODS BEFORE ME.

Take a few moments to think quietly and prayerfully about ways you follow the first commandment. These questions may help you.

Do I try to love God above all things?

Do I really believe in, trust, and love God?

Do I pray to God sometime each day?

How do I encourage others to trust in God?

How do I take an active part in the worship of God, especially in the Mass and the other sacraments?

How do I try to learn more about the Catholic faith?

Trusting in God at all times is not always easy. There are times when we may lose sight of his love for us. Think about these situations:

- We pray to God and ask for help. Yet when we do not get the answer we want, we may doubt God. We begin to think that he is not listening. We worry that God has forgotten us.
- We have so many other interests that God loses importance. We forget about God's place in our lives.
- We are so happy and things are going so well that we forget that we need God.

Call on God! Ask him to help you to always place your hope and trust in him. God will always help you when you ask. He will help you to remember how important he is. He will help you to remember that you need him. God will give you the grace to trust in him and to hope in his goodness.

WE RESPOND

How can you show God that you are living out the first commandment?

Circle any activity that shows trust in God. Use the space provided to explain why you did not circle an activity.

- Participating in Mass
- Wishing on a star
- Celebrating the sacrament of Reconciliation
- Making the sign of the cross
- Listening to a fortune teller
- Relying on a lucky charm
- Praying

115

Chapter 9 • Day 4

ACTIVITY BANK

Faith and Media

Promoting Trust in God

Activity Materials: magazines or newspapers with advertisements, construction paper, markers or crayons

Show the students a few examples of advertisements in magazines or newspapers. Discuss the important ways that advertising influences our lives. Encourage the students to write and design their own advertisements for trusting in God or taking time for God. Encourage them to think of a slogan or logo to use in promoting either concept. Display the students' work.

ask a volunteer to read aloud the fifth paragraph. Remind the students that God is there to help us, if only we trust and believe in him.

Reflect on the First Commandment Have the students make an examination of conscience by reflecting prayerfully on the questions listed on page 115. Remind the students that this is a quiet time and that they are to think only about their own actions.

Quick Check

✔ *What does it mean to trust in God?* (We believe in his love for us.)

✔ *What does putting our hope in God mean?* (We are confident in God's blessings in our lives.)

WE RESPOND

___ minutes

Connect to Life Ask the *We Respond* question. Encourage the students to share their ideas. Then have the students complete the activity. Discuss the reasons the students give for circling or not circling each activity listed.

Pray Invite the students to pray the following:

O God, we trust you.
We hope in you.
We love you above all things.
Amen.

Plan Ahead for Day 5

Catechist Goal: To review chapter ideas and their relationship to our faith life

Preparation: Make copies of Chapter 9 Test in the Grade 4 Assessment Book (option).

Chapter 9 • **Day 5**

Catechist Goal

- To review chapter ideas and their relationship to our faith life

Our Faith Response

- To apply what has been learned to our lives

CHAPTER TEST

The Chapter 9 Test is provided in the Grade 4 Assessment Book.

Review

Grade 4
Chapter 9

Circle the correct answer.

1. Giving worship to a creature or thing instead of God is ______.
   lying   (**idolatry**)   laziness
2. Through prayer and worship we can ______ God.
   (**honor**)   deny   forget
3. The Israelites worshiped ______.
   the sun   the moon   (**the one true God**)
4. Giving God thanks and praise is ______.
   (**worship**)   love   idolatry

Match each phrase on the left with its definition on the right.

5. to set up a false god — 6 to believe in God's love for us
6. to trust in God — 8 to give God thanks and praise
7. to pray to God — 5 to worship a person or thing instead of God
8. to worship God — 7 to listen and talk to God with our minds and hearts

Complete the following:

9–10. The Shema is See pages 108–109.

Choose and complete one of the following projects:

- Write a poem or song to remind people that God should be first in their lives.
- Interview some adults. Ask them whether they think people today worship false gods. If so, what are those false gods?

116

Lesson Plan

___ minutes

Chapter Review Allow time for the students to complete questions 1–4. Allow them to look back in the chapter, if necessary. Invite volunteers to provide the correct answers. Clear up any misconceptions that arise. Then have the students complete the matching section, numbers 5–8, and complete the sentence in question 9–10.

Assessment Activity This activity can be done as a homework assignment. Invite a volunteer to read aloud the three project choices and remind the students that each of them should choose one project. When they have completed their projects, invite them to share them with the class.

___ minutes

Reflect & Pray Invite a volunteer to read aloud the *Reflect & Pray* text. Help the students to reflect on the words of Saint Matthew by sharing your own thoughts.

Key Words To review the *Key Words* from the chapter, write them on the board and allow the students time to define each one in their own words. When the students have completed this task, invite them to share their definitions. Clear up any misconceptions or misunderstandings.

Remember Review the key ideas in the chapter by inviting the students to highlight one or two main words in each of the four *We Believe* statements. After they have finished, have volunteers share their words.

We Respond in Faith

Reflect & Pray

We all have favorite things and times in life that we treasure. Reflect on these words: "For where your treasure is, there also will your heart be" (Matthew 6:21).

What do you think these words mean? ______________________

____

My God, I believe in you, I trust you, I love you.

Key Words

prayer (p. 110)
worship (p. 110)
idolatry (p. 112)

Remember

- We believe in the one true God.
- We honor the one true God.
- We love God above all things.
- We place our hope and trust in God.

Our Catholic Life

The Monastic Life

Keeping the first commandment means that we put God first in our lives. Some Catholic men and women are called to live the first commandment by living in communities of prayer. They live the monastic life. Each monastic community lives in a building called a monastery.

These men and women give their lives to God in prayer for the world. They work to support themselves in various ways, such as farming or making bread to sell. All that they do is offered to God in prayer. This shows us that anything we do can be offered to God in prayer, too.

Home Connection

Sharing Faith with My Family

Make sure to send home the family page (text page 118).

Encourage the students to pray the family prayer together with their families. Review the "Putting God First" game.

For additional information and activities, encourage families to visit Sadlier's

www.WEBELIEVEweb.com

Help them to see that the main words in these four sentences are *believe, honor, love, hope,* and *trust.* Point out that doing these things will help them follow the first commandment. Discuss how each photo or illustration in this chapter relates to the first commandment.

Our Catholic Life Choose volunteers to read aloud the two paragraphs. Help the students to see that there are many ways that people try to keep the first commandment. Everything we do can be offered to God in prayer. Discuss ways that the students can offer their lives or work to God.

Chapter 10 The Second Commandment

Overview

In Chapter 9 the students learned about ways we follow the first commandment. In this chapter the students will learn that we follow the second commandment by respecting and honoring the name of God.

Doctrinal Content	For Adult Reading and Reflection *Catechism of the Catholic Church*
The students will learn:	Paragraph
• God's name is holy.	2143
• We respect God's name.	2144
• We call upon God's name.	2153
• We respect and honor sacred places.	1186

psalm (p. 120)
reverence (p. 123)
bless (p. 124)
sacred (p. 126)

Catechist Background

What does your name mean to you?

Names are an essential part of who we are. When God appeared to Moses, and Moses asked what God's name was, the answer was Yahweh, "I am the One who is." The Israelites believed that when people gave their names, they offered themselves and welcomed the possibility of friendship. By revealing his name, God sent a clear sign to his people that his friendship was open to them.

The second commandment directs us to use God's name only with respect. Christians are urged to show that same respect for the name of Jesus, the Son of God. Additionally, we owe respect to all whose names we use in prayers, such as Mary and the saints.

The second commandment is widely ignored, even by Christians. We may say to ourselves that we intend no disrespect, but disrespect is nonetheless given, and our faith is dishonored.

The *Catechism of the Catholic Church* teaches us a positive approach. "The gift of a name belongs to the order of trust and intimacy. 'The Lord's name is holy.' For this reason man must not abuse it. He must keep it in mind in silent, loving adoration. He will not introduce it into his speech except to bless, praise, and glorify it" (2143).

How can you use God's name in a more prayerful and worthy manner?

Lesson Planning Guide

Lesson Focus	Presentation	Materials
Day 1		
page 119 **We Gather in Prayer** **pages 120–121** *God's name is holy.*	• Praise God together. Respond in song. • Discuss ways of getting to know someone in the **We Gather** questions. • Read and discuss the **We Believe** text about the second commandment. Sing a psalm of praise. Write a psalm for the **We Respond** activity.	For the prayer space: Bible, poster of the Ten Commandments "Lord, I Lift Your Name on High," Rick Founds, #9 Grade 4 CD "Psalm 103: The Lord Is Kind," Carey Landry, #10 Grade 4 CD
Day 2		
pages 122–123 *We respect God's name.*	• Discuss the **We Gather** question. • Read and discuss using God's name in the **We Believe** text.  Write titles for God. • Reflect on the **We Respond** statement about praying to God. • Read and discuss the *As Catholics* text.	• Bible
Day 3		
pages 124–125 *We call upon God's name.*	• Discuss the **We Gather** questions. • Read and discuss the **We Believe** text about calling upon God's name to bless us and to witness our truthfulness. Write and design a public service message in the **We Respond** activity.	• colored pencils or markers
Day 4		
pages 126–127 *We respect and honor sacred places.*	• Discuss the **We Gather** statements. • Discuss the sacred in the **We Believe** text. • Reflect on the second commandment. Complete the **We Respond** activity.	• picture of the Temple in Jerusalem • copies of Reproducible Master 10, guide page 119G
Day 5		
page 128 **Review** **pages 129–130** **We Respond in Faith**	• Complete questions 1–10. Work on the *Assessment Activity.* • Complete the *Reflect & Pray* activity. • Review *Remember* and *Key Words.* • Read and discuss *Our Catholic Life.* • Discuss the **Sharing Faith with My Family** page.	• index cards, a basket • Chapter 10 Test in Assessment Book, pp. 19–20 • Chapter 10 Test in Test Generator • Review & Resource Book, pp. 25–27 • Family Book, pp. 30–32

For additional ideas, activities, and opportunities: Visit Sadlier's **www.WEBELIEVEweb.com**

Enrichment Ideas

Chapter Story

José and his mother were on their way to the store. José thought, "Now would be a good time to talk to her about Marcos."

José said, "Mom, would you like it if people just called you by your last name? What if they said, 'Santos, let's go to the store. Santos, are you coming to practice? Santos, hurry up or we're going to be late?'"

José's mother answered, "I don't think I would like that at all. What's going on that you are asking me this?"

José explained, "Marcos and I have been friends since first grade, but now he's treating me like everybody else. He's calling everybody by their last names. When he talks about Father Finn or our teachers, he only uses their last names. I guess he thinks it makes him seem older, but it doesn't to me."

José's mother said, "Well, I hope you don't start doing this. Only using last names is a sign of disrespect. Try not answering Marcos a few times when he calls you Santos. If he asks what's the matter, you can tell him you didn't hear your name. You only respond to your first name."

▶ *If you were José, what would you do?*

FAITH and MEDIA

▶ On Day 3, if the students do the optional *Respectful Television* activity (Activity Bank), come prepared to suggest some suitable television programs and/or bring videotapes of such programs for the students to watch.

▶ On Day 4, after you show a picture or pictures of the Temple in Jerusalem, you might direct the students to specific Web sites where they can find additional pictures and information about the Temple.

CHAPTER PROJECT: A LITANY BOOK

A traditional prayer of the Church is the Litany of the Holy Name of Jesus in which we call upon Jesus, using different titles to ask him to have mercy on us. Each day with your students, call upon Jesus, Son of the Living God; Jesus, Prince of Peace; Jesus, model of goodness; Jesus, Good Shepherd; Jesus, the true light. Have the students make litany books. On each page have the students copy one of Jesus' titles. You may want to make prayer books that contain litanies available to them. Invite the students to illustrate the pages and encourage them to add their own prayerful titles for Jesus to their books. Provide opportunities in the coming weeks for the students to use their litany books in quiet prayer and reflection.

Connections

To Scripture

Throughout this chapter the students will study biblical passages in which a variety of titles are used to address God. As they read from and listen to Scripture, encourage them to look for the different ways God is described or named. For example, when the students read the verses from Psalm 103, encourage them to list the titles the psalmist uses to address and describe God. Invite the students to highlight these words or write them in the margins of their books. Encourage them to use some of these titles to address God when they pray.

To Catholic Social Teaching

Life and Dignity of the Human Person
As Catholics we believe all human life is sacred and deserving of respect. In this chapter the students learn that following the second commandment requires that we have a deep respect for everyone. We show our respect for God and others by treating them respectfully. For example, being courteous shows respect. Calling others insulting names does not show respect. Whenever possible, commend students for situations in which they treat others with respect.

To Liturgical Music

Encourage the students to listen carefully to the music used during Mass. Ask them to consider how we use music to call upon the Lord. What titles for God do you hear in the music? Some titles used in liturgical music include "Heavenly King," "God of Life and of the Living," "Our Father," "Lamb of God," and "Almighty Father." Invite the students to note some of these titles after they next participate in Mass.

Meeting Individual Needs

Students with Visual Needs

Allow students with visual needs to sit close to the board or wherever the focus of the class is centered. Also consider alternate ways for these students to learn the message of the lesson. In this week's lesson, for example, the students are studying the different names used to address God. Having all students use clay to form the letters of one of these names and keep the letters on their desks could be especially helpful for the student with visual needs.

ADDITIONAL RESOURCES

Book *Praise God,* Gunvor Edwards, Liturgical Press, 1999. Children learn how important it is to show God proper respect.

Video *The Golden Calf,* CCC of America, 1995. From the series, In the Beginning, this animated video tells the story of the Golden Calf and Moses' reaction to it. (30 minutes)

To find more ideas for books, videos, and other learning material, visit Sadlier's

www.WEBELIEVEweb.com

Catechist Development

Developing a Liturgical Sense in Children

by Sister Linda L. Gaupin, CDP, Ph.D.

Sister Linda L. Gaupin, CDP, is Diocesan Director for Religious Education for the Diocese of Orlando. She is the project director for the text, The Spirit Sets Us Free *and is the former Associate Director for the Secretariat for the Liturgy at the USCCB. She has a Ph.D. from the Catholic University of America.*

One of the most enjoyable tasks of catechetical ministry is forming children into the liturgical life of the Church.

Liturgical prayer has such tremendous power to form us in the faith. It is no wonder that it is one of the primary sources for catechesis. However, this rich source of formation is sometimes overlooked in catechesis. In fact, the *General Directory for Catechesis* identifies a weak link between catechesis and liturgy as one of the problems affecting the vitality of catechesis in recent years [*GDC* 30].

As catechists, we can develop a liturgical sense in children by celebrating the rich treasury of liturgical prayer, directing catechesis on liturgical symbols, keeping the liturgical year, and respecting repetition.

Liturgical prayer includes Mass and the sacraments, morning and evening prayer, liturgies of the word, blessings, and many other ritual celebrations. Encourage children to become familiar with all types of liturgical prayer throughout their catechetical formation.

By directing catechesis on liturgical symbols, children become aware of the symbols' beauty and placement within the liturgy. The assembly, water, oil, cross, laying on of hands, light, white garment, and bread and wine are the dominant symbols in our liturgical rites that mark and shape us as a people. Catechesis on the symbols and gestures, which go along with these symbols, opens up their many levels of meaning, and using the symbols and gestures in prayer forms us in the faith.

Catechist Development Topics (Topic and Guide Page)

By keeping the liturgical year, the children learn the major truths of the faith that are unfolded throughout the liturgical year. Celebrating various liturgical prayers appropriate to a season, catechesis on the season, and respecting the integrity of the season form children in the major teachings of the Church.

Good liturgical prayer is repetitious. Repetition allows us to make the liturgy our own, to participate fully.

Resources

Huck, Gabe. *Preparing Liturgy for Children and Children for Liturgy.* Chicago: Liturgy Training Publications, 1989.

Mazar, Peter. *School Year, Church Year: Activities and Decorations for the Classroom.* Chicago: Liturgy Training Publications, 2001.

Ways to Implement Developing a Liturgical Sense in Children

- Incorporate a liturgical calendar within the program calendar. Schedule Masses on significant days. Include blessings from the *Book of Blessings* that address special seasons and/or events in the life of children. Plan special seasonal celebrations (such as in Advent and Lent). Celebrate the sacrament of Reconciliation on appropriate days in the calendar as well as during significant seasons.

- Attend to the environment. Ensure that the dominant symbols pervade (cross, light, water, etc.) and are not overshadowed by secondary symbols. Use the colors of the various liturgical seasons throughout the environment. Set aside a special area in each room for prayer. Include the word of God and dominant liturgical and seasonal symbols of the season.

- Form a liturgy committee. Good liturgy does not just happen! Form a committee of adults and older children in the school or parish to prepare the various liturgical celebrations.

- Get Scripture in the picture. Prominence should be given to enthronement of the word of God. A decorative Bible or lectionary should always be prominently displayed. Set aside time for proclamation and catechesis of the Scripture readings for the coming Sunday. Empower children to learn how to reflect on the readings and share their reflections.

- Make a liturgy and life connection. Our liturgical prayer, symbols, and seasons give meaning to all areas of our life. It is important to make a connection between liturgy and the other subjects that we teach.

For additional ideas, activities, and opportunities, visit Sadlier's

www.WEBELIEVEweb.com

With thanks to:
Mary Birmingham
Director of Liturgy/Music
Our Savior Parish
Cocoa Beach, Florida

Under Mary's direction, the children in Our Savior's Catholic parish community begin their liturgical formation very early. The children come together to prepare the liturgy in accord with the liturgical seasons. They prepare the environment and plan processions. The children are readers and cantors. They select the music. They prepare a reflection on the readings from their religion class. They give an explanation of the saints or feasts appointed for a given day. Everyone is involved in the process. By January, the third grade classes are ready to join the other children in the preparation of the weekly program. Mary has found that the children in the parish are as at home in the celebration of liturgy "as fish are to water." It is an integral part of their spiritual formation.

Notes

CHAPTER 10 GRADE 4

Name ______________________________

Write a prayer to:

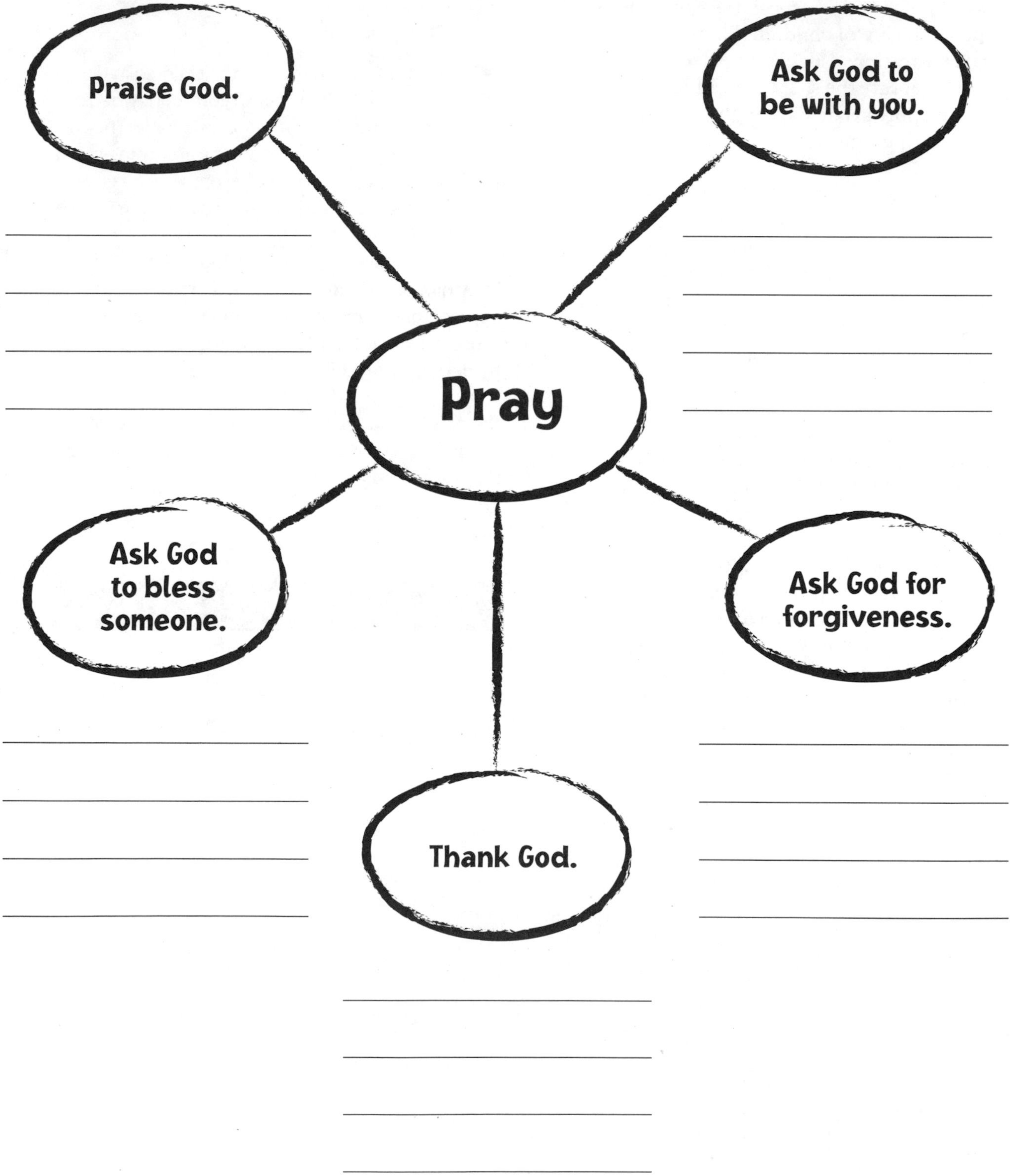

Pray

Praise God.

____
____
____
____

Ask God to be with you.

____
____
____
____

Ask God to bless someone.

____
____
____
____

Ask God for forgiveness.

____
____
____
____

Thank God.

____
____
____
____

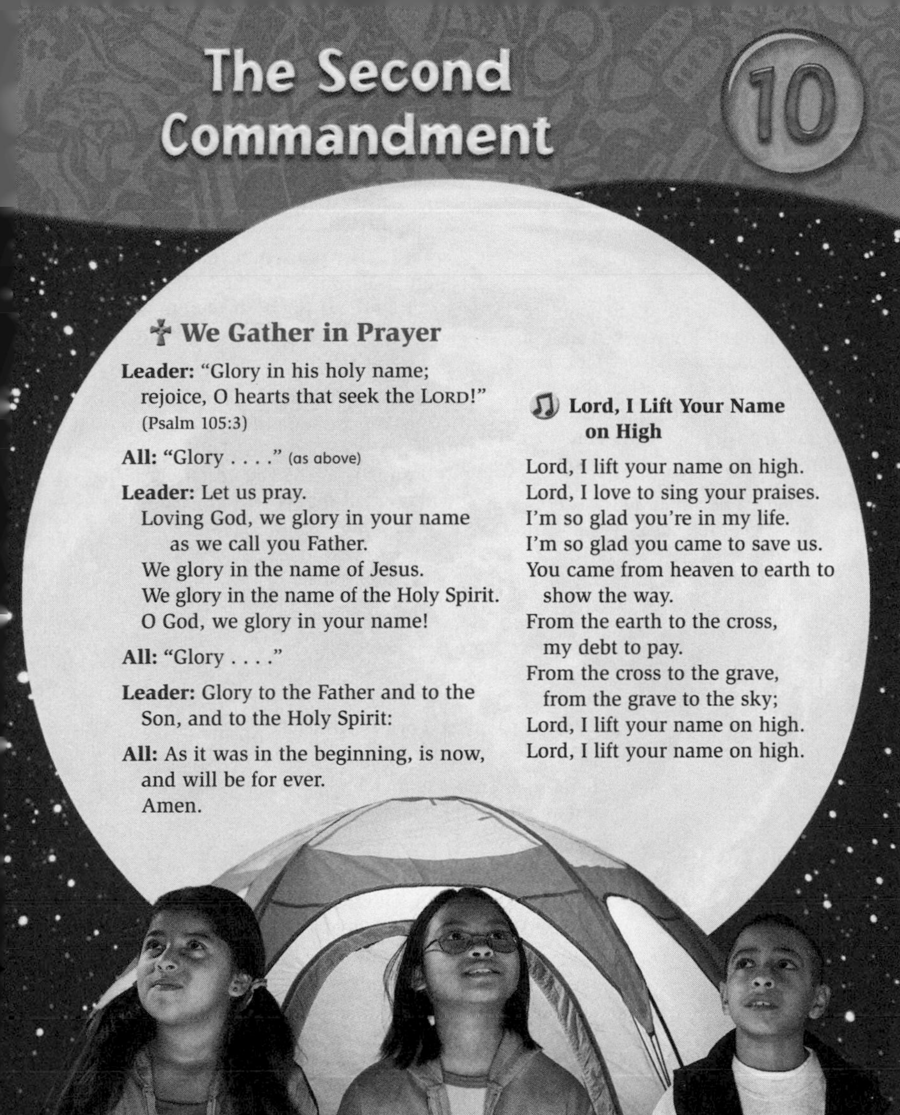

The Second Commandment
10
We Gather in Prayer
Leader: "Glory in his holy name;
rejoice, O hearts that seek the LORD!"
(Psalm 105:3)
All: "Glory . . . ." (as above)
Leader: Let us pray.
Loving God, we glory in your name
as we call you Father.
We glory in the name of Jesus.
We glory in the name of the Holy Spirit.
O God, we glory in your name!
All: "Glory . . . ."
Leader: Glory to the Father and to the
Son, and to the Holy Spirit:
All: As it was in the beginning, is now,
and will be for ever.
Amen.
Lord, I Lift Your Name on High
Lord, I lift your name on high.
Lord, I love to sing your praises.
I'm so glad you're in my life.
I'm so glad you came to save us.
You came from heaven to earth to
show the way.
From the earth to the cross,
my debt to pay.
From the cross to the grave,
from the grave to the sky;
Lord, I lift your name on high.
Lord, I lift your name on high.
119

PREPARING TO PRAY

In this gathering prayer the students give glory to God and raise their voices in song to God.

• Invite a volunteer to be the prayer leader. Have this student practice the part.

• Give the students time to practice the song "Lord, I Lift Your Name on High," Rick Founds, #9 Grade 4 CD.

Prayer Space

• Place a Bible on the prayer table. Open it to the Book of Psalms.

• Display a poster or plaque of the Ten Commandments on the prayer table. Set off the second commandment from the others by taping a gold ribbon or cord around it.

This Week's Liturgy

Visit **www.webelieveweb.com** for this week's liturgical readings and other seasonal material.

Lesson Plan

We Gather in Prayer ___ minutes

Pray

• Invite the students to gather in the prayer space. When the students are settled, signal the prayer leader to begin.

• After the Glory to the Father has been prayed, lead the students in singing "Lord, I Lift Your Name on High."

Home Connection Update

Invite the students to share the ways their families used the "Putting God First" game piece from the Chapter 9 family page. Ask the students what questions their families may have had about the first commandment.

Chapter 10 • Day 1

Catechist Goal

- To emphasize that God's name is holy

Our Faith Response

- To give praise to God's holy name

psalm

Lesson Materials

- Grade 4 CD

Teaching Tip

Honoring Students' Names

To teach the students about honoring God's name, it is important to honor the students' names. There are many ways to do this. Take time early on to learn their names. Be sure to find out their preferred names. For example, Peter may prefer Pete, Guadalupe may prefer Lupe, and so on. Make an effort to memorize a student's name and pronounce it correctly. Also, resist the temptation to call a student by his or her last name or to use a form of address that may be offensive to the student.

God's name is holy.

WE GATHER

✝ *Lord God, holy is your name.*

How do you get to know someone? What are some ways you can learn about that person?

WE BELIEVE

God revealed himself to his people. He made himself known to Abraham, to Isaac, to Jacob, to Moses and the Israelites. When Moses asked God what God's name was, God answered, "I am who am" (Exodus 3:14). The Hebrew letters of God's response form the name Yahweh.

The Israelites knew that God was holy and understood that his name was holy, too.

Out of respect for God's holiness, the Israelites did not say the name Yahweh aloud. Instead they called upon God as Lord. They praised the name of the Lord often. For instance, the Israelites prayed, "From the rising of the sun to its setting let the name of the LORD be praised" (Psalm 113:3).

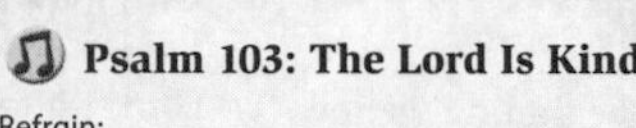

The Israelites wrote many psalms like this one to the Lord. A **psalm** is a song of praise to honor the Lord. The Book of Psalms is in the Old Testament. The writers of the psalms praised God's holy name.

Here is one of these psalms of praise.

Psalm 103: The Lord Is Kind

Refrain:

The Lord is kind and merciful,
kind and merciful.

Bless the LORD, O my soul;
all my being, bless his holy name.
Bless the LORD, O my soul;
forget not all his benefits. (Refrain)

Like the Israelites, we believe that God's name is holy. The second commandment reminds us that God is holy and so is his name. It reminds us to honor God and to honor his name.

Key Word
psalm a song of praise to honor the Lord

120

Lesson Plan

WE GATHER ___ minutes

✝ **Pray** Pray together the Sing of the Cross and the *We Gather* prayer.

Focus on Life Discuss the *We Gather* questions. Help the students understand that a name is often the first thing we want to know about a person. Knowing someone's name and calling that person by name gives us a connection to him or her. Tell the students that in this lesson they will learn that God's name is holy.

WE BELIEVE ___ minutes

Learn About God's Name Ask the students what words come to mind when they think of the word *holy*. Then read together the *We Believe* statement. On the board write the name *Yahweh*. Explain that this name for God is pronounced *Yah-way*. Then ask volunteers to read aloud the first two *We Believe* paragraphs.

Discuss the Psalms Ask the students to read together the words of the Israelites' prayer at the end of the second paragraph. Explain that this is a verse from Psalm 113.

Then have the students read the third *We Believe* paragraph. Ask: *When do we most often pray aloud or sing psalms?* (during our celebration of Mass and the sacraments)

Sing the Psalm Ask a volunteer to read aloud the words of Psalm 103 from page 120. Explain that songwriters have long used the psalms as a basis for hymns and songs. Play "Psalm 103: The Lord Is Kind," from

WE RESPOND

Be a psalm writer. Write your own psalm of praise to the Lord.

Share your psalm with your class.

121

ACTIVITY BANK

Multiple Intelligences

Musical, Visual, Bodily-Kinesthetic

Activity Materials: cassette tape recorder, blank cassette tapes, poster board, markers

Invite the students to take part in a musical project. Prepare a psalm prayer experience that can be shared with others. Have the students work together to write a song based on the words of Psalm 113, verse 3. Ask a group of volunteers to make up dance movements for the song and another group to illustrate the song on poster board. Invite a group of younger children to share the psalm prayer experience with the class.

the Grade 4 CD. Then replay it and invite the students to sing along.

Quick Check

✔ *Why did the Israelites not say the name Yahweh aloud?* (The Israelites did not say God's name because of their respect for his holiness.)

✔ *What is a psalm?* (A psalm can be a song of praise to honor the Lord.)

WE RESPOND

___ minutes

Connect to Life Invite the students to complete the *We Respond* psalm-writing activity. Encourage them to express their love for God and their awe of his greatness. Tell the students who are having difficulty that they may write their own words for Psalm 113:3. If possible, put up a Web page on which to display the students' psalms.

Pray Pray Psalm 113:3 together.

Plan Ahead for Day 2

Catechist Goal: To teach that we call upon God's name with respect

Preparation: Have available a list of titles for God for the *We Respond* activity.

Catechist Goal

- To teach that we call upon God's name with respect

Our Faith Response

- To call upon God's name and recall his presence among us

reverence

Lesson Materials

- Bible

As Catholics...

We Are Given a Christian Name

After the lesson is completed, form small groups and have the students read the *As Catholics* text to one another. Encourage the students to share what their names mean to them and to discuss with their parents how their names were chosen.

YOU SHALL NOT TAKE THE NAME OF THE LORD YOUR GOD IN VAIN.

We respect God's name.

WE GATHER

✝ *God, we will bless your name forever.*

Do you know people who have a title, for example, Dr. for a doctor or Mrs. for a married woman? Write some titles of people you know.

____

____

____

WE BELIEVE

The second commandment states, "You shall not take the name of the LORD your God in vain." To take God's name in vain means to use it in a disrespectful or unnecessary way. Respecting God's name and the name of Jesus is a sign of the respect we owe to God. Each time that we use God's name, we are calling on the all-powerful God.

We call on God by using one of his many titles. These titles come from ways that God works in our lives today. They come from ways God has acted in the lives of his people.

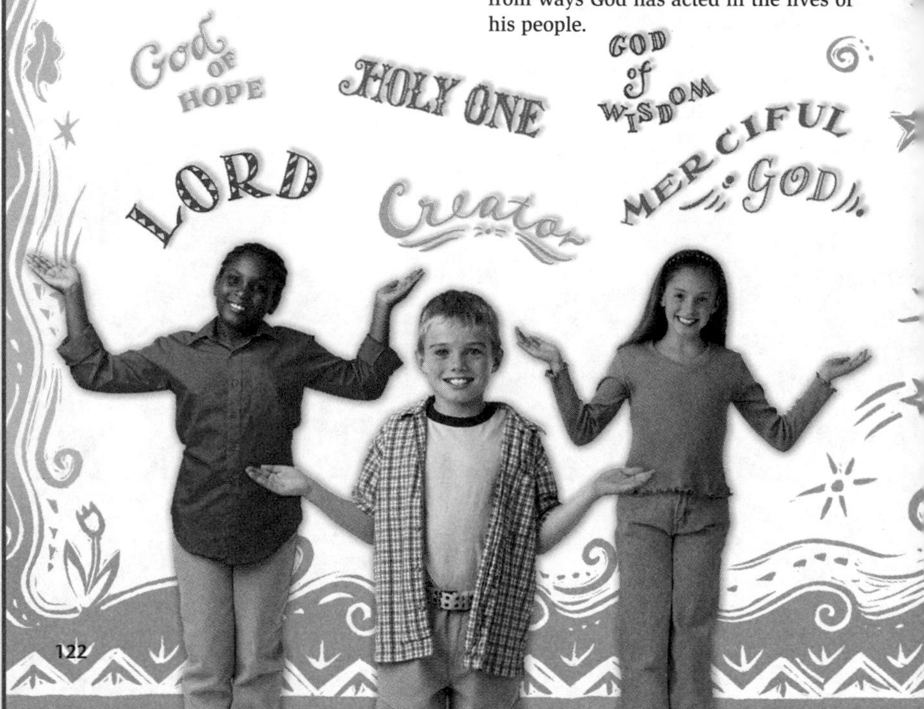

122

Lesson Plan

WE GATHER ___ minutes

✝ **Pray** Pray together the Sign of the Cross. Then invite the students to pray the *We Gather* prayer several times, beginning with a whisper, gradually and prayerfully getting louder and louder, and ending with an exclamation of joy.

Focus on Life Give the students time to think of the people they know who have titles. Have them write the titles on the line provided. Ask: *Why do we call people by titles such as Mrs. or Dr.?* Help the students to understand that we call people by their titles as a sign of respect. Tell the students that in this lesson they will learn that we follow the second commandment when we respect God's name.

WE BELIEVE ___ minutes

Read About the Commandment Have the students read aloud the second commandment. Ask: *What do you think it means to take God's name in vain?* Invite a few volunteers to share their responses. Then have volunteers read aloud the first two *We Believe* paragraphs.

Do the Activity Invite the students to read aloud the list of God's titles. Go over the *We Believe* activity directions. Have the students work in pairs. After they have had time to complete their lists, invite each pair to share their titles for God. The partners might alternate saying their titles. Encourage the students to speak the titles in a manner that reflects their understanding of the second commandment.

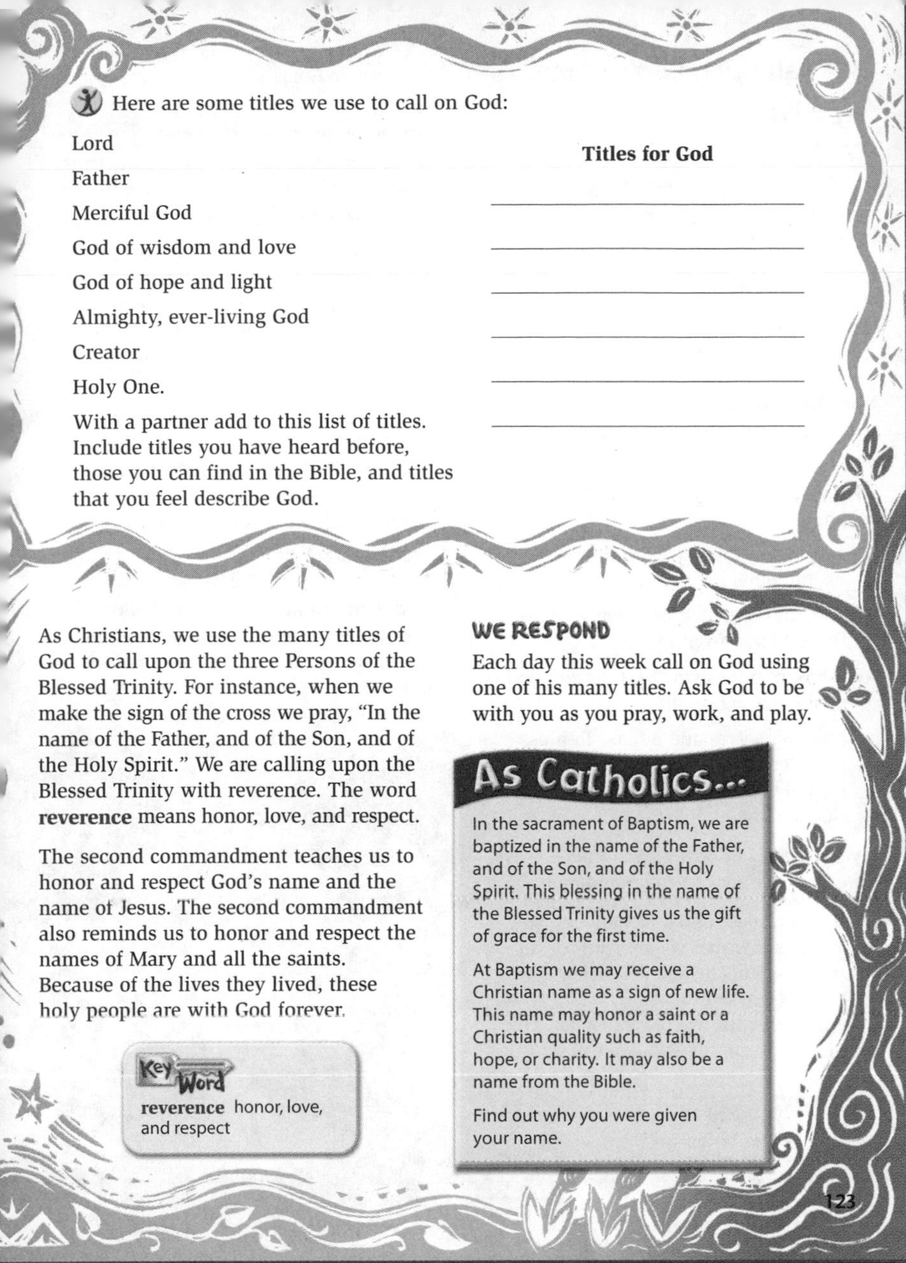

Here are some titles we use to call on God:

Lord
Father
Merciful God
God of wisdom and love
God of hope and light
Almighty, ever-living God
Creator
Holy One.

With a partner add to this list of titles. Include titles you have heard before, those you can find in the Bible, and titles that you feel describe God.

Titles for God

____
____
____
____
____
____

As Christians, we use the many titles of God to call upon the three Persons of the Blessed Trinity. For instance, when we make the sign of the cross we pray, "In the name of the Father, and of the Son, and of the Holy Spirit." We are calling upon the Blessed Trinity with reverence. The word **reverence** means honor, love, and respect.

The second commandment teaches us to honor and respect God's name and the name of Jesus. The second commandment also reminds us to honor and respect the names of Mary and all the saints. Because of the lives they lived, these holy people are with God forever.

Key Word
reverence honor, love, and respect

WE RESPOND

Each day this week call on God using one of his many titles. Ask God to be with you as you pray, work, and play.

As Catholics...

In the sacrament of Baptism, we are baptized in the name of the Father, and of the Son, and of the Holy Spirit. This blessing in the name of the Blessed Trinity gives us the gift of grace for the first time.

At Baptism we may receive a Christian name as a sign of new life. This name may honor a saint or a Christian quality such as faith, hope, or charity. It may also be a name from the Bible.

Find out why you were given your name.

123

Activity Bank

Parish

Making a Connection with the Names

Activity Materials: parish directory

Encourage the students to learn the names of parish members who are homebound or residents of nursing homes. Ask the person in the parish who ministers to these members for the names of people who would appreciate correspondence from the students. The students might also write to retired priests or religious. Invite the students to write letters to these parish members. Remind the students to use respectful language and proper titles, such as *Mr., Mrs., Miss, and Ms.*, or *Father, Deacon, Sister,* and *Brother.* Encourage the students to share what they have been learning in class.

Learn About Reverence Choose volunteers to read aloud the last two *We Believe* paragraphs. Emphasize the meaning of the key word *reverence*. Explain that we must speak the names of the Persons of the Blessed Trinity, Mary, and all the saints with reverence.

Quick Check

✔ *Why do we treat God's name with respect?* (because God's name is holy and worthy of our respect)

✔ *What does the word reverence mean?* (honor, love, and respect)

WE RESPOND

___ minutes

Connect to Life Read the *We Respond* text with the class. Then have the students work in small groups. Ask each group to think of three times during the day when they might call upon God. Then have them think of different titles for God (examples: praying to God as Great Creator; thanking our Faithful Provider at mealtime).

Pray Pray together: *O God, we bless your name.*

Plan Ahead for Day 3

Catechist Goal: To describe ways to follow the second commandment

Preparation: Invite a priest or permanent deacon to bless your students and the classroom.

Chapter 10 • Day 3

Catechist Goal

- To describe ways to follow the second commandment

Our Faith Response

- To show respect for the name of God in our speech

 **bless**

Lesson Materials

- colored pencils or markers

Teaching Tip

Respectful Speech in the Classroom

You will help the students to speak respectfully by always addressing them respectfully. Additionally, you should maintain a consistent policy of "zero tolerance" for lack of respect, either spoken or shown.

We call upon God's name.

YOU SHALL NOT TAKE THE NAME OF THE LORD YOUR GOD IN VAIN.

WE GATHER

✝ *Holy Spirit, make our words holy.*

The words we use show others the way we think and feel about them. What are the different ways you talk to your classmates, teachers, neighbors, and family members?

How do you show respect for these people by the way you speak to them?

WE BELIEVE

We honor God by using his name with respect. We can use God's name to

- praise him and give him our love and respect
- call upon him and ask him to be with us and others
- ask him to forgive us when we have turned away from him
- thank him for being with us and giving us all that we need
- bless ourselves and others. To **bless** is to dedicate someone or something to God or to make something holy in God's name.

When we use God's name in these ways, we obey the second commandment.

We also respect God's name when we use it to show that we are truthful. In some courts of law and in other situations, we may be asked to take an oath. When we take an oath, we place our hand on a Bible and call on God. We call on God to witness that we are speaking the truth. If what we are saying is not true, then we are using God's name in vain.

Sometimes in anger people may use God's name to curse, or call harm on, others. They may even curse others just to get attention. When they do these things, they are using God's name in vain.

To follow the second commandment, we must always honor God's name. Jesus honored God's name as holy. He taught us to pray, "Father, hallowed be your name" (Luke 11:2). Each time we call on God with love and respect or use his name in truth, we keep his name holy.

God is the Father of all of us. Following the second commandment also requires us to have a deep respect for all of his children. We should use their names, too, with respect.

Key Word
bless to dedicate someone or something to God or to make holy in God's name

124

Lesson Plan

WE GATHER ___ minutes

✝ **Pray** Remind the students that the Holy Spirit is our helper. Then pray the Sign of the Cross and *We Gather* prayer.

Focus on Life Have a volunteer read aloud the *We Gather* statement and first question. Give the students time to think about their answers and encourage them to share their responses. Then ask the students to respond to the second question. Guide the discussion to include not only words that show respect but also the tone of voice that we use when we speak. At this point you might also want to share the *Chapter Story*. Tell the students that in this lesson they will learn to call on God respectfully.

WE BELIEVE ___ minutes

Call Upon God Read together the *We Believe* statement. Ask: *What does it mean to "call upon" someone?* Help the students understand that when you call upon someone, you get that person's attention so that you can converse with him or her.

Act It Out Form two groups. Have them alternate reading the list of ways we can use God's name respectfully. Then have each group choose one way of calling upon God and act out various ways in which to do it. Note the art that shows calling upon God in prayer and through prayer circles.

Complete the Text Have volunteers read aloud the remaining *We Believe* paragraphs. Emphasize:

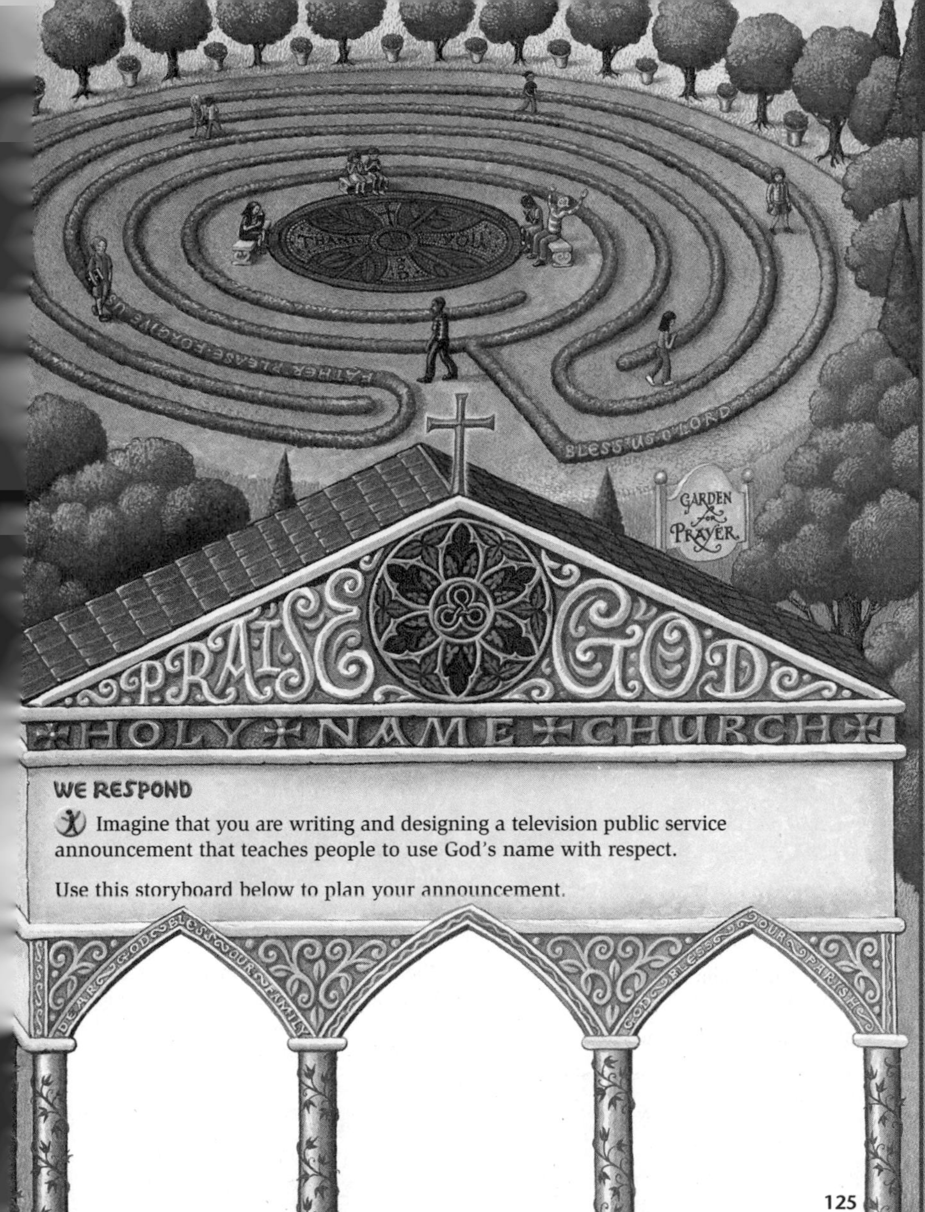

WE RESPOND

Imagine that you are writing and designing a television public service announcement that teaches people to use God's name with respect.

Use this storyboard below to plan your announcement.

125

Activity Bank

Curriculum Connection

Language Arts–Vocabulary

Activity Materials: a children's thesaurus

Encourage the students to use a thesaurus to build their vocabularies. Show the students how to look up the word *respect* and have them make a list of other words that have the same meaning. Then have the students write prayers or short paragraphs advising other young people about living the first two commandments. Encourage the students to use several different words for respect in their prayers or advice paragraphs.

- When we place our hand on the Bible to take an oath, we are calling on God to witness that we are speaking the truth.
- When we use God's name to curse, we are not following the second commandment.
- Jesus said God's name is holy when he prayed, "hallowed be your name" (Luke 11:2).
- We need to use the names of every person with respect.

Quick Check

✔ *What is one way we honor God?* (We honor God by calling on him using respectful words and in a respectful tone of voice.)

✔ *What are some reasons we call upon God?* (Accept reasons listed on page 124.)

WE RESPOND

___ minutes

Connect to Life Provide time for the *We Respond* activity. Explain that a public service announcement is designed to inform or educate people about something rather than to sell them something. Have the students share their storyboards.

Pray Pray: *God, our heavenly Father, we praise and give glory to your name with reverence and respect. Amen.*

Plan Ahead for Day 4

Catechist Goal: To underscore that keeping God's name holy includes respecting the places where we worship him

Preparation: Bring in a picture of the Temple in Jerusalem; make copies of Reproducible Master 10.

Chapter 10 • Day 4

Catechist Goal

• To underscore that keeping God's name holy includes respecting the places where we worship him

Our Faith Response

• To respect sacred places that honor God's name

 **sacred**

Lesson Materials

• picture of the Temple in Jerusalem
• copies of Reproducible Master 10

Teaching Tip

In Your Parish Church

If possible, make arrangements to visit your parish church after you have presented this lesson. Remind the students that while they are in the church they are to be respectful in their tones of voice and in their actions. When you arrive at the church, encourage the students to sit separately. Have them reflect quietly about keeping the second commandment.

YOU SHALL NOT TAKE THE NAME OF THE LORD YOUR GOD IN VAIN.

We respect and honor sacred places.

WE GATHER

✝ *Lord, may we praise your name forever.*

Your parish church is a special place where you go to honor and praise God. Discuss what the church is like:

• before the community gathers to worship
• during the Mass or other celebrations
• after the community has worshiped together.

WE BELIEVE

Jesus taught his followers to honor God and to speak respectfully when using God's name. But he also taught his followers to honor places that are dedicated to God. These places are sacred. **Sacred** is another word for holy.

The following story shows how serious Jesus was about respecting and honoring the house of God.

The Temple in Jerusalem was a very holy place. Once Jesus saw that some people were selling and buying things in a certain part of the Temple. Jesus then "overturned the tables of the money changers and the seats of those who were selling doves." Jesus used the words of a prophet, saying, "'My house shall be a house of prayer,'
but you are making it a den of thieves" (Matthew 21:12, 13).

Why do you think Jesus acted the way he did in the Temple?

Jesus was angry at the disrespect people were showing toward God's holy place. How do Jesus' actions in the Temple help us to understand the second commandment?

The second commandment helps us to keep God's name holy. It also reminds us that places where we worship God and honor his name are holy, too.

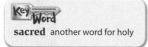

sacred another word for holy

126

Lesson Plan

WE GATHER ___ minutes

✝ **Pray** Pray together the Sign of the Cross and the *We Gather* prayer.

Focus on Life Invite the students to discuss what the parish church is like at the three times listed in the *We Gather* section. Have volunteers record their descriptions on the board. Tell the students that in this lesson they will learn about respecting and honoring sacred places.

WE BELIEVE ___ minutes

Learn About Sacred Places Read aloud the *We Believe* statement. Ask the students to tell you what they think the word *sacred* means. Then invite a volunteer to read aloud the first two paragraphs in the *We Believe* section.

Read About the Temple Show the students a picture of the Temple in Jerusalem. Then read the story of Jesus in the Temple (Matthew 21:12, 13). Pause for a moment of silence after reading the story. Then ask: *Why do you think Jesus acted the way he did in the Temple?* (Possible answer: Jesus is angry because people are using the Temple as a place of business instead of a place of prayer and worship.) Encourage the students to share their ideas. Then read the remaining *We Believe* text.

Reflect on the Second Commandment As an examination of conscience, read aloud the questions in the chart. Pause after each one to give the students time for reflection. Remind them that an examination of conscience is an important part of preparing for the sacrament of Reconciliation.

Take a few moments to think quietly and prayerfully about the ways of keeping the second commandment. These questions may help you.

Do I respect God's name and the name of Jesus?

How have I used God's name?

Have I called on God and asked him to be with me?

How do I use the names of Mary and all the saints?

Have I respected the names of my family members, friends, and teachers?

Do I have respect for all the places where God is worshiped?

How do I act when I am in church?

WE RESPOND

What are some other sacred places besides your parish church?

We need to respect the sacred places where we honor God. We do this when we

- ______________________________
- ______________________________
- ______________________________

127

ACTIVITY BANK

Multicultural Connection

Holy Places Around the World

Activity Materials: Internet access and other research resources

Invite the students to do research on holy places around the world. Form the class into groups and ask each group to research a particular place. For example, one group might research the Holy Land; another might research Saint Peter's Basilica in Vatican City; another, Lourdes; and another, the Shrine of Our Lady of Guadalupe. Encourage the groups to find information about any special religious feasts celebrated at the places they are researching. Invite the groups to share what they learn with the rest of the class.

Quick Check

✔ *What does the word sacred mean?* (Sacred is another word for holy.)

✔ *How should we treat places that are dedicated to God?* (We should respect sacred places.)

WE RESPOND ___ minutes

Connect to Life Read aloud the *We Respond* question and invite the students to share their answers. Then have the students complete the *We Respond* activity by naming ways we show respect in sacred places. Encourage the students to share their responses. Point out that both the cathedral on page 126 and the simple church on page 127 are sacred places.

Pray Distribute copies of Reproducible Master 10 and read the directions aloud. Remind the students that they learned the kinds of prayer in Grade 3, Chapter 10 of *We Believe*: praise, thanksgiving, petition, blessing, and intercession. Tell the students to use the prayers they write as the concluding prayer.

Plan Ahead for Day 5

Catechist Goal: To review chapter ideas and their relationship to our faith life

Preparation: Make copies of Chapter Test 10 in the Grade 4 Assessment Book (option). Bring index cards or small pieces of paper and a basket or other container.

Chapter 10 • **Day 5**

Catechist Goal

- To review chapter ideas and their relationship to our faith life

Our Faith Response

- To apply what has been learned to our lives

CHAPTER TEST

Chapter 10 Test is provided in the Grade 4 Assessment Book.

Review

Grade 4
Chapter 10

Circle the correct answer.

1. We ______ something when we make it holy in God's name.

dishonor curse (bless)

2. We ______ God, his name, and the places where we worship him.

(honor) curse disrespect

3. The word ______ means honor, love, and respect.

magic (reverence) cursing

4. We believe that God's name is ______.

a psalm (holy) an oath

Complete the following:

5. When Moses asked God what his name was, God answered

"I am who am."

6. Taking God's name in vain means

to use it in a disrespectful or unnecessary way.

7. We honor and respect the names of Mary and all of the saints because

these holy people are with God forever. (See page 123.)

8. To follow the second commandment we must

always honor God's name and respect the names of all. (See page 124.)

9–10. How can we show respect for sacred places?

See pages 126–127.

During the week make a list of people, places, or things that help you to remember God's holy name. Be ready to share your list with the class.

128

Lesson Plan

___ minutes

Chapter Review Have the students answer questions 1–10. Then ask volunteers to share their answers. As the students' answers will vary in this section, allow time for several students to read their answers. Clear up any misconceptions that might arise.

Assessment Activity Give the students time to work on their lists. Then invite the students to share the people, places, and things that help them remember God's holy name. Combine the students' ideas into a class list.

___ minutes

Reflect & Pray Read aloud the *Reflect & Pray* text. Allow the students time to reflect and write.

Key Words Provide each student with four index cards or small pieces of paper. Invite the students to write their own meanings for the *Key Words,* each on its own piece of paper, without the word that is being defined. Collect the definitions and place them in a basket or other container. Have the students take turns drawing a definition, reading it aloud, and calling on someone to give the *Key Word.*

Remember Invite the students to reflect on the four *We Believe* statements by asking themselves: *What do*

We Respond in Faith

Reflect & Pray

We have many opportunities to call upon God to bless us. When will you ask for God's blessing this week?

____

Think of someone you know who might need God's blessing, too. Ask God to bless this person.

Key Words

psalm (p. 120)
reverence (p. 123)
bless (p. 124)
sacred (p. 126)

Remember

- God's name is holy.
- We respect God's name.
- We call upon God's name.
- We respect and honor sacred places.

Our Catholic Life

The Jesus Prayer

Christians have a special prayer called the Jesus Prayer. This prayer has been prayed for centuries. The Jesus Prayer is easy to pray. Begin by closing your eyes and being still, as still as you can. Then, as you breathe in, say very quietly, "Jesus." As you breathe out, say "Savior" or "Peace" or another short word that reminds you of Jesus. When we call on the name of Jesus, we ask him to be with us in a special way.

Home Connection

Sharing Faith with My Family

Make sure to send a copy the family page home with each student (text page 130).

Explain that the words of the family prayer are the words of a traditional hymn of the Church.

For additional information and activities, encourage families to visit Sadlier's

www.WEBELIEVEweb.com

the statements have to do with the second commandment? Encourage them students to share their insights with the class.

Our Catholic Life Read aloud the text about the Jesus Prayer. Help the students to understand that prayer does not have to be talking to God in complete sentences. Prayer can also be a reflective, meditative experience in which we draw closer to God and enjoy the warmth of his presence. For example, the Jesus Prayer, with its few words to say, may help us to focus on Jesus' presence. Encourage the students to pray the name of Jesus with reverence.

CHAPTER 10 GRADE 4

SHARING FAITH with My Family

Sharing What I Learned

Discuss the following with your family:
- the second commandment
- God's holy name
- the psalms
- sacred places.

A Family Prayer

Lead your family in this prayer.

Holy God, we praise thy name!
Lord of all, we bow before thee;
All on earth thy scepter claim,
All in heav'n above adore thee;
Infinite thy vast domain,
Everlasting is thy reign.
(from *Catholic Household Blessing and Prayers*)

Putting God First

"Putting God First" is a game that tests your knowledge of Unit 2. Chapters 8–12 Family Pages each have a part of the game board that your family will put together after Chapter 12. Save this board piece. Learn the answers to the questions in red. Be ready to play the game!

Visit Sadlier's www.WEBELIEVEweb.com

Connect to the Catechism
For adult background and reflection, see paragraphs 2143, 2144, 2153, and 1186.

130

PUPIL PAGE 130

Chapter 11 The Third Commandment

Overview

In chapter 10 the students learned about the second commandment and the respect and honor due to God's name. In this chapter they will learn about the third commandment and ways we observe the Lord's Day.

Doctrinal Content	For Adult Reading and Reflection *Catechism of the Catholic Church*
The students will learn:	Paragraph
• God gave us a special day to rest and worship him.	2172
• We keep the Lord's Day holy by participating in the Sunday Mass.	2177
• The Lord's Day is a day for rest and relaxation.	2185
• We keep the Lord's Day holy by caring for the needs of others.	2186

Sabbath (p. 133)
synagogue (p. 135)
holy day of obligation (p. 135)
Corporal Works of Mercy (p. 139)
Spiritual Works of Mercy (p. 139)

Catechist Background

What good memories do you have of Sundays?

The third commandment states: "Remember to keep holy the sabbath day. Six days you may labor and do all your work, but the seventh day is the sabbath of the LORD, your God" (Exodus 20:8–10). The sabbath recalls the story of creation. "In six days the Lord made the heavens and the earth, the sea and all that is in them; but on the seventh day he rested. That is why the Lord has blessed the sabbath day and made it holy" (Exodus 20:11).

Christians believe that Jesus was raised from the dead on the day after the Sabbath. We, therefore, set aside Sunday as the Lord's Day. So today Jews gather to worship on the traditional Sabbath, while Catholics and most other Christians, of course, gather for worship on Sunday. (Since Vatican II, Catholics may also participate in the celebration of Sunday Mass on Saturday evening.)

Sunday is meant to be different. *The Code of Canon Law* states: "On Sundays . . . the faithful are bound . . . to abstain from those labors and business concerns which impede the worship to be rendered to God, the joy which is proper to the Lord's Day, or the proper relaxation of mind and body" (Canon 1247). The Lord's Day, then, provides us an opportunity to worship God, set time aside for our families, and renew and refresh our bodies, spirits, and hearts.

What further steps can you take to keep holy the Lord's Day?

Lesson Planning Guide

Lesson Focus	Presentation	Materials
ay 1		
age 131 **We Gather in Prayer** **ages 132–133** *od gave us a special day to rest nd worship him.*	Pray together by singing. • Respond in prayer. • Discuss the **We Gather** text and questions. • Read and discuss the **We Believe** text about the third commandment. Write and plan ways to honor God on Sunday in the **We Respond** activity.	For the prayer space: calendar and markers; Bible "Open Our Hearts" Christopher Walker, #11 Grade 4 CD • chart paper • markers
Day 2		
pages 134–135 *We keep the Lord's Day holy by participating in the Sunday Mass.*	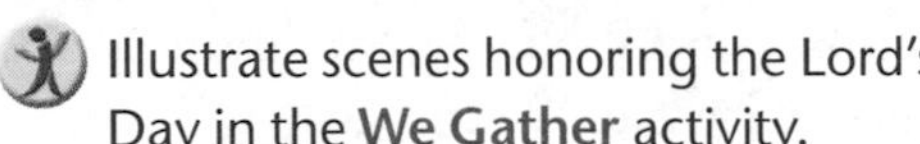 Illustrate scenes honoring the Lord's Day in the **We Gather** activity. • Read and discuss Sabbath, and the Lord's Day in the **We Believe** text. Write ways families can participate at Mass. • Discuss holy days of obligation. • Answer the **We Respond** question.	• drawing paper • crayons or markers • Grade 4 CD
Day 3		
pages 136–137 *The Lord's Day is a day for rest and relaxation.*	 Complete the **We Gather** activity. • Read and discuss the **We Believe** text. Fill in chart in the **We Respond** activity. • Read and discuss the *As Catholics* text.	
Day 4		
pages 138–139 *We keep the Lord's Day holy by caring for the needs of others.*	• Answer the **We Gather** questions. • Discuss the Works of Mercy in the **We Believe** text. • Write stories about photos. • Reflect on the third commandment. List ways to perform Works of Mercy in the **We Respond** activity. • Read and discuss Saint Brigid in the *Blessed are they . . .* text.	• copies of Reproducible Master 11, guide page 131G
Day 5		
Page 140 **Review** **pages 141–142** **We Respond in Faith**	• Complete questions 1–10. Work on the *Assessment Activity.* • Complete the *Reflect & Pray* activity. • Review *Remember* and *Key Words.* • Read and discuss *Our Catholic Life.* • Discuss the **Sharing Faith with My Family** page.	• poster board, magazines and news-papers for clipping • Chapter 11 in Assessment Book, pp. 21–22 • Chapter 11 Test in Test Generator • Review & Resource Book, pp. 28–30 • Family Book, pp. 33–35

For additional ideas, activities, and opportunities: Visit Sadlier's **www.WEBELIEVEweb.com**

Enrichment Ideas

Chapter Story

Nicole had been going many places with her friends. When she wasn't with them, she was talking to them on the phone.

Nicole's dad had been working on a special project for work. The project was finally finished. Nicole's dad decided he needed to spend some time with his daughter. He called her from work to set up a special afternoon.

Nicole was very surprised when she heard her dad's voice on the phone. "I can't believe you're calling me, Dad." Nicole was even more surprised when her dad said, "Nicole, I'm inviting you to spend Saturday afternoon with me. We can go wherever you would like and do whatever you would like to do. Of course, I want you to be reasonable. Just let me know tonight after dinner."

Nicole was so happy. She started thinking about what she and her dad could do during their special time together.

▶ *If you were Nicole, how would you feel about your dad's invitation? What would you choose to do?*

FAITH and MEDIA

▶ After reading the list of holy days of obligation on page 135 suggest to the students that they make use of the Internet to research each holy day. You might bookmark a few suitable Web sites, or tell them where to find the information online if they will be doing their research outside of class.

▶ On Day 4, in connection with your discussion of the Corporal and Spiritual Works of Mercy, direct the students to the Web site of your parish, your diocese, Catholic social service agencies such as Catholic Charities USA and Catholic Relief Services. Discover some of the ways that Catholics are working together to perform acts of mercy every day.

CHAPTER PROJECT: GIFT EXCHANGE

Explain that God has given us Sunday as a day to rest, to enjoy being with our family, and to worship him. Also explain that every time we do as he asked and keep the Lord's Day holy, we are giving a gift to God. Remind the students that every day that we live, God gives us the gift of life. Provide the students with a very large gift box. Cut a slit in the top and have volunteers make special gift wrap to wrap around the box. Then write or print *Sunday* or *The Lord's Day* on each side of the box. Keep the box near the prayer table. Each day this week, after the students have completed the *We Respond* activity or discussion, have them record on slips of paper one thing they plan to do next Sunday to honor God. Then invite the students to put their papers in the box during the *We Respond* prayer.

Connections

To Liturgy

Explain to the students that Catholics all around the world gather every Sunday for the celebration of the Mass. This has been happening since the beginning of the Church, and the fundamental structure of the Mass has remained unchanged throughout the centuries. As the Church, we are all united as the one Body of Christ, and thus we keep holy the Lord's Day by participating in the Eucharist. We are united with one another no matter how far apart we may be.

To Catholic Social Teaching

Solidarity of the Human Family
Help the students recognize that we are one human family and that people of different cultures and those who live in different countries are our neighbors, too. God calls all Catholics to use their time, strength, and resources to help people everywhere. Explore with the students the many ways their parishes and dioceses help people all around the world. Invite the students to find out what organizations are offering the help. Encourage the students to find opportunities to do volunteer work for these organizations.

To Family

Invite the students to discuss ways that the Lord's Day and holy days of obligation are observed in their families. Ask them to share prayers that they pray with their families on these days, or Sunday traditions in which their families may participate. Share ways of enjoying the leisure of the Lord's Day. Encourage the students to plan to celebrate holy days with their families.

Meeting Individual Needs

Students with Auditory Needs

Students with auditory needs may have difficulty participating in discussions. Using a variety of approaches to explain a lesson will reinforce the message. For example, when explaining the Corporal Works of Mercy, consider asking the students to act out different ways we can meet the physical needs of people. Students with auditory needs will be glad to participate in the lesson and not have to worry about missing out on discussions.

ADDITIONAL RESOURCES

Books *Serve the Lord with Gladness; A Manual for Servers,* David Phillipart, Liturgy Training Publications, 1998. This shows the privilege of serving God and includes why and how.

Teach Me About the Mass, Paul S. Plum, Our Sunday Visitor, 2001. This bilingual book explains how attending Mass is an important way of worshiping God.

To find more ideas for books, videos, and other learning material, visit Sadlier's

www.WEBELIEVEweb.com

Catechist Development

Appreciating Diverse Cultures

by Allan Figueroa Deck, SJ, Ph.D., S.T. D.

Father Allan is a Jesuit who has worked for more than 25 years in the Hispanic community as parish priest, teacher, and writer. He is currently director of the Loyola Institute for Spirituality in Orange, CA and adjunct professor of theology at Loyola Marymount University in Los Angeles, CA.

Pope Paul VI's *On Evangelization in the Modern World says*, "Evangelization loses much of its force and effectiveness if it does not take into consideration the actual people to whom it is addressed, if it does not use their language, their signs and symbols, if it does not answer the questions they ask, and if it does not have an impact on their concrete life."

Since the Second Vatican Council the Church has stressed the basic role that cultural awareness plays in its mission. The target of all the Church's teaching activity is specifically *culture*. Catechesis cannot occur when teachers are unfamiliar with culture—their own and that of their students.

Culture refers to the underlying values, ways of thinking and feeling of a people. Understanding culture does not rely on merely recognizing the *externals* such as customs, dress, food, or music, etc. as much as it does on appreciating and understanding the *internals*, a people's *core of meaning*: *What is life all about? Where are we going? What is right and wrong?* When viewed this way, culture is close to religion. Culture and religion both deal with matters that are of great, even ultimate, importance.

The process by which the gospel message engages cultures is called *inculturation*. The questionable ideal of the "melting pot" in the United States has led some to even think that one can legitimately ignore culture in communicating the faith. The Church teaches differently. Not incidentally, the teaching style of Jesus Christ in the parables demonstrated a keen sense of cultural awareness.

Catechist Development Topics (Topic and Guide Page)

As catechists, we must engage the unspoken values that underlie one's own way of life, pursuits, and passions. At the heart of all cultures are narratives or stories, powerful symbols, and rituals. If you want to know your core culture, do a little self-analysis. What stories move you? What symbols elicit a response? Which rituals are most meaningful?

The same analysis must be made of the cultures represented in the classroom or parish setting. Saint Augustine in his treatise on Christian

(continued on next page)

Resources

Arbuckle, Gerald A. *Earthing the Gospel: An Inculturation Handbook for the Pastoral Worker.* Maryknoll, NY: Orbis Books, 1990.

Gallagher, Michael Paul. *Clashing Symbols: An Introduction to Faith and Culture.* Mahwah, NJ: Paulist Press, 1997.

education insists that one must *love* his or her students. If you know nothing about their culture or, even worse, find nothing lovable in it, your effectiveness as a teacher is limited.

The basic challenge of catechesis is "getting beneath the skin" and loving those we teach. Of course, the final and most important task of the catechist is communicating the gospel message. To do that effectively one must know the *difference* between one's culture and the Christian faith. The gospel and Church teaching are rooted in cultures but always go beyond them.

Ways to Implement Appreciating Diverse Cultures

- Identify the various cultural backgrounds in the class or group. Stress the *catholicity* (universalism) of the Church by sharing examples of how Catholics come in all cultural varieties. Encourage the children to learn that God is the creator of difference.

- Point out the stories, symbols, and rituals of Jesus' own Jewish culture, which was more rural than urban. Use this as springboard for discussion for students to give examples of anything similar in their culture.

- Plan a celebration of diversity by asking your class or group to play music or sing songs in languages from other countries, dress in ethnic clothing, make and share an ethnic food dish, retell a folktale or story that is from another culture, etc.

- If possible, ask your students to explain how they celebrate special days like *quinceañeras*, or Baptisms. Have them research special feasts or days celebrated in other cultures.

- Ask your students whether all the customs or ways of doing things in their culture are consistent with the gospel requirement that we love God, neighbor, and ourselves.

For additional ideas, activities, and opportunities, visit Sadlier's

www.WE BELIEVE web.com

With thanks to:

Deborah Quirke
St. Philip and James School
Bronx, New York

Deborah helps her students appreciate diversity by using magazine pictures of people from around the world. Under Deborah's direction, the children talk about the ways the people are different, and the ways they are alike. This activity helps everyone to remember that we are all God's children. Deborah uses a camera to take a photograph of each child in her group. Then using these photographs and the magazine pictures, the children help to make a class bulletin board that helps them to celebrate the diversity of all God's children.

Notes

Name ____

Read the following list. Place a **C** in front of a Corporal Work of Mercy. Place an **S** in front of a Spiritual Work of Mercy.

______ **1.** Be kind when your little sister scribbles on your homework.

______ **2.** Cheer up your uncle who broke his leg.

______ **3.** Help a friend understand a science project.

______ **4.** Encourage your friends who wonder if they should tell the truth.

______ **5.** Pray for the leaders of our country.

______ **6.** Donate food to the parish food drive.

______ **7.** Help out at the car wash to raise funds for the homeless shelter.

______ **8.** Give clothes that you have outgrown to children who need them.

______ **9.** Accept apologies when they are offered to you.

______ **10.** Comfort someone who is crying.

Show your family the Corporal and Spiritual Works of Mercy on page 138. Decide on one work that you could do together as a family.

The Third Commandment

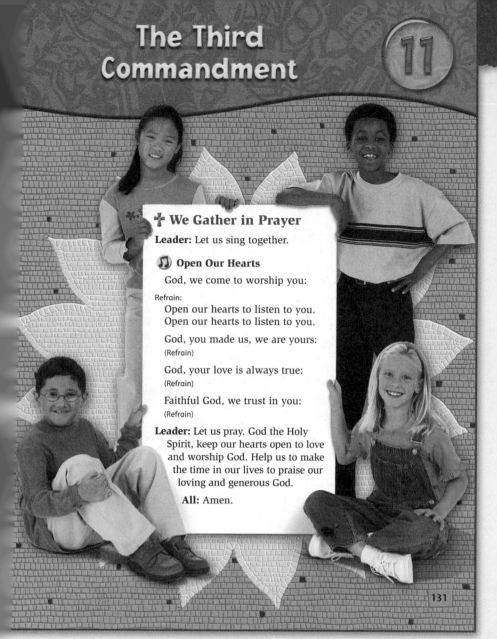

11

We Gather in Prayer

Leader: Let us sing together.

Open Our Hearts

God, we come to worship you:

Refrain:
Open our hearts to listen to you.
Open our hearts to listen to you.

God, you made us, we are yours:
(Refrain)

God, your love is always true:
(Refrain)

Faithful God, we trust in you:
(Refrain)

Leader: Let us pray. God the Holy Spirit, keep our hearts open to love and worship God. Help us to make the time in our lives to praise our loving and generous God.

All: Amen.

131

Preparing to Pray

In this gathering prayer, the students will call on God through song, asking him to open their hearts.

- Invite a volunteer to be the prayer leader. Have this student practice the part.
- Using a calendar page for this month, have volunteers mark each Sunday by drawing in the space for that day something to represent Jesus' Resurrection (cross with burst of light, flowers, butterfly).

The Prayer Space

- On the table place a Bible and the decorated calendar page for this month.
- If you have chosen to do the *Chapter Project*, place the Sunday gift box near the table.

This Week's Liturgy

Visit **www.webelieveweb.com** for this week's liturgical readings and other seasonal material.

Lesson Plan

We Gather in Prayer ___ minutes

Pray

- Invite the students to gather in the prayer space.
- Pause for a moment of silence. Then ask the leader to begin to pray.
- Play the song "Open Our Hearts," #11 from the Grade 4 CD. Ask the students to read the lyrics silently.

Home Connection Update

Review the activities on the Chapter 10 Family Page. Ask: *What do your design panels look like for "Putting God First"? What question did you add to the game?*

Chapter 11 • Day 1

Catechist Goal

- To explain the meaning of the Sabbath

Our Faith Response

- To express the ways we can honor God on Sundays

 **Sabbath**

Lesson Materials

- chart paper
- markers

Teaching Tip

Leading by Example

A teacher's example is an important educational tool. In these lessons concerning the holiness of the Lord's Day, be prepared to share your experiences of Sunday worship and rest. Describe the benefits you have derived from participating in Mass. Be sensitive to the students who, through no fault of their own, are unable to participate in the celebration of Mass. Also, describe the ways you keep the Lord's Day holy by taking time for rest and charitable work.

A Jewish family remembers and celebrates at a special meal.

God gave us a special day to rest and to worship him.

WE GATHER

✝ *Faithful God, we praise and thank you for your love.*

Think of a time you spent a day doing something special with a good friend or someone in your family.

What made the day special? What made it different from other days?

WE BELIEVE

How well do you remember the story of creation? In six days God created the heavens, the earth, and all that is in them, but what did God do on the seventh day?

"He rested on the seventh day from all the work he had undertaken. So God blessed the seventh day and made it holy." (Genesis 2:2–3)

The Israelites set apart the seventh day of the week, known today as Saturday, to rest and to honor God in a special way. They kept this day as their **Sabbath**.

Sabbath is a Hebrew word that means "rest." It is written in the Book of Exodus that God told his people: "Remember to keep holy the sabbath day" (Exodus 20:8).

The Sabbath day was different from other days. On the Sabbath day the Israelites praised God for creation. They thanked God for freeing them from slavery in Egypt. They remembered the special covenant God made with them. They took time to think about the ways they were following God's law.

שבת

132

Lesson Plan

WE GATHER ___ minutes

✝ **Pray** Pray together the Sign of the Cross and *We Gather* prayer.

Focus on Life Have the students reflect on the *We Gather* questions. Invite volunteers to share their responses. You may want to read aloud the *Chapter Story* now. Tell the students that in this lesson they will learn that we set apart the Lord's Day to rest and to worship God.

WE BELIEVE ___ minutes

Learn About the Sabbath Together, read aloud the *We Believe* statement and the third commandment. Invite a volunteer to read aloud the first *We Believe* paragraph and scriptural quote. Discuss what it means to *rest*. Have a volunteer record the students' responses on the board or on chart paper.

Ask the students to read silently as you read aloud the next three *We Believe* paragraphs. Then have the students look at the list of meanings for the word *rest*. Ask: *Does anything written on the board remind you of what the Israelites did on the Sabbath?*

Discuss Sunday Have the students form small groups. Tell the groups to read the last two *We Believe* paragraphs. Then ask the groups to discuss what work and activities might keep them from making the Lord's Day holy. Explain: *In today's world many adults have to work on Sunday. If we have family members who work on Sundays, we can help them have time for rest and prayer.*

REMEMBER TO KEEP HOLY THE LORD'S DAY.

Key Word

Sabbath the day of rest set apart to honor God in a special way

Like the Israelites and later the Jews, Christians have a day dedicated to God. On that day we worship God in a special way. Unlike the Israelites, we celebrate our holy day on the first day of the week. It was on the first day of the week that Christ rose from the dead. This is why we call Sunday, the first day of the week, the Lord's Day.

In the third commandment we are told, "Remember to keep holy the Lord's Day." Every Sunday we gather to celebrate that Jesus died and rose to save us. We rest from any work or activities that keep us from making the Lord's Day holy.

WE RESPOND

Plan some specific ways that your family can honor God this Sunday. Write them here.

____

____

____

____

____

Why do you think it is important to set aside time for God? What can you do to honor God this week?

Sabbath

A Catholic family remembers and celebrates at Sunday Mass.

Chapter 11 • Day 1

ACTIVITY BANK

Multiple Intelligences

Interpersonal

Have the students calculate the number of hours they might spend in different activities on Sundays. Have them list in one column the activity and in a second column how much time they might spend enjoying the activity. For example:

Activity	*Time*
hiking	4 hours
playing soccer	3 hours

Ask the students to total up the hours spent in these recreational activities. Then invite them to consider how these activities help them relax and, at the same time, keep holy the Lord's Day.

We can try not to make extra work for them. We can watch our behavior during their free time. Invite the sudents to explain how the people in the photos could be honoring the third commandment.

Quick Check

✔ *Why do Christians celebrate the Lord's Day on the first day of the week?* (Christians celebrate the first day of the week as the Lord's Day because Christ rose from the dead on Sunday.)

✔ *What is the third commandment?* (It is "Remember to keep holy the Lord's Day.")

WE RESPOND

___ minutes

Connect to Life Invite the students to complete the *We Respond* activity. Ask volunteers to share what they have written. Then discuss the *We Respond* questions.

Pray To conclude the lesson pray together: *God, we thank you for your gift of creation. We thank you for your commandments. We want to honor you every week by setting aside time to make the Lord's Day holy. Amen.*

Plan Ahead for Day 2

Catechist Goal: To present the Mass as the most important way we keep the Lord's Day holy

Preparation: If possible, obtain several copies of the *We Believe* Grade 3 text.

Chapter 11 • Day 2

Catechist Goal

- To present the Mass as the most important way we keep the Lord's Day holy

Our Faith Response

- To identify the ways we can participate in Mass and keep the Lord's Day holy

synagogue
holy day of obligation

Lesson Materials

- drawing paper
- crayons or markers
- Grade 4 CD

Teaching Tip

Volunteers

When asking for volunteers, take your time in making your choices. Some students take longer to process a direction or request. Pause for a few moments to give them some time to think and respond.

We keep the Lord's Day holy by participating in Sunday Mass.

REMEMBER TO KEEP HOLY THE LORD'S DAY.

WE GATHER

✝ *Lord, we honor you every day.*

Think about Sundays. Illustrate a scene that shows Sunday as the Lord's Day.

WE BELIEVE

We learn from the Bible that the Jewish day of rest is a day of joy, prayer, and family meals.

In the gospels we read that Jesus went to the synagogue on the Sabbath. The **synagogue** is the gathering place where Jewish people pray and learn about God. Jesus kept the Sabbath holy by praying and by doing good things for others. He also spent time with his family and friends on the Sabbath.

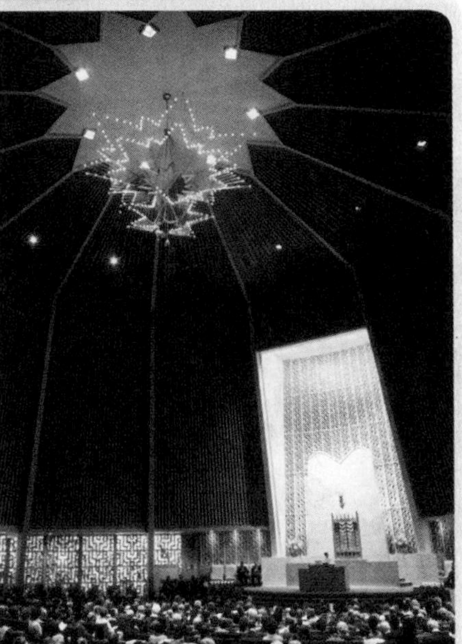

A Jewish community worshiping in the synagogue on the Sabbath

The first Christians continued to set apart a day for rest and for worship of God. They came together in their homes to celebrate the Lord's Day. On this day, "They devoted themselves to the teaching of the apostles and to the communal life, to the breaking of the bread and to the prayers" (Acts of the Apostles 2:42).

We, too, come together to celebrate the Lord's Day. On Sundays we gather as a Church community to celebrate the Mass. Participating in the Mass is the most important thing that we do to keep the Lord's Day holy. This is because the Eucharist is at the very center of our life and worship.

In the celebration of the Eucharist, we

- praise and thank God
- listen to God's word
- remember and celebrate Jesus' life, death, and Resurrection
- celebrate Jesus' gift of himself in the Eucharist
- receive Jesus Christ in Holy Communion
- go out to share Jesus' love, serve others, and build a better community.

Each time that we participate in Mass we are obeying the words of Jesus: "Do this in memory of me" (Luke 22:19).

Lesson Plan

WE GATHER ___ minutes

✝ **Pray** Pray together the *We Gather* prayer.

Then remind the students that we should take time to pray to God every day, either with others or by ourselves.

Focus on Life Invite the students to complete the *We Gather* activity. While the students are drawing, play some of the songs on the Grade 4 CD. When the students have finished, provide time for them to share their drawings with the class. Tell them that in this lesson they will learn that participating in Mass keeps the Lord's Day holy.

WE BELIEVE ___ minutes

Discuss "Keep Holy" Ask a volunteer to read aloud the *We Believe* statement. Ask: *What does it mean to keep something holy? How do you think Jesus kept the Sabbath holy?* Write the word *synagogue* on the board. Read aloud the first *We Believe* paragraph and explain that Jesus gathered there with other Jews on the Sabbath.

Present Key Concepts Divide the class into three groups, and assign one of the next three paragraphs to each group. Ask each group to read and discuss its assigned paragraph and then present the main ideas to the rest of the class.

Read About the Mass Emphasize the importance of participating in the parish celebration of Mass. Have the students read silently the two lists of ways we can participate. Then allow time for the students to complete the *We Believe* activity and share their answers.

Priests leading the assembly at Sunday Mass

It is important that every person take part in the Mass. Here are some ways you can participate:

- Arrive on time for Sunday Mass.
- Listen carefully to the readings.
- Pray aloud with the rest of the assembly.

In what other ways can you and your family be more involved in the celebration of Mass?

- ______________________
- ______________________

As Catholics we must participate in Mass on Sundays. In many parishes this Mass is celebrated on Saturday evenings, too.

We also must participate in Mass on holy days of obligation. A **holy day of obligation** is a day set apart to celebrate a special event in the life of Jesus, Mary, or the saints.

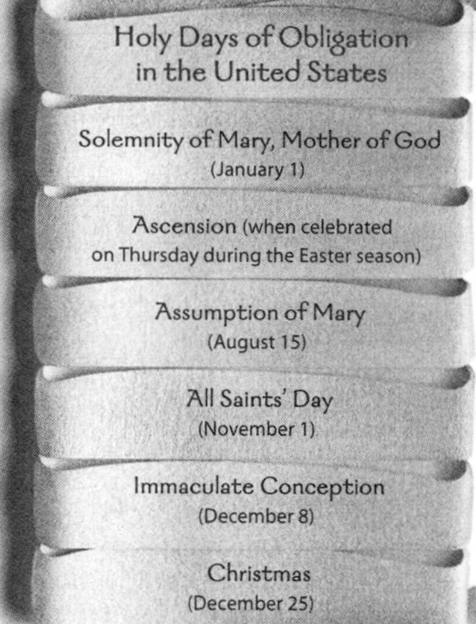

Holy Days of Obligation in the United States
Solemnity of Mary, Mother of God (January 1)
Ascension (when celebrated on Thursday during the Easter season)
Assumption of Mary (August 15)
All Saints' Day (November 1)
Immaculate Conception (December 8)
Christmas (December 25)

We "keep holy the Lord's Day" by taking part in Mass, by resting from work, by remembering our friendship with God, and by doing kind and loving things for others.

WE RESPOND

What can you and your family do to set aside Sunday as a special day?

synagogue the gathering place where Jewish people pray and learn about God

holy day of obligation a day that is set apart to celebrate a special event in the life of Jesus, Mary, or the saints

135

ACTIVITY BANK

Liturgy

Guest Speaker

Invite a member of the parish liturgy committee to speak to the students. Beforehand, have the students write down any questions they may have about the preparation for or celebration of Sunday Mass. Give these questions to the guest speaker prior to his or her presentation. Have the speaker answer the questions and discuss what the parish committee does to help with the parish's celebration of Sunday Mass.

Remember Holy Days Ask the students to recall what they have learned about holy days of obligation. Read aloud the list of holy days in the chart. Remind the students that in previous grades they learned about these events in Jesus' and Mary's lives. If possible, provide a few *We Believe* Grade 3 texts to help the students.

Quick Check

✔ *What is the most important thing we do to keep the Lord's Day holy?* (We participate at Mass.)

✔ *In addition to Sundays, when must we also participate in the celebration of Mass?* (We must attend Mass on holy days of obligation.)

WE RESPOND

___ minutes

Connect to Life Invite the students to reflect quietly upon the *We Respond* question. Encourage them to take steps to make Sundays extra special days of worship.

Pray Pray together: *God, help us to remember our friendship with you. We want to do kind and loving things for others every day of the week. Amen.*

Plan Ahead for Day 3

Catechist Goal: To describe ways to observe the Lord's Day

Preparation: Decide how you will group the students for the *We Believe* activity.

Catechist Goal

- To describe ways to observe the Lord's Day

Our Faith Response

- To help others keep the Lord's Day holy

As Catholics...

The Lord's Day

After you have completed the lesson, have two volunteers to read aloud the text. Then write on the board the different names mentioned in the text. (the First Day, the Eighth Day, The Day of Light) Ask a volunteer to explain why they think the Church uses each name.

REMEMBER TO KEEP HOLY THE LORD'S DAY.

The Lord's Day is a day for rest and relaxation.

WE GATHER

✝ *Lord, we praise you and thank you for your love and friendship.*

Check the things you like to do.

- ☐ Read a book.
- ☐ Visit a museum.
- ☐ Listen to music.
- ☐ Play sports.
- ☐ Spend time on a hobby.
- ☐ Enjoy the outdoors.

What are other things you like to do?

Would it be good to do these things on Sunday? Why or why not?

WE BELIEVE

Doing things that we enjoy helps us to rest and relax. Doing things we enjoy together strengthens our families and friendships. Rest and relaxation are an important part of following the third commandment. Relaxing can help us to be more aware of God's presence and goodness.

136

Lesson Plan

WE GATHER ___ minutes

✝ **Pray** Have the students think about ways we experience God's love and friendship. Pray together the *We Gather* prayer.

Focus on Life Invite a volunteer to read aloud the directions for the *We Gather* activity and the list of things to do. Allow a few minutes for the students to check what they like to do. Then engage them in a discussion about other things they like to do. Have them think about which things could help them to make Sunday a special day. Tell them that in this lesson they will learn that the Lord's Day is a day for rest, relaxation, and communion with God.

WE BELIEVE ___ minutes

Identify Main Ideas Read aloud together the *We Believe* statement. Then have the students form small groups. Ask the groups to read the three *We Believe* paragraphs. Then ask the groups to have their members decide on three main points of the lesson.

Make Lists Have the groups list things they might do on the Lord's Day to bring them closer to God. After an appropriate amount of time, invite the groups to compare their lists. Display their lists around the classroom. Also discuss each photo in the chapter and decide why each activity is appropriate for Sunday.

The Lord's Day is a good time to share the gifts God has given us. We can share a meal with our family and enjoy one another's company. We can spend time reading from the Bible and praying as a family. We can get together with friends. We can take time to visit people who are sick or unable to leave their homes. We can take part in parish activities to help others.

All the things that we do should bring us closer to God and remind us that God has given us many gifts. Being thankful brings us closer to God and to one another. In this way we keep the Lord's Day holy all day long.

As Catholics...

The Church has different names for the Lord's Day. The Lord's Day has been called the *First Day*. This is because Jesus rose from the dead on the first day of the week.

Another name for the Lord's Day is the *Eighth Day*. Calling this day the *Eighth Day* reminds us that the Lord's Day is the first day of the new creation. The new creation, brought about by Jesus, brings us the hope of living forever with God in heaven.

The *Day of Light* is also a name for the Lord's Day. We know that God created light and that Jesus is the Light of the World. Because of Jesus we can see and know God's love.

Ask your family members if they know of other names for the Lord's Day.

WE RESPOND

Sundays are days of relaxation and praise of God. Read the first column below. Use the second column to explain how each activity can help people to keep the Lord's Day holy. Share your answers.

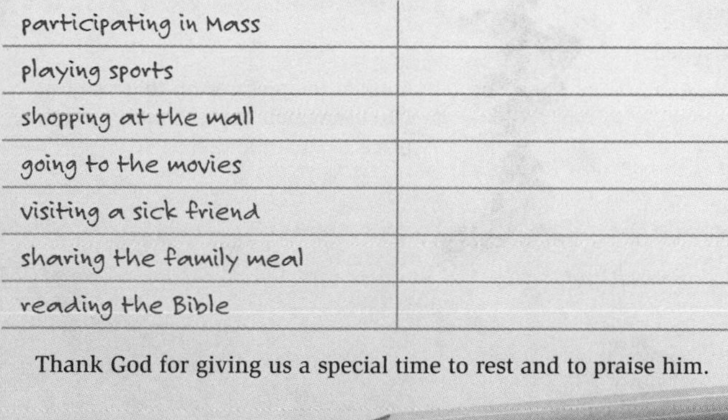

participating in Mass	
playing sports	
shopping at the mall	
going to the movies	
visiting a sick friend	
sharing the family meal	
reading the Bible	

Thank God for giving us a special time to rest and to praise him.

137

Activity Bank

Multicultural Connection

Mariachi Music at Mass

Activity Materials: the video *Mariachi Mass* (produced by the International Folk Cultural Center)

Explain to the students that in Mexico and in parts of the United States, Mariachi Masses are a popular form of worship. Mariachi musicians play violins, guitars, basses, *vihuelas* (five-string guitars), and trumpets to accompany parts of the Mass. The joyful music moves the worshipers to give God praise and thanksgiving. Invite the class to watch the video *Mariachi Mass* and to pay close attention to the special role the music plays in the celebration. Encourage the students to share their feelings about the Mariachi Mass.

Quick Check

✔ *What is the Lord's Day?* (The Lord's Day is a day for rest and relaxation.)

✔ *Why do we relax with our families on the Lord's Day?* (Spending time with our families helps us to be more aware of God's presence and goodness.)

WE RESPOND ___ minutes

Connect to Life Allow the students time to complete the *We Respond* activity. Have them share and compare their answers as a group. Ask volunteers to lead the discussion and write their answers on the board.

Pray Invite the students to pray quietly, thanking God for the many gifts he has given us.

Plan Ahead for Day 4

Catechist Goal: To explain that we keep the Lord's Day holy by performing works of mercy

Preparation: Make copies of Reproducible Master 11.

Catechist Goal

- To explain that we keep the Lord's Day holy by performing works of mercy

Our Faith Response

- To express our love for God by performing the works of mercy

Corporal Works of Mercy
Spiritual Works of Mercy

Lesson Materials

- copies of Reproducible Master 11

Blessed are they...

Saint Brigid

After the lesson has been completed, have volunteers read aloud the text. Ask if the students know anyone who is doing the same kind of work today. Remind the students that the saints show us ways to live out the Beatitudes.

We keep the Lord's Day holy by caring for the needs of others.

REMEMBER TO KEEP HOLY THE LORD'S DAY.

WE GATHER

✝ *God, strengthen us to serve you.*

Many people in the world are in need. What are some things they need? How can we help them?

WE BELIEVE

At the end of Mass, we are sent out to share Jesus' love and to serve others. Doing good things for others in Jesus' name helps us to make Sunday holy. The Works of Mercy are things we do that help us care for the needs of others.

People have different kinds of needs. We can care for the physical needs of people. *Corporal* means "of the body." The things that we do to care for the physical needs of others are the **Corporal Works of Mercy**.

We can care for the spiritual needs of people. *Spiritual* means "of the spirit." The things that we do to care for the minds, hearts, and souls of others are the **Spiritual Works of Mercy**.

Corporal Works of Mercy

Feed the hungry.
Give drink to the thirsty.
Clothe the naked.
Visit the imprisoned.
Shelter the homeless.
Visit the sick.
Bury the dead.

Spiritual Works of Mercy

Admonish the sinner.
(Give correction to those who need it.)
Instruct the ignorant.
(Share our knowledge with others.)
Counsel the doubtful.
(Give advice to those who need it.)
Comfort the sorrowful.
(Comfort those who suffer.)
Bear wrongs patiently.
(Be patient with others.)
Forgive all injuries.
(Forgive those who hurt us.)
Pray for the living and the dead.

Look at the pictures on these pages. Discuss which work of mercy is taking place in each picture.

138

Lesson Plan

WE GATHER ___ minutes

✝ **Pray** Pray the Sign of the Cross and the *We Gather* prayer.

Focus on Life Ask the students to think about things they need, such as food, water, love, and support. Ask them how they would feel if they did not have these needs met. Based on this answer, have the students think about ways they can help meet the needs of others. Tell the students that in this lesson they will learn that we keep the Lord's Day holy by caring for the physical and spiritual needs of others.

WE BELIEVE ___ minutes

Learn About the Works of Mercy Have a volunteer read aloud the *We Believe* statement and the first paragraph. Then read aloud the second paragraph and explain the differences between *corporal* and *spiritual.*

Have the students read the lists of Corporal Works of Mercy and Spiritual Works of Mercy. Ask the students to circle the Spiritual Works that they can do now.

Describe the Photos Have the students form groups. Have the groups identify the work of mercy illustrated in each photograph on pages 138–139. Then assign a photograph to each group and ask the members to write a story about what is being shown. When all are finished, invite the groups to share their stories.

Reflect on the Third Commandment Allow a few minutes of quiet time for an examination of con-

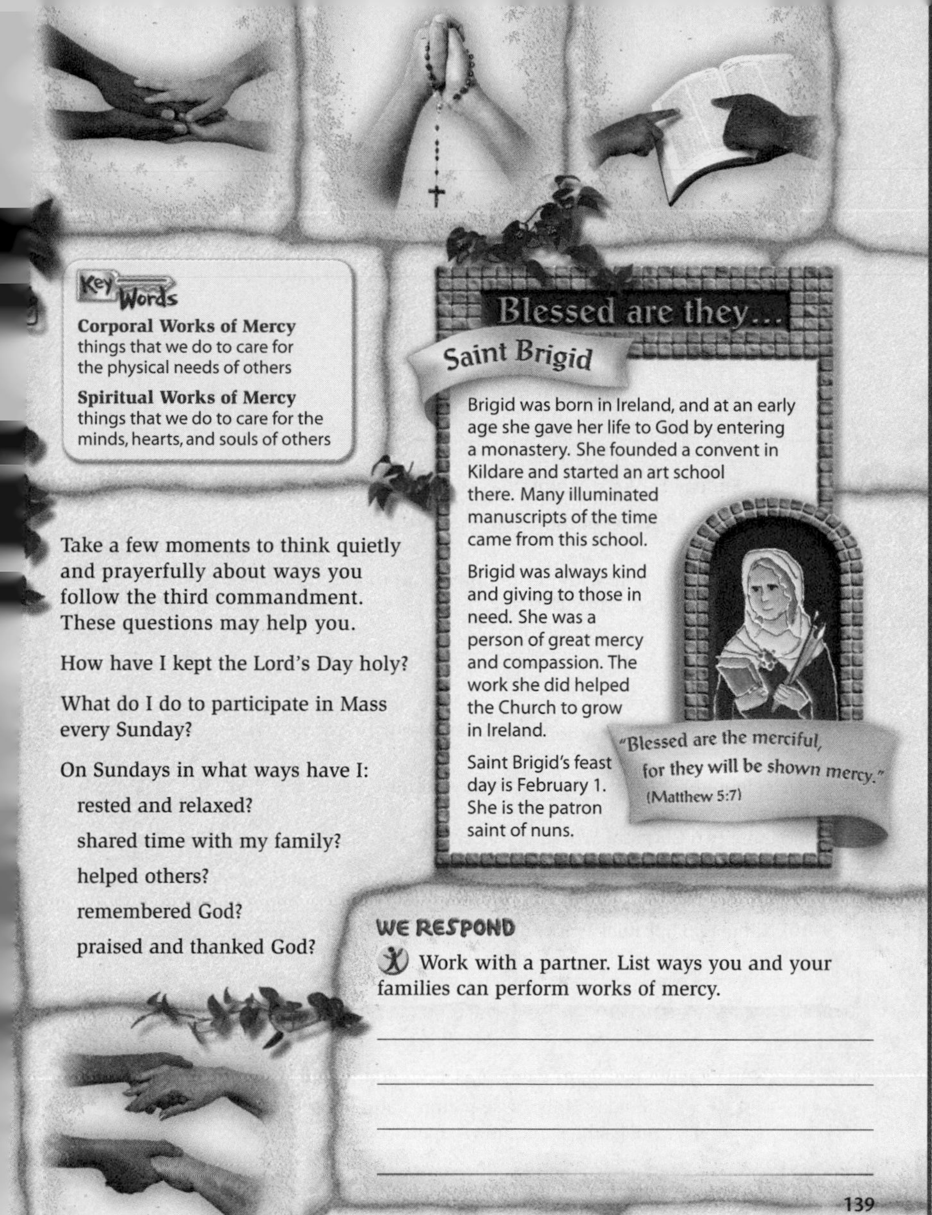

Key Words
Corporal Works of Mercy
things that we do to care for the physical needs of others
Spiritual Works of Mercy
things that we do to care for the minds, hearts, and souls of others
Take a few moments to think quietly and prayerfully about ways you follow the third commandment. These questions may help you.
How have I kept the Lord's Day holy?
What do I do to participate in Mass every Sunday?
On Sundays in what ways have I:
rested and relaxed?
shared time with my family?
helped others?
remembered God?
praised and thanked God?
Blessed are they...
Saint Brigid
Brigid was born in Ireland, and at an early age she gave her life to God by entering a monastery. She founded a convent in Kildare and started an art school there. Many illuminated manuscripts of the time came from this school.
Brigid was always kind and giving to those in need. She was a person of great mercy and compassion. The work she did helped the Church to grow in Ireland.
Saint Brigid's feast day is February 1. She is the patron saint of nuns.
"Blessed are the merciful, for they will be shown mercy." (Matthew 5:7)
WE RESPOND
Work with a partner. List ways you and your families can perform works of mercy.
139

Activity Bank

Catholic Social Teaching

Call to Family, Community, and Participation

To extend this lesson's focus on the Corporal and Spiritual Works of Mercy, encourage the students to join together as a group to collect food for the parish food pantry or a local food depository. Check with the parish outreach committee director about the kinds of food that are most needed. Help the students organize the drive. Enlist the help of a few parents or older students in the collection process. Be sure that every student has an opportunity to participate in this corporal work of mercy.

science. Have the students use the questions to reflect on the ways they have kept the third commandment.

Quick Check

✔ *What are the Corporal Works of Mercy?* (The Corporal Works of Mercy are things we do to care for the physical needs of others.)

✔ *What are the Spiritual Works of Mercy?* (The Spiritual Works of Mercy are things we do to care for the minds, hearts, and souls of others.)

We Respond ___ minutes

Connect to Life Distribute copies of Reproducible Master 11. Read the directions aloud. Have the students work independently to complete the activity. (Place a C in front of 2, 6, 7, and 8; an S in front of 1, 3, 4, 5, 9, and 10.) Then have the students work in pairs to complete the *We Respond* activity. Invite the pairs to share their answers.

Pray Invite the students to pray with you, thanking God for all of creation and asking God to help us all care for other people. As you pray, invite the students to add specific examples. *God, we thank you for all you have created. We hope to honor you by helping others by* (showing kindness, working in the parish, contributing clothing, and so on).

Plan Ahead for Day 5

Catechist Goal: To review chapter ideas and their relationship to our faith life

Preparation: Have magazines and newspapers available; make copies of Chapter 11 Test in the Grade 4 Assessment Book (option).

Catechist Goal

- To review chapter ideas and their relationship to our faith life

Our Faith Response

- To apply what has been learned to our lives

CHAPTER TEST

Chapter 11 Test is provided in the Grade 4 Assessment Book.

Grade 4
Chapter 11

Write True or False for the following sentences. Then change the false sentences to make them true.

1. True Catholics must participate in Mass on Sundays and holy days of obligation.

2. False *Sabbath* is a word that means "honoring the Lord's name."
Sabbath is a word that means "rest."

3. False Sunday is like any other day of the week.
Sunday is the first day of the week, the Lord's Day.

4. True Spending time with our families is an important part of keeping the Lord's Day holy.

Complete the following:

5. The third commandment tells us to keep holy the Lord's Day.

6. We celebrate Sunday as the Lord's Day because Christ rose from the dead on the first day of the week.

7–8. Name two Corporal Works of Mercy. See page 138.

9–10. Name two Spiritual Works of Mercy. See page 138.

Make a display called "The Top Ten Ways to Keep Sunday Holy." Use pictures and photos from magazines and newspapers. Write your own captions.

140

Lesson Plan

___ minutes

Chapter Review Have the students complete questions 1–10 of the review. Once they have finished, ask them to say aloud each of the correct answers. Ask the questions in turn, and be sure all students understand the correct answers and why they are correct.

Assessment Activity Have the students work in pairs. Ask them to think about the top ten ways, in their opinion, to keep Sunday a holy day. Have them illustrate their ideas using scenes from magazines or newspapers.

___ minutes

Reflect & Pray Provide quiet time for the students to complete the prayer.

Key Words Write the *Key Words* on the board. Ask the students to use their own words to explain the meaning of each.

Remember Organize the class into four groups. Assign each group one of the *We Believe* statements. Have each group plan a brief skit that displays its members' understanding of the statement. For example, for the Day 2 statement, the students might develop a skit in which they are participating at Mass. Encourage the members of all the groups to give suggestions and comments on the other groups' skits.

We Respond in Faith

Reflect & Pray

Lord, may we enjoy the gift of your love and share it with others.

Lord, I want to keep your day holy. Help me ______________

____

____

Key Words

Sabbath (p. 133)
synagogue (p. 135)
holy day of obligation (p. 135)
Corporal Works of Mercy (p. 139)
Spiritual Works of Mercy (p. 139)

Remember

- God gave us a special day to rest and to worship him.
- We keep the Lord's Day holy by participating in Sunday Mass.
- The Lord's Day is a day for rest and relaxation.
- We keep the Lord's Day holy by caring for the needs of others.

Our Catholic Life

Altar Servers

Today boys and girls are encouraged to participate at Mass as altar servers. They are trained to assist the priest at the celebration of Mass. They often lead the assembly in procession with the cross, and they light the altar candles. Because of what they do, altar servers behave in a reverent way. It is an honor to be an altar server.

Home Connection

Sharing Faith with My Family

Be sure to send home the family page (text page 142).

Read together the family prayer. Ask: *Why is this an appropriate prayer for Sunday?* (because it mentions the Blessed Trinity and resting with God) You may want to tell your students that this prayer is taken from the book *Catholic Household Blessings and Prayers.*

For additional information and activities, encourage families to visit Sadlier's

www.WEBELIEVEweb.com

Our Catholic Life Have a volunteer read aloud the text about altar servers. Invite the students to identify altar servers they may know in the parish and tell what they do during the celebration of the Eucharist. Then ask the students to think of ways they can help out at school and at home, and suggest that they can also help out at church.

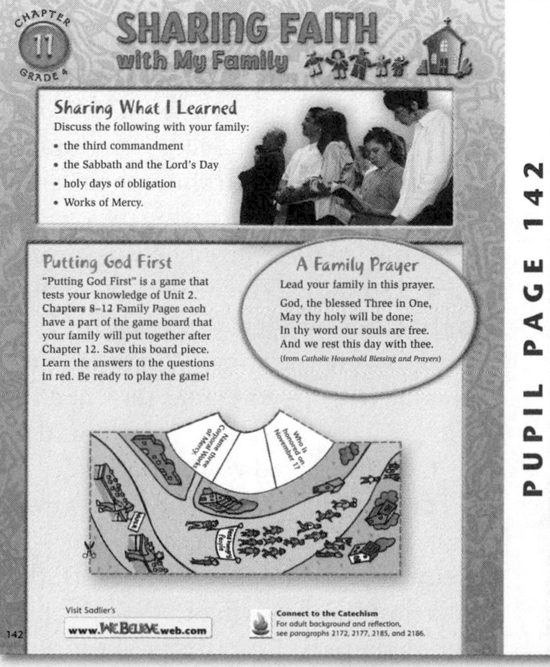

CHAPTER 11 GRADE 4

SHARING FAITH with My Family

Sharing What I Learned

Discuss the following with your family:

- the third commandment
- the Sabbath and the Lord's Day
- holy days of obligation
- Works of Mercy.

Putting God First

"Putting God First" is a game that tests your knowledge of Unit 2. Chapters 8–12 Family Pages each have a part of the game board that your family will put together after Chapter 12. Save this board piece. Learn the answers to the questions in red. Be ready to play the game!

A Family Prayer

Lead your family in this prayer.

God, the blessed Three in One,
May thy holy will be done;
In thy word our souls are free.
And we rest this day with thee.

(from *Catholic Household Blessing and Prayers*)

Visit Sadlier's www.WEBELIEVEweb.com

Connect to the Catechism
For adult background and reflection, see paragraphs 2172, 2177, 2185, and 2186.

142

PUPIL PAGE 142

Chapter 12 Strengthened by the Eucharist

Overview

In Chapter 11 the students learned about the third commandment. In this chapter they will focus on the Eucharist and will learn that receiving the Body and Blood of Christ nurtures and strengthens them to be active followers of Christ.

Doctrinal Content	For Adult Reading and Reflection *Catechism of the Catholic Church*
The students will learn:	Paragraph
• The Introductory Rites unite us and prepare us for worship.	1348
• During the Liturgy of the Word, we hear the word of God.	1349
• During the Liturgy of the Eucharist, we offer gifts of bread and wine and receive the Body and Blood of Jesus Christ.	1355
• In the Concluding Rite we are sent to live as disciples of Jesus.	1397

Mass (p. 145)
assembly (p. 145)
Liturgy of the Word (p. 147)
homily (p. 147)
Liturgy of the Eucharist (p. 149)
eucharistic prayer (p. 149)
consecration (p. 149)

Catechist Background

What is something for which you are most grateful?

Jesus was traveling to Jerusalem. Upon entering a village, he was greeted by ten lepers. Standing far from Jesus, the lepers shouted "Master, have mercy on us!" And, indeed, Jesus showed them mercy. He told them to show themselves to a priest and while they walked away, they were healed. One of the lepers realized he was cleansed and returned to Jesus. The healed man fell at Jesus' feet and thanked him. Jesus then said, "Ten were cleansed, were they not? Where are the other nine? Has none but this foreigner returned to give thanks to God?" Then he said to him, 'Stand up and go; your faith has saved you" (Luke 17: 17–19).

The meaning of the word *Eucharist* gives us insight into what it is about. It comes from the Greek word for thanksgiving. Thus, the Eucharist is an act of thanksgiving to God. By participating in the eucharistic liturgy, the Mass, we are acting like the leper who returned to thank Jesus for being cleansed of his leprosy. Like the leper, we realize that Jesus has healed us. Like the leper, we are deeply grateful for the opportunity to live free from the effects of sin. And like the leper, we have chosen to return to express our gratitude to God for his many gifts.

The Eucharist is also known as the *Holy Sacrifice* "because it makes present the one sacrifice of Christ the Savior" (*CCC* 1330). Again like the leper, we turn to Jesus for mercy and receive it through this memorial of his Passion and Resurrection.

In what ways do you show your gratitude to God?

Lesson Planning Guide

Lesson Focus	Presentation	Materials
Day 1		
page 143 **We Gather in Prayer** **pages 144–145** *The Introductory Rites unite us and prepare us for worship.*	• Listen to Scripture. • Respond in song. • Discuss the **We Gather** questions. • Discuss the Mass and its Introductory Rites in **We Believe** text. • Unscramble the words in the activity. • Answer the **We Respond** question.	For the prayer space: items that represent people and things for which the students are thankful • index cards "Come to the Feast/Ven al Banquete," #12, Grade 4 CD
Day 2		
pages 146–147 *During the Liturgy of the Word, we hear the word of God.*	• Discuss effects of words on people in the **We Gather** statements. • Discuss the **We Believe** text about the Liturgy of the Word. • Act out the story about Jesus that was chosen in the **We Respond** activity. • Read and discuss the *As Catholics* text.	• Lectionary and the Book of the Gospels (option)
Day 3		
pages 148–149 *During the Liturgy of the Eucharist, we offer gifts of bread and wine and receive the Body and Blood of Jesus Christ.*	 Discuss the **We Gather** question. • Read and discuss the Liturgy of the Eucharist in the **We Believe** text. • Discuss the gifts presented at the Mass in the **We Respond** questions.	• index cards
Day 4		
pages 150–151 *In the Concluding Rite we are sent to live as disciples of Jesus.*	• Discuss actions and listening in the **We Gather** questions. • Read and discuss the Concluding Rite in the **We Believe** text. • Complete the activities. • For the **We Respond** section, respond in song and answer question.	• copies of Reproducible Master 12, guide page 143G "Take the Word of God with You," #13, Grade 4 CD
Day 5		
page 152 **Review** **pages 153–154** **We Respond in Faith**	• Complete questions 1–10. • Work on the *Assessment Activity.* • Complete the *Reflect & Pray* question. • Review *Remember* and *Key Words.* • Read and discuss the Blessed Sacrament in *Our Catholic Life.* • Discuss the **Sharing Faith with My Family** page.	• index cards • Chapter Test 12 in the Assessment Book, pp. 23–24 • Chapter 12 Test in Test Generator • Review & Resource Book, pp. 31–33 • Family Book, pp. 36–38

For additional ideas, activities, and opportunities: Visit Sadlier's **www.WEBELIEVEweb.com**

Enrichment Ideas

Chapter Story

Gracie's dad hung up the phone and beamed with excitement. "Well, that's wonderful news! It looks like our whole family will be getting together for our family reunion. Everybody's coming!"

"What about Uncle Tim and Aunt Elaine and my cousins, Mark and Marianne? They live far away," said Gracie, a hint of doubt creeping into her voice.

"Just as I said, Gracie. Everybody in the family is really coming! Grandma and Grandpa will stay with us, and the others plan to stay with your other aunts and uncles. But there's so much to do to get ready, and I'm going to depend on you and your sister to help your mom and me. What do you say to that?"

"Sure!" Gracie exclaimed. "Mom can make one of her famous to-do lists. I'm sure everyone else will do what they can to help."

"I'm glad to hear your enthusiasm, Gracie," chuckled Mom. "There will be quite a crowd, and they will all be hungry. We'll have to make a lot of food. And, of course, everyone has a favorite dish."

Mom smiled as she started to make her to-do list. "It will be wonderful for the family to be together. What a special time it will be!"

▶ *What things did Gracie's family do to prepare for the family reunion? When your family gathers for a celebration, how do you contribute?*

FAITH and MEDIA

▶ On day 5, after the students have compiled and answered their list of frequently asked questions (FAQs) about the celebration of the Mass, you might work with the class to set up a *Mass FAQ* Web page on the parish or school Web site. As you do so, remind the students that the Church urges us to use the Internet to communicate the good news of Jesus.

CHAPTER PROJECT: A MASS CHART

Attach a large sheet of white paper to the wall. Make four vertical columns. Write the following headings at the top of the columns: *The Introductory Rites, The Liturgy of the Word, The Liturgy of the Eucharist, and The Concluding Rite.* During each day's lesson invite the students to use colored pencils or markers to fill in under the appropriate heading what they have learned about that part of the Mass. Encourage them either to write about or to draw a picture to show what they have learned. For example, under *The Introductory Rites* a student could write, "The Introductory Rites unite me with the other members of the parish." Another student could represent this unity by drawing people singing and smiling together. When the columns under all four headings have been filled in, review with the students what they have learned.

Connections

To Mission

The Church's celebration of the Eucharist cannot be separated from its missionary mandate to bring the good news of Christ to others. When we remember others' needs in the general intercessions, we pray not only for God to be with them but also for God to strengthen us to act as Christ would to them. And at the conclusion of the Mass, we are sent out to serve the Lord, to bring his peace to others. Use these two examples to connect worship and our daily lives of discipleship.

To Catholic Social Teaching

Dignity of Work and the Rights of Workers
The Catholic Church teaches that work is a duty in which we invest our God-given talents for the good of all. Work has dignity because through it we participate in building up God's kingdom on earth. Sunday is an appropriate time to consider the ways our work contributes to this process. Suggest that the students talk with their parents or other adults after Mass. Have the students ask: What skills does your work require? How does your work help others? Are your rights as a worker respected? Have the students record the adults' responsibilities and then share them with the class.

To Family

The Church encourages the faithful to receive Holy Communion regularly and frequently. Just as sharing at least one meal a day together strengthens the bond linking family members, participating as a family in the act of sharing the Body and Blood of Christ strengthens the fabric of our parish family life. Encourage the students to make "Come to the Banquet" invitations for their family members. Have the students invite their family members to receive Holy Communion with them at Mass.

Meeting Individual Needs

English-Language Learners

Students with a limited use of English will benefit from the use of flash cards. Flash cards with the key words or terms on one side and a simple explanation or picture (a chalice, for example, or an open Bible) can be shared with an English-proficient partner. Allow the students time to quiz one another with the cards.

ADDITIONAL RESOURCES

Book *The Holy Eucharist,* Lawrence G. Lovasik, Catholic Book Publishing, 1995. This book uses simplified language to explain the Eucharist to students.

Video *The Mass for Children; A Middle-Grader's Guide to Understanding the Mass,* Liguori Publications, 1993. A priest helps unruly children see Mass as more than an obligation. (33 minutes)

To find more ideas for books, videos, and other learning material, visit Sadlier's

www.WEBELIEVEweb.com

Religious Education Assessment

by Sr. Marie Pappas, CR

Sister Marie Pappas, CR, a Sister of the Resurrection, is currently associate superintendent for religious education for the office of the Superintendent of Schools for the Archdiocese of New York. She is also an adjunct professor of Catechetics at Dunwoodie Seminary.

The catechist asks, "Have I effectively imparted what I intended?" The student asks, "Do I know and understand?" Assessment in religious education measures both catechist and student: "Have we, together, achieved the goal for this lesson?"

The *General Directory for Catechesis* reminds us of the fundamental tasks of catechesis: knowledge of the faith, liturgical education, moral formation, prayer and missionary initiation. (73) Religious education is a formation in all of these dimensions of discipleship. It is an awesome responsibility to evaluate our catechizing and the students' progress. Yet, we cannot improve our catechizing nor facilitate the students' growth if we do not measure results and plan accordingly.

The content of religious education necessitates progressive development of higher order thinking skills, opportunities for practical application, and regular assessment by which the religious educator can determine whether or not, and to what degree, progress is happening. Assessment not only measures multi-faceted student faith knowledge and skills, but also redirects the efforts and effectiveness of the religious educator.

Religious education assessment should measure recognition of content, comprehension, capacity for reflection, critical thinking, problem-solving, and application. Religious education assessment should also include a capacity for creative meaningful construction that provides feedback for the catechist. These measure the students' assimilation, appropriation, and application of the doctrinal, spiritual, liturgical, and relational content of Catholic belief. Assessment can be done through quizzes and tests; discussions; projects; research; portfolios; charitable service and social action; liturgical planning and participation; retreats for personal reflection.

Only through assessment can we know if the students and we are working effectively together. Only if we work effectively can we, with the Holy Spirit, continue to fully form disciples who can share the good news.

Catechist Development Topics (Topic and Guide Page)

Resources

Convey, John J. *Assessment of Catholic Religious Education.* Washington, D.C.: NCEA, 1999.

Wiggins, Grant P. *Assessing Student Performance: Exploring the Purpose and Limits of Testing.* San Francisco: Jossey–Bass, 1999.

Ways to Implement Religious Education Assessment

- Compile a computer bank of objective questions, true and false, multiple choice, matching, definitions, or completions that reflect each key topic. These items can be used to create quizzes and tests.
- Have students design their own assessment to test one another.
- Use life situations for discussion and problem-solving activities. This enables students to practice applying faith to life.
- Have students conduct surveys or interviews related to key topics. Their ability to prepare appropriate questions will demonstrate what they have mastered. Interviewing people will foster the relational aspects of faith.
- Design a checklist related to the curriculum as a student self-inventory. Use these checklists to assess concepts that have been mastered. These checklists can also help you to assess what needs further work, and what students want to learn more about.

With thanks to:
Donna Grosso
Curé of Ars Parish
Merrick, New York

Donna assesses her fourth grade group in a fun format called "The Game." At the beginning of the year, teams of four children are randomly assigned. "The Game" is played in three phases. *Phase 1:* The team is read an answer and responds in the form of a question after huddling for one minute. *Phase 2:* The team is asked a question and responds with the answer after huddling for one minute. *Phase 3:* The team chooses either the question or answer format and responds accordingly. Points for each correct response are assigned. Donna has found that by using "The Game" on a weekly basis, she can assess her group and note their individual strengths and weaknesses regarding content. Donna also gives her students take-home sets of "The Game" to share with their families and to use as study guides during the year.

Notes

For additional ideas, activities, and opportunities, visit Sadlier's

www.WEBELIEVEweb.com

Name ____

Work with a partner to answer the following questions.

At what part of the Mass:

- do we become united as the Body of Christ on earth?

  ____

- do we pray the Lord's Prayer?

  ____

- are we sent out to do God's work?

  ____

- do we listen to and respond to God's word?

  ____

In which reading do we hear about the words and actions of Jesus during his ministry?

____

Write the four parts of the Mass in the correct order.

1. ____________________ **2.** ____________________

3. ____________________ **4.** ____________________

Strengthened by the Eucharist

Chapter 12 • **Day 1**

✝ We Gather in Prayer

Reader: A reading from the first Letter of Saint Paul to the Corinthians.

"For I received from the Lord what I also handed on to you, that the Lord Jesus, on the night he was handed over, took bread, and, after he had given thanks, broke it and said, 'This is my body that is for you. Do this in remembrance of me.' In the same way also the cup, after supper, saying, 'This cup is the new covenant in my blood. Do this, as often as you drink it, in remembrance of me.' For as often as you eat this bread and drink the cup, you proclaim the death of the Lord until he comes." (1 Corinthians 11:23–26)

The word of the Lord.

All: Thanks be to God.

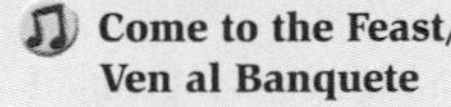

Come to the Feast/ Ven al Banquete

Ven, ven al banquete.
Ven a la fiesta de Dios.
Here the hungry find plenty,
here the thirsty shall drink.
Ven a la cena de Cristo,
come to the feast.

143

Preparing to Pray

In this gathering prayer the students will hear the story of the Last Supper read from Scripture and will respond in song.

- Invite a volunteer to be reader. Give him or her time in a quiet place to prepare for the reading.
- Have the students listen to "Come to the Feast/Ven al Banquete," from the Grade 4 CD. Then have them sing along with the music as practice

The Prayer Space

- In keeping with the meaning of the word *Eucharist* (thanksgiving), gather two or three items that represent people and things for which the students are thankful. Items might include a crucifix, photos of families or friends, and objects representing talents and abilities, such as dancer's shoes, paintbrushes, or sports equipment.

This Week's Liturgy

Visit **www.webelieveweb.com** for this week's liturgical readings and other seasonal material.

Lesson Plan

We Gather in Prayer ___ minutes

✝ Pray

- Invite the students to the prayer space and signal the reader to begin.
- After the reading is complete, play "Come to the Feast/Ven al Banquete," from the Grade 4 CD.

Home Connection Update

Invite the students to share the ways their families used the Chapter 11 family page. Ask: *What did your family do with the page?*

Catechist Goal

- To teach that the Introductory Rites unite us

Our Faith Response

- To rejoice as individuals in our parish assembly and seek closer union with other parishioners

Mass

assembly

Lesson Materials

- index cards

Teaching Note

Getting Ready for Mass

Today's lesson teaches that the Introductory Rites of the Mass unite us as the Body of Christ. This is an opportunity to discuss ways to get ready for Mass. Invite students to prepare for Mass by praying during the week for the grace to be united with Jesus in the Eucharist. Encourage them to greet other members of Christ's Body and to visit with God in silent prayer.

The Introductory Rites unite us and prepare us for worship.

WE GATHER

✝ *Lord, hear the prayers of your people.*

What are some things you are thankful for? In what ways do you show others your thanks?

WE BELIEVE

The word *eucharist* means "giving thanks." Whenever we participate in the Eucharist, we thank God for creating the world, for saving us from sin, and for making us a holy people.

The celebration of the Eucharist is also called the **Mass**. The Mass has four parts: the Introductory Rites, the Liturgy of the Word, the Liturgy of the Eucharist, and the Concluding Rite.

The Introductory Rites unite us as the Body of Christ. The Church is the Body of Christ on earth. Jesus is the head of the body, and he is with us always. We are united by Jesus' presence among us.

Like the human body, the Church has many parts, or members. Different members have different gifts and talents. Each member is important. All the members are united by the same love for and belief in Jesus Christ.

It is the Body of Christ that gathers to celebrate the Mass. This community of people gathered to worship in the name of Jesus Christ is called the **assembly**. We are part of the assembly. The assembly offers thanks and praise to God throughout the Mass.

The Introductory Rites also prepare us to hear God's word and to celebrate the Eucharist.

Unscramble these words. Then use them to complete the sentences.

caerutsih eucharist

hrhcuc church

etniu unite

msalsyeb assembly

When we join with a community of people to worship in the name of Jesus, we are part of the assembly.

The Mass is another name for the celebration of the Eucharist.

We are the Body of Christ. We are the Church.

The Introductory Rites unite us as the Body of Christ.

144

Lesson Plan

WE GATHER

___ minutes

✝ **Pray** Remind the students that God always listens to us when we pray. Pray the Sign of the Cross and the *We Gather* prayer.

Focus on Life Have the students respond to the *We Gather* questions. Encourage them to share their descriptions of the people and things for which they give thanks. Invite them to use the items on the prayer table as prompts. Tell the students that in this lesson they will learn that we gather together for Mass to worship God and to thank him for his goodness and love.

WE BELIEVE

___ minutes

Read aloud the *We Believe* statement. Then explain that during the Introductory Rites—the first part of the Mass—we gather together for worship and prepare to celebrate the Eucharist.

Learn About the Introductory Rites Have volunteers read aloud the *We Believe* text. Emphasize the following points:

- The Church is the Body of Christ on earth.
- The Introductory Rites unite the many members of the Church into one body.
- The Introductory Rites prepare the people to hear God's word and to celebrate the Eucharist.

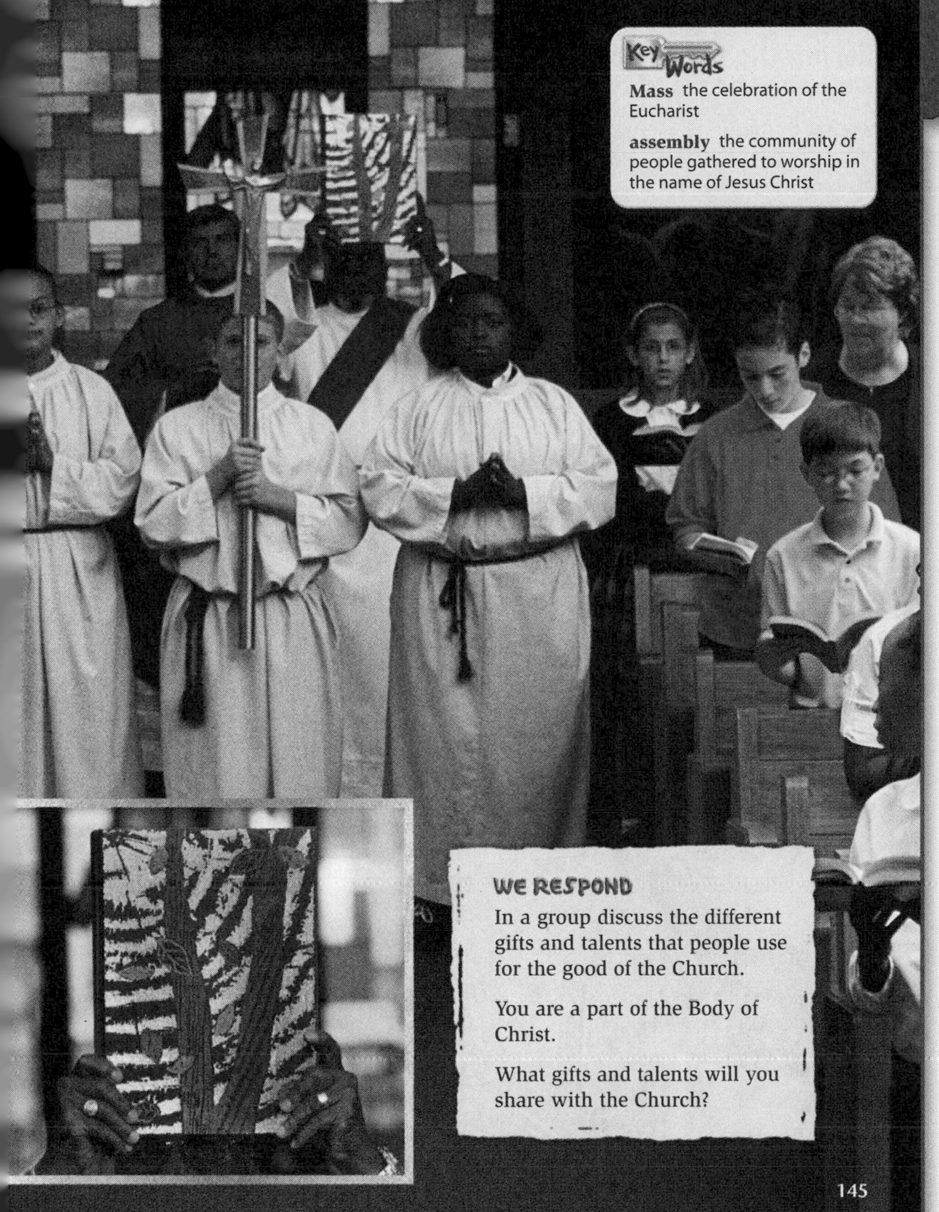

Key Words
Mass the celebration of the Eucharist
assembly the community of people gathered to worship in the name of Jesus Christ
WE RESPOND
In a group discuss the different gifts and talents that people use for the good of the Church.
You are a part of the Body of Christ.
What gifts and talents will you share with the Church?
145

ACTIVITY BANK

Community

Talent Show

Activity Materials: colored paper, crayons or markers

Invite the students to share their talents and gifts with the community by putting on a talent show. Emphasize that there will be no judging or prizes. Encourage the students to think about what they will do. For example, one group of students might sing a song they learned in class. Another group might accompany the singers on musical instruments. Some students might perform a skit illustrating a point from this week's lesson. Encourage artistic students to design and make flyers advertising the talent show. Post the flyers around the community. Invite one student to emcee the show. Have that student welcome the audience and explain that God blesses us all with special gifts and talents. Take pictures during the show and post them on a bulletin board or poster with the title *God Blesses Us with Special Gifts and Talents.*

Record the Key Words Have the students write all the *Key Words* and their definitions on index cards.

Chart the Diversity Make a chart on the board listing the diverse members and talents in the parish. For example, some parishioners may be fluent in languages. They might use this talent to minister to someone who has recently moved to this country and the parish.

Do the Activity The word scramble activity reinforces the lesson's main concepts.

Quick Check

✔ *What does the word Eucharist mean?* ("giving thanks")

✔ *What are the Introductory Rites?* (They unite us as the Body of Christ and prepare us to hear God's word and celebrate the Eucharist.)

WE RESPOND ___ minutes

Connect to Life Read and discuss the *Chapter Story* on page 143C. Form groups to discuss the talents that they and others can use for the good of the Church.

Pray Pray aloud: *Lord, help us to use our talents. Amen.*

Plan Ahead for Day 2

Catechist Goal: To examine the importance of the Liturgy of the Word at the Mass

Preparation: Decide how you will group students for the *We Respond* activity.

Chapter 12 • Day 2

Catechist Goal

• To examine the importance of the Liturgy of the Word at the Mass

Our Faith Response

• To listen and respond to the word of God

Liturgy of the Word
homily

Lesson Materials

• Lectionary and Book of the Gospels (option)

As Catholics...

The Living Word of God

After presenting the lesson, have volunteers read the text aloud. Invite the students to share ways the Bible helps them to know and understand God's presence with us today.

During the Liturgy of the Word, we hear the word of God.

WE GATHER

✝ *Lord, you have the words of everlasting life.*

People's words affect us in different ways. Their words may comfort us or move us to do something. Think of a time when someone's words affected you.

WE BELIEVE

After the Introductory Rites unite us as the Body of Christ, the Liturgy of the Word begins. The **Liturgy of the Word** is the part of the Mass when we listen and respond to God's word. We grow in faith as we hear about God's great love for his people. We hear how God is present among us today.

On Sundays and holy days of obligation, there are three readings. The first two readings are read from a special book called the lectionary. The lectionary is a collection of readings from the Bible. The first reading is usually taken from the Old Testament. In this reading we hear about God's love and mercy for his people. After the first reading we sit in silence. Then we pray by singing a psalm.

The second reading is taken from the New Testament. It is usually taken from a letter written by one of Jesus' first disciples. In this reading we are encouraged to live together as followers of Jesus.

146

Lesson Plan

WE GATHER ___ minutes

✝ **Pray** Organize the class into three groups. Ask each group to pray aloud the *We Gather* prayer, putting emphasis on the word you assign to that group. One group will emphasize *you;* another group will emphasize *words;* the third group will emphasize *life.* Ask each group in turn to pray aloud. Then invite all three groups to pray together while continuing to emphasize their assigned words.

Focus on Life Have the students read the *We Gather* text silently. Then invite them to consider how words can affect a person. Encourage volunteers to describe times when someone's words affected them in a positive way. Tell the students that in this lesson the students will learn about listening and responding to God's word.

WE BELIEVE ___ minutes

Learn About the Readings Ask a volunteer to read aloud the *We Believe* statement and the first *We Believe* paragraph. Then form the class into three groups. Assign one of the next three paragraphs about the readings at Mass to each group. Allow time for each group to read its paragraph quietly and prepare a presentation of the paragraph's main ideas.

Have each group make its presentations. Place the Lectionary and the Book of the Gospels on the prayer table. Have the groups look through them.

Discuss the Homily Write the word *homily* on the board. Ask volunteers to define it. Then have the students read the paragraph about the homily. Read the last *We Believe* paragraphs together.

Before the third reading, we stand to show that we are ready to listen to the good news of Jesus Christ. The third reading, always from one of the four gospels of the New Testament, is read from the Book of the Gospels. The deacon or priest proclaims this reading. In this reading we hear about the words and actions of Jesus during his ministry. We hear about the ways Jesus wants his disciples to live.

Then the priest or deacon gives a homily. The **homily** is a talk that helps us to understand the readings and to grow as faithful followers of Jesus.

Next we state what we believe by saying the creed. We then remember the needs of all God's people by praying the general intercessions. We pray for the Church and its leaders. We pray for world leaders and those they lead. We pray for those who are in need, those who are sick, and those who have died.

As Catholics...

The Bible is the word of God. It is also called Sacred Scripture. This is because God the Holy Spirit guided the human writers of the Bible. They wrote what God wanted to share with us.

God speaks to us through the words of the Bible. The Bible is God's living word to us. It is a record of the ways God has acted in the lives of his people. It is also about the ways we are called to live and respond to God. The Bible helps us to know and understand that God is with us today.

Plan a time this week to read from the Bible with your family.

Liturgy of the Word the part of the Mass when we listen and respond to God's word

homily a talk given by the priest or deacon that helps us to understand the readings and to grow as faithful followers of Jesus

WE RESPOND

Think about a favorite story you know concerning Jesus and his work among the people.

Work with a partner or in a group. Choose one story and act it out for the class.

How do Jesus' words and actions in this story apply to your life?

147

Chapter 12 • Day 2

ACTIVITY BANK

Multiple Intelligences

Visual-Spatial

Activity Materials: illustrations or replicas of illuminated manuscripts, parchment-colored paper, colored pens and pencils, glitter glue, copies of current liturgical readings

Invite the students to imagine themselves as scribes. Show them pictures of illuminated manuscripts that feature decorated capital letters. The beauty of these works shows how highly the word of God is valued. Explain that in the Middle Ages scribes spent countless hours copying the Scriptures. Hand out copies of the coming week's liturgical readings. Invite each student to choose a one- or two-verse portion of one of the readings and write it on his or her parchment sheet. Then invite the student "scribes" to use colored pens or pencils to illuminate the initial capital letters of their chosen texts. The students might also use glitter glue to decorate their manuscripts. Display the manuscript pages in a prominent place.

Quick Check

✔ *What readings are included in the Liturgy of the Word?* (an Old Testament reading, a New Testament reading, a responsorial psalm, and a Gospel reading)

✔ *What do you hear in the homily?* (We hear a talk that helps us understand the readings and helps us grow as faithful followers of Jesus.)

WE RESPOND ___ minutes

Connect to Life Have the students work in small groups to choose a story from one of the gospels and act it out for the class. Suggestions might include the story of the lost sheep (Luke 15:4–7); the story of the good Samaritan (Luke 10:29–37) or the story of the Pharisee and the tax collector (Luke 18:9–14). After each group has presented its skit, invite the students to reflect privately on the *We Respond* question.

Pray Invite volunteers to pray intercessions similar to those at Mass. Invite all to respond *Lord, hear our prayer* after each intercession.

Plan Ahead for Day 3

Catechist Goal: To describe the words and actions of the Liturgy of the Eucharist

Preparation: Be prepared to discuss the ways our bodies are nourished.

Catechist Goal

- To describe the words and actions of the Liturgy of the Eucharist

Our Faith Response

- To identify and participate in the Liturgy of the Eucharist

Liturgy of the Eucharist
eucharistic prayer
consecration

Lesson Materials

- index cards

Teaching Tip

Liturgical Actions

During the Liturgy of the Eucharist, many actions are occurring. Point out and explain these actions. For example, there is the collection, the presentation of gifts, the washing of the priest's hands, the elevation of the Host during the eucharistic prayer, and the Great Amen.

During the Liturgy of the Eucharist, we offer gifts of bread and wine and receive the Body and Blood of Jesus Christ.

WE GATHER

✝ *Jesus, you give us the gift of yourself.*

There are many things that we would *like* to have in our lives. What are the things that we *need* to have in our lives?

____

____

____

WE BELIEVE

To grow and be strong, we need nourishment for our bodies. We also need to be nourished to live as Christians. In the Liturgy of the Word, we are nourished as we listen to God's living word. In the Liturgy of the Eucharist, we are nourished by the Body and Blood of Christ.

During the Liturgy of the Eucharist, we present the gifts of bread and wine. The eucharistic prayer is prayed, and the bread and wine become the Body and Blood of Christ. We receive Jesus in Holy Communion. We are united to Jesus and one another as the Body of Christ. The **Liturgy of the Eucharist** is the part of the Mass in which the death and Resurrection of Christ are made present again; our gifts of bread and wine become the Body and Blood of Christ, which we receive in Holy Communion.

Here is what happens during the Liturgy of the Eucharist:

- At the beginning of the Liturgy of the Eucharist, members of the assembly bring forward gifts of bread and wine. The gifts represent all the blessings God has given to us. At this time money and other offerings are also brought forward. This shows our concern for our parish and for those in need.
- The priest prays the eucharistic prayer in our name. The **eucharistic prayer** is the Church's greatest prayer of praise and thanksgiving to God. It joins us to Christ and one another.

148

Lesson Plan

WE GATHER

___ minutes

✝ **Pray** Invite the students to pray a silent prayer of thanks for the word of God. Then pray together the *We Gather* prayer.

Focus on Life Ask the students to consider the *We Gather* statement and question. Have volunteers name some things they would *like* to have. Encourage them to think about whether these things are essential to life and health or are just fun to have or fashionable. Then have the students write down things that they *need*. Tell the students that in this lesson they will learn that we are nourished by the Body and Blood of Christ.

WE BELIEVE

___ minutes

Read the Text Read aloud the *We Believe* statement. Then invite a volunteer to read the first two *We Believe* paragraphs. Write the word *nourish* on the board and ask volunteers to define it. Do the same with *nourishment*. Discuss with the students how their bodies are nourished. Explain that we need to nourish our faith life. Encourage the students to name ways they can do this.

Learn About the Liturgy of the Eucharist Read aloud the remaining *We Believe* text and chart. Have the students to compose three questions about the readings. Invite the students to work in pairs. Each partner should ask the other for answers to the questions. Circulate among the students to resolve any disputes or to clarify any answers.

- After the eucharistic prayer we pray the Lord's Prayer together. We call on God the Father to give us the things we need and to forgive us. As a sign of our love and unity, we offer one another a sign of peace. The priest then breaks the Host while we pray the "Lamb of God."
- Then the assembly comes forward to receive Holy Communion. We sing to show our joy and thankfulness. After we receive Holy Communion, we quietly thank God the Father for the gift of his Son. We ask the Holy Spirit to help us to act like Christ each day. Holy Communion makes the life of God in us stronger. It strengthens us to be Christ to one another.

Many important things happen during the eucharistic prayer:

- We honor God for all the wonderful things he has done for us. We join with the angels to give God praise.
- The priest asks the Holy Spirit to come upon our gifts of bread and wine and make them holy. Then he says and does what Jesus said and did at the Last Supper. The priest takes the bread and says, "This is my body." Taking the cup of wine, the priest says, "This is my blood." This part of the eucharistic prayer is called the **consecration**. By the power of the Holy Spirit and through the words and actions of the priest, the bread and wine become the Body and Blood of Christ. Jesus is truly present in the Eucharist. This is called the *real presence*.
- We proclaim the mystery of faith by calling to mind the death, Resurrection, and coming of the risen Lord in glory.
- We pray that the Holy Spirit will unite the Church in heaven and on earth. The eucharistic prayer ends with our great Amen. We are saying yes to the prayer the priest has prayed in our name. We remember the needs of the Church.

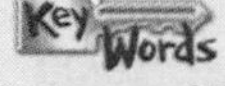

Liturgy of the Eucharist the part of the Mass in which the death and Resurrection of Christ are made present again; our gifts of bread and wine become the Body and Blood of Christ, which we receive in Holy Communion

eucharistic prayer the Church's greatest prayer of praise and thanksgiving to God

consecration the part of the eucharistic prayer when, by the power of the Holy Spirit and through the words and actions of the priest, the bread and wine become the Body and Blood of Christ

WE RESPOND

At Sunday Mass in your parish, what gifts are brought forward at the beginning of the Liturgy of the Eucharist? What do these gifts represent?

149

ACTIVITY BANK

Visit Parish Church

Plan a trip to a parish church, and invite the students to point out and explain anything that reminds them of the Liturgy of the Eucharist. Look for gospel stories or images of wheat, bread, grapes, or chalice in stained-glass windows and in posters or banners in the northax or vestibule. Ask the students where the Holy Eucharist is reserved in the church. (tabernacle)

Remember the Key Words Once again, encourage the students to write the *Key Words* and definitions from today's lesson on individual cards for future reference.

Quick Check

✔ *What gifts are offered during the Liturgy of the Eucharist?* (The gifts of bread and wine are offered.)

✔ *What is the Church's greatest prayer of praise and thanksgiving to God?* (The eucharistic prayer is the Church's greatest prayer of praise and thanksgiving.)

WE RESPOND

___ minutes

Connect to Life Have the students to answer the *We Respond* questions. Help them understand that the gifts of bread and wine were given to us as part of God's creation and that we offer them back to God in thanks.

Pray Then pray or sing together:
Christ has died,
Christ is risen,
Christ will come again.

Plan Ahead for Day 4

Catechist Goal: To present that at the end of Mass, we are sent out to live as Jesus' disciples

Preparation: Make copies of Reproducible Master 12.

Chapter 12 • **Day 4**

Catechist Goal

• To present that at the end of Mass, we are sent out to live as Jesus' disciples

Our Faith Response

• To name ways of living as disciples of Jesus

Lesson Materials

• copies of Reproducible Master 12

In the Concluding Rite we are sent to live as disciples of Jesus.

WE GATHER

✝ *Jesus, we listen to your words.*

Sometimes your parents or teachers say, "You didn't listen to me." How do they know that you did not listen? What do our *actions* have to do with *listening*?

WE BELIEVE

The final part of the Mass is the Concluding Rite. The priest blesses us in God's name. Once again we answer, "Amen." The deacon or priest's final words to the assembly are, "Go in peace to love and serve the Lord." He sends us out to do God's work every day.

We usually sing a final hymn before we leave the church.

Think about the situations pictured. Then write how you could love and serve the Lord in each situation.

150

Teaching Tip

Singing Together

Do not take a lot of time when teaching the songs in the *We Believe* text. Play the CD song track twice. The first time, have the students read the words silently as they listen; the second time, have the students join in the singing.

Lesson Plan

WE GATHER ___ minutes

✝ **Pray** Pray the Sign of the Cross and the *We Gather* prayer.

Focus on Life Read aloud the *We Gather* questions. You may want to share your own experiences to begin the discussion. Then invite volunteers to share experiences when *not* listening caused problems. Also, ask volunteers to tell about times when listening *well* produced positive results. Tell the students that in this lesson they will learn about being sent to love and serve the Lord.

WE BELIEVE ___ minutes

Learn About the Concluding Rite Invite a student to read aloud the *We Believe* statement. Then explain that in today's lesson the students will learn about living according to the words they have heard.

Invite volunteers to read the first two *We Believe* paragraphs. Explain that *concluding* refers to "the end," and that the Concluding Rite ends the Mass. Select another student to go to the board and write the deacons or priest's final words to the assembly (Go in peace to love and serve the Lord). Point out how these words encourage us to go and do God's work.

Do the Activities Guide the students to the first *We Believe* activity. Invite volunteers to describe each situation. Clarify what is happening in each case. Have the students write a way that they could show love in each situation. Then extend the activity. Have the students illustrate on page 151 one way they can love and serve God this week.

Now illustrate a way you will love and serve God this week.

WE RESPOND

Take the Word of God with You

Take the word of God with you as you go.

Take the seeds of God's word and make them grow.

Go in peace to serve the world, in peace to serve the world.

Take the love of God, the love of God with you as you go.

Today, what will you do to try to make the world a better place?

At the end of Mass, we are sent out to live as the Body of Christ. We try to be signs of God's love and presence in the world.

We leave the Eucharist filled with grace and peace. We have been nourished by God's word and by the Body and Blood of Christ. We have been united with Christ and with one another. We have been strengthened to perform Works of Mercy for others.

We act as disciples of Jesus. We share our gifts, our talents, and our time with others. We work for peace and justice in our homes, our schools, and our neighborhoods. We try to make the world a better place.

151

ACTIVITY BANK

Community

Stewardship

Activity Materials: materials to make bird feeders (for example, pinecones, peanut butter, and birdseed)

In bringing offerings of bread and wine in the Liturgy of the Eucharist, we acknowledge God as creator of all things good and thank him for his creation. Invite the students to consider ways that they can serve as stewards of God's creation. One way they can do this is by setting up a bird feeder, stocking it regularly with birdseed, and supplying fresh water. This project shows an appreciation of creation, kindness motivated by God's love, and a desire for service. Invite the students to make bird feeders by covering pinecones with peanut butter and then rolling the coated pinecones in birdseed. Encourage the students to hang their birdfeeder in a tree at home or near the school. Remind them that caring for creation is one way we show our thanks to God.

Learn How the Eucharist Motivates Have volunteers read the last two *We Believe* paragraphs. Discuss ways that the Eucharist can strengthen and help us to become better disciples of Christ.

Review Main Ideas Distribute copies of Reproducible Master 12 and read the directions aloud. (Answers: Introductory Rites, Liturgy of the Eucharist, Concluding Rite, Liturgy of the Word, Gospel; order: 1 Introductory Rites, 2 Litury of the Word, 3 Liturgy of the Eucharist, 4 Concluding Rite)

Quick Check

✔ *What are the deacon or priest's words as he sends us out to do God's work?* (Go in peace to love and serve the Lord.)

✔ *How can we act as disciples of Christ?* (Answers will vary.)

WE RESPOND ___ minutes

Connect to Life Play "Take the Word of God with You," from the Grade 4 CD. Read and discuss the lyrics. Sing the song together.

Pray Invite a volunteer read the *We Respond* question. Have the students quietly reflect on their responses.

Plan Ahead for Day 5

Catechist Goal: To review chapter ideas and their relationship to our faith life

Preparation: Make copies of Chapter 12 Test in the Grade 4 Assessment Book (option).

Catechist Goal

- To review chapter ideas and their relationship to our faith life

Our Faith Response

- To apply what has been learned to our lives

Lesson Materials

- index cards

CHAPTER TEST

The Chapter 12 Test is provided in the Grade 4 Assessment Book.

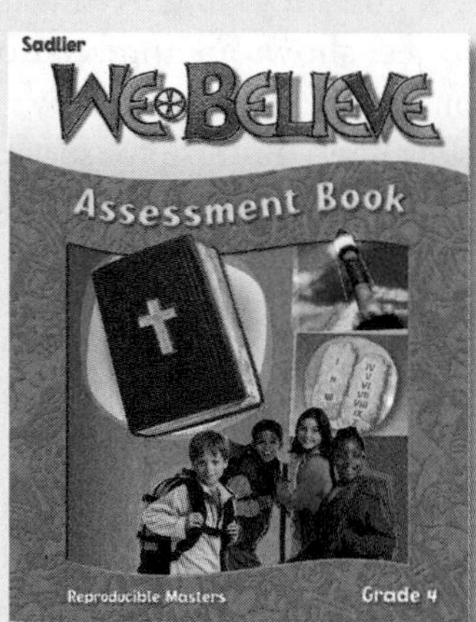

Circle the correct answer.

1. The part of the eucharistic prayer when the bread and wine become the Body and Blood of Christ is called the ______.

   creed (consecration) song

2. The ______ offers thanks and praise to God throughout the Mass.

   homily (assembly) Bible

3. The Introductory Rites, the Liturgy of the Word, the Liturgy of the Eucharist, and the Concluding Rite are the four parts of the ______.

   Gloria (Mass) Bible

4. We hear about the words and actions of Jesus during his ministry when the ______ is proclaimed.

   (gospel) psalm creed

Write True or False for the following sentences. Then change the false sentences to make them true.

5. True Jesus is truly present in the Eucharist.

6. False The creed and the general intercessions are part of the Introductory Rites.

   The creed and the general intercessions are part of the Liturgy of the Word

7. True God speaks to us through the words of the Bible.

8. False The first two readings at Mass are taken from the Book of the Gospels.

   The first two readings at Mass are read from the Lectionary.

Complete the following:

9–10. The eucharistic prayer is See pages 148–149.

Work with your classmates to make a list of frequently asked questions about the celebration of the Mass. Then individually answer the questions.

152

Lesson Plan

___ minutes

Chapter Review Have the students complete questions 1–4. Then invite the students to read aloud the completed statements. Use this opportunity to reinforce a correct response or clarify any misunderstanding. Next, ask the students to complete the true/false questions, 5–8. Remind the students to rewrite the false statements to make them true. Then invite volunteers to read each statement, correcting false statements as necessary. Finally, have the students complete question 9–10.

Assessment Activity Read aloud the activity directions. Then form small groups and allow enough time for the groups to make their lists of frequently asked questions. Have someone from each group share the group's questions. Invite responses.

___ minutes

Reflect & Pray Read aloud the introduction and ask the students to write their responses. Remind the students that we always want to act so that others can see that Christ lives in us.

Key Words Write each of the *Key Words* or phrases on an index card and shuffle the cards. Invite a volunteer to select a card at random and then read the card aloud and give a definition in his or her own words. The students may decide by a show of hands if they agree. If the definition is incorrect, ask a volunteer to correct it. The students may refer to the *Key Words* box in the appropriate lesson to check the answers. Write the correct definitions on the board.

We Respond in Faith

Reflect & Pray

When we leave the church after Mass, how can we act to show that Christ lives in us?

______________________________.

Jesus, always keep me close to you.

Key Words

Mass (p. 145)
assembly (p. 145)
Liturgy of the Word (p. 147)
homily (p. 147)
Liturgy of the Eucharist (p. 149)
eucharistic prayer (p. 149)
consecration (p. 149)

Remember

- The Introductory Rites unite us and prepare us for worship.
- During the Liturgy of the Word, we hear the word of God.
- During the Liturgy of the Eucharist, we offer gifts of bread and wine and receive the Body and Blood of Jesus Christ.
- In the Concluding Rite we are sent to live as disciples of Jesus.

Our Catholic Life

Adoration of the Blessed Sacrament

During and after Mass, Catholics honor Jesus' real presence in the Eucharist. After Holy Communion, the remaining consecrated Hosts are put in a special place in the Church called the *tabernacle*. The Eucharist in the tabernacle is known as the *Blessed Sacrament*. The Blessed Sacrament is taken as Holy Communion to people who are dying and to those who are sick.

We adore Jesus in the Blessed Sacrament. We can visit the Blessed Sacrament to show our love and devotion to Jesus. We pray before the Blessed Sacrament alone or as a community at devotional prayers and solemn processions.

Home Connection

Sharing Faith with My Family

Remember to send home the family page (text page 154) with each student.

Here are the directions for the completed "Putting God First" game:

- Determine the order of play.
- Have players place their game markers (pennies, buttons, or checkers) on the board.
- Use dice or make a spinner to determine the players' moves around the board.

For additional information and activities, encourage families to visit Sadlier's

www.WEBELIEVEweb.com

Remember Read aloud the four statements. Form the class into four groups, one for each statement. Ask each group to select a student to list the points the group decides are most essential about its statement. Tell the students they may refer to their books. When all groups have finished, invite the scribes to share each group's work. Clarify or reinforce the responses as necessary.

Our Catholic Life Read the text aloud. Encourage the students to show their love for Jesus by visiting the Blessed Sacrament. If possible, take the students on a visit. Encourage an attitude of quiet adoration as they pray silently to thank Jesus for his presence. Afterward, invite the students to share how they feel, knowing that Christ himself is present with them. Encourage them to visit the Blessed Sacrament often.

Chapter 12 Grade 4

SHARING FAITH with My Family

Sharing What I Learned

Discuss the following with your family:

- the Introductory Rites
- the Liturgy of the Word
- the Liturgy of the Eucharist
- the Concluding Rite.

Putting God First

"Putting God First" is a game that tests your knowledge of Unit 2. Connect all the game board pieces from Chapters 8–12. Give each family member a button or bean. Take turns throwing a number marker to count squares to play the game. If someone gets a right answer to a question, he or she gets another throw. Enjoy as everyone puts God first!

A Family Prayer

Lead your family in this prayer.

Soul of Christ, sanctify me.
Body of Christ, heal me.
Blood of Christ, drench me.
Water from the side of Christ, wash me.
Passion of Christ, strengthen me.

(from *Catholic Household Blessing and Prayers*)

Visit Sadlier's www.WEBELIEVEweb.com

Connect to the Catechism
For adult background and reflection, see paragraphs 1348, 1349, 1355, and 1397.

154

PUPIL PAGE 154

Chapter 13 Advent

Advent | Christmas | Ordinary Time | Lent | Triduum | Easter | Ordinary Time

Advent

Advent has a twofold character: as a season to prepare for Christmas when Christ's first coming to us is remembered; as a season when that remembrance directs the mind and heart to await Christ's Second Coming at the end of time.

(Norms Governing Liturgical Calendars, 39)

Overview

In this chapter the students will learn that in Advent we prepare for the coming of the Lord.

For Adult Reading and Reflection
You may want to refer to paragraphs 524 and 671 of the *Catechism of the Catholic Church*.

Catechist Background

What do you need this Advent seaon?

The season of Advent begins with somber reflection on the end time when Christ will come again and the reign of God will be fulfilled. The season culminates with our joyful celebration of Christ's coming in history as the Word made flesh. Like the ancient Hebrew prophets, we proclaim and practice a joyful anticipation of the coming of the Day of the Lord.

"When the Church celebrates the liturgy of Advent each year, she makes present this ancient expectancy of the Messiah, for by sharing in the long preparation for the Savior's first coming, the faithful renew their ardent desire for his second coming" (*CCC* 524). The liturgical readings of the season look forward to the day when "the wolf shall be a guest of the lamb, and the leopard shall lie down with the kid" (Isaiah 11:6a), and God's peace will reign on the earth.

In many parts of the world, the annual celebration of the sister seasons of Advent and Christmas occur in the darkness of winter when the world is most in need of hope and light. The Church prays fervently with Isaiah, "O house of Jacob, come let us walk in the light of the Lord!" (2:5).

Although Christ's reign is already present in the Church, it has yet to be fulfilled "with power and great glory" at the second coming. "That is why Christians pray, above all in the Eucharist, to hasten Christ's return by saying to him: "*Marana tha*! 'Our Lord, come!'" (CCC 671).

How will you be a sign of Christ's reign in your life?

Lesson Planning Guide

Lesson Focus	Presentation	Materials
Day 1		
Guide page 155C **Text page 155** **Introduce the Season**	• Read the *Chapter Story*. • Introduce the Advent season. • Proclaim the words on the banner.	
Day 2		
Guide and Text pages 156–157 **We Gather** **We Believe**	• Discuss in the **We Gather** question. • Read and discuss the meaning of Advent and the comings of Christ in the **We Believe** text. Plan an Advent play and act it out.	• colored chalk
Day 3		
Guide and Text page 158 **We Respond**	• Read about the appearance of Our Lady of Guadalupe to Saint Juan Diego. • Reflect on ways to imitate Mary in **We Respond**.	
Day 4		
Guide and Text page 159 **We Respond in Prayer**	Respond in song. • Listen to Scripture and respond in prayer.	• prayer space items: Advent wreath and candles, image of Our Lady of Guadalupe, purple tablecloth "Somos el Cuerpo de Cristo/We Are the Body of Christ," Jaime Cortez, #14 Grade 4 CD
Day 5		
Guide and Text pages 160A–160B **We Respond in Faith**	• Explain the individual Advent project. • Explain the Advent group project. • Discuss the **Sharing Faith with My Family** page.	• copies of Reproducible Master 13, guide page 160A • scissors, markers

For additional ideas, activities, and opportunities: Visit Sadlier's **www.WEBELIEVEweb.com**

Focus on Life

Chapter Story

Christmas was still weeks away, but Mark and Alicia Lee were already letting their parents know what what they wanted for Christmas. "There's just one thing I absolutely have to have," said Mark, pointing to a magazine ad for a skateboard. "All my friends are getting these for Christmas." His sister, Alicia, put in her request for a new video game. "It was designed especially for girls like me," she remarked. Their parents sighed and went on preparing for dinner.

At the dinner table Mr. Lee put down his fork and said he had some surprising news. "This Christmas we going to have some cousins from Bejing visit with us."

"When will we get to meet them? " Alicia asked. "Sooner than you think," her mother replied. Then Mrs. Lee told the Mark and Alicia that their cousins had counted on staying with friends until they got settled in an apartment. But now the friends had lost their jobs and the whole plan has fallen through. "So," their mother paused for a moment, "your father and I invited them to stay with us!" Mr. Lee added, "I know you realize that each of us will have to make some real adjustments. Our cousins will be staying until after Christmas and we must provide for their needs. That means fewer presents and you will have to share your rooms with your cousins."

Mark and Alicia looked at each other. They realized that skateboards and video games would be out of the question this year. But they also realized that their parents were counting on them.

"No problem, Dad," Mark replied. "Alicia and I can store our extra stuff in the garage and there will be plenty of room." His sister grinned and added, "That's for sure. Besides, we don't want to be like that innkeeper in Bethlehem."

▶ *What was the meaning of Alicia's comment about the innkeeper in Bethlehem? If you were Mark or Alicia, how do you think you would have responded to your father's surprising news? Why?*

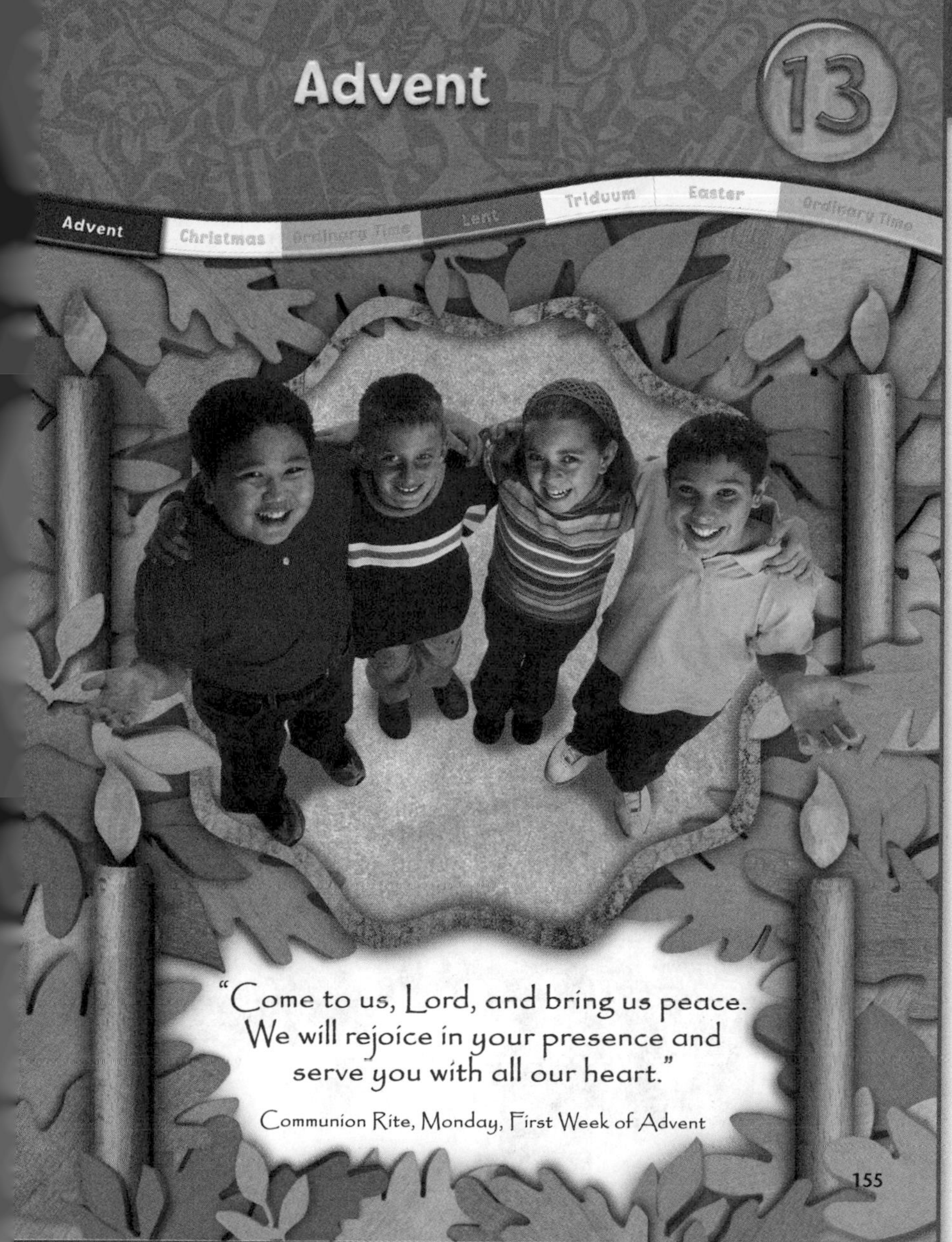

Advent
13
Advent
Christmas
Ordinary Time
Lent
Triduum
Easter
Ordinary Time
"Come to us, Lord, and bring us peace.
We will rejoice in your presence and
serve you with all our heart."
Communion Rite, Monday, First Week of Advent
155

Catechist Goal

- To emphasize that in Advent we prepare for the coming of the Lord

Our Faith Response

- To offer our Advent prayers with Mary in preparing for the coming of Jesus

ADDITIONAL RESOURCES

Videos *Advent with Saint Nicholas: Customs from Around the World,* Twenty-Third Publications, 2000. Saint Nicholas helps Holly learn about various Advent customs. (12 minutes)

The First Christmas, Billy Budd Films, Inc., 1998. This video uses clay animation to tell the story of the birth of Jesus. (21 minutes)

To find more ideas for books, videos, and other learning material, visit Sadlier's

www.WEBELIEVEweb.com

Lesson Plan

Introduce the Season ___ minutes

• **Pray** the Sign of the Cross and the prayer "Come to us, Lord, and bring us peace."

• **Read** Have a student read aloud the *Chapter Story* on guide page 155C. Discuss the students' responses to the accompanying questions. Stress the importance of sharing what we have with others and adjusting our expectations.

• **Have** the students read aloud the chapter title. Explain: *Advent is the first season of the Church year. During Advent we prepare for the coming of the Lord.*

• **Invite** the students to look at and discuss the photo. Ask: *What reminds you about getting ready to celebrate the birth of Jesus?* Invite volunteers to share some family preparations made during Advent.

• **Proclaim** together the words on the banner under the photo.

Lesson Materials
- colored chalk
- Grade 4 CD
- copies of Reproducible Master 13
- markers and scissors

Teaching Tip
Empathetic Teachers

Veteran teachers often list empathy as a vitally important quality of successful teachers. When the teacher is able to identify with the students' difficulties, rather than resenting or ignoring them, stress is reduced and learning is enhanced. The empathetic teacher gives positive feedback to all students. He or she is not easily angered or depressed. Relying on the Holy Spirit's guidance, he or she recognizes the Spirit's presence in each child.

In Advent we prepare for the coming of the Lord.

WE GATHER

✠ *Mary, help us to prepare for the coming of Jesus.*

What are some things you anticipate, or look forward to, with excitement?

WE BELIEVE

The season of Advent is a time of preparation. It is a season of joyful hope and anticipation. During the four weeks of Advent we prepare ourselves for the coming of the Lord. In fact, the word *Advent* means "coming."

During the season of Advent, we hope for Christ's coming in the future, and we prepare by being his faithful followers today. We celebrate that Jesus is with us today, and we prepare to celebrate that he first came to us over two thousand years ago in Bethlehem.

We begin Advent by praying for Jesus Christ to come again at the end of time. We know that Jesus will return because he told us that he would. We do not know exactly when Christ will come again. Yet as people of faith, we trust that he will. We do know that Jesus wants us to be ready. He wants us to prepare by living a life that shows that we are his disciples. When Jesus comes again, he will comfort his people: "He will wipe every tear from their eyes" (Revelation 21:4). He will come to bring us into his kingdom of peace, joy, and love. We get ready by following the commandments and following Jesus' teachings. We prepare our hearts.

156

Lesson Plan

WE GATHER ___ minutes

Focus on Life Have the students respond to *We Gather* question. Have a volunteer list student responses on the board in colored chalk. Explain to the students that today's lesson describes a very different kind of anticipation in which the entire Church takes part.

WE BELIEVE ___ minutes

• **Read** aloud the *We Believe* statement. Ask the students what they think "coming of the Lord" refers to. Listen to their ideas.

• **Have** the students work with partners reading and underlining important ideas in the text on pages 156–157. Call on the partners to share their ideas. Emphaszie the following:

- We celebrate Jesus' first coming.
- We celebrate Jesus' coming and being with us today.
- We prepare for Christ's final coming in the future by living as his disciples.

• **Remind** the student that Jesus is always with us, especially in his eucharistic presence. It is with Mary and the entire Church that we anticipate and wait for the coming of the Savior, Jesus Christ.

In Advent we celebrate more than the future coming of Jesus. We also celebrate his coming in our world and his presence in the world today. When we pray, "Come, Lord Jesus" with the Church during Advent, we pray knowing that Jesus is always with us. Jesus tells us, "For where two or three are gathered together in my name, there am I in the midst of them" (Matthew 18:20). Jesus comes to us every day in the celebration of the Eucharist, in all the sacraments, and in the love we have for one another.

In our world today many people are hungry or homeless. Many people are suffering from war and disease. When we pray, "Come, Lord Jesus," we pray that Jesus will come to those who need him most, and to us that we may share his love with others.

As Advent comes to an end, we focus our waiting and preparing on Jesus' first coming. We prepare as Mary prepared for the birth of her Son. We share her anticipation as we wait for the coming of the Savior.

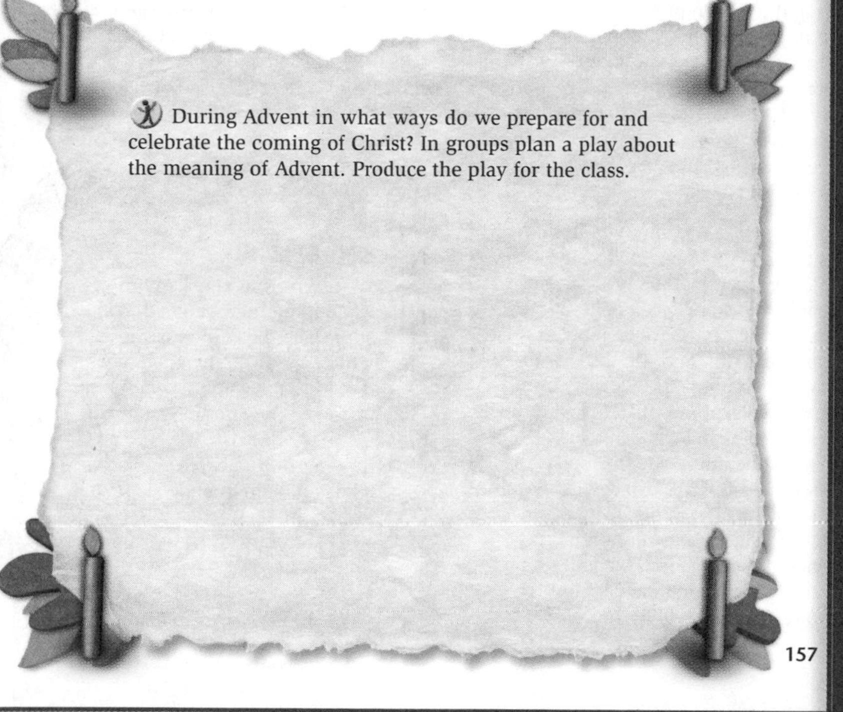

During Advent in what ways do we prepare for and celebrate the coming of Christ? In groups plan a play about the meaning of Advent. Produce the play for the class.

Activity Bank

Liturgy

Feast of the Immaculate Conception

Activity Materials: Bible

The feast of the Immaculate Conception of the Virgin Mary is celebrated on December 8. Explain that this holy day of obligation honors Mary because she was born free from sin. Long before Mary was conceived by her parents, God had already prepared her to become the mother of our Savior. Have a student proclaim Luke 1:26-32, 34-35, 38. Invite responses on what this gospel reading reveals about Mary. Encourage the students to imitate Mary's desire to do whatever God wants.

Read aloud the directions on page 157 for producing a play. Encourage the groups to be creative in their scripts. If there is time, have groups present their plays.

Quick Check

✔ *What do we prepare for during Advent?* (We prepare for the coming of the Lord in the future by being faithful followers.)

✔ *As Advent ends, what do we prepare for?* (We prepare for our celebration of Jesus' first coming as our Savior.)

CONNECTION

Multicultural Connection

Our Lady of Guadalupe

Explain that Our Lady of Guadalupe is the Patroness of the Americas. The people of both North and South America honor her in a special way and ask for her prayers. We know that she especially cares for those who are poor and oppressed. The scriptural readings of the Advent season are filled with humanity's longing for the fulfillment of God's reign of peace and justice. Mary's appearance to Juan Diego reminds us that we are all brothers and sisters in her son, Jesus Christ. On the feast day of Our Lady of Guadalupe (December 12), people gather for Mass. Often they join in procession into their parish church in honor of Mary, Mother of our Savior.

Statue of Saint Juan Diego and Our Lady of Guadalupe

During the season of Advent we have feast days that help us prepare for Christ's coming. These two Advent feasts are related. On December 12 we honor Mary as Our Lady of Guadalupe, the patroness of the Americas. On December 9 we remember Saint Juan Diego, to whom Our Lady of Guadalupe appeared.

Juan Diego was a farmer who lived outside of a city known today as Mexico City. There were not many Christians in this area, but Juan Diego believed in Christ. Every day he walked fifteen miles to participate in Mass. On his way to Mass the morning of December 9, 1531, Juan passed Tepeyac Hill. He heard music and saw a glowing cloud. When he got to the top of the hill, a young woman dressed like an Aztec princess was there. She spoke to Juan in his own language and said that she was the Virgin Mary. She asked that a church be built on the hill so that she could give her love, compassion, and help to the people.

Juan went to the bishop with this news. The bishop kindly listened to Juan, but could not believe that this really happened. Then on December 12 the Virgin Mary appeared to Juan again as the Aztec Lady. She told him to climb the hill where they had met. When he did, Juan found flowers growing in the frozen soil. They were roses which did not even grow in Mexico. He gathered them in his cloak and went at once to the bishop. When Juan opened his cloak the flowers fell to the ground. And on the inside of Juan's cloak was a glowing image of the Lady. She became known as Our Lady of Guadalupe.

Soon after, a church was built on this hill where our Lady had appeared. Since that time a special devotion to Mary as Our Lady of Guadalupe has grown, and millions of Native Mexicans have been baptized as followers of her son, Jesus Christ.

WE RESPOND

We learn from Our Lady of Guadalupe that we need to appreciate the culture of those to whom we bring the good news. If it were not for Mary, millions of people may not have known the love of Christ. We, too, need to understand people so that we can help them to understand and know Christ. What is one way you can follow Mary's example this week?

158

Lesson Plan

WE BELIEVE (continued) ___ minutes

• **Celebrate** the fact that during Advent we remember Saint Juan Diego on December 9 and on December 12 we honor Mary as Our Lady of Guadalupe. Read aloud the remaining *We Believe* text. Stress that Mary's appearance to Juan Diego is of special significance to the people of Mexico.

WE RESPOND ___ minutes

Connect to Life Use the *We Respond* paragraph to connect the example of Our Lady of Guadalupe with our daily lives as followers of Christ. Point out that Mary's appearance to Juan Diego revealed her love and respect for the Native Mexicans. Let students know that we will explore ways of following Mary's example in another lesson. Ask a volunteer to read *We Respond* text aloud. Give the students a few minutes to reflect on ways they can follow Mary's example. (We can respect everyone we meet.)

• **Pray** Gather in the prayer space, with the Advent wreath. Offer the following prayer:

May this wreath remind us that Jesus
is ever coming into our lives, and his love
for us has no end. Amen.

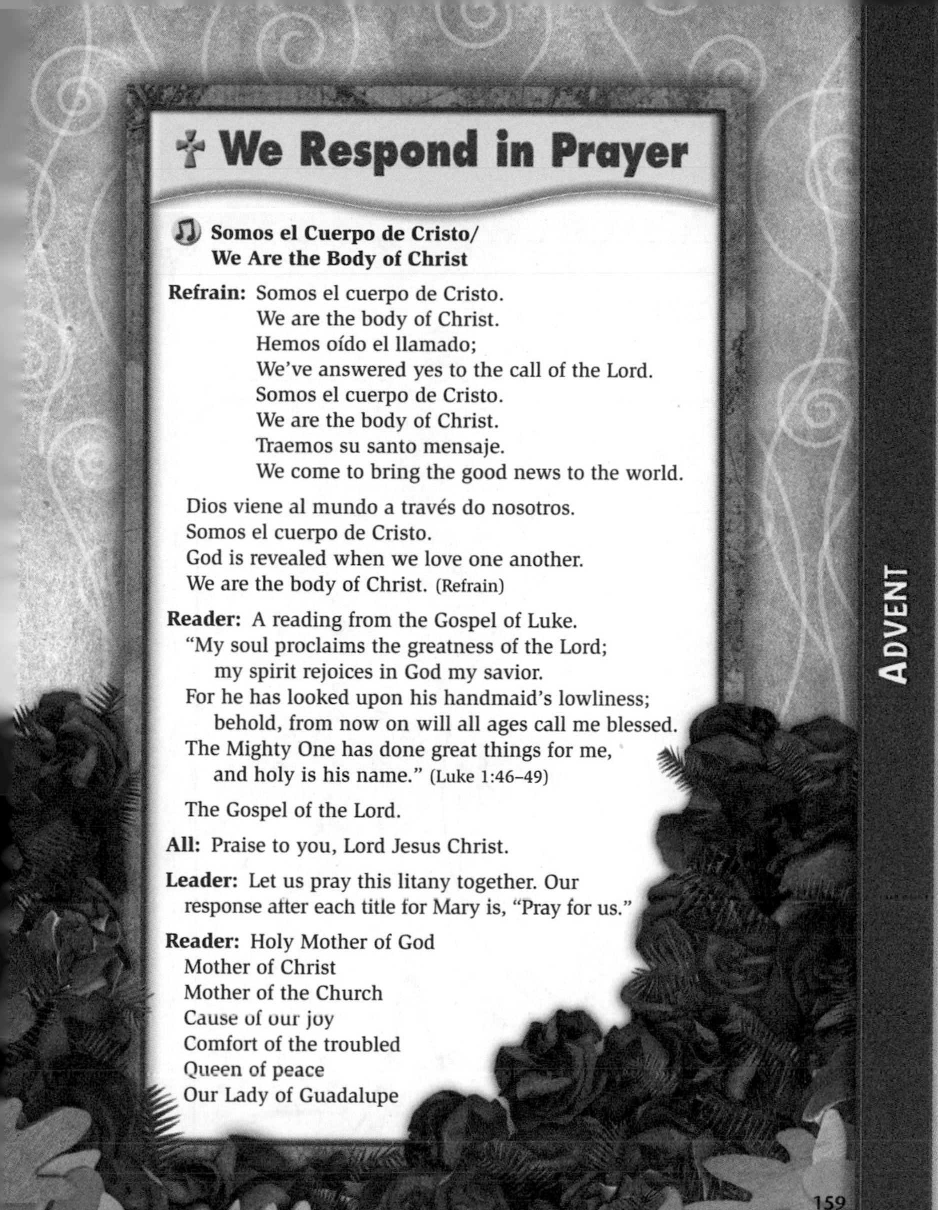

We Respond in Prayer
Somos el Cuerpo de Cristo/ We Are the Body of Christ
Refrain: Somos el cuerpo de Cristo.
We are the body of Christ.
Hemos oído el llamado;
We've answered yes to the call of the Lord.
Somos el cuerpo de Cristo.
We are the body of Christ.
Traemos su santo mensaje.
We come to bring the good news to the world.
Dios viene al mundo a través do nosotros.
Somos el cuerpo de Cristo.
God is revealed when we love one another.
We are the body of Christ. (Refrain)
Reader: A reading from the Gospel of Luke.
"My soul proclaims the greatness of the Lord;
my spirit rejoices in God my savior.
For he has looked upon his handmaid's lowliness;
behold, from now on will all ages call me blessed.
The Mighty One has done great things for me,
and holy is his name." (Luke 1:46–49)
The Gospel of the Lord.
All: Praise to you, Lord Jesus Christ.
Leader: Let us pray this litany together. Our response after each title for Mary is, "Pray for us."
Reader: Holy Mother of God
Mother of Christ
Mother of the Church
Cause of our joy
Comfort of the troubled
Queen of peace
Our Lady of Guadalupe
159
ADVENT

Preparing to Pray

The students will open with a song in both Spanish and English. They will listen to a reading from Scripture and respond with a litany in honor of Mary.

- Assume the role of prayer leader.
- Choose a reader to proclaim both the Scripture and the litany.
- Practice the song and the response after each title for Mary.

The Prayer Space

- Have an Advent wreath with four candles; statue or picture of our Lady of Guadalupe; purple table covering

This Week's Liturgy

Visit **www.webelieveweb.com** for this week's liturgical readings and other seasonal material.

We Respond in Prayer ___ minutes

- **Pray** the Sign of the Cross.
- **Sing** the song, "Somos el Cuerpo de Cristo/ We Are the Body of Christ" on the Grade 4 CD.
- **Have** the reader proclaim the Scripture.
- **Conclude** with the litany in honor of Mary.

Name ____

Make this Advent sign to put on one of your doorknobs at home.

Come, Lord Jesus!

We Respond in Faith

Individual Project

Distribute copies of Reproducible Master 13, scissors, and markers. Explain that the students will decorate the door hangers to remind them that Jesus is the reason that we celebrate the season of Christmas. Call on volunteers to share ideas about where to hang the completed project.

Group Project

Display a long stretch of butcher paper across the board. Have the students work with partners on the Advent prayer board. Distribute markers and assign partners to one of the following tasks:

• Copy the first petition of the prayer on page 155, "Come to us Lord, and bring us peace," and illustrate it on the first panel of the prayer board.

• Copy the first half of the second petition, "We will rejoice in your presence," and illustrate it on the second panel.

• Copy the last part of the prayer, "and serve you with all our heart," and illustrate it on the third part.

• When finished, display the students' work in a prominent place in the school or parish hall.

Home Connection

Sharing Faith with My Family

Make sure to send home the family page (text page 160).

Encourage the students to share "A Family Prayer for Advent" and use it as a grace before meals.

For additional information and activities, encourage families to visit Sadlier's

www.WEBELIEVEweb.com

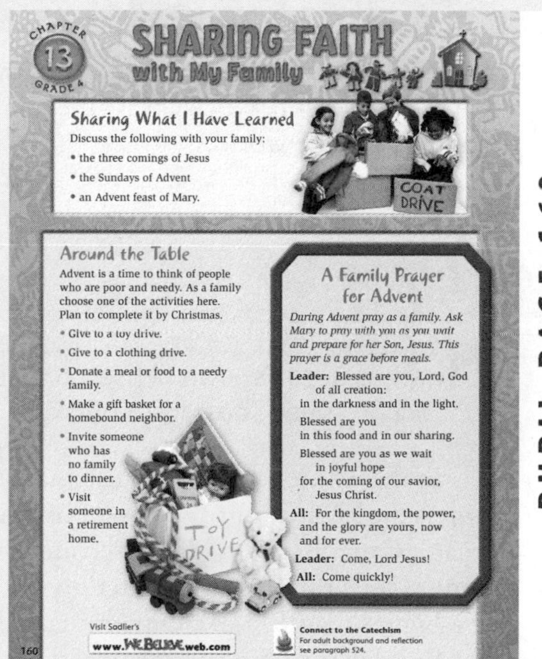

Chapter 13 Grade 4

SHARING FAITH with My Family

Sharing What I Have Learned

Discuss the following with your family:

- the three comings of Jesus
- the Sundays of Advent
- an Advent feast of Mary.

Around the Table

Advent is a time to think of people who are poor and needy. As a family choose one of the activities here. Plan to complete it by Christmas.

- Give to a toy drive.
- Give to a clothing drive.
- Donate a meal or food to a needy family.
- Make a gift basket for a homebound neighbor.
- Invite someone who has no family to dinner.
- Visit someone in a retirement home.

A Family Prayer for Advent

During Advent pray as a family. Ask Mary to pray with you as you wait and prepare for her Son, Jesus. This prayer is a grace before meals.

Leader: Blessed are you, Lord, God of all creation:
in the darkness and in the light.
Blessed are you
in this food and in our sharing.
Blessed are you as we wait in joyful hope
for the coming of our savior, Jesus Christ.

All: For the kingdom, the power, and the glory are yours, now and for ever.

Leader: Come, Lord Jesus!

All: Come quickly!

Visit Sadlier's www.WEBELIEVEweb.com

Connect to the Catechism
For adult background and reflection see paragraph 524.

160

PUPIL PAGE 160

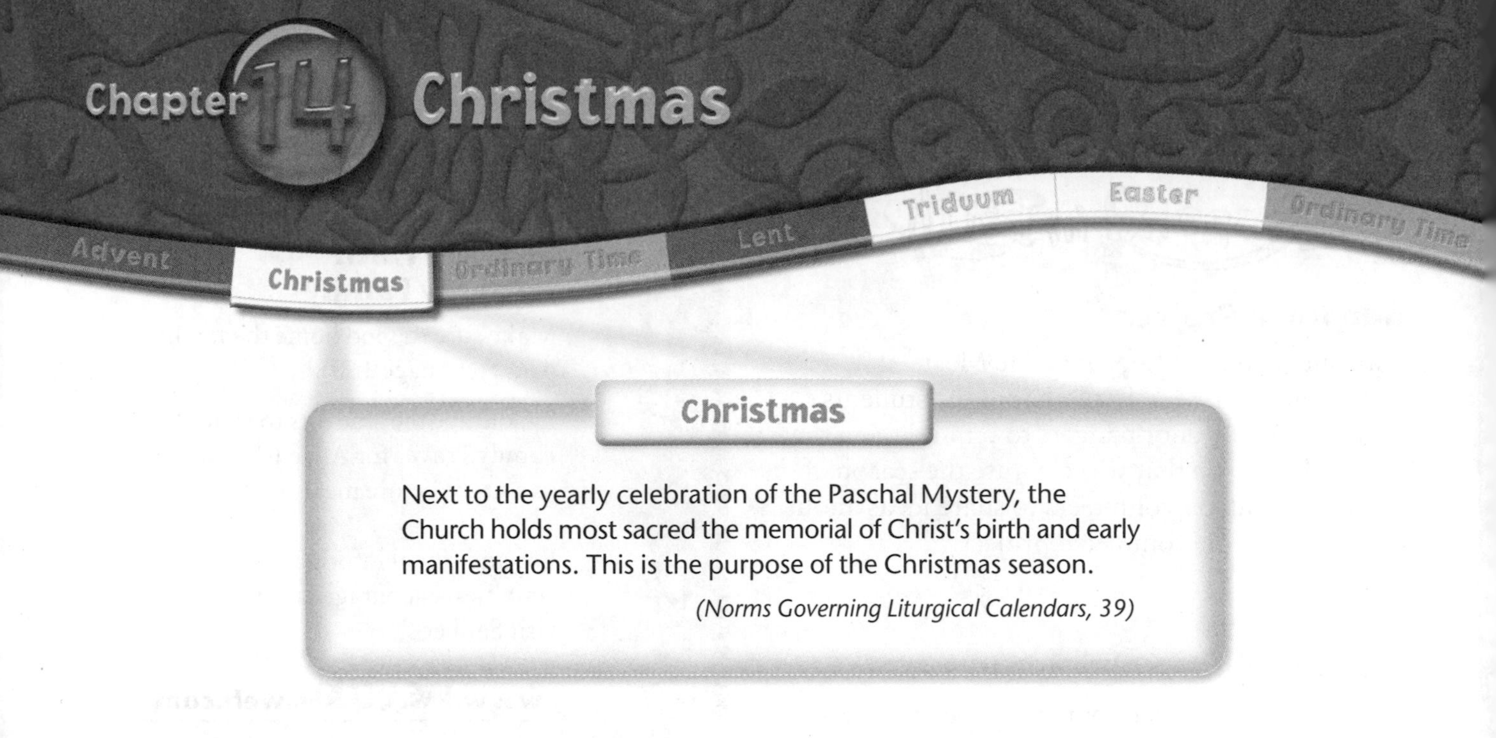

Christmas

Next to the yearly celebration of the Paschal Mystery, the Church holds most sacred the memorial of Christ's birth and early manifestations. This is the purpose of the Christmas season.

(Norms Governing Liturgical Calendars, 39)

Overview

In this chapter the students will learn that during the Christmas season, we celebrate the Son of God's coming into the world.

For Adult Reading and Reflection
You may want to refer to paragraphs 457 and 528 of the *Catechism of the Catholic Church*.

Catechist Background

How has Jesus shown himself to you in the Christmas seasons of your life?

In the Church year, the Christmas season "celebrates the birth of our Lord and His epiphanies (magi, Cana, Baptism). [It is] second only to the annual celebration of the Easter mystery" [2](*Sharing the Light of Faith*, 144). Our annual celebration of the Word made flesh commemorates the beginning of our redemption. Out of love for humanity, the Father sent the Son as the Savior of the world.

By his Incarnation, the Son of God made us sharers in his divinity. "For the Son of God became man so that we might become God" (*CCC* 460). It is this oneness between God and people, this reconciliation with the Father effected by the Son, that lies at the heart of our celebration of the Christmas season.

At the Epiphany, the Church celebrates the manifestation of the Son of God as the Savior and Messiah. The adoration by the magi from the East represents the welcoming of the good news of salvation by all nations. All who seek as they did the "messianic light of the star of David" will receive from the Jews the "messianic promise of the Old Testament" (*CCC* 528).

As he was manifested to the magi, the Son of God was also manifested to the world at his Baptism. The Holy Spirit came upon him and a voice from heaven proclaimed him "my beloved Son" (Matthew 3:17).

At the third of his epiphanies, Jesus Christ was manifested as the Son of God at the wedding feast at Cana. Transforming the water into choice wine, Jesus "revealed his glory, and his disciples began to believe in him" (John 2:11).

How will you witness to others the true meaning of this Christmas season in your home or at work?

Lesson Planning Guide

Lesson Focus	Presentation	Materials
Day 1		
Guide page 161C **Guide and Text page 161** **Introduce the Season**	• Read the *Chapter Story*. • Introduce the Christmas season. • Proclaim the words on the banner.	• parish hymnal
Day 2		
Guide and Text pages 162–163 **We Gather** **We Believe** *Matthew 2:1–12*	• Discuss what people share in common for **We Gather**. • Read the **We Believe** text. • Dramatize Scripture story.	• props: large foil-covered star and dowel; fabric pieces for headdresses and costumes; drums, maracas and bells (option)
Day 3		
Guide and Text page 164 **We Respond**	Read and discusss the special ways people celebrate the feast of the Epiphany in **We Respond**.	
Day 4		
Guide and Text page 165 **We Respond in Prayer**	• Listen to Scripture. Respond in song.	• prayer space items: manger scene with magi; gold foil crown; white table covering "Praise Him with Cymbals," Janet Vogt, #15, Grade 4 CD • paper cutouts of light symbols
Day 5		
Guide pages 166A–166B **We Respond in Faith**	• Explain the individual Christmas project. • Explain the Christmas group project. • Discuss **Sharing Faith with My Family** page.	• copies of Reproducible Master 14, guide page 166A

For additional ideas, activities, and opportunities: Visit Sadlier's **www.WE BELIEVE web.com**

Focus on Life

Chapter Story

The students were restless after lunch. So Mrs. Perez decided to tell a story she called "The Most Dangerous Carol of All."

In sixteenth-century England Catholics were not allowed to practice their faith. If they were caught learning about their religion, they were imprisoned or even put to death. To make sure that young Catholics could learn the basics of their faith, two Jesuit priests had a brilliant idea. They composed a carol called "The Twelve Days of Christmas." For each of the twelve days from Christmas to Epiphany, the composers devised a code for a basic truth of the Catholic faith. "On the first day of Christmas," the song began, "my true love gave to me." When English Catholics heard those words, they knew that God was speaking to them. They were God's true love. The first gift, "a partridge in a pear tree," was the most important. It meant Jesus Christ the King, reigning from the cross.

The "two turtle doves" represented the Old and New Testaments. The "three French hens" meant the three gifts of the magi. The "four calling birds" symbolized the four gospels. The "five golden rings" represented the first five books of the Bible, and the "six geese-a-laying" equaled the six precepts of the Church. The "seven swans a-swimming" represented the seven sacraments. The "eight maids a-milking" signified the Beatitudes. The "nine ladies dancing" were the nine choirs of angels. And the "ten lords a-leaping" were the Ten Commandments. Finally, the "eleven pipers piping" stood for the apostles—after the death of Judas. And the "twelve drummers drumming" represented the twelve basic beliefs we name when we pray the Apostles' Creed.

"So," said Mrs. Perez, "whenever we sing 'The Twelve Days of Christmas,' we should remember those young brave Catholics."

▶ *Why did Mrs. Perez call this carol "dangerous"?*

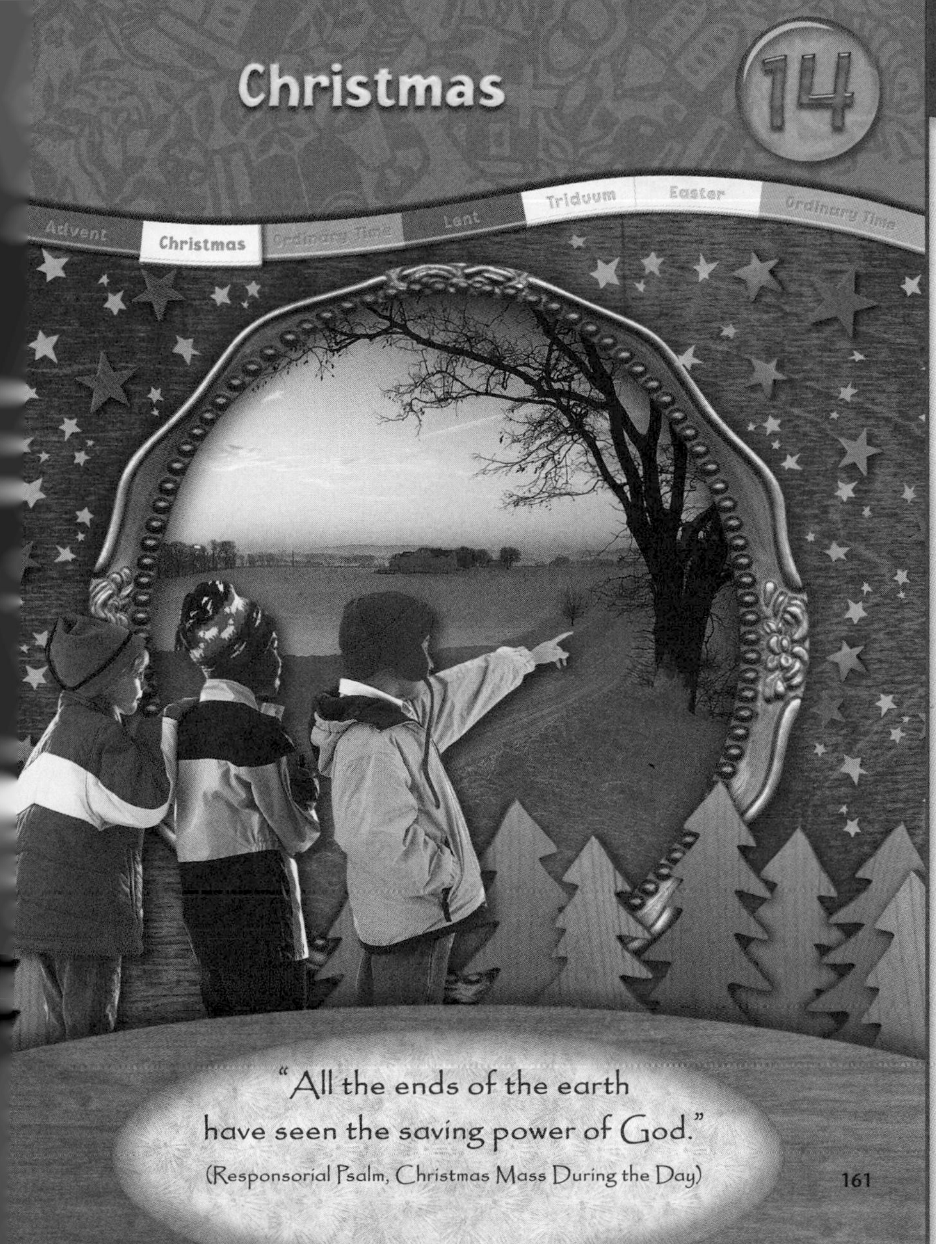
Christmas
14
Advent
Christmas
Ordinary Time
Lent
Triduum
Easter
Ordinary Time
"All the ends of the earth
have seen the saving power of God."
(Responsorial Psalm, Christmas Mass During the Day)
161

Catechist Goal

- To understand that during the Christmas season, we celebrate the Son of God's coming into the world

Our Faith Response

- To plan a special way of celebrating the Christmas season

ADDITIONAL RESOURCES

Book *Joy to the World: Christmas Celebrations, Customs and Crafts,* Phyllis Wezeman and Jude Dennis Fournier, Ave Maria Press, 1992. This book offers customs from twelve countries.

Video *McGee and Me! Twas the Fight Before Christmas,* Tyndale Christian Video, 1990. Loving people who are hard to love is the lesson for Nicholas and his friend, McGee. (30 minutes)

To find more ideas for books, videos, and other learning material, visit Sadlier's

www.WEBELIEVEweb.com

Lesson Plan

Introduce the Season ___ minutes

• **Invite** the students to gather in the prayer space. If possible, teach the melody of the Responsorial Psalm for Christmas Mass During the Day from the parish hymnal. Sing together the verse from text page 161.

• **Read** aloud the *Chapter Story* on guide page 161C. Use the closing question to point out the courageous faith and ingenuity of the priests who wrote the carol and the young Catholics who learned about their faith by singing it.

• **Invite** the students to comment on the photo. Ask them to make up a story to go along with the photo.

• **Proclaim** together the words on the banner under the photo.

Lesson Materials

- props for play (option)
- Grade 4 CD
- copies of Reproducible Master 14

Teaching Note

Forming Disciples

Help students appreciate their call to be Christ-lights for others. Affirm that discipleship is not a future possibility but a present privilege. Pray for each student before the lesson. Be aware that you are participating in a process of "Catechesis [that] shapes the minds, hearts, and spirits of believers, forming them as disciples" (GDC #87).

During the Christmas season we celebrate the Son of God's coming into the world.

WE GATHER

✝ *You came that we might have the fullness of life.*

Name some countries in different parts of the world. What are some things people in different parts of the world have in common?

WE BELIEVE

Over two thousand years ago Jesus was born in Bethlehem of Judea. But his mission went far beyond that small town in a small country. The Son of God lived among us so that the whole world could know his Father's love. He came for everyone, and he lived for everyone. Jesus Christ died and rose to new life for all people.

During the Christmas season, we celebrate the wonderful event of the Incarnation: that God the Son, the second Person of the Blessed Trinity, became man. We celebrate that Jesus came to be the light for all nations.

One feast during the season of Christmas, the feast of the Epiphany, reminds us of this in a special way. We celebrate Jesus' *epiphany*, or Jesus' showing of himself to the whole world. We read about this event in the Gospel of Matthew.

Matthew 2:1–12

Narrator: When Jesus was born in Bethlehem, magi, or wise men, traveled from the east to find him. They arrived in Jerusalem, saying:

Magi: "Where is the newborn king of the Jews? We saw his star at its rising and have come to do him homage" (Matthew 2:2).

Narrator: When King Herod and the others in Jerusalem heard this, they were very troubled. King Herod asked the magi where the Messiah was born, and they answered:

Magi: "In Bethlehem of Judea, for thus it has been written through the prophet" (Matthew 2:5).

162

Lesson Plan

WE GATHER ___ minutes

Focus on Life Have the students answer the *We Gather* question. Have volunteers make a Venn diagram on the board illustrating different countries and what they have in common. Suggest that the students consider these categories: language, religion, government, holiday customs, climate, and clothing.

WE BELIEVE ___ minutes

• **Invite** a volunteer read aloud the *We Believe* statement at the top of page 162. Explain to the students that today they will explore what the Church celebrates in the Christmas season and how the Son of God comes to all the people of the earth.

• **Read** aloud the first two *We Believe* paragraphs. Write the word *Incarnation* on the board. Give the definition: *The event in which the Son of God, the second Person of the Blessed Trinity, became man.* Have a volunteer write the definition on the board. Ask: *Why did the Son of God come to live among us?* (to save us and to show us the Father's love)

• **Give** the students the opportunity to dramatize the reading of Matthew 2:1–12. Write the term *epiphany* on the board and have students find the meaning in the third *We Believe* paragraph (Jesus' showing of himself to the world). If available, distribute costume pieces for turbans and shawls to volunteers who will portray the magi, King Herod, and Mary. If available, distribute the rhythm instruments to be used for special effects between the speeches

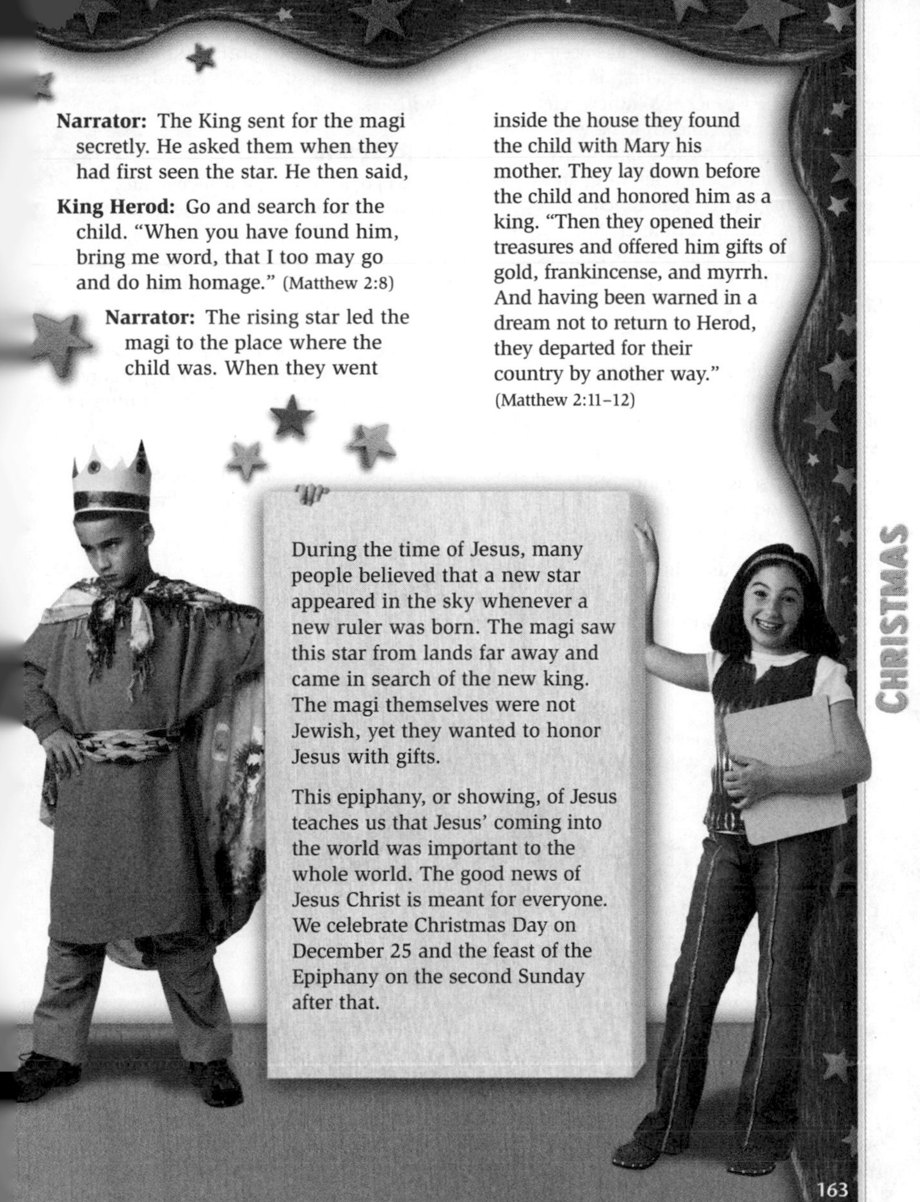

Narrator: The King sent for the magi secretly. He asked them when they had first seen the star. He then said,
King Herod: Go and search for the child. "When you have found him, bring me word, that I too may go and do him homage." (Matthew 2:8)
Narrator: The rising star led the magi to the place where the child was. When they went inside the house they found the child with Mary his mother. They lay down before the child and honored him as a king. "Then they opened their treasures and offered him gifts of gold, frankincense, and myrrh. And having been warned in a dream not to return to Herod, they departed for their country by another way." (Matthew 2:11–12)
During the time of Jesus, many people believed that a new star appeared in the sky whenever a new ruler was born. The magi saw this star from lands far away and came in search of the new king. The magi themselves were not Jewish, yet they wanted to honor Jesus with gifts.
This epiphany, or showing, of Jesus teaches us that Jesus' coming into the world was important to the whole world. The good news of Jesus Christ is meant for everyone. We celebrate Christmas Day on December 25 and the feast of the Epiphany on the second Sunday after that.
CHRISTMAS
163

Activity Bank

Parish

Merry Christmas Messages

Organize the students into groups of three. Invite each group to make a Christmas card with a message to lift people's spirits during this season. Tell them to be creative in their efforts. Suggest that they think of their audience: children in hospitals, seniors in nursing homes, service men and women away from home. Encourage the students to use the words of the evangelists, especially Saints Matthew and Luke. After groups have finished, collect the cards and read aloud messages to the whole group. Then send their messages to their intended recipients. Congratulate the students on their work.

of the narrator and the characters. Assign the roles and have students enact the drama.

• **Invite** a volunteer to read aloud the copy on the banner the students are holding. Ask the students what the appearance of a new star meant to many people who lived at the time of Jesus. (a new ruler had been born) Make sure the students understand the significance of the feast of the Epiphany. (that the good news of Jesus Christ is meant for everyone)

Quick Check

✔ *What does the Church celebrate during the Christmas season?* (The Church celebrates the Son of God's coming into the world.)

✔ *What does Jesus' epiphany teach us?* (Jesus' epiphany teaches us that his good news was meant for the whole world.)

CONNECTION

Multicultural Connections

Christmas Celebrations Around the World

On Christmas Eve the people of Ukraine end their day of fasting with a Holy Supper at which twelve dishes are served. Each dish represents an apostle, as well as the produce of the earth. In Ecuador native peoples who live in the mountains form a procession and ride their colorfully decorated llamas down to the ranches in the valley below. There they present farm products to the Christ Child in the manger, and the children ask the Holy Infant for blessings on their families and their animals. Encourage the fourth graders to look up Christmas customs in other parts of the world. Have them record meal customs on white index cards. (These may include recipes.) On green cards have them record other customs like special family or parish activities. Make a Christmas Around the World reference file.

The story of the magi's visit has been a part of our Christmas celebrations for centuries. The Gospel of Matthew refers to magi, who were known to be wise men, but does not include how many traveled to honor Jesus. Yet, through the years, the magi have been called the three kings. And over time the kings were given names. Your parish may sing the hymn "We Three Kings" during the Christmas season. This song is actually about the magi.

Throughout history people have also taken an interest in the treasure the magi offered: frankincense, myrrh, and gold. It is said that the:

- frankincense was in honor of Christ being divine because incense is used at the liturgy and for other times of prayer.
- myrrh, a spice used in burials, was in honor of Christ's humanity, because Jesus would die and be buried like all human beings.
- gold was a sign of Christ's kingship because, in Jesus, God's Kingdom is with us.

WE RESPOND

Many people from Spanish-speaking countries have parades to celebrate the Epiphany. Three men dress as kings. They give candy and small presents to the children, just as the magi shared what they had with Jesus.

Some people celebrate Epiphany with a special cake. A bean is baked into it, and whoever finds the bean is king or queen for the day!

Is there a special way that you can celebrate, too? This week celebrate Jesus' birth and his presence in your life!

____

____

Children looking for the bean in the king cake.

164

Lesson Plan

WE BELIEVE (continued) ___ minutes

• **Ask** the students to share what they know about the magi. Then have volunteers read aloud the remaining *We Believe* paragraphs on page 164. Make sure that the students understand the symbolism of the three gifts. If the students know the words to "We Three Kings," sing it together.

WE RESPOND ___ minutes

Connect to Life Read aloud the *We Respond* paragraphs. Review the epiphany customs described there. If students have recipes or stories about Three Kings' cakes to share, invite them to do so.

Describe briefly some of the Christmas season customs from around the world. Use the following:

• In Nicaragua (Central America), the Three Kings bring gifts to the children on the feast of the Epiphany. The Christmas season concludes with a splendid fireworks display.

• In Wales (Europe) an annual Christmas carol competition is held with each village choir providing a different melody for the same words.

• **Read** aloud the *We Respond* activity directions. Invite volunteers to share ways their families celebrate Jesus' birth and presence. Have the students choose one way and write it in their books.

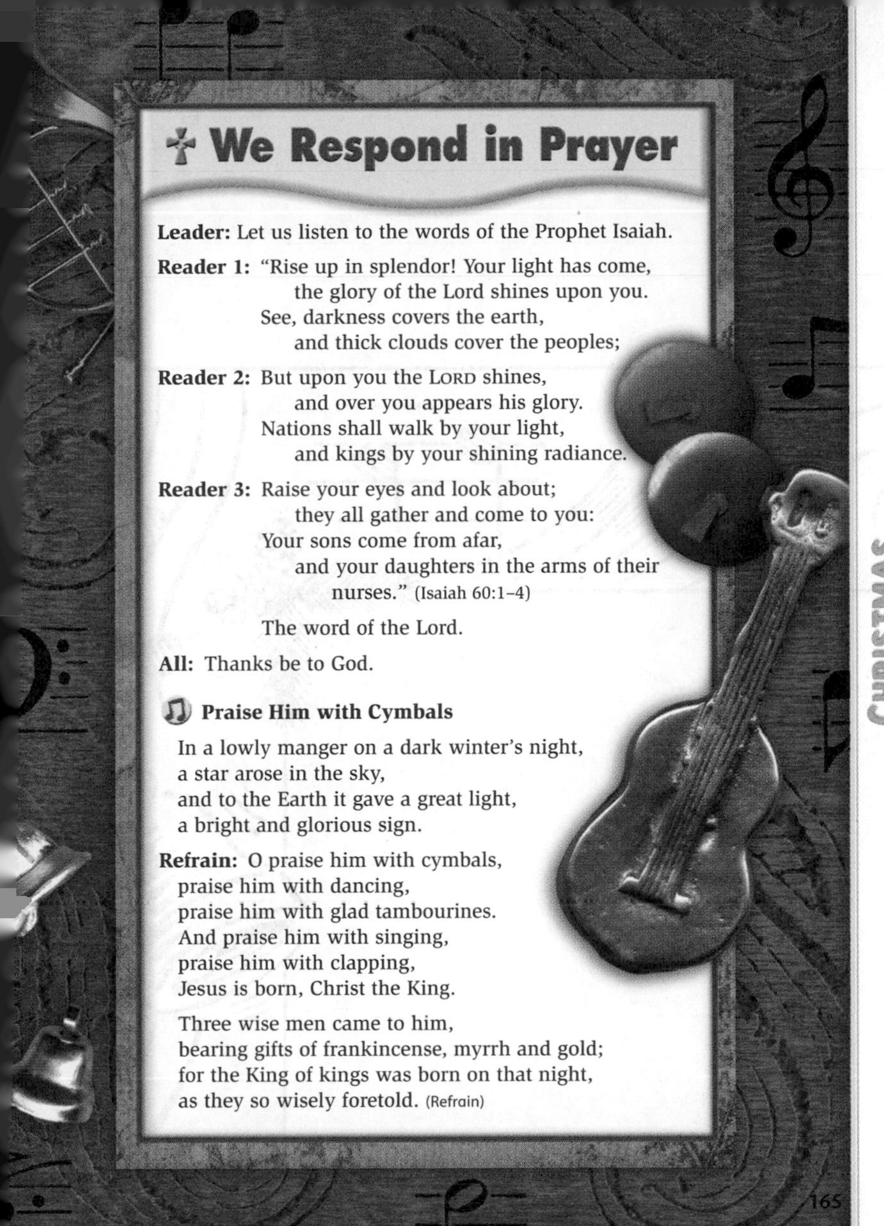
We Respond in Prayer

Leader: Let us listen to the words of the Prophet Isaiah.

Reader 1: "Rise up in splendor! Your light has come,
the glory of the Lord shines upon you.
See, darkness covers the earth,
and thick clouds cover the peoples;

Reader 2: But upon you the LORD shines,
and over you appears his glory.
Nations shall walk by your light,
and kings by your shining radiance.

Reader 3: Raise your eyes and look about;
they all gather and come to you:
Your sons come from afar,
and your daughters in the arms of their
nurses." (Isaiah 60:1–4)

The word of the Lord.

All: Thanks be to God.

Praise Him with Cymbals

In a lowly manger on a dark winter's night,
a star arose in the sky,
and to the Earth it gave a great light,
a bright and glorious sign.

Refrain: O praise him with cymbals,
praise him with dancing,
praise him with glad tambourines.
And praise him with singing,
praise him with clapping,
Jesus is born, Christ the King.

Three wise men came to him,
bearing gifts of frankincense, myrrh and gold;
for the King of kings was born on that night,
as they so wisely foretold. (Refrain)

CHRISTMAS

165

Preparing to Pray

In this prayer the students will proclaim God's word and will praise God in song.

- Invite three students to serve as readers and provide them time to prepare.
- Practice the song, "Praise Him with Cymbals," Janet Vogt, #15, Grade 4 CD.
- Distribute light symbols (stars, sun, moon, candle, lighthouse) and have students each write one way they will be a light for others.

The Prayer Space

- Gather the following items: a manger scene with figures of the magi, gold foil crown; white table covering

This Week's Liturgy

Visit **www.webelieveweb.com** for this week's liturgical readings and other seasonal material.

We Respond in Prayer ___ minutes

- **Pray** the Sign of the Cross and opening words of the prayer.
- **Have** the readers proclaim the scriptural verses from the prophet Isaiah.
- **Conclude** with singing "Praise Him with Cymbals," from Grade 4 CD. Process around the room and return to the prayer space.

Name ____

Write an original Christmas carol.

We Respond in Faith

Individual Project

Talk with the students about some of their favorite Christmas carols and why they like them. Distribute copies of Reproducible Master 14 and have a volunteer read the directions aloud. Suggest that the students write lyrics to any melody they already know. Their carols should communicate some truth about the Incarnation or the feast of the Epiphany of Jesus. As time allows, invite the students to recite the lyrics of their carols or sing them for the class. Commend their creative work, and suggest that they share their carols with family and friends.

Group Project

Making "Twelve Days" Props

As a follow-through of the *Chapter Story* and an extension of the Christmas season, invite small groups or partners to make "Twelve Days" props. Distribute copies of the carol. Assign one of the twelve days to each of the groups. Make available a variety or materials such as: fabrics, filter and basic sewing supplies for the partridge and other birds; cardboard; poster board and foil for stand-up figures like the lords and ladies; yellow play dough for the rings, and so on. Have the students use the props to teach younger students the carol and its meaning.

HOME CONNECTION

Sharing Faith with My Family

Make sure to send home the family page (text page 166).

Encourage the students to use "A Family Prayer for the Christmas Season" with a ritual of house blessing on the Feast of the Epiphany. The family might walk from one room to another, sprinkling holy water from a bowl with an evergreen branch.

For additional information and activities, encourage families to visit Sadlier's

www.WEBELIEVEweb.com

CHAPTER 14 GRADE 4

SHARING FAITH with My Family

Sharing What I Learned

Discuss the following with your family:

- Christ's coming
- the visit of the magi
- Epiphany today.

Around the Table

How can your family show Jesus to the world? Make sure each room has something that expresses your faith, like a crucifix, a picture, or a holy water font. As a family make your own symbol. You might color the symbol in a rainbow of colors, each family member choosing one color. Put the symbol in a window to show Jesus to the world!

A Family Prayer for the Christmas Season

The feast of Epiphany is a day for the blessing of a home. Pray this blessing with your family.

Leader: Peace be to this house!

All: Both now and forever. Amen.

Leader: Lord Jesus, you came to live among us. We ask your blessing on this place where we live. May we live here in peace and love, and may we share your blessings with all who come to our door.

All: Amen.

166 Visit Sadlier's www.WEBELIEVEweb.com

Connect to the Catechism
For adult background and reflection see paragraph 528.

PUPIL PAGE 166

ASSESSMENT

In the *We Believe* program each core chapter ends with a review of the content presented, and with activities that encourage the students to reflect and act on their faith. The review is presented in two formats, standard and alternative.

Each unit is also followed by both standard and alternative assessment. The standard test measures basic knowledge and vocabulary assimilation. The alternative assessment allows the students another option—often utilizing another learning style—to express their understanding of the concepts presented.

Using both forms of assessment, perhaps at different times, attends to the various ways students' learning can be measured. You can also see the Grade 4 *We Believe* Assessment Book for:

- standard assessment for each chapter
- alternative assessment for each chapter
- standard assessment for each unit
- alternative assessment for each unit
- a semester assessment which covers material presented in Units 1 and 2
- a final assessment which covers material presented in Units 1, 2, 3, and 4.

For answers to Assessment questions: **17–18**, see Chapter 8, pages 102–103; **19–20**, see Chapter 12, pages 148–149.

Grade 4
Unit 2

Choose a word from the box to complete the sentence.

bless	Jesus	Corporal	vain	Eucharist
idolatry	covenant	reverence	Spiritual	worship

1. Jesus lived his life according to the __covenant__ God made with his people.
2. To take God's name in __vain__ is to use it in a disrespectful or unnecessary way.
3. To give God thanks and praise is to __worship__ him.
4. It is an act of __idolatry__ to put someone or something before God.
5. When we show honor, love, and respect to God, we are showing him __reverence__.
6. To __bless__ something or someone is to dedicate that thing or that person to God.
7. Feeding the hungry and caring for the sick are __Corporal__ Works of Mercy.
8. Comforting the suffering and forgiving those who hurt us are __Spiritual__ Works of Mercy.
9. The celebration of the __Eucharist__ is the most important way we keep the Lord's Day.
10. On the Lord's Day we gather to celebrate that __Jesus__ died and rose to save us.

167

Write the letter of the Scripture verse that matches each of the following:

11. __d__ the Shema
12. __c__ the Great Commandment
13. __a__ the New Commandment
14. __b__ the First Commandment
15. __f__ the Second Commandment
16. __e__ the Third Commandment

a. "As I have loved you, so you also should love one another." (John 13:34)

b. "I, the LORD, am your God. . . . You shall not have other gods besides me." (Exodus 20:2, 3)

c. "You shall love the Lord, your God, with all your heart, with all your soul, and with all your mind." (Matthew 22:37)

d. "Hear, O Israel! The LORD is our God, the LORD alone!" (Deuteronomy 6:4)

e. "Remember to keep holy the sabbath day." (Exodus 20:8)

f. "You shall not take the name of the LORD, your God, in vain." (Exodus 20:7)

Answer the questions.

17–18. God calls us to respect the human dignity of all people. What can a fourth grader do to show respect for basic human rights?

18–20. At the consecration of the Mass, by the power of the Holy Spirit and through the words of the priest, the bread and wine become the Body and Blood of Christ. Why is this important?

168

The Commandments Help Us to Love Others
UNIT 3
169

UNIT 3 SHARING FAITH as a Family

Five Ways to Improve Communication in Your Home

Here are five ideas to help you improve communication within your family:

1. **Speak up!** You can't expect others to know what your needs, hurts, or concerns are unless you tell them.
2. **Watch for underlying messages.** Words *do not* say it all. Pay attention to body language, style of speech, and what is left *un*said.
3. **Back off.** Pressing another person to resolve a conflict before he or she is ready can lead to greater resistance and resentment. Cooling down, thinking things through, and reconnecting are essential parts of the equation.
4. **Get rid of distractions.** When engaging in an important conversation, turn off the TV, shut down the computer, and let the answering machine handle phone calls. Focus on being present to one another.
5. **Ask questions.** *Active* listening entails asking questions that clarify what the speaker is trying to say. It makes him or her feel "heard."

Communication is a give-and-take process that, in the end, can build strong bonds of love and mutual respect.

Media Matters

In this unit, the children learn that keeping the fourth commandment means: honoring their parents and guardians; honoring those who help them to know what God wants them to do; listening with respect to teachers, pastors, bishops, and the pope; obeying the laws of their city, state, and nation.

Watch either a nightly news program or an entertainment program with your child. Point out the stories (or story lines) that show people following the fourth commandment. You might see stories that do not. As a family, discuss your findings.

From the Catechism

"The family should live in such a way that its members learn to care and take responsibility for the young, the old, the sick, the handicapped, and the poor."

(Catechism of the Catholic Church, 2208)

What Your Child Will Learn in Unit 3

Unit 3 continues the presentation of the Ten Commandments with the fourth through the eighth commandments. In this unit, the children learn the need for being a responsible member of their family and society in general. Family responsibilities and respect for authority are highlighted as is the sacredness of all human life. Children are encouraged to commit themselves to protecting life, respecting their bodies, and working for the dignity of all human beings. The children are called to appreciate that they are made in God's own image.

The meaning of virtue and specifically the meaning of chastity and what it entails are next explained. The joys of friendship, married love, and faithfulness in all relationships are also highlighted. The meaning of justice and respect for the property of others is stressed. Respect for creation, caring for the poor, and appreciating the Works of Mercy are included here. The unit concludes with an emphasis on God as the source of all truth, the importance of giving witness to the truth, telling the truth, and respecting the truth.

Did You Know?

These statistics come from a group that monitors television viewing habits.

- Children watch 2.1 hours of television per day, second only to the time they spend sleeping.
- Over half (55.8%) of secondary-school-aged young people have a television set in their room.
- Children with television sets in their bedrooms watch 2.5 more hours of television per week than children without sets in their bedrooms.

(from *Television in the Home: The 1997 Annenberg Survey of Parents and Children*)

Plan & Preview

- ▶ Remember to have scissors on hand so that the "Scripture Picture" on each family page can be cut out.
- ▶ Have markers and crayons available so that you can draw the "Scripture Picture."

170

Class Connection

Point out the unit title to the students. Ask them what they think they will be learning more about in this unit. Have a class discussion, preparing the students for this unit.

Home Connection

Sharing Faith as a Family

Sadlier *We Believe* calls on families to become involved in:

- learning the faith
- prayer and worship
- living their faith.

Highlighting of these unit family pages and the opportunities they offer will strengthen the partnership of the Church and the home.

For additional information and activities, encourage families to visit Sadlier's

www.WEBELIEVEweb.com

Chapter 15 The Fourth Commandment

Overview

In Chapter 12 the students learned about the celebration of the Mass. In this chapter they will learn that the fourth commandment teaches us to respect and honor our parents, guardians, and all people in authority.

Doctrinal Content	For Adult Reading and Reflection *Catechism of the Catholic Church*
The students will learn:	Paragraph
• God wants us to love and respect others.	2199
• In our families we learn to love God and others.	2207
• In our families we have the responsibility to love and respect one another.	2206
• Citizens and leaders work together for peace.	2238

domestic church
(p. 175)

Catechist Background

Whom do you honor?

Obedience is not a popular concept in today's individualistic society. Yet, obedience is a central discipline for the Christian who believes that "God has willed that, after him, we should honor our parents and those whom he has vested with authority for our good" (*CCC* 2248).

The fourth commandment calls for honoring one's parents. For children this is often translated as obeying parents and guardians. And, perhaps, we think of the fourth commandment as being specifically directed toward children. But this commandment calls sons and daughters of all ages to honor their parents. "As much as they can, they must give them material and moral support in old age and in times of illness, loneliness, or distress" (*CCC* 2218).

The commandment includes honoring members of the extended family, elders, and ancestors. It also includes "the duties of pupils to teachers, employees to employers, subordinates to leaders, citizens to their country and to those who administer or govern it" (*CCC* 2199). Thus, honoring those who have legitimate authority is a lifelong responsibility and challenge.

We can follow the example of Jesus. Often, when the fourth commandment is discussed, the story of the young Jesus being lost in the Temple is told. You will recall that it recounts how Jesus returned to Nazareth with Mary and Joseph "and was obedient to them" (Luke 2:51). But the incident also shows that Jesus' first obedience was to his Father in heaven. In fact, Jesus taught us to call God our Father and by doing so was reminding us that our first obedience also is to God.

Whom do you find it difficult to honor? How do you pray for that person?

Lesson Planning Guide

Lesson Focus	Presentation	Materials
Day 1		
page 171 **We Gather in Prayer** **pages 172–173** *God wants us to love and respect others.* *Luke 2:46–52*	• Listen to Scripture. • Respond in prayer. • Discuss the **We Gather** questions. • Read and discuss the Ten Commandments in **We Believe.** Complete the **We Respond** activity. • Pray together.	For the prayer space: statue or picture of the Holy Family, gift-wrapped box with open top
Day 2		
pages 174–175 *In our families we learn to love God and others.*	• For the **We Gather** question, define *family*. • Read and discuss the **We Believe** text about family as community and domestic church.  Do the **We Respond** activity. • Read and discuss the Feast of the Holy Family in *As Catholics*. • Pray together.	• strips of construction paper, glue or tape, crayons or markers • pictures of the students' family members (option)
Day 3		
pages 176–177 *In our families we have the responsibility to love and respect one another.*	• Reflect on family roles and responsibilities in the **We Gather** question. • Read and discuss the **We Believe** text. Complete the **We Respond** activity. Respond by singing.	• copies of Reproducible Master 15, guide page 171G "We Are the Family," Ray Repp, #16, Grade 4 CD
Day 4		
pages 178–179 *Citizens and leaders work together for peace.*	Complete the **We Gather** activity. • Read and discuss respect for those in authority in the **We Believe** text. • Reflect on the **We Respond** question. • Pray together.	• magazines containing photographs of family groups, world leaders, and people working for peace around the world • construction paper, tape, or glue
Day 5		
page 180 **Review** **pages 181–182** **We Respond in Faith**	• Complete questions 1–10. Work on the *Assessment Activity*. • Complete the *Reflect & Pray* activity. • Review *Remember* and *Key Word*. • Read and discuss *Our Catholic Life.* • Discuss **Sharing Faith with My Family**.	• Chapter 15 Test in Assessment Book, pp. 31–32 • Chapter 15 Test in Test Generator • Review & Resource Book, pp. 34–36 • Family Book, pp. 43–45

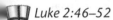

For additional ideas, activities, and opportunities: Visit Sadlier's **www.WEBELIEVEweb.com**

Enrichment Ideas

Chapter Story

Jill's mom glanced out the window again. In a worried voice she said, "If this rain keeps up and the river keeps rising, we may have to evacuate." Jill shuddered. Her whole family loved their riverside home in Sunnyvale, and to think of it covered with water frightened her.

After supper that night Gran and mom moved the family albums and Gran's silverware up to the second floor. "The river's flooded before, but it's not likely to come up that high," said Gran. Jill made sure her backpack was full of her school folders, her favorite books, and her art supplies.

They were awakened at dawn by a loudspeaker. "Everyone must evacuate now! The fire department will assist you with rowboats. Repeat: Wait for assistance to evacuate immediately!"

Suddenly the men and women from Sunnyvale's fire and rescue service were at the door. They helped Jill's mother and grandmother into the boat. Then, when someone lifted Jill in with a big swoop, she felt as if she was flying.

Jill wondered whether this was like the city bus, and they were expected to pay something. "Is this a free ride?" she asked one rescuer.

The rescuer grinned. "Your tax dollars at work! You can thank the good citizens of Sunnyvale," he said. "I couldn't afford to work full time for free, but I like helping people like you."

Jill smiled. She wondered why people complained about paying taxes. She thought about other good things in Sunnyvale: the town library, the recreation center where all the kids played basketball after school, and the beautiful town park with its playground and duck pond. Being a good citizen was really about taking care of everyone! Right then and there Jill prayed a little prayer of thanksgiving for the good citizens of Sunnyvale, and for the fire and rescue team.

▶ *What are some good things in your town or city? How can you be a good citizen?*

FAITH and MEDIA

▶ Day 1 offers an opportunity to point out the connection between faith and media. As the students do the video storyboard activity, remind them of the power that writers, directors, actors, and animators have to influence the public. A well-written, well-acted, or cleverly animated video about the fourth commandment is a valuable teaching tool. Additionally, it can reach those who cannot read and who are unaffected by the printed word.

CHAPTER PROJECT: A PARISH FAMILY TREE

Ask the students to work in groups to complete the chapter project. Using a large piece of white paper or poster board, invite them to develop a "family tree" for the parish that shows the many different families that make up the parish family. Encourage them to decide how they would like the tree organized. What parts of the parish make up the tree's roots, trunk, and branches? Invite the students to think of the many different types of families that exist in the parish as they draw the tree. Encourage them to develop a parish tree that reflects the idea that the Church is a community just as a family is a community, and that we are all part of the human family.

Connections

To Mary

On Day 1 the students will learn about the Holy Family and Jesus' respect for his mother. Explain that we do not have much information about Jesus' early life. We do know, however, that Jesus valued and honored Mary and Joseph. We also know that at his death Jesus instructed the apostle John to love Mary as his own mother. The Church venerates Mary as our mother, too. We honor Mary as the Mother of God and the Mother of the Church.

To Saints

Among the saints whose feasts are celebrated each year are numerous examples of faithful parents, siblings, sons, and daughters. Make available to the students library and Internet sources on the lives of the saints. Examples include Thérèse of Lisieux and her entire family, Benedict and Scholastica, Elizabeth Ann Seton, Thomas More, and King Louis of France. Have the students write brief reports on how these saints lived the fourth commandment.

To Community

The students are reminded in this chapter that God wants us to love and respect others in our families and communities. Guide the students to understand that "community" includes our own families, the parish and Church family, the greater community of neighbors, and, ultimately, the community of all people everywhere. Encourage the students to reach out within the community of the parish and their neighborhoods to show someone that they care. Remind the students of the positive influence individuals in the parish can have on the community around them.

Meeting Individual Needs

English Language Learners

Students for whom English is a second language may not be reading at the same level as their peers. Invite those for whom English may be difficult to read the passages silently. Then have them read the text back to you or to another student. Offer assistance with unfamiliar words, and have the students underline or list key information as they work through the chapter.

ADDITIONAL RESOURCES

Book *Willie Wins*, Almira Astudillo Gilles, Lee & Low Books, Inc., New York, NY, 2001. This story tells of a Filipino boy's struggle between what his classmates might think and the honor and respect he holds for his father. He learns the depth of his father's love.

Video *The Boy Jesus in the Temple,* CCC of America, 1997. From the series *A Kingdom Without Frontiers,* this video depicts a young Jesus found preaching to the temple elders. (30 minutes)

To find more ideas for books, videos, and other learning material, visit Sadlier's

www.WEBELIEVEweb.com

Using Children's Art

by Renée McAlister

Renée McAlister is an author and national creative consultant for William H. Sadlier, Inc. She received her B.S. and M.S. in early childhood development and education from Louisiana State University in Baton Rouge, LA.

In his 1999 *Letter to Artists*, Pope John Paul II wrote, "With loving regard, the divine Artist passes on to the human artist a spark of his own surpassing wisdom, calling him to share in his creative power." (No. 1) The catechist is in a unique position to foster artistic expression and to call forth this "spark of the divine" in children.

All children are naturally attracted to art. Given the chance, children will effortlessly produce artistic works. Children use art as a basic tool of expression. They paint, draw, color, and create with self-confidence, ease, and pleasure. Art activities are more than just fun for children. Art plays a major role in their development.

Cognitive Development Knowledge becomes permanent when the information is processed in an artistic way. Abstract faith concepts can be imagined and concretized through art. Using graphs, drawings, paintings, collage, coloring, and other art media strengthens the creative part of the brain. Through art, children explore the real world and invent their own meaningful sets of symbolic marks and colors. Their conceptual understanding of the world around them is depicted in their art.

Motor Development Creating art improves motor skills and eye-hand coordination. Spatial awareness is also developed through art experiences.

Emotional Development Art provides a unique avenue of expression for children of all ages. Their artistic creations represent not only their interpretation of experiences, but also of emotions relevant to these experiences. Art gives a voice to their feelings and to their beliefs.

Social Development Art provides expression for children who are deficient in social skills. Children will often verbalize as they create expressions of art. Sharing faith through art helps develop self-confidence by offering children a safe environment for socialization.

Catechist Development Topics (Topic and Guide Page)

Resources

Costello, Gwen. *School Year Activities for Religion Classes*. Mystic, CT: Twenty-Third Publications, 2000.

Hurwitz, Albert *Children and Their Art*. New York: Harcourt Brace College Publishing, 1994.

Ways to Implement Using Children's Art

- Provide a special area for art activities. In this area, provide a table, easel, or covered floor space for independent art exploration.
- Collect a variety of art supplies and materials, such as crayons, markers, scissors, glue, different sizes and types of paper, clay, paints, brushes, and various other craft items. The greater the variety of supplies, the more creative the art projects. Have paper towels and/or rags available for clean up.
- Encourage the use of liturgical colors and symbols in artwork to express the Church seasons. Display children's art where parishioners can appreciate it.
- Send ideas for family art projects home to begin a liturgical season or to celebrate a feast.
- Respect children's expression of emotions, ideas, and thoughts. Refrain from changing the children's work into a more "perfect picture." Allow the children to direct the progress of their artistic projects. Ask, "Tell me about your artwork," rather than "What is that?" Encourage the children to share their artwork with the group.
- Call the children's attention to the variety of art in *We Believe*. Have them discuss what they see and how it makes them feel. You can also ask them how they would draw the same scene.

For additional ideas, activities, and opportunities, visit Sadlier's

www.WEBELIEVEweb.com

With thanks to:
Bobette Robideaux
Our Lady of Fatima School
Lafayette, Louisiana

By blending art, religion, and technology, children in Bobette's class use the Internet to find instant visuals and Web sites devoted to famous artists. These visuals then become a springboard to discuss the artist's life, artistic style, and subject matter. Later, one-of-a-kind "masterpieces" begin to emerge from the group. A student uses Matisse's cut-paper technique to display something special from God's universe. Other students paint Van Gogh-stylized self portraits with cotton swab brushes. Adventuresome students may even attach art paper to the bottom of their desks and crawl under to paint in the style of Michelangelo and his Sistine Chapel ceiling. Using art helps Bobette become closer to her students. "Watching youngsters accept their unique artistic gifts from God is a constantly inspiring experience."

Notes

Name ____________________

Pretend you are writing episodes for a television show about the fourth commandment. Give a name to the show and titles to the first three episodes.

The Fourth Commandment

✝ We Gather in Prayer

Leader: In the Gospel of Luke, we read about a journey that Jesus, Mary, and Joseph made to the Temple in Jerusalem. When it was time to leave, Mary thought Jesus was with Joseph. Joseph thought Jesus must have gone with Mary. They left Jerusalem without him! For a whole day, they did not realize that he was not with the group. When they did, they went back to look for him. This is where we begin our reading.

Reader 1: "After three days they found him in the temple, sitting in the midst of the teachers, listening to them and asking them questions, and all who heard him were astounded at his understanding and his answers.

Reader 2: When his parents saw him, they were astonished, and his mother said to him, 'Son, why have you done this to us? Your father and I have been looking for you with great anxiety.'

Reader 3: And he said to them, 'Why were you looking for me? Did you know that I must be in my Father's house?' But they did not understand what he said to them.

Reader 4: He went down with them and came to Nazareth, and was obedient to them; and his mother kept all these things in her heart.

Reader 5: And Jesus advanced [in] wisdom and age and favor before God and man." (Luke 2:46–52)

Leader: Let us pray. God our Father, you gave your Son a family to help him grow. May we, like Jesus, listen to our parents and obey them, so that we too may grow in wisdom, age, and favor before you and all people. We ask through Jesus Christ, our Lord.

All: Amen.

171

Preparing to Pray

In this gathering prayer the students proclaim the Scripture story of the finding of Jesus in the Temple. The students will read and reflect on this story.

• Tell the students you will read the part of the leader. Ask five volunteers to take the parts of the readers. Give them time to prepare what they will read.

The Prayer Space

• If possible, display a picture or statue of the Holy Family in the prayer space; place a gift-wrapped box with an open top in the area.

This Week's Liturgy

Visit **www.webelieveweb.com** for this week's liturgical readings and other seasonal material.

Lesson Plan

We Gather in Prayer ___ minutes

✝ Pray

• Invite the students to gather together in the prayer space. Say, *We gather in prayer.*

• Pray the Sign of the Cross. Read the opening leader's part. Invite the first volunteer to start reading.

• Read the leader's closing prayer and have everyone pray *Amen.*

• Invite the students to reflect silently on the readings.

Home Connection Update

Review the activities on the Chapter 12 family page. Ask: *In what ways did you and your family honor God and show your love for one another over the weekend?*

Catechist Goal

• To introduce the fourth commandment

Our Faith Response

• To seek to practice the fourth commandment in our families

As Catholics...

The Feast of the Holy Family

At the conclusion of the lesson read the text on page 175 to the students. Ask them to think about their own families. Discuss ways their families show love for God and one another.

God wants us to love and respect others.

WE GATHER

✝ *Lord, help us to see you in one another.*

Who do you rely on in your family and neighborhood? Why do you rely on them?

WE BELIEVE

The Ten Commandments remind us of our relationship with God. God is always with us. We respond to God by the ways we live out the commandments. The Ten Commandments help us to know how to love God, ourselves, and others. They help us to judge good from evil, right from wrong. Following the Ten Commandments gives us the happiness that comes from a relationship with God. Living by the Ten Commandments also helps us to be active members of the Church community.

In the Great Commandment Jesus told us that the Ten Commandments are all about love.

When we follow the first three commandments, we show our love for God. We love God by honoring him and praising him. We believe that he is the one true God. We use his name with respect. We keep his day holy. When we follow the fourth through the tenth commandments, we show love for others. All people are made in God's image. Whenever we respect and honor one another, we honor God.

The Great Commandment

"You shall love the Lord, your God, with all your heart, with all your soul, and with all your mind." (Matthew 22:37)

"You shall love your neighbor as yourself." (Matthew 22:39)

The Ten Commandments

1. I am the Lord your God: you shall not have strange gods before me.
2. You shall not take the name of the Lord your God in vain.
3. Remember to keep holy the Lord's Day.
4. Honor your father and your mother.
5. You shall not kill.
6. You shall not commit adultery.
7. You shall not steal.
8. You shall not bear false witness against your neighbor.
9. You shall not covet your neighbor's wife.
10. You shall not covet your neighbor's goods.

Lesson Plan

WE GATHER ___ minutes

✝ **Pray** Pray the Sign of the Cross and the *We Gather* prayer.

Focus on Life Ask the students to share their answers to the *We Gather* questions. Tell the students that in this lesson they will learn that God wants us to love and respect others.

WE BELIEVE ___ minutes

Read the Text Have a volunteer read aloud the *We Believe* statement; then, invite a volunteer to read aloud the first *We Believe* paragraph. Discuss the Ten Commandments. Emphasize the following:

• The Ten Commandments help us to know how to love God and others.

• The Ten Commandments help us to distinguish good from evil and right from wrong.

• Following the Ten Commandments gives us the happiness that comes from a relationship with God, and it helps us in the Church community.

Have the students complete the reading independently. Ask volunteers to identify ways we are called to follow the fourth commandment.

Use a Fishbone Organizer Draw a "fishbone" graphic organizer on the board with three lines on one side of the organizer for the first three commandments and seven lines on the other. Use *Jesus' Great Commandment* as a title for the organizer. Invite students to write a commandment on each line to fill in the ten lines on the board. Assist them to recall which

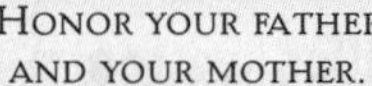
HONOR YOUR FATHER AND YOUR MOTHER.

The fourth commandment is: "Honor your father and your mother" (Exodus 20:12). It teaches us to appreciate and obey our parents, our guardians, and all those who lead and serve us. We value and listen with respect to our parents, guardians, teachers, pastors, bishops, the pope, and all those who help us to see God's will for us. We also obey the laws of our city, state, and nation.

Jesus showed us how to live out the fourth commandment. He himself was obedient to his mother, Mary, and his foster father, Joseph. Jesus did the things that God his Father wanted. Jesus showed respect for religious leaders—priests, teachers, and leaders who helped to bring people closer to the Father.

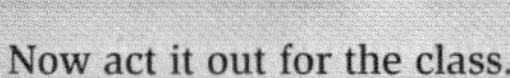
WE RESPOND

Imagine you are producing a series of videos to teach people about the Ten Commandments.

In a group use this storyboard to plan what you would talk about and show on the video "The Fourth Commandment."

Now act it out for the class.

173

Chapter 15 • **Day 1**

ACTIVITY BANK

Faith and Media

TV-Video Viewing Project

Activity Materials: television

Invite the students to see how the fourth commandment is treated in television shows and movies. Encourage them to think about the fourth commandment to see whether anything in the program or film is related to it. The characterizations may include people who break this commandment. What are the consequences of doing so? Have the students write a summary of the program or film. Then ask them to explain how the story relates to the fourth commandment.

commandments help us to love God and which commandments help us to love ourselves and others.

Quick Check

✔ *When we follow the fourth through the tenth commandments, what are we doing?* (We are showing our love and respect for others.)

✔ *What does the fourth commandment teach us?* (to honor our father and mother, and also to respect and honor all those who help us see God's will for us: teachers, pastors, bishops, the pope, and other leaders and authorities)

WE RESPOND ___ minutes

Connect to Life Have the students work in groups to complete the video storyboards. Invite the students to share their ideas for the fourth commandment videos. In discussion encourage the students to say what they think it means to honor their parents or guardians. Ask: *How can we thank God for the gift of our families?*

Pray Conclude by praying the Sign of the Cross and the following: *Dear God, we thank you for the gift of our families and the gift of your commandments. Help us to see you in one another so that we may share our love for you with other people. Amen.*

Plan Ahead for Day 2

Catechist Goal: To explain ways that Christian families live out the fourth commandment

Preparation: Have available strips of construction paper, tape or glue, crayons or markers; ask the students to bring in snapshots of family members (option).

Catechist Goal

- To explain ways that Christian families live out the fourth commandment

Our Faith Response

- To appreciate our families for teaching us about loving God and others

 **domestic church**

Lesson Materials

- strips of construction paper
- tape or glue
- crayons or markers
- snapshots of students' family members (option)

Teaching Tip

Families

Today's lesson focuses on the definition of *family* and our individual responsibilities to our families. Use the opportunity to reinforce that our families are communities. Within each family community we have the responsibility to love and respect one another, just as God calls us to love and respect others.

In our families we learn to love God and others.

HONOR YOUR FATHER AND YOUR MOTHER.

WE GATHER

✝ *Jesus, help us to live in peace by following your loving example.*

How would you define the word *family*?

WE BELIEVE

A family is a community. It may be large or small. It may include parents and grandparents, brothers and sisters, aunts and uncles, and cousins. Family members share love and spend time together. They try to live in peace, helping one another. They support one another in good times and in bad. The fourth commandment reminds family members of their duties to one another.

The Holy Family lived out the fourth commandment. They honored and respected one another. Jesus, Mary, and Joseph shared both happy and sad times with their relatives and friends. They worked and prayed together. They honored and loved God.

Through Baptism the members of every Christian family share the very life of God—the Father, the Son, and the Holy Spirit. As Christian families we can pray and worship together. We try to live so that all people will know the love of God. We help and comfort those who are in need. We share our faith in God and love for one another with all those we meet. In these ways, Christian families work together to spread God's kingdom here on earth. As Christian families, we are called to be communities of faith, hope, and love.

174

Lesson Plan

WE GATHER ___ minutes

✝ **Pray** Pray the Sign of the Cross and the *We Gather* prayer.

Focus on Life Begin by inviting the class to describe the many and varied ways the word *family* can be defined. Help the students to understand that single-parent households, homes with several generations under one roof, and other living arrangements are all families—communities of people who love and respect one another. Tell the students that in this lesson they will learn that it is in our families that we learn to love God and others.

WE BELIEVE ___ minutes

Make a Love Chain Have a volunteer read aloud the *We Believe* statement; then, invite a volunteer to read aloud the first *We Believe* paragraph. Ask the students to list all the members of their families. Have each student write the names from his or her list on separate slips of construction paper and glue or tape the strips in joined rings to form a chain of love. Once each student has completed his or her chain, use strips on which you have written words such as *love, family, community, peace,* and *respect* to connect the chains into one long love chain.

Learn About Families Once the love chain has been placed on display in the prayer space, have volunteers take turns reading aloud the remainder of the *We Believe* text. After each paragraph is read, pause to discuss it.

Remember the Key Word Encourage the students to look at the key word for this lesson. The idea of a domestic church may elicit new suggestions about what it means to be a Christian family.

Every Christian family is called to be a **domestic church**, or a "church in the home." Within our families we learn about and experience work, forgiveness, and discipline. We grow in our faith and ability to choose what is good. We learn to take part in the Church community.

Jesus Christ is present in every Christian family. Christian families help the Church to grow stronger. Families work with other families to help build neighborhoods, parishes, nations, and a better world.

Key Word
domestic church the church in the home, which every Christian family is called to be

As Catholics...

Jesus, Mary, and Joseph are called the Holy Family. Each year on the Sunday after Christmas, the Church celebrates the Feast of the Holy Family. On this day we recall the love that Jesus shared with Mary, Joseph, his other relatives, and his friends. We thank God for the gift of our own families. We ask God to help all families.

How can you and your family show love for God and one another?

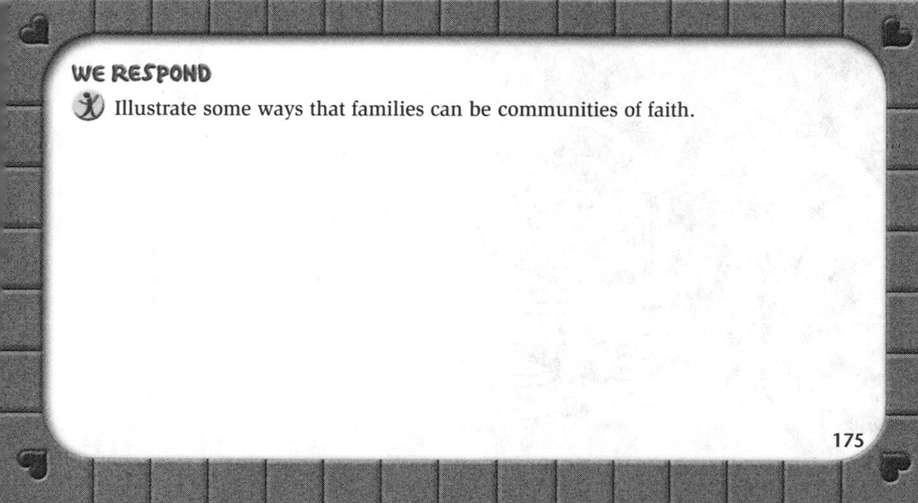

WE RESPOND

Illustrate some ways that families can be communities of faith.

175

Chapter 15 • Day 2

ACTIVITY BANK

Multicultural Connection

Families Around the World

Activity Materials: Internet and other research sources

Invite the students to use classroom encyclopedias, the school library, or Catholic Web sites to learn how Catholic families in other countries honor the Holy Family. For example, students might research the Mexican custom of Las Posadas, in which families reenact the Holy Family's search for an inn in Bethlehem. If students have Catholic pen pals in other countries, this would be a good opportunity for them to ask their friends the ways their families teach them the meaning of the fourth commandment.

Quick Check

✔ *How did the Holy Family live out the fourth commandment?* (They loved and honored God, and they honored and respected one another.)

✔ *How do Christian families share in the life of God the Father, the Son, and the Holy Spirit?* (Through Baptism the members of every Christian family share in the life of God.)

WE RESPOND

___ minutes

Connect to Life Have the students complete the *We Respond* activity. Discuss "communities of faith" and the things we can do to show love for God and others in the communities of our families, parish, and neighborhood.

Revisit the Prayer Space Invite the class to gather in the prayer space with their family snapshots. Ask them to pray a silent prayer of thanks for God's gift of a family. Then have the students add their photos to the gift box in the prayer space (option).

Pray Pray the Sign of the Cross and this prayer: *Dear God, please help us to live as Jesus did, loving and honoring our families and all of the people in our community. Amen.*

Plan Ahead for Day 3

Catechist Goal: To emphasize the responsibilities parents and children have toward one another

Preparation: Make copies of Reproducible Master 15; have available the Grade 4 CD.

Catechist Goal

- To emphasize the responsibilities parents and children have toward one another

Our Faith Response

- To identify our responsibilities in our families

Lesson Materials

- copies of Reproducible Master 15
- Grade 4 CD

Teaching Tip

Using Music in the Classroom

Today's lesson includes a song. Music can be a highly effective teaching tool, especially for auditory learners. Singing in unison also encourages a positive group dynamic. Let the students listen to the recorded song once or twice before joining in. Set the volume high enough to assist shy students and those who have difficulty following a tune, but not so high that they cannot hear themselves singing.

HONOR YOUR FATHER AND YOUR MOTHER.

In our families we have the responsibility to love and respect one another.

WE GATHER

✝ *Jesus, son of Mary, teach us to love and honor one another.*

Discuss the different roles and responsibilities of members of a family.

What are some of the responsibilities you have in your family?

WE BELIEVE

Parents and guardians have many responsibilities in their families. They try to make sure that their children have the things they need. They care for and protect their children. They teach them about the world in which they live. They help them to learn to work and play with other children. They show them ways to respect other people and to respect the property of others.

Catholic parents have a special responsibility to help their children grow in faith. They are to:

- share their love for and belief in God
- teach their children about God the Father, God the Son, and God the Holy Spirit
- teach their children about Jesus and the Church
- teach their children how to pray and worship with them at Sunday Mass
- help their children to learn the difference between good and evil
- show their children the importance of sharing and caring for the needs of others.

Parents and guardians share these responsibilities with the whole Church.

Lesson Plan

WE GATHER ___ minutes

✝ **Pray** Invite the students to take their family photographs from the gift box and name the people in the snapshots. Pray the Sign of the Cross and the *We Gather* prayer.

Focus on Life Use the *We Gather* questions and discussion to initiate a role-playing activity. Ask volunteers to act out different responsibilities adults and children have within a family. Tell the students that in this lesson they will learn that members of families have the responsibility to love and respect one another.

WE BELIEVE ___ minutes

Read the Text Have a volunteer read aloud the *We Believe* statement. Invite the students to read silently the *We Believe* text. Move around the room and offer help as the students read.

Do the Activity Ask a volunteer to read aloud the activity directions. Divide the class into groups. When the groups have finished, draw a three-column chart on the board. At the top of the first column write *children*; at the second, *teenagers*; and at the third, *adults.* Invite the groups to take turns writing their ideas on the chart. Discuss which photos in the chapter show people who are honoring the fourth commandment.

Work with a Partner Distribute copies of Reproducible Master 15. Ask a volunteer to read the directions aloud. When all the pairs are ready, invite them to share their ideas for the television show.

Children have responsibilities to their families, too. An important way to honor our parents and guardians is to obey them. Obedience is doing the just and good things that are asked of us. We keep the fourth commandment when we obey and respect our parents, cooperate with them, and appreciate them.

Our caring can become a way of thanking our parents or guardians for all they have done for us. As we grow older, the ways that we show our care for our parents will change. We may have to make sure that our parents have all that they need. Our visits, our phone calls, and our e-mails to our parents may become more important than ever.

Work with a group. Brainstorm situations in which children, teenagers, and adults follow the fourth commandment in different ways.

WE RESPOND

We Are the Family

Refrain:

We are the fam'ly and we
are the home.
We are the mountain where love
can be known.
We are the voices and we are
the hands
for bringing peace to our land.

And in our fam'ly all are welcome,
doesn't matter who you are.

In our home there's always room,
so plan to stay.

On our mountain where we labor
there's much work that's left to do,
and your talents would be helpful
if you stay. (Refrain)

Activity Bank

Curriculum Connection

Language

Activity Materials: a children's thesaurus

Encourage the students to use a thesaurus to build their vocabularies. Show the students how to look up the words *responsibility* and *respect.* Then have them make lists of other words that have similar meanings. Invite the students to write prayers or short paragraphs for younger children about living the fourth commandment. Encourage the writers to use several different words for responsibility and respect in their prayers and advice paragraphs.

Quick Check

✔ *What special responsibility do Catholic parents have?* (They are called to help their children grow in faith.)

✔ *As we become older, how can we thank our parents or guardians for all they do for us now?* (We can thank them by caring for them.)

WE RESPOND ___ minutes

Connect to Life Emphasize that by living up to our responsibilities to one another, we are showing our love and respect for God and for our families. Remind the students that we are all children in God's family. Play "We Are the Family," #16 on the Grade 4 CD. Then play it again and invite the students to sing along.

Pray Invite the students to gather in the prayer space. Pray: *Jesus, we thank you for the gift of our families. Please help us to meet our responsibilities to them with your love and guidance. Amen.*

Plan Ahead for Day 4

Catechist Goal: To highlight the importance of showing respect for leaders and authority figures

Preparation: Have available magazines, construction paper, and tape or glue.

Chapter 15 • Day 4

Catechist Goal

- To highlight the importance of showing respect for leaders and authority figures

Our Faith Response

- To choose to respect the authority figures in our community

Lesson Materials

- magazines containing photographs of family groups, world leaders, and people working for peace around the world
- construction paper
- tape or glue

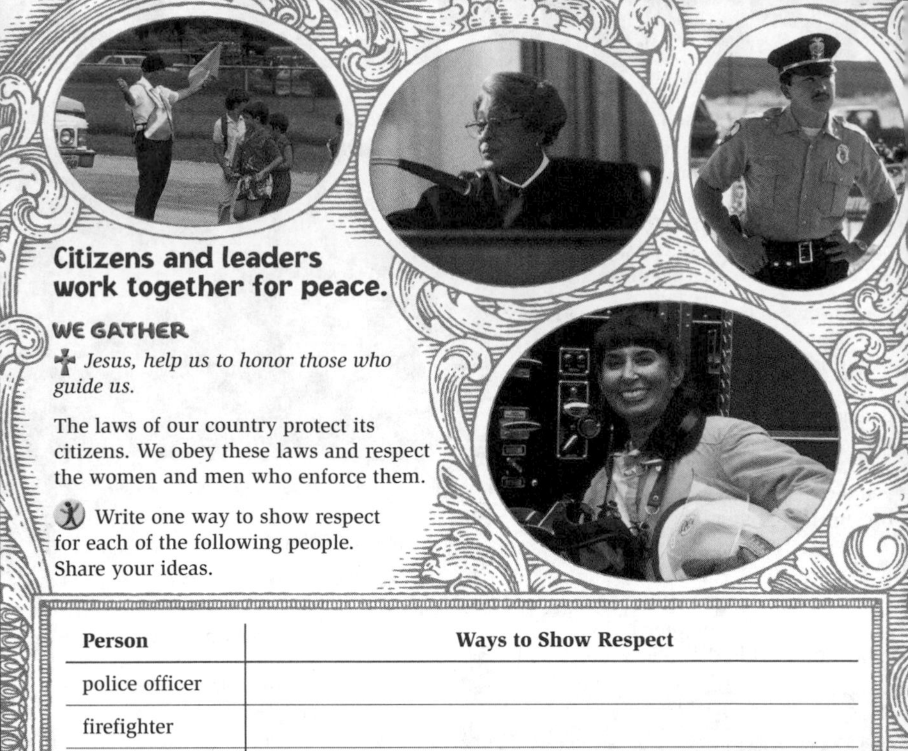

Citizens and leaders work together for peace.

WE GATHER

✝ *Jesus, help us to honor those who guide us.*

The laws of our country protect its citizens. We obey these laws and respect the women and men who enforce them.

Write one way to show respect for each of the following people. Share your ideas.

Person	Ways to Show Respect
police officer	
firefighter	
crossing guard	
judge	

WE BELIEVE

We are called to respect all people. The fourth commandment requires us to respect those who have a responsibility for us.

We should have respect for our teachers, church leaders, and all government leaders. These people are in positions of authority. Those in authority are called to respect the dignity of all people. They are asked to make sure that all people are treated fairly. They are called to work for peace. The only time we should not obey people who are responsible for us is when they ask us to do something that is wrong or unjust.

In the Gospel of Matthew we find Jesus respecting law and authority. After he cured a man's skin disease, Jesus said, "See that you tell no one, but go show yourself to the priest, and offer the gift that Moses prescribed" (Matthew 8:4).

178

Teaching Tip

Good Leadership

As a teacher you are an authority figure. Be an example of good leadership. Make your classroom a safe and supportive environment. Treat students fairly. Emphasize confidentiality and acceptance of students' ideas. Respect your students' individuality. Let them know that you will listen to them.

Lesson Plan

WE GATHER ___ minutes

✝ **Pray** After praying together the *We Gather* prayer, ask the students to select magazine photographs of people working for peace. Mount these photographs on sheets of construction paper. Invite the students to add the photographs to the gift box, explaining each photo as they do so.

Focus on Life Ask volunteers to read aloud the *We Gather* text and activity directions. Then have the students complete the activity and share their ideas. Tell the students that in this lesson they will learn ways citizens and leaders work together to help one another and to promote peace. Share the *Chapter Story* on guide page 171C.

WE BELIEVE ___ minutes

Read the Text Ask volunteers to read aloud the *We Believe* text. After each paragraph is read, encourage discussion of the main ideas in it. Emphasize the following:

- Citizens and leaders are called to follow God's commandments.
- As citizens we are called to honor just laws and leaders.
- As citizens we are called to participate and work together with our leaders for peace.

Reflect on the Fourth Commandment Explain to the students that the questions in their texts can help them examine their consciences in preparation for the sacrament of Reconciliation. Guide the students in making an examination of conscience by reading aloud the questions in the box.

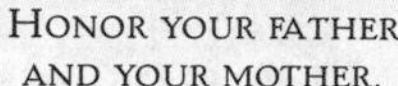

HONOR YOUR FATHER AND YOUR MOTHER.

Jesus showed respect for authority by telling the man to go to the priest. Jesus honored the law of Moses by telling the man to offer the gift.

Learning about and obeying the just laws of our country, state, city, or town is an important way to keep the fourth commandment. As citizens, another way is to participate in our government, especially by voting and paying taxes. We want our government to be just and fair, and to do good for the people of our country and the world. So we can write and talk to people who make decisions for our community. We can ask them to work for justice and peace.

We pray for our own leaders and lawmakers, and for the leaders of governments throughout the world. We work together for peace.

Take a few moments to think quietly and prayerfully about ways you follow the fourth commandment. These questions may help you.

Do I obey my parents in all that they ask of me?

Have I thanked my parents or guardians for all that they do?

Do I respect my brothers and sisters?

Do I help them?

Do I settle disagreements without fighting or arguing?

Do I obey my grandparents and respect them?

How have I showed respect for older people?

Do I obey my teachers and others in authority?

Do I obey police officers, crossing guards, firefighters, and other officials?

Have I followed the laws of my city, state, and country?

WE RESPOND

What can you do this week to be a peaceful person at home?

179

Chapter 15 • Day 4

ACTIVITY BANK

Curriculum Connection

Social Studies

Activity Materials: Internet and other research sources

Invite the students to use classroom encyclopedias, the school library, or Internet references to investigate Nobel Peace Prize winners whose faith inspired them to work for peace. Organize the class into groups to prepare reports on Mother Teresa (1979 winner), Archbishop Desmond Tutu (1984), and Bishop Carlos Filipe Ximenas Belo (1996). Explain to the groups that their reports might include answers to the following questions: *For what efforts to bring about world peace was this person noted? What role did his or her faith play in this person's work for peace? What can we learn from this person's example?*

Quick Check

✔ *Why do we give respect to our teachers, church leaders, and all government leaders?* (We are called to respect all people; the fourth commandment requires us to respect those who have responsibility for us.)

✔ *In what ways do we follow the fourth commandment in respect to law and authority?* (We learn about and obey just laws; we participate as citizens; we pray for our leaders and work with them for peace.)

WE RESPOND

___ minutes

Connect to Life After the students have written their answers to the We *Respond* question, invite them to share their answers with the class. Discuss how each photo on the page relates to authority.

Pray Together, pray again the *We Gather* prayer. Invite the students to offer silent prayers for peace.

Plan Ahead for Day 5

Catechist Goal: To review chapter ideas and their relationship to our faith life

Preparation: Make copies of Chapter 15 Test in the Grade 4 Assessment Book (option).

Chapter 15 • Day 5

Catechist Goal

- To review chapter ideas and their relationship to our faith life

Our Faith Response

- To apply what has been learned to our lives

CHAPTER TEST

Chapter 15 Test is provided in the Grade 4 Assessment Book.

Write True or False for the following sentences. Then change the false sentences to make them true.

1. True The fourth commandment is: "Honor your father and your mother."

2. True The domestic church is the church in the home.

3. True Children honor their parents by obeying them.

4. False The fourth commandment reminds us to get enough sleep.
The fourth commandment reminds us to honor our fathers, mothers, guardians, and all those who lead and serve us.

Write the letter of the phrase that completes each of the following:

5. c	The fourth commandment	a. are called to respect the dignity of all people.
6. d	Christian families	b. is doing the just and good things that are asked of us.
7. a	People in authority	c. teaches us to honor our parents, guardians, and all those who lead and serve us.
8. b	Obedience	d. are called to be communities of faith, hope, and love.

Write a sentence to answer the question.

9–10. How does the Great Commandment teach us about the Ten Commandments?
See page 172.

Make an idea bank about the ways people can live out the fourth commandment at home, school, and in the community.

180

Lesson Plan

___ minutes

Chapter Review Explain to the students that they are now going to check their understanding of what they have learned. Have the students complete questions 1–8. Ask volunteers to read aloud each correct answer. Have the students write their responses to question 9–10.

Assessment Activity Read the directions with the students. As appropriate, allow the class to review the chapter text as they complete the activity.

___ minutes

Reflect & Pray Read aloud the introduction. Allow the students time to write their prayers. Invite volunteers to share their responses.

Key Word Write the *Key Word, domestic church,* on the board. Ask the students to define the word, then invite them to suggest additional definitions to expand and enhance the meaning of the phrase.

Remember Form the students into groups of four. Assign one of the statements to each group. Have each group discuss its statement. Then allow time for the groups to share what they have learned.

We Respond in Faith

Reflect & Pray

When we show respect for others we show respect for God, too! What does this mean to you?

Holy Spirit, help us ______________________________

____

Key Word
domestic church (p. 175)

Remember

- God wants us to love and respect others.
- In our families we learn to love God and others.
- In our families we have the responsibility to love and respect one another.
- Citizens and leaders work together for peace.

Our Catholic Life

Call to Family, Community, and Participation

We live our Catholic faith in communities. The family is the most basic and important community to which we belong. Families are the center of our society. A society is a group of people or communities that share common experiences and laws.

Being a member of a family teaches us ways to take part in our communities and in society. The Church calls us to make our families strong. We need to help families that struggle. We need to support programs and laws that benefit family life.

Home Connection

Sharing Faith with My Family

Make sure to send home the family page (text page 182).

Encourage the students to read and discuss the Scripture quote with their families and to work with family members on their "Scripture Pictures."

For additional information and activities, encourage families to visit Sadlier's

www.WEBELIEVEweb.com

Our Catholic Life Read aloud the text. Encourage discussion of each paragraph. Ask: *In what ways can we live our faith in our communities? In what ways can we help at school, at home, and in the parish?* Share ways that you work to support the parish community in the school and suggest ways the students' parents work for them.

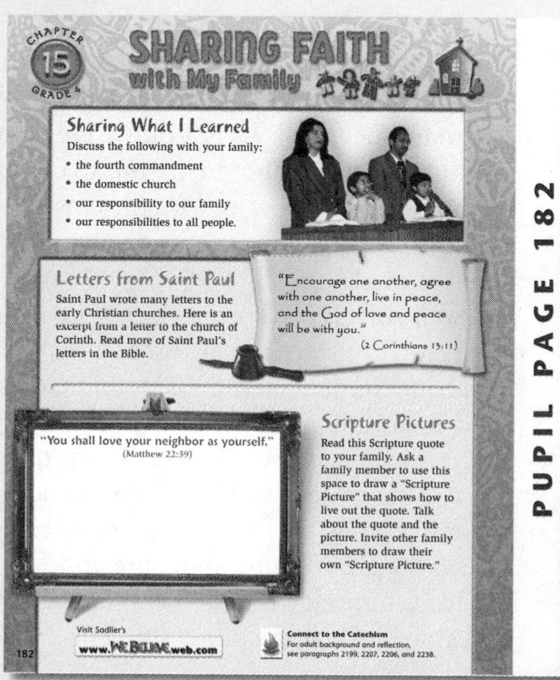

Chapter 15 Grade 4

SHARING FAITH with My Family

Sharing What I Learned

Discuss the following with your family:

- the fourth commandment
- the domestic church
- our responsibility to our family
- our responsibilities to all people.

Letters from Saint Paul

Saint Paul wrote many letters to the early Christian churches. Here is an excerpt from a letter to the church of Corinth. Read more of Saint Paul's letters in the Bible.

"Encourage one another, agree with one another, live in peace, and the God of love and peace will be with you."
(2 Corinthians 13:11)

"You shall love your neighbor as yourself."
(Matthew 22:39)

Scripture Pictures

Read this Scripture quote to your family. Ask a family member to use this space to draw a "Scripture Picture" that shows how to live out the quote. Talk about the quote and the picture. Invite other family members to draw their own "Scripture Picture."

Visit Sadlier's
www.WEBELIEVEweb.com

Connect to the Catechism
For adult background and reflection, see paragraphs 2199, 2207, 2206, and 2238.

182

PUPIL PAGE 182

Chapter 16 The Fifth Commandment

Overview

In Chapter 15 the students learned that the fourth commandment teaches us to honor and respect our parents, guardians, and all people in authority. In this chapter the students will learn what it means to live the fifth commandment by respecting all human life.

Doctrinal Content	For Adult Reading and Reflection *Catechism of the Catholic Church*
The students will learn:	Paragraph
• Human life is sacred.	2258
• The right to life is the most basic human right.	2270
• We respect the gift of life.	2288
• Promoting peace is a way to respect life.	2304

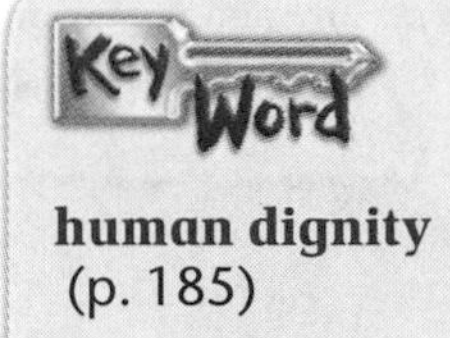

human dignity
(p. 185)

Catechist Background

Has anyone "saved your life," either literally or figuratively?

"You shall not kill." The fifth commandment teaches that "no one can under any circumstance claim for himself the right directly to destroy an innocent human being" (CCC 2258). In an age that knows violence and terrorism, the fifth commandment needs to be proclaimed clearly. This commandment calls us not only to refrain from harming innocent human life but to champion it—from the unborn new and fragile existence to the lives of those who experience the ravages of serious illness and old age.

Some of us one day may be involved in the life and death decisions that affect another person. The fifth commandment reminds us that God alone is Lord of life and death. However, on a daily basis we are responsible for words and actions that either nurture life or devalue life. We can be compassionate or uncaring; we can respond or reject; we can spread the gospel or promote the opposite message.

Jesus himself expanded and deepened the meaning of the fifth commandment. In Matthew's Gospel Jesus says: "You have heard it said to your ancestors, 'You shall not kill; and whoever kills will be liable to judgment.' But I say to you, whoever is angry with his brother will be liable to judgment" (5:21–22). Jesus recognized that anger often is the motive behind murder. Thus he stops us far short of killing and asks us not to use hurtful words or name-calling as weapons against others.

Through the fifth commandment God the Father calls us individually and as a community of faith to be peacemakers and preservers of life. In fact, the commandment might read: You shall not kill: you shall enhance life! As disciples of his Son we must be vigilant for and work against those things that destroy the life and dignity of the human person: scandal, injustice, prejudice, hatred, oppression of any kind, and war.

How do you in your own life contribute to peace-making and work for life issues?

Lesson Planning Guide

<table>
<tr><th>Lesson Focus</th><th>Presentation</th><th>Materials</th></tr>
<tr><td colspan="3">Day 1</td></tr>
<tr><td>Page 183
We Gather in Prayer

pages 184–185
Human life is sacred.</td><td>• Listen to Scripture.
Respond in song.
• Discuss persons who protect life in the We Gather questions.
• Read and discuss the We Believe text about human life as God's gift.
Do the We Respond activity.
• Read and discuss the As Catholics text.
• Pray together.</td><td>For the prayer space: basket, strips of colored paper, pictures of various people
"You Are Near," Dan Schutte, #17, Grade 4 CD</td></tr>
<tr><td colspan="3">Day 2</td></tr>
<tr><td>pages 186–187
The right to life is the most basic human right.</td><td>• In We Gather discuss the value of human life as treated in media.
• Read and discuss the We Believe text.
Do the We Respond activity.
• Pray together.</td><td>• several Bibles</td></tr>
<tr><td colspan="3">Day 3</td></tr>
<tr><td>Pages 188–189
We respect the gift of life.</td><td>Do the We Gather activity.
• Read and discuss the We Believe text.
Complete the activity.
Reflect on ways to respect the body in the We Respond question.
• Pray together.</td><td>• a Bible</td></tr>
<tr><td colspan="3">Day 4</td></tr>
<tr><td>pages 190–191
Promoting peace is a way to respect life.

Matthew 5:43–45</td><td>• Discuss the We Gather question.
• Read and discuss the We Believe text.
Complete the questions.
• Reflect on the fifth commandment.
Sing the We Respond song.
• Read and discuss Blessed are they . . .</td><td>• copies of Reproducible Master 16, guide page 183G (option)
"Prayer of Saint Francis," Sebastian Temple, #19, Grade 4 CD</td></tr>
<tr><td colspan="3">Day 5</td></tr>
<tr><td>page 192
Review

pages 193–194
We Respond in Faith</td><td>• Complete questions 1–10.
Work on the Assessment Activity.
• Complete the Reflect & Pray activity.
• Review Remember and Key Word.
• Read and discuss Our Catholic Life.
• Discuss Sharing Faith with My Family.</td><td>• magazine pictures
• Chapter 16 Test in Assessment Book, pp. 33–34
• Chapter 16 Test in Test Generator
• Review & Resource Book, pp. 37–39
• Family Book, pp. 46–48</td></tr>
</table>

For additional ideas, activities, and opportunities: Visit Sadlier's **www.WEBELIEVEweb.com**

Enrichment Ideas

Chapter Story

Mother Teresa was born in 1910 in Macedonia. She loved being in church, praying and singing. When she was nine years old her father died. Her mother worked hard to support the family. She taught Teresa and her other two children the importance of helping those who are poor or in need.

When she was 18 years old, Teresa decided to become a nun. She joined the Sisters of Our Lady of Loretto, who were very active in India. In 1928 she began her journey to India.

In India she became a teacher. She cared for and loved her poor students so much that they began to call her Ma. In 1948 Teresa had a moment that changed her life. While walking the streets of Calcutta she came across a half-dead woman lying in front of a hospital. She stayed with the sick woman until she died. From that moment Mother Teresa dedicated her life to helping the poorest of the poor. In Calcutta she founded an order of nuns known as the Missionaries of Charity. As Mother Superior Teresa led and directed the work of these nuns, who are dedicated to serving the poor.

In 1952 Mother Teresa organized a home where those who were dying in the streets of Calcutta could come to die in peace, with dignity and respect. She recognized the human dignity of these poor people whom society had forgotten. She saw that the lives of all people are valuable and important because God has created us all.

In 1979 Mother Teresa won the Nobel Peace Prize for her devotion to those in need. On September 5, 1997, Mother Teresa died, having given her life to the service of the poorest of the poor.

▶ *What can you learn from the life of Mother Teresa? How can you follow her example in living the fifth commandment?*

FAITH and MEDIA

▶ To help the students with the *Chapter Project,* gather a selection of Catholic periodicals and both local and national magazines and newspapers for the students' use. These print media might contain a news story that will help illustrate the effects of violence and the efforts of peacemakers.

▶ On Day 2 the students are asked to think about whether the television programs they watch and the computer games they play show respect for human life. Come prepared with a few examples of shows and games that exhibit a positive attitude toward the value of human life.

CHAPTER PROJECT: LOOKING CLOSER AT OUR WORLD

Living the fifth commandment means respecting the lives of all people. Emphasize that there are peacemakers in the world who try to bring respect and peace to many people. Bring in current newspaper and magazine articles and ask the students to find stories that deal with violence and peace. Take time to discuss some of the news stories with the students. Point out the effects of violence and the ways peacemakers work to counteract those effects and fulfill the fifth commandment. Ask each student to choose one article and write a short reflection on it. The reflection should include what the student has learned from the article, whether or not the people described followed the fifth commandment, and the ways the actions of the people affect others. Collect the news articles and the students' reflections and display them on a bulletin board. This will allow students to apply what they are learning.

Connections

To Scripture

Saint Paul writes in Romans 13:9 that the fifth commandment and all other commandments "are summed up in this saying, 'You shall love your neighbor as yourself.'" Read this passage to the students to help them understand that loving others is a fulfillment of the fifth commandment. Help the students to see that their everyday actions are a way of keeping the commandments. This will make following God's law more relevant to them.

To Stewardship

Students can keep the fifth commandment through acts of stewardship. Explain that when we donate our time through volunteer work, give money to the parish and to charity, and share our talents with others, we are showing respect for the dignity, life, and needs of our neighbors. Provide opportunities for the students to be stewards: Volunteer to help a kindergarten class, choose a charitable organization and start a classroom coin-collection jar; or encourage the students to share their talents at a local nursing home.

To Saints

The saints showed their love for God and others by keeping the Ten Commandments. One saint who lived her life in fulfillment of the fifth commandment was Elizabeth of Portugal. Present the students with the following information about her. Elizabeth was a queen who worked for peace in her family and in her country. When resentment between her husband and her son turned to war, Elizabeth rode between the fighting armies and brought about peace. She devoted her life to promoting peace and preserving the sanctity of life. Her feast day is July 4.

Meeting Individual Needs

Students with ADD

Students with Attention Deficit Disorder (ADD) may benefit from structure. Provide these students with a schedule of the day's activities. This will allow them to check off what they have accomplished and know what is coming up next. The schedule will help them focus on the activities for the day, and checking off finished activities will provide them with a sense of completion.

ADDITIONAL RESOURCES

Books *Saint Francis of Assisi: Gentle Revolutionary,* Mary Emmanuel Alves, FSP, Pauline Books and Media, 2000. This is a story of the sacredness of all life.

Saint Edith Stein: Blessed by the Cross, Mary Lea Hill, FSP, Pauline Books and Media, 2000. Edith Stein is a heroic model for young people.

Video *John the Baptist,* CCC of America, 1997. From the series *A Kingdom Without Frontiers,* this video presents an animated life of the saint. (30 minutes)

To find more ideas for books, videos, and other learning material, visit Sadlier's

www.WEBELIEVEweb.com

Sharing Catholic Social Teaching

by Joan Rosenhauer

Joan Rosenhauer is Special Projects Coordinator for the U.S. Conference of Catholic Bishops' Department of Social Development and World Peace. She has been a lead staff person for the bishops' program on Catholic Social Teaching and Catholic Education.

"The sharing of our social tradition is a defining measure of Catholic education," the U.S. bishops wrote in their statement, *Sharing Catholic Social Teaching*, page 3.

The Church's social teaching includes thought *and* action—both of which are essential elements of Catholic education. The Church has applied the lessons of the Scriptures to the world around us through a series of documents. This body of thought is known as Catholic Social Teaching. There are seven key themes of Catholic Social Teaching. These are:

Life and Dignity of the Human Person Every human is a precious gift from God and must be protected. People must be treated with respect. Public policies must be measured by whether they enhance human life and dignity.

Call to Family, Community, and Participation Human beings are social beings. Our relationships must reflect the values of our faith. This begins with supporting and sustaining the family. In society, all people have both a right and a responsibility to participate in economic, social, and political life.

Rights and Responsibilities of the Human Person A healthy society can be achieved only if basic human rights are protected and responsibilities are met.

Option for the Poor and Vulnerable We care especially for those who are in greatest need. A moral test of our society is how our most vulnerable members are doing.

Dignity of Work and the Rights of Workers Work is one way we participate in God's creation. If the dignity of work is to be protected, the rights of workers must be respected.

Solidarity of the Human Family We are our brothers' and sisters' keepers no matter where they live throughout the world.

Care for God's Creation We respect the gift of creation by protecting God's people and the environment in which we live.

(continued on next page)

Catechist Development Topics (Topic and Guide Page)

Resources

Himes, Kenneth R. *Responses to 101 Questions on Catholic Social Teaching.* Mahwah: Paulist Press, 2001.

Sharing Catholic Social Teaching: Challenges and Directions. Washington, D.C.: United States Catholic Conference, 1998.

As catechists, our teaching about the Catholic social tradition must include practicing charity *and* working for justice and peace. Through our words and actions, we can encourage our students to build a more just world and to promote the good of all people, especially those who are in greatest need.

Ways to Implement Sharing Catholic Social Teaching

- When teaching about the Eucharist, remind your students that we are called to recognize Christ in the consecrated host and in the "least" of his brothers and sisters.
- When teaching about the Blessed Trinity, discuss the Church's understanding of human beings as social beings (created in the image of God) with important responsibilities to our families and the obligation to participate in society.
- Involve students in service projects such as collecting food or clothing for people in need. For each project, identify one of the seven themes of Catholic Social Teaching to teach in connection with the effort.
- Read about saints, heroes, public leaders, etc. who practiced charity and pursued justice and peace. Also read articles about people who do this today. Discuss how their lives reflect themes from Catholic Social Teaching.
- Work with your diocesan social action office to conduct an "Offering of Letters." Families can be invited to write a letter to a public official about an issue of justice and peace. Students can bring them to a parish or school Mass and include them in the offering. Those who choose not to prepare a letter can write a prayer intention on an index card and include it in the offering.
- If members of your parish belong to a legislative network or participate in a pro-life march or "lobby day" in the state capital, invite them to speak to your students about what they do and why it's important in light of Catholic Social Teaching.

For additional ideas, activities, and opportunities, visit Sadlier's

www.WEBELIEVEweb.com

With thanks to:
Eileen Scheibner
St. Thomas More Parish
Convent Station, New Jersey

Under Eileen's direction, the children in her parish are mindful of Catholic Social Teaching. One important activity is participating in making a yearly "Giving Tree." Eileen and the children compile a list of supplies for people in need throughout the parish community and surrounding areas. These are then illustrated as ornaments and placed on the "Giving Tree" by the children. Each family in the parish is encouraged to fulfill a request on the "Giving Tree." The children actively participate in the process of sorting food, clothes, etc. With the assistance of a social worker and other members of the parish community, Eileen and the children help to deliver the supplies to people in need. The children are eager to share their experiences which naturally leads to discussions on the broader themes of Catholic Social Teaching.

Notes

Name ______________________________

In each column list ways that the individual, group, or nation works for peace and justice.

Individual	Group	Nation

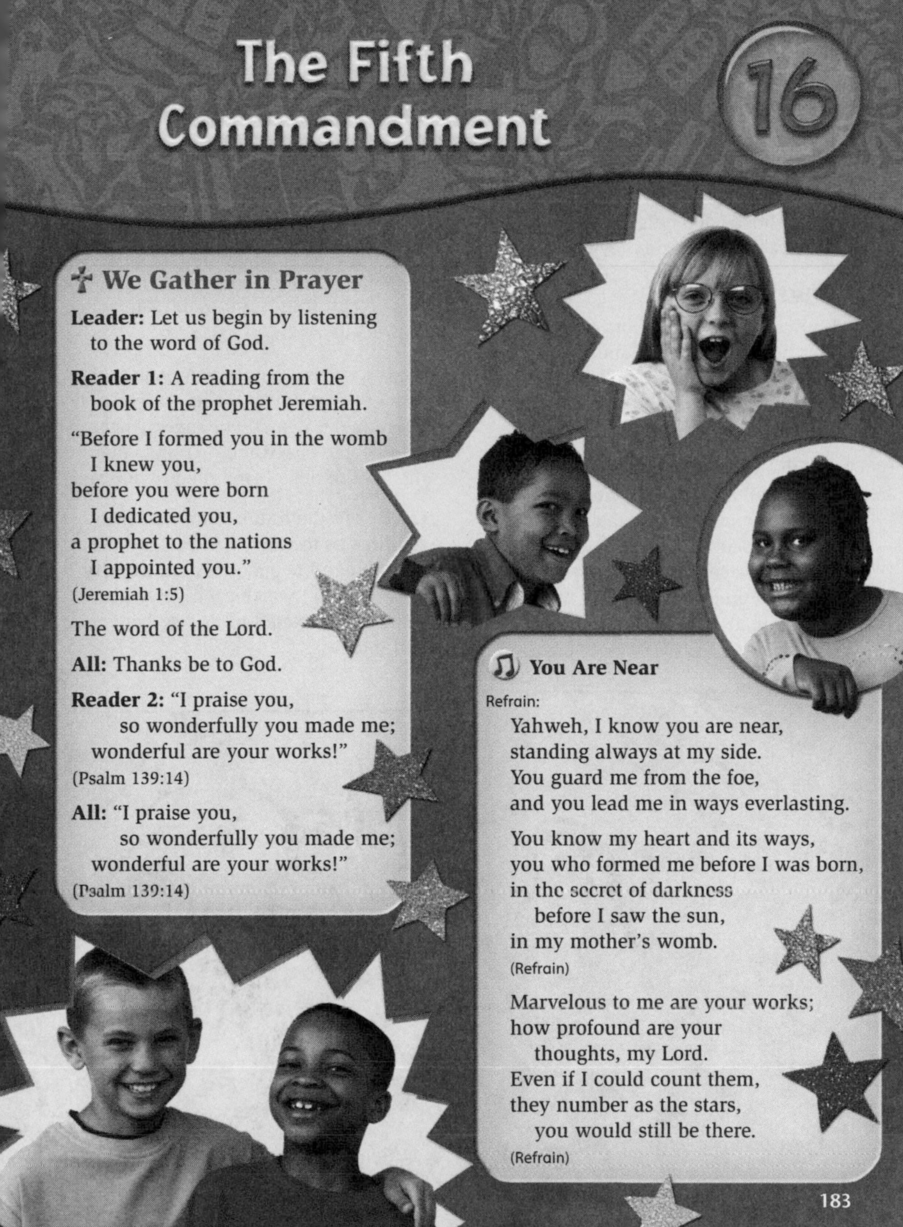

The Fifth Commandment 16

We Gather in Prayer

Leader: Let us begin by listening to the word of God.

Reader 1: A reading from the book of the prophet Jeremiah.

"Before I formed you in the womb
I knew you,
before you were born
I dedicated you,
a prophet to the nations
I appointed you."
(Jeremiah 1:5)

The word of the Lord.

All: Thanks be to God.

Reader 2: "I praise you,
so wonderfully you made me;
wonderful are your works!"
(Psalm 139:14)

All: "I praise you,
so wonderfully you made me;
wonderful are your works!"
(Psalm 139:14)

You Are Near

Refrain:
Yahweh, I know you are near,
standing always at my side.
You guard me from the foe,
and you lead me in ways everlasting.

You know my heart and its ways,
you who formed me before I was born,
in the secret of darkness
before I saw the sun,
in my mother's womb.
(Refrain)

Marvelous to me are your works;
how profound are your
thoughts, my Lord.
Even if I could count them,
they number as the stars,
you would still be there.
(Refrain)

183

PREPARING TO PRAY

Through proclamation of Scripture and song, the students will praise God for his wonderful works.

• Tell the students that you will take the leader's part.

• Assign two readers and allow them time to read and rehearse their parts.

• Practice the group responses.

• Play "You Are Near," Dan Schutte, #17, Grade 4 CD, once or twice to let the students learn the song.

The Prayer Space

• Gather the following items: a basket holding small pictures of people of different backgrounds at various stages of life: babies, children, young adults, and middle-aged and older adults. The pictures should illustrate the value of every person's life at each stage of life.

This Week's Liturgy

Visit **www.webelieveweb.com** for this week's liturgical readings and other seasonal material.

Lesson Plan

We Gather in Prayer ___ minutes

Pray

• Invite the students to the prayer space with the words *We gather in prayer.* Give the students a few quiet moments to prepare their hearts for prayer.

• Ask volunteers to place the basket and the pictures in the prayer space.

• Pray together the Sign of the Cross and the opening prayer.

• After the prayer, play "You Are Near," and encourage the students to sing along.

Home Connection Update

Invite the students to share the ways they used the Chapter 15 family page. Ask: *Did you talk about the fourth commandment, the domestic church, and our responsibilities to our families and others?* Invite volunteers to share descriptions of what their family members drew for the "Scripture Pictures."

Chapter 16 • Day 1

Catechist Goal

• To explain that all human life is sacred

Our Faith Response

• To seek ways we can respect and protect life in our daily activities

 **human dignity**

Lesson Materials

• Bibles for the students

As Catholics...

About Our Feelings

After you have finished the lesson, invite volunteers to read aloud the text. Emphasize that hearts filled with peace help us to follow the fifth commandment and live as Jesus taught.

Human life is sacred.

YOU SHALL NOT KILL.

WE GATHER

✝ *Dear God, all life comes from you and will return to you.*

Who are the people in our neighborhoods and cities who work to protect life? What do they do?

WE BELIEVE

All human life is a gift from God. God shares his life with each and every one of us. Of all God's creation, only we are made to love God and grow in his friendship.

The fifth commandment is based on the belief that all life is sacred, created by God. The fifth commandment states, "You shall not kill" (Exodus 20:13; Deuteronomy 5:17). To follow this commandment we must respect and protect human life. We must value life in all that we say and do.

During the Sermon on the Mount, Jesus taught about the fifth commandment. He said, "You have heard that it was said to your ancestors, 'You shall not kill; and whoever kills will be liable to judgment.' But I say to you, whoever is angry with his brother will be liable to judgment" (Matthew 5:21–22).

Jesus gave us a new way to look at the fifth commandment. Jesus asks us to have peace in our hearts, not anger. Anger can lead people to say and do things that hurt the lives of others, and their own lives.

Living out the fifth commandment requires us to respect all life and the dignity of all people. **Human dignity** is the value and worth each person has from being created in God's image and likeness.

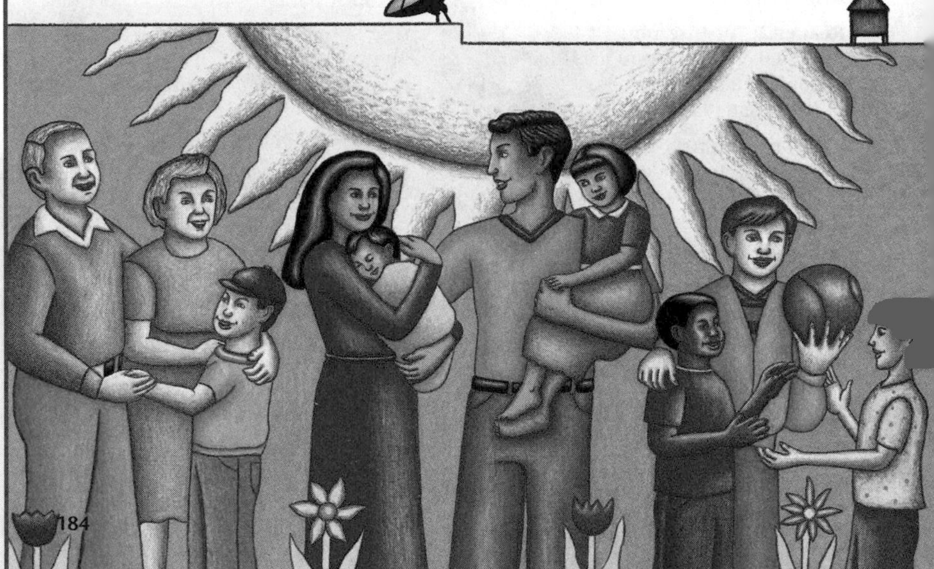

184

Lesson Plan

WE GATHER ___ minutes

✝ **Pray** Pray the Sign of the Cross and the *We Gather* prayer.

Focus on Life As they respond to the *We Gather* questions, encourage the students to discuss workers such as police officers and firefighters who, by their actions every day, acknowledge the value of every human life. Tell the students that in this lesson they will learn that God creates human life and that all human life is therefore sacred.

WE BELIEVE ___ minutes

Learn About Life Invite a volunteer to read aloud the *We Believe* statement. Then ask volunteers to read aloud the *We Believe* paragraphs. Emphasize the following:

• God gives each of us the gift of life.

• The fifth commandment calls us to recognize, by our words and our actions, the value of every human life.

• God creates people of different races, ages, genders, and abilities. All people are equal because all are created by God.

Take a Closer Look In the third *We Believe* paragraph, the students read about Jesus' Sermon on the Mount. Organize the class into small groups of three or four students each. Provide each group with a Bible. Ask each group to read and reflect on Jesus' Sermon on the Mount as described in the Gospel of Saint Matthew, Chapter 5. After a few minutes invite each group to present one of its ideas to the class, and have all the students discuss what they have learned from Jesus' words.

This gift gives us the ability to think, to make choices, and to love. Human dignity makes us someone, not something. It makes us all equal with one another.

Differences of race, sex, age, and ability do not change how God treats us. These differences should not change how we treat one another. We are called to respect all people because each and every person is created by God.

WE RESPOND

What are the gifts of life for which you are thankful?

Design a mural to show the different ways we can respect and protect life:

- at home and in the neighborhood
- in class and on the playground
- in sports and activities.

As Catholics...

When Jesus taught about the fifth commandment, he told us not to have anger in our hearts. Anger is a feeling that can lead us to act in harmful or hurtful ways. However, sometimes anger can lead us to speak out for what is right and to help others change unjust situations. Feelings themselves are not right or wrong. However, the way we deal with or act on our feelings can be. Learning how to deal with our feelings in a Christian way is an important part of growing in faith.

This week try to think before you act on your feelings.

Key Word

human dignity the value and worth each person has from being created in God's image

ACTIVITY BANK

Multicultural Connection

Celebrating Our Differences

Activity Materials: Internet or other research sources

Differences of ethnic background do not affect the way God treats us, and they should not affect the way we treat each other. Invite the students to research their own ethnic backgrounds and write one-page reports about one aspect of their heritage. A Mexican American student might choose to write about the special place Our Lady of Guadalupe has in his or her home; an Irish American student might write about Saint Patrick and his place in Irish history. Allow the students time to share their reports in small groups, then lead the whole class in a discussion of our differences as something to celebrate rather than as something to separate us. Display the student's reports on a bulletin board under the heading *God's Love Makes Us Equal.*

iscuss Human Dignity Invite a volunteer to read loud the definition of the key word *human dignity.* oint out the ways we can treat other people with espect. Say: *We treat all people with love, kindness, and nderstanding. We treat all people as equals.* Then read loud the *Chapter Story* and ask the students to think of ays to follow Mother Teresa's example in living the fth commandment.

uick Check

✓ *What does Jesus ask us to have in our hearts?* (Jesus asks us to have peace in our hearts.)

✓ *What is human dignity?* (Human dignity is the value and worth each person has from being created in God's image.)

WE RESPOND ___ minutes

Connect to Life Invite the students to read the directions for the activity. Have them work in small groups to design their murals. When all have finished, ask the groups to share their murals with the class. Emphasize the importance of respecting and protecting life in our neighborhood, in our school, and in our community.

Pray Invite the students to offer individual prayers of gratitude for the gift of life.

Plan Ahead for Day 2

Catechist Goal: To teach that the right to life is the most basic human right

Preparation: Come prepared with a few examples of television shows and video games that exhibit a positive attitude toward the value of human life.

Chapter 16 • Day 2

Catechist Goal

- To teach that the right to life is the most basic human right

Our Faith Response

- To understand that the right to life is the most basic human right

The right to life is the most basic human right.

WE GATHER

✝ *Jesus, you give us life.*

Think about the television shows you have seen or computer games you have played lately. In what ways did they show human life being valued? being harmed? Explain your answers.

WE BELIEVE

The fifth commandment teaches us about the right to life. The right to life is the most basic human right. We all share this right. Unfortunately, not all the things that people do value and protect human life. For example, people are sometimes violent. They act in ways that destroy things or harm and injure others. Violence against people can lead to a disregard for human life.

Because our own life is sacred, we have the right to protect and defend ourselves. We also have a special responsibility to protect the lives of those who cannot defend themselves.

The deliberate killing of an innocent person is a very serious sin. It takes away that person's life. Each of us has the right to life from the moment of conception to the moment of death.

- Unborn children deserve protection and respect as all people do. They have the right to life. The deliberate killing of an unborn human being is a very serious sin.

- Our lives are a gift from God. We must value our own lives. To take one's own life is called suicide. It is a very serious sin.

Teaching Tip

Discussing Sensitive Topics

In this lesson students are confronted with controversial topics. Be sensitive to the feelings of your students when discussing these topics. Help guide the students' minds and hearts by underscoring the importance of respecting all life. Remind the class that our Church family helps guide us when we are faced with these grave issues.

Lesson Plan

WE GATHER ___ minutes

✝ **Pray** Pray the *We Gather* prayer.

Focus on Life Have the students read silently the *We Gather* text. Ask them to share their answers. Encourage the students to take a critical look at the often violent images they see in the media. Tell the students that in this lesson they will learn that God calls us to respect the right to life.

WE BELIEVE ___ minutes

Discuss the Value of Life Invite a volunteer to read aloud the *We Believe* statement; then, ask a volunteer to read aloud the first *We Believe* paragraph. Emphasize:

- The fifth commandment establishes the basic right to life for all people.
- Violence denies the human dignity of another person.

Invite the students to talk with a partner about the violence they see in their community and around the world. Ask: *How does this violence affect others? How does violence make us feel? What do you wish were different about the world?* Explain that by respecting life in their own words and actions, the students can help make their community and the world a better place.

Learn About Respecting and Protecting Life Have the students read the second and third *We Believe* paragraphs. Explain that the right to life is a very controversial issue in our society and that people have strong opinions about it. Point out that all people are created by God and that killing another person, except in self-defense, is a very serious sin. Human life is sacred from the moment of conception until the moment of death.

- People who are sick, disabled, elderly, or dying have the same right to life as all people. They deserve our care and protection. The deliberate killing of someone who is suffering or slowly dying is a very serious sin.

God's mercy is greater than the actions of any person. In his great love, God calls those who have sinned to come back to him. We believe that God will show mercy and love to those who are truly sorry.

We Respond

With a group develop a radio commercial. Focus on the positive message of protecting and respecting all life. Your commercial might be a song, a poem, or even a speech.

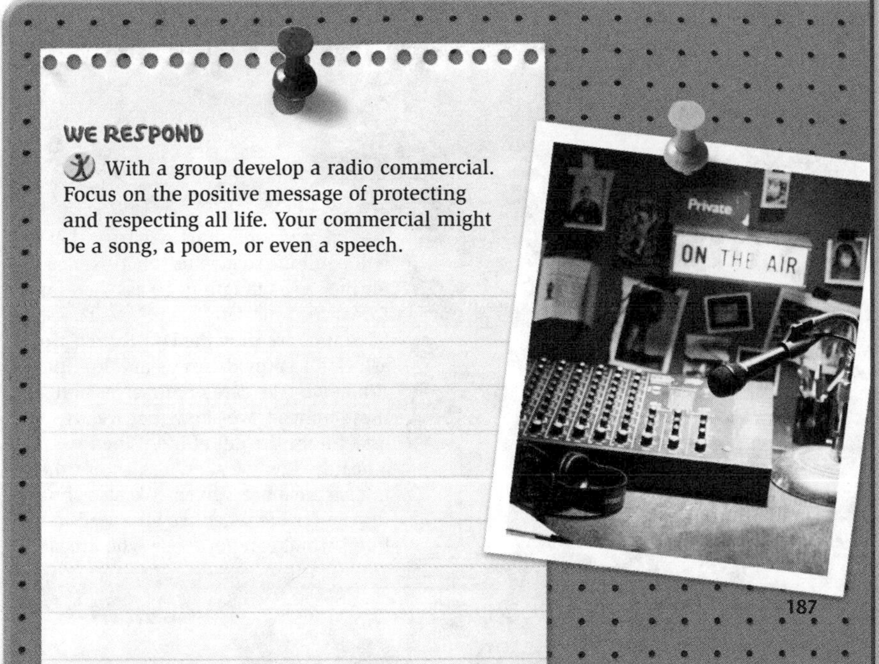

Activity Bank

Catholic Social Teaching

Life and Dignity of the Human Person

Catholic social teaching states that human life is sacred and should be protected. Various Catholic and public agencies provide needed services for families and their children. Help the students organize a diaper or baby-food drive, either as a class or as a school. By collecting needed supplies, the students will show their respect for life.

The Church teaches us that the lives of unborn children and the elderly should be respected and protected.

Read aloud the rest of the *We Believe* text. Brainstorm ways that we can help protect all human life. (Care for the sick, the elderly, and children in need; help the homeless and victims of domestic violence; minister to prisoners on death row.) Invite the students to comment on each photo.

Quick Check

✔ *What is the most basic human right?* (The right to life is the most basic human right.)

✔ *What is greater than the actions of any person?* (God's mercy)

We Respond

___ minutes

Connect to Life Help the students to recall effective radio commercials, and ask them to explain why these commercials worked. Then read the directions and organize the class into small groups. Allow each group to present its commercial to the class. Discuss the message of each commercial.

Pray Invite the students to look again at the pictures in the basket in the prayer space. Pray a special prayer of petition for respect for life in our community, our society, and our world.

Plan Ahead for Day 3

Catechist Goal: To examine ways we can respect the gift of life

Preparation: Be prepared to discuss ways to live a healthy life.

Catechist Goal

• To examine ways we can respect the gift of life

Our Faith Response

• To respect life in our words and actions

Lesson Materials

• a Bible

We respect the gift of life.

WE GATHER

✝ *God, you are the creator of all life.*

What are some things that you can do to promote healthy living?

____

____

____

WE BELIEVE

God created each of us. We trust that he will continue to give us what we need for life. Jesus taught us to ask God our Father for "our daily bread" (Matthew 6:11). Each time we pray the Our Father, we ask God to provide for us and for others. When we take care of ourselves and those in need, we show that we are grateful for the gift of life. When we live a healthy life, we show respect for the life we have been given. We also show respect for life when we give food to the hungry and care for those who are sick.

188

Teaching Tip

Role-Playing

In today's lesson the students will have the opportunity to engage in role-playing. To help make this activity run smoothly, discuss your behavioral expectations with the class beforehand. Explain that you would like them to remain "in character" as much as possible, but that they should not begin to act in inappropriate ways. You may also wish to establish a closing signal to alert the role-players that it is time to end their skit.

Lesson Plan

WE GATHER ____ minutes

✝ **Pray** Invite the students to think about the many good things God has created. Pray aloud the *We Gather* prayer.

Focus on Life Ask volunteers to read aloud the *We Gather* question. Invite the students to share their answers. Tell the students that in this lesson they will learn how we show respect for the life given to us by God.

WE BELIEVE ____ minutes

Live a Healthy Life Invite volunteers to read aloud the *We Believe* statement and the *We Believe* text. Emphasize the following:

• God gives life to all of us.

• God does not create us and then leave us. He continues to provide for us and watch over us. We can ask God for help as we do when we pray the Our Father.

• We can show God our thanks for the gift of life by taking good care of our lives and the lives of others.

• People who are poor, hungry, and vulnerable are in need of our care and help. God calls us to respect the lives of all those in need.

Do the Activity Remind the students that God asks us to live out the fifth commandment in our daily lives. Read aloud the directions for the activity. When all have finished, invite volunteers to share their answers.

Act It Out Organize the class into four or five groups. Ask each group to prepare and perform a skit in which a person or people are caring for those in need. Allow

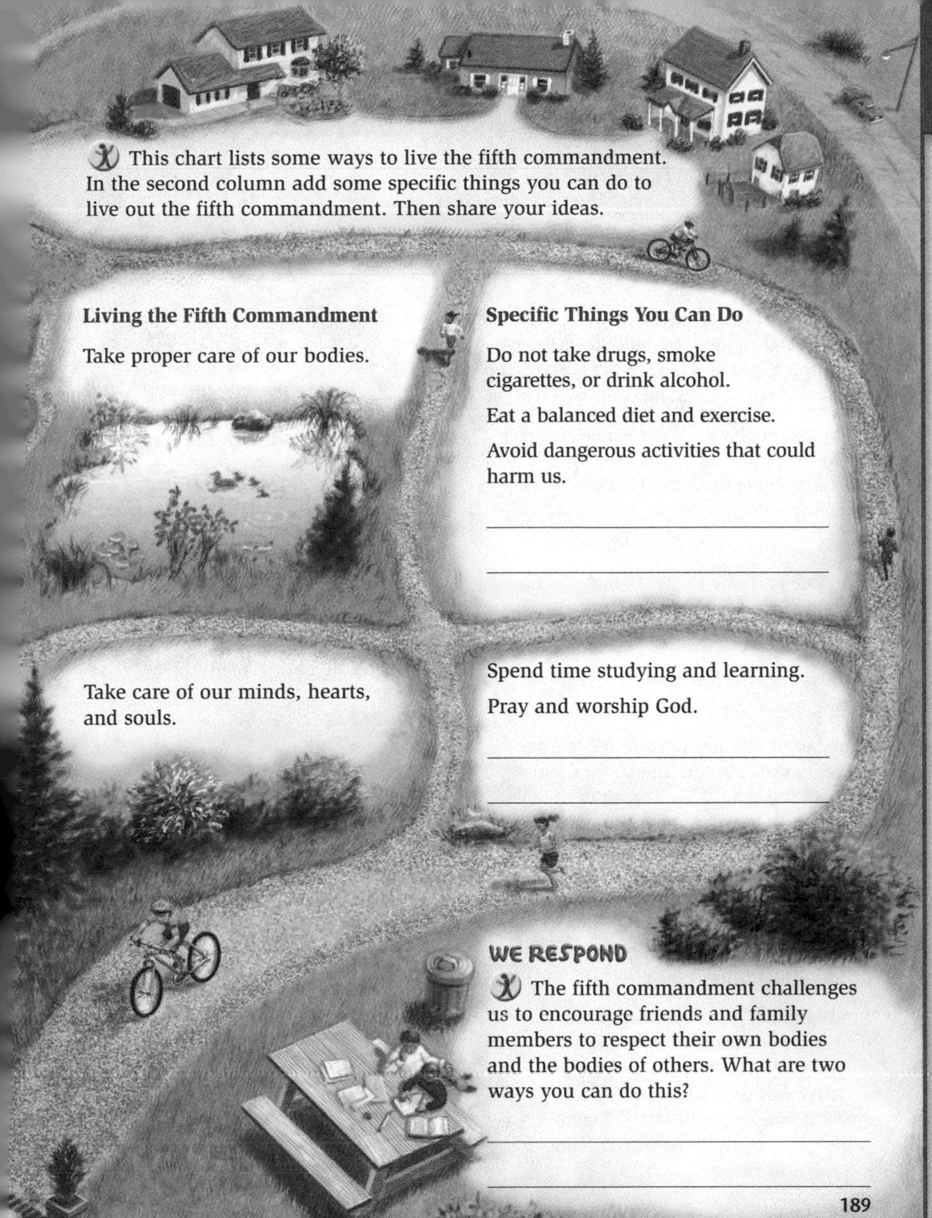

This chart lists some ways to live the fifth commandment. In the second column add some specific things you can do to live out the fifth commandment. Then share your ideas.
Living the Fifth Commandment
Specific Things You Can Do
Take proper care of our bodies.
Do not take drugs, smoke cigarettes, or drink alcohol.
Eat a balanced diet and exercise.
Avoid dangerous activities that could harm us.
Take care of our minds, hearts, and souls.
Spend time studying and learning.
Pray and worship God.
WE RESPOND
The fifth commandment challenges us to encourage friends and family members to respect their own bodies and the bodies of others. What are two ways you can do this?
189

Chapter 16 • **Day 3**

ACTIVITY BANK

Curriculum Connection

Science

Activity Materials: illustration of the food pyramid, markers or colored pencils

Eating a balanced diet is a specific way to live a healthy life and thus live out the fifth commandment. Remind the students about the four food groups and show them an illustration of the USDA food guide pyramid. Discuss the number of servings from each food group that we should eat every day. Invite the students to design a "spiritual food pyramid." Praying and worshiping God might be at the base of the pyramid, with such recommendations as studying and learning on the other levels.

each group time to present its skit. Remind the students that when we care for those in need, we show God our gratitude for the gift of life.

Write About Creation The first *We Believe* sentence, "God created each of us," recalls the words of Jeremiah 1:5. Read this verse to the class; then invite the students to write a brief paragraph describing God who loves us from the very first moment of our conception.

Quick Check

✔ *What do we ask for when we pray the Our Father?* (We ask God to provide for us and for others.)

✔ *How do we show respect for life?* (by living a healthy life and by caring for the hungry and the sick)

WE RESPOND ___ minutes

Connect to Life Have the students read the *We Respond* paragraph. Remind them that we have been given the mission to spread the good news of God's message. Invite them to share their responses.

Pray Recall that we pray the Our Father to ask for the daily bread we need to sustain our lives. Invite the class to pray the Our Father together.

Plan Ahead for Day 4

Catechist Goal: To describe ways the Church works toward peace

Preparation: Make copies of Reproducible Master 16 (option). Have the Grade 4 CD available.

Chapter 16 • Day 4

Catechist Goal

- To describe ways the Church works toward peace

Our Faith Response

- To identify ways we can work for peace and justice

Lesson Materials

- copies of Reproducible Master 16 (option)
- Grade 4 CD

Blessed are they...

Saint Edith Stein

After the lesson has been presented, invite volunteers to read aloud the text. Explain to the students that Edith, who took the name Teresa when she became a nun, wanted to bring hope and comfort to God's people. We also know Edith Stein as Saint Teresa Benedicta of the Cross.

Promoting peace is a way to respect life.

YOU SHALL NOT KILL.

WE GATHER

✝ *God, our heavenly Father, help us to care for and protect one another.*

What does the word *peace* mean to you?

WE BELIEVE

God cares for all people, no matter what they do. God's grace strengthens us to love and respect others. Love and respect lead to peace in our hearts and in our world.

Peace comes about when people truly love one another and work together. The Church community works toward peace by making sure people:

- have the things they need to live
- feel free and safe to talk to one another
- respect the dignity of individuals and societies
- follow Jesus' command to love others as he has loved us.

Jesus taught his disciples to value love above all else. He told them, "You have heard that it was said, 'You shall love your neighbor and hate your enemy.' But I say to you, love your enemies, and pray for those who persecute you, that you may be children of your heavenly Father, for he makes his sun rise on the bad and the good, and causes rain to fall on the just and the unjust" (Matthew 5:43–45).

If individuals, groups, and nations work for peace and justice, we will have a world of love, not hatred and violence. We trust that God will help us to be strong witnesses to his love. Together as the Church, we hope in God's mercy and pray for peace.

PEACE

With a partner answer the following questions. Then share your answers with the class.

What can you do to keep your home peaceful?

____

____

What can your class do to make your school a safe and peaceful place?

____

____

What can your parish do to encourage peace and discourage violence in your neighborhood?

____

____

What can our nation do to promote peace in the world?

____

____

190

Lesson Plan

WE GATHER ___ minutes

✝ **Pray** Pray the Sign of the Cross and the *We Gather* prayer.

Focus on Life Invite a volunteer to read aloud the *We Gather* question. Ask the students to share their answers. Write some of the responses on the board. Explain that to be a person of peace means to value the life of every human being. Tell the students that in this lesson they will learn that respecting life also means working for peace and justice.

WE BELIEVE ___ minutes

Identify the Main Points After a volunteer has read aloud the *We Believe* statement, organize the students into pairs. Ask the pairs to read the *We Believe* text together and list three main points. Then invite each pair to share one point. Write the responses on the board and discuss the main points.

Promote Peace and Justice Have groups of students work together to complete the *We Believe* activity. When all have finished, invite them to share their answers. Include the students' responses in a class "peace pact." Explain that this pact will remind them of ways to promote peace among themselves, in their words and in their actions. Post a copy of the pact in the classroom.

Reflect on the Fifth Commandment Invite the students to use the chart on page 190 and the questions on page 191 to help them make an examination of conscience. Encourage them to think about ways to honor this commandment more fully.

Chapter 16 • **Day 4**

Take a few moments to think quietly and prayerfully about ways you follow the fifth commandment. These questions may help you.

Have I respected the dignity of all people?

Have I shown by my actions that all people have the right to life?

Have I lived each day in a healthy way?

Have I done anything that could harm myself or others?

Have I spoken out against violence and injustice?

Have I lived in peace with my family and neighbors?

Blessed are they...

Saint Edith Stein

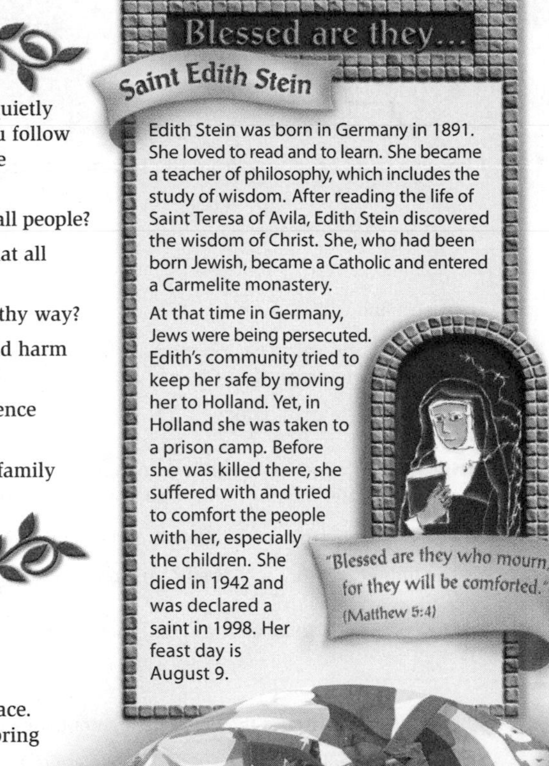

Edith Stein was born in Germany in 1891. She loved to read and to learn. She became a teacher of philosophy, which includes the study of wisdom. After reading the life of Saint Teresa of Avila, Edith Stein discovered the wisdom of Christ. She, who had been born Jewish, became a Catholic and entered a Carmelite monastery.

At that time in Germany, Jews were being persecuted. Edith's community tried to keep her safe by moving her to Holland. Yet, in Holland she was taken to a prison camp. Before she was killed there, she suffered with and tried to comfort the people with her, especially the children. She died in 1942 and was declared a saint in 1998. Her feast day is August 9.

"Blessed are they who mourn, for they will be comforted." (Matthew 5:4)

WE RESPOND

♫ **Prayer of St. Francis**

Make me a channel of your peace.
Where there is hatred, let me bring your love.
Where there is injury, your pardon, Lord,
And where there's doubt, true faith in you.

Make me a channel of your peace.
Where there's despair in life, let me bring hope.
Where there is darkness only light,
And where there's sadness ever joy.

World Youth Day

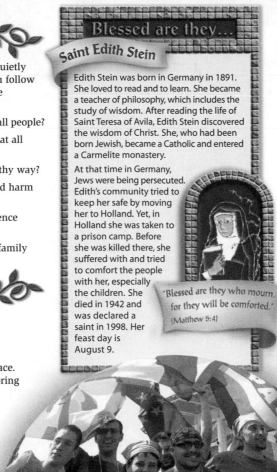

191

Activity Bank

Faith and Media

Peacemakers on the Web

Activity Materials: Internet

When individuals, groups, and nations work for peace and justice, they help transform our world into a place of peace. Organize the students into small groups and guide them as they use the Internet to research peacemakers. Distribute copies of Reproducible Master 16. Explain: *You can use this chart to outline ideas for your presentation.* Offer a list of subjects like Mother Teresa, Archbishop Oscar Romero, Dorothy Day, Mohandas Gandhi, Archbishop Desmond Tutu, President Nelson Mandela, Pax Christi, Amnesty International, the U.S., and the UN. Ask each group to prepare a short presentation on their research.

Quick Check

✔ *How does peace come about?* (Peace comes about when people truly respect one another and work together to solve problems.)

✔ *What did Jesus teach his disciples to value above all else?* (Jesus taught us to love.)

WE RESPOND ___ minutes

Connect to Life Invite the students to tell what they have learned about respecting life. Explain that God helps us to spread peace. Ask the class to share reasons why promoting peace is important to our community and our world. Explain that Saint Francis wrote a prayer to express our call to promote peace. Ask the students to read the "Prayer of Saint Francis" in the *We Respond* text.

Pray Conclude by playing and singing the "Prayer of Saint Francis," #19, Grade 4 CD.

Plan Ahead for Day 5

Catechist Goal: To review chapter ideas and their relationship to our faith life

Preparation: Have available magazines and newspapers. Make copies of Chapter 16 Test in the Grade 4 Assessment Book (option).

Chapter 16 • Day 5

Catechist Goal

- To review chapter ideas and their relationship to our faith life

Our Faith Response

- To apply what has been learned to our lives

Choose a word or phrase from the box to complete each sentence.

sacred	protect	human dignity	peace

1. We have the responsibility to respect and protect life.
2. The value and worth each person has from being created in God's image is human dignity.
3. All human life should be cared for and protected because it is sacred.
4. Peace comes about when people truly love one another and work for justice.

Write True or False for the following sentences. Then change the false sentences to make them true.

5. False The fourth commandment teaches us to love and respect human life.
The fifth commandment teaches us to love and respect human life.
6. True The deliberate killing of an innocent person is a very serious sin.
7. False We can respect the gift of life by not taking care of our bodies.
We can respect the gift of life by taking care of our bodies.
8. True Peace comes about when people truly love one another.
(A more complete statement can be made by adding "and work for justice.")

Write a sentence to answer the question.

9–10. Why is human life sacred? See pages 184–185.

ASSESSMENT Use pictures from magazines or other sources to make a photo display with captions to illustrate respect for life and human dignity.

192

Chapter Test

Chapter 16 Test is provided in the Grade 4 Assessment Book.

Lesson Plan

___ minutes

Chapter Review Explain to the students that they are going to check their understanding of what they have learned. Have them answer questions 1–8. Then invite volunteers to read aloud each correct answer. Have the students write responses to question 9–10.

Assessment Activity Have a volunteer read aloud the directions for the *Assessment Activity.* Provide the students with newspapers and magazines in which to find photos for the display. You may want to have the students work in small groups of three or four. Encourage the students to write captions explaining how each picture expresses respect for life or shows human dignity. Post the finished display on a bulletin board.

___ minutes

Reflect & Pray Guide the students to write individual prayers asking God for help in respecting their own lives. Explain that by respecting our own lives, we show our gratitude for the gift of life. Remind the students that God is always with us to help us.

 **Key Word** Invite a volunteer to read aloud the definition of *human dignity.* Have the students discuss what it means to treat others with human dignity, and why God calls us to respect life.

Remember Review the important ideas of the chapter by discussing the four *We Believe* statements. Organize the class into four groups and assign each group one statement. Invite each group to write as

We Respond in Faith

Reflect & Pray

Think about the value of your own life as a child of God. In what ways do you respect your own life?

Loving Creator, help me to

____

____

____

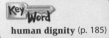

Key Word
human dignity (p. 185)

Remember

- Human life is sacred.
- The right to life is the most basic human right.
- We respect the gift of life.
- Promoting peace is a way to respect life.

Our Catholic Life

Life and Dignity

Every year, the Church in the United States holds special events to promote respect for life. For example, on the first Sunday of October, Respect Life Sunday, we reflect together on all the ways we can respect the sacredness of human life.

Every year on January 22 we are asked to participate in the National Prayer Vigil for Life. Many Catholics go to Washington, D.C. to pray together. Our parish churches may be open for special times of prayer. We promise again to protect and respect all human life, especially unborn children.

Many parishes have Respect Life Committees that work to make people more aware of the life and dignity of all people.

Home Connection

Sharing Faith with My Family

Make sure to send home the family page (text page 194).

Encourage the students to use the chapter photos and artwork when telling their families what they have learned.

For additional information and activities, encourage families to visit Sadlier's

www.WEBELIEVEweb.com

many ideas as possible about its statement. Allow time for the groups to share their ideas.

Our Catholic Life Read aloud the text. Help the students realize that the Church works to protect and recognize the right to life of the unborn child. Invite the students to share ways they can help the Church promote the right to life of all human beings.

Chapter 16 Grade 4

SHARING FAITH with My Family

Sharing What I Learned
Discuss the following with your family:
- living out the fifth commandment
- valuing human dignity
- respecting the gift of life
- taking care of our bodies, minds, and souls.

Letters from Saint Paul
Saint Paul wrote many letters to the early Christian churches. Here is an excerpt from a letter to the church of Rome. Read more of Saint Paul's letters in the Bible.

"Do not be conquered by evil but conquer evil with good." (Romans 12:21)

"Give us today our daily bread." (Matthew 6:11)

Scripture Pictures
Read this Scripture quote to your family. Ask a family member to use this space to draw a "Scripture Picture" that shows how to live out the quote. Talk about the quote and the picture. Invite other family members to draw their own "Scripture Picture."

Visit Sadlier's www.WEBELIEVEweb.com

Connect to the Catechism
For adult background and reflection, see paragraphs 2258, 2270, 2288, and 2304.

194

PUPIL PAGE 194

Chapter 17 The Sixth Commandment

Overview

In Chapter 16 the students learned that the fifth commandment calls us to respect all human life. In this chapter they will learn about the sixth commandment and ways we show and share love with others.

Doctrinal Content	For Adult Reading and Reflection *Catechism of the Catholic Church*
The students will learn:	Paragraph
• God creates each person with the ability to show and share love.	2331
• We are all called to chastity.	2348
• Friendships are one way we grow in love.	2347
• The love between a husband and wife is very special.	2361

virtue (p. 199)
chastity (p. 199)

Catechist Background

Who is an example of self-control for you?

The sixth commandment states, "You shall not commit adultery" (Exodus 20:14). To a culture awash in images that denigrate the human body and promote the misuse of human sexuality, this commandment is particularly relevant.

The Church derives from this commandment two important principles that are seldom mentioned in popular culture: chastity and self-mastery.

The *Catechism of the Catholic Church* defines chastity as "the successful integration of sexuality within the person and thus the inner unity of man in his bodily and spiritual being" (2337). Chastity, then, is using our sexuality in a way that reflects the integrity of our physical and spiritual natures. People violate chastity when they are sexually active outside of marriage, lead double lives, indulge in pornography, or give in to uncontrolled or illicit sexual desires.

Self-mastery is learning the ways to use our God-given freedom that lead to holy and peaceful lives. The alternative is clear: governance of our passions leads to peace; domination by them results in unhappiness (see *CCC* 2339). Here are but a few of the many ways we can practice self-mastery: being present to God in prayer, receiving the grace of the sacraments, practicing self-denial, developing good moral habits, and obeying the commandments.

In what ways can you strengthen self-mastery in your life?

Lesson Planning Guide

Lesson Focus	Presentation	Materials
Day 1		
page 195 **We Gather in Prayer** **pages 196–197** *God creates each person with the ability to show and share love.*	• Listen to Scripture. Respond in song. • Discuss the **We Gather** questions. • Read and discuss the **We Believe** text about the sixth commandment. Do the bumper sticker activity. • Reflect on the **We Respond** question. • Pray together.	For the prayer space: collage of pictures of family and friends showing love for one another; basket containing strips of colored construction paper "I Am Special," Bernadette Farrell, #20, Grade 4 CD
Day 2		
pages 198–199 *We are all called to chastity.*	• Discuss habits with the **We Gather** questions. • Read and discuss the virtue of chastity in the **We Believe** text. Do the **We Respond** media activity. • Read and discuss vocations in the *As Catholics* text. • Pray together.	
Day 3		
pages 200–201 *Friendships are one way we grow in love.*	• Reflect on showing care for friends with the **We Gather** statement. • Read and discuss the **We Believe** text. • Answer the **We Respond** question. Respond in song as prayer.	• strips of colored paper from the basket in the prayer space, glue or stapler "Though We Are Many/Make Us a Sign," Bernadette Farrell, #27, Grade 4 CD
Day 4		
pages 202–203 *The love between a husband and wife is very special.*	• Discuss how families show love with the **We Gather** question. • Read and discuss Matrimony in the **We Believe** text. • Reflect on the sixth commandment. • Answer the **We Respond** question. • Pray together.	• copies of Reproducible Master 17, guide page 195G • heart-shaped paper cutouts
Day 5		
page 204 **Review** **pages 205–206** **We Respond in Faith**	• Complete questions 1–10. Work on the *Assessment Activity.* • Complete the *Reflect & Pray* activity. • Review *Remember* and *Key Words.* • Read and discuss *Our Catholic Life.* • Discuss **Sharing Faith with My Family**.	• Chapter 17 Test in Assessment Book, pp. 35–36 • Chapter 17 Test in Test Generator • Review & Resource Book, pp. 40–42 • Family Book, pp. 49–51

For additional ideas, activities, and opportunities: Visit Sadlier's **www.WEBELIEVEweb.com**

Enrichment Ideas

Chapter Story

Jamie couldn't wait to meet the new neighbors. He was happy that a new family with a boy his age was moving in.

A moving van pulled into the driveway next door, and Jamie watched as several adults unloaded boxes and furniture. Where was the boy? Jamie decided to find out for himself. He introduced himself to a woman carrying a lamp. "Hi, I'm Jamie. I heard that you have a son who's in fourth grade, just like me."

The woman smiled and said, "That's right. Michael will be very glad to have a new friend right next door." She called to her son to come and meet Jamie. A boy with light brown hair came racing toward them. Jamie held up his hand to give Michael a high five, but when Michael came closer, Jamie dropped his hand and looked at the ground. He mumbled about being late for dinner and ran back home.

Jamie's dad saw that he was upset and asked him what was wrong. Jamie blurted out, "The new boy is different! We can't be friends." His dad gave him a hug and said, "Michael has Down Syndrome, but that doesn't mean you can't be friends. God made him special, just as God made you special."

Just then the doorbell rang, and Jamie went to answer it. Michael was standing on the front step. He was holding a soccer ball. "Would you like to play?" he asked, smiling. Jamie nodded, and the two boys went outside and began kicking the ball around the backyard.

The boys began to play soccer together every afternoon. Michael always had a smile for Jamie, and Jamie looked forward to their soccer matches.

One night, before saying his bedtime prayers, Jamie's dad asked him whether there was anyone for whom he was especially thankful. Jamie smiled and said, "Michael."

▶ *What did Jamie learn about the special way God creates each of us?*

FAITH and MEDIA

▶ On Day 1 the students will design "friendship and love" bumper stickers. Remind the students that bumper stickers—like billboards, magazine ads, radio and television commercials, pictures of performers on T-shirts, and team logos on sporting goods —are forms of advertising and therefore examples of media. A T-shirt, backpack, or bumper sticker can be used to promote the respect we have for ourselves and others just as it can be used to advertise a sports team or a popular singer.

▶ On Day 2, as you discuss the *We Respond* activity, point out to the students that there are positive and negative aspects to the media. It has the power to influence people to do right as well as to do wrong.

CHAPTER PROJECT: THE GREATEST OF THESE IS LOVE

In this chapter the students will learn about the sixth commandment. At the beginning of the week read 1 Corinthians 13:13: "So faith, hope, love remain, these three; but the greatest of these is love." Provide the students with markers or colored pencils and six heart-shaped pieces of construction paper in various colors. Invite them to write "The Greatest of These Is Love" on one of the hearts. After each day's lesson ask students to reflect on what they have learned. Encourage them to write a few sentences on one of the hearts about how they will keep the sixth commandment. At the end of the week staple the hearts together so the students will have a "book of love." Remind them that every day we are called to love God, one another, and ourselves. Encourage the students to keep these books as a reminder of the importance of love in their lives.

Connections

To Scripture

In Matthew 5:27–28 we read that Jesus also taught about the sixth commandment. Students may not understand the idea of committing adultery in one's heart. Explain that not only are we called to keep the sixth commandment in our actions but also in our hearts and minds. God wants our thoughts and feelings to be loving and respectful. As you teach this chapter, emphasize the idea that our thoughts and feelings are as important as our actions.

To Saints

As the students learn about the meaning of marriage and married love, point out that an important part of the relationship between a husband and wife is their commitment to love and serve Christ and others. Many married followers of Christ have been named saints by the Church; for example, Saint Margaret of Scotland. In some cases, both a husband and a wife have been honored, such as Saints Isidore and Maria. Encourage the students to learn about these saints and to research others who have given witness to Christ through their married lives.

To Family

Marriage is a sacrament and a sacred institution of the Church. This chapter explores the special relationship between a husband and wife. Encourage the students to think about their own families in connection to the sixth commandment. Be sensitive to the fact that students may have parents who are separated, divorced, or have a difficult relationship. Establish a safe and nurturing environment in which the students feel comfortable sharing their family situations.

Meeting Individual Needs

Students with Visual Needs

Students with visual needs may have difficulty seeing notes, bulletin boards, or text from the lesson. Make sure your teaching method incorporates ways of reaching these students. For example, when writing on the board, say aloud what you are writing. You may also provide students with copies of overheads or outlines of what is written on the board. When handing out worksheets or outlines, avoid clutter on the page. Taking such steps will ensure that students with visual needs feel included in the classroom, and it will enrich their learning.

ADDITIONAL RESOURCES

Video *Lazarus Lives,* Nest Family Entertainment, 2000. From the series *Animated Stories from the New Testament*. Lazarus shows he is a compassionate friend to Jesus and others. (30 minutes)

To find more ideas for books, videos, and other learning material, visit Sadlier's

www.WEBELIEVEweb.com

Catechist Development

Using Scripture

by Rev. Donald Senior, CP, Ph.D., S.T.D.

Donald Senior entered the Passionist Religious Congregation in 1960 and was ordained a Catholic priest in 1967. He has been president of Catholic Theological Union, Chicago, Illinois, since 1987 where he has also served as Professor of New Testament. He lectures and conducts workshops throughout the United States and abroad.

The use of Scripture in the Church's catechesis has been a new and exciting emphasis since the Second Vatican Council. There are several ways that Scripture plays a role in effective catechesis.

First of all, the Bible traces the overarching story of God's love for his people Israel (Old Testament) and the continuing story in the life of Jesus and the founding and spread of the early Church (New Testament). Even though we are separated in time and culture from the biblical peoples, they are our ancestors in the faith. Their experience of God sets the pattern for our own faith.

From God's creation of the world and the human person in God's own image, to the remarkable stories of Jesus and his disciples as the fulfillment of Israel's dreams, and culminating with the explosive power of God's Spirit bringing the gospel into the world, your students' knowledge of the biblical story gives them a share in this great heritage of faith.

The Scriptures also provide us with a rich set of symbols that, like great poetry, help put our experience of God into words. Crossing the Red Sea, climbing the mountain of Sinai, looking for a promised land, being tempted in the desert, following in the footsteps of Jesus, being a doubting Thomas or a confused Peter, saying "yes" like Mary, standing at the foot of the cross, the Church as the body of Christ—all these and a thousand other biblical metaphors and symbols capture the experience of faith. Communicating these images to young Christians gives them a common language of faith with other Christians across the world.

Finally, the biblical stories also transmit the moral and spiritual wisdom of our faith. This is particularly true of Jesus' parables but also extends to many other stories. The parable of the prodigal son teaches us about the unlimited forgiveness of God, just as the parable of the Good Samaritan reminds

(continued on next page)

Catechist Development Topics (Topic and Guide Page)

Resources

Catoir, John T. *Joyfulling Living the Gospels Day by Day: Minute Meditations for Every Day*. Catholic Book Publishing Company, 2001.

Cavalletti, Sofia, et al. *The Religious Potential of the Child: Experiencing Scripture and Liturgy with Young Children.* Chicago, IL: Liturgy Training Publications, 1993.

us that authentic charity is determined by what we do and not by our status. The stories of the Bible can help inform the imagination and the conscience of all students while affording them values to live by.

Ways to Implement Using Scripture

- Put a Scripture quote in a prominent place before beginning each lesson. It could be from your *We Believe* chapter, or the coming Sunday's liturgy. Invite students to reflect on the quote and to share what it means for their lives.
- Engage students in Scripture drama. Have them "try on" the characters and sense what it felt like to be one of the prophets or the first disciples called by Jesus, a leper, or Mary or Joseph on the journey to Bethlehem. To become the characters helps your students to remember them and their stories of faith.
- Emphasize the connections between what Jesus did in the Scriptures and the work of the Church today: healing, forgiving sin, standing for justice and against oppression.
- Encourage students to explore the Holy Land on appropriate Web sites. This stirs their imagination to "see" where the stories of our heritage happened as they study them.
- Compare today's news headlines to events that happened in Scripture. Do people today worship false idols as some people in the Old Testament did? Are there people today who are looked down on as the Samaritans were in the New Testament?

For additional ideas, activities, and opportunities, visit Sadlier's

www.WEBELIEVEweb.com

With thanks to:
Sue Juliano, DRE
St. Therese of Lisieux Parish
Shelby Township, Michigan

One catechist reviews the Scripture Cake recipe (see below) with her students before asking them to bring in an ingredient in order to make the cake at the next class. They are asked to find the ingredients in each Scripture passage. The catechist then uses the kitchen in the parish hall to prepare the cake with her students. She has discovered that they enjoy finding the "ingredients" in the Bible as much as they enjoy eating the Scripture Cake!

Scripture Cake

$^1/_2$ cup **Judges 5:25** (curds-use butter)
$1^1/_2$ tbsp. **1 Samuel 14:25** (honey)
2 cups **1 Kings 4:22** (flour)
$^1/_2$ tsp. **Leviticus 2:13** (salt)
1 tsp. **1 Corinthians 5:6** (yeast-use baking powder)
1 tsp. **2 Chronicles 9:9** (spices-use 1 tsp. each of cinnamon, ginger, and cloves)
$^1/_2$ cup **Judges 4:19** (milk)
1 cup **1 Samuel 30:12** (raisins)
1 cup **Nahum 3:12** (figs, dried and chopped)
1 cup **Genesis 43:11** (almonds)
4 **Isaiah 10:14** (eggs, beaten well)

Cream first two ingredients together in a mixing bowl. In separate bowl, sift flour, salt, baking powder, and spices together. Add dry ingredients alternately with milk to mixing bowl. Add raisins, figs, and almonds mixing well. Fold in beaten eggs. Bake in a 9 x 13 pan at 350° F for 45 to 60 minutes. Let cool, cut and enjoy!

Notes

Name ____

Use the code to find out some things that the sixth commandment teaches us.

A	1
B	2
C	3
D	4
E	5
F	6
G	7
H	8
I	9
J	10
K	11
L	12
M	13
N	14
O	15
P	16
Q	17
R	18
S	19
T	20
U	21
V	22
W	23
X	24
Y	25
Z	26

1. Our

19	5	24	21	1	12	9	20	25

is a gift from God

2. The sixth commandment

16	18	15	20	5	3	20	19

marriage vows.

3.

3	8	1	19	20	9	20	25

helps us to respect our bodies.

4. God asks us to be good and

6	1	9	20	8	6	21	12

friends.

5. Human

4	9	7	14	9	20	25

makes us all equal.

The Sixth Commandment

17

✝ We Gather in Prayer

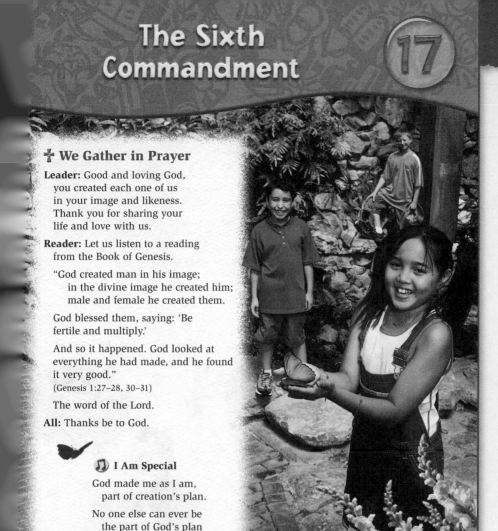

Leader: Good and loving God, you created each one of us in your image and likeness. Thank you for sharing your life and love with us.

Reader: Let us listen to a reading from the Book of Genesis.

"God created man in his image;
in the divine image he created him;
male and female he created them.

God blessed them, saying: 'Be fertile and multiply.'

And so it happened. God looked at everything he had made, and he found it very good."
(Genesis 1:27–28, 30–31)

The word of the Lord.

All: Thanks be to God.

I Am Special

God made me as I am,
part of creation's plan.
No one else can ever be
the part of God's plan
that's me.

195

Preparing to Pray

In the gathering prayer the students will hear the word of God and sing about God's special creation.

- Explain to the students that you will be the leader. Appoint a reader and tell the students that they will respond *Thanks be to God* at the conclusion of the prayer.
- Play the song "I Am Special," #20 on the Grade 4 CD.
- Allow time for the reader and the other students to practice the prayer, the response, and the song.

The Prayer Space

- Make a collage of pictures showing families and friends expressing love for one another. Display it in the prayer space.
- Place narrow strips of colored construction paper in a basket in the prayer space. Encourage the students to write special prayers for family and friends on the strips of paper during the week.

This Week's Liturgy

Visit **www.webelieveweb.com** for this week's liturgical readings and other seasonal material.

Lesson Plan

We Gather in Prayer ___ minutes

✝ Pray

- Invite the students to the prayer table by saying, *We gather in prayer*. Give the students a few moments to get settled into a prayer circle.
- Pray the Sign of the Cross and the opening prayer. After the proclamation of Scripture, quietly play the song "I Am Special," #20 on the Grade 4 CD, as the students sing.

Home Connection Update

Invite the students to share their experiences using the Chapter 16 family page. Ask: *How did drawing the Scripture Pictures with your family help you to understand the way that good overcomes evil?*

Catechist Goal

• To explain that God creates each person with human sexuality

Our Faith Response

• To express love and respect for our gift of human sexuality

Teaching Note

The Creation Story

The Book of Genesis presents two different stories of creation. The first story, in Genesis 1:1–2:1–4, offers a general account of human creation; the second story, in Genesis 2:5–25, gives us more details. Discuss both stories with your students to provide a deeper understanding of the creation of man and woman. You may wish to focus on Genesis 2:18, in which it is explained that God wanted to create a "suitable partner" for man. Ask the students what being a partner entails. Emphasize the equality of the relationship between man and woman and the ways men and women help and rely on each other.

God creates each person with the ability to show and share love.

WE GATHER

✝ *Loving Creator, we praise you.*

How would you describe yourself to a friend or classmate? What makes you who you are?

WE BELIEVE

From the Old Testament we learn the stories of creation. Of all of God's wonderful creation, humans are the most special. We are made in God's image and likeness and share the same human dignity. Human dignity is a gift from God that makes us all equal. Because of our human dignity, we are free to think and love and make choices.

God also creates each person with human sexuality. Human sexuality is the gift of being able to feel, think, choose, love, and act as the person God created us to be. Human sexuality makes us female or male. It is a part of everything about us.

Although males and females are different, we are all equal. These differences come from God. They are good and beautiful and are an important part of who we are.

196

Lesson Plan

WE GATHER ___ minutes

✝ **Pray** Pray the Sign of the Cross and the *We Gather* prayer.

Focus on Life Invite the students to read the *We Gather* questions and share their responses. Read aloud the *Chapter Story* and ask what Jamie learned about his new friend. Tell the students that in this lesson they will learn that God creates each person to show and share love.

WE BELIEVE ___ minutes

Learn About the Sixth Commandment Invite volunteers to read aloud the *We Believe* statement and the *We Believe* text. Emphasize:

• God created human beings in his image and likeness.

• God created them male and female, with human sexuality. Each of us is able to feel, think, choose, love, and act as the male or female God created us to be.

• Males and females are different but equal.

• The sixth commandment asks us to honor the love and faithfulness of a husband and wife and to love ourselves, our bodies, and our family and friends.

Explore Meaning Organize the class into small groups to explore the meaning and importance of the sixth commandment. Assign each group a part of living out the commandment, such as honoring the love of a husband and wife, respecting and controlling our bodies, or showing love for family and friends. Invite each group to share its ideas.

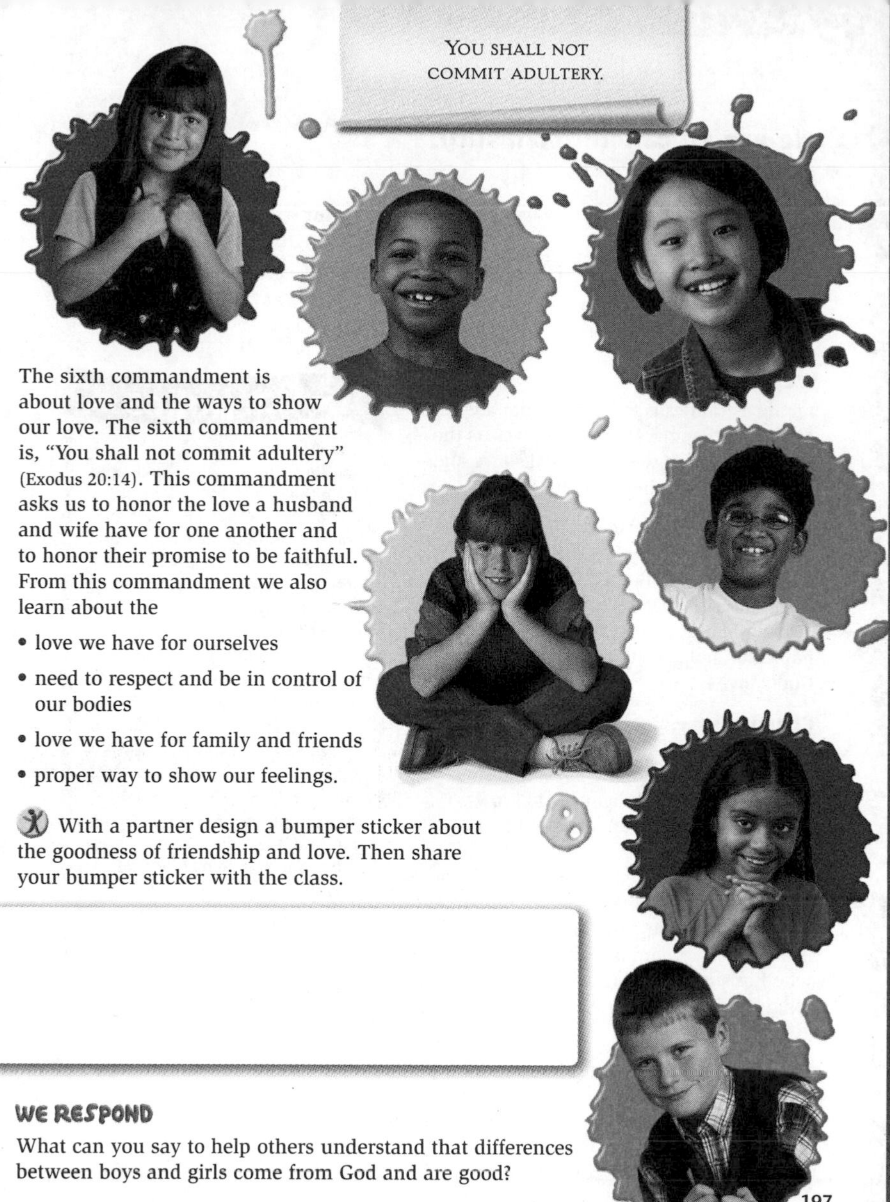
You shall not commit adultery.

The sixth commandment is about love and the ways to show our love. The sixth commandment is, "You shall not commit adultery" (Exodus 20:14). This commandment asks us to honor the love a husband and wife have for one another and to honor their promise to be faithful. From this commandment we also learn about the

- love we have for ourselves
- need to respect and be in control of our bodies
- love we have for family and friends
- proper way to show our feelings.

With a partner design a bumper sticker about the goodness of friendship and love. Then share your bumper sticker with the class.

We Respond

What can you say to help others understand that differences between boys and girls come from God and are good?

197

Activity Bank

Curriculum Connection

Reading

Activity Materials: Bibles

Help the students learn about the special role of women in the Bible. Prepare a list of biblical women and corresponding Bible passages. This list might include Ruth (Ruth 1:1–18), Esther (Esther 7:1–8), the Virgin Mary (Luke 1:26–56), and Mary Magdalene (John 20:1–18). You might also give the students some background information to help provide a sense of context. Provide the class with Bibles. Invite the students to choose one woman from the list, read her story, and write a brief paragraph about her. When all have finished, have the students share their paragraphs.

Do the Activity Have pairs of students work together to design a bumper sticker. Invite each pair to share its work.

Quick Check

✔ *What is the sixth commandment?* (The sixth commandment is "You shall not commit adultery.")

✔ *What is the meaning of the sixth commandment?* (It asks us to honor the love and faithfulness shared by a husband and wife and to love ourselves, respect and control our bodies, and love family and friends.)

We Respond

___ minutes

Connect to Life Invite the students to celebrate and be thankful for the differences between males and females. Emphasize that these differences are good, complementary, and a gift from God. Invite volunteers to share their responses to the *We Respond* question.

Pray Invite the students to pray a prayer of gratitude for God's creation of men and women, and to reflect on the beauty and goodness of these differences and the uniqueness of every human being.

Plan Ahead for Day 2

Catechist Goal: To present the meaning of a chaste life

Preparation: Have suggestions available to help the students compose the concluding prayer.

Catechist Goal

- To present the meaning of a chaste life

Our Faith Response

- To appreciate the virtue of chastity in our relationships

virtue
chastity

We are all called to chastity.

WE GATHER

✝ *God, we want to grow as your children.*

What are some things you do every day? Do you plan to do them, or are they things you do by habit?

Jesus is our friend. He asks us to love others as he has loved us. Jesus asks us to show our friends and family that God is loving.

WE BELIEVE

Living as God calls us to live is not always easy. However, the Holy Spirit gives us the grace to do so. If we accept God's love and help, we grow as his children.

The more often we choose to follow God's law, the better we live as God's children. We get into a habit of choosing to act in ways that show love for God, ourselves, and others. A **virtue** is a good habit that helps us to act according to God's love for us.

Chastity is the virtue by which we use our human sexuality in a responsible and faithful way. Chastity helps us to respect our whole bodies. It helps us to grow in appreciation and understanding of ourselves and our bodies. Through our Baptism we are called to live by the virtue of chastity. Chastity is an important part of being a child or a young adult. Chastity is an important part of being an adult whether single or married, a priest or a religious sister or brother.

We look to Jesus as our model of chastity. He followed the Ten Commandments faithfully and completely. In his activities, friendships, and family relationships Jesus showed love for God and others.

As Catholics...

God first shared his love and goodness with us when he created us. In the sacrament of Baptism, God gives us a share of his life and holiness. Throughout our lives God calls us to holiness. He asks us to grow in love for him and one another. We are called to become more like Jesus Christ. We are called to bring the good news of Jesus to others so that they will love and follow him, too.

God also calls each of us to love and serve him in a certain way. This call is a vocation. We may be called to the married life, the single life, the priesthood, or the religious life. All of these vocations are important to the life of the Church community. Together we try to love as Jesus did and grow in holiness.

What are some questions you have about different vocations?

As Catholics...

Vocations

After you have presented the lesson, read aloud the *As Catholics* text. Answer any questions the students may have. Discuss what it means to be called to love and serve God. Encourage them to think about the faithfulness to their vocations of people that they know.

Lesson Plan

WE GATHER ___ minutes

✝ **Pray** Invite the students to pray silently the *We Gather* prayer. Then pray the Sign of the Cross and pray aloud, *Lord, help us to follow your example of loving others. Amen.*

Focus on Life Ask the students to read the *We Gather* questions silently and then share their thoughts with one classmate. Tell the students that in this lesson they will learn that we are all called to keep the virtue of chastity.

WE BELIEVE ___ minutes

Explain Virtue Have one volunteer read aloud the *We Believe* statement and have others read aloud the five *We Believe* paragraphs. Explain that God gives us the gifts of grace and free will. These gifts enable us to accept God's love for us. If we choose to follow God's love and God's laws we are better able to lead a life of virtue—a life of good habits that help us to act according to God's love. Emphasize the following points:

- A virtue is a good habit that helps us to act according to God's love for us.
- Chastity is the virtue by which we use our human sexuality in a responsible and faithful way. Chastity helps us to respect and love our bodies and ourselves.

Key Words

virtue a good habit that helps us to act according to God's love for us

chastity the virtue by which we use our human sexuality in a responsible and faithful way

WE RESPOND

List an example for each category in column A. Draw a line from each example to all the points in Column B that apply to it.

Column A	Column B
• a television show ______ •	• appreciated the differences between male and female as a gift from God.
• an advertisement ______ •	• honored the love between a husband and wife.
• a magazine ______ •	• showed that it is important to respect our bodies by the things we do and say.
	• encouraged people to think well of and love themselves.
	• included people showing their feelings in a proper way.

Chapter 17 • Day 2

Activity Bank

Faith and Media

Sending Positive Messages

Activity Materials: poster board, markers

In today's lesson the students explore various media for positive messages that reflect God's will. The students may discover that the messages we find in the media do not always reflect God's message. Invite the students to design advertisements to send positive messages about keeping the sixth commandment. Have the students work in groups to write, design, and draw their ads with markers on poster board. The ads might include slogans or catch phrases such as "Chastity is everyone's call."

- Through his model of friendship, family relationships, and chastity, Jesus taught us about love of others.
- Jesus asks us to love one another as God loves us.

Talk About Families Draw the students' attention to the artwork of the Holy Family on page 174 and the photo on page 175. Discuss ways that each shows loving God and others.

Quick Check

✔ *What is chastity?* (the virtue by which we use our human sexuality in a responsible and faithful way)

✔ *How did Jesus model chastity?* (Jesus followed the Ten Commandments faithfully and completely. He showed love for God and others through his friendships and family relationships.)

WE RESPOND

___ minutes

Connect to Life Explain to the students that in the *We Respond* activity they will name specific examples of ways that God's message has been expressed in various media. If the students cannot name many positive examples, discuss the fact that today's media do not always offer messages that reflect God's will. Encourage the students to think carefully about the sort of messages we get from the media.

Pray Pray: *Jesus, help us to show others that God is loving.*

Plan Ahead for Day 3

Catechist Goal: To emphasize that friendships are one way we grow in love

Preparation: Have available strips of colored paper, glue or staples, and the Grade 4 CD.

Chapter 17 • Day 3

Catechist Goal

- To emphasize that friendships are one way we grow in love

Our Faith Response

- To express our love for our family and friends

Lesson Materials

- strips of colored paper
- glue or stapler

Teaching Note

Friendship

In the Gospel of John we read about one of Jesus' friendships. When Jesus' friend Lazarus was ill, Jesus "remained for two days in the place where he was" (John 11:6). Jesus wanted to be with Lazarus in his time of need and comfort Mary and Martha, the sisters of Lazarus. When Lazarus died, Jesus wept (John 11:35). As the Son of God Jesus was able to perform a miracle and raise Lazarus from the dead. We cannot do this for our friends, but we can follow Jesus' example of caring friendship.

YOU SHALL NOT COMMIT ADULTERY.

Friendships are one way we grow in love.

WE RESPOND

✝ *Lord, bless our families and our friends.*

Think about ways you show a friend that you care for her or him.

WE BELIEVE

Friendship is a very important part of growing and learning about love and trust. Our friendships have an important place in our lives. God asks us to be good and faithful friends to the people in our lives. Those good friendships also prepare us to be the adults God calls us to be.

From the time that we are little children until the time that we are very old, we learn ways to show our love for others. We learn to express our friendship. We show respect for our family and friends by the way we listen to them and by the way we speak to them. We share our love and care for others by smiles and handshakes and hugs. We say a kind word when someone is hurt. We pat each other on the back after a good game. We kiss our parents good night and hug our relatives when they visit.

God made our bodies to show our love for him and for one another. We harm our human dignity and our relationship with God if we use our bodies in an improper way. The sixth commandment asks us to express love in all of our relationships in the proper way.

200

Lesson Plan

WE GATHER ___ minutes

✝ **Pray** Invite the students to recall the importance of family and friends in their lives and to pray the *We Gather* prayer silently for these people.

Focus on Life Invite the students to read and think about the *We Gather* text. Ask them to name the ways they show friends that they care. Tell the students that in this lesson they will learn that friendship is one way we grow in love.

WE BELIEVE ___ minutes

Read the Text Ask volunteers to read aloud the *We Believe* statement and the *We Believe* text. Pause after each paragraph to emphasize the following points:

- God calls us to be good and faithful friends to the people in our lives.
- There are many ways to show and share love with our family and friends.
- The sixth commandment asks us to express love in our relationships in the proper way.

Describe a Good Friend Invite the students to reflect on the idea of friendship as expressed in the text and in the photos. Ask the students to list reasons why friendship is important in their lives. Then have volunteers share their lists.

Act It Out Invite each student to choose a partner with whom to discuss the meaning of friendship. Encourage the pairs to role-play ways to show friendship in situations such as the following:

WE RESPOND

During the next week what will you do to show your family members how much you care about them?

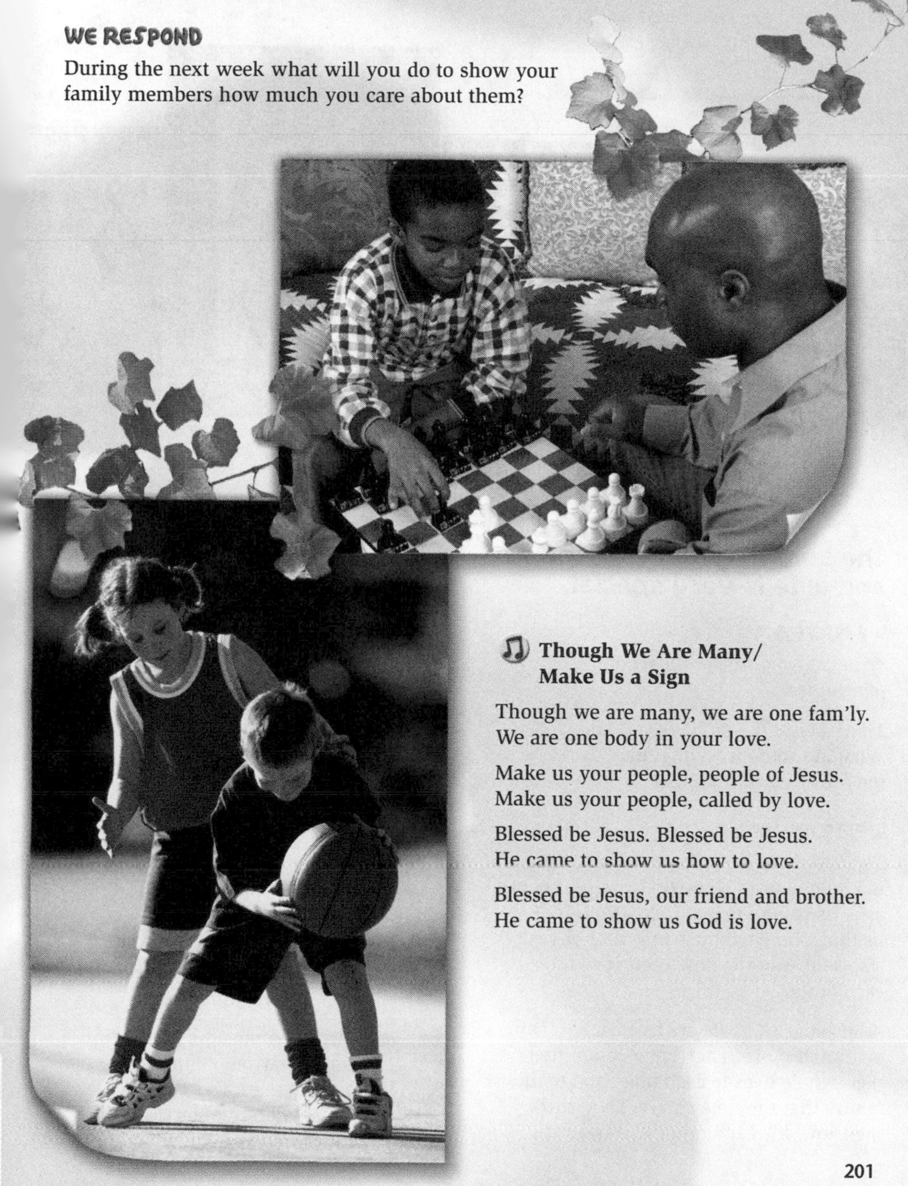

Though We Are Many/ Make Us a Sign

Though we are many, we are one fam'ly.
We are one body in your love.

Make us your people, people of Jesus.
Make us your people, called by love.

Blessed be Jesus. Blessed be Jesus.
He came to show us how to love.

Blessed be Jesus, our friend and brother.
He came to show us God is love.

201

ACTIVITY BANK

Curriculum Connection

Arts and Crafts

Activity Materials: string, multicolored beads (If possible, use beads showing such religious symbols as a cross or a dove.)

Invite the students to discuss the importance of friendships and family relationships in our lives and the different ways we can express love and care for people. Then give each student a supply of string and beads with which to make a friendship bracelet for a friend or family member. Explain that this gift from the heart will be a symbol of love and care. Encourage the students to give the finished bracelets to someone special as a symbol of love and friendship.

- One student is being left out of a game.
- A friend has suffered a loss or a failure.
- A friend wants to celebrate a special event.
- A new student seems lost on the first day at school.

Quick Check

✔ *What kind of friend does God ask us to be?* (a good and faithful friend to the people in our lives)

✔ *How does the sixth commandment relate to friendship?* (The sixth commandment asks us to express love in all of our relationships in the proper way.)

WE RESPOND ___ minutes

Connect to Life Have the students read and discuss the *We Respond* question. Then invite the students to read and listen to the song "Though We Are Many/Make Us a Sign," #27 on the Grade 4 CD.

Pray Invite those students who have not done so to write prayers for family and friends on the strips of paper in the basket in the prayer space. Then, glue or staple the strips into links to form a prayer chain. Display the chain in the prayer space, and invite the students to pray silently for all the intentions offered in the chain. Conclude by praying aloud the Our Father.

Plan Ahead for Day 4

Catechist Goal: To describe the special relationship between a husband and wife

Preparation: Make copies of Reproducible Master 17 and heart-shaped cutouts.

Chapter 17 • Day 4

Catechist Goal

- To describe the special relationship between a husband and wife

Our Faith Response

- To appreciate the sacrament of Matrimony

Lesson Materials

- copies of Reproducible Master 17
- heart-shaped paper cutouts

YOU SHALL NOT
COMMIT ADULTERY.

The love between a husband and wife is very special.

WE GATHER

✝ *Jesus, you are our model of faithfulness.*

Think about the families you know. What are some ways that they show their love for one another?

WE BELIEVE

The love between a husband and wife is a unique love. The sixth commandment asks us to honor that love. It reminds us that God gave husbands and wives a special way to show their love for each other.

A husband and wife are friends, but they are much more. They have committed their whole lives to each other and to the family that they may start. They show their love for each other in a beautiful, physical way that belongs only in marriage. A husband and wife are to share this love only with each other.

In the sacrament of Matrimony, the husband and wife make a vow, or promise, to each other. When they marry, they vow to love and honor each other. They vow to be loyal and trustworthy. They vow to be faithful, or true to each other, for the rest of their lives.

The sixth commandment protects the marriage vows. The sixth commandment is, "You shall not commit adultery" (Exodus 20:14). Adultery is being unfaithful to one's husband or wife. It is a very serious sin against the dignity of marriage and the sixth commandment.

The grace of the sacrament of Matrimony strengthens the married couple to live out their Christian marriage. The Church prays that those who are married will remain faithful and true to one another.

202

Teaching Tip

Using Guest Speakers

Invite one or two married couples to speak to the class about the sacrament of Matrimony. Ask the couples to explain the different parts of the marriage rite and the symbolism of each. Encourage the students to ask questions and to describe weddings they have attended. During the discussion remind the students of the importance of the marriage vows and the relationship between husband, wife, and God.

Lesson Plan

WE GATHER ___ minutes

✝ **Pray** Pray together the Sign of the Cross and the *We Gather* prayer.

Focus on Life Invite the students to reflect aloud on the *We Gather* question. Tell the students that in this lesson they will learn about the special love between a husband and wife.

WE BELIEVE ___ minutes

Read the Text Invite volunteers to read aloud the *We Believe* statement and the *We Believe* text. Stress:

- The sixth commandment asks us to honor the unique love between a husband and wife.
- A husband and wife show their love for one another in a beautiful, physical way that belongs only in marriage.
- In the sacrament of Matrimony a husband and wife vow to love, honor, and be faithful and loyal to each other for the rest of their lives.
- Adultery is the act of being unfaithful to one's wife or husband.

Discuss the Sacrament of Matrimony Have the students share their thoughts about the sacrament of Matrimony.

Do the Activity Distribute copies of Reproducible Master 17 and read the directions aloud. When all the students have uncoded the words, review the answers. (1, sexuality; 2, protects; 3, chastity; 4, faithful; 5, dignity)

Take a few moments to think quietly and prayerfully about ways you follow the sixth commandment. These questions may help you.

Do I appreciate the differences among my classmates and family members?

Do I honor myself as special and created by God?

Do my actions show love and respect for myself and others?

Do I use my body in responsible and faithful ways?

In what ways do I express my affection for friends and family?

Do I value my friendships?

WE RESPOND

Being loyal and trustworthy is an important part of being a member of a family and being a good friend. How can you show others that you are loyal to them?

203

Activity Bank

Multicultural Connection

Marriage Customs Around the World

Activity Materials: Internet or other research resources

Invite students to research Catholic marriage customs around the world. For this activity you might organize the class into several groups and assign each group a different country. These might include more easily researched, traditionally Catholic countries such as Italy or Mexico or less traditionally Catholic countries in Asia and Africa. Encourage the students to focus on the religious aspects of the ceremony, but also have them find out such things as what the bride and groom traditionally wear and what type of celebration is held after the religious ceremony. Have each group prepare a short report to share with the class.

Reflect on the Sixth Commandment Introduce the examination of conscience by inviting the students to reflect quietly and prayerfully on the questions in the on page 203.

Quick Check

✔ *What is the sacrament of Matrimony?* (Matrimony is a sacrament in which a husband and wife make a promise to love, honor, and be loyal and faithful to each other for the rest of their lives.)

✔ *How does the sixth commandment relate to marriage?* (The sixth commandment protects the marriage vows of loyalty and faithfulness between a husband and wife.)

WE RESPOND

___ minutes

Connect to Life Invite the students to read the *We Respond* text and the question. Invite responses. Then hand out heart-shaped paper cutouts and invite each student to write on a heart one specific way he or she can show loyalty and trust in a relationship. Have the students place the hearts in the basket in the prayer space.

Pray Invite the students to pray silently to Jesus to help them follow the sixth commandment. Conclude by praying together the Our Father.

Plan Ahead for Day 5

Catechist Goal: To review chapter ideas and their relationship to our faith life

Preparation: Make copies of Chapter 17 Test in the Grade 4 Assessment Book (option).

Chapter 17 • Day 5

Catechist Goal

- To review chapter ideas and their relationship to our faith life

Our Faith Response

- To apply what has been learned to our lives

CHAPTER TEST

Chapter 17 Test is provided in the Grade 4 Assessment Book.

Grade 4
Chapter 17

Choose a word or phrase from the box to complete each sentence.

human sexuality	virtue	chastity	Matrimony

1. In the sacrament of Matrimony, the bride and groom make a vow to be faithful to each other.
2. Using our human sexuality in a responsible way is called chastity.
3. A virtue is a good habit that helps us to act according to God's love for us.
4. Through human sexuality, we express and show our love and affection.

Write the letter of the phrase that completes each of the following:

5. c The sixth commandment
6. b Friendship is
7. d To be faithful is
8. a We look to Jesus

a. as our model of chastity.
b. one way we grow in love.
c. teaches us about the ways to show our love.
d. to be true to each other.

Write a sentence to answer the question.

9–10. Why is it important to love and respect ourselves?

See pages 196–197.

Make a list of ways you can express your love and friendship to the people in your life. Then write a song, short poem, or story about the importance of caring for others.

204

Lesson Plan

___ minutes

Chapter Review Explain to the students that they are going to review what they have learned. Have them complete questions 1–8. Ask volunteers to read aloud each correct answer. Then have the students write their responses to question 9–10.

Assessment Activity Have a volunteer read aloud the directions to the *Assessment* activity. Encourage the students, as they make their lists, to explore expressions of love in both friendships and family relationships. Allow the students time to reflect on the ideas in their lists and complete their songs, poems, and stories. Then invite volunteers to share their writings with the class.

___ minutes

Reflect & Pray Read the introduction and the question aloud. After the students have reflected on the importance of being created in God's image and on why each individual is a special part of God's creation, pray again together the Day 1 *We Gather* prayer. Say: *All the boys and girls in these photos can praise God because they are special.*

Key Words Write the *Key Words* on the board. Ask volunteers to define each word and explain how it relates to the sixth commandment. Then invite the students to share their thoughts. During the discussion emphasize the importance that the concepts described by these two words should play in our lives.

We Respond in Faith

Reflect & Pray

You are created in God's image. What does this mean to you?

God, I am a special part of your creation.

I ____

____

Key Words

virtue (p. 199)
chastity (p. 199)

Remember

- God creates each person with the ability to show and share love.
- We are all called to chastity.
- Friendships are one way we grow in love.
- The love between a husband and wife is very special.

Our Catholic Life

Rights and Responsibilities

The gift of human dignity gives us the ability to think, choose, and love. Certain rights and responsibilities come with this gift. We all have the right to the things we need for life. Among these rights is the right to live by and practice one's faith. We also all have the responsibility to respect and protect the rights of others. We have the responsibility to act so that the rights of others are being met.

Home Connection

Sharing Faith with My Family

Make sure to send home the family page (text page 206).

Invite the students to reflect on Scripture with their families and to complete the Scripture Picture.

For additional information and activities, encourage families to visit Sadlier's

www.WEBELIEVEweb.com

Remember Organize the students into four groups and assign each group one of the four *We Believe* statements. Ask each group to devise a word web or make a list that expands on the statement and shows ways the statement relates to the sixth commandment. Then invite each group to present its thoughts to the class.

Our Catholic Life Read aloud the text. Remind the students that Catholic social teaching emphasizes the rights and dignity of the human person, and that this teaching is meant to protect the sanctity and value of human life. Connect this teaching to the sixth commandment. Encourage the students to protect the sacredness of all life by practicing respect and responsibility in all their relationships.

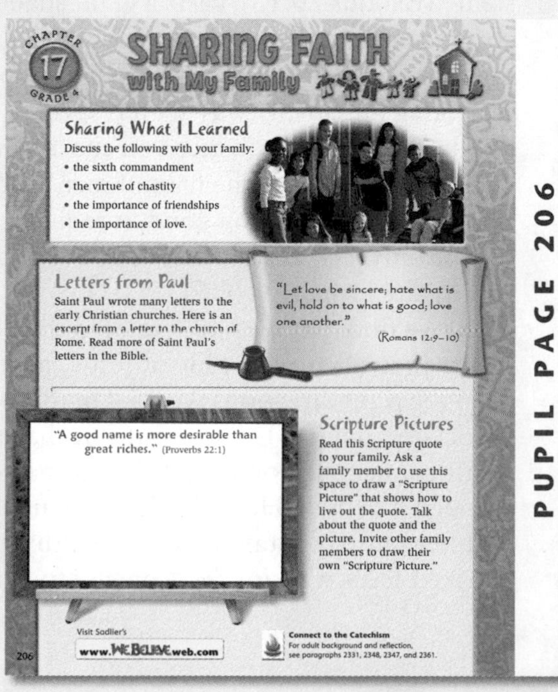
Chapter 17, Grade 4

SHARING FAITH with My Family

Sharing What I Learned

Discuss the following with your family:

- the sixth commandment
- the virtue of chastity
- the importance of friendships
- the importance of love.

Letters from Paul

Saint Paul wrote many letters to the early Christian churches. Here is an excerpt from a letter to the church of Rome. Read more of Saint Paul's letters in the Bible.

"Let love be sincere; hate what is evil, hold on to what is good; love one another." (Romans 12:9–10)

"A good name is more desirable than great riches." (Proverbs 22:1)

Scripture Pictures

Read this Scripture quote to your family. Ask a family member to use this space to draw a "Scripture Picture" that shows how to live out the quote. Talk about the quote and the picture. Invite other family members to draw their own "Scripture Picture."

Visit Sadlier's www.WEBELIEVEweb.com

Connect to the Catechism: For adult background and reflection, see paragraphs 2331, 2348, 2347, and 2361.

206

PUPIL PAGE 206

Chapter 18 The Seventh Commandment

Overview

In Chapter 17 the students learned that the sixth commandment teaches us to show and share love with others. In this chapter the students will learn that the seventh commandment calls us to live out the peace and justice of Jesus Christ. They will also discover that God wants us to respect the property and dignity of all people.

Doctrinal Content	For Adult Reading and Reflection *Catechism of the Catholic Church*
The students will learn:	Paragraph
• We are called to act with justice	2401
• We respect the property of others	2412
• God's creation is meant for all people	2415
• We are called to help all people meet their basic needs	2446

stewards of creation (p. 213)

Catechist Background

How would you define the word stealing?

The seventh commandment, "You shall not steal" (Exodus 20:15), casts a giant shadow that covers a multitude of sins. It "forbids unjustly taking or keeping the goods of one's neighbor and wronging him in any way with respect to his goods. It commands justice and charity in the care of earthly goods and the fruit of men's labor. For the sake of the common good, it requires respect for the universal destination of goods and respect for private property" (CCC 2401).

If we find that we have violated this commandment, an incident in the life of Jesus can help guide us in the right direction. We read in the Gospel of Luke (see Luke 19:1–10) about Zacchaeus, a wealthy tax collector. One day Jesus passed through his town. He hailed Zacchaeus and said that he wanted to stay with the wealthy man, who received Jesus with joy. Zacchaeus stood in front of Jesus and said that he would give half of his possessions to the poor and would repay four times over anyone that he had defrauded. Jesus then spoke, "Today salvation has come to this house. . . . For the Son of Man has come to seek and to save what was lost" (Luke 19:9–10).

If we have taken something that belongs to another, we are obliged to return it or make restitution for it. If we have in any way benefited from theft or fraudulent activity, we must repay in direct proportion to what we have gained. If we have profited from the unjust treatment of others, we must, like Zacchaeus, look for a way to make amends.

How can you show greater respect for the goods of others?

Lesson Planning Guide

Lesson Focus	Presentation	Materials
Day 1		
page 207 **We Gather in Prayer** **pages 208–209** *We are called to act with justice.*	• Listen to Scripture. Respond in song. • Discuss the **We Gather** situation. • Read and discuss the **We Believe** text about the seventh commandment. Do the **We Respond** activity. • Discuss the *As Catholics* text.	For the prayer space: Bible with passages marked; banner of the seventh commandment "New Heart and New Spirit," John Schiavone, #22, Grade 4 CD • markers (regular, fabric, and glitter) • plain white T-shirts (option)
Day 2		
pages 210–211 *We respect the property of others.*	Write a thank-you poem or song for the **We Gather** activity. • Read and discuss the **We Believe** text. Respond to the situations in the activity. • Reflect on the **We Respond** question.	• recording of soft classical music • pictures that show willfully damaged property
Day 3		
pages 212–213 *God's creation is meant for all people.*	• Discuss the **We Gather** questions. • Read and discuss being stewards of creation in the **We Believe** text. Complete the chart. • Discuss the **We Respond** question.	• photographs showing scenes of natural beauty, library card–sized piece of cardboard for each student • school photo of each student (option)
Day 4		
pages 214–215 *We are called to help all people meet their basic needs.*	• Discuss basic human needs in the **We Gather** questions. • Read and discuss the **We Believe** text. Design a mural on the Works of Mercy (refer to Chapter 11). • Reflect on the seventh commandment. Sing a song for **We Respond**. • Read and discuss the *Blessed are they . . .* text.	• Bible • copies of Reproducible Master 18, guide page 207G "New Heart and New Spirit," John Schiavone, #22, Grade 4 CD
Day 5		
page 216 **Review** **pages 217–218** **We Respond in Faith**	• Complete questions 1–10. Work on the *Assessment Activity.* • Complete the *Reflect & Pray* activity. • Review *Remember* and *Key Word.* • Read and discuss *Our Catholic Life.* • Discuss **Sharing Faith with My Family.**	• sentence strips and metal fasteners • Chapter 18 Test in Assessment Book, pp. 37–38 • Chapter 18 Test in Test Generator • Review & Resource Book, pp. 43–45 • Family Book, pp. 52–54

For additional ideas, activities, and opportunities: Visit Sadlier's **www.WEBELIEVEweb.com**

Enrichment Ideas

Chapter Story

Jessica looked out the bus window as the bus pulled up to Amanda's house. Jessica and Amanda were in fourth grade together. Amanda sat down next to Jessica on the bus and asked her what she had done last night. "I finished my vocabulary homework," Jessica replied. "Oh," said Amanda. "I went to the mall with my sister."

School had always been easy for Jessica. What was hard for Jessica was making friends, because her family moved so often. She didn't have any brothers or sisters, either, so sometimes she felt a little lonely.

At school the fourth-grade teacher, Ms. Green, reminded them that their vocabulary unit was due tomorrow. "Don't forget that report cards are only a week away. Your work has to be handed in on time."

Amanda suddenly sat up very straight in her seat. "What am I going to do?" she thought. "I haven't even started that unit. Even if I tried to do it all tonight, I'd probably get everything wrong!"

Then she glanced over at Jessica. Jessica was pretty nice—kind of quiet, but smart. She was the newest student in fourth grade, and Amanda knew that she wanted a friend.

At lunchtime Amanda walked over to the table where Jessica was sitting by herself. "Hi, Amanda!" Jessica said. "Have a seat."

"I . . . I have a favor to ask you, Jessica," Amanda said quietly. "It's about that vocabulary unit. I haven't started it yet, and I know you're already finished. Could I take your book home with me tonight? No one would ever know."

Jessica didn't know what to say. She wanted Amanda to be her friend. Maybe Amanda was right—no one would ever know. "What should I do?" Jessica thought.

▶ *What do you think Jessica should do? What action shows faithfulness to the seventh commandment?*

FAITH and MEDIA

▶ On Day 2, in the *We Gather* activity, students are asked to write a prayer, poem, or song thanking God for the good things in their lives. Take the opportunity to remind the students that prayers, poems, and songs are all forms of media. As such, they carry messages of comfort and inspiration to those who pray, say, sing or read them.

▶ Similarly, on Day 4 remind the students that murals such as the ones they are designing for the *We Believe* activity are also examples of media. Through the ages artists have been commissioned to paint murals on the walls of churches and other public buildings to instruct, inform, and inspire viewers as well as please their eyes.

CHAPTER PROJECT: NEW HEART AND NEW SPIRIT

Give the students an opportunity to live out their Catholic faith by helping others. Make a list of volunteer opportunities that are suitable for fourth graders. These could include activities such as collecting gently used toys for a homeless shelter, gathering school supplies for a school in need, or stocking the shelves of a community food pantry. Enlist the help of parents and staff to supervise the fourth grade volunteers, and be sure to obtain parental permission for each student to participate in these activities. After the students have completed their service, encourage them to describe ways their work helped them to help others and honor the seventh commandment. Explain to the students that such service should not be a one-time occurrence, but an ongoing part of their lives. Encourage them to serve others, especially those who need their help the most.

Connections

To Scripture

On Day 4 the students will hear these words of Saint James: "So also faith of itself, if it does not have works, is dead" (James 2:17). Remind the class that the seventh commandment requires us to work for justice. Encourage the students to imitate Jesus' example of caring for the poor and for those who are persecuted or excluded by society. Urge the students to share their gifts with others and aid those who lack life's basics.

To Stewardship

As the students learn more about the responsibilities given to us in the seventh commandment, encourage them to be good stewards. Explain that God has entrusted us with the gift of creation and it is our duty to care for this gift. Tell the students that good stewardship includes conserving natural resources. Encourage the students to think of ways to do this. Examples might include conserving water by turning off the faucet while brushing our teeth, taking shorter showers, or not watering the lawn when rainfall has been scarce and water supplies are below normal.

To Vocations

As the students learn about the importance of living out their faith by giving to others, encourage them to learn more about the priests, brothers, and sisters who give so freely of themselves to others. Use Catholic newspapers, biographies of the saints, and other religious publications to introduce the students to different types of religious orders whose members work to live out the message of the seventh commandment.

Meeting Individual Needs

Students with Auditory Needs

Be aware of students who may have auditory needs. Seat students who have difficulty hearing at the front of the class. Speak clearly, slowly, and distinctly. Be sure to situate yourself directly in front of a student who lip-reads. If a student has an American Sign Language interpreter, be sure to speak directly to the student, not to the interpreter. Make the student feel respected and valued. Through your example show the other students how to respect and include students with auditory needs.

ADDITIONAL RESOURCES

Video *The Story of Zacchaeus,* CCC of America, 1997. From the series *A Kingdom Without Frontiers.* Jesus praises Zacchaeus, who admits stealing and promises to repay his debt. (30 minutes)

To find more ideas for books, videos, and other learning material, visit Sadlier's

www.WEBELIEVEweb.com

Developing an Appreciation of Mary

by M. Jean Frisk, ISSM, M.A., S.T.L.

M. Jean, a Schoenstatt Sister of Mary, teaches Marian catechesis at The Marian Library/International Marian Research Institute in Dayton, Ohio. Sr. Jean also authors Marian works and co-develops the Mary Page at the Institute. She received her STL from the International Marian Research Institute affiliated with the Marianum in Rome.

"Today as ever, all laborers of catechesis, trusting in her intercession, turn to the Blessed Virgin Mary, who saw her Son grow '[in] wisdom, age and grace' (Luke 2:52). They find in her the spiritual model for carrying out and strengthening the renewal of contemporary catechesis, in faith, hope and love." [*GDC* 291]

As catechists, we can help our students develop an appreciation for Mary by considering the following in our lessons:

Mary's relation to the Blessed Trinity Mary said yes to the Father, accepted her mission for the Son, and was formed and overshadowed by the Holy Spirit.

Mary's relation to Jesus Christ Mary's story is irrevocably linked with Jesus. When we learn about Mary, we learn more about God the Son who became man. Mary was Jesus' most faithful follower and remains with him now to help show us the hope and fulfillment of our baptism into Christ.

Mary as model and mother of the Church Mary is "the Church's model of faith and charity. Thus she is a 'preeminent and . . . wholly unique member of the Church'" (*CCC* 967), "the symbol and the most perfect realization of the Church" (*CCC* 507), "a mother to us in the order of grace" (*CCC* 968).

The story of Mary based on Scripture All the gospels include Mary. She is part of the early Church after the Resurrection.

Catechist Development Topics (Topic and Guide Page)

The Church's Marian feasts Liturgy honors Mary's role in salvation and her role as our spiritual mother who teaches us the faith. The Church teaches us how to ask Mary for her assistance in prayer.

Mary's humanness Mary listens. She helps her family and others. She works gladly and sees the needs of others. She prays. She praises God by

(continued on next page)

Resources

"Mother of the Christ, Mother of the Church." *Papal Documents on the Blessed Virgin Mary* edited by Marianne Lorraine Trouvé. Boston: Pauline Books, 2001.

http://www.udayton.edu/mary *The Mary Page* is an extensive resource for videos, art on loan, activities, book lists, devotions, prayers, etc. produced by the University of Dayton's Marian Library/International Marian Research Institute.

singing hymns. Mary questions things respectfully. Mary does what Jesus tells us to do. Mary shows us the integrity of a human person filled with divine life.

Mary and the hope for Christian Unity There are ecumenical dimensions to devotion to Mary. Her life, words, and example teach us how to love Jesus and what Christians can do to remain faithful to him. (See *Marialis Cultis*, 32.)

Ways to Implement Developing an Appreciation of Mary

- Include a picture or statue of Mary in the prayer space. Teach and pray Marian prayers: Hail Mary, Magnificat, Memorare, the Litany of the Blessed Virgin Mary.
- Honor Mary. Celebrate the Church's Marian devotions with a May crowning. Honor her in October, the month of the rosary, by teaching and praying the rosary. Various cultures have specific devotions. Invite students to share their unique ways of honoring Mary.
- Have a "Mary Day" once a month. Invite your students to learn Mary hymns. In preparation for Mary Day, let students select a project to help people who are poor, sick, or lonely in your area (food basket, brownies for workers, cards for shut-ins, pennies for the missions). Bring the fruits of that project to the liturgy, and find ways to distribute these afterwards.
- In Advent, have a Mary Festival between the Immaculate Conception (8th), Patroness of the United States, and Our Lady of Guadalupe (12th), Patroness of the Americas. Encourage the children to find ways to be like Mary and bring Christ's light to others. Plan liturgies and charities. Discuss ways to create a peaceful pre-Christmas atmosphere at school, in the parish, and at home.

With thanks to:
Karen Mackley
St. John the Baptist School
New Brighton, Minnesota

Under Karen's direction, her students develop an appreciation for Mary by participating in an activity called, "Following in Mary's Footsteps." As an ongoing idea throughout the year, Karen reads Scripture passages about Mary, and the group discusses the sacrifices and great things that Mary has done. The students brainstorm ways they can try to be more like Mary in their daily lives. Each time that Karen observes a student "following in Mary's footsteps," she gives the student a sticker on a chart or an inexpensive charm for a bracelet. (Paper bracelets work as well.) At the end of the year, all the students participate in a special way in a celebration of Mary.

Notes

Name ______________________________

Place a ✔ in front of each headline that shows people honoring the seventh commandment.

_____ 1. Water Levels Rise as People Cut Back on Water Usage

_____ 2. Deliberate Fire Damages Garage

_____ 3. Local Man Arrested for Breaking Neighbor's Arm

_____ 4. Family Donates Money to Keep Homeless Shelter Open

_____ 5. Corporation "Adopts" Local Highway to Keep It Clean

_____ 6. Bookkeeper Charged with Stealing from Car Dealership

_____ 7. Student Receives Award for Returning Lost Wallet

_____ 8. High School Garden Club Raises Vegetables for the Needy

_____ 9. Drunken Driver Hits Teenager on Bike

Explain one way people in your community honor the seventh commandment.

____

____

____

The Seventh Commandment

✝ We Gather in Prayer

Leader: Let us listen to the words of the prophet Isaiah as he teaches the people about justice.

Reader 1: "Do you call this a fast,
a day acceptable to the LORD?
This, rather, is the fasting that I wish:

Reader 2: releasing those bound unjustly,
untying the thongs of the yoke;

Reader 3: Setting free the oppressed,
breaking every yoke;

Reader 4: Sharing your bread with the hungry,
sheltering the oppressed and the homeless;

Reader 5: Clothing the naked when you see them,
and not turning your back on your own." (Isaiah 58:5–7)

♫ **New Heart and New Spirit**

Refrain:

New heart and new spirit
give us, O God,
New heart and new spirit,
to live in love.

Your word gives us hope
that there is a way to live
in your justice and peace each day.
(Refrain)

207

Chapter 18 • Day 1

PREPARING TO PRAY

In this prayer the students will proclaim the meaning of true justice as described by the prophet Isaiah.

• Assign five readers and allow them time to rehearse. Tell the students that you will read the leader's part and everyone will sing the song.

• Play the song "New Heart and New Spirit," #22 on the Grade 4 CD, and allow time for practice.

The Prayer Space

• Display a banner with the words *You shall not steal* in the prayer space.

• Place a Bible in the center of the prayer space and bookmark the following passages: Isaiah 58:5–7; James 2:15–17; Luke 19:8; Exodus 20:15, and Matthew 5:1–12.

This Week's Liturgy

Visit **www.webelieveweb.com** for this week's liturgical readings and other seasonal material.

Lesson Plan

We Gather in Prayer ___ minutes

✝ Pray

• Say: *God asks us to have new hearts filled with peace and justice.* Then invite the students to gather in the prayer space with their books open to the opening prayer.

• Point out the scriptural passages that are marked in the Bible. Say: *Each of these passages relates to this chapter. If you have the time, please feel free to read them.*

• After praying the Sign of the Cross, begin the opening prayer.

• At the end of the prayer, play and sing "New Heart and New Spirit."

Home Connection Update

Invite the students to share the ways their families used the Chapter 17 family page. Ask: *What did you learn from the Scripture Pictures activity about the value of a good name?*

Chapter 18 • Day 1

Catechist Goal

• To teach what the seventh commandment calls us to do

Our Faith Response

• To identify the responsibilities of the seventh commandment

Lesson Materials

• markers (regular, fabric, and glitter varieties)

• a plain, white, cotton T-shirt for each student

As Catholics...

Saint John the Baptist

After presenting the lesson, have volunteers read aloud the text. Invite the students to name other saints who have worked for peace and justice. As you ask the students to identify other cities named for saints, name one or two, such as San Francisco, California, and Saint Louis, Missouri.

We are called to act with justice.

YOU SHALL NOT STEAL.

WE GATHER

✝ *Lord, your ways lead to justice.*

Think about a space that is yours. It may be your room at home or a desk or locker at school. Talk about the ways that others can show respect for your space.

WE BELIEVE

God wants us to love him and to respect one another. He gave us the Ten Commandments to help us do this. The seventh commandment is about the ways we treat other people and the things that belong to them. The seventh commandment is, "You shall not steal" (Exodus 20:15). It is based on justice. Justice means respecting the rights of others and giving them what is rightfully theirs.

The seventh commandment calls us to:

- care for the gifts of creation
- care for the things that belong to us and respect what belongs to others
- not take things that are not ours
- show respect for the goods and property of others
- work to help all people share the gifts of the earth.

The seventh commandment challenges us to live with one another in love. We are all part of one human family. We need to be aware of the ways our decisions affect others. What we do to help one another shows our love for God, who created all of us.

We are called to make sure that all people can share in the goodness of creation. The goods of creation were given to the entire human race. We are asked to share the earthly goods that we have with other people who may be in need. We help others to find ways to meet their basic needs. It is our common responsibility to work so that all people can have the things they need.

As Catholics...

Saint John the Baptist prepared people for the coming of Jesus, the Messiah. John the Baptist was a prophet. His preaching is like a bridge between the Old and New Testaments. John preached about justice and how to practice it. He told the crowd, "Whoever has two cloaks should share with the person who has none. And whoever has food should do likewise" (Luke 3:11).

We think about John the Baptist especially during Advent, when we prepare to celebrate the birth of Jesus. The city of San Juan, Puerto Rico, was named for John the Baptist. The birthday of John the Baptist is celebrated by the whole Church on June 24.

Do you know any other cities that are named for saints?

208

Lesson Plan

WE GATHER ___ minutes

✝ **Pray** Pray the Sign of the Cross and the *We Gather* prayer.

Focus on Life Read aloud the *We Gather* text and invite the students' comments. As they discuss what it means to respect another's space, ask: *What sort of reaction might we have when someone fails to respect our personal space or property?* Tell the students that in this lesson they will learn how we are called to act with justice.

WE BELIEVE ___ minutes

Ask What If? Read aloud the *We Believe* statement. Then ask volunteers to read aloud the *We Believe* paragraphs. Review the bulleted points explaining what the seventh commandment calls us to do, and explain to the students what a chain reaction is. Help the students understand that not living by the seventh commandment has a chain reaction effect by asking "what if" questions based on the bulleted points. For example, ask: *What might happen if we take things that are not ours? Who gets hurt? How do they get hurt? How do we get hurt if we steal or willfully damage the property of others? How is our relationship with God affected if we break the seventh commandment?* Diagram one such chain reaction on the board.

Think About Justice Write the word *justice* vertically on the board. With the students write an acrostic. You might start with *J is for Jesus, who wants us to treat others fairly,* and move on to *U is for Understanding how others feel about their property, S is for Showing respect to others,* and so on.

WE RESPOND

Work with a partner to design a T-shirt that shows what you can do to live the seventh commandment. Use catchy phrases and bright colors to really get your message across to others.

209

Chapter 18 • Day 1

ACTIVITY BANK

Faith and Media

Learning to Help Others

Activity Materials: Internet and other research materials

Help the students learn about organizations such as Catholic Relief Services, the Peace Corps, and Habitat for Humanity that work to make people's lives better. Organize the students into small groups and have each group research the work of one organization. Have each group give an oral report describing the ways its assigned organization honors the seventh commandment in its work. Then ask the students to think of ways that fourth graders can work for peace and justice. You may also wish to have the whole class visit the Catholic Relief Service Web site. The site offers news and activities for students and also provides resources for teachers.

Quick Check

✔ *What is the seventh commandment?* (The seventh commandment is "You shall not steal.")

✔ *What is the seventh commandment based on?* (The seventh commandment is based on justice, which is respecting the rights of others and giving them what is rightfully theirs.)

WE RESPOND ___ minutes

Connect to Life Read aloud the *We Respond* directions. Encourage the student pairs to use their imaginations as they design their T-shirts. If the students are working on real shirts, provide them with a variety of brightly colored markers, including fabric and glitter markers. Arrange a special time for the students to wear their T-shirts and share their messages of peace and justice.

Pray Conclude by praying, *Dear God, help us to live in your peace and justice each day. Strengthen us to practice our faith as did the preacher John the Baptist. Amen.*

Plan Ahead for Day 2

Catechist Goal: To explore what it means to respect the property of others

Preparation: Have available a CD of soft classical music and pictures of willfully damaged property.

Catechist Goal

- To explore what it means to respect the property of others

Our Faith Response

- To name ways that we can show respect for the property of others

Lesson Materials

- CD of soft classical music
- pictures of damaged property

Teaching Tip

Making Restitution

The classroom is an excellent arena in which to teach about respecting the property of others. Help the students understand that they are to respect others' property exactly as they want their own respected. Explain that we show disrespect when we abuse, belittle, or steal another person's property. Our property is an extension of ourselves, and disrespect for our property can be seen as disrespect for us.

We respect the property of others.

YOU SHALL NOT STEAL.

WE GATHER

✝ *Father, all that we have comes from you.*

Think about the good things that you and your family have. Write a prayer, poem, or song to thank God for these things.

____

____

____

____

WE BELIEVE

God wants us to show respect for the property or the goods that belong to others. When we follow the seventh commandment, we do not take things that belong to others. Stealing is any action that unjustly takes away the property or rights of others.

Sometimes people take things from others because they decide the owners do not need them. Some people may think that taking little things does not matter. Others may think that if they borrow things they do not have to give them back. Sometimes people may pick up things while shopping, and then not pay for these things. In all of these situations people are taking things from others. They are stealing.

However, following the seventh commandment is about more than not stealing the belongings of other people. For example, people should not damage a neighbor's property on purpose. Nor should people take up other people's time unnecessarily. Doing so does not honor the importance of the other things that people need to do. Sometimes people cheat on a test, copy homework, or use the ideas of others as their own. All of these kinds of acts also take something that belongs to another. Often these acts hurt others as much, or more, than taking their possessions.

Jesus lived a life of justice and fairness. He asked his disciples to do the same. He wanted them to use what they had to help others.

From the Gospel of Saint Luke we also learn that Jesus wanted people to repay debts and to live up to their promises. Jesus praised a man named Zacchaeus after Zacchaeus promised that if he had taken anything from anyone he would "repay it four times over" (Luke 19:8). The seventh commandment requires people to give back what they have unjustly taken from others.

Lesson Plan

WE GATHER ___ minutes

✝ **Pray** Pray the Sign of the Cross and the *We Gather* prayer.

Focus on Life Play classical music softly in the background as you read aloud the *We Gather* text and invite the students to write their prayer, poem, or song of thanks. Tell the students that in this lesson they will learn that we must respect the property of others.

WE BELIEVE ___ minutes

Talk About the Meaning Many students might think that the seventh commandment deals only with stealing. Read aloud the *We Believe* statement. Divide the class into three groups and have each group read and discuss one of the first three *We Believe* paragraphs. Then have each group present the main point of its paragraph. Make sure these points include such things as not returning borrowed things, cheating, failing to keep promises, and wasting other people's time. Then read aloud the *Chapter Story* and ask the questions that follow.

Write a Happy Ending Invite the students to write short scenarios in which someone has to make a choice that involves the seventh commandment. Then have the students exchange papers and write endings to each others' scenarios.

Learn from Jesus Read aloud the last two *We Believe* paragraphs and the activity directions. Ask a volunteer to read aloud each situation and invite the whole class to discuss ways to repay each loss.

Read these situations. How can each person give back what he or she has taken from someone else?

Tisha puts her sister's hair brush in her own backpack. She keeps it with her and uses it.

____

____

____

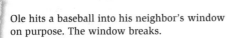

Janis cheats at a game of checkers with Jeremy.

____

____

____

Willa gets her father to buy her new sneakers after she "loses" her old ones on purpose.

____

____

____

Ole hits a baseball into his neighbor's window on purpose. The window breaks.

____

____

____

WE RESPOND

How will you show respect for the property of others this week?

211

Chapter 18 • Day 2

ACTIVITY BANK

Community

The Seventh Commandment and Business

Activity Materials: list of community contacts

Invite a local store manager, small-business owner, or police officer to speak about the importance of honesty in business and the negative effects of shoplifting. Before the speaker arrives, have the students prepare a list of questions. They may ask how stealing hurts the shoplifter, his or her family, other consumers, and the business.

Respect Property Show the students pictures of willfully damaged property such as graffiti-covered walls, a littered park, or broken windows. Ask the students to name ways to help prevent this sort of vandalism and lack of respect for property.

Quick Check

- ✔ *What are some ways that people break the seventh commandment?* (They may fail to respect the rights or property of others, take things from a store, fail to keep promises, keep borrowed things, cheat on a test, or copy homework.)
- ✔ *What does the story of Zacchaeus teach us?* (It is important to repay our debts.)

WE RESPOND

___ minutes

Connect to Life Read aloud the *We Respond* question and ask the students to reflect quietly on their responses.

Pray Form a prayer circle. Pray: *Dear God, please help us to respect the property of others. Let us imitate your Son, Jesus, who lived a life of justice and fairness. Amen.*

Plan Ahead for Day 3

Catechist Goal: To underscore that the seventh commandment calls us to care for God's creation

Preparation: Bring photos of natural beauty, library card–sized pieces of cardboard, and, if possible, school photos of the students.

Chapter 18 • Day 3

Catechist Goal

- To underscore that the seventh commandment calls us to care for God's creation

Our Faith Response

- To express thanks for the many gifts of creation

stewards of creation

Lesson Materials

- photos of natural beauty
- library card–sized pieces of cardboard
- school photo of each student (option)

Teaching Tip

Cooperative Learning Groups

In today's lesson the students will work in cooperative learning groups. When organizing such groups, seek balance by grouping together students whose strengths, challenges, and personalities complement one another. Vary such groups often to give the students opportunities to work with a variety of classmates. Try to use activities that encourage team building.

God's creation is meant for all people.

WE GATHER

✝ *God our creator, you have given us wonderful gifts.*

What are some places that your teacher might suggest for a class trip? Who takes care of these places? Why?

WE BELIEVE

"God looked at everything he had made, and he found it very good." (Genesis 1:31) God gave humans everything he created so that we would have the things that we need to live. The seventh commandment teaches us to use in the proper ways all that God has given us. We all have a responsibility to use the good things of the earth and not to abuse them. The seventh commandment calls us to care for God's creation.

Stewards are people who take care of things. God asks us to be stewards of his creation. **Stewards of creation** are those who take care of everything that God has given them.

Together as stewards of God's creation, we must protect our environment. Every day we use some of God's gifts for our food, our shelter, our work, and even for our relaxation. The words of the seventh commandment, "You shall not steal" (Exodus 20:15), are a reminder to use these gifts in a responsible way. People, communities, and nations should not use so much food, water, energy, and other gifts from God that there is not enough for others. The goods of creation are to be shared.

We are challenged to care for the world. It is not only God's gift to us but to the generations of people to come. We must work together for the good of all God's creation.

212

Lesson Plan

WE GATHER ___ minutes

✝ **Pray** Pray together the Sign of the Cross and the *We Gather* prayer.

Focus on Life Show the students photos of beautiful places. Have the students read and answer the *We Gather* questions. Ask the students to describe what happens when such places are abused or neglected. Tell the students that in this lesson they will learn that God's creation is meant for all people.

WE BELIEVE ___ minutes

Learn How to Be a Caretaker Have volunteers read aloud the *We Believe* statement and the four *We Believe* paragraphs. Emphasize the following:

- The seventh commandment calls us to care for God's creation.
- It is our responsibility to protect the environment.
- We must use our resources wisely and conserve God's gifts for those who will come after us.

Talk About the Key Word Discuss the kinds of things that God wants us to take care of in creation.

Complete the Chart Have the students work in groups to complete the chart. Ask a volunteer from each group to name disrespectful actions. Invite suggestions for ways to remedy each wrong. Write them on the board.

Make an ID Card Give each student a piece of cardboard about the size of a library card. Have the students label the cards *Steward of Creation ID Card*.

Work in groups to complete this chart. Then as a class discuss what can be done to change the disrespectful actions.

YOU SHALL NOT STEAL.

Actions that show respect for creation	Actions that show disrespect for creation

WE RESPOND

This week be a steward of creation. What will you do?

Key Word

stewards of creation those who take care of everything God has given them

Heal the Bay.

HEAL THE BAY! WE WERE HERE FIRST!

213

Chapter 18 • Day 3

ACTIVITY BANK

Curriculum Connection

Science

Activity Materials: lima beans or flower seeds, potting soil, small containers such as milk cartons or plastic cups

Give each student some seeds to germinate on a wet paper towel. When the seeds begin to sprout, have the students place them in small containers that have been lined with soil and have a drainage hole in the bottom. Cover the sprouts with more soil. Place the seedlings in sunlight and encourage the students to water them. Have the students measure their plants' growth and record it in a logbook. Encourage the students to reflect in their logbooks about what caring for these plants teaches us about being stewards of creation.

Have each student paste a school photo or draw a self-portrait on the card and write and sign a short, personal pledge telling how he or she will care for God's creation.

Quick Check

✔ *What does it mean to be a steward of creation?* (It means to take care of God's gifts and use them wisely.)

✔ *Why must we care for the world?* (because it is God's gift for all people and future generations)

WE RESPOND

___ minutes

Connect to Life Read aloud the *We Respond* text. Examples might include saving water or electricity, tending a garden, picking up litter, or taking reasonable rather than too-large helpings of food.

Pray Ask the students to join you in praying: *We praise you, Lord, for the beauty of the earth. We honor you, Lord, by valuing creation's worth. Amen.*

Plan Ahead for Day 4

Catechist Goal: To present that Jesus expects his disciples to help all people meet their basic needs

Preparation: Have available the Grade 4 CD; make copies of Reproducible Master 18.

Catechist Goal

• To present that Jesus expects his disciples to help all people meet their basic needs

Our Faith Response

• To identify ways that we can help people in need

Lesson Materials

• Bible
• copies of Reproducible Master 18
• Grade 4 CD

Blessed are they...

Saint Vincent do Paul and Saint Louise de Marillac

After you have completed the lesson, direct the students to this text. Remind them that *righteousness* is another word for *justice*. Have volunteers read the text and discuss ways Saints Vincent and Louise worked for justice.

We are called to help all people meet their basic needs.

WE GATHER

✝ *God, your mercy endures forever!*

What are the basic things that people need to live? Does everyone have these things? Discuss your answers.

WE BELIEVE

In the Beatitudes Jesus calls us to "hunger and thirst for righteousness" (Matthew 5:6). *Righteousness* is another word for justice. We work for justice when we imitate Jesus. As disciples of Jesus we share Jesus' concern for others. We help the people whose basic needs are not being met.

Jesus expects his disciples to share and to be generous toward others, especially the poor. Jesus showed care and love for those who were suffering. He showed mercy to people, especially those who were poor and powerless. We are asked to do more than pray for the poor. We must respond to their needs.

Saint James made this point very clear in his letter to some of the first disciples of Jesus. He said, "If a brother or sister has nothing to wear and has no food for the day, and one of you says to them, 'Go in peace, keep warm, and eat well,' but you do not give them the necessities of the body, what good is it? So also faith of itself, if it does not have works, is dead" (James 2:15–17).

Every person is created in God's image. This makes all people equal, sharing the same human dignity. We need to respect the human rights of all people. We need to stand up for those who do not have the things that are basic to life.

The Church calls us to work together so that all people are treated justly. By performing the Works of Mercy, we care for the needs of others. The Works of Mercy are things that we do to care for the physical and spiritual needs of others. Our acts of love may help people meet their basic needs.

Design a mural that illustrates the Works of Mercy.

Lesson Plan

WE GATHER ___ minutes

✝ **Pray** Pray aloud together the Sign of the Cross and the *We Gather* prayer.

Focus on Life Ask the students to read the *We Gather* questions. Invite responses. Remind the class of the difference between *needing* and *wanting*. Someone may *want* a new bicycle, for example, but not *need* it. Tell the students that in this lesson they will learn that as followers of Jesus we are called to help all people meet their basic needs.

WE BELIEVE ___ minutes

Recall the Beatitudes Read aloud the *We Believe* statement. Remind the students that Jesus gave us the Beatitudes as a blueprint for living. Read aloud the account of the Sermon on the Mount in Matthew 5:1–12.

Read the Text Have volunteers read aloud the *We Believe* paragraphs. Emphasize these points:

• In the Beatitudes Jesus tells us that we should "hunger and thirst for righteousness."

• Throughout his life Jesus worked to help the poor. Saint James explains in his letter that it is not enough merely to sympathize. We must act.

• The Church calls us to care for people's physical and spiritual needs by performing the Works of Mercy.

Do the Activity Direct the students to the Works of Mercy charts on page 138. Invite the students to review the charts and then design a mural on page 214. Call on volunteers to share their work.

Take a few moments to think quietly and prayerfully about ways you follow the seventh commandment. These questions may help you.

Have I cared for the gifts of creation?

Have I taken care of my belongings?

Have I taken things that do not belong to me?

Have I respected the property of others?

Have I been honest in taking tests and playing games?

Have I shared what I have with those who are in need?

Have I worked with my family, parish, or school to care for those who are poor or to make their lives better?

Have I performed Works of Mercy?

Blessed are they...

Saint Vincent de Paul and Saint Louise de Marillac

To "hunger and thirst" for something means to want something very badly. Vincent de Paul knew what it was to want justice since he had once been forced into slavery by pirates. When he escaped, he began to care for those who were poor and in need. He asked Louise de Marillac to help him, and together they founded the Daughters of Charity. The sisters of this community still serve the poor today. The sisters work in schools and hospitals, in services to children and the elderly, and in parishes. Saint Louise is the patroness of social workers.

Vincent also founded the Congregation of the Mission. This is a community of priests and brothers who preach, give retreats, work in parishes, and teach in schools. Saint Vincent's feast day is September 27. Saint Louise's feast day is March 15.

"Blessed are they who hunger and thirst for righteousness, for they will be satisfied." (Matthew 5:6)

WE RESPOND

New Heart and New Spirit

Refrain:

New heart and new spirit
give us, O God,
New heart and new spirit,
to live in love.

Your word gives us hope
that there is a way to live
in your justice and peace each day.
(Refrain)

Activity Bank

Multicultural Connection

Working for Peace and Justice

Activity Materials: mission magazines and Web sites

Invite the students to learn about the work of Catholic missionaries around the world by reading mission magazines and visiting appropriate Web sites. Help the students identify the kinds of problems—poverty, illness, illiteracy, and unemployment—facing people in developing countries. Discuss the ways Catholic missionaries are living out the seventh commandment as they care for the poor and powerless. Then ask the students to suggest ways for young people in the United States to help missionaries in their work.

Find Ways to Honor the Seventh Commandment Distribute copies of Reproducible Master 18, and read the directions aloud. Invite the students to work independently. When all the students are ready, review the answers. (Numbers 1, 4, 5, 7, and 8 should have checks.)

Reflect on the Seventh Commandment Invite the students to use the questions on page 215 as an examination of conscience. Encourage the students to think about ways to honor this commandment more fully.

Quick Check

✔ *What does Jesus mean when he says that we should "hunger and thirst for righteousness"?* (He means that we should work to see that all the people in the world receive justice.)

✔ *Which are the Works of Mercy?* (The Works of Mercy are things we do to care for the physical and spiritual needs of others.)

WE RESPOND ___ minutes

Connect to Life Have the students think of ways to share God's peace and justice with their classmates, their families, and all the people in God's family.

Pray Gather in the prayer space. Play and sing "New Heart and New Spirit," #22, Grade 4 CD.

Plan Ahead for Day 5

Catechist Goal: To review chapter ideas and their relationship to our faith life

Preparation: Make copies of Chapter 18 Test in the Grade 4 Assessment Book (option). Have available sentence strips and metal fasteners.

Catechist Goal

- To review chapter ideas and their relationship to our faith life

Our Faith Response

- To apply what has been learned to our lives

CHAPTER TEST

Chapter 18 Test is provided in the Grade 4 Assessment Book.

Grade 4
Chapter 18

Write True or False for the following sentences. Then change the false sentences to make them true.

1. True As stewards of God's creation, we are called to protect the world.
2. False The seventh commandment teaches us to show respect for our bodies.
The seventh commanments teaches us to show respect for the goods and property of others.
3. True Justice requires respecting the rights of others.
4. False Jesus' disciples are generous to others, especially the rich.
Jesus' disciples are generous to others, especially the poor.

Choose a word or phrase from the box to complete each sentence.

stealing	creation	justice	seventh commandment

5. Justice requires giving others what is rightfully theirs.
6. Any action that unjustly takes away the property or rights of others is stealing.
7. God's gifts of creation are for all people.
8. The seventh commandment requires people to give back what they have unjustly taken.

9–10. Write a short paragraph about the importance of the seventh commandment.

Watch the news with your family. Choose one story that relates to the seventh commandment. Write a summary of the story, describing how the seventh commandment is being lived out.

216

Lesson Plan

___ minutes

Chapter Review Explain to the students that they are now going to check their understanding of what they have learned. Have the students complete questions 1–8. Invite volunteers to provide the correct answers. Then allow time for the students to respond to question 9–10.

Assessment Activity This activity offers another opportunity to review what the students have learned about living out the seventh commandment. In this case, you might suggest that the students watch one of the weekend news programs with family members. They can present their news story summaries to the class next week along with their reports on their families' use of this week's family page.

___ minutes

Reflect & Pray Read the incomplete sentence aloud. Ask the students to think about what the term *justice* means to them as they write their responses. When all have finished, invite the students to gather in the prayer space to pray silently to God that all the world's people might be treated with justice.

Key Word Give each student a sentence strip. Ask the students to write on the strip one way to act as a steward of creation. Collect the strips and punch a hole in each one. Assemble the strips into sets of five and join each set with a metal fastener. Organize the class into small groups and give each group a set of sentence strips. Have the groups use the sentence

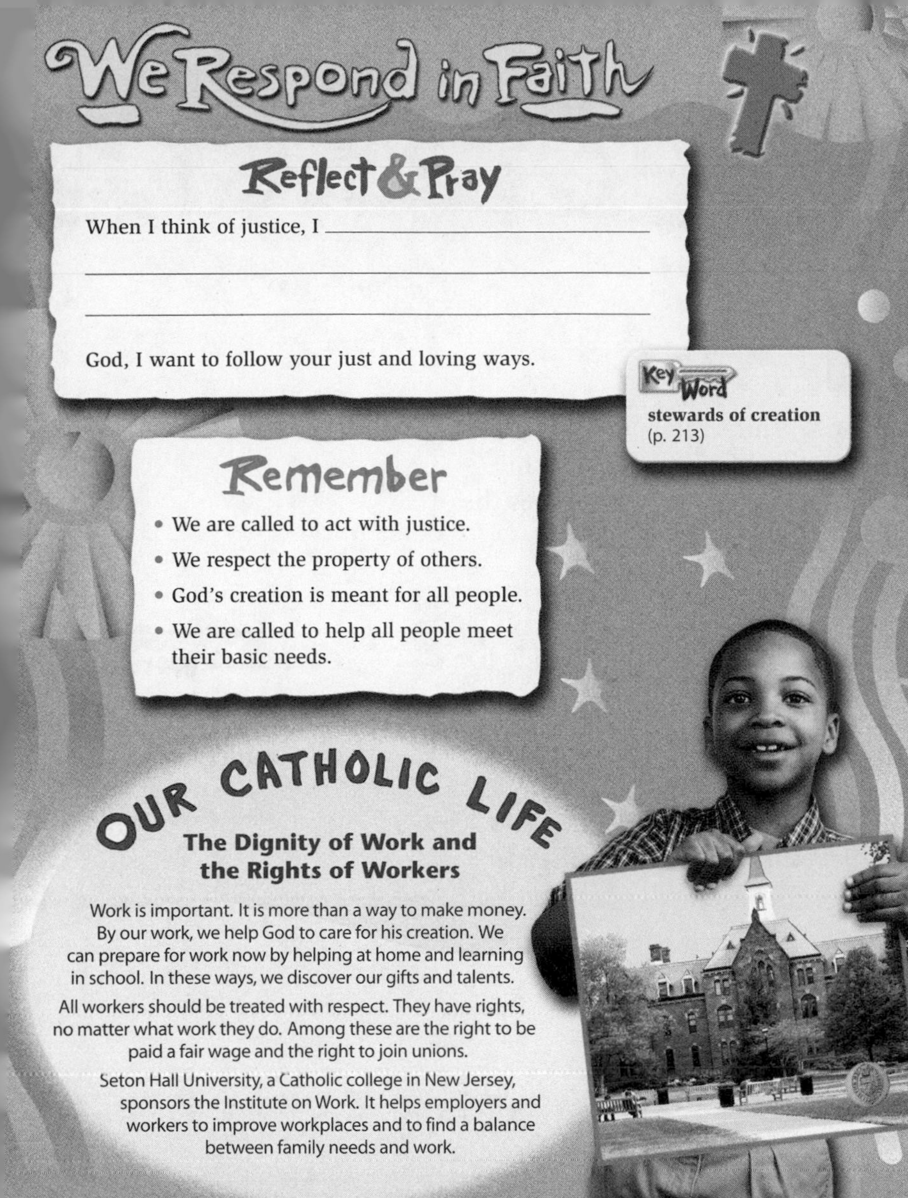

We Respond in Faith

Reflect & Pray

When I think of justice, I ______________________

____

____

God, I want to follow your just and loving ways.

Key Word
stewards of creation
(p. 213)

Remember

- We are called to act with justice.
- We respect the property of others.
- God's creation is meant for all people.
- We are called to help all people meet their basic needs.

Our Catholic Life

The Dignity of Work and the Rights of Workers

Work is important. It is more than a way to make money. By our work, we help God to care for his creation. We can prepare for work now by helping at home and learning in school. In these ways, we discover our gifts and talents.

All workers should be treated with respect. They have rights, no matter what work they do. Among these are the right to be paid a fair wage and the right to join unions.

Seton Hall University, a Catholic college in New Jersey, sponsors the Institute on Work. It helps employers and workers to improve workplaces and to find a balance between family needs and work.

Home Connection

Sharing Faith with My Family

Make sure to send home the family page (text page 218).

Remind the students to share what they have learned by doing the family page activities with their families. Read aloud the "Letters from Paul" verse and point out this week's Scripture Pictures quote.

For additional information and activities, encourage families to visit Sadlier's

www.WEBELIEVEweb.com

strips to review the different ways we can be stewards of God's creation.

Remember Read aloud each of the four *We Believe* statements. Help the students understand the difference that living out the seventh commandment in each of these ways will make in their lives and in the life of the Church.

Our Catholic Life Read aloud the text. Invite the students to express their feelings about work and the rights of workers. Ask them to describe some of the rights that workers deserve. Ask: *Why is the mission of the Institute on Work important?*

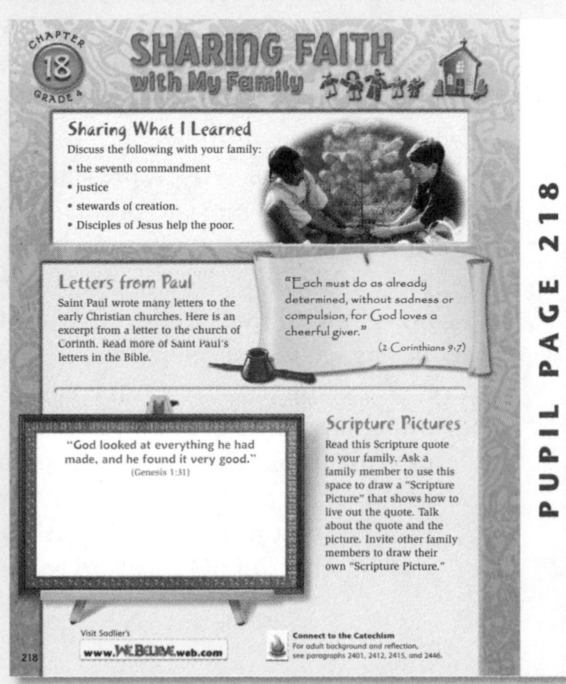

Chapter 18 Grade 4

SHARING FAITH with My Family

Sharing What I Learned
Discuss the following with your family:
- the seventh commandment
- justice
- stewards of creation.
- Disciples of Jesus help the poor.

Letters from Paul
Saint Paul wrote many letters to the early Christian churches. Here is an excerpt from a letter to the church of Corinth. Read more of Saint Paul's letters in the Bible.

"Each must do as already determined, without sadness or compulsion, for God loves a cheerful giver." (2 Corinthians 9:7)

"God looked at everything he had made, and he found it very good." (Genesis 1:31)

Scripture Pictures
Read this Scripture quote to your family. Ask a family member to use this space to draw a "Scripture Picture" that shows how to live out the quote. Talk about the quote and the picture. Invite other family members to draw their own "Scripture Picture."

Visit Sadlier's www.WEBELIEVEweb.com

Connect to the Catechism
For adult background and reflection, see paragraphs 2401, 2412, 2415, and 2446.

218

PUPIL PAGE 218

Chapter 19 The Eighth Commandment

Overview

In Chapter 18 the students learned that the seventh commandment calls us to respect others, their property, and the world God created. In this chapter the students will learn that the eighth commandment teaches the importance of learning and living the truth that comes from God.

Doctrinal Content	For Adult Reading and Reflection *Catechism of the Catholic Church*
The students will learn:	Paragraph
• God teaches us what it means to be true.	2465
• We are called to witness to the truth of our faith.	2472
• We have a responsibility to tell the truth.	2483
• We have a responsibility to respect the truth.	2469

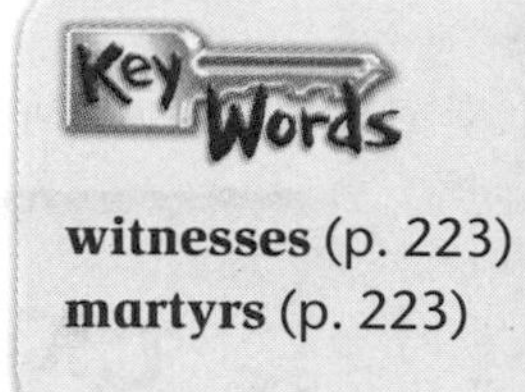

witnesses (p. 223)
martyrs (p. 223)

Catechist Background

Have you ever been hurt by another person's lie?

The eighth commandment is "You shall not bear false witness against your neighbor" (Exodus 20:16). Jesus commented on this commandment by saying, "Let your 'Yes' mean 'Yes' and your 'No' mean 'No.' Anything more is from the evil one" (Matthew 5:37). By saying this, Jesus was calling his followers to be truthful.

Christians are the living representatives of Christ. We bear his name and proclaim his message. We have been anointed through the gift of the Holy Spirit at Baptism. We express our belief in God who is "the source of all truth" (CCC 2465). When we engage in dishonesty and lies, we betray our deepest calling because truth is one of the most important characteristics of a Christian.

Jesus is identified with truth. "In Jesus Christ, the whole of God's truth has been made manifest" (CCC 2465). In testimony to this, John's gospel describes Jesus as "full of grace and truth" (1:14) and Jesus calls himself "the way and the truth and the life" (14:6). The devil is identified with lying. "There is no truth in him. When he tells a lie, he speaks in character, because he is a liar and the father of lies" (John 8:44).

When we choose to speak a falsehood with the intention of misleading or deceiving, we are lying. Lies may seem to be small "twists of the truth," but inexorably they edge us away from Christ and closer to the father of lies. Truthfulness often is difficult, but ultimately it is rewarding. As Jesus promised, "you will know the truth, and the truth will set you free" (John 8:32).

What can you do today to be a witness of the truth?

Lesson Planning Guide

Lesson Focus	Presentation	Materials
Day 1		
age 219 **We Gather in Prayer**	• Pray the psalm. Respond in song.	For the prayer space: Bible, basket "Come Follow Me," Barbara Bridge, #23, Grade 4 CD • slips of paper
pages 220–221 *God teaches us what it means to be true.*	• Discuss the **We Gather** question. • Read and discuss the eighth commandment in the **We Believe** text. • Discuss the **We Respond** questions. • Pray together.	
Day 2		
pages 222–223 *We are called to witness to the truth of our faith.*	• In **We Gather** name easy and difficult times to tell the truth. • Read and discuss the **We Believe** text. • Answer the **We Respond** question. Role-play the witness activity. • Read the *Blessed are they . . .* text. • Pray together.	• blank note cards
Day 3		
pages 224–225 *We have a responsibility to tell the truth.*	• Discuss the **We Gather** question. • Read and discuss the **We Believe** text. • Answer the **We Respond** question. Do the storyboard activity. • Pray together.	
Day 4		
pages 226–227 *We have a responsibility to respect the truth.*	• Discuss the **We Gather** pictures. • Read the **We Believe** text. Do the activity about being truthful. • Reflect on the eighth commandment. • Answer the **We Respond** questions. • Read the *As Catholics* text. • Pray together.	• copies of Reproducible Master 19 guide page 219G • slips of paper for each student
Day 5		
page 228 **Review** **pages 229–230** **We Respond in Faith**	• Complete questions 1–10. Work on the *Assessment Activity.* • Complete the *Reflect & Pray* activity. • Review *Remember* and *Key Words.* • Read and discuss *Our Catholic Life.* • Discuss **Sharing Faith with My Family**.	• Chapter 19 Test in Assessment Book, pp. 39–40 • Chapter 19 Test in Test Generator • Review & Resource Book, pp. 46–48 • Family Book, pp. 55–57

For additional ideas, activities, and opportunities: Visit Sadlier's **www.WEBELIEVEweb.com**

Enrichment Ideas

Chapter Story

Will slammed the back door shut and stomped up the stairs to his bedroom. He had attended rehearsal that afternoon, and things hadn't gone well. He hadn't known any of his lines. When Mr. Benson, the teacher directing the play, had asked what was wrong, Will had said that he had been sick all weekend and wasn't able to practice.

Mr. Benson had smiled at Will and told him he hoped he felt better. After rehearsal Will met his friend Eric by his locker. Just then Mr. Benson walked by and stopped to talk to the boys. He asked Eric if he'd had a good weekend. Eric said, "It was great! Will and I went hiking on Saturday, and on Sunday we rode our bikes by the lake." Mr. Benson didn't say anything to Will.

Will was so embarrassed he ran home as fast as he could. His mom heard him slam the door. She came to his room to ask him what was wrong. Will told her what had happened, and his mom asked him what he planned to do. "I guess I should tell Mr. Benson the truth." His mom smiled and said, "You know that's the right thing to do. Lies only lead to more problems."

The next morning Will went to school early and knocked on Mr. Benson's door. Mr. Benson told him to come in and asked Will what he wanted to talk about. Will looked at the floor and said, "I know you know I lied about being sick this weekend. I'm sorry I didn't tell the truth."

Mr. Benson smiled and said, "I'm glad you decided to tell me, Will. I know it isn't always easy to tell the truth, but it's the right thing to do. When people don't tell the truth, it hurts their relationship with other people. People stop trusting them."

Will practiced his lines all the next weekend. At Monday's rehearsal he knew his part perfectly. Mr. Benson patted him on the back and said, "Great job! You learned your lines, and you learned an important lesson."

▶ *What did Will learn from this experience?*

FAITH and MEDIA

▶ On Day 3 there is a discussion about gossip and rumors. This is an opportunity to remind the students that the Internet and e-mail make it very easy for people to spread gossip, rumors, and false information. With a few clicks of a mouse, someone can forward a rumor via e-mail to thousands of people around the world. And when a lie about a person's reputation is posted on a Web site, it can stay there for years, causing damage every time someone types the person's name into a search engine.

CHAPTER PROJECT: MODERN MARTYRS

In this chapter the students learn that martyrs are those Christian witnesses who have died for their faith. Although many faithful witnesses were martyred during the early years of Christianity, there are also Catholics in today's world who are martyred for their faith. Invite the students to research a modern martyr; that is, someone who died for his or her faith within the last 100 years. Have the students work in small groups. They may use Catholic Web sites or other research sources to gather information. You may wish to consult Robert Royal's book *Catholic Martyrs of the Twentieth Century* for ideas. Research subjects could include Maximilian Kolbe, Edith Stein, Archbishop Oscar Romero, Padre Miquel Pro, and the missionary martyrs of El Salvador. Encourage the students to use different presentation methods—essays, artwork, or other—to share what they have learned.

Connections

To Liturgy

During Mass, at the penitential rite, we confess that we have not always followed God's will. Encourage the students to have a truthful heart as they pray this prayer during Mass. Explain that God wants us to repent for our sins, that is, to feel truly sorry for our wrongdoing and to strive to live according to God's will. Tell the students that in Psalm 15 we are told that whoever speaks truth from the heart will be blessed.

To Saints

Tell the story of Saint Stephen, the first Christian martyr. Stephen was put on trial for preaching about Jesus and then was executed by stoning. Even as he faced death, Stephen did not abandon his faith. He called out, "Lord Jesus, receive my spirit" (Acts 7:59). Although we may never have to make such a sacrifice, we can follow Saint Stephen's example of being a faithful witness. Nothing should deter us from proclaiming the truth of our Savior.

To Family

Encourage the students to understand that telling the truth is essential to family life. Explain that if their parents or guardians were never truthful, it would be hard for the students to trust them. In the same way, emphasize that the students must be truthful with family members in order to gain their trust. Telling the truth helps build strong, healthy relationships.

Meeting Individual Needs

Students with Speech Impediments

Work with students who have speech impediments to devise learning arrangements suited to their needs. A student with a speech impediment might find giving a presentation in front of the class difficult or even embarrassing. If such a student is to give a presentation, offer a variety of options. The student might videotape the presentation and show the tape to the class. Allow these students to work in small groups and in one-on-one situations in which they can experience success.

ADDITIONAL RESOURCES

Videos

In the Beginning: Journey to the Promised Land, CCC of America, 1995. God keeps His promise to the Israelites to lead them to the promised land after they wander in the desert. (30 minutes)

Veggie Tales: Larry-Boy and the Rumor Weed, Big Idea Productions, Inc., 1999. A whopping rumor is spreading like a weed. Larry-Boy tries to stop it before someone gets hurt. (30 minutes)

To find more ideas for books, videos, and other learning material, visit Sadlier's

www.WEBELIEVEweb.com

Fishing in a Sea of Multimedia

by Caroline Cerveny, SSJ, D. Min.

Sister Caroline, director of educational technology for William H. Sadlier, Inc., is a nationally recognized speaker and leader in interactive media ministry for faith formation. She holds a D. Min. in Parish Revitalization from McCormick Seminary (Chicago), MA in religious studies from St. Mary's College (Winona) and an MA in educational technology from Governor's State University (Chicago).

Catechists today are challenged to proclaim the gospel in a world where tools, communication, children, and learning are different. Today, technology stands at the center of this very different world. Using the integration of sound, video, text, and graphics in a digital environment, multimedia is set to become the medium of choice for the 21st century.

Alert to the shifting patterns in all areas of life and culture, the Church recognizes the importance of her own incorporation of technology into all arenas of teaching and ministry. Pope John Paul II, in his May, 2002 Communications Day letter reminds us that online multimedia technology offers "magnificent opportunities" for evangelization, especially among young people who increasingly use the Web as a "window on the world."

While we can sometimes feel like we are drowning in the endless possibilities software companies offer, the following suggestions present "user-friendly" paths for incorporating multimedia into the learning experience of young Catholics of all ages.

Identify available technology. You will need at least one computer. Presentation software (e.g., Microsoft PowerPoint) or authoring tools like Hyperstudio can be used for creating multimedia projects for your lesson. These programs allow you or your students to turn an outline into a work of art using display type, graphics, animation, and even video clips. You can present this technology-driven creation on screen using a computer that is connected to a television converter and large TV monitor [usually affordable and thus available in schools] or connected to a LCD panel and overhead projector. Or you may print color transparencies that may be used with an overhead projector.

Choose multimedia resources. Sources of religious information may be located in books, CD-ROMs, and on the Internet. What is important to remember is that finding quality and theologically correct

(continued on next page)

Catechist Development Topics (Topic and Guide Page)

Resources

Druin Allison (editor). *The Design of Children's Technology.* Morgan Kaufmann Publishers, 1998.

Foley, Kim. *Using and Creating Virtual Field Trips.* Persistent Vision, 2001. If you'd like to order the book, please send email to info@field-trips.org.

material may be a challenge using Internet resources. In today's interactive environment, it is possible for anyone to publish his or her thoughts and beliefs. A search engine does not discern if the material you find represents true Catholic theology. It simply finds information for you. Often you will need to take time to find material that reflects Catholic Tradition. If you are in doubt, check with your parish DRE, pastor, or someone whose theology and ministry you respect to verify that the material you are using from the Internet represents what the Catholic Church teaches.

Ways to Implement Fishing in a Sea of Multimedia

- Here are multimedia projects you or your students can create using a combination of media and format: prayer reflection; chapter summary of a lesson; interactive games ; pop quizzes; interpretations of words of the Our Father, Hail Mary, and other traditional prayers; weekly vocabulary words.

- Using *Printmaster Gold 4.0 and HP Restickables* Large Round Inkjet Stickers, invite students to create stickers to represent their favorite saints. They can share these stickers with their friends so that they can add them to their notebooks or bookbags.

- Multimedia projects lend themselves to team efforts. If you want to do a prayer reflection for your class that consist of five or more slides, assign one slide to a mini-team of two persons. They can work on the project and bring their diskette back to you as their completed assignment. You can then assign a student to merge these slides together to create one multimedia presentation.

For additional ideas, activities, and opportunities, visit Sadlier's

www.WEBELIEVEweb.com

With thanks to:
Bill Beebe
St. Helena's Parish
Edison, New Jersey

Bill takes advantage of the fact that his older students know more about technology than many of the adults in the parish. Each year, Bill invites his students to mentor younger students in a "Safe Faith Day." During this time, the older students present ways to safely use the Internet to learn more about Jesus and the Catholic faith and tradition. A week before, Bill meets with his students to review Web sites and search engines that will be presented during the day. The theology presented as well as the links offered on each site are evaluated. On the actual "Safe Faith Day," Bill says, "I walk around and monitor the interaction between students. I am always amazed at what a positive, evangelizing experience it is!"

Notes

Name ____

Explain why each drawing relates to the eighth commandment.

The Eighth Commandment

We Gather in Prayer

Leader: Let us pray Psalm 119.

Side 1: "Your word, LORD, stands forever;
it is firm as the heavens.

Side 2: Through all generations your truth
endures;
fixed to stand firm like the earth."
(Psalm 119:89, 90)

Side 1: "Your justice is forever right,
your teaching forever true."
(Psalm 119:142)

Side 2: "I call with all my heart, O LORD;
answer me that I may observe your
laws."
(Psalm 119:145)

Side 1: Glory to the Father, and to the
Son, and to the Holy Spirit:

Side 2: As it was in the beginning, is now,
and will be for ever. Amen.

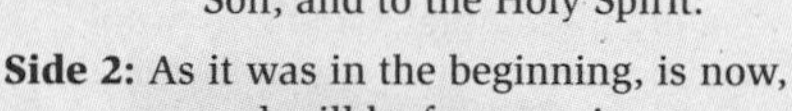

Come, Follow Me

Refrain:
Come, follow me, come, follow me.
I am the way, the truth, and the life.
Come, follow me, come, follow me.
I am the light of the world, follow me.

You call us to serve with a generous
heart;
in building your kingdom each one
has a part.
Each person is special in your
kingdom of love.
Yes, we will follow you, Jesus!
(Refrain)

219

Chapter 19 • Day 1

Preparing to Pray

Through presentation of psalms and singing, the students will give glory to God who is forever true and just.

• Play the song "Come, Follow Me," #23 on the Grade 4 CD. Allow the students time to practice.

• Organize the class into two groups. Assign one group the Side 1 readings and the other group the Side 2 readings. Allow time for each group to look over its readings.

• Invite one student to be the prayer leader.

The Prayer Space

• Gather the following items: a Bible opened to Psalm 119, a basket.

This Week's Liturgy

Visit **www.webelieveweb.com** for this week's liturgical readings and other seasonal material.

Lesson Plan

We Gather in Prayer ___ minutes

Pray

• Invite the students to gather in a circle in the prayer space with their books open to the opening prayer.

• When all have assembled, pray the Sign of the Cross and the words *We gather in prayer.* Invite the leader to begin.

• Pray the opening prayer.

• Play and sing together "Come, Follow Me."

Home Connection Update

Ask volunteers to present their seventh commandment news story summaries (the Chapter 18 *Assessment Activity*) to the class. Then invite the students to share their experiences using the Chapter 18 family page with their families. Ask: *What did you learn from the Scripture Picture exercise?*

Chapter 19 • Day 1

Catechist Goal

- To describe the ways God remained true to the Israelites

Our Faith Response

- To live out the eighth commandment and be true to God

Lesson Materials

- slips of paper

Teaching Note

Living the Commandment

There are many opportunities to help students apply the eighth commandment to their lives. Encourage the students to be honest and fair when working and playing with one another. Explain that they have a responsibility to one another, as well as to themselves, to tell the truth.

God teaches us what it means to be true.

You shall not bear false witness against your neighbor.

We Gather

✝ *God, we promise to be true to you.*

Imagine a courtroom scene where the witness is called to the stand. What does the witness promise?

We Believe

A witness is someone who has seen or heard something. To witness means to have personal knowledge and to truthfully tell what is known. To give false witness can harm others. It can harm the whole community.

The eighth commandment states: "You shall not bear false witness against your neighbor" (Exodus 20:16). Like all of the commandments, it tells us something about the relationship between God and the Israelites. God has been true to his people since the very beginning.

God promised Abraham that he would become the father of a great nation. Abraham believed God, yet Abraham and his wife, Sarah, grew old and had no children. But God kept his promise and Sarah gave birth to a son, Isaac. Through Isaac, God's people the Israelites began. God's word was true.

Many years later God heard the prayers of his people asking for freedom from their slavery in Egypt. God sent Moses to lead them to freedom and eventually made a covenant with them. God promised to be their God. The Israelites promised to be his people and to live by the Ten Commandments.

220

Lesson Plan

We Gather ___ minutes

✝ **Pray** Pray the Sign of the Cross and the *We Gather* prayer.

Focus on Life Read aloud the *We Gather* question. Invite the students to recall trial scenes they may have seen on television or in a movie where a person swears to tell the truth. Tell the students that in this lesson they will learn that God teaches us what it means to be true.

We Believe ___ minutes

Read the Text Ask volunteers to read aloud the *We Believe* statement and the *We Believe* text. Pause to discuss the ways that God showed his commitment and truthfulness to the Israelites. Emphasize the following points:

- God has been true to his people from the beginning.
- God kept his promise to Abraham and Sarah, and their descendants were the people of Israel.
- God freed his people from slavery in Egypt and gave them laws by which they should live.
- The eighth commandment helped the Israelites to be truthful to God and to one another.

At the end of the reading ask: *What did God expect in return from his people?* (faithfulness and true witness of their faith)

Act Out the Eighth Commandment Ask the students to think about what it means to be true. Invite them to name different situations in which a person can demonstrate that he or she is true to a family member, to a friend, or to another person. Have the

The Old Testament is full of stories showing that God was faithful and true. The Israelites were starving in the desert, and God sent them food. They needed help against their enemies, and God sent them leaders. And when they forgot to live their part of the covenant, God sent prophets to remind them to be faithful and true to him.

By living out the Ten Commandments, the Israelites gave witness to the truth of God's great love for them. They sang hymns in honor of God's faithfulness:

"For the LORD's word is true;
all his works are trustworthy"
(Psalm 33:4).

Because God was true to his people, they learned to be true to God and one another. The eighth commandment helped them to be true and truthful.

WE RESPOND

How can you be true to God and one another? What will you do to show your family members that you are trustworthy and truthful?

221

ACTIVITY BANK

Faith and Media

The Eighth Commandment in Action

Activity Materials: basic props and costumes, video camera (option)

Invite groups of students to write and act out skits illustrating situations in which young people are having difficulty following the eighth commandment. If possible, videotape the skits. Encourage the students to devise a variety of scenarios and solutions to demonstrate the many ways we can find to uphold God's word. Invite family members to watch the skits.

students work in small groups to act out situations showing faithfulness and commitment to God and other people. Allow time for the groups to present their skits.

Reflect on the Prayer Ask the students to reread silently the *We Gather* prayer. Encourage them to reflect on what it means to be true to God.

Quick Check

✔ *What does the eighth commandment tell us?* (The eighth commandment tells us, "You shall not bear false witness against your neighbor.")

✔ *What did God promise Abraham?* (God promised Abraham that he would become the father of a great nation.)

WE RESPOND

___ minutes

Connect to Life Have the students quietly read the *We Respond* questions and then respond. Hand a slip of paper to each student. Have the students write two ways they can apply the eighth commandment to their lives, fold the papers, and put them in the basket in the prayer space. Ask the students to pray that they succeed in living the eighth commandment.

Pray Ask the students to turn to page 326 and pray the Act of Faith.

Plan Ahead for Day 2

Catechist Goal: To present that we are called to witness to the truth of our faith

Preparation: Be prepared to share examples of people who have demonstrated their commitment to their faith.

Chapter 19 • Day 2

Catechist Goal

• To present that we are called to witness to the truth of our faith

Our Faith Response

• To listen to the Holy Spirit and seek to be faithful witnesses to our faith

martyrs
witnesses

Lesson Materials

• blank note cards

Blessed are they...

The Martyrs of Uganda

Ask a volunteer to read aloud the *Blessed are they* text. Have the groups consider the following questions: *Why would the chief feel threatened by the faith these people? Would you find it difficult to stay true to your faith in the face of a difficult situation?* Remind the students that they can rely on the Holy Spirit for strength.

YOU SHALL NOT BEAR FALSE WITNESS AGAINST YOUR NEIGHBOR.

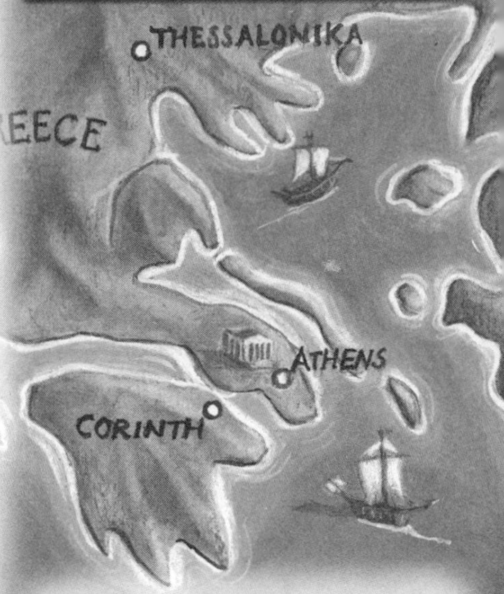

We are called to witness to the truth of our faith.

WE GATHER

✝ *Jesus, we look to you to show us the truth.*

It sometimes takes courage to tell the truth. Name some times when it is easy to tell the truth. Name some times when it is difficult.

WE BELIEVE

We learn from the New Testament that Jesus is the way, the truth, and the life. God the Father sent his Son to help us live in truth. Jesus told us, "For this I was born and for this I came into the world, to testify to the truth. Everyone who belongs to the truth listens to my voice" (John 18:37). We live in the truth when we listen to Jesus and follow the example of his life.

The first disciples had personal knowledge of Jesus. They witnessed his life, death, and Resurrection. Jesus knew that his disciples would need help to become good witnesses. So after Jesus rose from the dead and before he ascended into heaven, he promised his disciples that the Holy Spirit would come to them. "You will receive power when the holy Spirit comes upon you, and you will be my witnesses in Jerusalem, throughout Judea and Samaria, and to the ends of the earth" (Acts of the Apostles 1:8). Once Jesus returned to his Father, it was up to these first disciples to share the truth about Jesus with others.

At Pentecost the disciples received the Holy Spirit and were filled with courage. At once they spoke to the crowds, and the people understood them in their own languages.

The disciples began to teach the good news of Jesus, but not everyone believed them. Some people became angry and threw stones at them. Others sent the disciples to jail. However, the Holy Spirit made the disciples strong. They remained faithful to the truth about the risen Christ.

Faith in Jesus spread throughout the world. However, in some areas people were not allowed to believe in Jesus. In Rome Christians faced death if they would not worship false gods. Many Christian women and men were witnesses to their faith.

222

Lesson Plan

WE GATHER ___ minutes

✝ **Pray** Pray the Sign of the Cross and the *We Gather* prayer.

Focus on Life Ask the students to read silently the *We Gather* text. Invite volunteers to respond. Tell the students that in this lesson they will learn that we are called to be witnesses to the truth of our faith.

WE BELIEVE ___ minutes

Learn About the Holy Spirit Have volunteers read aloud the *We Believe* statement and the first three *We Believe* paragraphs. Stress the following points:

• We live the way God wants when we listen to Jesus and follow his example.

• At Pentecost the disciples were filled with the Holy Spirit. This enabled them to proclaim the gospel to people of all nations.

Consider the Martyrs Ask the students to read the fourth through the sixth *We Believe* paragraphs. Emphasize: *The martyrs died because of their faith in Jesus, which they would not abandon.* Encourage the students to imagine the dangers and persecutions faced by the disciples as they preached the good news. Remind the students that the disciples were filled with the Holy Spirit and that this gave them courage.

Write About Witnesses Have a volunteer read aloud the final *We Believe* paragraphs. Ask students to think of people they know who are faithful witnesses.

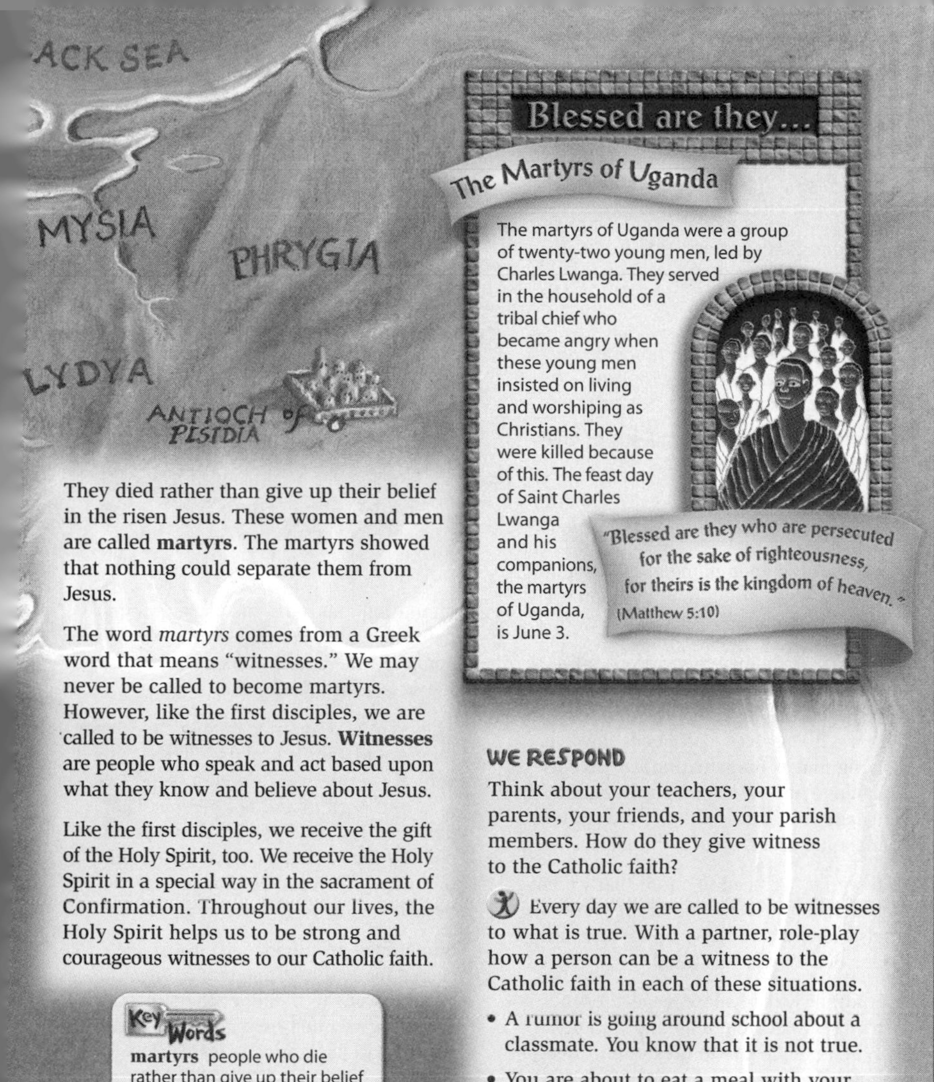

Blessed are they...

The Martyrs of Uganda

The martyrs of Uganda were a group of twenty-two young men, led by Charles Lwanga. They served in the household of a tribal chief who became angry when these young men insisted on living and worshiping as Christians. They were killed because of this. The feast day of Saint Charles Lwanga and his companions, the martyrs of Uganda, is June 3.

"Blessed are they who are persecuted for the sake of righteousness, for theirs is the kingdom of heaven." (Matthew 5:10)

They died rather than give up their belief in the risen Jesus. These women and men are called **martyrs**. The martyrs showed that nothing could separate them from Jesus.

The word *martyrs* comes from a Greek word that means "witnesses." We may never be called to become martyrs. However, like the first disciples, we are called to be witnesses to Jesus. **Witnesses** are people who speak and act based upon what they know and believe about Jesus.

Like the first disciples, we receive the gift of the Holy Spirit, too. We receive the Holy Spirit in a special way in the sacrament of Confirmation. Throughout our lives, the Holy Spirit helps us to be strong and courageous witnesses to our Catholic faith.

Key Words

martyrs people who die rather than give up their belief in the risen Jesus

witnesses people who speak and act based upon what they know and believe about Jesus

WE RESPOND

Think about your teachers, your parents, your friends, and your parish members. How do they give witness to the Catholic faith?

Every day we are called to be witnesses to what is true. With a partner, role-play how a person can be a witness to the Catholic faith in each of these situations.

- A rumor is going around school about a classmate. You know that it is not true.
- You are about to eat a meal with your family in a local restaurant.
- A community official does not support laws that respect life.

223

ACTIVITY BANK

Curriculum Connection

Language Arts

Invite the students to write stories about a situation in which a person decides to make a change in his or her life based on the eighth commandment. Ask the students to describe the life of the person, his or her actions before deciding to follow the eighth commandment, the person's reasons for making the change, and the way the person came to his or her decision to change. The stories should also include the effects that the change had on the person's life and on the lives of others. When all have finished, have the students share their stories.

Have the students write the names on blank note cards with descriptions of the ways these people live their lives as witnesses and place the cards in the basket in the prayer space.

Quick Check

✔ *What is Pentecost?* (the day when the Holy Spirit came to the disciples and filled them with courage)

✔ *What are witnesses?* (people who speak and act based upon what they know and believe about Jesus)

WE RESPOND ___ minutes

Connect to Life Read aloud the *We Respond* text and invite responses. Read aloud the directions for the activity. Organize the students into pairs and have them enact the situations. Allow time for discussion.

Pray Invite the students to pray silently for the people whose names have been placed in the basket in the prayer space. Remind the students to call on the Holy Spirit for strength in times of adversity.

Plan Ahead for Day 3

Catechist Goal: To emphasize that the eighth commandment requires telling the truth

Preparation: Decide on a "secret" to share in *We Believe*.

Catechist Goal

- To emphasize that the eighth commandment requires telling the truth

Our Faith Response

- To strive to always tell the truth

Teaching Note

Using Scripture

The example of Peter in Mark 14:66–72 shows us that even the disciples were capable of dishonesty. Peter often acted as the spokesperson for the disciples and boldly proclaimed the message of Jesus as Messiah. Still, on the night of Jesus' betrayal, Peter three times denied knowing Jesus. Tell the students that we will not always find it easy to tell the truth. However, like Peter, we need to repent for the times we are untruthful, and make amends.

We have a responsibility to tell the truth.

WE GATHER

✝ *Holy Spirit, give us the strength to always tell the truth.*

Imagine that everyone was truthful. How would this change the world?

WE BELIEVE

From the eighth commandment we learn about the need for the truth. This commandment teaches us to

- witness to the truth of Jesus by the things we say and do
- tell the truth
- respect the privacy of others
- honor the good name of others and to avoid anything that would harm their reputation.

To lie is to deliberately make a false statement. People sometimes lie to avoid responsibility or punishment or even to make themselves look good. However, lying makes the situation worse. Lies damage our own good name, and they usually hurt other people as well. Lies make us lose respect for ourselves.

If we lie, we need to admit that we have lied. Then we need to tell the truth. We also must try to make up for any harm our lies may have caused.

Another way to show respect for the truth is to avoid gossip and rumors. When people gossip they often spread untruths about other people. Gossip leads to rumors. A rumor is information that we hear yet we do not know if it is true. Spreading rumors can hurt a person's reputation and harm his or her good name. We read from the words of a wise person in the Old Testament: "Never repeat gossip" (Sirach 19:6).

The eighth commandment also addresses the need to handle promises in the correct way. If we promise to keep a secret, we give our word to another person. That person trusts us. If we break the promise and tell the secret, we have gone back on our word. We have broken the person's trust.

Sometimes people may ask us to keep a secret about something that is harmful or dangerous to them or others. In this situation we must help them. We have the duty to tell someone we trust: a parent, a teacher, a school nurse, or a priest. To get help for people in danger is not "telling on them." It takes courage and it is an act of great friendship.

224

Lesson Plan

WE GATHER ___ minutes

✝ **Pray** Pray the Sign of the Cross and the *We Gather* prayer.

Focus on Life Read aloud the *We Gather* question. Invite responses and write them on the board. Tell the students that in this lesson they will learn that God has given us a responsibility to tell the truth.

WE BELIEVE ___ minutes

Describe a Truthful World Have a volunteer read aloud the *We Believe* statement. Then ask the students to look at the *We Gather* responses. Invite the students to share details of this imagined world.

Learn About the Eighth Commandment
Have volunteers read aloud the *We Believe* text. Pause to emphasize the following:

- Lies may let us briefly avoid responsibility or punishment, but lies will ultimately make things worse.
- If we lie, we damage our own good name.
- We need to admit that we have lied and try to make up for any harm we may have caused.
- Gossip and rumors are to be avoided.
- If we give our word to keep a secret, we should do so unless the information involved is harmful to others.

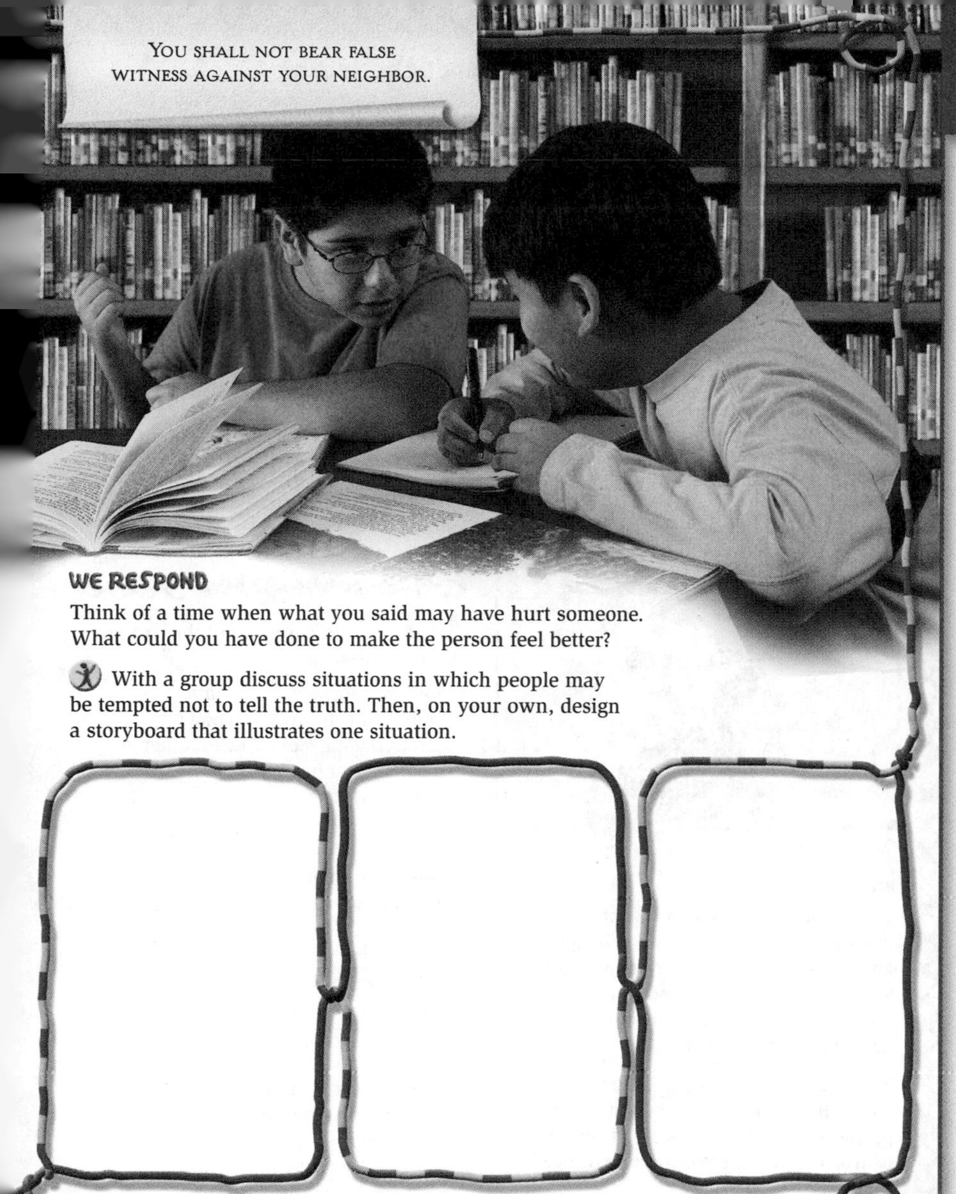

YOU SHALL NOT BEAR FALSE
WITNESS AGAINST YOUR NEIGHBOR.

WE RESPOND

Think of a time when what you said may have hurt someone. What could you have done to make the person feel better?

With a group discuss situations in which people may be tempted not to tell the truth. Then, on your own, design a storyboard that illustrates one situation.

225

Chapter 19 • Day 3

ACTIVITY BANK

Multiple Intelligences

Bodily-Kinesthetic

Activity materials: CDs of varied instrumental music, percussion instruments, simple props and costume pieces

Have the students work in small groups to devise and perform silent scenarios depicting situations in which people are lying or being truthful. Ask the students to use facial expressions, body movements, costumes, props, music, and sound effects—but not words—to convey the message and portray the emotions of each situation. Invite each group to perform for the class, and encourage post-performance discussion.

Confusing the Message Invite the students to gather with you in a circle. Whisper a "secret" to the student on your right, who will then pass it to the student on his or her right, and so on around the circle. When the last person has heard the secret, ask that student to repeat it aloud. Explain that this is how rumors are spread.

Quick Check

✔ *What does the eighth commandment require us to do?* (Live the truth that comes from God.)

✔ *When do we need to keep a secret, and when should we tell a secret to someone else?* (We keep the secrets that we have given our word to keep, unless the secret is harmful to someone. Then we need to tell someone who can help.)

WE RESPOND ___ minutes

Connect to Life Have the students read the *We Respond* text. Invite responses. Organize the class into small groups to read and discuss the *We Respond* activity. Then have the students complete their storyboards individually. Share the storyboards.

Pray Conclude by praying the Our Father together.

Plan Ahead for Day 4

Catechist Goal: To explain the importance of telling the truth

Preparation: Have available slips of paper for each student; make copies of Reproducible Master 19.

Catechist Goal

- To explain the importance of telling the truth

Our Faith Response

- To identify times we need to be more truthful

Lesson Materials

- slips of paper for each student
- copies of Reproducible Master 19

As Catholics...

The Golden Rule

After the lesson is completed, have a volunteer read aloud the text and the question. Invite responses and discuss them with the class. Then suggest different situations and ask for ways the Golden Rule might be applied. For example, how might students apply the Golden Rule when a new student joins their class? Help the students understand that to act in a kind, fair way is to uphold the teachings of Jesus.

We have a responsibility to respect the truth.

WE GATHER

✝ *Holy Spirit, guide us to the truth.*

Look at the pictures below. Discuss what they have in common.

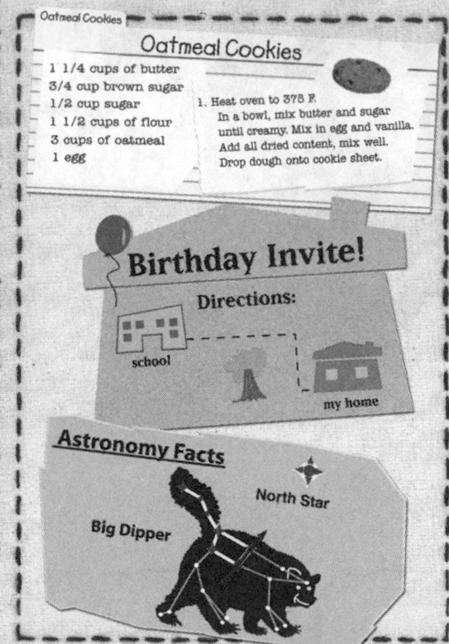

WE BELIEVE

When your Mom tells you what you are having for dinner, why do you believe her? When a traffic officer motions for you to cross a street, why do you believe it is safe? Why is it that you trust some people but do not trust others?

From many experiences that you have had in life, you have learned that some people are true to their word. They can be trusted. When they say something, they mean it. These people are honoring the eighth commandment because they are being truthful. They are living out the truth in their lives.

Once, when Jesus was teaching about the eighth commandment, he explained it very simply. He said, "Let your 'Yes' mean 'Yes,' and your 'No' mean 'No'" (Matthew 5:37). Jesus expects our words to be true. When we follow Jesus' teachings, we learn what is true and how to live out the truth.

Sometimes the truth will hurt someone's feelings or make them sad. At these times, unless it is necessary to share the information, we show respect and love for those involved by not saying anything.

How could you live out the truth in these situations?

- You are supposed to be doing your homework, but you are playing a video game in your room. Your mother asks whether you have finished your homework or not.

____

- You borrow something from a friend and lose it.

____

- When you buy some candy, the clerk gives you an extra dollar in your change.

____

- You promise to go to a party, but something comes up that you would rather do.

____

226

Lesson Plan

WE GATHER

___ minutes

✝ **Pray** Pray the Sign of the Cross and the *We Gather* prayer.

Focus on Life Share the *Chapter Story* on guide page 219C. Invite the students to read silently the *We Gather* text and study the pictures. Guide the students to realize that each picture shows the communication of factual—that is, truthful—information. Tell the students that in this lesson they will learn that we have a responsibility to be true to our word.

WE BELIEVE

___ minutes

Learn About the Truth Ask volunteers to read aloud the *We Believe* statement and paragraphs. Stress:

- We trust people who are known for being truthful.
- Jesus taught that he expects us to be truthful and to keep our word.
- If the truth will be hurtful to another person, and it is not necessary to share the information, we should show respect for others by not saying anything at all.

Do the Activity Invite the students to read aloud the text and discuss how to handle each situation truthfully and respectfully. Then form the class into small groups and have each group choose one situation to role-play.

Explain Examples Distribute copies of Reproducible Master 19. Have a volunteer read the directions aloud. Invite the students to work in pairs. Call on each pair to share their reasoning. (Accept reasonable answers.)

YOU SHALL NOT BEAR FALSE WITNESS AGAINST YOUR NEIGHBOR.

Take a few moments to think quietly and prayerfully about ways you follow the eighth commandment. These questions may help you.

Have I spoken and acted upon my belief in Jesus?

Have I trusted in God's word?

Have I been true to the teachings of the Catholic faith at home and in school?

Have I taken responsibility for my words and been truthful?

Have I respected the privacy of others?

Have I done the things I said I would do?

Have I made promises that I did not keep?

Have I thanked those who are trustworthy and faithful?

WE RESPOND

How important is it to be truthful in your family and with your friends? What will you do this week to show others how important the truth is?

As Catholics...

In talking to others and about others, we must be guided by Jesus' words: "Do to others whatever you would have them do to you" (Matthew 7:12). This teaching of Jesus is often called "The Golden Rule." We should always remember these words of Jesus. They help us to act in a fair and just way towards one another. They also help us to speak about others in a respectful, caring way.

How can you practice the Golden Rule this week?

227

ACTIVITY BANK

Catholic Social Teaching

Rights and Responsibilities Toward One Another

Catholic social teaching reminds us that we have rights and responsibilities to one another, to our families, and to society. One of these responsibilities is to tell the truth. Ask the students to remember that God calls us to be truthful to ourselves, to our families, and to our communities. Organize the class into three groups and have each group discuss one of the following topics: being true to ourselves, being true to our families, and being true to our society. Have each group present a summary of its discussion to the class.

Reflect on the Eighth Commandment
Encourage the students to complete the examination of conscience. Allow sufficient time for them to read and reflect prayerfully on each of the questions.

Quick Check

- ✔ *How do we learn what is true?* (We learn what is true by following Jesus' teachings.)
- ✔ *What is our reason to trust people?* (We often trust people who mean what they say and are true to their word.)

WE RESPOND ___ minutes

Connect to Life Have a volunteer read aloud the *We Respond* questions. After a brief class discussion, have each student write on a slip of paper one way that he or she will demonstrate the importance of telling the truth this week. Ask the students to put these slips in the basket in the prayer space as reminders to pray for the grace to be faithful to the eighth commandment.

Pray Ask the students to pray silently to God for the grace to help them live the eighth commandment. Then pray aloud: *Holy Spirit, help us to tell the truth. Guide our hearts and our tongues and remind us of our commitment to tell the truth.*

Plan Ahead for Day 5

Catechist Goal: To review chapter ideas and their relationship to our faith life

Preparation: Make copies of Chapter 19 Test in the Grade 4 Assessment Book (option).

Chapter 19 • Day 5

Catechist Goal

- To review chapter ideas and their relationship to our faith life

Our Faith Response

- To apply what has been learned to our lives

CHAPTER TEST

Chapter 19 Test is provided in the Grade 4 Assessment Book.

Grade 4
Chapter 19

Write True or False for the following sentences. Then change the false sentences to make them true.

1. True God teaches us what it means to be true.

2. True The eighth commandment teaches us to tell the truth.

3. True Lies make us lose respect for ourselves.

4. False Jesus expects our words to be false.
   Jesus expects our words to be true.

Write the letter of the phrase that defines each of the following:

5. c lie — **a.** people who speak and act based upon what they know about Jesus
6. d martyr — **b.** information we hear but do not know to be true
7. a witnesses — **c.** deliberately make a false statement
8. b rumor — **d.** people who die rather than give up their belief in Jesus

9–10. Write a short paragraph about the importance of the eighth commandment.

Imagine that you have been asked to write an advice column for the school newspaper. What are some examples of letters you might receive? How could you use Jesus' words, "Let your 'Yes' mean 'Yes,' and your 'No' mean 'No'" (Matthew 5:37)?

228

Lesson Plan

___ minutes

Chapter Review Explain to the students that they are going to review what they have learned. Ask them to complete questions 1–8. Invite volunteers to provide the correct answers. Then give the students time to write their answers to question 9–10.

Assessment Activity Invite a volunteer to read aloud the activity directions. Have the students work in small groups to devise sample letters and appropriate responses using Jesus' words. Then have each group share its letters and responses with the class.

___ minutes

Reflect & Pray Read aloud the questions. Invite volunteers to name examples of truthful and trustworthy people and say why they have chosen them. Allow time for the students thoughtfully to complete their prayers. Then invite the students to pray their prayers silently.

Key Words Write the two key words on the board and ask volunteers to define the key words in their own words. Write the student's definitions on the board as they give them; then add the definitions from the text.

We Respond in Faith

Reflect & Pray

Who do you think is a good example of a truthful and trustworthy person? Why?

Jesus, I want to witness to your life. Help me

____

____

Key Words

martyrs (p. 223)
witnesses (p. 223)

Remember

- God teaches us what it means to be true.
- We are called to witness to the truth of our faith.
- We have a responsibility to tell the truth.
- We have a responsibility to respect the truth.

Our Catholic Life

Option for the Poor and Vulnerable

All Catholics are encouraged to make a choice to help the poor and those who cannot care for themselves. We are to care for those who have been hurt by poverty, sickness, or homelessness. In this way we follow Jesus who said that, in his kingdom, "The last will be first" (Matthew 19:30).

One group that puts the last first is the Saint Vincent de Paul Society. This society was founded by a layman, Frederic Ozanam, in France. The members look for ways to help those in need. Many parishes work with the Saint Vincent de Paul Society.

Home Connection

Sharing Faith with My Family

Make sure to send home the family page (text page 230).

Remind the students to share what they have learned with their families, and encourage them to do this week's "Scripture Pictures" activity. Read aloud the quote from Saint Paul.

For additional information and activities, encourage families to visit Sadlier's

www.WEBELIEVEweb.com

Remember Review and discuss the four *We Believe* statements. Invite four volunteers to give brief explanations of the four statements.

Our Catholic Life Read aloud the text. Discuss our responsibility to help the poor and vulnerable. Invite the students to share experiences they might have had working with the Saint Vincent de Paul Society or with other charitable organizations that help people in need.

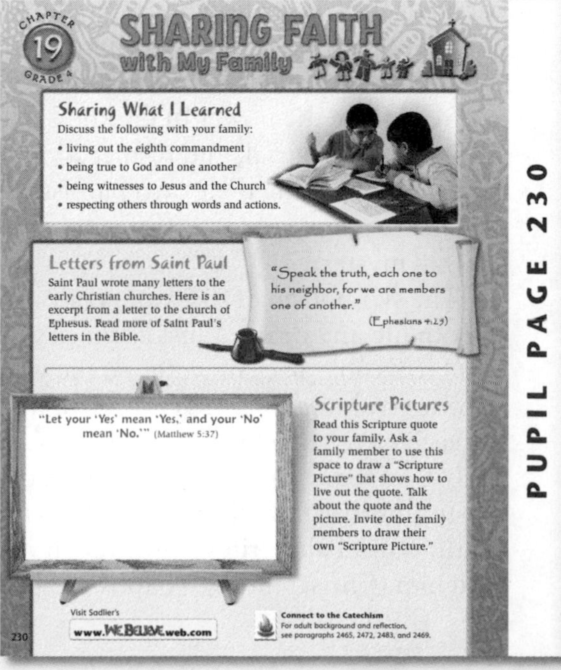

Chapter 19 Grade 4

SHARING FAITH with My Family

Sharing What I Learned

Discuss the following with your family:

- living out the eighth commandment
- being true to God and one another
- being witnesses to Jesus and the Church
- respecting others through words and actions.

Letters from Saint Paul

Saint Paul wrote many letters to the early Christian churches. Here is an excerpt from a letter to the church of Ephesus. Read more of Saint Paul's letters in the Bible.

"Speak the truth, each one to his neighbor, for we are members one of another." (Ephesians 4:25)

"Let your 'Yes' mean 'Yes,' and your 'No' mean 'No.'" (Matthew 5:37)

Scripture Pictures

Read this Scripture quote to your family. Ask a family member to use this space to draw a "Scripture Picture" that shows how to live out the quote. Talk about the quote and the picture. Invite other family members to draw their own "Scripture Picture."

Visit Sadlier's www.WEBELIEVEweb.com

Connect to the Catechism

For adult background and reflection, see paragraphs 2465, 2472, 2483, and 2469.

230

PUPIL PAGE 230

Chapter 20 Lent

Advent | Christmas | Ordinary Time | Lent | Three Days | Easter | Ordinary Time

Lent

Lent is a preparation for the celebration of Easter. For the Lenten liturgy disposes both catechumens and the faithful to celebrate the Paschal Mystery: catechumens, through the several stages of Christian initiation; the faithful, through reminders of their own baptism and through penitential practices.

(Norms Governing Liturgical Calendars, 27)

Overview

In this chapter the students will learn that Lent is the season of preparation for Easter.

For Adult Reading and Reflection
You many want to refer to paragraphs 540 and 613 of the *Catechism of the Catholic Church*.

Catechist Background

How have times of deep personal reflection changed you?

During the forty days of Lent, the Church prepares for the celebration of Easter, the greatest feast of the liturgical year. The catechumens prepare to receive the sacraments of initiation by which "we are freed from the power of darkness and joined to Christ's death, burial, and resurrection" (*The Rites*, 1:1,1). By renewing their own baptismal promises at Easter, the people of God reaffirm their faith in the paschal mystery.

The symbolism of the waters of Baptism speaks of both life and death. "Just as the gestation of our first birth took place in water, so the water of Baptism truly signifies that our birth into the divine life is given to us in the Holy Spirit" (*CCC* 694). Early Christian baptismal pools were often shaped like tombs to signify that our baptism is also a death. Saint Paul writes: "We were indeed buried with him [Christ] through baptism into death, so that, just as Christ was raised from the dead by the glory of the Father, we too might live in newness of life" (Romans 6:4).

Throughout the season of Lent, we prepare to renew our Baptism by means of prayer, penance, fasting, and almsgiving. By our time in the desert, we are made ready to sing at the Easter Vigil:

> This is the night when Christians everywhere,
> washed clean of sin
> and freed from all defilement, are restored to
> grace and grow together in holiness.
> (*Exsultet*, "Easter Proclamation")

How do you hope to be changed during this Lenten season?

Lesson Planning Guide

Lesson Focus	Presentation	Materials
Day 1		
Guide page 231C **Guide and Text page 231** **Introduce the Season**	• Read the *Chapter Story*. • Introduce the season of Lent. • Proclaim the words on the banner.	
Day 2		
Guide and Text pages 232–233 **We Gather** **We Believe**	• Discuss what is needed for growth in the **We Gather** questions. • Read and discuss the **We Believe** text about the focus of Lent. Complete the Lenten plans.	
Day 3		
Guide and Text page 234 **We Respond**	• Read the text about Saint Joseph and the way people honor him. • Discuss the **We Respond** question.	
Day 4		
Guide and Text page 235 **We Respond in Prayer**	• Listen to Scripture. • Respond in prayer.	• prayer space items: a large cactus, a basin of holy water, an alms basket, a statue or picture of Saint Joseph, a purple candle and table cloth
Day 5		
Guide pages 236A–236B **We Respond in Faith**	• Explain the individual Lenten project. • Explain the group Lenten project. • Discuss the **Sharing Faith with My Family** page.	• copies of Reproducible Master 20, guide page 236A

For additional ideas, activities, and opportunities: Visit Sadlier's **www.WEBELIEVEweb.com**

Focus on Life

Chapter Story

It was Mara's first day in the new school. She felt as nervous as a mouse facing a hungry cat. "Why did mom have to start her new job in a new city in the middle of the year?" she wanted to know. "Everyone will be staring at me because I'm the new kid," she told herself. "I can't wait for this day to be over with."

Mrs. Caputo, the principal, introduced Mara to her new teacher, Mrs. O'Toole. Mrs. O'Toole escorted Mara to her new classroom and said, "Boys and girls, I want you to meet Mara Boyle. Please do your best to make her feel at home here."

Somewhat nervous and dry in the throat, Mara made her way to her seat. At that moment, she felt like she was walking through a desert. Mara still longed for her old school where everything and everyone was so familiar.

The class was about to read a story. Someone placed an open book on Mara's desk. She looked up to see a freckle-faced boy smiling at her. "That's my reading book," he said. "You can use it until Mrs. O'Toole gets you one. I'm Rick Amato," introducing himself with a quick smile.

By lunchtime, three more of Mara's classmates had introduced themselves. They invited her to sit with them during lunch. By dismissal time, Mara discovered that Rick, Lisa, and Cindy lived within a few blocks of her house.

As she walked home with Cindy, Mara thought maybe this new school won't be such a bad place after all.

▶ *What changed Mara's negative attitude about attending the new school? Be specific.*

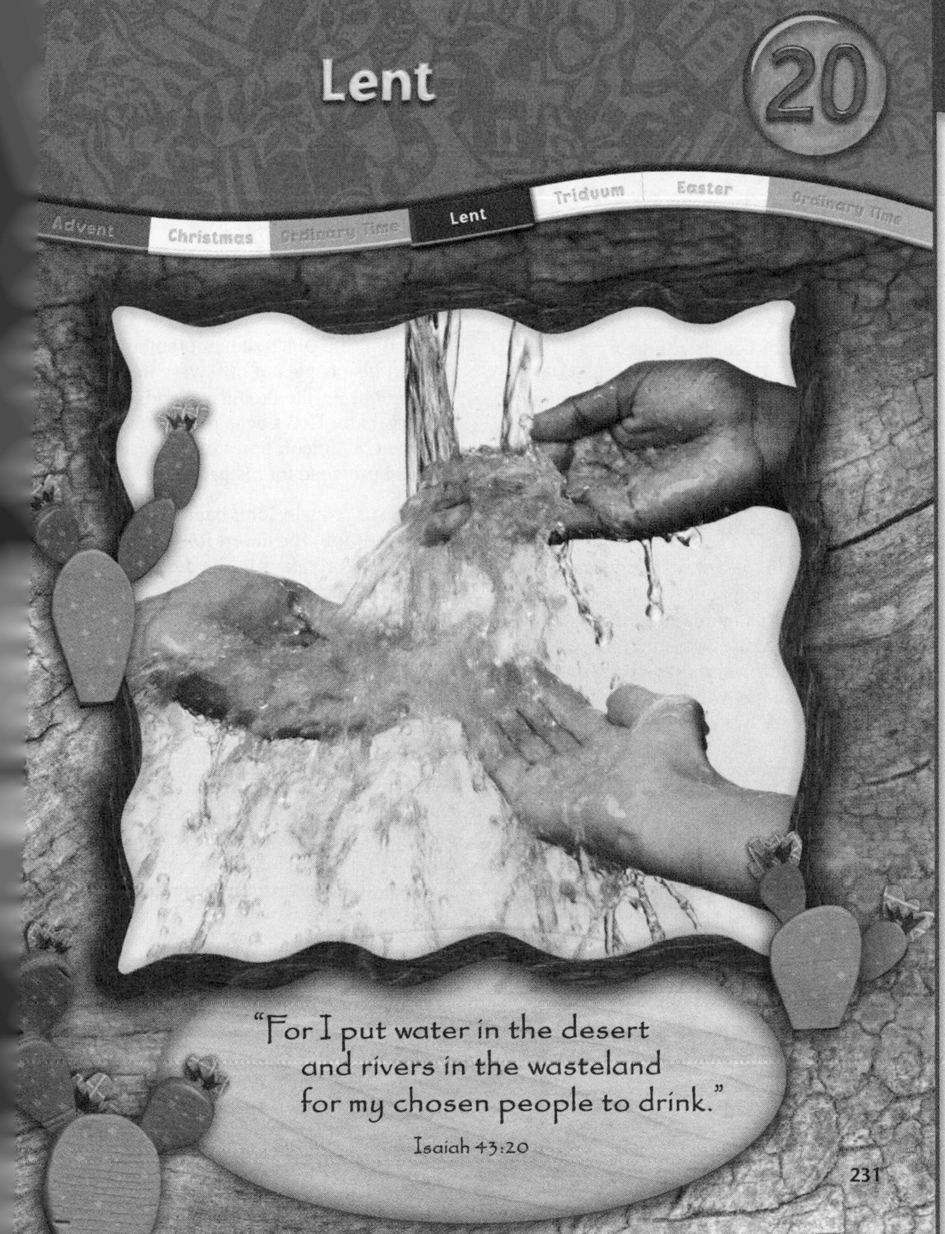
Lent
20
Advent
Christmas
Ordinary Time
Lent
Triduum
Easter
Ordinary Time
"For I put water in the desert
and rivers in the wasteland
for my chosen people to drink."
Isaiah 43:20
231

Chapter 20 • Lent

Catechist Goal

- To present that Lent is the season of preparation for Easter

Our Faith Response

- To choose a way to follow Jesus during Lent

ADDITIONAL RESOURCES

Book *Bible Stories for the 40 Days,* Melissa Musick Nussbaum, Liturgy Training Publications, 1997. This book has a story for each day of Lent from Ash Wednesday to Holy Thursday.

Video *The Angel's Lenten Lesson,* Twenty-Third Publications, 1995. The angel helps Danny remember the heart of the Lenten message—to follow Jesus. (14 minutes)

To find more ideas for books, videos, and other learning material, visit Sadlier's

www.WEBELIEVEweb.com

Lesson Plan

Introduce the Season ___ minutes

• **Pray** the Sign of the Cross and the words of Isaiah 43:20 on page 231.

• **Read** aloud the *Chapter Story* on guide page 231C. Discuss the change in Mara's attitude toward the new school. Ask: *Why is adjusting to new surroundings or experiencing any kind of change so difficult for people?* Encourage the students to understand that other people can help us to go through the adjustment and change. They make us feel welcome.

• **Have** a student read aloud the chapter title. Explain: *Lent is our season of preparation for Easter. It is a time to be reconciled with God and with others.*

• **Invite** the students to discuss the photo. Ask: *How does the photo relate to the quote?*

• **Proclaim** together the words on the banner under the photo.

Lesson Materials
- copies of Reproducible Master 20

Teaching Note
The Desert

The desert, as image and reality, has deep significance in both the Old and New Testaments. It is the place where the chosen people were tested for forty years on their journey to the Promised Land. Elijah spends forty days on his passage through the desert to Mount Horeb when he flees from Queen Jezebel. And Jesus spends that same period of time in the desert after his baptism. These are the symbolic precedents for the forty days of Lent.

Lent is the season of preparation for Easter.

WE GATHER

✝ *Lord Jesus, help us grow.*

What do plants and animals need to grow? What do you need to grow?

WE BELIEVE

The season of Lent is a time of preparation. Those who will celebrate the sacraments of initiation—Baptism, Confirmation, and Eucharist—at Easter are preparing for their reception into the Church. The Church prays for and encourages them. All of us get ready to renew our Baptism at Easter.

This preparing is a way to grow as Jesus' disciples. During Lent we focus on what Jesus did for us by his suffering, death, and Resurrection. We thank God for his mercy. We think and pray about the new life Christ shares with us in Baptism. We know that we live now by grace, the life of God within us. We can live forever with God because Jesus died and rose to bring us God's life.

Lent, which begins on Ash Wednesday, lasts forty days. The number forty has special meaning for us.

We read in the Old Testament that after God led his people out of slavery in Egypt, they set out for the Promised Land. It took forty years for God's people to get there. These were difficult times in the desert, but God provided for his people.

After Jesus' cousin John baptized him, Jesus went into the desert for forty days. During his forty days in the desert, Jesus prayed and fasted from food. The Holy Spirit was with Jesus as he prepared for his work. During the forty days of Lent, we go "into the desert" with Jesus. Lent is a desert time for the whole Church, the time in which we prepare for the waters of Baptism at Easter.

Lent is a season of simple living. We make a special effort to pray, to do penance, and to do good works. We are called to do these things all year long. However, during Lent they take on special meaning as we prepare to renew our Baptism.

232

Lesson Plan

WE GATHER ___ minutes

Focus on Life Have the students discuss and answer the *We Gather* questions. List on the board what plants and animals need to grow. Then add things human beings need in order to grow. Stress the human need for spiritual and intellectual nourishment as well as the physical nourishment.

WE BELIEVE ___ minutes

• **Have** a volunteer read aloud the *We Believe* statement. Have students read silently and underline important points in the *We Believe* paragraphs. Stress that the focus of Lent is on what Jesus did for us. Explain that the forty days of our Lenten journey echo that of the Israelites in the desert and Jesus' forty days and nights in the wilderness.

How will you make Lent a time of simple living focused on God and the needs of others?

In groups, come up with ways your family, parish, and class can follow Jesus during Lent.

Pray

During Lent we try to give more time to God, and prayer helps us to do this. Prayer is our conversation with God. In prayer we open our hearts and minds to God. In Lent we may devote extra time to daily prayers and worship. The Church's liturgy reminds us of God's great love and mercy for his people throughout history. It reminds us that in his love God gave us his own Son. It draws us closer to Jesus and unites us with one another. Many parishes gather for the stations of the cross (p. 329) and have special celebrations of the sacrament of Reconciliation. We pray especially for those who are preparing for the sacraments of initiation.

Do Penance

You know that penance is an important part of the sacrament of Reconciliation. Doing penance is a way to show that we are sorry for our sins. Our penance repairs our friendship with God that has been hurt by our sins. It also helps us to refocus on God and on the things that are important in our lives as Christians. Doing penance can help us focus on Christ and his willingness to give so freely of himself. This helps us to act as a true disciple of Christ.

During Lent we may do penance by giving up things we enjoy, like a favorite food or activity. We may go out of our way to practice a work of mercy or to give of our time in a special way. Catholics of a certain age do penance by fasting from food or not eating meat on specific days during Lent.

Do Good Works

During Lent we also show special concern for those in need. We follow Jesus' example of providing for the hungry and caring for the sick. We try to help other people get the things they need and make sure that people have use of the goods of creation that are rightfully theirs. Many parishes have food and clothing drives during this time of year. Families may volunteer at soup kitchens, visit those who are sick, and practice other works of mercy.

233

LENT

Activity Bank

Mission

Our Baptismal Call

Activity Materials: list of web sites, e-mail or other addresses for Catholic missionaries; copies of mission magazines

Let students know that at their Baptism, the celebrant prayed the following or similar words: "You call those who have been baptized to announce the Good News of Jesus Christ to people everywhere" (*The Rites*, 1:154). Because Lent is our season of preparing to renew our Baptism at Easter, it is a fitting time to support Catholic missionaries around the world. Distribute the magazines and have partners find a particular mission or missionary they will write to, pray for, and help in whatever ways are possible. Have the students use the web sites and addresses to follow through on their decisions. Remind the students that they can also announce the good news in their daily lives by word and example.

• **Ask** three volunteers to read aloud the *We Believe* paragraphs concerning praying, doing penance, and doing good works.

Do the *We Believe* activity. Have students work in groups to show ways their families, their parish, and their class can follow Jesus during Lent. Invite each group to share its ideas. Then decide on one meaningful action the class will do together.

Quick Check

✔ *What are we preparing for during Lent?* (We are preparing to renew our Baptism at Easter.)

✔ *How do we prepare during Lent?* (We pray, do penance, and do good works.)

Connection

Parish

Rite of Christian Initiation of Adults

Consult the pastor or the director of the RCIA about ways the students can show their support for the catechumens and candidates who are journeying toward the Easter sacraments of Baptism, Confirmation and Eucharist. The students and their families might sponsor a coffee after Mass to meet and welcome the catechumens and the candidates. They might want to write them letters of support or compose prayers for their intentions.

Saint Joseph

In many countries around the world, Catholics have traditions and customs for the feast of Joseph, husband of the Blessed Virgin Mary. The feast of Saint Joseph is celebrated on March 19.

We learn from the gospels that Joseph, the foster father of Jesus, was a carpenter. Joseph trusted God when he learned that Mary was to be the mother of the Son of God. Joseph provided a home for Mary and the child Jesus, and he loved and cared for them. Joseph shared his Jewish faith with Jesus, and Joseph made sure that the family traveled to Jerusalem each year for the Passover feast. All of this helps us to know that Joseph "was a righteous man" (Matthew 1:19).

Italians and Italian-Americans have a special devotion to Saint Joseph. Their Saint Joseph's Day tradition began centuries ago in Sicily, Italy. There the people were suffering from a drought, and they called on Saint Joseph for help. They asked him to pray to God for rain. The people promised to honor Saint Joseph with a feast if the rains came. The tradition says that rain soaked the area, and the people were true to their word. In a public area they set up large tables piled high with food. All those who were in need were invited to come and eat.

In many places today this tradition continues with a Saint Joseph's altar. The altar is usually made of donated materials and has three stairs as a sign of the Blessed Trinity. On the altar are flowers, food—including specially baked bread—and statues. Food collected is shared with those present and brought to those in need. There are many different Saint Joseph's Day customs, but caring for those who are poor or in need is always an important part of the day.

WE RESPOND

Talk about some special Lenten customs or traditions in your family, parish, and neighborhood. What are some ways you would like to honor Saint Joseph this Lent?

234

Lesson Plan

WE BELIEVE (continued) ___ minutes

• **Have** the students read silently the *We Believe* paragraphs about Saint Joseph. Stress that Saint Joseph showed strength of character in his firm trust in God's word. Point out that Italian and Italian-American devotion to Saint Joseph is only one example of the many Catholics around the world who honor Saint Joseph.

WE RESPOND ___ minutes

Connect to Life Read aloud the *We Respond* text on page 234. Have the students discuss Lenten customs and traditions of their families or neighborhoods. List on the board ways in which the students would like to honor Saint Joseph during this Lent. Suggest that they could follow his example of trust in God, love for family, religious devotion, or using his talents as a carpenter to help others.

• **Pray** together: *Lord, prepare us to renew our Baptism at Easter. Help us to welcome those entering the Church through the sacraments of Baptism, Confirmation and Eucharist. Help us to trust in you as Saint Joseph did during his life. Amen.*

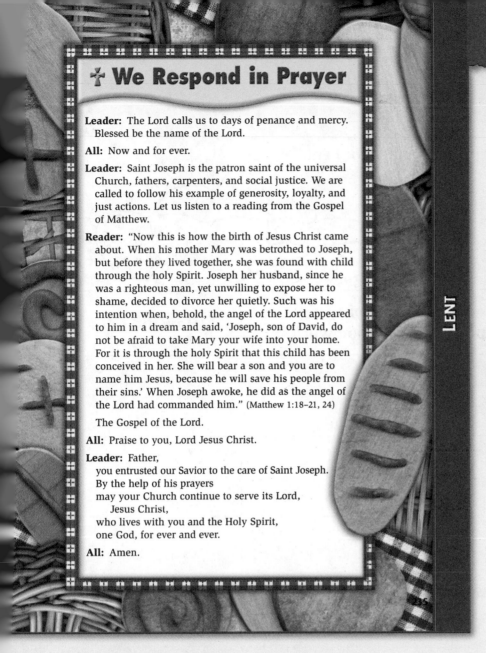

✝ We Respond in Prayer

Leader: The Lord calls us to days of penance and mercy. Blessed be the name of the Lord.

All: Now and for ever.

Leader: Saint Joseph is the patron saint of the universal Church, fathers, carpenters, and social justice. We are called to follow his example of generosity, loyalty, and just actions. Let us listen to a reading from the Gospel of Matthew.

Reader: "Now this is how the birth of Jesus Christ came about. When his mother Mary was betrothed to Joseph, but before they lived together, she was found with child through the holy Spirit. Joseph her husband, since he was a righteous man, yet unwilling to expose her to shame, decided to divorce her quietly. Such was his intention when, behold, the angel of the Lord appeared to him in a dream and said, 'Joseph, son of David, do not be afraid to take Mary your wife into your home. For it is through the holy Spirit that this child has been conceived in her. She will bear a son and you are to name him Jesus, because he will save his people from their sins.' When Joseph awoke, he did as the angel of the Lord had commanded him." (Matthew 1:18–21, 24)

The Gospel of the Lord.

All: Praise to you, Lord Jesus Christ.

Leader: Father,
you entrusted our Savior to the care of Saint Joseph.
By the help of his prayers
may your Church continue to serve its Lord,
Jesus Christ,
who lives with you and the Holy Spirit,
one God, for ever and ever.

All: Amen.

Preparing to Pray

The students will listen to a reading from the Gospel of Saint Matthew and respond in prayer.

- Select volunteers to place the items on the prayer table at the beginning of the prayer.
- Tell the students you will be the prayer leader.
- Choose a student to read aloud the scriptural passage.

The Prayer Space

- Gather the following items: a large cactus, a basin of holy water, an alms basket, a statue or picture of Saint Joseph, a purple candle, and a purple table covering.

This Week's Liturgy

Visit www.webelieveweb.com for this week's liturgical readings and other seasonal material.

✝ We Respond in Prayer ___ minutes

- **Pray** the Sign of the Cross and opening words.
- **Read** aloud the introductory paragraph about Saint Joseph.
- **Have** the reader proclaim the scriptural passage from the Gospel of Saint Matthew.
- **Conclude** with the prayer.

Name ______________________________

Fill in the chart. Use it as your personal guide for Lent.

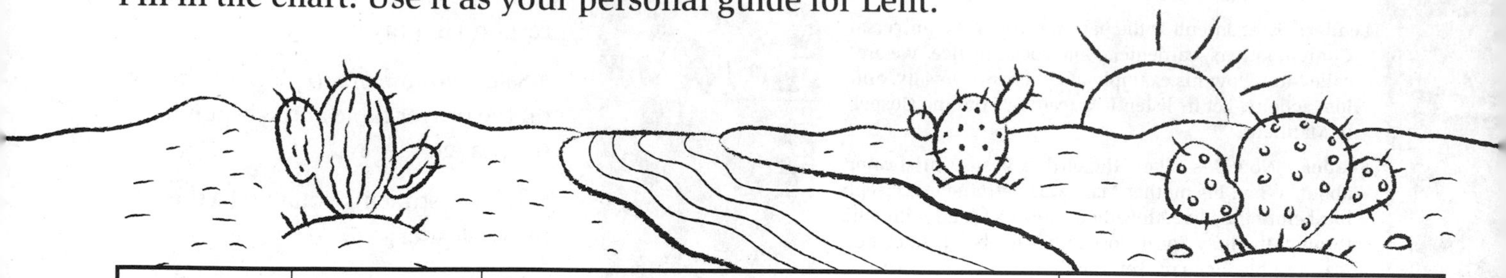

Week	Dates	My plan for prayer, penance, and good works	How did I do?

We Respond in Faith

Individual Project

Distribute Reproducible Master 20. Read the directions aloud. Explain that there are six weeks in Lent, and help the students fill in the dates in column two. Ask the students for suggestions for column three, and list them on the board. Encourage the students to plan something different each week. Have them complete columns two and three in class; then bring the charts home. At the end of each week, remind the students to see how they did. Have them reward themselves by adding a smiley face or star in column four.

Group Project

The traditional Lenten practice of fasting has many contemporary interpretations. Catholics might fast from eating junk food, watching TV sitcoms, playing video games, or going shopping. Each of these activities might distract a person's attention away from God. In more positive ways, Catholics might also decide to fast for special intentions such as world peace and justice, an end to world hunger, respect of human life and dignity, or for an increase in harmony in families and the larger community. Form small groups of students to mount a daily poster campaign called *40 Ways to Fast*. Each poster will advertise one way to fast on a particular day of Lent. Display the posters in a prominent place in the school or parish hall.

HOME CONNECTION

Sharing Faith with My Family

Make sure to send home the family page (text page 236).

Encourage the students to tell their families about the season of Lent, the three ways of following Jesus during this season, and how we honor Saint Joseph on his Lenten feast day. Discuss some charities that could benefit from the family's "Raindrop Box."

For additional information and activities, encourage families to visit Sadlier's

www.WEBELIEVEweb.com

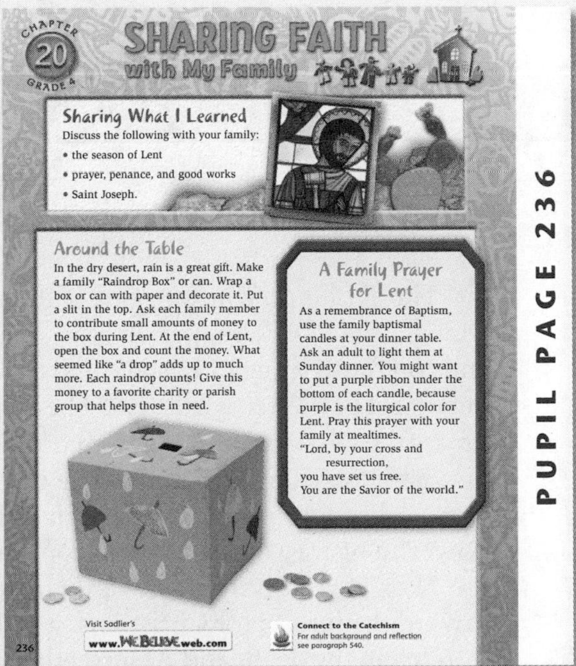

CHAPTER 20 GRADE 4

SHARING FAITH with My Family

Sharing What I Learned

Discuss the following with your family:

- the season of Lent
- prayer, penance, and good works
- Saint Joseph.

Around the Table

In the dry desert, rain is a great gift. Make a family "Raindrop Box" or can. Wrap a box or can with paper and decorate it. Put a slit in the top. Ask each family member to contribute small amounts of money to the box during Lent. At the end of Lent, open the box and count the money. What seemed like "a drop" adds up to much more. Each raindrop counts! Give this money to a favorite charity or parish group that helps those in need.

A Family Prayer for Lent

As a remembrance of Baptism, use the family baptismal candles at your dinner table. Ask an adult to light them at Sunday dinner. You might want to put a purple ribbon under the bottom of each candle, because purple is the liturgical color for Lent. Pray this prayer with your family at mealtimes.

"Lord, by your cross and
resurrection,
you have set us free.
You are the Savior of the world."

Visit Sadlier's www.WEBELIEVEweb.com

Connect to the Catechism
For adult background and reflection see paragraph 540.

236

PUPIL PAGE 236

Chapter 21 Triduum

Advent | Christmas | Ordinary Time | Lent | Triduum | Easter | Ordinary Time

Easter Triduum

Christ redeemed us all and gave perfect glory to God principally through his paschal mystery: dying he destroyed our death and rising he restored our life. Therefore the Easter Triduum of the passion and resurrection of Christ is the culmination of the entire liturgical year.

(Norms Governing Liturgical Calendars, 18)

Overview

In this chapter the students will learn that the Easter Triduum celebrates the joy of the cross.

For Adult Reading and Reflection
You may want to refer to paragraphs 1168 and 1165 of the *Catechism of the Catholic Church*.

Catechist Background

How have you experienced "the joy of the cross" in your life?

The Triduum, which begins with the Evening Mass of the Lord's Supper on Holy Thursday and ends on the evening of Easter Sunday, is the preeminent feast of the liturgical year. The Church celebrates the Passover of Jesus from death to life, and his victory over sin and death. The original meaning and celebration of Passover in derived from the powerful history of the Jewish people.

"For Jews, it is the Passover of history, tending toward the future; for Christians, it is the Passover fulfilled in the death and Resurrection of Christ, though always in expectation of its definitive consummation" (CCC 1096).

The historical events by which Christ Jesus accomplished our salvation are not simply recalled in a passive observance by the faith community. The celebration of these events exerts "a special sacramental power and influence which strengthens Christian life" [3](*Sharing the Light of Faith*, 144). Through our active participation in the liturgy of the Easter Triduum, we are filled with the grace of these saving mysteries.

At the heart of the Triduum, which illuminates the entire Church year, is the Church's experience and ongoing remembrance of Christ's dying and rising. The Church enters into these saving events and is transformed by them. As Jesus assured his disciples at the Last Supper, their grief at his passing would be changed into joy at his rising. "But I will see you again, and your hearts will rejoice, and no one will take your joy away from you" (John 16:22).

In what ways will you open yourself more deeply to the joy of the cross during this Triduum?

Lesson Planning Guide

Lesson Focus	Presentation	Materials
Day 1		
Guide page 237C **Guide and Text page 237** **Introduce the Season**	• Read the *Chapter Story*. • Introduce the Easter Triduum. • Proclaim the words on the banner.	
Day 2		
Guide and Text pages 238–239 **We Gather** **We Believe**	• Discuss the **We Gather** questions. • Read and discuss the **We Believe** text about Holy Thursday, Good Friday, Holy Saturday, and Easter Sunday.	
Day 3		
Guide and Text page 240 **We Respond**	Write about ways to celebrate the Easter Triduum. • Write a prayer of praise for the **We Respond** activity.	• instrumental music
Day 4		
Guide and Text page 241 **We Respond in Prayer**	• Listen to Scripture. • Respond in prayer.	• prayer space items: cross, large white candle, seasonal flowering plant, two table coverings (one white, one red, if possible)
Day 5		
Guide pages 242A–242B **We Respond in Faith**	• Explain the individual Triduum project. • Explain the Triduum group project. • Discuss the **Sharing Faith with My Family** page.	• copies of Reproducible Master 21, guide page 242A • Grade 4 CD

For additional ideas, activities, and opportunities: Visit Sadlier's **www.WEBELIEVEweb.com**

Focus on Life

Chapter Story

Many young men wanted to marry Clare Offreduccio. She was beautiful, wealthy, and kind as well. What more could they want? However, it was Clare herself who wanted more. She had been listening to the powerful preaching of Francis of Assisi. He too had led a privileged life. But he had given up everything to follow Jesus and live among the poor. Clare dreamed of dedicating her life to Jesus as Francis had done.

On the night of Palm Sunday in the year 1212, Clare waited until her parents were asleep. Then she crept out of the house. She and a servant went to meet Francis and his brown-robed followers. They walked in a torch-lit procession to a chapel called the "Little Portion." There Clare exchanged her brocade gown for a rough brown robe with a rope for a belt. Before placing a veil over her head, Francis cut off Clare's long, blonde hair. She promised to live the rest of her life in gospel poverty, purity, and obedience.

Later Francis led Clare to a convent where she would be safe until he could provide a home for her. A few days later, in Holy Week, her family and some of the young men who wanted to marry her, came to get her. Clare pulled off her veil. Horrified at the sight of her boyish, close-cropped hair, they realized that Clare's decision was final.

A few months later Clare's sister Agnes came to join her. They were the first two members of a new religious community that Francis would call the Poor Ladies. They would live in an enclosed convent or monastery where everything they did could be focused on God. Clare would spend her life praying for the world she had left behind.

Saints Francis and Clare remained close friends who helped each other to follow Christ. Francis traveled from place to place, preaching the gospel. Clare remained in her monastery, working and praying for all those in need. Both saints were especially devoted to Jesus on the cross.

▶ *How might the example of Saint Clare or Saint Francis help young people today to follow Jesus?*

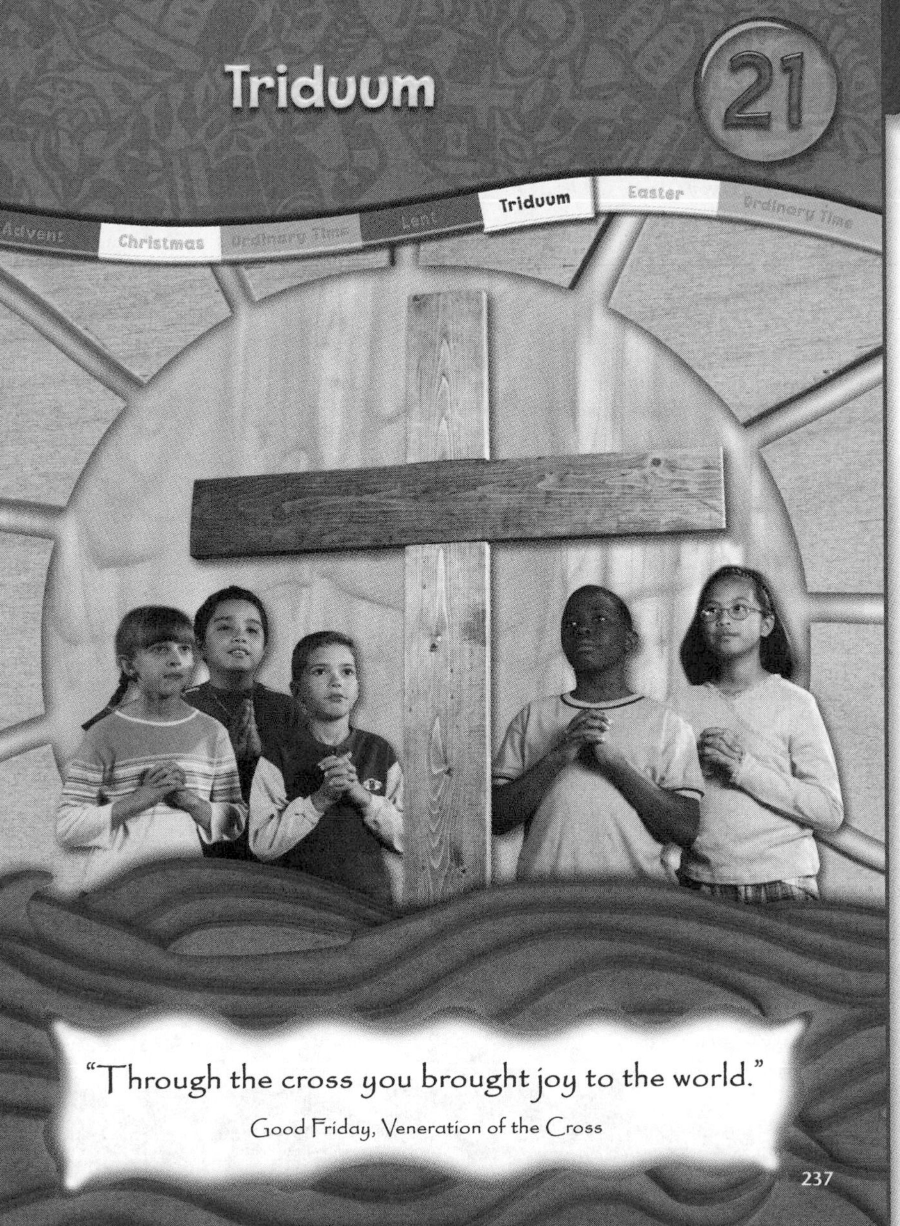

Triduum
21
Advent
Christmas
Ordinary Time
Lent
Triduum
Easter
Ordinary Time
"Through the cross you brought joy to the world."
Good Friday, Veneration of the Cross
237

Chapter 21 • Triduum

Catechist Goal

- To explain that the Easter Triduum celebrates the joy of the cross

Our Faith Response

- To appreciate and participate in the liturgical celebration during the days of the Easter Triduum

ADDITIONAL RESOURCES

Videos *Stations of the Cross for Children,* Twenty-Third Publications, 1997. Father Stan describes the stations in simple clear children's terms, reflecting on their application to life today. (15 minutes)

Visual Bible for Kids: The Story Behind the Cross, Thomas Nelson, Inc., 1998. A girl throwing rocks at a cross learns the true story of Jesus' crucifixion and Resurrection. (30 minutes)

To find more ideas for books, videos, and other learning material, visit Sadlier's

www.WEBELIEVEweb.com

Lesson Plan

Introduce the Season ___ minutes

• **Pray** the Sign of the Cross and the words *Through the cross you brought joy to the world.*

• **Read** aloud the *Chapter Story* on guide page 237C. Discuss the lives and example of Saints Clare and Francis. Explain that both saints followed the way of the cross with joy and in the hope of rising to new life in the crucified but risen Jesus.

• **Have** the students open their text to page 237. Read aloud the chapter title. Explain: *The Easter Triduum is the greatest celebration of the year. We remember Jesus' passing from death to new life. Jesus Christ changed our lives forever.*

• **Invite** the students to look at the photo. Ask: *What are the people doing to prepare for the celebration of the Easter Triduum?* Invite volunteers to share what they recall about the Easter Triduum and its ceremonies.

• **Proclaim** together the words on the banner under the photo.

Lesson Materials
- instrumental music
- cross
- copies of Reproducible Master 21
- Grade 4 CD

Teaching Note
Stations of the Cross

The traditional devotion of praying the Stations of the Cross began in the 12th century at the time of the Crusades to the Holy Land. Their original purpose was to serve Christians who were unable to make a pilgrimage to Jerusalem. The Stations enabled them to walk more closely with the suffering Christ from his judgment by Pilate to his burial in the tomb provided by Joseph of Arimathea. There are most often fourteen stations. However, some parish churches and shrines also have a fifteenth station depicting the Resurrection.

The Easter Triduum celebrates the joy of the cross.

WE GATHER

✠ *Jesus, by your death you bring us new life. Glory to you!*

What are some things you do that last for several days? What joins, unites, or connects the days?

WE BELIEVE

Triduum is a Latin word that means "three days." The Easter Triduum is the greatest celebration of the year. It is during these three great days that we remember Jesus' passing from death to new life. It is an amazing thing that joy can come from death. But by dying, and then rising, the Son of God changed our lives forever.

We count the days of the Easter Triduum from evening to evening. The Easter Triduum begins on the evening of Holy Thursday and ends on the evening of Easter Sunday. The Church's liturgical year continues the Jewish tradition of counting days from evening to evening. We spend these three days in prayer and worship. Because we cannot celebrate one day without the others, we celebrate them as one special liturgy.

Holy Thursday

The Evening Mass of the Lord's Supper begins the Easter Triduum. Many things happen at this celebration. We remember what happened at the Last Supper. At the Last Supper, Jesus gave the gift of himself in the sacrament of the Eucharist. The Eucharist is a promise that we will share God's life forever.

We remember Jesus' teachings to serve others and the example of service he gave us by washing his disciples' feet. "He took a towel and tied it around his waist. Then he poured water into a basin and began to wash the disciples' feet and dry them with the towel around his waist." (John 13:4–5) We also have a special collection for those who are in need.

As the parish community leaves this celebration, they are not actually dismissed with the usual "Go in peace to love and serve the Lord." This reminds us that Holy Thursday and Good Friday are connected in a special way.

238

Lesson Plan

WE GATHER ___ minutes

Focus on Life Have the students respond to the *We Gather* questions. Write their responses on the board to show the connections between the days and the activities. Point out that the Easter Triduum commemorates and celebrates the three most important days in the liturgical year of the Church.

WE BELIEVE ___ minutes

• **Read** aloud the *We Believe* statement and the first two *We Believe* paragraphs. Explain that although the Triduum extends over three days, it is celebrated as one continuing liturgy in which the entire Church participates.

• **Divide** the class into four groups. Assign each group one of the days outlined on pages 238 and 239. Have each group read about its day and explain it to the rest of the class. Clarify any questions that might arise during the presentations.

Holy Saturday

On Holy Saturday, we spend time thinking and praying. We remember that Jesus died for us and was laid in a tomb. We prepare to celebrate Jesus' new life. We gather with our parish at night for the Easter Vigil. This is the most beautiful and exciting night of the whole year!

On Good Friday, we watched as the cross was carried out of the church. Now, as we wait in darkness at the Easter Vigil, we turn to see something carried into our midst. It is no longer the cross of Christ, but a single bright flame of joy and life. It is the paschal candle. It is lit at the Easter Vigil as a symbol of Jesus' Resurrection.

"Christ our light," the deacon sings.

"Thanks be to God," we sing in response.

Good Friday

On Good Friday, the Church remembers the death of Jesus on the cross. The cross is the sign of Christ's suffering and death. But it is also the great sign of his Easter victory. When Jesus died on the cross, he was not defeated. He rose from death, and in doing so won over sin and death forever.

In church, the altar is bare, without cloths, candles, or even a cross. We honor the cross with a prayerful procession during the liturgy. We listen to the Scripture readings about what happened to Jesus on the day of his death. We remember that Jesus was the faithful servant of God who suffered and died so that we might have new life. We also pray for the whole world on this day, since Jesus died and rose for the whole world. And, as with Holy Thursday's liturgy, the Good Friday liturgy does not actually end but extends into Saturday.

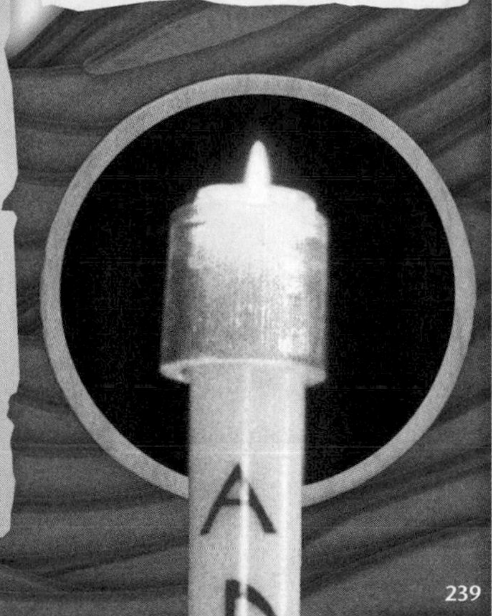

Activity Bank

Multiple Intelligences

Interpersonal

Activity Materials: interviewer's notebooks, Bible

Explain to the students that in his letter to the Christians in Rome Saint Paul says that he longs to see them so that they may be mutually encouraged by one another's faith, theirs and his. (See Romans 1:12.) Invite the students to think of a person whose faith might encourage them to be more loyal disciples of Jesus during this Triduum season. Suggest talking with a parent or grandparent, a teacher or parish minister, a teenager who is active in the parish, a priest, or religious. Have the students write three interview questions that they ask the interviewee. Suggest these questions: *How do you pray? Who or what helps you to be a good Christian? How do you cope with sadness or suffering?* Have the students write the responses they receive.

Quick Check

✔ *What does the Easter Triduum celebrate?* (The Triduum celebrates the joy of the cross and Jesus' passing from death to new life.)

✔ *What are the three holy days we celebrate with one special Triduum liturgy?* (The three holy days are Holy Thursday, Good Friday, and Holy Saturday [the Vigil] that anticipates the celebration of Easter Sunday and the glory of Jesus' Resurrection.)

Connection

Multicultural Connection

Celebrating the Easter Triduum
Activity Materials: library and Internet resources

Invite the students to explore the various ways Catholics of different ethnic groups and rites (Byzantine, Armenian, Alexandrian, Chaldean, and Antiochene) celebrate the Easter Triduum. Students may decide to examine customs associated with the season, or research various liturgical practices. An example of the former would be the Hispanic Catholic custom of the Holy Thursday afternoon "blessing of the bread." The loaves are blessed in the church and are considered a sacramental. Families share the bread during the Triduum. An example of the latter would be the Ukrainian Byzantine Good Friday practice of the Procession of the Holy Shroud. The shroud is a cloth with an image of Christ in the tomb. Have the students illustrate their findings with drawings to be displayed in a prominent place.

At this vigil, we listen to many readings from the Bible. We remember all the great things God has done for us. We sing Alleluia with joy to celebrate that Jesus rose from the dead. And those preparing to become members of the Church celebrate the sacraments of initiation and receive the new life of Christ. We welcome them and once again renew our own Baptism.

Easter Sunday

On this day we proclaim, "The Lord has indeed risen, alleluia. Glory and kingship be his for ever and ever."
(Entrance Antiphon, Easter Sunday)
We gather with our parishes and families to celebrate this most important Sunday of the year. We know that Jesus is with us always.

Make notes about the ways you can celebrate the days of the Triduum.

Holy Thursday	Good Friday	Holy Saturday	Easter Sunday

We Respond

Make up your own prayer of praise and thanksgiving for Jesus our risen Savior. Pray it often.

240

Lesson Plan

We Believe (continued) ___ minutes

Ask a volunteer to read aloud the directions for the *We Believe* activity. Explain that the students can use ideas that they heard during the presentation, that they read in the text, or ideas of their own. Encourage the students to be creative. Provide time for the students to share their ideas.

We Respond ___ minutes

Connect to Life Have the student read the *We Respond* directions. Play quiet instrumental music. Encourage the students to compose their own prayers of praise and thanks to Jesus. Allow ample time for reflection and writing.

• **Have** the students decide whether they would like to have their prayers duplicated and published as a Triduum prayer booklet for families and friends. Enlist a committee of volunteers to help with this project.

• **Gather** in the prayer space. Invite volunteers to share their original prayers.

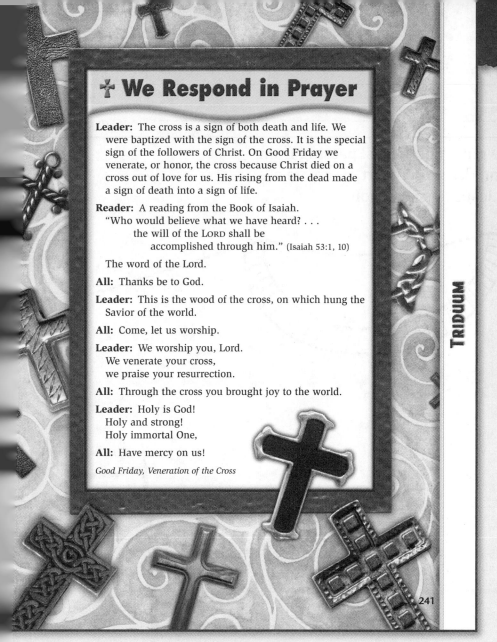

We Respond in Prayer

Leader: The cross is a sign of both death and life. We were baptized with the sign of the cross. It is the special sign of the followers of Christ. On Good Friday we venerate, or honor, the cross because Christ died on a cross out of love for us. His rising from the dead made a sign of death into a sign of life.

Reader: A reading from the Book of Isaiah.
"Who would believe what we have heard? . . .
the will of the LORD shall be
accomplished through him." (Isaiah 53:1, 10)

The word of the Lord.

All: Thanks be to God.

Leader: This is the wood of the cross, on which hung the Savior of the world.

All: Come, let us worship.

Leader: We worship you, Lord.
We venerate your cross,
we praise your resurrection.

All: Through the cross you brought joy to the world.

Leader: Holy is God!
Holy and strong!
Holy immortal One,

All: Have mercy on us!

Good Friday, Veneration of the Cross

PREPARING TO PRAY

The students will listen to a scriptural passage from the prophet Isaiah and respond in prayer.

- Assume the role of prayer leader.
- Choose a reader to proclaim the Scripture.

The Prayer Space

- Gather the following items: cross, large white candle, seasonal flowering plant, two table coverings (one white, one red, if possible).

This Week's Liturgy

Visit **www.webelieveweb.com** for this week's liturgical readings and other seasonal material.

We Respond in Prayer ___ minutes

- **Pray** the Sign of the Cross and opening prayer.
- **Have** the reader proclaim the passage from Isaiah 53:1,10.
- **Conclude** by venerating the cross. Lead the students in this prayer: *We adore you, O Christ, and we bless you, because by your holy cross you have redeemed the world.*

Name ____

During the Easter Triduum we remember Jesus' passing from death to new life. Write a poem, design a T-shirt, or create a symbol to express your joy in Jesus' Resurrection.

We Respond in Faith

Individual Project

Distribute the Reproducible Master 21. Invite a volunteer to read the directions aloud. Have the students suggest designs or symbols and list these on the board. Play the Grade 4 CD as the students work. Provide time for them to share their work.

Group Project

The students can serve their school and parish by making an Easter Vigil banner on which the nine dominant symbols of our faith are represented. These symbols are: the assembly of the faithful, the cross; the Paschal candle; holy oil; the laying on of hands; the white garment; salt; baptismal water, and the bread and wine. Have the students design large, carefully-drawn symbols to be arranged on a white background. Beneath the banner, they could display brief explanation of each symbol. Display the banner in the church's entrance or a prominent place at school.

Home Connection

Sharing Faith with My Family

Make sure to send home the family page (text page 242).

Invite them to consider what they will relate to their families about the Easter Triduum, the veneration of the cross, and the celebration of the three great days.

For additional informatio+n and activities, encourage families to visit Sadlier's

www.WEBELIEVEweb.com

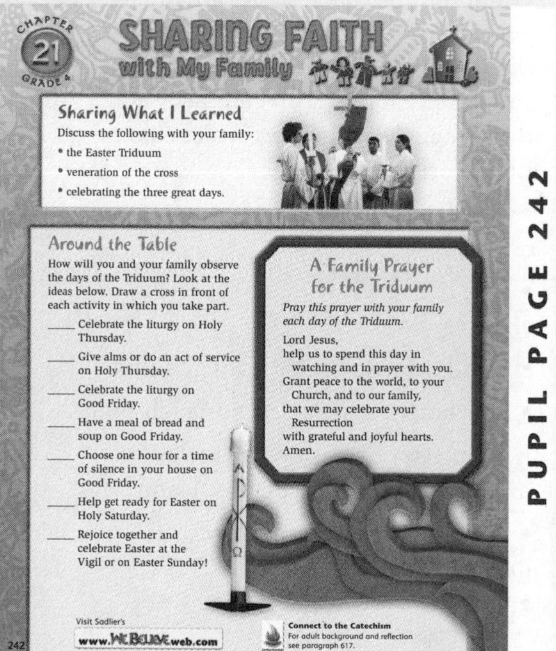

Chapter 21 Grade 4

SHARING FAITH with My Family

Sharing What I Learned

Discuss the following with your family:

- the Easter Triduum
- veneration of the cross
- celebrating the three great days.

Around the Table

How will you and your family observe the days of the Triduum? Look at the ideas below. Draw a cross in front of each activity in which you take part.

_____ Celebrate the liturgy on Holy Thursday.

_____ Give alms or do an act of service on Holy Thursday.

_____ Celebrate the liturgy on Good Friday.

_____ Have a meal of bread and soup on Good Friday.

_____ Choose one hour for a time of silence in your house on Good Friday.

_____ Help get ready for Easter on Holy Saturday.

_____ Rejoice together and celebrate Easter at the Vigil or on Easter Sunday!

A Family Prayer for the Triduum

Pray this prayer with your family each day of the Triduum.

Lord Jesus,
help us to spend this day in
watching and in prayer with you.
Grant peace to the world, to your
Church, and to our family,
that we may celebrate your
Resurrection
with grateful and joyful hearts.
Amen.

Visit Sadlier's
www.WEBELIEVEweb.com

Connect to the Catechism
For adult background and reflection see paragraph 617.

242

PUPIL PAGE 242

ASSESSMENT

In the *We Believe* program each core chapter ends with a review of the content presented, and with activities that encourage the students to reflect and act on their faith. The review is presented in two formats, standard and alternative.

Each unit is also followed by both standard and alternative assessment. The standard test measures basic knowledge and vocabulary assimilation. The alternative assessment allows the students another option—often utilizing another learning style—to express their understanding of the concepts presented.

Using both forms of assessment, perhaps at different times, attends to the various ways students' learning can be measured. You can also see the Grade 4 *We Believe* Assessment Book for:

- standard assessment for each chapter
- alternative assessment for each chapter
- standard assessment for each unit
- alternative assessment for each unit
- a semester assessment which covers material presented in Units 1 and 2
- a final assessment which covers material presented in Units 1, 2, 3, and 4.

For answers to Assessment questions: **17–18**, see Chapter 15, pages 178–179; **19–20**, see Chapter 18, pages 212–213.

Grade 4
Unit 3

Fill in the circle beside the correct answer.

1. Every Christian family is called to be a ______.
   - ● domestic church ○ private community ○ lawful authority
2. When we obey our parents and guardians, we are living by the ______.
   - ○ eighth commandment ○ sixth commandment ● fourth commandment
3. ______ is the value and worth each person has from being created in God's image.
   - ○ Divine mercy ● Human dignity ○ Loving respect
4. ______ are women and men who died rather than give up their belief in Jesus.
   - ○ Stewards ○ Guardians ● Martyrs
5. The virtue of ______ helps us to respect ourselves and our bodies.
   - ○ hope ● chastity ○ faith
6. Stewards of creation are those who ______ everything that God has given them.
   - ○ use up ● take care of ○ do not appreciate
7. Throughout our lives, the ______ helps us to be strong and courageous witnesses to our Catholic faith.
   - ○ fifth commandment ● Holy Spirit ○ virtue of obedience
8. If individuals, groups, and nations work for ______, we will have a world of love, not hatred and violence.
   - ● justice and peace ○ safety and security ○ strength and freedom

243

Write True or False for the following sentences. Then change the false sentences to make them true.

9. False Our friendships are not that important in our lives.
   Our friendships are a very important part of growing and learning about love and trust.
10. True Each of us has the right to life from the moment of conception to the moment of death.
11. False When we speak out against violence and injustice, we honor the sixth commandment.
    When we speak out against violence and injustice, we honor the fifth commandment.
12. False When we obey the just laws of our nation, we honor the first commandment.
    When we obey the just laws of our nation, we honor the fourth commandment.
13. False When we make promises but do not keep them, we fail to honor the fifth commandment.
    When we make promises but do not keep them, we fail to honor the eighth commandment.
14. True Copying homework or using someone else's ideas as our own is stealing.
15. False The fifth commandment requires people to give back to others the things that were unjustly taken from them.
    The seventh commandment requires people to give back to others the things that were unjustly taken from them.
16. True When we work to help all people share the gifts of the world, we honor the seventh commandment.

Answer the questions.

17–18. Our government leaders are called to respect the dignity of all people. What should we do if our leaders pass laws that are wrong or unjust?

19–20. As stewards of God's creation, what can we do now to make sure that our own children will be able to share in God's gifts in the future?

244

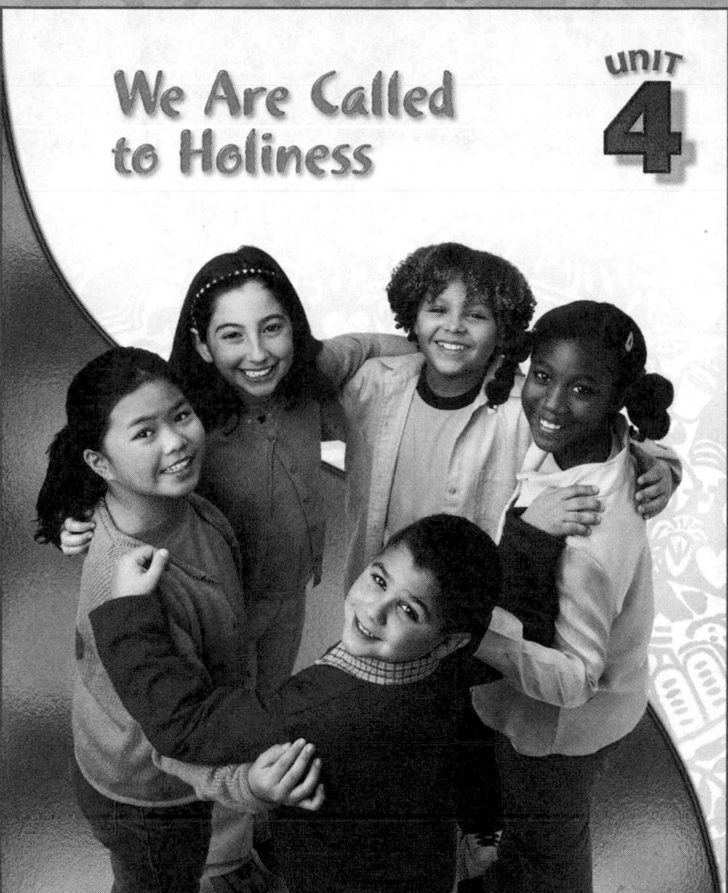

A Fourth Grader's Concept of Justice

Three little words. "It's not fair!" They may sound trivial, but when they are exclaimed by children as a whining complaint, these three little words can become almost intolerable.

It can be very tempting to respond in frustration, "Life's not fair." A much more helpful approach would be to recognize that "It's not fair" is symptomatic of growth. It's a normal, and healthy, way for children to behave. They have entered a stage of moral development in which they are attuned to rules and to the evaluation of their good and bad behavior in light of those rules. Rather than just doing what someone in authority tells them, children are thinking about how they—and others—should behave. As children continue to grow, they hopefully will one day move to a stage in which the welfare of others is more important to them than simply an adherence to rules.

The next time you hear your child protest the fairness of something, remind yourself that it is a sign that he or she is growing up.

From the Catechism

"Becoming a disciple of Jesus means accepting the invitation to belong to *God's family*, to live in conformity with His way of life."

(Catechism of the Catholic Church, 2233)

What Your Child Will Learn in Unit 4

This last unit of the Grade 4 We Believe program is meant to inspire the children to live out the Ten Commandments in their daily lives. It begins with a presentation of the ninth commandment as the children become more aware that they are growing up and experiencing all kinds of feelings. God creates all of us to share love and relationships. This discussion leads to the benefits of purity of heart and the virtue of modesty. The tenth command ment is presented in the context that trust in God counters greed and envy while promoting generosity of heart.

The Ten Commandments are summarized as the children are called to grow in holiness, to be the Church, and to be disciples of Jesus. As members of the Church, they are called to respect the laws, or precepts, of the Church as well as Church leaders who guide and help them. The children end their Grade 4 textbook with an inspiring call to discipleship. Here, the Blessed Virgin Mary is presented as our model of discipleship.

Plan & Preview

- A beautiful portrait of a saint, entitled "Our Family of Saints," is found on each family page in this unit. Cut it out and put it in a place where the family can see it.
- Have markers and pencils available to fill in the "Holiness Hall of Fame."

Holiness Hall of Fame

We nominate Terrence Farrell because Terry answered God's call to holiness

Terry and his son

(Photo courtesy of the Farrell family)

A Story in Faith

Terrence Patrick Farrell Called to Holiness

He looked like he had been born a New York City firefighter. His looks didn't lie. Saving lives was Terrence Patrick Farrell's business. He was a firefighter with one of city's most elite units, and a volunteer firefighter near his home in Huntington, Long Island.

Thus, it was no surprise that Terry always responded to a "call to duty." When his brother's son was diagnosed with leukemia, Terry had his blood tested as a possible bone marrow donor. He later received word that his blood matched that of a young girl in Nevada who was dying of t-cell lymphoma. Terry flew to Nevada to undergo the painful process of bone marrow extraction. A year later, he learned that the operation had been a success and the girl had been cured.

Terry and the girl's family finally met at a restaurant high atop the World Trade Center. As the little group celebrated Terry's wonderful act of selflessness and kindness, little did anyone know that this extraordinary man would lose his life in that very spot years later.

On September 11, 2001, Terrence Patrick Farrell was one of the many New York City firefighters who answered the call to duty. A member of Rescue 4, he rushed to the call at the World Trade Center. He lost his life in the crumbling giant towers.

No one who knew Terry Farrell will ever forget his kindness and dedication to others. Terry is a true member of the Holiness Hall of Fame.

246

Class Connection

Point out the unit title to the students. Ask them what they think they will be learning more about in this unit. Have a class discussion, preparing the students for this unit.

Home Connection

Sharing Faith as a Family

Sadlier *We Believe* calls on families to become involved in:

- learning the faith
- prayer and worship
- living their faith.

Highlighting of these unit family pages and the opportunities they offer will strengthen the partnership of the Church and the home.

For additional information and activities, encourage families to visit Sadlier's

www.WEBELIEVEweb.com

Chapter 22 The Ninth Commandment

Overview

In Chapter 19 the students learned from the eighth commandment that God calls us to respect and tell the truth. In this chapter the students will learn that by following the ninth commandment we can live out the virtue of modesty.

Doctrinal Content	For Adult Reading and Reflection *Catechism of the Catholic Church*
The students will learn:	Paragraph
• Feelings are a gift from God.	2516
• God created us to share love.	2520
• God calls us to be pure of heart.	2519
• The virtue of modesty helps us to be pure of heart.	2524

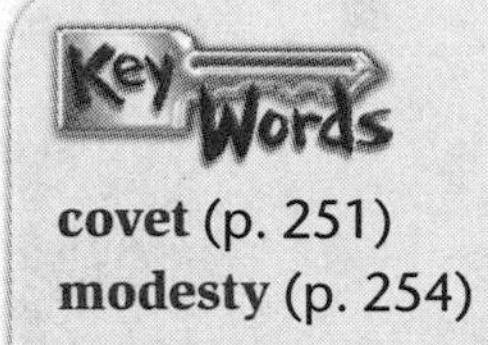

covet (p. 251)
modesty (p. 254)

Catechist Background

Have you ever strongly desired something you could not have?

The ninth commandment requires us not to covet our neighbor's wife. At first glance the commandment does not seem to apply to many of us. Yet, when we study the commandment more carefully, we realize it offers us other timely challenges.

The commandment directs us toward purity of heart. Jesus said, "For from the heart come evil thoughts, murder, adultery, unchastity, theft, false witness, blasphemy. These are what defile a person" (Matthew 15:19–20). Jesus may have been reiterating his teaching from the Beatitudes: "Blessed are the clean of heart, for they will see God" (Matthew 5:8). There is an old expression, "Garbage in, garbage out." If we focus our heart's desire on things that are not ours to have, we are filling our hearts with garbage. If we focus out hearts on God and his kingdom, we "will see God."

The ninth commandment also directs us toward modesty, a virtue that "guides how one looks at others and behaves toward them in conformity with the dignity of persons and their solidarity" (CCC 2521). We practice modesty in many ways. We keep hidden what should remain hidden. We act respectfully toward our own body and those of others. We approach life with discretion, refusing to meddle in other people's business and treating our neighbors in a decent and courteous manner. And we register our discontent when it becomes clear to us that people are being exploited.

How can you grow more pure of heart?

Lesson Planning Guide

Lesson Focus	Presentation	Materials
Day 1		
page 247 **We Gather in Prayer** **pages 248–249** *Feelings are a gift from God.*	• Listen to Scripture. Respond in song. • Discuss the **We Gather** question. • Read and discuss the **We Believe** text. Complete the activity based on pictures. • Reflect on the **We Respond** statement and respond in prayer.	For the prayer space: statue of the Blessed Virgin Mary, picture of a couple standing at the altar being married  "We Are Yours, O Lord," Janet Vogt, #24, Grade 4 CD
Day 2		
pages 250–251 *God created us to share love.*	• Discuss the **We Gather** questions. • Read and discuss the gift of human sexuality in the **We Believe** text. Complete the song activity. • Reflect on the **We Respond** question. • Pray together.	
Day 3		
pages 252–253 *God calls us to be pure of heart.*	• Discuss the **We Gather** questions. • Decorate the paper hearts. • Read and discuss the **We Believe** text. Complete the **We Respond** activity. • Read and discuss Mary as our model in the *As Catholics* text. • Pray together.	• paper hearts with the word *God* written on one side • markers • copies of Reproducible Master 22, guide page 247G
Day 4		
pages 254–255 *The virtue of modesty helps us to be pure of heart.*	 Do the **We Gather** activity. • Read and discuss the **We Believe** text.  Complete the activity based on situations. • Reflect on the ninth commandment. • Discuss the **We Respond** question. • Pray for courage.	• markers • butcher paper
Day 5		
page 256 **Review** **pages 257–258** **We Respond in Faith**	• Complete questions 1–10. Work on the *Assessment Activity.* Complete the *Reflect & Pray* activity. • Review *Remember* and *Key Words.* • Read and discuss *Our Catholic Life.* • Discuss **Sharing Faith with My Family.**	• "Letters to the Editor" and corresponding articles • Chapter 22 Test in Assessment Book, pp. 43–44 • Chapter 22 Test in Test Generator • Review & Resource Book, pp. 49–51 • Family Book, pp. 62–64

For additional ideas, activities, and opportunities: Visit Sadlier's **www.WEBELIEVEweb.com**

Enrichment Ideas

Chapter Story

Adam had a great birthday. He received many gifts. He couldn't help, however, feeling a small pang of disappointment that no one had given him the new handheld video game that he wanted.

When Adam arrived at school on Monday, he learned that there was a new student in his class. The new boy came into the classroom and he went straight to an empty desk. When Adam looked over at the new boy, he couldn't believe his eyes—the boy was playing the video game Adam wanted so much! Adam felt so jealous he didn't know what to do.

Just then the teacher came in. Ms. Andrews introduced the new boy and asked everyone to be helpful and friendly to Miguel. Ms. Andrews noticed Miguel's video game and told him that games weren't allowed in school. She took the video game and put it on her desk, telling Miguel that he could have it back at the end of the day.

Finally the day was over. As the students left the classroom, Adam noticed that, even though Ms. Andrews and Miguel had both left the room, Miguel's video game was still on the teacher's desk. No one would notice if Adam just put it into his bag and left.

Adam really wanted that game. Just as he started to reach for it, however, his conscience won out over temptation. Instead of taking the game, Adam went to the door of the classroom. He looked down the hall and saw that Miguel was still there. Adam called to Miguel that he had forgotten his game.

Miguel ran back and thanked Adam, saying that he didn't know what he would have told his parents if he had come home without it. Miguel then asked Adam if he would like to come to his house to play the game. "You bet I would!" said Adam. He had made a good choice and a new friend.

▶ *What did Adam learn about temptation? What can we do to avoid temptation?*

FAITH and MEDIA

▶ This week the students are asked to think about whether the lyrics of their favorite songs show respect to others (Day 2) and whether television commercials present people speaking and acting in a respectful manner (Day 4). The students are also asked to find a positive newspaper story and write a letter to the editor about it (Day 5). This week, then, provides an excellent opportunity to remind students that songs, commercials, newspaper articles, and letters to the editor are examples of media. Point out that the media can be used both to promote Christian values and to undermine them.

CHAPTER PROJECT: NIGHTLY REVIEW

Explain to the students that they will be learning about the ways our feelings become more complex as we grow older, and about the ways we must choose to respond to our feelings in a loving and respectful manner. Emphasize that feelings are natural because they are a gift from God. Help the students to see that understanding our feelings is an important part of making good choices about our actions. Encourage the students to review their day every night before they go to bed. Invite them to think about the feelings they experienced, the temptations they faced, and the choices they made during the day. Have the students write prayers asking God to help them act in loving and respectful ways. Urge them to pray their prayers each night after their nightly review.

Connections

To Prayer

As the class discusses ways to resist temptation, remind the students that we ask God for help in overcoming temptation when we pray the Our Father. Tell the students that Jesus understands that we encounter difficult situations. He wants us to be reminded, each time we pray the Our Father, that we do not have to resist temptation alone. Encourage the students to pray the Lord's Prayer whenever they are faced with a challenge and they need to rely on their conscience to make a decision.

To Catholic Social Teaching

Life and Dignity of the Human Person
In this chapter the students will learn that practicing the virtue of modesty honors their own dignity and the dignity of others. Catholic social teaching reinforces this idea with the theme of the life and dignity of the human person. This theme reminds us that we are called to protect and respect the dignity of every human being. Have the students consider whether they always dress in ways that reflect for their dignity. Encourage them also to think and act modestly so that they may honor the dignity of others.

To Mary

At times we are tempted to express our feelings in unloving and disrespectful ways. God understands this and wants us to ask for help. Encourage the students to pray to Mary, our model for chastity and purity of heart, for the strength to resist temptation. Help the students understand that following Mary's example and practicing the virtue of chastity will help us show our love for others in an honest and respectful way.

Meeting Individual Needs

Students with Mobility Needs

Students who use wheelchairs view the classroom from a different perspective. Consider this perspective as you arrange desks and set out student resources and materials. Wide aisles, low shelves, and convenient placement of everyday materials will help you make your classroom accessible and inviting for all.

ADDITIONAL RESOURCES

Videos *Saints for Kids, Volume 5: Mary, the Mother of Jesus,* Pauline Books and Media, 1999. This is a brief video sketch of Mary, the model of purity of heart. (4-minute segment of 16-minute tape)

Close Encounters with the Beatitudes, Oblate Media and Communications, 2000. An angel shows Jimmy how his schoolmates help build God's Kingdom by living out the Beatitudes. (13 minutes)

To find more ideas for books, videos, and other learning material, visit Sadlier's

www.WEBELIEVEweb.com

Forming Evangelizing Catechists

by Rev. John E. Hurley, CSP, D.Min.

Father John Hurley, a Paulist priest, is Executive Director of the Secretariat for Evangelization at the United States Conference of Catholic Bishops in Washington, D.C.

In the document *On Evangelization in the Modern World,* Pope Paul VI declared that "the task of evangelizing all people constitutes the essential mission of the Church." In fact, he went on to declare, "She exists in order to evangelize." (EN 14) One of the fundamental moments in evangelization is catechesis. After the initial proclamation of the gospel, catechesis deepens the understanding of the truths of faith and fosters the relationship of the believer to Jesus and to the Church.

It is not surprising then that the *General Directory for Catechesis* notes that among the six central tasks of catechesis is "missionary initiation." (*GDC* 86) Catechists are called to equip those whom they catechize to be evangelizers who are able and excited to share their faith. In *Go and Make Disciples, A National Plan and Strategy for Catholic Evangelization in the United States*, the U.S. bishops challenge us to be enthusiastic messengers of the gospel. Our enthusiasm can become contagious and invite others to know the Lord who is the source of our joy. This can be achieved when we:

- are enthusiastic about the message that we are inviting others to hear and accept,
- are contagious witnesses to the gospel so that others will invite us to tell the story,
- invite others to join us in public acts that help to transform society.

The vocation of the catechist is to be a formator of disciples. Therefore, our own discipleship to Jesus must be rooted in a profoundly religious catechesis that is nourished by the gospel. As catechists, we are first of all living witnesses of the good news of Jesus. To be such witnesses requires more than a cognitive grasp of theology and Scripture; it means we have experienced a conversion of heart, and that the deep joy of that turning to God then impels us to share the gospel message with others.

Catechist Development Topics (Topic and Guide Page)

Resources

General Directory for Catechesis. Washington, D.C. United States Catholic Conference, 1997.

Go and Make Disciples: A National Plan and Strategy for Catholic Evangelization in the United States. Washington, D.C.: National Conference of Catholic Bishops, 1992.

Our Hearts Were Burning Within Us: A Pastoral Plan for Adult Faith Formation in the United States. Washington, D.C.: United States Catholic Conference, 1999.

Ways to Implement Forming Evangelizing Catechists

- Sharing the good news means that we know our faith and are able to articulate what we believe. Encourage the development of the vocabulary of faith with games and activities which reinforce key terms.
- Help the students to understand the connection between assessments of their learning and their ability to help others learn the Catholic faith.
- Give students opportunities to share their knowledge of Jesus with younger children. They can dramatize a gospel story or help to teach a prayer. Let them choose something they are enthusiastic about.
- Have students identify ways they can be evangelizers at home, at school, on the playground, with teams or other specific areas of their lives. Help them to name behaviors, decisions, and attitudes as well as words that will witness to Jesus.
- Invite members of the parish evangelization team to share their work with the students.
- Ask students to name people they know who share the message of Jesus in their lives. Make a list and name those people during prayer. The children might make cards or certificates to affirm and encourage these evangelizers.

For additional ideas, activities, and opportunities, visit Sadlier's

www.WeBelieveweb.com

With thanks to:
Barbara Occhipinti
St. William the Abbot
Seaford, New York

Barbara invites her students to produce a sixty-second video message, "We can evangelize!" Students brainstorm the ways we can share the good news of Jesus Christ. The group enlists the help of the school art department, music teachers, and a few parents with video equipment and expertise. Students design background scenes, choose (and sometimes write!) music, and craft a script. Once the message is honed to fit the time restraint, the actual taping takes place. Usually, the video message is taped several times, with different students being on camera to give everyone a chance. The finished tapes are used at parish events, and open houses in school, in the religious education program, and even for the adult evangelization committee.

Notes

Name ____

Use the code to discover an important message.

A	B	C	D	E	F	G	H	I	J	K	L	M
7	15	10	1	20	23	13	26	3	17	25	19	8

N	O	P	Q	R	S	T	U	V	W	X	Y	Z
2	12	16	4	21	9	6	18	24	11	22	5	14

13	12	1 ’ 9

13	21	7	10	20

9	6	21	20	2	13	6	26	20	2	9

18	9

6	12

15	20

16	18	21	20

12	23

26	20	7	21	6

The Ninth Commandment

✝ We Gather in Prayer

Leader: Let us ask God to look into our hearts and fill them with his goodness and love.

Reader: A reading from the Book of the Prophet Ezekiel.

"I will give you a new heart and place a new spirit within you, taking from your bodies your stony hearts and giving you natural hearts. I will put my spirit within you and make you live by my statutes, careful to observe my decrees. You shall live in the land I gave your fathers; you shall be my people, and I will be your God." (Ezekiel 36:26–28)

The word of the Lord.

All: Thanks be to God.

Leader: Glory to the Father, and to the Son, and to the Holy Spirit:

All: As it was in the beginning, is now, and will be for ever. Amen.

We Are Yours, O Lord

Refrain:

Help us to remember who and what we are:
We are yours, O Lord.

Teach us in your ways for all of our days. Let us hear your unspoken voice. (Refrain)

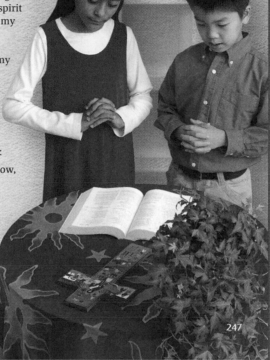

247

Chapter 22 • Day 1

PREPARING TO PRAY

During this prayer the students will hear the words of the prophet Ezekiel and through song will call on God to teach us his ways.

• Invite a volunteer to be the reader, and allow time for him or her to practice the reading.

• Select two volunteers to place the items in the prayer space at the appropriate time.

• Tell the students that you will read the leader's part and that everyone will read the parts marked "All" and sing the song together.

• Play "We Are Yours, O Lord," #24 on the Grade 4 CD, and allow time for the students to practice.

The Prayer Space

• Gather the following items: a statue of the Virgin Mary and a picture of a couple standing at the altar as they marry.

This Week's Liturgy

Visit **www.webelieveweb.com** for this week's liturgical readings and other seasonal material.

Lesson Plan

We Gather in Prayer ___ minutes

✝ Pray

• Invite the students to gather in the prayer space with their books open to the gathering prayer.

• Have the volunteers place the items in the prayer space as you explain their significance: Mary is our greatest example of purity of heart; husbands and wives are called to be faithful to each other, and all people are called to respect the love between a husband and wife.

• Pray the Sign of the Cross and begin the opening prayer.

• Signal the beginning of the musical portion of the gathering prayer by saying, *We are yours, O Lord.*

Home Connection Update

Invite volunteers to discuss the ways their families shared the Chapter 19 family page. Ask: *Did you do the "Scripture Pictures" activity? Did you discuss the quote from Saint Paul?* Encourage the students to talk about attending Mass with their families and about other family activities over the weekend.

Chapter 22 • Day 1

Catechist Goal

• To explain that feelings are a gift from God

Our Faith Response

• To identify ways to express our feelings that show our love and respect for God

Teaching Tip

Modeling Academic Behavior

Not only do the students pay attention to the material you present, they also pay attention to you. Use this attention as a teaching opportunity by modeling academic behavior during today's lesson. As you and the students work together to outline the main points of the *We Believe* text, model careful reading skills by referring often to specific parts of the text.

Feelings are a gift from God.

WE GATHER

✝ *Lord, may we always grow closer to you.*

Think about the ways your life is different now than when you were in first grade. What are some of the things that have changed?

WE BELIEVE

As we grow older many things change. We look different. We may enjoy different television shows and games. The kind of music we listen to usually changes, too.

We may be given more responsibilities at home and in school. We may take part in different sports or belong to different clubs. We might make new friends.

As we grow up we begin to understand more about the ways we think and feel. Feelings are natural. They are a gift from God. We all have feelings from the youngest age. Love, anger, joy, fear, and sadness are some of the feelings we may have. It is important to understand that people can have different feelings about the same thing. For example, a ride on a roller coaster may make one person happy and another person afraid.

Jesus had feelings, too. Look at these pictures. Under each picture is the Scripture passage that goes with it. How do you think Jesus felt in each situation? Why?

• "He came and took her by the hand, and the little girl arose." (Matthew 9:25)

love, joy

• "He overturned the tables of the money changers." (Mark 11:15)

angry

248

Lesson Plan

WE GATHER ___ minutes

✝ **Pray** Pray the Sign of the Cross and the *We Gather* prayer.

Focus on Life Have a volunteer read aloud the *We Gather* question. Invite responses. Tell the students that in this lesson they will learn that feelings change, too, and that we must learn to respond to them in healthy and respectful ways.

WE BELIEVE ___ minutes

Read the Text Ask a volunteer to read aloud the *We Believe* statement. Then have other volunteers read aloud the first three *We Believe* paragraphs. Emphasize:

• As we grow older, many things change.

• Feelings are natural, a gift from God.

Highlight an Idea After reading about different responses to a roller-coaster ride, ask the students to name other examples of things that might cause different responses in different people.

Do the Activity Discuss that Jesus, the Son of God, was fully human and fully divine and that he experienced many of the same feelings we do. Read the directions aloud. (Answers: He felt love in picture 1, anger in picture 2, joy in picture 3, and sadness in picture 4.)

Invite volunteers to read aloud the last three *We Believe* paragraphs. Pause to emphasize the following:

• We have choices in the way we deal with and act on our feelings.

• We should express our feelings in loving and respectful ways and not give in to temptation.

• "After Jesus was baptized, he came up from the water and behold, the heavens were opened [for him], and he saw the Spirit of God descending." (Matthew 3:16)

joy

• "And Jesus wept." (John 11:35)

sad

As we grow older, the things that cause us to feel certain ways may change. And the ways we express our feelings change, too. Feelings themselves are not good or evil, but the way we deal with or act on our feelings can be good or evil.

The way we express a feeling either shows love and respect for God and others, or does not show love and respect. We should not express feelings that might lead us to act in unloving or disrespectful ways. We should not give in to temptation. A temptation is an attraction to choose sin. A temptation is not a sin, but giving in to temptation is a sin.

We can call on the Holy Spirit to strengthen us and guide us to make good choices about the ways we act. The gift of conscience, the ability to know the difference between good and evil, helps us to choose actions that show love for God, ourselves, and others. We can also call on people we trust to help us to make good decisions.

WE RESPOND

Take a few moments to think quietly and prayerfully about the different feelings you may have. Ask Jesus to help you to understand these feelings. Ask for the strength to express your feelings in a way that shows love for God and others.

249

Activity Bank

Multiple Intelligences

Bodily-Kinesthetic

Activity materials: a Bible and some simple props

Have the students read silently the story of Jesus feeding the five thousand (Matthew 14:13–21) as an example of Jesus' showing compassion for others. Then invite the whole class to act out the story. Select one student to be the narrator, and have other students take the roles of Jesus, the disciples, the sick people whom Jesus cures, and other individuals in the crowd—men, women, and children. Encourage everyone to imagine the feelings of the person he or she is portraying and to act out those feelings as if he or she really were that person in that situation.

• We can call on the Holy Spirit, our conscience, and people we trust to help us make good decisions.

Read the *Chapter Story* Read the *Chapter Story* and discuss the questions that follow.

Quick Check

✔ *What does the gift of conscience help us to do?* (to choose actions that show love for God, ourselves, and others)

✔ *When should we show restraint in expressing our feelings?* (We should not express feelings that might lead us to act in unloving or disrespectful ways.)

WE RESPOND ___ minutes

Connect to Life Invite the students to read the *We Respond* text and pray silently to Jesus. Emphasize that feelings are never sinful, but remind the students that the ways we express our feelings can affect our own lives and our relationships with others and with God.

Pray Pray together the Our Father.

Plan Ahead for Day 2

Catechist Goal: To teach what the ninth commandment means

Preparation: Consider your response to the *We Gather* questions and prepare for discussion.

Catechist Goal

• To teach what the ninth commandment means

Our Faith Response

• To name ways of acting that honor the ninth commandment

 **covet**

Teaching Tip

Desk Placement

The arrangement of desks in a classroom can either help or hinder the educational objectives you want to accomplish as you teach a specific lesson. For example, placing desks in rows may be appropriate when the students are to work independently but inappropriate when the students are to work cooperatively. Consider rearranging the desks whenever doing so will enhance an activity. Before teaching today's lesson, you might consider how best to arrange the desks for a fruitful class discussion.

God created us to share love.

WE GATHER

✝ *Holy Spirit, help us to show love for ourselves and others.*

How do you feel when someone compliments you? As you are growing up, compliments may seem more important to you. Has anyone ever given you a compliment that surprised you? If so, why were you surprised?

WE BELIEVE

Part of growing up is becoming more aware of the gift of human sexuality that God has given us. God creates each of us male or female. He gave us this gift of human sexuality so we can show others love and affection.

The sixth commandment teaches us the proper ways to show love and affection. It teaches us to respect and be in control of our bodies.

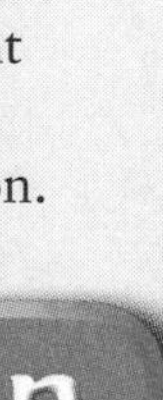

Name your favorite song.

____

Why do you like this song?

____

____

Does this song respect both women and men? How does it make you feel about yourself?

250

Lesson Plan

WE GATHER ___ minutes

✝ **Pray** Pray together the Sign of the Cross and the *We Gather* prayer.

Focus on Life Read and discuss the *We Gather* questions. Tell the students that in this lesson they will learn some ways that can help our feelings and thoughts when it comes to loving others.

WE BELIEVE ___ minutes

Read the Text Ask volunteers to read aloud the *We Believe* statement and the first two *We Believe* paragraphs. Discuss how each of the pictures shows giving love and affection. Emphasize the following:

• Part of growing up is becoming more aware of the gift of human sexuality.

• God gives us the gift of human sexuality so we can show others love and affection.

Do the Activity Have the students complete the *We Believe* activity. Ask volunteers to share their answers to the questions. Discuss the responses. Explain that some songs exploit human feelings about sexuality. Help the students understand that we must surround ourselves with things that will help us to respect and be in control of our bodies and our feelings.

Consider the Ninth Commandment Ask volunteers to read aloud the final two *We Believe* paragraphs. Emphasize the following:

• To covet means to wrongly desire something that is someone else's.

YOU SHALL NOT COVET YOUR NEIGHBOR'S WIFE.

The ninth commandment is also about love and affection. The ninth commandment is, "You shall not covet your neighbor's wife." To **covet** means to wrongly desire something that is someone else's. When we desire, or want, something unreasonably, our thoughts and feelings can lead us to do things we should not do.

Husbands and wives are called to be faithful to one another. They are asked to be loyal to each other. The ninth commandment calls all people to respect the love between a husband and a wife. It helps all of us to know the proper ways to feel and think about loving others.

Key Word

covet to wrongly desire something that is someone else's

WE RESPOND

Think about all the things that you wanted this week. Do you think your wishes brought you closer to God? Ask God to help you want the things that will bring you closer to him.

251

Chapter 22 • Day 2

ACTIVITY BANK

Multicultural Connection

Wedding Songs Around the World

Activity Materials: Internet or compact discs/cassettes

Invite the students to research the kinds of songs that are sung at Catholic weddings around the world. Ask: *Why is music a popular way to express love?* Encourage the students to do their research on the Internet, or check out CDs or cassettes of such music from the library. For example, students might research the mariachi songs played at Mexican weddings. Encourage the students to find English translations of the songs to enable the class to study the lyrics. In each case ask: *How does this song promote honoring the ninth commandment? Does the song celebrate love in a way that is pleasing to God?*

• The ninth commandment calls all people to respect the love between a husband and wife.

Invite the students to share their thoughts about weddings, marriage, and the love and fidelity between husbands and wives. Be sensitive to the fact that some students may have parents who are single, widowed, separated, or divorced. Remind the students that God understands the difficulties that can occur in a marriage.

Quick Check

✔ *Why does God give us the gift of human sexuality?* (so that we can show others love and affection)

✔ *What does the ninth commandment help us to do?* (to know the proper ways of feeling and thinking when it comes to loving others)

WE RESPOND ___ minutes

Connect to Life Read aloud the *We Respond* text and give the students time for personal reflection. Encourage the students to ask God to help them want appropriate things.

Pray Invite the students to thank God for the gifts of their feelings and their bodies.

Plan Ahead for Day 3

Catechist Goal: To present what it means to be pure of heart

Preparation: Have available paper hearts with the word *God* written on one side; make copies of Reproducible Master 22.

Catechist Goal

- To present what it means to be pure of heart

Our Faith Response

- To choose to be pure of heart

Lesson Materials

- paper hearts with the word *God* written on one side
- markers
- copies of Reproducible Master 22

Mary, Our Model

After presenting the lesson, have volunteers read aloud the *As Catholics* text. Help the students understand that we can learn how to practice purity of heart by following the example of Mary.

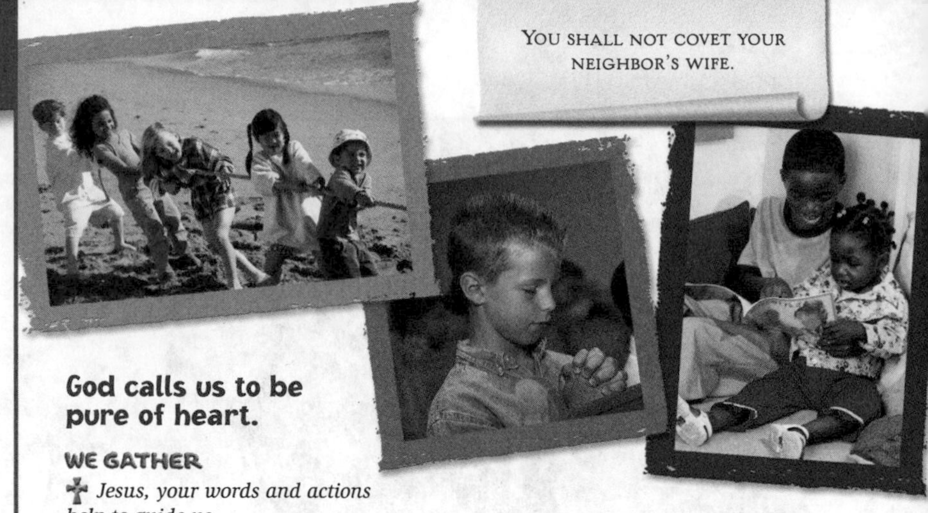
YOU SHALL NOT COVET YOUR NEIGHBOR'S WIFE.

God calls us to be pure of heart.

WE GATHER

✝ *Jesus, your words and actions help to guide us.*

Some phrases in our language have interesting meanings, for example, "I have a heavy heart." This does not mean that your heart weighs too much. What do you think it does mean? What are some things that may cause someone to have a "heavy heart"?

WE BELIEVE

Jesus understood that the human heart could be filled with love of God and the ways of God. He also knew that our hearts could be turned away from God. By his words and actions, Jesus taught us how to focus our hearts on God. In his Sermon on the Mount, Jesus gave us the Beatitudes. The Beatitudes are teachings that describe the way to live as disciples of Jesus. In the Beatitudes Jesus promises us happiness if we love God and trust in God. One of the beatitudes is:

"Blessed are the clean of heart,
for they will see God" (Matthew 5:8).

Living by the ninth commandment means being clean of heart, or pure of heart. When we are pure of heart, we live as God calls us to live. We love others and believe in God's love for us. Our thoughts and feelings lead us to trust in God's ways and to value our human sexuality.

How can our hearts be made pure? God first gives us a pure heart in Baptism. Throughout our lives we work to make our hearts pure by

- practicing the virtue of chastity, which helps us to show love for others in an honest and faithful way
- trying to know and follow God's will
- avoiding thoughts and feelings that lead us away from following God's commandments
- praying, celebrating the sacraments, and keeping our hearts focused on God.

In all these ways, God's grace strengthens us to be pure of heart.

252

Lesson Plan

WE GATHER ___ minutes

✝ **Pray** Pray together the Sign of the Cross and the *We Gather* prayer.

Focus on Life Ask a volunteer to read aloud the *We Gather* text. Invite responses to the questions. Tell the students that in this lesson they will learn that we must be pure of heart to live as God calls us to live.

WE BELIEVE ___ minutes

Decorate the Hearts Distribute markers and paper hearts with the word *God* printed on one side. As the students decorate the hearts, help them understand that we can learn how to focus our hearts on God.

Read the Text Ask a volunteer to read aloud the *We Believe* statement. Then have the students read aloud the *We Believe* paragraphs. Emphasize the following:

- Jesus taught us how to focus our hearts on God.
- The Beatitudes are teachings that help us live as disciples of Jesus.
- Living by the ninth commandment means being clean, or pure, of heart.
- When we are pure of heart, we are living as God calls us to live.
- God's grace strengthens us to be pure of heart by practicing the virtue of chastity; by trying to know and follow God's will; by avoiding thoughts and feelings that might lead us into temptation; and by praying, celebrating the sacraments, and focusing our hearts on God.

WE RESPOND

On the recipe card, write your own recipe for a pure heart. How can you "serve" this recipe for a pure heart to others?

RECIPE

Sample:

2 cups of love for God and others

1 cup of joy

6 heaping tablespoons of prayer

Mix with a dash of good humor.

Serve to all you meet!

As Catholics...

Mary was pure of heart. She lived as God wanted her to live. When the angel of the Lord appeared to Mary and asked her to become the mother of Jesus, she said, "May it be done to me according to your word" (Luke 1:38). Mary was ready to do what God asked. She said yes to God because her heart was open to God's call.

Mary is our greatest example of a chaste person. She shows us how to speak and act with a pure heart. She was a loving wife to Joseph. She was a loving mother to Jesus. As Catholics we believe that Mary is our mother, too. Mary wants to see us live as devoted children of God. We can ask Mary to pray for us. We can imitate her love for God and his ways.

This week ask Mary to help you.

Chapter 22 • Day 3

Activity Bank

Meeting Individual Needs

Gifted and Talented Students

Activity Materials: *New American Bible*

Students learn in different ways and at different paces. Invite those students who might benefit from an enrichment activity to read the Beatitudes in Matthew 5:1–12. Ask the students to consider the reasons these teachings are so important to people who try to follow the will of God. Encourage the students to write their own versions of the Beatitudes.

Complete the Reproducible Master Distribute Reproducible Master 22 and ask the students to complete the activity. (Answer: God's grace strengthens us to be pure of heart.)

Quick Check

✔ *What are the Beatitudes?* (The Beatitudes are teachings that describe the way to live as disciples of Jesus.)

✔ *What happens when we are pure of heart?* (We live as God calls us to live.)

WE RESPOND ___ minutes

Connect to Life Read aloud the directions to the *We Respond* activity. Write the sample recipe on the board. Provide time for the students to write their recipes. When all have finished, ask volunteers to present their recipes and answer the *We Respond* question. Discuss what recipe the people in the pictures might be following.

Pray Conclude by praying together the Hail Mary.

Plan Ahead for Day 4

Catechist Goal: To examine the meaning of the virtue of modesty

Preparation: Have markers and butcher paper available.

Chapter 22 • Day 4

Catechist Goal
- To examine the meaning of the virtue of modesty

Our Faith Response
- To appreciate the virtue of modesty in our relationships

 **modesty**

Lesson Materials
- markers
- butcher paper

Teaching Tip
Clarity

Clear communication of instructions and expectations is an essential component of effective teaching. When directions are clear and precise, the momentum of the lesson is preserved and students move quickly to the next task or activity. But when directions are vague, momentum is interrupted and students move off task. As you teach today's lesson, be clear and precise when giving instructions for classroom activities.

YOU SHALL NOT COVET YOUR NEIGHBOR'S WIFE.

The virtue of modesty helps us to be pure of heart.

WE GATHER

✝ *God, guide us in our thoughts, words, and actions to respect ourselves and others.*

Think of some television advertisements you have seen recently. Did they include people speaking and acting in ways that showed respect for themselves and others? Why or why not?

WE BELIEVE

Being pure of heart requires modesty. **Modesty** is the virtue by which we think, speak, act, and dress in ways that show respect for ourselves and others.

Being modest is an important part of living out the ninth commandment. Modesty is about honoring our own dignity and the dignity of others. When we are modest we protect our bodies. Modesty guides how we look at others and behave toward them.

modesty the virtue by which we think, speak, act, and dress in ways that show respect for ourselves and others

How do you think the virtue of modesty could be practiced in each of these situations?

Barry has just received his grade on a very difficult test. He is very happy because he did very well. His best friend did not do as well. How can Barry practice the virtue of modesty?

____

____

254

Lesson Plan

WE GATHER ___ minutes

✝ **Pray** Pray the Sign of the Cross and the *We Gather* prayer.

Focus on Life Read aloud the directions for the *We Gather* activity. Have the students work independently. Then give butcher paper and markers to two students and have them record responses as volunteers share their thoughts. Ask the students whether their behavior has been influenced by advertisements. Tell the students that in this lesson they will learn that the practice of modesty helps us to be pure of heart.

WE BELIEVE ___ minutes

Read the Text Have a volunteer read aloud the *We Believe* statement. Then pair the students and have the pairs quietly read the first two *We Believe* paragraphs.

Do the Activity Ask the pairs of students to read and complete the *We Believe* activity. Encourage them to think of several different responses for each scenario. Remind them that we always have the choice to act modestly. Allow time for everyone to finish. Then ask volunteers to share their responses.

Reflect on the Ninth Commandment Draw the students' attention to the questions in the box. Explain that these questions can help them make an examination of conscience. Invite the students to reflect quietly, prayerfully, and individually on the questions.

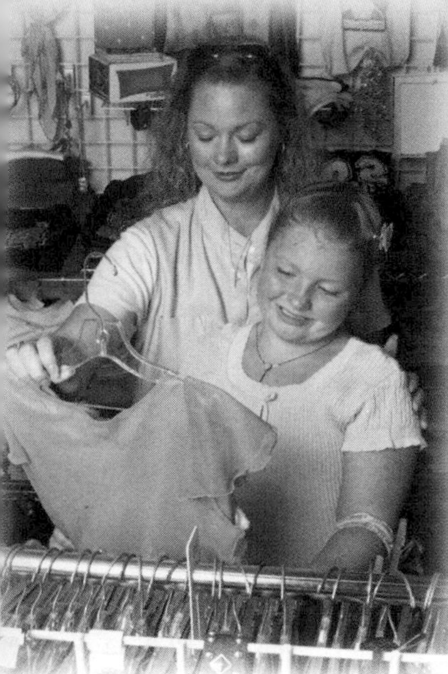

Yana is going to a birthday party. Her mother lets her pick out a new outfit for the party. How can Yana practice the virtue of modesty?

Take a few moments to think quietly and prayerfully about ways you follow the ninth commandment. These questions may help you.

Do I always act on my feelings? Should I?

Do I try not to give in to temptation?

Do I pray for strength and guidance in making good choices?

Have I been responsible about the things that I want?

Do I stay away from things and people who do not value human sexuality?

Do I try to show my feelings in a respectful way?

Do I try to do the things God wants me to do?

In what ways do I practice the virtue of modesty?

WE RESPOND

Imagine that you need to explain the ninth commandment to someone who has never heard about it. What would you tell him or her?

Ask God for the courage to respect yourself and others always.

255

ACTIVITY BANK

Faith and Media

Promoting Modesty

Activity Materials: television

Practicing the virtue of modesty is part of keeping the ninth commandment. Today's media often send a contrary message, however. Invite the students, with their parents' or guardians' permission, to watch a particular television program. Ask the students to note the ways the program presents issues of modesty or immodesty. Have the students ask: Do the people on this program promote the ninth commandment, or do they break it? Encourage the students to write letters to local television stations or to the networks explaining why it is important for television programs to promote and respect the dignity of all people.

Quick Check

✔ *What is modesty?* (Modesty is the virtue by which we think, speak, act, and dress in ways that show respect for ourselves and others.)

✔ *How does modesty help us live out the ninth commandment?* (Modesty guides the way we look at others and behave toward them.)

WE RESPOND

___ minutes

Connect to Life Ask the students to read silently the *We Respond* text and answer the question.

Pray Encourage the students to ask God for the courage to respect themselves and others; then pray together Psalm 51:12:

A clean heart create for me, God;
renew in me a steadfast spirit.
Amen.

Plan Ahead for Day 5

Catechist Goal: To review chapter ideas and their relationship to our faith life

Preparation: Make copies of Chapter 22 Test in the Grade 4 Assessment Book (option); have available "Letters to the Editor" pages and articles referred to in the letters.

Catechist Goal

- To review chapter ideas and their relationship to our faith life

Our Faith Response

- To apply what has been learned to our lives

CHAPTER TEST

Chapter 22 Test is provided in the Grade 4 Assessment Book.

Grade 4
Chapter 22

Choose a word or phrase from the box to complete each sentence.

feelings	pure of heart	respect	human sexuality

1. ___Human sexuality___ is a gift from God so that we can show others love and affection.

2. We can be ___pure of heart___ by loving others and believing in God's love for us.

3. ___Feelings___ are a gift from God and should be respected by ourselves and others.

4. It is important to show ___respect___ for God and the feelings of others.

Write the letter of the phrase that defines each of the following:

5. ___d___ covet
6. ___a___ chastity
7. ___b___ ninth commandment
8. ___c___ modesty

a. virtue that helps us to show love for others in an honest and faithful way

b. calls all people to respect the love between a husband and wife

c. the virtue by which we show respect for ourselves and others

d. to wrongly desire something that is someone else's

9–10. Write a short paragraph about the importance of the ninth commandment.

See pages 250–251.

Read the newspaper with your family. Find a story that illustrates people who are pure of heart. Write a "Letter to the Editor" explaining the ways the people in this story live in God's love.

256

Lesson Plan

___ minutes

Chapter Review Explain to the students that they will now check their understanding of what they have learned. Ask them to complete questions 1–8. Invite volunteers to share the correct answers. Then have the students write their responses to question 9–10.

Assessment Activity Have the students read the directions. Show the students examples of actual "Letters to the Editor" in newspapers and magazines; if possible, also show the students the articles the letter writers are responding to. Ask the students to write their "Letters to the Editor" over the weekend, perhaps in response to an article in the Sunday paper or a magazine. Invite the students to share their letters—and, if possible, the original articles—in class after the weekend.

___ minutes

Reflect and Pray Read aloud the introduction to this activity. Remind the students of the difference between the behaviors and actions we show "on the outside" and the thoughts and feelings we have inside our hearts. Allow time for everyone to reflect privately on the Scripture reading and write his or her prayer.

Key Words Write the two *Key Words* on the board, each at the center of a large circle. Invite the students to name other words or phrases that come to mind when they think of each key word. Write these words and phrases in the circle around the key word to which each relates. Then ask volunteers to recall the definitions of the key words.

We Respond in Faith

Reflect & Pray

Sometimes people do everything right "on the outside," but their hearts are not filled with love for God and others. This is what Jesus has to say: "Hypocrites, well did Isaiah prophesy about you when he said:

'This people honors me with their lips,
but their hearts are far from me'"
(Matthew 15:7–8).

God, help me to be pure of heart. Help me to

____

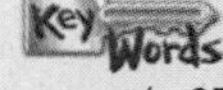

Key Words
covet (p. 251)
modesty (p. 254)

Remember

- Feelings are a gift from God.
- God created us to share love.
- God calls us to be pure of heart.
- The virtue of modesty helps us to be pure of heart.

Our Catholic Life

Solidarity of the Human Family

We believe in the solidarity of the human family. This means that no matter where in the world we live, we are all united by God as brothers and sisters. We may have many different ideas, different religions and customs, and different systems of government. Yet, because God created each one of us, we are all one family.

We especially care for people around the world when they are in need. One group that helps is Catholic Relief Services. In times of flood, famine, earthquake, or war, Catholic Relief is there to help. This group gives Catholics the chance to support people in other countries and to work for laws that end poverty around the world.

Chapter 22 • Day 5

Home Connection

Sharing Faith with My Family

Make sure to send home the family page (text page 258).

Encourage the students to discuss the work of Saint Katharine Drexel with their families. Then read the directions for the *Holiness Hall of Fame* and explain that there will be four more opportunities in the coming weeks to nominate people for this honor.

For additional information and activities, encourage families to visit Sadlier's

www.WEBELIEVEweb.com

Remember Review the four *We Believe* statements. Ask the students to list two things they learned from the lesson that went with each statement. Ask volunteers to share their answers.

Our Catholic Life Invite two volunteers to read aloud the text. Emphasize that all people everywhere are brothers and sisters despite our differences. Help the students understand that this membership in the human family carries responsibilities. Explain that poverty, hunger, and homelessness exist not only in faraway places but also in our own neighborhoods. Encourage the students to name ways we can care for our brothers and sisters in need.

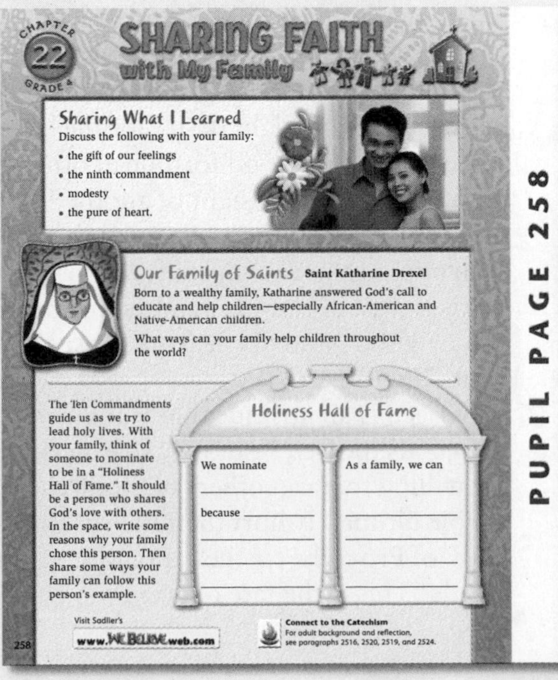

Chapter 22 Grade 4

Sharing Faith with My Family

Sharing What I Learned
Discuss the following with your family:
- the gift of our feelings
- the ninth commandment
- modesty
- the pure of heart.

Our Family of Saints Saint Katharine Drexel
Born to a wealthy family, Katharine answered God's call to educate and help children—especially African-American and Native-American children.
What ways can your family help children throughout the world?

The Ten Commandments guide us as we try to lead holy lives. With your family, think of someone to nominate to be in a "Holiness Hall of Fame." It should be a person who shares God's love with others. In the space, write some reasons why your family chose this person. Then share some ways your family can follow this person's example.

Holiness Hall of Fame
We nominate ______ because ______
As a family, we can ______

Visit Sadlier's www.WEBELIEVEweb.com

Connect to the Catechism
For adult background and reflection, see paragraphs 2516, 2520, 2519, and 2524.

258

PUPIL PAGE 258

Chapter 23 The Tenth Commandment

Overview

In Chapter 23 the students learned positive ways to follow the ninth commandment and be pure of heart. In this chapter the students will learn that our hearts are to be filled with love and generosity, not with envy or greed.

Doctrinal Content	For Adult Reading and Reflection *Catechism of the Catholic Church*
The students will learn:	Paragraph
• We are called to have generous hearts.	2538
• Jesus taught us to trust in God above all things.	2544
• Depending upon God brings happiness.	2547
• Jesus teaches us that God's law is love.	1970

envy (p. 260)
greed (p. 263)
poor in spirit (p. 264)

Catechist Background

How do you feel when a friend is praised or receives an award?

According to the tenth commandment we are not to covet our neighbor's goods. This commandment rises from the Decalogue like a red flag warning us against envy, greed, and avarice.

Envy is a capital sin, and a particularly nasty one at that. It is a feeling of resentment or begrudging esteem or outright desire for the belongings, achievements, or good fortune of others. "It refers to the sadness at the sight of another's goods and the immoderate desire to acquire them for oneself, even unjustly. . . . From envy are born hatred, detraction, calumny, joy caused by the misfortune of a neighbor, and displeasure caused by his prosperity" (*CCC* 2539).

Greed is an attitude that leads us to want material goods, power, or money so excessively that we are willing to harm others to attain them. Greedy people ultimately hurt themselves. This is what the Book of Proverbs teaches about the effects of greed: "This is the fate of everyone greedy for loot: unlawful gain takes away the life of him who acquires it" (1:19) and "He who is greedy of gain brings ruin on his own house" (15:27). Avarice, greed's first cousin, is miserliness, an insatiable and inordinate desire to possess and hoard wealth.

Saint Paul in his letter to the Colossians offers a powerful antidote to envy, greed, and avarice. "Put on then, as God's chosen ones, holy and beloved, heartfelt compassion, kindness, humility, gentleness, and patience, . . . And over all these put on love, that is, the bond of perfection. And let the peace of Christ control your hearts, the peace into which you were also called in one body. And be thankful" (3:12–15).

How can you focus on gratitude in your life?

Lesson Planning Guide

Lesson Focus	Presentation	Materials
Day 1		
page 259 **We Gather in Prayer**	• Listen to Scripture. Respond in song.	For the prayer space: small cans of food and bottles of water, Bible, basket
pages 260–261 *We are called to have generous hearts.*	• Discuss the **We Gather** question. • Read and discuss the tenth commandment and envy in the **We Believe** text. Do the role-play activity. • Discuss the **We Respond** question. • Pray together.	"Pescador de Hombres/Lord, You Have Come," Cesareo Gabarain, #25, Grade 4 CD • copies of Reproducible Master 23, guide page 259G
Day 2		
pages 262–263 *Jesus taught us to trust in God above all things.*	• Discuss just or unjust situations in the **We Gather** text. • Read and discuss the **We Believe** text. Do the rewrite activity. • Answer the **We Respond** questions. • Read and discuss the *As Catholics* text. • Pray together.	• chart paper, markers
Day 3		
pages 264–265 *Depending upon God brings happiness.* *Acts of the Apostles 20:33–35*	• Discuss the **We Gather** questions. • Read and discuss the **We Believe** text. • Discuss being poor in spirit. Complete the **We Respond** activity. • Discuss Saint Thérèse of the Child Jesus in *Blessed are they. . .*	copy of the song "Blest Are They," David Haas, #2, Grade 4 CD
Day 4		
pages 266–267 *Jesus teaches us that God's law is love.*	Do the **We Gather** activity. • Read and discuss the **We Believe** text. Compose a song for the **We Respond**.	• large self-stick labels, markers
Day 5		
page 268 **Review** **pages 269–270** **We Respond in Faith**	• Complete questions 1–10. Work on the *Assessment Activity.* • Complete the *Reflect & Pray* activity. • Review *Remember* and *Key Words.* • Read and discuss in *Our Catholic Life.* • Discuss **Sharing Faith with My Family**.	• magazines, newspapers, folders, poster board • Chapter 23 in the Assessment Book, pp. 45–46 • Chapter 23 Test in the Test Generator • Review & Resource Book, pp. 52–54 • Family Book, pp. 65–67

For additional ideas, activities, and opportunities: Visit Sadlier's **www.WEBELIEVEweb.com**

Enrichment Ideas

Chapter Story

As a girl in Italy Frances Xavier Cabrini wanted nothing more than to devote herself to God. She wanted to become a nun. Since she was physically weak, she was told that she was not strong enough for the religious life. She did not become discouraged but trusted that God had a plan for her. She helped her parents with work on their farm and began teaching in a school for girls. A few years went by and Frances finally was able to take her religious vows and become a nun. However, things still did not turn out as Frances had planned.

Frances longed to do missionary work in China, but God had another plan for her. In 1889 the Church sent her to New York City to help the many Italian immigrants living there. She did not know much English when she arrived in New York, but with God's help she was able to do great things. She founded schools, hospitals, and orphanages. She knew that true happiness is found in helping others, and she devoted her life to helping the poor.

Twenty years after coming to the United States, Frances became an American citizen. She traveled throughout the United States doing God's work, and she founded more than sixty-five organizations to help those in need. She died in Chicago in 1917. In 1946 she was made a saint, the first American citizen to be canonized. Because of all the help she gave to those who made the United States their new home, she is the patron saint of immigrants.

Saint Frances Xavier Cabrini obeyed the tenth commandment. She trusted in God and did not doubt that God had a plan for her. Instead of insisting on going to China, she was open to going to New York. Even though she didn't know much English, she did not worry about life in a new country. She did not desire material things but devoted her life to caring for the poor. She showed us how to live a life that is poor in spirit.

▶ *From the example of Saint Frances Cabrini, what have you learned about placing your trust in God?*

FAITH and MEDIA

▶ On Day 5 the students will be asked to look through magazines and newspapers and search the Internet with their families for pictures and articles that show people living out the Ten Commandments. This attention to the media is both deliberate and necessary. Since students are exposed to the media every day, it is important to provide them with tools to differentiate information that supports the Ten Commandments from information that does not. Students can then use these tools to make good moral decisions rather than being misdirected by the attractive but occasionally unsavory influences offered by some elements of the media.

CHAPTER PROJECT: A "GOOD LIFE" COLLAGE

Have the students make a collage to show the difference between living a good life according to the gospel and living "the good life" as it is promoted in our society. Have the students look for pictures of things, such as luxury cars and fancy houses, that society says people need to be happy. Have the students also look for pictures showing the happiness that comes from living according to God's will, such as scenes of people helping others. Have the students assemble the collage on a large piece of poster board or chart paper. Print a title such as *What Is a Good Life?* in the center. Then, on one side place the things society says are necessary for "the good life"; on the other place the ways to lead a good life according to the gospel. Display the collage in the classroom or a hallway.

Connections

To Saints

Explain that many saints are known for rejecting worldly ideals. Many of them lived and worked among the poor. Invite the students to read the lives of the saints. Then encourage the students to follow the example of these saints by looking for ways to help those who are less fortunate.

To Stewardship

Remind the students that being generous can mean more than simply giving money or gifts. Being generous can also take the form of donating one's time or sharing one's talents. Encourage the students to open their hearts to others. Encourage them to show their generosity by listening to a grandparent or helping to take care of a younger brother or sister. Invite the students to think of new ways to be generous.

To Family

Encourage the students to be supportive of their siblings and other family members. Explain that they might sometimes feel envious of a sister, a brother, or a cousin's achievements. To counteract this feeling of envy, encourage the students to react in a positive, loving way the next time a family member is successful.

Meeting Individual Needs

Students with Visual Needs

Be aware of your students with visual needs. Some of these students may be sensitive to light, for example. Find out whether fluorescent lighting bothers these students and, if possible, arrange to have different lighting in the classroom. Similarly, when the class is working on a hands-on project such as the collage, allow the students with visual needs an opportunity to explore the materials. Give these students verbal directions if necessary, but avoid taking their hands and placing them on an object.

ADDITIONAL RESOURCES

Video *Veggie Tales: Madame Blueberry,* Big Idea Productions, Inc., 1993. This video shows why we should be thankful for the things we have, not resentful about the things we do not have. (30 minutes)

To find more ideas for books, videos, and other learning material, visit Sadlier's

www.WEBELIEVEweb.com

Developing an Understanding of Mission

by Most Rev. Gregory M. Aymond D.D.

Bishop Gregory M. Aymond, D.D. is the Chair of the U.S. Bishops' Committee on World Mission and the Bishop of the Diocese of Austin, Texas. He has been involved in the missionary work of the Church since 1976 and has visited numerous missionary countries.

At the end of his time on earth, Jesus commanded his apostles: "Go, therefore, and make disciples of all nations, baptizing them in the name of the Father, and of the Son, and of the holy Spirit" (Matthew 28:19). As Catholics, this, too, is our call. To be Catholic and to be a catechist is to be a missionary. To be a missionary is to take seriously Jesus' command to share our faith with others.

Through our Baptism, we become members of the Catholic Church. We receive the Light of Christ and are called to live our lives embracing Jesus and his message. Throughout the gospels, Jesus encourages us to share his message and his light with all people. Pope John Paul II reminds us, "Faith is not a private matter, it is to be shared with others." (*Redemptoris Missio*, December 7, 1990) It is through this sharing of our faith that we not only respond to Jesus' command, but also model him and continue his work on earth.

Catholic means "universal." Two thirds of the world's population do not know Jesus. Jesus' command to make disciples of all nations calls us to bring his message and open our hearts to not only our families and communities, but also to those

- who have never heard of Christ.
- who know Jesus and suffer persecution for their Christian beliefs.
- who live in developing countries where they hunger for food, justice, and a deeper faith in Christ and the Church.
- whom we will never meet but are nonetheless our sisters and brothers in the global Church.

Catechist Development Topics (Topic and Guide Page)

As catechists we have a privileged ministry helping to expand the minds and hearts of our students in order for them to live fully the call of Baptism. It is our responsibility to teach our students the message of Jesus and to challenge them to embrace and live this message, not only in our homes and communities, but also throughout the whole world.

Resources

Written and video educational materials regarding one aspect of our mission as Catholics can be obtained from the Society for the Propagation of the Faith/Holy Childhood Association at 1-800-431-2222.

Redemptoris Missio (the Mission of the Redeemer) by Pope John Paul II

To the Ends of the Earth. Washington, D.C.: U.S. Catholic Conference.

Ways to Implement Developing an Understanding of Mission

- Invite your students to read passages from various books of the New Testament and to list any references to mission and evangelization.
- Take time to have your students, as a class, pray regularly for missionaries and for the people they serve.
- Teach students about other nations' cultures and religions. Take advantage of the cultural diversity that exists in your room. Explain that our mission is to *all* people.
- Provide the opportunity for your class or group to write to a missionary requesting information about his/her ministry in a developing country. This can be done by regular mail or on the Internet.
- Invite the students to communicate as "pen pals" with children in developing countries.
- Invite a missionary to visit your room and share his/her experiences of "making disciples of all nations." Possibly, this person could show photos or videos of his or her work to the people of God.
- Sponsor parish and school activities that encourage students to give of their time and talents to those in the mission world.
- Use education programs from the Holy Childhood Association and the Society for the Propagation of the Faith. Their address is 366 Fifth Avenue, New York, NY 10001.

For additional ideas, activities, and opportunities, visit Sadlier's

www.WEBELIEVEweb.com

With thanks to:
Thomas Doyle
All Souls Catholic School
Sanford, FL

Thomas joins other teachers and staff for a program called "IHS," or "In His Steps." Students and staff nominate students who have done a kind act for another. It might be a student who helps another student with learning computer skills. It might be a student who shares his or her book stickers with another. Or a student might help a teacher set up a class project. When a student does what Jesus would do in that situation, he or she receives a pin that is in the form of three footprints with the words "In His Steps." The students' names and kind acts are read out in the morning as everyone gathers for prayer.

Notes

Name ____

Draw or write how you would complete the statements.

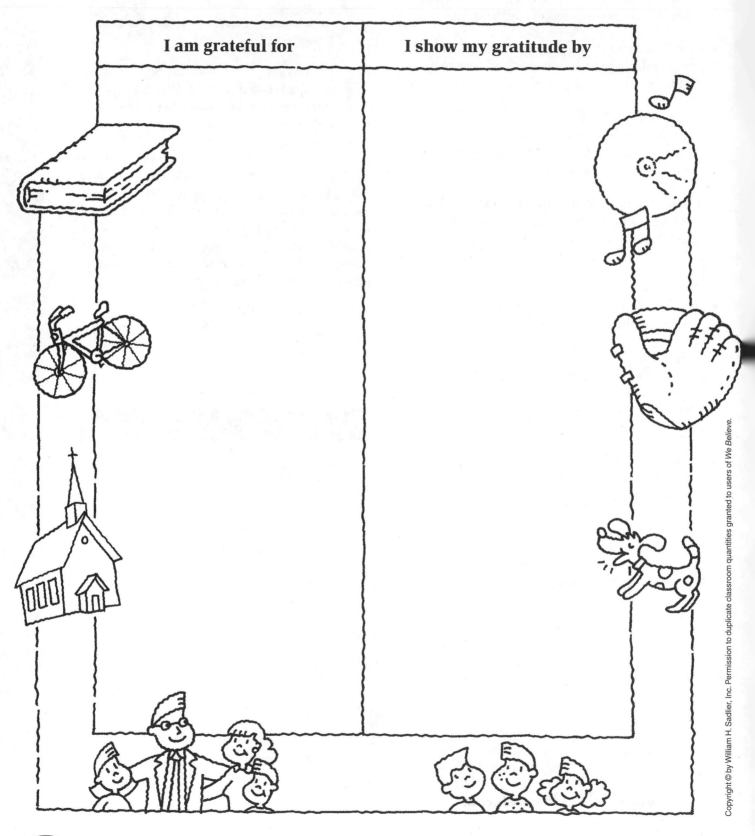

I am grateful for	I show my gratitude by

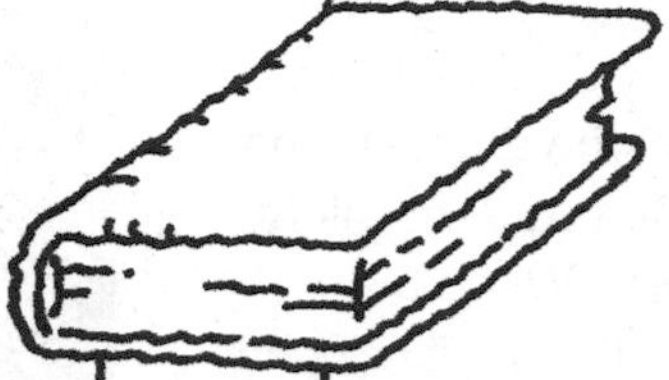

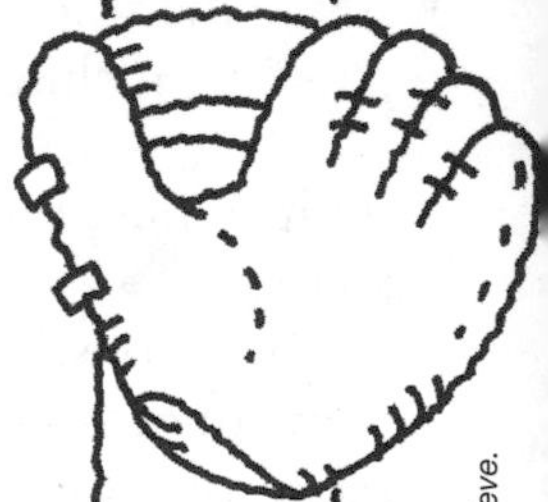

The Tenth Commandment

We Gather in Prayer

Leader: Let us listen to the words of Jesus as he teaches us about important things in life.

Reader: A reading from the holy Gospel according to Luke.

All: Glory to you, Lord.

Reader: Jesus said, "Therefore I tell you, do not worry about your life and what you will eat, or about your body and what you will wear. For life is more than food and the body more than clothing. Notice the ravens: they do not sow or reap; they have neither storehouse nor barn, yet God feeds them. How much more important are you than birds!" (Luke 12:22–24)

The Gospel of the Lord.

All: Praise to you, Lord Jesus Christ!

Pescador de Hombres/ Lord, You Have Come

Lord, you have come to the seashore,
neither searching for the rich nor the wise,
desiring only that I should follow.

Refrain:
O Lord, with your eyes set upon me,
gently smiling, you have spoken my name;
all I longed for I have found by the water,
at your side, I will seek other shores.

Tú has venido a la orilla,
no has buscado ni a sabios ni a ricos;
tan sólo quieres que yo te siga.

Refrain:
Señor, me has mirado a los ojos,
son riendo has dicho mi nombre,
en la arena he dejado mi barca,
junto a ti buscaré otro mar.

259

Chapter 23 • Day 1

Preparing to Pray

In this prayer the students will put their trust in God and sing about following Christ.

- Tell the students that you will be the leader, and that everyone will pray the parts marked "All."
- Invite a volunteer to be the reader and give him or her time to rehearse.
- Assign students to carry items to the prayer space at the appropriate time.
- Decide whether you will sing "Pescador de Hombres/Lord, You Have Come," #25 on the Grade 4 CD, in English or Spanish. Play the song for the students and allow time for rehearsal.

The Prayer Space

- Have available small cans of food and small bottles of water to represent God's caring for our needs, a basket, and a Bible with a marker at Luke 12:22–24.

This Week's Liturgy

Visit **www.webelieveweb.com** for this week's liturgical readings and other seasonal material.

Lesson Plan

We Gather in Prayer ___ minutes

Pray

- Invite the students to gather together in the prayer space. Explain that the food and water represents God's caring for our needs.
- Have the students open their books to the opening prayer. Then pray the Sign of the Cross and begin the opening prayer.
- Have several students bring forward the cans and bottles of food and water and place them in the basket as the song is sung.

Home Connection Update

Invite the students to share their experiences using the Chapter 22 family page. Ask: *Who did you nominate to the "Holiness Hall of Fame"?* Then invite volunteers to read the "Letters to the Editor" they wrote for the Chapter 22 Assessment Activity.

Chapter 23 • Day 1

Catechist Goal

- To present the reasons why it is wrong to be envious

Our Faith Response

- To explore ways to overcome being envious of others

 envy

Lesson Materials

- copies of Reproducible Master 23

We are called to have generous hearts.

WE GATHER

✝ *Holy Spirit, help us to know our hearts.*

Think of a time when you did something, and then had to explain your actions. Was it difficult to think about why you had acted that way?

WE BELIEVE

The tenth commandment is, "You shall not covet your neighbor's goods." Like the ninth commandment, the tenth commandment teaches us to look into our hearts and to examine our thoughts and feelings. We try to understand our feelings toward the things that others have.

The tenth commandment also relates to the seventh commandment. Both of these commandments deal with the property of others. We do not take things that do not belong to us. We also do not wrongly desire those things. When we live out the tenth commandment, we do not covet, or wrongly desire, the goods and property of others.

Living out the tenth commandment keeps us from spending too much time wishing for the things we do not have. Instead, we should be thankful for what we have. We should work for what we need and work to help others to have what they need.

Are we happy that people have what they need? Are we happy that people have many things that they want? **Envy** is a feeling of sadness when someone else has the things we want for ourselves. Envy can lead to taking what belongs to someone else.

You shall not covet your neighbor's goods.

People who are envious think mostly about themselves. They are not happy for the success of other people. Instead, they want success, power, or money for themselves. Envious people have a hard time seeing what they already have and being grateful for it. However, when people rely on God and are grateful for the many gifts he has given them, envy does not become a part of their lives. People who think of others in a loving and giving way develop a generous heart, not an envious one.

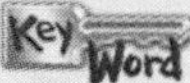

envy a feeling of sadness when someone else has the things we want for ourselves

260

Teaching Tip

Generosity

Encourage the students to have generous hearts. Remind them that a generous heart is forgiving, slow to anger, and not envious. Encourage them to ask God for a generous heart, and remind them that God listens to their prayers. Share with the students the words of the prophet Ezekiel: "I will give you a new heart and place a new spirit within you" (36:26).

Lesson Plan

WE GATHER ___ minutes

✝ **Pray** Pray together the Sign of the Cross and the *We Gather* prayer.

Focus on Life Invite the students to read the *We Gather* question and share their responses. Tell the students that in this lesson they will learn that God asks us to have generous hearts.

WE BELIEVE ___ minutes

Read the Text Invite a volunteer to read aloud the *We Believe* statement. Write the tenth commandment on the board. Then invite several volunteers to read aloud the first five *We Believe* paragraphs. Pause between paragraphs to emphasize the following:

- The tenth commandment is related to the seventh commandment in that it deals with the property of others.
- People who are envious think mostly about themselves.
- People who think of others in a loving and giving way develop a generous heart.

Do the Activity Organize the students into three groups, and assign each group one of the situations. Allow the groups time to prepare, then invite them to perform their scenes.

Invite a volunteer to read aloud the final *We Believe* paragraph. Then ask the students to think about the scenes they have just enacted. Emphasize that the tenth commandment calls us not only to act justly but also to think justly.

Read each situation. Act it out to show how the boys and girls can follow the tenth commandment.

- Darryl helped his father all summer. At the start of the school year, his father gave him a new bike as a reward for his hard work. Vinny sees the new bike and thinks, "I want that bike."
- As an only child, David has been the center of attention for his family. Last March, David's parents adopted a beautiful baby girl. Now David has to share the attention with his new baby sister.
- Roberta and Carlos were finalists in the school spelling bee. Carlos misspelled a word that Roberta spelled correctly. Roberta won.

The tenth commandment reminds us not only to act justly but also to think justly. It reminds us to look into our hearts. We should not be so worried about what others have that we lose sight of what is important. God and his love are important. People and their needs are important. The Church community in which we worship and grow in faith is important. God's gifts of creation are important. These are the things that should fill our hearts.

WE RESPOND

How can you show that you have a generous heart?

Ask Jesus to help you to be generous as he was.

261

ACTIVITY BANK

Faith and Media

Wants and Needs

Activity Materials: magazines, newspapers, and videotaped television commercials (optional)

Have the students examine some examples of contemporary advertising, either in print or on television, to determine what messages the ads are sending about wants and needs. Encourage the students to ask themselves such questions as, *Do any of these ads make me feel envious of others? Do I want things more because of what I see in ads?* Have the students discuss what they found in the advertisements. Explain that advertisers are trying to persuade us that we need certain things. Encourage the students to remember the difference between wants and needs and to be aware of the advertiser's message whenever they look at an ad.

Quick Check

✔ *What does the tenth commandment state?* ("You shall not covet your neighbor's goods.")

✔ *What is envy?* (Envy is a feeling of sadness when someone else has the things we want for ourselves.)

WE RESPOND ___ minutes

Connect to Life Read aloud the *We Respond* text. Call on volunteers to share their answers. (We can show a generous heart by donating food, money, or clothing; by praying for people in need; by writing letters to government officials asking them to support programs for those in need.) Distribute copies of Reproducible Master 23. Ask the students to read the directions silently; clarify any questions. Provide time for the students to complete the activity.

Pray Ask the students to bring their books and to gather in the prayer space. Invite the students ask Jesus silently to help them to be generous as he was. Then ask the students to open their books to page 327. Pray together "Prayer for Peace."

Plan Ahead for Day 2

Catechist Goal: To explain that greed blinds us to true happiness

Preparation: Have available chart paper and markers.

Chapter 23 • Day 2

Catechist Goal

- To explain that greed blinds us to true happiness

Our Faith Response

- To choose one way to overcome greed

 **greed**

Lesson Materials

- chart paper
- markers

As Catholics...

Religious Vows

After you have completed the lesson, read aloud the *As Catholics* text. Invite the students to respond to the question about ways to help religious communities in their work. Encourage the students to ask family members to help them learn about religious communities serving in the area. Remind the students, too, that they can learn more about religious communities on the Internet.

Jesus taught us to trust in God above all things.

WE GATHER

✝ *Lord, teach us what is important to you.*

Discuss each of these situations. How is the person being just or unjust?

When tickets to a concert go on sale, Mr. Maddie buys as many as he can. Then he sells the tickets to others at a much higher price.

Rella's aunt visits her and brings her a box of candy. Rella places the box on the kitchen table so the whole family can enjoy the candy.

A company hires six new workers as word processors. Three are given medical plans.

Now talk about the opposite of each of these situations.

WE BELIEVE

"You shall not covet your neighbor's house . . . nor anything else that belongs to him" (Exodus 20:17) reminds us not to get caught up in wanting things. We all need certain things to have a happy and healthy life. God hopes that we have those things. He calls us to help others have the things they need, too. However, when people are greedy they want more and more of something—for example, money or clothing. **Greed** is an excessive desire to have or own things.

262

Lesson Plan

WE GATHER ___ minutes

✝ **Pray** Pray together the Sign of the Cross and the *We Gather* prayer.

Focus on Life Organize the students into small groups to discuss the three *We Gather* situations and their opposites. After a few minutes invite volunteers to explain how the person in each situation is being just or unjust and to describe the opposite situation. Tell the students that in this lesson they will learn that Jesus taught us to trust in God above all things.

WE BELIEVE ___ minutes

Explore the Text Have the students silently read the *We Believe* statement. Then have volunteers read aloud the *We Believe* text. Emphasize the following:

- God wants us to have the things we need in order to live a happy and healthy life.
- God also wants us to help others to have the things they need.
- Greed can cause people to forget what is really important in life.
- Jesus taught us that trusting in God is more important than thinking about money and success.

Complete the Sentence Write the following sentence on the board: *I can guard against greed by* ________. Ask the students to write down the sentence and complete it. Invite volunteers to share their responses.

Do the Activity Have the students work with partners to rewrite for today Jesus' teaching in Luke 12:22–24. To

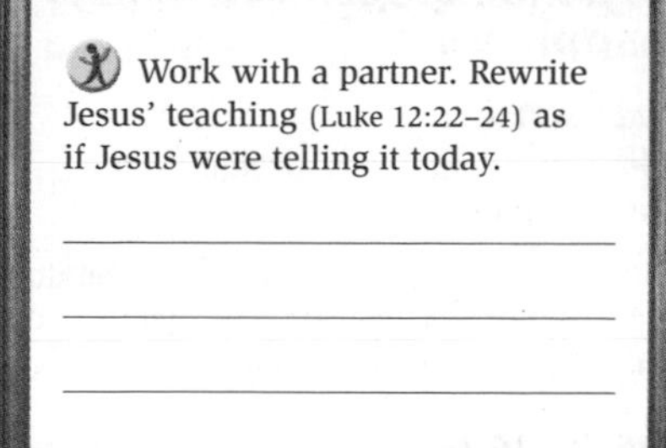

Work with a partner. Rewrite Jesus' teaching (Luke 12:22–24) as if Jesus were telling it today.

Think about these words of Jesus: "Take care to guard against all greed, for though one may be rich, one's life does not consist of possessions" (Luke 12:15).

When people are greedy they want things so much that they can forget the things that are important in life. They forget about the happiness that comes from loving God and others. They forget about living the way that Jesus taught us to live. Jesus taught us that trusting in God is more important than thinking about money and success.

Jesus said, "Therefore I tell you, do not worry about your life and what you will eat, or about your body and what you will wear. For life is more than food and the body more than clothing. Notice the ravens: they do not sow or reap; they have neither storehouse nor barn, yet God feeds them. How much more important are you than birds!" (Luke 12:22–24).

Talk about what Jesus' teaching means to you.

Key Word

greed an excessive desire to have or own things

WE RESPOND

What is important to you in your life? Why is it important? Does it help you to love God and others? What could you do to make God more important in your life?

As Catholics...

Some men and women devote their lives to Christ and to the Church. They become religious sisters, brothers, or priests. As members of religious communities, they make vows, or promises, to God. These vows are poverty, chastity, and obedience. In their religious communities they share everything for the common good. Their way of life gives them great freedom to serve God and their neighbors. They are not distracted by the desire for material things or power or fame.

With your family check to find out which religious communities are serving in or near your town or city. Find out more about them and their work. Is there any way that you can help in their work?

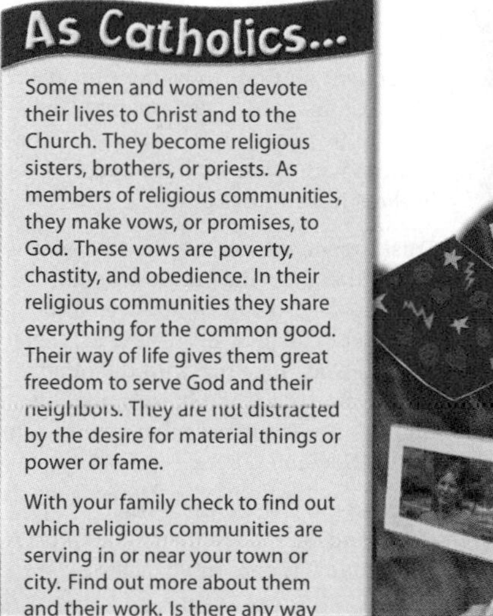

263

ACTIVITY BANK

Curriculum Connection

Social Studies

Activity Materials: map showing the Amazon rainforest, Internet and other research resources, poster board

The Amazon rainforest is the largest rainforest on earth. It supplies more than twenty percent of the oxygen we breathe. It is also home to a great variety of plants and animals. The rainforest is rapidly disappearing, however, due in part to people's greed. Invite the students to research ways to balance the needs of ranchers and farmers with the need to keep the rainforests from disappearing. Ask the students to consider the way the tenth commandment applies to our use of the world's natural resources as well as to money and other possessions. Have the students make posters describing ways that people can help preserve the rainforest.

spark the students' imagination, offer an example, such as, *Look at the caterpillars; they do not worry about designer clothes, yet God gives them butterfly wings!*

Quick Check

✔ *What is greed?* (Greed is an excessive desire to have or own things.)

✔ *Why does greediness interfere with loving God?* (When people are greedy, they want things so much that they forget the things that are important, such as loving God and others.)

WE RESPOND ___ minutes

Connect to Life Ask the students to read silently the *We Respond* questions, and allow time for them to formulate their responses. Pin up a large piece of chart paper and ask volunteers to name the things that are important to them and to say why. Write each response on the chart. Then encourage a discussion of the ways these things do or do not help us to love God and others. Finally, invite volunteers to say what they might do to make God more important in their lives.

Pray Gather in the prayer space. Invite volunteers to name things that God has provided for them. After each response, pray: *Lord, we thank you.*

Plan Ahead for Day 3

Catechist Goal: To describe what it means to be poor in spirit

Preparation: Be prepared to give examples of ways your parish gives and receives love.

Catechist Goal

- To describe what it means to be poor in spirit

Our Faith Response

- To explore ways to be poor in spirit

poor in spirit

Lesson Materials

- Grade 4 CD

Blessed are they...

Saint Thérèse of the Child Jesus

After you have completed the lesson, ask the students to read silently and think about the text. Point out that to be a flower in God's garden is to depend completely on him for everything—that is, to be poor in spirit. Then invite volunteers to name some of the things a fourth grader today might do to live as a flower in God's garden.

Depending upon God brings happiness.

YOU SHALL NOT COVET YOUR NEIGHBOR'S GOODS.

WE GATHER

✝ *God, we praise you for filling our hearts with joy.*

What makes you happy? What do you do when you are happy? How can you share that happiness with others?

WE BELIEVE

Jesus tells us that true happiness comes from loving God and living as Jesus did. Jesus said,

"Blessed are the poor in spirit,
for theirs is the kingdom of heaven"
(Matthew 5:3).

We are **poor in spirit** when we depend on God completely. Just as a child depends on her or his parents, so we should be dependent on God. To be poor in spirit we must be trusting and open to God's will. To be poor in spirit we need to be content with what we have and find joy in the simple things of life.

Trust, openness, and joy are the very words that describe people who are poor in spirit. They do not need a lot of things. The poor in spirit place their trust in God. Together with the other members of the Church, they are able to find the true happiness that comes from loving God and others.

People who live by the tenth commandment place their trust in God. They follow the example of Jesus.

poor in spirit those who depend on God completely

264

Jesus placed his trust in his Father. Jesus gave to those who were in need and cared for people who were sick or alone. Jesus asks all of his disciples to do the same. The Church shows that it is poor in spirit when it helps people who are in need.

Parish fair for the missions

Saint Paul was one of Jesus' disciples. He tried to help people believe in Jesus and live as Jesus did:

"I have never wanted anyone's silver or gold or clothing. You know well that these very hands have served my needs and my companions. In every way I have shown you that by hard work of that sort we must help the weak, and keep in mind the words of the Lord Jesus who himself said, 'It is more blessed to give than to receive'" (Acts of the Apostles 20:33–35).

Saint Paul did not waste time wishing that he had the money that some other people had. Saint Paul helped those in need because he followed the words of Jesus, "It is more blessed to give than to receive" (Acts of the Apostles 20:35). As long as we also follow these words of Jesus, we too will be honoring the tenth commandment.

Lesson Plan

WE GATHER ___ minutes

✝ **Pray** Pray the Sign of the Cross and the *We Gather* prayer.

Focus on Life Have the students read and respond to the *We Gather* questions. Introduce the *Chapter Story*. Tell the students that in this lesson they will learn that depending upon God brings happiness.

WE BELIEVE ___ minutes

Read the Text Read aloud the *We Believe* statement and the first *We Believe* paragraph. Then have volunteers read aloud the rest of the *We Believe* text. Emphasize the following:

- True happiness comes from loving God.
- We are called to be poor in spirit, which means we must be trusting and open to God's will.
- It is better to give than to receive.

Listen to the Music Play the refrain of the song "Blest Are They" on Grade 4 CD. Point out to the students that the lyrics of the song are based on the Beatitudes. Invite the students to relate the lyrics to the theme of this lesson.

Understand the Key Word Check the students' understanding of the word by asking them to name ways we can be poor in spirit. Examples might include trusting that God has a plan for us; loving God and others; not wanting an excess of material possessions.

Reflect on the Tenth Commandment Invite the students to use the questions as an examination of

Take a few moments to think quietly and prayerfully about ways you follow the tenth commandment. These questions may help you.

Do I wish that I had things that belong to others?

Am I sad when others have things that I would like?

Do I trust in God?

Am I willing to share with others?

When I get money as a gift or for my allowance, do I give some of it to the poor and needy in my community?

Am I happy with what I have or am I always asking for more things?

Blessed are they...

Saint Thérèse of the Child Jesus

Being poor in spirit means depending on God for everything. Even as a little girl, Thérèse knew that everything she had came from God. She loved God as much as she could. She thought of herself as a little flower in God's garden.

When she was only fifteen, she entered a monastery of religious sisters. There she prayed for the whole world. Before she died, she promised to spend her heaven in doing good upon earth. Her feast day is October 1.

"Blessed are the poor in spirit, for theirs is the kingdom of heaven." (Matthew 5:3)

WE RESPOND

Complete the chart by writing examples of ways you and your parish give and receive time, love, and gifts.

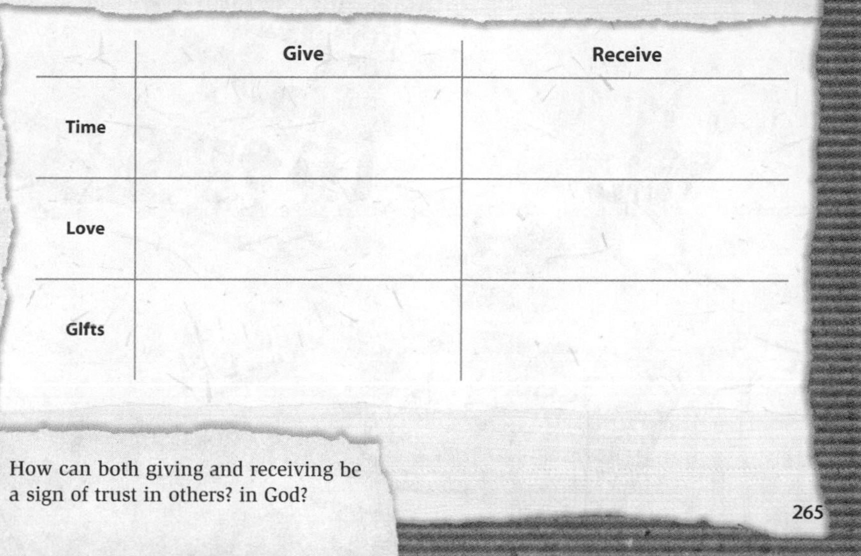

	Give	Receive
Time		
Love		
Gifts		

How can both giving and receiving be a sign of trust in others? in God?

ACTIVITY BANK

Mission

The Poor in Spirit

Activity Materials: mission materials

Missionaries try to lead lives that are truly poor in spirit. They often leave behind their family and friends. They may live in a country whose language and culture are unfamiliar to them. They must depend on God completely. Invite the students to research a mission society and to support the missions in some way. If your parish supports a specific mission society, obtain information about it and share the information. Ask the students to conduct research on the Internet to learn more about mission work. Invite the students to write letters to missionaries.

conscience. Encourage the students to think about ways to honor this commandment more fully.

Quick Check

✔ *What does it mean to be poor in spirit?* (To be poor in spirit is to depend upon God completely, to trust in God and find joy and happiness in the simple things in life.)

✔ *What did Jesus say was more important than receiving?* (Jesus said it is better to give than to receive.)

WE RESPOND

___ minutes

Connect to Life Read aloud the *We Respond* activity directions and draw the chart on the board. Give the students time to fill in their own charts. Then invite volunteers to share their responses. Write the students' comments in the appropriate boxes on the chart on the board. Finally, ask the students to share their responses to the final two questions.

Pray Gather in the prayer space and pray: *Lord, you taught us it is better to give than to receive. Help us to share what we have with others. Amen.*

Plan Ahead for Day 4

Catechist Goal: To emphasize that love of God and neighbor sums up the Ten Commandments

Preparation: Have available large self-stick labels and markers.

Chapter 23 • Day 4

Catechist Goal

- To emphasize that love of God and neighbor sums up the Ten Commandments

Our Faith Response

- To follow Jesus' example of loving God and others

Lesson Materials

- large self-stick labels
- markers

Teaching Note

The Writings of Saint Paul

Saint Paul encouraged Christians to keep the commandments but also challenged the followers of Christ to do everything in love. Paul tells us that it is not enough just to live by the rules. We are called by Jesus to show our love for God and our love for others in everything we do. Paul's famous passage in 1 Corinthians 13:2–5 eloquently describes true love.

Jesus teaches us that God's law is love.

WE GATHER

Christ, we want to love as you do.

Look at the sticker on the notebook—"God's law makes us happy!" It encourages others to live out the Ten Commandments.

Design your own stickers here to do the same.

God's Law is LOVE

GOD's Law Makes US HAPPY!

266

Lesson Plan

WE GATHER ___ minutes

Pray Pray together the Sign of the Cross and the *We Gather* prayer.

Focus on Life Have a volunteer read aloud the *We Gather* activity directions. Invite the students to sketch a design in the space provided. Then hand out large self-stick labels and markers and have the students make their own stickers. Tell the students that in this lesson they will learn that love is the fulfillment of God's law.

WE BELIEVE ___ minutes

Study the Text Have a volunteer read aloud the *We Believe* statement. Then have four volunteers read aloud the *We Believe* paragraphs. Pause to emphasize the following:

- Jesus' life is a perfect model of fulfilling God's law.
- We must follow the commandments with love for God, for ourselves, and for others.
- Love of God and neighbor sums up the Ten Commandments.

Quick Check

✔ *How did Jesus fulfill the law?* (Jesus lived the law with complete love for God and others.)

✔ *What sums up the Ten Commandments?* (Love of God and neighbor sums up the Ten Commandments.)

We Believe

In Jesus' life we see the perfect way to live God's law. Jesus followed the Ten Commandments. He was always faithful to God's law. Jesus said, "Do not think that I have come to abolish the law or the prophets. I have come not to abolish but to fulfill" (Matthew 5:17).

Jesus fulfilled the law by living it with complete love for God and others. Jesus showed that following the Ten Commandments brings the happiness that comes from friendship with God. When we follow the commandments, we must do so with love for God, ourselves, and others. Jesus said and did things that showed God's love. His life was one of holiness, complete love of his Father, and service to others. Jesus' life showed that the Holy Spirit was active and working in the world.

Jesus cared for those who were poor and comforted those who were sick. He accepted all people and helped them to feel God's love and care. Jesus called all people to look into their hearts, to be more giving, to go beyond their own needs to the needs of others. His life and his words showed us that we must love God above all things and our neighbor as ourselves.

We believe that love of God and neighbor sum up the Ten Commandments. In one of his letters to the early Christian community, Saint Paul wrote, "Love is the fulfillment of the law" (Romans 13:10).

We Respond

Each day this week watch for people who are living out the Ten Commandments. Family members, friends and classmates, and people in your parish and neighborhood are among those who can show us how to love God and neighbor.

With a partner, make up a song to describe ways people live out the Ten Commandments.

____

____

____

____

____

What will you do this week to be an example to others?

Activity Bank

Meeting Individual Needs

Students with Attention Deficit Disorder

Students with attention deficit disorder benefit from activities that involve movement. Invite the students to play charades. Ask them to act out ways of keeping God's law. These role-plays should relate to living any of the commandments. Allow the students to perform these role-plays individually, with a partner, or in small groups. Have the student or students who are first to guess the theme of each role-play take the next turn.

Curriculum Connection

Art

Activity Materials: drawing paper, markers, crayons, or paints

Have the students work individually or in pairs to draw comic strips showing people following the tenth commandment. You may wish to show students a variety of sample comic strips from the daily or Sunday newspaper to stimulate their imagination.

We Respond

___ minutes

Connect to Life Read aloud the *We Respond* paragraph and the activity directions. Form the class into pairs to work on the songs. As a help you might suggest that the students set new words to familiar tunes or write rhythmic recitations that do not depend on music. Allow time for composition; then invite the pairs to perform their songs for the class. When all have finished, read the final question and invite responses.

Pray Gather in the prayer space and pray Psalm 40:9:

To do your will is my delight;
My God, your law is in my heart.
Amen.

Plan Ahead for Day 5

Catechist Goal: To review chapter ideas and their relationship to our faith life

Preparation: Make copies of Chapter 23 Test in the Grade 4 Assessment Book (option); have available magazines and newspapers, folders, and pieces of poster board for the Assessment activity.

Chapter 23 • **Day 5**

Catechist Goal

- To review chapter ideas and their relationship to our faith life

Our Faith Response

- To apply what has been learned to our lives

CHAPTER TEST

Chapter 23 Test is provided in the Grade 4 Assessment Book.

Grade 4
Chapter 23

Write the letter of the phrase that defines each of the following:

1. __c__ envy
2. __d__ greed
3. __a__ poor in spirit
4. __b__ tenth commandment

a. those who depend on God completely

b. teaches us to examine our thoughts and feelings about the goods of this world

c. a feeling of sadness when someone else has the things we want for ourselves

d. an excessive desire to have or own things

Write True or False for the following sentences. Then change the false sentences to make them true.

5. __True__ True happiness comes from loving God and living as Jesus did.

6. __False__ People who are loving and giving develop an envious heart.
People who are loving and giving develop a generous heart.

7. __True__ Trust in God is more important than money and success.

8. __True__ We must follow God's law by loving God, self, and others.

9–10. Write a short paragraph about the importance of the tenth commandment.

With your family, find pictures and articles of people, groups, or organizations who are living out the Ten Commandments. Design a display highlighting the good works of people living as Jesus taught us.

Lesson Plan

___ minutes

Chapter Review Ask the students to complete questions 1–8, and ask volunteers to read aloud the correct answers. Then read aloud question 9–10. Allow time for the students to complete their sentences. Then invite volunteers to share what they have written.

Assessment Activity Read aloud the Assessment activity directions. Provide magazines and newspapers to the students and let them search for and cut out appropriate pictures and articles. Give each student a manila folder for the clippings and a piece of poster board. Encourage the students to take these materials home and to work on their displays with their families. Invite the students to bring the finished displays to class after the weekend.

___ minutes

Reflect & Pray Read aloud the paragraph and invite the students to complete and write out their individual prayers to Jesus. Suggest that they take these prayers home to pray each day.

Key Words Write the three *Key Words* on the board. Invite volunteers to define each one and use it in a sentence.

Remember Ask the students to read silently the *We Believe* statements and think of two ways to live out each statement. Invite volunteers to share their responses.

We Respond in Faith

Reflect & Pray

Jesus tells us that true happiness comes from trusting God and depending upon him as Jesus did. This is what it means to be poor in spirit.

Jesus, I want to be poor in spirit. Help me to

____

____

Key Words

envy (p. 260)
greed (p. 263)
poor in spirit (p. 264)

Remember

- We are called to have generous hearts.
- Jesus taught us to trust in God above all things.
- Depending upon God brings happiness.
- Jesus teaches us that God's law is love.

Our Catholic Life

Care for God's Creation

Care for God's creation is an important part of our faith. God gave us a beautiful world, and it is up to all of us to protect God's gifts. We are to treat every part of creation with respect: people, animals, plants, land, water, and air. We must make sure that animals are cared for properly, not neglected or treated cruelly. Plants and trees are very important to a healthy environment, and we must take care of them.

Saint Isidore and Saint Maria are the patron saints of farmers and agricultural workers. They were a married couple who were farmers in Spain. They cared respectfully for animals and were generous in helping those who were poor.

Chapter 23 • Day 5

Home Connection

Sharing Faith with My Family

Invite the students to read and discuss the story of Blessed Pope John XXIII with their families. Encourage the students to ask family members who are old enough to remember this pope and the council he called to recall those exciting days.

Remind the students to take home the materials for their "Living the Commandments" displays, and make sure to send home the family page (text page 270).

For additional information and activities, encourage families to visit Sadlier's

www.WEBELIEVEweb.com

Our Catholic Life Ask two volunteers to read aloud the *Our Catholic Life* paragraphs. Emphasize that caring for animals is another way to show respect and love for God's creation. Encourage the students to visit the library or the Internet to learn more about Saint Isidore and Saint Maria.

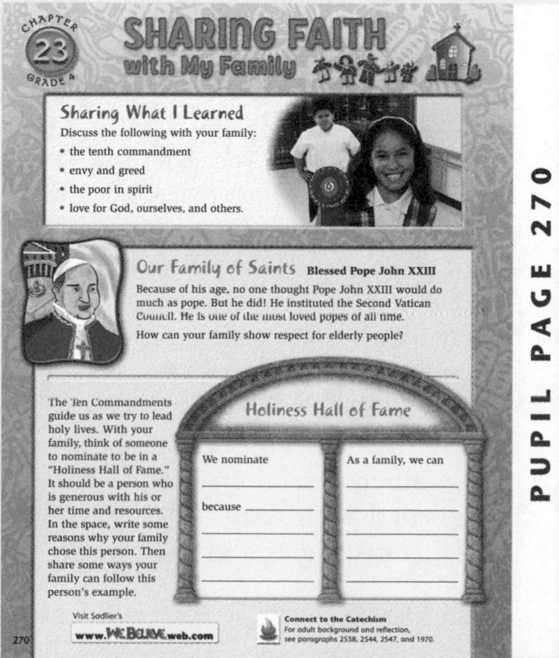

Chapter 23 Grade 4

SHARING FAITH with My Family

Sharing What I Learned

Discuss the following with your family:
- the tenth commandment
- envy and greed
- the poor in spirit
- love for God, ourselves, and others.

Our Family of Saints **Blessed Pope John XXIII**

Because of his age, no one thought Pope John XXIII would do much as pope. But he did! He instituted the Second Vatican Council. He is one of the most loved popes of all time.

How can your family show respect for elderly people?

The Ten Commandments guide us as we try to lead holy lives. With your family, think of someone to nominate to be in a "Holiness Hall of Fame." It should be a person who is generous with his or her time and resources. In the space, write some reasons why your family chose this person. Then share some ways your family can follow this person's example.

Holiness Hall of Fame

We nominate ____________ because ____________

As a family, we can ____________

Visit Sadlier's www.WEBELIEVEweb.com

Connect to the Catechism
For adult background and reflection, see paragraphs 2538, 2544, 2547, and 1970.

270

PUPIL PAGE 270

Chapter 24 We Grow in Holiness

Overview

In Chapter 23 the students learned that the tenth commandment calls us to have thankful hearts and to not envy other people or desire their things. In this chapter the students will learn that we grow in holiness through prayer, the sacraments, and the gifts of the Holy Spirit.

Doctrinal Content	For Adult Reading and Reflection *Catechism of the Catholic Church*
The students will learn:	Paragraph
• Jesus is our model of holiness.	1698
• We open our hearts and minds in prayer..	2766
• The sacraments draw us closer to God.	1123
• The Holy Spirit shares special gifts with us.	1831

liturgy (p. 276)
sacrament (p. 276)
gifts of the Holy Spirit (p. 279)
fruits of the Holy Spirit (p. 279)

Catechist Background

What would happen if the world were suddenly deprived of air?

The Holy Spirit is to our spiritual existence what air is to our physical existence. In fact, the Spirit is sometimes referred to as the breath of God and is represented by wind or moving air.

The Holy Spirit enables us to proclaim "Jesus is Lord" (1 Corinthians 12:3). The Spirit wells up in our hearts and bursts out with the words " Abba! Father!" (Galatians 4:6). The Spirit offers us the grace to know the only true God and the one whom he sent, Jesus Christ (John 17:3). The Holy Spirit gives us our knowledge of the faith and touches us first so that we may touch Christ. And through Baptism, the Spirit communicates with us in a manner both intimate and personal.

The Holy Spirit is the life force of the Church. The Spirit inspires the Scriptures, through which "the Church constantly finds her nourishment and her strength" (CCC 104). The Holy Spirit makes Christianity a living and vibrant religion by continually renewing the Church throughout history. The Spirit guides the Church and preserves her in truth until Jesus returns at the end of time. The Spirit puts us into communion with Christ through the sacramental liturgy.

We can appreciate God the Holy Spirit by seeing the results, or fruits, of the Spirit. We see these in the lives of Christian people who strive to live by the gospel of Jesus Christ. Through their lives we find the fruits of the Spirit as promised in the letter to the Galatians: "love, joy, peace, patience, kindness, generosity, faithfulness, gentleness, self-control" (5:22–23).

In what ways is the Holy Spirit working in your life today?

Lesson Planning Guide

Lesson Focus	Presentation	Materials
Day 1		
page 271 **We Gather in Prayer** **pages 272–273** *Jesus is our model of holiness.*	• Pray to the Holy Spirit. Respond in song. Complete the **We Gather** activity. • Read and discuss Jesus as our perfect model of holiness in the **We Believe** text. Do the map activity. • Answer the **We Respond** questions. • Pray together.	For the prayer space: basket; slips of paper for prayer petitions; picture or statue of Jesus; Bible "You Call Us to Live," Christopher Walker, #26, Grade 4 CD
Day 2		
pages 274–275 *We open our hearts and minds in prayer.*	• Discuss the **We Gather** questions. • Read and discuss the **We Believe** text. Match Jesus' ways and words of praying in the activity. Complete the **We Respond** activity. • Pray the Our Father.	
Day 3		
pages 276–277 *The sacraments draw us closer to God.*	• Discuss the **We Gather** questions. • Read about the liturgy and sacraments in the **We Believe** text. Write song titles for sacraments in the activity. • Answer the **We Respond** questions. • Read and discuss *As Catholics.*	
Day 4		
pages 278–279 *The Holy Spirit shares special gifts with us.*	• Discuss the **We Gather** questions. • Read and discuss gifts of the Holy Spirit in **We Believe** and complete chart. • Read about fruits of the Holy Spirit. Plan a short play for the activity. • For the **We Respond**, pray together.	• copies of Reproducible Master 24, guide page 271G (option)
Day 5		
page 280 **Review** **pages 281–282** **We Respond in Faith**	• Complete questions 1–10. Work on the *Assessment Activity.* • Complete the *Reflect & Pray* activity. • Review *Remember* and *Key Words.* • Read and discuss *Our Catholic Life.* • Discuss **Sharing Faith with My Family**.	• Chapter 24 in the Assessment Book, pp. 47–48 • Chapter 24 Test in the Test Generator • Review & Resource Book, pp. 55–57 • Family Book, pp. 68–70

For additional ideas, activities, and opportunities: Visit Sadlier's **www.WEBELIEVEweb.com**

Enrichment Ideas

Chapter Story

For as long as Tony could remember, it had always been Dad, Gram, and Tony. Tony's dad was a police officer and sometimes had to work long hours. So, most of the time, it was just Tony and Gram who did things together.

When Tony was little, some of his classmates thought it was funny that Gram practiced baseball with him and took him to his scouting meetings. But by fourth grade, all of the kids had got used to Gram. Some of them called her "Gram," too.

Today Tony was rushing to get ready for his basketball game. "Come on, Tony, we have to hurry," Gram said. "There probably will be a lot of traffic. It's rush hour, you know."

"Yeah, Gram, I know. Did you find my jersey?" Tony asked. "I sure did! It was under your bed!" Gram replied.

At the game Gram, in her baseball cap and sneakers, sat with the parents. It was always easy to pick Gram out of the crowd. She was the one cheering the loudest for Tony's team, the Falcons.

"That was a great game!" Gram said when it was over, even though the Falcons had lost. Tony felt bad because he had missed a couple of shots, but Gram never mentioned things like that. She talked only about the things Tony did well.

"Tony, don't forget that we have to tackle that long division tonight," Gram reminded him. "I promised Mrs. Chen, your math teacher, that we'd work on it a little each night. Do you have any other homework?"

"I do. For religion I have to write about someone I know who follows the example of Jesus' life. Mr. Olson wants us to tell what makes this person holy."

"That sounds like a hard assignment," Gram said. "Whom will you write about?" "It's not really hard," Tony replied. "I'm going to write about you!"

▶ *Why did Tony chose to write about Gram for his religion homework?*

FAITH and MEDIA

▶ On Day 3 the students read an *As Catholics* text about the Liturgy of the Hours and talk about their favorite times of prayer. This is a good time to remind the students that cyberspace can be a place for prayer. To do this, bookmark a variety of prayer-centered Web sites for the students to visit. Several sites offer all the prayers of the Liturgy of the Hours. There are also a number of Web sites, such as the Irish Jesuits' *Sacred Space*, that offer daily prayers, reflections, and Scripture readings in a variety of languages.

CHAPTER PROJECT: A CLASS QUILT OF THE SACRAMENTS

Provide the students with squares of fabric and fabric markers. Ask each student to select one sacrament. Then invite the students to use the fabric squares and markers to design symbols that will remind people of their chosen sacraments. Remind the students of such symbols as water (Baptism), a dove or flame (Confirmation), a chalice and host (the Eucharist), a peace sign (Reconciliation), holy oil (Anointing of the Sick), wedding rings (Matrimony), and a stole (Holy Orders). Encourage the students to think of other symbols as well. Design a center square for the quilt that reads *The Seven Sacraments*. Place the sacrament squares on a cloth backing and glue or sew them together. Display the quilt in a school hallway or in the church.

Connections

To Liturgy

Keep the students and their families informed about liturgies and seasonal observances celebrated by the parish. Encourage the students and their families to attend. Check with the parish's director of liturgy to find out about other opportunities for prayer with members of the parish community.

To Community

The gifts of the Holy Spirit help us to follow the example of Jesus' life. Encourage the students to use these gifts. For example, we can use the gift of understanding to show love for members of the community who feel neglected. We can visit people who cannot leave their homes and the elderly and listen to them. Invite the students to think of additional ways to use these gifts to serve others.

To Vocations

Talk to the students about religious orders and communities that people can join to serve God in a special way. Tell the students about contemplative orders. Explain that these cloistered women and men have chosen to serve God by devoting their lives to prayer. Share stories with students about contemplative saints such as Thérèse of the Child Jesus, Benedict of Nursia, and Brigid of Kildare.

Meeting Individual Needs

Students with Developmental Needs

Fourth grade is a turning point for many students. In every classroom there are probably a few students who are struggling with the academic and social demands of the middle grades. The developmental needs of these students may range from coping with developmental demands to more serious challenges such as language and processing deficits. Be patient with these students and work with them to achieve their full potential.

ADDITIONAL RESOURCES

Books *Prayers and Practices for Young Catholics,* William H. Sadlier, 1997. On pages 5–6 the young Catholic is guided through traditional prayers and various forms of prayer.

A Quiet Place with Jesus, Anne Joan Flanagan and Sheila Anne Smith, Pauline Books and Media, 1996. This book of meditations helps children grow in holiness.

To find more ideas for books, videos, and other learning material, visit Sadlier's

www.WEBELIEVEweb.com

Using Music

by Jack Miffleton

Jack Miffleton is a composer and teacher, known internationally for his work in children's religious education. His songs are sung in classrooms and churches around the world. Currently, he teaches music at St. Jarlath's School in Oakland, California.

"Among the many signs and symbols used by the Church to celebrate its faith, music is of preeminent importance." *(Music in Catholic Worship §23)*

It is difficult to imagine catechesis with primary and middle grade children without music, movement and song. It is a natural and spontaneous way that children express themselves. Punctuating a lesson with songs and acclamations is good pedagogy, good religion, and children like it!

Singing is good pedagogy. Young children have short attention spans. Movement and song are aids in helping them focus. Regular singing can help establish an easy rapport between catechist and child by allowing the catechist to enter the world of the child without being "childish." Singing the Scriptures adds a unique dimension to the process of hearing and learning about God's word. If students can sing it, they will remember it. Modern Catholic hymnals are filled with Scripture in song. Recorded songs or instrumental music can create an atmosphere of reverence during a quiet time or while your students are involved in individual or group projects.

Singing is good religion. "One who sings, prays twice," wrote Saint Augustine. Using music in a catechetical setting is not just a practical teaching device; it is also good religious education. The liturgies of the Church are sung prayers. From the beginning, children can benefit from an approach to prayer and catechesis that is modeled on liturgy. In liturgy, for example, a verbal proclamation is usually followed by a sung response. Acclamatory song can highlight a lesson or classroom activity. Beginning and ending a class with a seasonal psalm or song refrain can draw students into the liturgical year without preaching about it.

Singing is fun! An important aspect of catechesis is the socialization and friendships that take place among the children in your class or group. Singing with one voice strengthens this process of community building. Even when singing together just for fun, Christian children model what they are as one Body of Christ.

Catechist Development Topics (Topic and Guide Page)

Resources

Rise Up and Sing. (Second Edition) Young People's Music Resource. Portland: Oregon Catholic Press.

Singing Our Faith. A New Hymnal for Children. Chicago: GIA Publications, Inc.

Ways to Implement Using Music

- Select songs that express something to which the students can relate—nature, a joy, a sadness, a pet, a relative. Choose lyrics that contain something that parallels what the children are learning.

- For the primary grades, choose songs with movements and repetition. There are many catechetical songs that are developed to help children at the primary levels make connections between their everyday life and their faith.

- Middle grade children will enjoy and benefit from songs that pique their curiosity or require a challenge, for example, songs celebrating biblical personalities or a Bible story put to verse. Middle grade children will also relate more directly to the meaning of the words and can understand the place and flow of music in liturgy.

- Catechists can usually do more in song than they think. In planning a lesson first look at the music recommended by the *We Believe* program. The Scripture text or the topic of the lesson may suggest a song or refrain you already know. Get acquainted with some of the many musical resources developed for children.

- Teaching a song should not be tedious. When children like a song, they will take it over quickly. "Call and response" or "echo" style songs will have the children singing immediately. Songs that are more complicated or contain several verses can be learned a little at a time over several classes.

- The use of recorded music can be helpful in supporting the singing. Be sure to review the songs on the We Believe CD before class so that you can fully engage the children when leading the group in song.

- Remember—children will readily sing without accompaniment. Use movements and gestures to animate the song.

For additional ideas, activities, and opportunities, visit Sadlier's

www.WEBELIEVEweb.com

With thanks to:
Sister Maureen Viani, SNJM
Christ the King Church
Pleasant Hill, California

With the assistance of volunteer musicians singing is included within our faith sessions. The children gather bi-weekly in their respective grade levels for fifteen minutes of singing. The musicians involve the children in movement, gesture, and prayer using age-appropriate psalms, acclamations, and hymns, which support and enhance their sharing and reflecting around the Sunday readings. Besides allowing the children an opportunity to encounter God's presence through song, these sessions have helped build a repertoire of songs that continue to enhance and strengthen our prayer gatherings and Eucharistic celebrations.

Notes

Name ____

Unscramble the letters to find the gifts of the Holy Spirit.

1. DUNSERNAGTIND

___ ___ ___ ___ ___ ___ ___ ___ ___ ___ ___ ___ ___

2. DONWER DAN WEA

___ ___ ___ ___ ___ ___   ___ ___ ___   ___ ___ ___

3. GRITH TENGMUDJ

___ ___ ___ ___ ___   ___ ___ ___ ___ ___ ___ ___ ___

4. DOGKENWEL

___ ___ ___ ___ ___ ___ ___ ___ ___

5. VEERCREEN

___ ___ ___ ___ ___ ___ ___ ___ ___

6. MIDWOS

___ ___ ___ ___ ___ ___

7. ACEGORU

___ ___ ___ ___ ___ ___ ___

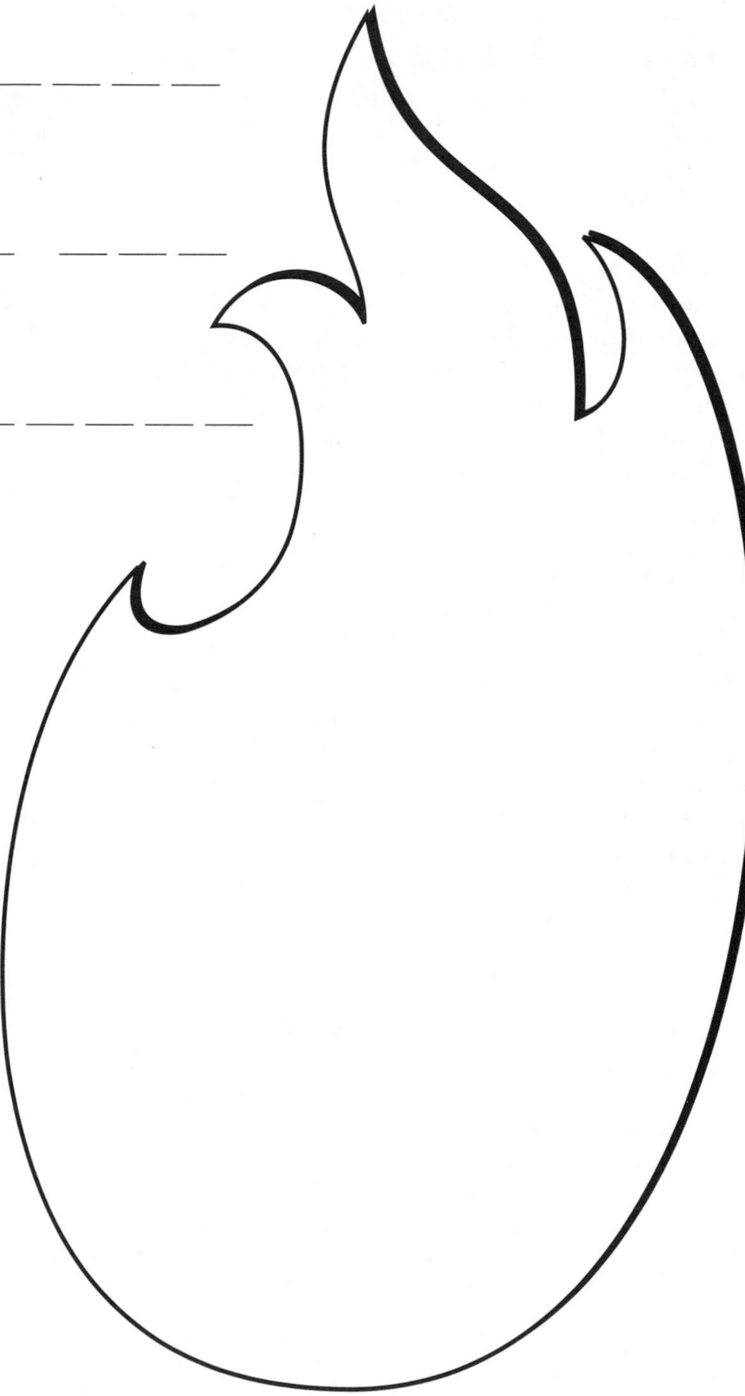

Choose one gift of the Holy Spirit.
In the flame, write or illustrate ways
you see people living out that gift.
Give a title to your work.

We Grow in Holiness 24

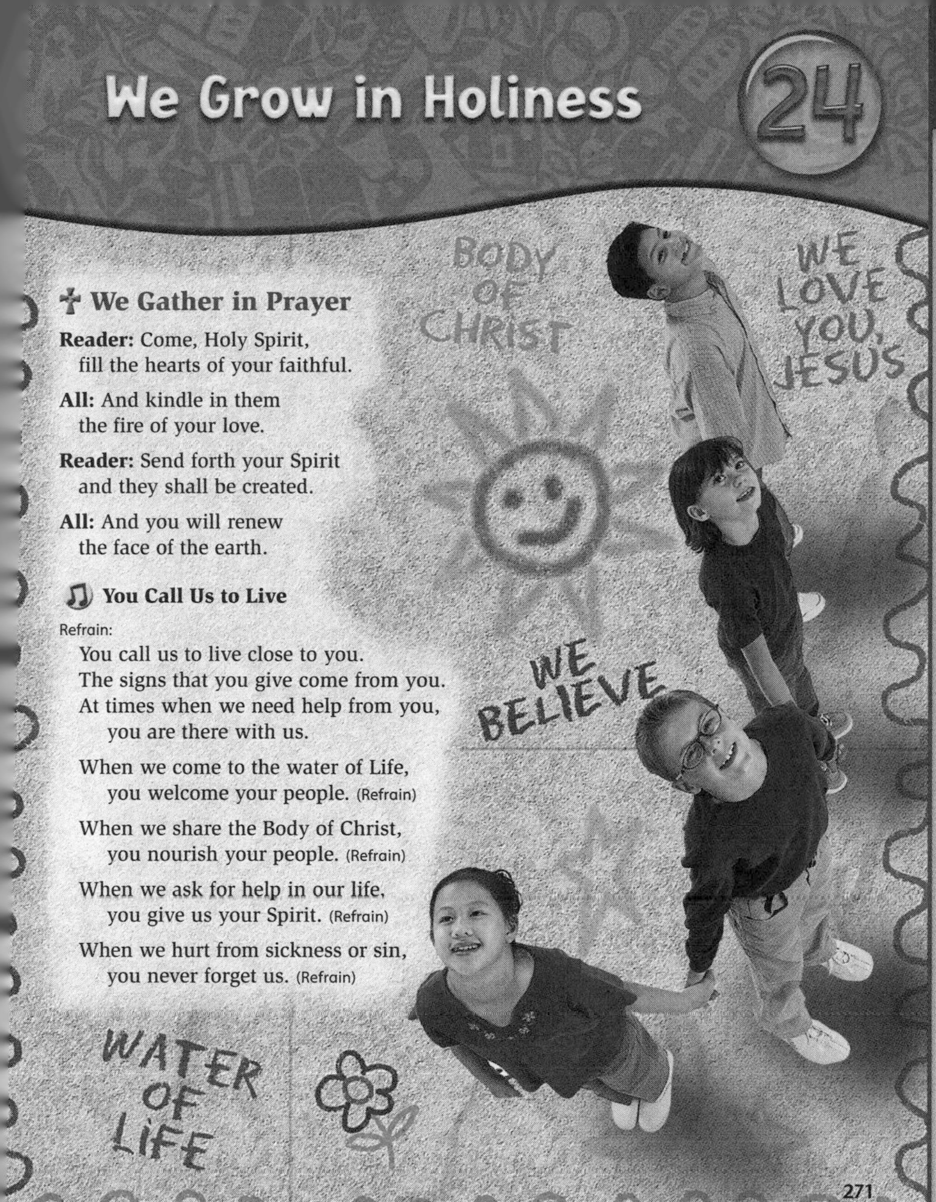

We Gather in Prayer
Reader: Come, Holy Spirit, fill the hearts of your faithful.
All: And kindle in them the fire of your love.
Reader: Send forth your Spirit and they shall be created.
All: And you will renew the face of the earth.
You Call Us to Live
Refrain:
You call us to live close to you.
The signs that you give come from you.
At times when we need help from you,
you are there with us.
When we come to the water of Life,
you welcome your people. (Refrain)
When we share the Body of Christ,
you nourish your people. (Refrain)
When we ask for help in our life,
you give us your Spirit. (Refrain)
When we hurt from sickness or sin,
you never forget us. (Refrain)
BODY OF CHRIST
WE LOVE YOU, JESUS
WE BELIEVE
WATER OF LIFE
271

PREPARING TO PRAY

In this prayer the students will call on the Holy Spirit to fill their hearts and strengthen them to live as disciples of Christ.

• Select a student to be the reader. Allow time for the reader and the other students to read over the prayer and the group responses.

• Play the song "You Call Us to Live" by Christopher Walker, #26 on the Grade 4 CD. Practice the song with the students.

• Invite the students to think about special petitions for which they would like to pray. Hand out small slips of paper and have the students write their intentions on the slips. Explain that they will place these in the basket in the prayer space at the end of the gathering prayer.

The Prayer Space

• In the prayer space place a basket and additional slips of paper for prayer petitions, a picture or statue of Jesus, and a Bible.

This Week's Liturgy

Visit **www.webelieveweb.com** for this week's liturgical readings and other seasonal material.

Lesson Plan

We Gather in Prayer ___ minutes

Pray

• Invite the students to gather in the prayer space with their books open to the gathering prayer.

• Pray the Sign of the Cross and signal the reader to begin the opening prayer.

• At the end of the service invite the students to place their prayer petition slips in the basket.

Home Connection Update

Invite volunteers to describe the ways they shared the Chapter 23 family page over the weekend. Ask: *What have you learned about Blessed Pope John XXIII?* Then invite the students to present the commandment displays they made for the Chapter 23 *Assessment* activity. Encourage the class to guess which commandments are being followed in each display.

Catechist Goal

- To present Jesus as our model of holiness

Our Faith Response

- To choose one way to be more like Jesus

Teaching Tip

Cooperative Learning Groups

When the students are collaborating in small group settings, ensure that everyone has an equal opportunity to participate. To do this, check that each member of a group has specific responsibilities. Holding each student accountable for a specific part of a project helps to ensure that the workload is divided. When you assess a group presentation, have each member describe, either orally or in writing, what part he or she had in the project. This will help you keep track of the way each person participated in the activity.

Jesus is our model of holiness.

WE GATHER

✝ *All holy, all loving God, keep us close to you.*

Answer these questions. Then share your answers with the class.

What does it mean to be holy?

____

____

What adjectives would you use to describe a holy person?

____

____

WE BELIEVE

God is all good and holy. He wants us to be holy, too. So God the Father sent his Son into the world to share his divine life with us. By his life, death, and Resurrection, Jesus frees us from sin and shares God's life and holiness with us.

Holiness is sharing in God's goodness and responding to God's love by the way we live. Being holy means being like God. Our holiness comes from grace, the gift of God's life that we first receive in Baptism. As members of the Church, we are called to grow in holiness. We grow in holiness when we

- believe in Jesus
- live as Jesus did, working for justice and peace
- pray
- celebrate the sacraments and respond to God's gift of himself.

Jesus Christ is the perfect model, or example, of holiness because he is the Son of God. Jesus put God his Father first in his life. The things Jesus did and the ways he treated others showed how important God was to him. Jesus trusted his Father completely and prayed to him often. Jesus lived by the commandments, loved others, and helped all those in need.

By his words and actions Jesus teaches us to be holy. He teaches us to love God and others, help those in need, and work for justice and peace. If we follow Jesus, he will lead us to holiness. We will grow in God's love.

272

Lesson Plan

WE GATHER

___ minutes

✝ **Pray** Pray the Sign of the Cross and the *We Gather* prayer.

Focus on Life Ask the students to read the *We Gather* questions. As a help, suggest that the students think of a person they consider to be holy. Invite them to think of the ways this person is like Jesus. Invite volunteers to share their responses. Tell the students that in this lesson they will learn that Jesus is our model of holiness.

WE BELIEVE

___ minutes

Discuss the Word Ask a volunteer to read aloud the *We Believe* statement. Then invite the students to define the word *model.* Explain that a role model is someone we follow and try to imitate. Read the *Chapter Story* and ask the question that follows. Then ask the students to name people whom they consider to be role models.

Read the Text Have volunteers read aloud the *We Believe* paragraphs. Pause to emphasize the following:

- Holiness is sharing in God's goodness.
- Our holiness comes from the gift of God's grace.
- Jesus is the perfect model of holiness because he is the Son of God.
- By his words and actions Jesus teaches us to be holy.

Design "Paths to Holiness" Maps Ask the students to read silently the directions to the *We Believe* activity. Remind the students that a map offers a set of directions or provides a process for doing something,

WE RESPOND

Who are some people who lead others to holiness?
In what ways are they an example to you?
What can you do to be an example of holiness, too?

273

ACTIVITY BANK

Multiple Intelligences

Linguistic

Activity Materials: Internet and other research resources

Review the bulleted list of ways we grow in holiness. Then invite the students to write "how-to" stories describing ways to live a holy life. Explain that a how-to story offers a set of directions or provides a process for doing something, and that writers of how-to stories often use transition words such as *first, second, next, then,* and *finally*. When all have had time to finish, invite volunteers to share their stories. Post the stories on the bulletin board.

but a map does it with diagrams and images rather than with words. Allow time for the students to complete and share their maps.

Quick Check

✔ *What is holiness?* (Holiness is sharing in God's goodness and responding to God's love by the way we live.)

✔ *How can we grow in holiness?* (We can grow in holiness by believing in Jesus, living as Jesus did, praying, and celebrating the sacraments.)

WE RESPOND ___ minutes

Connect to Life Invite a volunteer to read aloud the three *We Respond* questions and invite responses. Then ask the students to write down the names of saints, public figures, and people in their own lives who lead them to holiness and to tell the way each of these people serves as an example. Finally, have the students write what they can do to be examples of holiness. Encourage the students to take these lists home and review them regularly.

Pray Conclude by praying: *Dear God, you sent your Son, Jesus, to be a perfect example of holiness. Help us to imitate his example of peace, love, and justice. Amen.*

Plan Ahead for Day 2

Catechist Goal: To explain the benefits of prayer

Preparation: Be prepared to discuss the Lord's Prayer as the most perfect prayer and the summation of Jesus' teachings.

Chapter 24 • **Day 2**

Catechist Goal

- To explain the benefits of prayer

Our Faith Response

- To identify ways that we can talk and listen to God in prayer

Teaching Tip

Bulletin Board of Prayers

Post the heading *Prayers to Share* on a bulletin board. Tack a series of manila pocket folders to the board. Label the folders *Morning Prayers, Prayers Before Meals, Evening Prayers, Prayers to the Blessed Mother, Prayers for the Sick, Prayers for Peace*, and so on. Be sure to label one folder *Original Prayers* to allow the students to share their own prayers. Make copies of prayers that fit each category and place them in the appropriate folders. Invite the students to place copies of other prayers that they know in the folders, and encourage them to write their own prayers for the *Original Prayers* folder. Gather regularly to pray these prayers together.

We open our hearts and minds in prayer.

WE GATHER

✝ *Lord, teach us to pray.*

Think of someone you really like to spend time with. Is it easy for you to talk to this person? Why or why not?

WE BELIEVE

Prayer is a way that we communicate with God and a way that God communicates with us. We pray to God by listening and talking to him with our minds and hearts. When we open our minds and hearts to God, we respond to God's invitation to love him. We welcome God into our lives.

God the Holy Spirit helps us to pray and know what God wants us to do in our lives. The Holy Spirit helps us to be open to God's will for us.

Prayer is an important part of our call to holiness. Prayer helps us to be more trusting. It helps us to rely on God and to know what God wants us to do in our lives. Praying helps us to be strong believers. It strengthens us to follow Jesus' example. It helps us to live out our faith.

During his life on earth Jesus prayed often. In his family he learned the prayers of his Jewish faith. Jesus often prayed the psalms, and went to the synagogue to pray. In the gospels we find examples of different ways Jesus prayed.

Work with a partner. Match the way Jesus prayed to the words he used. Write **a, b, c,** or **d** on the line.

Ways Jesus Prayed

a. Jesus praised his Father as the source of all that is good.

b. Jesus asked to do the will of his Father.

c. Jesus trusted his Father to show mercy to others.

d. Jesus thanked his Father.

Words of Jesus

__c__ "Father, forgive them, they know not what they do." (Luke 23:34)

__a__ "I give praise to you, Father, Lord of heaven and earth." (Matthew 11:25)

__d__ "Father, I thank you for hearing me. I know that you always hear me." (John 11:41–42)

__b__ "Father, if you are willing, take this cup away from me; still, not my will but yours be done." (Luke 22:42)

274

Lesson Plan

WE GATHER ___ minutes

✝ **Pray** Pray the Sign of the Cross and the *We Gather* prayer together.

Focus on Life Read aloud the *We Gather* questions. Encourage volunteers to describe the activities—sports, games, and hobbies—they share with the person they have named, and the feelings they have when they talk with this person. Tell the students that in this lesson they will learn that we can open our hearts and minds to God in prayer.

WE BELIEVE ___ minutes

Learn About Prayer Invite a student to read aloud the *We Believe* statement. Then ask volunteers to read aloud the first three *We Believe* paragraphs. Pause to emphasize the following:

- In prayer we listen and talk to God. We communicate with him, and he communicates with us.
- The Holy Spirit helps us to be open to God's will for us.
- Prayer is an important part of our call to holiness. It helps us to follow Jesus' example and to live our faith.

Pray As Jesus Prayed Organize the students into pairs. Ask the pairs to read the fourth *We Believe* paragraph quietly together and then to read and complete the activity. Allow time for the pairs to finish; then have volunteers read aloud the correct answers. Ask: *Can you think of times when we might pray these words of Jesus? What are those times?* Invite responses.

Jesus' disciples wanted to pray as he did. So Jesus taught them the Lord's Prayer. The Lord's Prayer is also called the Our Father. The Lord's Prayer sums up Jesus' teachings. When we pray the Lord's Prayer, we are reminded that God is a loving Father. We turn to God in trust and hope. We call on God the Father because Jesus his Son did.

The Lord's Prayer is the most perfect prayer and it is an important part of all of our liturgy. Every time we pray "thy will be done," we are promising to follow God's will in our daily lives just as Jesus did.

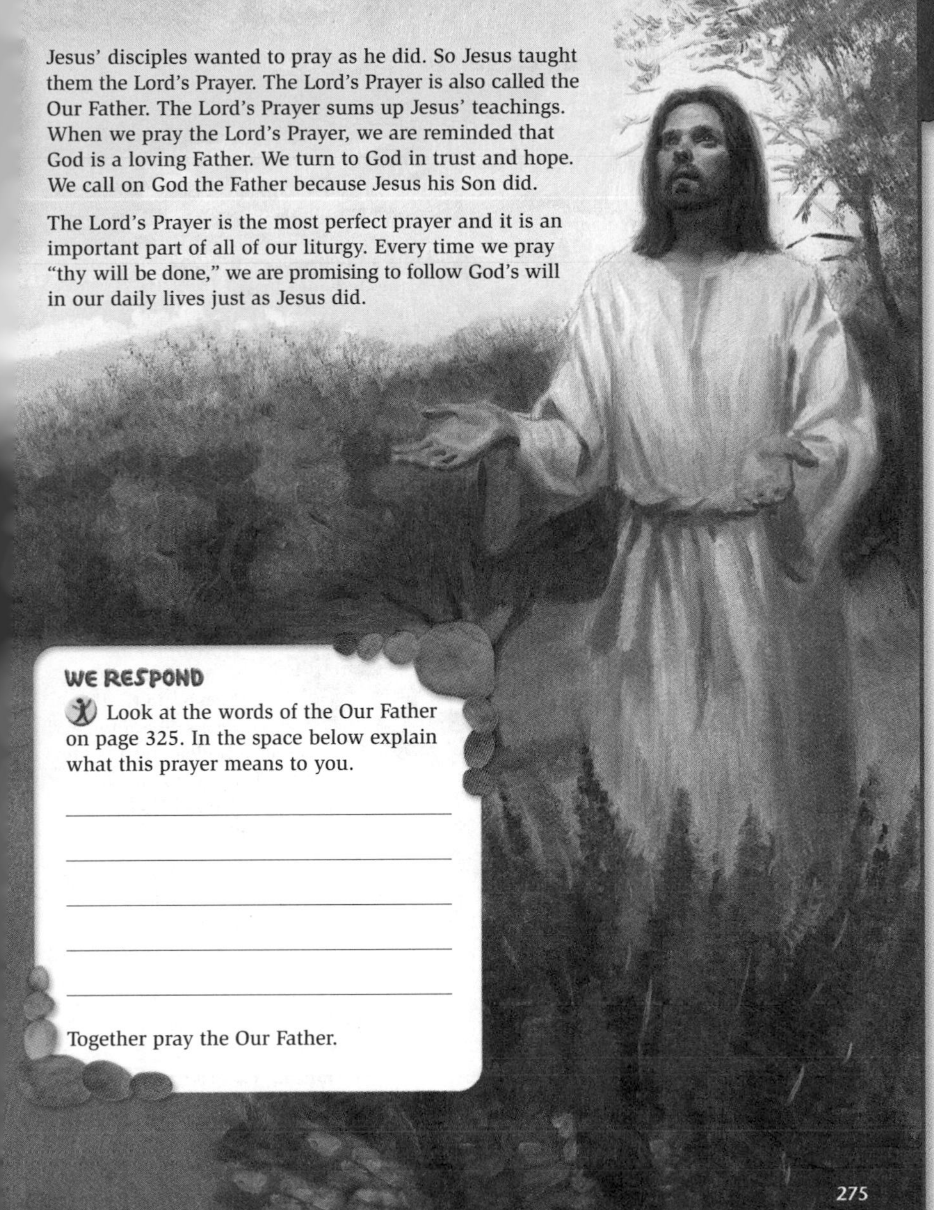

WE RESPOND

Look at the words of the Our Father on page 325. In the space below explain what this prayer means to you.

____

____

____

____

____

Together pray the Our Father.

275

Activity Bank

Multicultural Connection

The Our Father

Activity Materials: recordings of the Lord's Prayer in other languages

Obtain CDs or tapes of the Our Father as it is prayed or sung in a variety of languages, and play the recordings for the class. If you have students from various ethnic backgrounds in your class, try to find recordings of the prayer in these students' languages. You might also invite faculty, staff members, or students who know the Our Father in other languages to share their versions of the prayer with the class. Finally, you might let the students hear a recording of the Lord's Prayer as it is prayed or sung in Latin, the official language of the Church.

Ask volunteers to read aloud the last two *We Believe* paragraphs. Emphasize that the Lord's Prayer is the most perfect prayer and that it sums up Jesus' teachings.

Quick Check

- ✔ *What is prayer?* (Prayer is a way that we communicate with God and a way that God communicates with us.)
- ✔ *What did Jesus give his disciples so that they could pray as he did?* (He gave them the Lord's Prayer.)

WE RESPOND ___ minutes

Connect to Life Ask the students to read silently the *We Respond* text and to think prayerfully about each line of the Our Father as they write out their thoughts about this most perfect prayer. Encourage the students to pray the Our Father often.

Pray Invite the students to gather in a circle in the prayer space. Ask them to focus on the picture or statue of Jesus. Join hands and pray the Our Father together.

Plan Ahead for Day 3

Catechist Goal: To emphasize that we are enriched by the sacraments

Preparation: Be prepared to discuss ways to encourage others to participate in the liturgy.

Chapter 24 • Day 3

Catechist Goal

• To emphasize that we are enriched by the sacraments

Our Faith Response

• To name the ways the sacraments help us

 **liturgy**

sacrament

Lesson Materials

• index cards

As Catholics...

Liturgy of the Hours

After presenting the lesson, have a student read aloud the *As Catholics* paragraph and the questions that follow. As volunteers share their favorite times to pray and the reasons they like to pray at these times, encourage the students also to tell where they like to pray and what prayers they say at their favorite times.

The sacraments draw us closer to God.

WE GATHER

✝ *Be with us, Lord, when we gather in your name.*

Think of times when your family celebrates. What are these celebrations like? How do these celebrations bring you closer together as a family?

WE BELIEVE

Jesus sometimes prayed by himself, and he sometimes prayed with others. His first disciples often gathered together to pray. Today the Church community does the same thing. We gather together in Jesus' name to pray. The **liturgy** is the official public prayer of the Church. The liturgy includes the celebration of the Mass and the sacraments, as well as special prayers called the Liturgy of the Hours.

Christ is with us always. So he is always present when we celebrate the liturgy. He promised his first disciples: "Where two or three are gathered together in my name, there am I in the midst of them" (Matthew 18:20). During the liturgy, Christ is joined in a special way with the Church, the Body of Christ on earth. We praise God the Father for all of his blessings. We thank the Father for creation and for the gift of his Son.

When we come together in Christ's name, the Holy Spirit is with us, too. The Holy Spirit prepares our hearts to hear and understand how Christ is living and acting among us. The Holy Spirit draws us together and unites us as the Body of Christ.

Christ lives and acts in the Church, especially through the seven sacraments. A **sacrament** is a special sign given to us by Jesus through which we share in God's life.

Through each sacrament God shares his life with us, and we grow in holiness. In each sacrament we celebrate God's love for us. We rejoice because God shares his life with us. The sacraments help us to be more aware of God's presence in our lives.

Discuss the sacraments you have already learned about this year: Baptism, Eucharist, and Reconciliation.

liturgy the official public prayer of the Church

sacrament a special sign given to us by Jesus through which we share in God's life

276

Lesson Plan

WE GATHER ___ minutes

✝ **Pray** Pray together the Sign of the Cross and the *We Gather* prayer.

Focus on Life Have the students read silently the *We Gather* text and the questions. Invite volunteers to share their responses. Then ask the students to think about the ways the Church celebrates. Tell the students that in this lesson they will learn that the sacraments draw us closer to God.

WE BELIEVE ___ minutes

Read About the Liturgy Read aloud the *We Believe* statement. Then organize the students into trios and ask the trios to read and discuss quietly together the first four *We Believe* paragraphs. Then discuss the text as a class, emphasizing the following:

• The liturgy, the official public prayer of the Church, includes the celebration of the Eucharist and the other sacraments as well as the Liturgy of the Hours.

• Jesus is always present when we celebrate the liturgy.

• During the liturgy the Holy Spirit helps us to understand that Jesus is living and acting among us.

• Christ lives and acts in the Church especially through the sacraments, the special signs through which God shares his life with us.

Talk About the Sacraments Read aloud the sixth *We Believe* paragraph. The three sacraments discussed are the ones that most of the students have received. Ask three volunteers to read aloud the

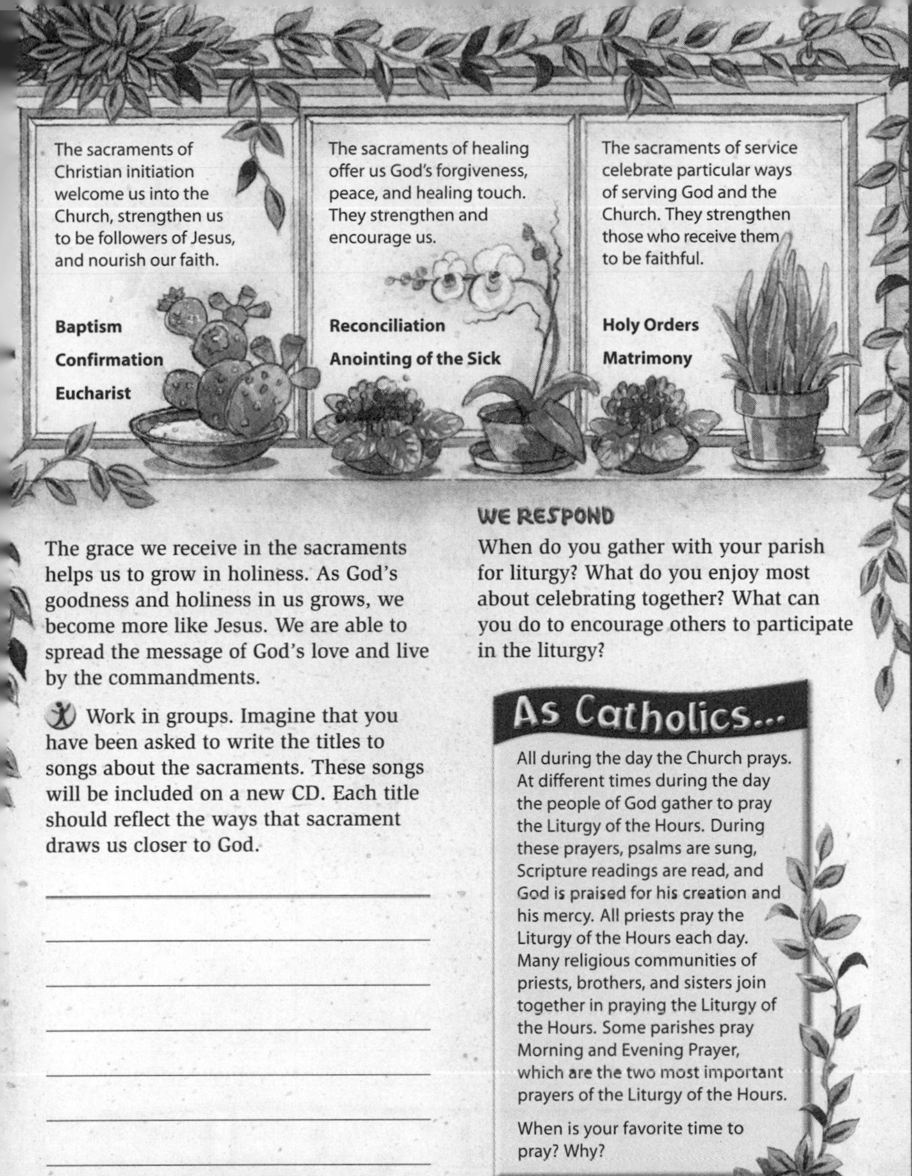

The sacraments of Christian initiation welcome us into the Church, strengthen us to be followers of Jesus, and nourish our faith.	The sacraments of healing offer us God's forgiveness, peace, and healing touch. They strengthen and encourage us.	The sacraments of service celebrate particular ways of serving God and the Church. They strengthen those who receive them to be faithful.
Baptism **Confirmation** **Eucharist**	**Reconciliation** **Anointing of the Sick**	**Holy Orders** **Matrimony**

The grace we receive in the sacraments helps us to grow in holiness. As God's goodness and holiness in us grows, we become more like Jesus. We are able to spread the message of God's love and live by the commandments.

Work in groups. Imagine that you have been asked to write the titles to songs about the sacraments. These songs will be included on a new CD. Each title should reflect the ways that sacrament draws us closer to God.

____

____

____

____

____

____

____

WE RESPOND

When do you gather with your parish for liturgy? What do you enjoy most about celebrating together? What can you do to encourage others to participate in the liturgy?

As Catholics...

All during the day the Church prays. At different times during the day the people of God gather to pray the Liturgy of the Hours. During these prayers, psalms are sung, Scripture readings are read, and God is praised for his creation and his mercy. All priests pray the Liturgy of the Hours each day. Many religious communities of priests, brothers, and sisters join together in praying the Liturgy of the Hours. Some parishes pray Morning and Evening Prayer, which are the two most important prayers of the Liturgy of the Hours.

When is your favorite time to pray? Why?

277

ACTIVITY BANK

Liturgy

Prepare a Class Mass

Activity Materials: missalettes, hymnals, banner-making materials

To allow the students to participate fully in a liturgical experience, help them to prepare a class Mass. Ask a parish priest to be the celebrant. Organize the students into committees to select the music, design a Mass booklet, write the petitions for the prayer of the faithful, and design and make a special banner. A group might also be formed to dramatize one or more of the Scripture readings for the Mass to illustrate the theme of the celebration. After this Mass has been celebrated, invite the celebrant to meet with the students to discuss what preparing and celebrating this Mass has taught them about the liturgy.

information in the chart. Then read aloud the final *We Believe* paragraph.

Do the Activity Read aloud the *We Believe* activity. Ask the students to re-form their earlier trios to work together. The songs can be ones that they know, or they can make up titles. Invite the trios to present their lists.

Quick Check

✔ *What is the liturgy?* (The liturgy is the official public prayer of the Church.)

✔ *What are the sacraments?* (The sacraments are special signs given to us by Jesus through which we share in God's life.)

WE RESPOND ___ minutes

Connect to Life Read aloud the *We Respond* questions and invite the students to share their answers. Discuss the many ways people take part in the liturgy, including praying, singing, and listening.

Pray Invite students to join you in the prayer space for the concluding prayer: *Dear God, you draw us closer to you through the celebration of the liturgy and the sacraments. Thank you for giving us these wonderful ways to praise and thank you. Amen.*

Plan Ahead for Day 4

Catechist Goal: To teach the seven gifts of the Holy Spirit

Preparation: Make copies of Reproducible Master 24.

Catechist Goal

- To teach the seven gifts of the Holy Spirit

Our Faith Response

- To appreciate the gifts of the Holy Spirit

Lesson Materials

- copies of Reproducible Master 24 (option)

Teaching Note

Getting to Know the Holy Spirit

Describe to the students the way the Holy Spirit works in each of us: *The Holy Spirit helps us to know God better and to follow his ways more fully.* Show the students different symbolic representations of the Spirit. Explain that the Holy Spirit is sometimes pictured as a dove, as tongues of fire, or as a rushing wind. You might also read and discuss scriptural passages such as Galatians 5:13–26, Ephesians 4:30–32, and 1 Corinthians 12:1–11.

The Holy Spirit shares special gifts with us.

WE GATHER

✝ *Send forth your Spirit, O Lord, and renew the face of the earth.*

Of all the gifts you have ever received, do you have a favorite? What makes the gift so special?

WE BELIEVE

As Catholics we answer God's call to holiness together, as a community of people who believe in and follow Jesus.

God the Holy Spirit helps the whole Church to grow. Together we grow in holiness as we celebrate the sacraments. Together we try to follow Jesus' example and lead lives of holiness. However, we need God's help. The Holy Spirit gives us that help and support.

The Holy Spirit is with us always. The Holy Spirit helps us to listen to our conscience and to make good choices. The seven **gifts of the Holy Spirit** help us to follow God's law and live as Jesus did. We receive these gifts in a special way in the sacrament of Confirmation.

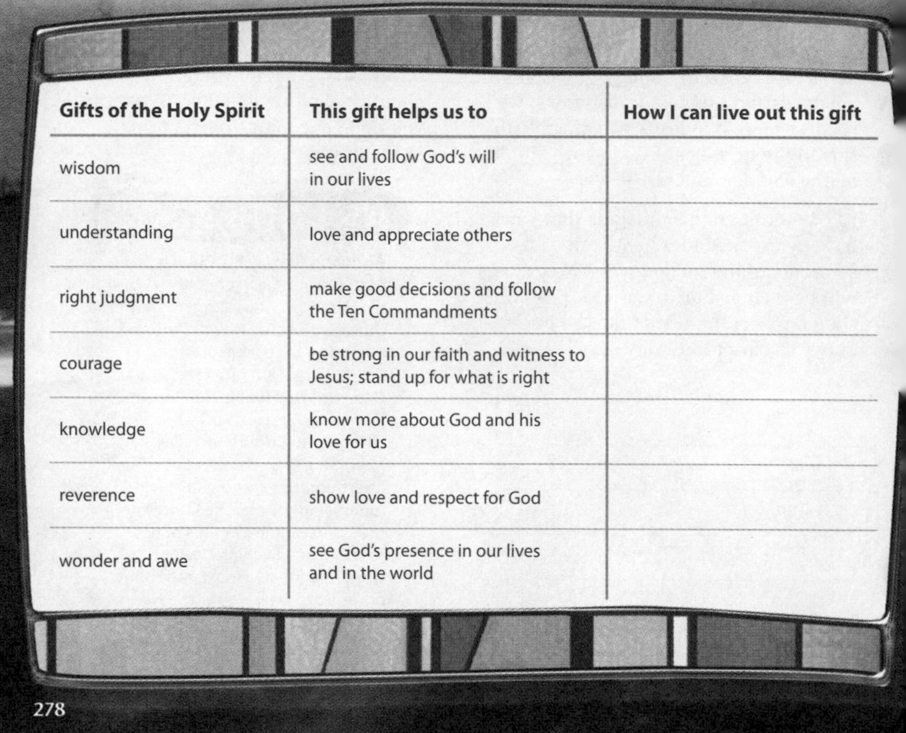

Gifts of the Holy Spirit	This gift helps us to	How I can live out this gift
wisdom	see and follow God's will in our lives	
understanding	love and appreciate others	
right judgment	make good decisions and follow the Ten Commandments	
courage	be strong in our faith and witness to Jesus; stand up for what is right	
knowledge	know more about God and his love for us	
reverence	show love and respect for God	
wonder and awe	see God's presence in our lives and in the world	

278

Lesson Plan

WE GATHER ___ minutes

✝ **Pray** Pray together the Sign of the Cross and the *We Gather* prayer.

Focus on Life Ask the students to read silently the *We Gather* questions. Invite responses. Tell the students that in this lesson they will learn that the Holy Spirit shares special gifts with us.

WE BELIEVE ___ minutes

Talk About the Holy Spirit Read aloud the *We Believe* statement. Invite volunteers to share what they think of when they hear the name "Holy Spirit." Write the students' responses on the board.

Read the Text Ask volunteers to read aloud the first two *We Believe* paragraphs. Emphasize these points:

- The Holy Spirit strengthens us so that we can listen to our consciences and make good choices.
- In the sacrament of Confirmation we receive the seven gifts of the Holy Spirit. These gifts help us to follow God's law and live as Jesus did.

Recognizing the Gifts and Fruits of the Holy Spirit Have the students read silently and complete the chart. Ask volunteers to share their responses.

Ask volunteers to read aloud the last two *We Believe* paragraphs. Pause to emphasize the fruits of the Holy Spirit are the good things that people can see in us when we respond to the gifts of the Holy Spirit.

Do the Activity Organize the students into groups to plan their short plays about the fruits of the Spirit in action. Have the students read the activity directions

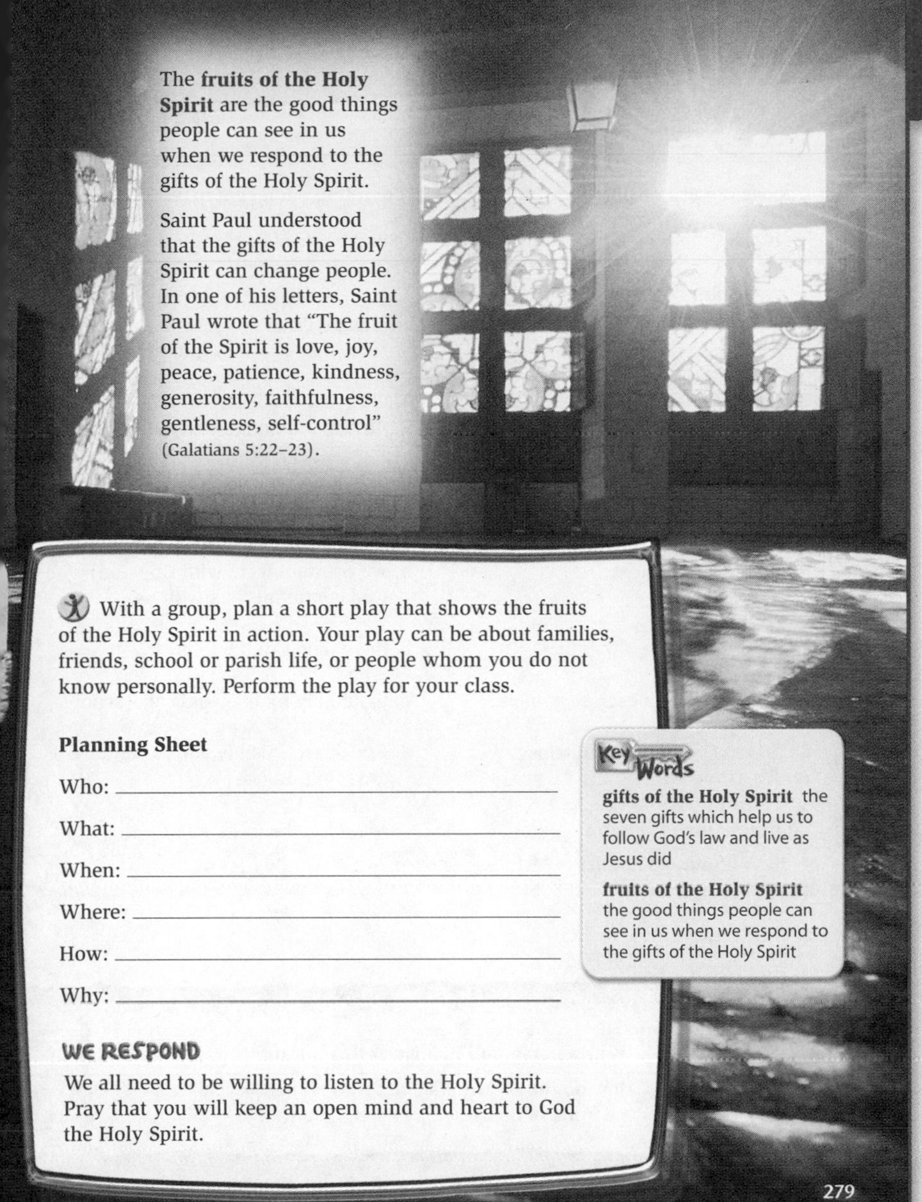

The **fruits of the Holy Spirit** are the good things people can see in us when we respond to the gifts of the Holy Spirit.
Saint Paul understood that the gifts of the Holy Spirit can change people. In one of his letters, Saint Paul wrote that "The fruit of the Spirit is love, joy, peace, patience, kindness, generosity, faithfulness, gentleness, self-control" (Galatians 5:22–23).
With a group, plan a short play that shows the fruits of the Holy Spirit in action. Your play can be about families, friends, school or parish life, or people whom you do not know personally. Perform the play for your class.
Planning Sheet
Who:
What:
When:
Where:
How:
Why:
Key Words
gifts of the Holy Spirit the seven gifts which help us to follow God's law and live as Jesus did
fruits of the Holy Spirit the good things people can see in us when we respond to the gifts of the Holy Spirit
WE RESPOND
We all need to be willing to listen to the Holy Spirit. Pray that you will keep an open mind and heart to God the Holy Spirit.
279

ACTIVITY BANK

Catholic Social Teaching

Call to Family, Community, and Participation

Have the students work together in small groups to list ways people can use the gifts of the Holy Spirit to help their families and members of their communities. Examples might include using the gift of understanding to forgive others, using the gift of courage to stand up to peer pressure, using the gift of knowledge to improve the lives of the less fortunate, and using the gift of right judgment to make good choices that benefit others. When everyone has finished, invite a volunteer from each group to share the group's list with the class.

and use the planning sheets to prepare their plays. Have each group perform its play for the class.

Distribute Reproducible Master 24 Read the directions aloud. Provide time for the students to unscramble the words, or have the students complete the activity at home. (Answers: 1, understanding; 2, wonder and awe; 3, right judgment; 4, knowledge; 5, reverence; 6, wisdom; 7, courage.) Schedule a time for the students to share the ways that they see others living out one of the gifts of the Holy Spirit.

Quick Check

✔ *What do the seven gifts of the Holy Spirit help us to do?* (The seven gifts of the Holy Spirit help us to follow God's law and live as Jesus did.)

✔ *What are the fruits of the Holy Spirit?* (They are the good things people can see in us when we respond to the gifts of the Holy Spirit.)

WE RESPOND

___ minutes

Connect to Life Read aloud the *We Respond* text. Have the students reflect on the Holy Spirit in their lives.

Pray Invite the students to pray to the Holy Spirit for help in keeping their minds and hearts open to God.

Plan Ahead for Day 5

Catechist Goal: To review chapter ideas and their relationship to our faith life

Preparation: Make copies of Chapter 24 Test in the Grade 4 Assessment Book (option).

Catechist Goal

- To review chapter ideas and their relationship to our faith life

Our Faith Response

- To apply what has been learned to our lives

CHAPTER TEST

Chapter 24 Test is provided in the Grade 4 Assessment Book.

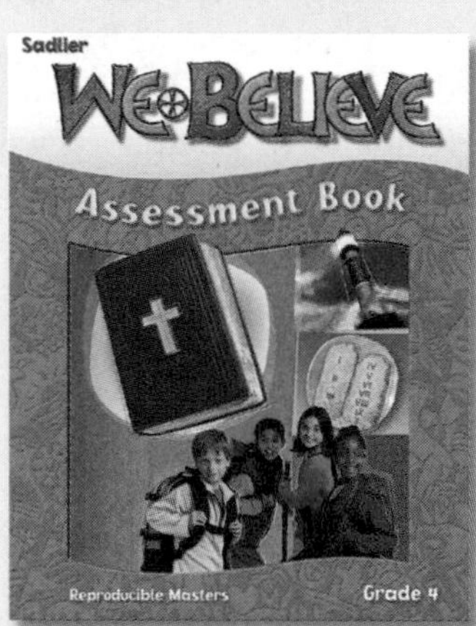

Grade 4
Chapter 24

Choose a word or phrase from the box to complete each sentence.

liturgy	sacrament	gifts of the Holy Spirit	fruits of the Holy Spirit

1. The gifts of the Holy Spirit help us to follow God's law and live as Jesus did.
2. The fruits of the Holy Spirit are the good things people can see in us when we respond to the gifts of the Holy Spirit.
3. A sacrament is a special sign given to us by Jesus through which we share in God's life.
4. The liturgy is the official public prayer of the Church.

Write the letter of the phrase that completes each of the following:

5. c Jesus teaches us
6. a Prayer is a way that
7. d Through each sacrament
8. b The Holy Spirit helps

a. we communicate with God and God communicates with us.
b. the whole Church to grow.
c. to be holy by his words and actions.
d. God shares his life with us and we grow in holiness.

Complete the following.

9–10. We grow in holiness See pages 272–273.

Write a paragraph to answer this question.
How do the sacraments, the gifts of the Holy Spirit, and the fruits of the Holy Spirit help you to live a holy life?

280

Lesson Plan

___ minutes

Chapter Review Remind the students that today they will check their understanding of what they have learned. Have them complete questions 1–8; then ask volunteers to read aloud the correct answers. Have the students write their responses to question 9–10.

Assessment Activity Encourage the students to include specific examples from their own lives as they list the ways the sacraments and the gifts and fruits of the Holy Spirit help them to live holy lives. When all have finished, invite volunteers to share their responses with the class.

___ minutes

Reflect & Pray Read aloud the introduction to the reflective activity. Ask the students to think about the many good works Jesus did while he lived on earth. Then provide time for the students to complete their prayer responses.

Key Words Invite the students to write sentences containing the words from the chapter but leave blanks where the *Key Words* would go. When all have finished, ask the students to trade papers with a partner and fill in their partner's blanks. Clarify any questions that arise.

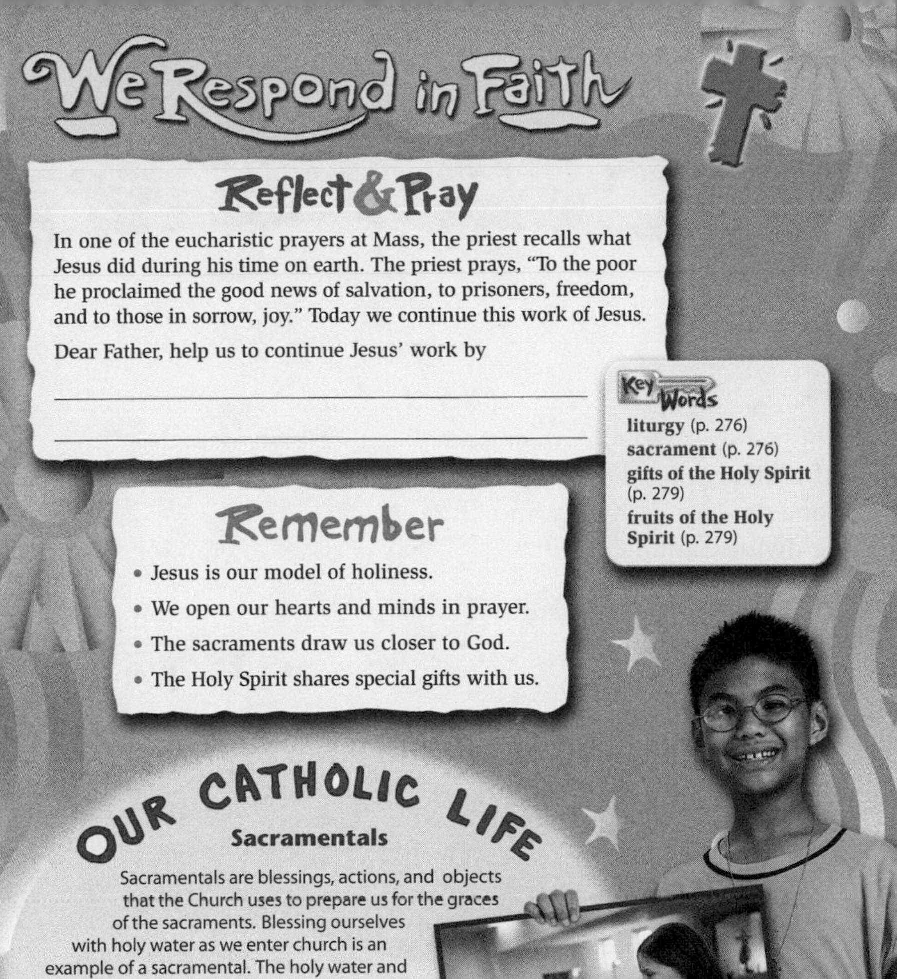

We Respond in Faith

Reflect & Pray

In one of the eucharistic prayers at Mass, the priest recalls what Jesus did during his time on earth. The priest prays, "To the poor he proclaimed the good news of salvation, to prisoners, freedom, and to those in sorrow, joy." Today we continue this work of Jesus.

Dear Father, help us to continue Jesus' work by

____

____

Key Words

liturgy (p. 276)
sacrament (p. 276)
gifts of the Holy Spirit (p. 279)
fruits of the Holy Spirit (p. 279)

Remember

- Jesus is our model of holiness.
- We open our hearts and minds in prayer.
- The sacraments draw us closer to God.
- The Holy Spirit shares special gifts with us.

Our Catholic Life

Sacramentals

Sacramentals are blessings, actions, and objects that the Church uses to prepare us for the graces of the sacraments. Blessing ourselves with holy water as we enter church is an example of a sacramental. The holy water and the sign of the cross help us to remember Baptism.

Blessings can be given to people, animals, places, food, and objects. Actions include making the sign of the cross, the laying on of hands, the sprinkling of water. Some objects that are sacramentals are statues, medals, rosaries, candles, and crucifixes.

Sacramentals remind us to praise God. They remind us of Jesus and the saints, and they help us to pray.

HOME CONNECTION

Sharing Faith with My Family

Make sure to send home the family page (text page 282).

Encourage the students to read the story of Saint Teresa de los Andes with their families, and remind the students to start thinking about this week's nominee for the "Holiness Hall of Fame."

For additional information and activities, encourage families to visit Sadlier's

www.WEBELIEVEweb.com

Remember Review the four *We Believe* statements. Remind the students that they can grow in holiness by following the model of Jesus, by celebrating the sacraments, and by keeping their minds and hearts open to the Holy Spirit.

Our Catholic Life Invite a volunteer to read aloud the text. Then point out some examples of sacramentals in the classroom. These might include statues, a crucifix, rosaries, or medals. Emphasize that these and other sacramentals remind us to praise God and help us to pray.

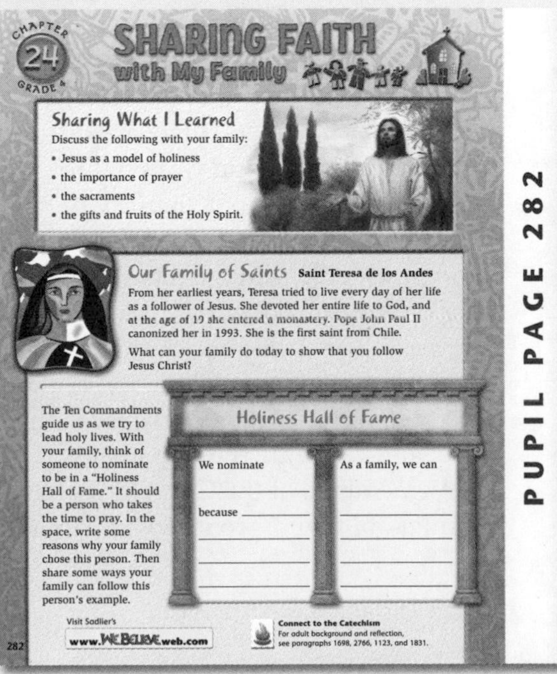

Chapter 24 Grade 4

SHARING FAITH with My Family

Sharing What I Learned

Discuss the following with your family:

- Jesus as a model of holiness
- the importance of prayer
- the sacraments
- the gifts and fruits of the Holy Spirit.

Our Family of Saints Saint Teresa de los Andes

From her earliest years, Teresa tried to live every day of her life as a follower of Jesus. She devoted her entire life to God, and at the age of 19 she entered a monastery. Pope John Paul II canonized her in 1993. She is the first saint from Chile.

What can your family do today to show that you follow Jesus Christ?

The Ten Commandments guide us as we try to lead holy lives. With your family, think of someone to nominate to be in a "Holiness Hall of Fame." It should be a person who takes the time to pray. In the space, write some reasons why your family chose this person. Then share some ways your family can follow this person's example.

Holiness Hall of Fame

We nominate ______ because ______

As a family, we can ______

Visit Sadlier's www.WEBELIEVEweb.com

Connect to the Catechism: For adult background and reflection, see paragraphs 1698, 2766, 1123, and 1831.

282

PUPIL PAGE 282

Chapter 25 We Are the Church

Overview

In Chapter 24 the students learned about holiness, prayer, sacraments, and the gifts and fruits of the Holy Spirit. In this chapter they will reflect on what it means to be an active member of a parish community and, in a more universal sense, a member of the worldwide Catholic Church.

Doctrinal Content	For Adult Reading and Reflection *Catechism of the Catholic Church*
The students will learn:	Paragraph
• The Church is a worldwide community.	814
• We have responsibilities as members of the Church.	2041
• We celebrate the sacraments.	2042
• We have an active role in the Church community.	2043

parish (p. 285)
pastor (p. 285)
deacon (p. 285)
diocese (p. 285)
bishops (p. 285)
pope (p. 285)
precepts of the Church (p. 286)

Catechist Background

To what organizations do you belong?

The Catholic Church is a complex, colorful, and diverse organization. "From its beginning, this one Church has been marked by a great *diversity* which comes from both the variety of God's gifts and the diversity of those who receive them. Within the unity of the People of God, a multiplicity of peoples and cultures is gathered together. Among the Church's members, there are different gifts, offices, conditions, and ways of life" (CCC 814).

Catholics participate in the Church in many ways, particularly at the local level, in our parish communities. Within the diocese the local embodiment of the global Church, the Body of Christ, is the parish. It is in the parish that we directly experience our life of faith. There we worship God, form communities of faith, share in the life of grace, and celebrate the sacraments.

As members of the Church, we have certain minimal obligations to it. To help us appreciate our responsibilities, the Church has given us principles or guidelines, known as precepts. "The precepts of the Church are set in the context of a moral life bound to and nourished by liturgical life. The obligatory character of these positive laws . . . is meant to guarantee to the faithful the very necessary minimum in the spirit of prayer and moral effort, in the growth of love of God and neighbor" (CCC 2041). The precepts teach us ways to act as members of our local Church communities and ways to ensure that the Church can be of service and grow.

What are some ways in which you can contribute to your parish's growth and development?

Lesson Planning Guide

Lesson Focus	Presentation	Materials
Day 1		
page 283 **We Gather in Prayer** **pages 284–285** *The Church is a worldwide community.*	• Pray in silence. Respond in song. • Discuss the **We Gather** questions. • Read and discuss the **We Believe** text. Design a flyer for the activity. • Read remaining paragraphs Complete the **We Respond** activity. • Pray together.	For the prayer space: copy of the latest parish bulletin, world map, copy of the Nicene Creed "Though We Are Many/Make Us a Sign," Bernadette Farrell, #27, Grade 4 CD • copies of parish bulletins • drawing paper
Day 2		
pages 286–287 *We have responsibilities as members of the Church.*	• Answer the **We Gather** questions. • Read and discuss the precepts of the Church the **We Believe** text. Complete the chart. • Discuss the **We Respond** question. • Pray together.	
Day 3		
pages 288–289 *We celebrate the sacraments.*	• Reflect on the **We Gather** questions. • Read about the sacraments and the first three precepts in **We Believe**. • Discuss the **We Respond** question and the pictures. • Pray together.	• copies of Reproducible Master 25, guide page 283G
Day 4		
pages 290–291 *We have an active role in the Church community.*	Complete the **We Gather** activity. • Read about the Church community and precepts 4–7 in **We Believe**. Write another precept. • Reflect on the **We Respond** question. • Read about the marks of the Church in *As Catholics.*	• copies of the Nicene Creed • notepaper, one piece per student
Day 5		
page 292 **Review** **pages 293–294** **We Respond in Faith**	• Complete questions 1–10. Work on the *Assessment Activity.* • Discuss the *Reflect & Pray* text. • Review *Remember* and *Key Words.* • Read and discuss *Our Catholic Life.* • Discuss **Sharing Faith with My Family**.	• sentence strips • Chapter 25 Test in the Assessment Book, pp. 49–50 • Chapter 25 Test in Test Generator • Review & Resource Book, pp. 58–60 • Family Book, pp. 71–73

For additional ideas, activities, and opportunities: Visit Sadlier's **www.WEBELIEVEweb.com**

Enrichment Ideas

Chapter Story

Francis Xavier was born near Pamplona, Spain, about five hundred years ago. He was an excellent student and began his career as a professor in Paris. There he met Saint Ignatius of Loyola, who convinced him to use his gifts to spread the gospel.

Francis became a Jesuit priest and was their first missionary. He preached the gospel to people throughout India and Japan. From letters to his fellow priests, we know that Francis Xavier was a very successful missionary. He baptized more than forty thousand people. In fact, in one month in India he baptized ten thousand people! Francis Xavier preached in the streets, worked with the sick, and taught young people their catechism.

It is easy to see how Francis Xavier was named patron of the missions. But how can it be that a young Frenchwoman, Saint Thérèse of Lisieux, who rarely traveled beyond her own hometown, was also named patron of the missions? From the age of fifteen, when she became a cloistered Carmelite sister, Thérèse never left the convent building.

When she was a child, Thérèse's father often gave her coins as a reward for excellent schoolwork. Thérèse saved the coins to help the poor children of China. As a young Carmelite Thérèse volunteered to work in the missions in Indochina but was denied permission because of poor health. When she knew she was dying, at age twenty-four, Thérèse told the other sisters not to buy flowers for her burial service, but to send the money to the missions in China and Africa.

Like all followers of Jesus, Thérèse was called to be a missionary. She offered her prayers, sacrifices and sufferings for missionaries serving around the world.

▶ *How can we be missionaries like Saint Francis Xavier and Saint Thérèse?*

FAITH and MEDIA

▶ This week remind the students of the many ways the Church uses media to serve its apostolic mission. Explain to them that the Church's mission takes place on many levels: in the parish, in the diocese, and worldwide. Have the students visit the Vatican Web site, where people around the world can access the words of the pope and the teachings of the Church in many languages. Visit the Web sites of your diocese and, if it has one, your parish. Bring to class some copies of your diocesan newspaper and a selection of other Catholic periodicals. Finally, bring in copies of your parish bulletin.

CHAPTER PROJECT: A MISSIONARY MAP

Use a large world map to help the students increase their understanding of our missionary mandate as Christians. Have the students work in small groups to research the Church's missionary activities in countries around the world. Have the students cut small triangles from construction paper (to represent flags) and label each one with a specific aspect of missionary work that would be beneficial in a particular place. Then have the students pin or tape these flags to the map at the appropriate locations. Ask the students also to make a short fact list about the people whom the Church's missionaries are serving in each of these places. Encourage the students to pray for the people and the missionaries in the places marked on the map.

Connections

To Scripture

Jesus tells us: "For where two or three are gathered together in my name, there am I in the midst of them" (Matthew 18:20). This statement underscores the integrity of the Christian community. Jesus did not intend that we be isolated from others. The missionary mandate is, above all, the call to form a Christian community. Ask the students to look for other passages in Scripture that highlight Jesus' call to serve and spread the message of his love.

To Catholic Social Teaching

Call to Family, Community, and Participation
In this chapter the students are introduced to the seven precepts of the Church. As you teach this chapter, pay particular attention to the fourth precept. Look for ways to help the students affirm that the family is the foundation of human society. Encourage the students to think of things that families can do to strengthen their commitment to this precept.

To Stewardship

In this chapter the students are asked to think about what it means to be part of a parish community. Discuss the ways that pastors, sisters, priests and deacons, altar servers, music directors, choir members and musicians, directors of religious education, parish council members, catechists, special ministers of the Eucharist, readers, ushers, visitors to the sick, and sacristans all serve the parish. Talk, too, about parish committees devoted to such ministries as food pantries, social action, and the right to life, that also exemplify stewardship.

Meeting Individual Needs

Students from Different Countries

If you have students from various countries in your class, invite them to describe how their families celebrate the sacraments of Baptism and First Eucharist. Ask them to include specific details about traditional celebrations, dress, food and music. Invite these students to share family photos that show the cultural practices they have described. Ask all the students to list ways that different customs help us appreciate the sacraments in different ways.

ADDITIONAL RESOURCES

Book *Call Me Little Theresa,* Susan Helen Wallace, FSP, Pauline Books and Media, 1996. This is a biography of St. Thérèse of Lisieux written in a fast-paced style with warm illustrations.

Video *Francis Xavier and the Samurai's Lost Treasure,* CCC of America, 1993. This video tells the story of the Saint's adventurous life carrying the gospel to India and Japan. (30 minutes)

To find more ideas for books, videos, and other learning material, visit Sadlier's

www.WEBELIEVEweb.com

Finding Value in Popular Culture

by Gloria Hutchinson

Gloria Hutchinson is an author of numerous books on religion and spirituality. She presents retreats and workshops across the country, often using popular videos and music in her presentations. Gloria has appeared in several Catholic Update videos.

While many dismiss "popular culture" as a wasteland, the wise catechist sees it as a field in which the wheat and the weeds grow side by side. Our task is to enable students to discern the difference and choose the good "grain" of spiritual nourishment.

The mass media, electronic, image-dominated culture of the twenty-first century exerts a compelling influence on youth. We cannot ignore the impact of MTV, the World Wide Web, cell phones and Walkmans, VCRs, DVDs and video games, super malls, fast-food chains, and logo-laden fashions. Religious education must take into account the expectations raised by popular culture. Our young people want to be entertained, stimulated, informed, and affected. And they want it all at a lively pace.

So how do we find value in a culture which has been described as "a competing religion"? We look with the eyes of faith rather than the glare of skepticism. We seek the good and enlist it in God's service. Pope John Paul II advises: "Contemporary reality demands a capacity to learn the language, nature and characteristics of mass media. Using the media correctly can lead to a genuine inculturation of the Gospel." (*Ecclesia in America,* 1999, #72)

The Holy Father's words apply to all aspects of popular culture. Whether we are evaluating a video game or a popular children's movie, we must "learn the language, nature and characteristics" of these products. What stories are they telling? Do they run counter to or parallel with the stories of Jesus?

Catechist Development Topics (Topic and Guide Page)

Like Jesus himself, catechists need to immerse themselves in their own culture in order to communicate effectively with the people of God.

As Jesus employed the fisherman's net and the mustard seed, the music of the day and the coin of the realm, we, too, must learn to press into service all creative and technological works that may feed the spirit. If we fail to do so, we lose the wheat along with the weeds.

Resources

Cardinal Roger Mahony. "Film Makers, Film Viewers: Their Challenges and Opportunities" On the Internet at http://cardinal.la-archdiocese.org

Adriacco, Dan. *Screen Saved: Peril and Promise of Media in Ministry.* Cincinnati: St. Anthony Messenger Press, 2000.

Malone, Peter with Sr. Rose Pacatte. *Lights, Camera . . . Faith! A Movie Lectionary*. Boston: Pauline Books and Media, 2001.

Ways to Implement Finding Value in Popular Culture

- Each week, take time to immerse yourself in one specific expression of popular culture such as: a youth-oriented radio station, family comic strips, video games, professional sports events, Web sites and chat rooms for the young.
- Teach children to analyze their favorite cultural works and products. Guide group dialogues on questions like these: How does this video game affect my feelings about violence? What is the key message of this song? How might this comic strip character help me to be a better disciple of Jesus?
- Involve groups of student film reviewers in choosing segments from popular videos for classroom use. Help them focus on characters who stand out as spiritual mentors or decision makers.
- Introduce age-appropriate role models from popular films. Have students decide how these role models show us gospel values in action.
- Design a popular culture bulletin board with a continuously updated display of symbols, photos, and articles on cultural works with spiritual values. Invite students to devise a ratings system for these works and to contribute to the display.

For additional ideas, activities, and opportunities, visit Sadlier's

www.WEBELIEVEweb.com

With thanks to:

Kim Suttie
Immaculate Heart of Mary Parish
Fairfield, Maine

Kim likes to use popular music as a form of prayer. When she is listening to a current song, she asks herself "Do the lyrics answer one of these questions: Could it be me talking to God, God talking to me, or a conversation between the two of us?" She notes that more often than not the song puts her thoughts and feelings into better words than she could ever come up with! Kim invites her students to bring in CDs of their favorite music to ask them the same questions she asks herself. She always has her students write out the lyrics to their favorite songs before she decides to play them for the entire group. It usually surprises the group how many of these songs spark spirited discussion and even thoughtful prayer.

Notes

Name ____

Use the clues to complete the puzzle.

Across

4. Community of believers who work and worship together

5. Baptism, Confirmation, Eucharist, Reconciliation, Anointing of the Sick, Holy Orders, and Matrimony

6. One holy, catholic, and apostolic are the ______ of the Church

8. Leaders of the Church and successors to the apostles

9. Man who preaches, baptizes, and assists the pastor

Down

1. Local area of the Church led by a bishop

2. Worldwide community united by Baptism

3. Seven laws or rules of the Church

4. Priest who leads a parish

7. Bishop of Rome and leader of the whole Church

We Are the Church 25

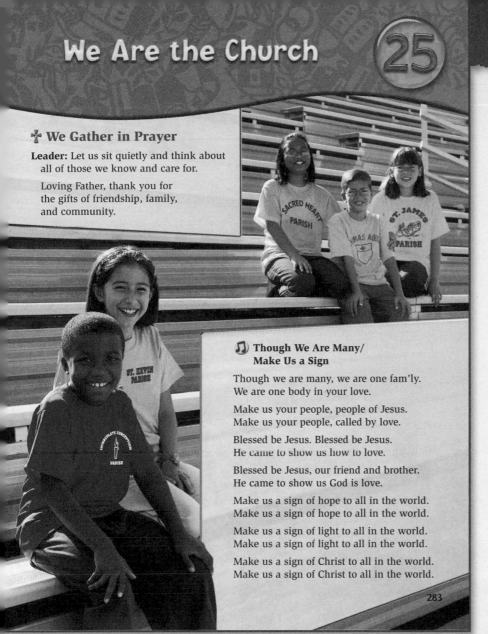

✝ We Gather in Prayer

Leader: Let us sit quietly and think about all of those we know and care for.

Loving Father, thank you for the gifts of friendship, family, and community.

♫ Though We Are Many/ Make Us a Sign

Though we are many, we are one fam'ly.
We are one body in your love.

Make us your people, people of Jesus.
Make us your people, called by love.

Blessed be Jesus. Blessed be Jesus.
He came to show us how to love.

Blessed be Jesus, our friend and brother.
He came to show us God is love.

Make us a sign of hope to all in the world.
Make us a sign of hope to all in the world.

Make us a sign of light to all in the world.
Make us a sign of light to all in the world.

Make us a sign of Christ to all in the world.
Make us a sign of Christ to all in the world.

283

Preparing to Pray

In this gathering the students sing of being united as the people of Jesus.

- Tell the students that you will be the prayer leader and that all will sing the song.
- Play "Though We Are Many/Make Us a Sign," #27 on the Grade 4 CD, and allow time for the students to practice. (The CD contains all the verses for the song. The first two verses do not appear in the student's text.)
- Select volunteers to place items in the prayer space at the appointed time.

The Prayer Space

- Have available this week's copy of the parish bulletin, a map of the world, and a copy of the Nicene Creed.

This Week's Liturgy

Visit **www.webelieveweb.com** for this week's liturgical readings and other seasonal material.

Lesson Plan

We Gather in Prayer ___ minutes

✝ Pray

- Invite the students to gather in the prayer space.
- Pray the Sign of the Cross and begin the opening prayer. Pause briefly after the first sentence to allow time for quiet reflection; then pray the end of the prayer.
- Play and sing together "Though We Are Many/Make Us a Sign."
- At the close of the song have the volunteers place the parish bulletin, the map, and the copy of the Nicene Creed in the prayer space.

Home Connection Update

Invite the students to share their experiences using the Chapter 24 family page. Ask: *Whom did your family nominate this week to the "Holiness Hall of Fame"?*

Chapter 25 • Day 1

Catechist Goal

- To explore what it means to be members of the Church

Our Faith Response

- To rejoice in our membership in the Church

parish **pastor**
deacon **diocese**
bishops **pope**

Lesson Materials

- copies of parish bulletins
- drawing paper

The Church is a worldwide community.

WE GATHER

Come, Holy Spirit, unite the Church.

As a member of your class, how do you help and encourage your classmates? What are some ways that they help and encourage you and one another?

WE BELIEVE

Catholics living all around the world share the same beliefs in Jesus and the Church. We celebrate the same seven sacraments and follow the commandments. We speak many different languages and have different customs, but we are united by our Baptism and our call to love God and others.

Living by the Ten Commandments is not something we do alone. As members of the Church, we support and encourage one another. We do this most often with our parish family. A **parish** is a community of believers who worship and work together. Catholics in nearby neighborhoods usually belong to the same parish. However, parishes vary in size and are made up of many different people.

Parish members gather for the celebration of Sunday Mass and for all of the sacraments. They come together to pray, study, and grow in faith. They work together for justice and peace in their parishes, neighborhoods, country, and world.

Many people serve their parishes through different ministries. These people take on different responsibilities in religious education, youth organizations, social outreach programs, and in the liturgy.

A **pastor** is the priest who leads the parish in worship, prayer, and teaching.

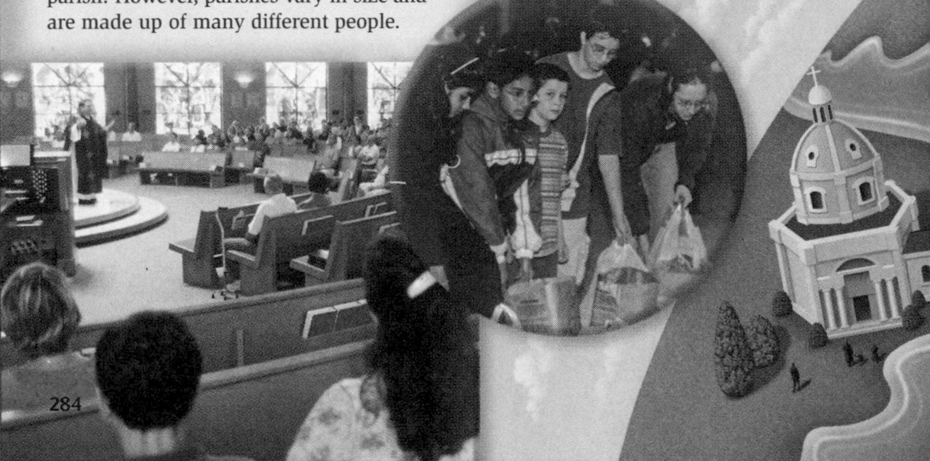

284

Teaching Note

Geographical Comparison

The concepts of parishes, dioceses, and the worldwide Church may be new to some of the students. One way to illustrate the Church community is to offer a comparison to a national community. Show the students that cities are located in states or provinces and that all of these are part of a larger community, their nation.

Lesson Plan

WE GATHER ___ minutes

Pray Pray together the Sign of the Cross and the *We Gather* prayer.

Focus on Life Ask a volunteer to read aloud the *We Gather* questions and invite responses. Tell the students that in this lesson they will learn that they are members of a nurturing, worldwide Church community.

WE BELIEVE ___ minutes

Read the Text After a volunteer has read aloud the *We Believe* statement, ask other volunteers to read aloud the *We Believe* text. Emphasize:

- All Catholics, no matter where they live or what language they speak, believe in Jesus and the Church.
- Our parish is our Church family. We come together to worship, to study, to help one another grow in faith, and to work for justice and peace.
- The pastor leads the parish; the bishop leads the diocese; the pope leads the whole Church.

Describe a Catholic Parish Hand out copies of the parish bulletin. Explain that every parishioner has an important role. Ask: *What are some parish ministries?* (Answers might include altar servers, music ministers, ushers, catechists and teachers, visitors to the sick.)

Design a Flyer Have a volunteer read aloud the activity directions. Distribute drawing paper and have pairs of the students sketch ideas. Help the students to recall examples and/or events that show the parish community in action.

A **deacon** serves the parish by preaching, baptizing, and assisting the pastor. All the members of the parish work together to continue Jesus' work.

Work with a partner. Design a flyer that illustrates a parish community in action. Your flyer can focus on your own parish or on many different parishes.

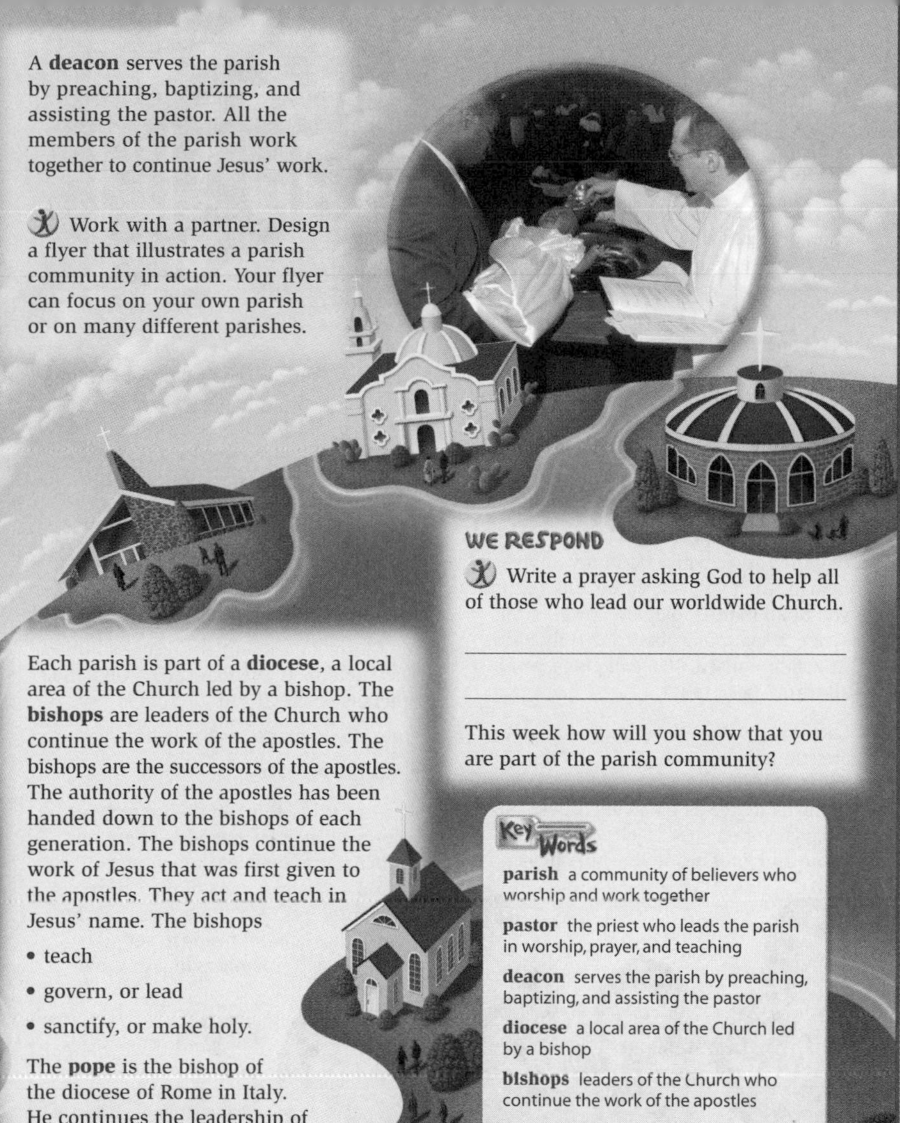

WE RESPOND

Write a prayer asking God to help all of those who lead our worldwide Church.

____

____

This week how will you show that you are part of the parish community?

Each parish is part of a **diocese**, a local area of the Church led by a bishop. The **bishops** are leaders of the Church who continue the work of the apostles. The bishops are the successors of the apostles. The authority of the apostles has been handed down to the bishops of each generation. The bishops continue the work of Jesus that was first given to the apostles. They act and teach in Jesus' name. The bishops

- teach
- govern, or lead
- sanctify, or make holy.

The **pope** is the bishop of the diocese of Rome in Italy. He continues the leadership of Saint Peter. Together with all the bishops, he leads and guides the whole Church.

Key Words

parish a community of believers who worship and work together

pastor the priest who leads the parish in worship, prayer, and teaching

deacon serves the parish by preaching, baptizing, and assisting the pastor

diocese a local area of the Church led by a bishop

bishops leaders of the Church who continue the work of the apostles

pope the bishop of Rome, who leads the whole Catholic Church

285

ACTIVITY BANK

Parish

The Parish Bulletin

Activity Materials: copies of current and recent parish bulletins from your parish and others; markers or colored pencils

Show the students copies of parish bulletins, and invite them to design their own. Have them work as if the parishioners will receive this copy of the bulletin at this coming weekend's liturgies. Suggest that the students focus on events and topics that are of interest to young people. They might include short articles about music or videos with Christian values, or listings of events for students. They might also include a cartoon or comic strip about parish life, a feature such as a catechism or Scripture "quest," or a brief description of a window, statue, or other artwork in the church.

Understand the Key Words Review and discuss the *Key Words* with the students. Ask volunteers to name their parish, the diocese to which their parish belongs, the bishop of that diocese, their pastor, any deacons that serve their parish and the pope.

Quick Check

✔ *In what ways are all Catholics united?* (by our Baptism and by our call to love God and others)

✔ *Describe what takes place in a parish.* (Answers will vary.)

WE RESPOND ___ minutes

Connect to Life Read aloud the *We Respond* activity directions. Have the students write their prayers and pray them silently. Then read aloud the question and invite responses. Look at each photo in the chapter and discuss ways the people are supporting the Church.

Pray Invite the students to pray for their parish.

Plan Ahead for Day 2

Catechist Goal: To explain that as baptized members of the Church we have certain responsibilities

Preparation: Be ready to discuss the seven precepts of the Church.

Chapter 25 • Day 2

Catechist Goal

- To explain that as baptized members of the Church we have certain responsibilities

Our Faith Response

- To choose ways to live out our responsibilities as members of the Church

precepts of the Church

Teaching Note

The Pope, Successor to Saint Peter

The word *pope* comes from the Greek word *papas*, meaning "father." The Holy Father, the pope, is the bishop of Rome, the successor to Saint Peter, and the Vicar of Christ. He speaks as the universal teacher in defining faith and morals. When a new pope must be chosen, all cardinals under the age of 80 come together in Rome in a meeting called a conclave to elect a pope by secret ballot.

We have responsibilities as members of the Church.

WE GATHER

✝ *Holy Spirit, be with us, the Church.*

Discuss what it is like to join a group, club, or organization. As a member do you promise to follow certain rules? Why?

WE BELIEVE

The pope and bishops are the successors of the apostles. Their authority comes from the authority Jesus gave to the first apostles. Jesus told the apostles, "Whoever listens to you listens to me" (Luke 10:16).

Jesus gave Peter and the apostles help in guiding the Church. At the Last Supper Jesus told the apostles, "The holy Spirit that the Father will send in my name—he will teach you everything and remind you of all that [I] told you" (John 14:26). When Jesus spoke about the Holy Spirit he also promised, "He will guide you to all truth" (John 16:13).

Like the apostles, the pope and bishops are strengthened and guided by the Holy Spirit. They help us to understand what it means to live as followers of Jesus in today's world. They teach us in Jesus' name and guide us to live holy lives.

The pope and bishops in St. Peter's Square, Vatican City

The Holy Spirit is with all of us, helping us to be Jesus' disciples. We can trust the pope and bishops to lead us. The pope and bishops have established some laws to help us know and fulfill our responsibilities as members of the Church. These laws are called the **precepts of the Church**.

The precepts of the Church remind us that growing in holiness and serving the Church are important responsibilities. They help us to see that loving God and others is connected to

- our life of prayer and worship
- our life of service.

It is helpful to think of the precepts as rules or principles intended as a guide for behavior. They teach us how we should act as members of the Church. These precepts also make sure that the Church has what it needs to serve its members and to grow.

Key Word

precepts of the Church laws to help us know and fulfill our responsibilities as members of the Church

286

Lesson Plan

WE GATHER ___ minutes

✝ **Pray** Pray together the Sign of the Cross and the *We Gather* prayer.

Focus on Life Ask a volunteer to read aloud the *We Gather* paragraph. Then have the students gather in groups of four to discuss the clubs or organizations to which they have belonged, their leaders, and their rules. Tell the students that in this lesson they will learn that the Church, like other organizations, has leaders. The Church also has rules, some of which are called *precepts*.

WE BELIEVE ___ minutes

Read the Text Ask a volunteer to read aloud the *We Believe* statement. Then have the students read silently the *We Believe* text. Allow time for all to finish reading; then discuss the following:

- Jesus gave the authority to lead the Church to the first apostles. That authority has been handed down through time to the pope and bishops of the Catholic Church today.
- Jesus promised that the Holy Spirit will teach us and guide us to all truth.
- The leaders of the Church have established the precepts of the Church to help us know and fulfill our responsibilities as members of the Church.

Do the Activity Invite one student to read aloud the activity directions. Remind the students that precepts, in general, are similar to the sort of rules that a member of any group promises to uphold. The precepts of the Church

Work in groups. Discuss what each precept is asking us to do. Talk about why you think the precept is important. What are some questions you might have about the precept? Record your thoughts and questions in the chart. Then as a class share what you have discussed.

The Precepts of the Church	Thoughts and Questions
1. Celebrate Christ's Resurrection every Sunday (or Saturday evening) and on holy days of obligation by taking part in Mass and avoiding unnecessary work.	
2. Lead a sacramental life. Receive Holy Communion frequently and the sacrament of Reconciliation regularly. We must receive Holy Communion at least once a year between the first Sunday of Lent and Trinity Sunday. We must celebrate Reconciliation once a year if we have committed mortal, or serious, sin.	
3. Study Catholic teaching throughout life, especially in preparing for the sacraments, and continue to grow in faith.	
4. Observe the marriage laws of the Church and give religious instruction and formation to one's children.	
5. Contribute to the support of the Church: one's own parish community, priests, the whole Church, and the pope.	
6. Do penance, including not eating meat and fasting from food on certain days.	
7. Join in the missionary work of the Church.	

WE RESPOND

Choose one precept. What will you do this week to follow the precept you selected? During the week explain that precept to someone else.

ACTIVITY BANK

Faith and Media

The Church and the Internet

Activity Materials: Internet access

The seventh precept calls us to join in the Church's missionary work. Discuss with the students the way the Internet can be used to help the Church in this work. Explain that Catholic Web sites have the potential to reach people all around the world. Let the students go online to look at their parish and diocesan Web sites and the Web sites of Catholic mission organizations such as the Society for the Propagation of the Faith (www.propfaith.org). Then visit the Vatican Web site (www.vatican.va). Discuss the ways the information on these Web sites might help lead people to the Church. Encourage the students to envision ways to use the Internet even more effectively to do the Church's missionary work.

tell us what we need to do to be loving members of the Church. Have the students stay in their groups of four to read and reflect on the information in the chart and record their thoughts and questions. Then discuss each precept in turn, inviting volunteers from each group to present the group's thoughts and questions on that precept.

Quick Check

✔ *From whom do the pope and bishops receive their authority?* (As the successors of the apostles, the pope and bishops receive their authority from Jesus.)

✔ *What are the precepts of the Church?* (The precepts of the Church are laws that help us know and perform our responsibilities as Catholics.)

WE RESPOND ___ minutes

Connect to Life Read and discuss the *We Respond* text. Encourage the students to write the precept they have chosen on a slip of paper and carry it with them during the week.

Pray Invite the students to gather in the prayer space. Pray again together the *We Gather* prayer. Then pray: *Holy Spirit, help us to know and fulfill our responsibilities as members of the Church. Amen.*

Plan Ahead for Day 3

Catechist Goal: To examine the ways the sacraments nourish us as we grow in age

Preparation: Have available copies of Reproducible Master 25.

Chapter 25 • Day 3

Catechist Goal

- To examine the ways the sacraments nourish us as we grow in age

Our Faith Response

- To receive the sacraments, especially the Eucharist

Lesson Materials

- copies of Reproducible Master 25

Teaching Note

The First Precept of the Church

It is easy to think that the students know what you know. This is not always the case. The first precept of the Church provides a good example. As you teach this lesson, you should be able to presume that the students know that participating at Mass on Sundays and holy days satisfies this obligation. Some students, however, might not understand that participating at Mass on Saturday evening or the evening before a holy day also satisfies this obligation. This is an ideal time to make that point.

We celebrate the sacraments.

WE GATHER

✝ *Jesus, your sacraments make us faithful disciples.*

What is one way that your life has changed since last year? How do you think this change has affected you?

WE BELIEVE

Many important things happen in Baptism. We are freed from original and personal sin, we receive the gift of grace, and we become children of God and members of the Church. Baptism changes us. It gives us new life in Christ. Baptism is like a door to the rest of the sacraments. It welcomes us to the Church and to celebrate the other sacraments. The sacraments strengthen, nourish, and heal the life of Christ in us.

The sacraments change our lives. Through the sacraments the life of Christ in us continues to grow. We are the Church, so when the life of Christ grows in each of us, the Church grows, too. As Catholics we worship together. We do this so that we can grow together in holiness. As active members of the Church, we receive the sacraments often so that God's love can grow in us.

Each time that we celebrate a sacrament we remember and celebrate Jesus' life, death, Resurrection, and Ascension. We honor the request of Jesus, "Do this in remembrance of me" (1 Corinthians 11:24). The first precept, or law, of the Church reminds us to celebrate the sacrament of the Eucharist. It tells us to participate in Mass on Sundays and holy days of obligation.

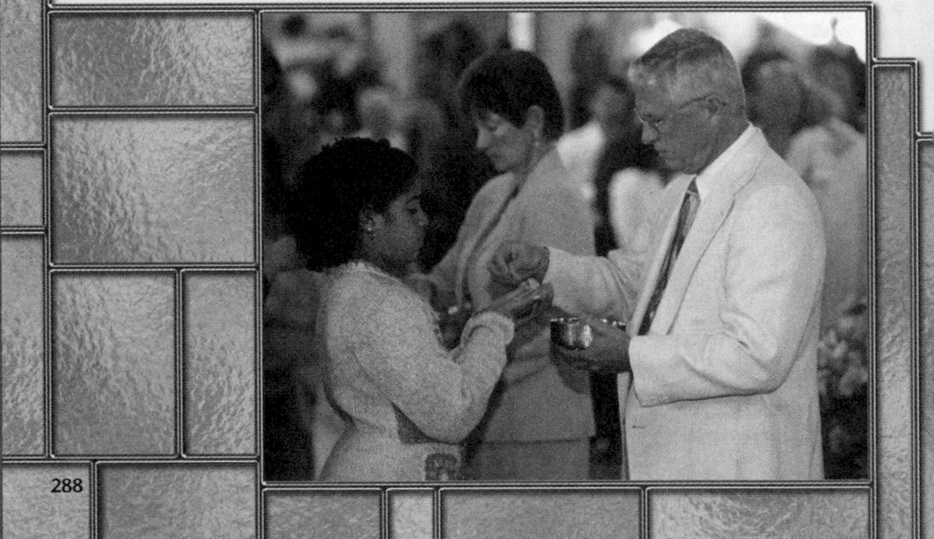

288

Lesson Plan

WE GATHER

___ minutes

✝ **Pray** Pray together the Sign of the Cross and the *We Gather* prayer.

Focus on Life Read aloud the *We Gather* questions and encourage responses. Tell the students that in this lesson they will learn that the sacraments nourish and strengthen us and keep us close to Jesus.

WE BELIEVE

___ minutes

Discuss the Sacraments Ask a volunteer to read aloud the *We Believe* statement. Then have other volunteers read aloud the first two *We Believe* paragraphs. Emphasize that the sacraments change our lives.

Identify Main Ideas Organize the students into three groups. Assign the third *We Believe* paragraph to the first group, the fourth and fifth paragraphs to the second, and the sixth paragraph to the third. Have the students in each group read the assigned text and present the main ideas to the class. Point out:

- The first precept of the Church reminds us to celebrate the sacrament of the Eucharist by participating at Mass on Sundays and holy days of obligation.
- The second precept calls us to lead a sacramental life through regular and frequent celebration of the sacraments of the Eucharist and Reconciliation.
- The third precept calls us to study our faith—to read the Bible and to learn more about the Church and the traditions of our faith.

The second law of the Church reminds us to keep our minds and hearts open to God by receiving Holy Communion and celebrating the sacrament of Reconciliation. This precept does require that we receive the Eucharist at least once during the season of Lent or of Easter. It also requires that we celebrate the sacrament of Reconciliation at least once a year, if we have committed serious sin. However, we can do more than this.

We are called to regular and frequent celebration of the sacrament of the Eucharist and the sacrament of Reconciliation. Receiving Holy Communion and God's forgiveness in Reconciliation are important ways of nourishing and healing the life of Christ in us. Our celebrating the sacraments strengthens the Church, too. We are united more closely to all the members of the Church.

The third law calls us to study our faith. This is an important part of preparing for the sacraments. Learning our faith is also a way to build up the community of faith. We need to read the Bible and learn more about Jesus. We need to have a better understanding of the Church and the traditions of our faith. We study not just to get answers to our own questions but also to discover how we can better live as Christ calls us to live. We learn how we can better serve Christ and all of God's people. We grow as faithful disciples of Jesus Christ.

WE RESPOND

What are some ways you and your family can follow the first three precepts of the Church?

Look at the pictures on these pages. Discuss the ways the people are following the precepts.

289

ACTIVITY BANK

A Sacrament Time Line

Mathematics

Activity materials: half sheets of white construction paper stapled together to make two- to three-foot-long horizontal graphs, one for each student; colored markers

Have the students make graphs to chart their sacramental lives. Give each student a pre-stapled graph strip. Have the students divide their graphs into spaces of equal width, one for each year of a student's life; and write the years, one to a space, across the bottom of the graph. Then have the students write the name of each sacrament they have celebrated in the space for the year in which they first celebrated it. Have the students also draw or paste pictures or symbols in the spaces—a drop of water to symbolize Baptism, for example, or a photo taken on the day of a First Eucharist. The students might also include pictures and symbols to mark the sacraments celebrated by other members of their families in the years shown on the graphs.

Distribute the Reproducible Master Hand out copies of Reproducible Master 25. Invite the students to complete the puzzle. When everyone has completed the puzzle, go over the answers. (Across: 4, parish; 5, sacraments; 6, marks; 8, bishops; 9, deacon; Down: 1, diocese; 2, Church; 3, precepts; 4, pastor; 7, pope)

Quick Check

✔ *What do the sacraments do for us?* (Answers might include that the sacraments strengthen, nourish, and heal the life of Christ in us.)

✔ *What do we remember and celebrate whenever we celebrate a sacrament?* (We remember and celebrate Jesus' life, death, Resurrection, and Ascension.)

WE RESPOND ___ minutes

Connect to Life Read aloud the *We Respond* question and the paragraph that follows. Invite the students to discuss ways they and their families can follow the precepts as well as the ways the people in the pictures are following the precept.

Pray Ask the students to gather in the prayer space. Then pray: *Help us, Lord, to follow your precepts.*

Plan Ahead for Day 4

Catechist Goal: To highlight the ways we can be active in the Church community

Preparation: Have available copies of the Nicene Creed.

Catechist Goal

- To highlight the ways we can be active in the Church community

Our Faith Response

- To take an active role in the Church community

Lesson Materials

- notepaper, one piece per student
- copies of the Nicene Creed

As Catholics...

Marks of the Church

After presenting the lesson, read aloud the *As Catholics* text. Explain that the word *marks* means "characteristics or features." Remind the students that the Church is *one* because it is one faith community united by Baptism. It is *holy* because all Catholics share in God's holiness through Baptism. It is *catholic*, or universal, because it welcomes everyone. It is *apostolic* because its leaders, the pope and the bishops, are the direct successors to the apostles.

We have an active role in the Church community.

WE GATHER

✝ *Jesus, help me to be a loving and generous member of the Church.*

Why is it important to take an active role in

- your family? ____________________
- your class and school? ____________________
- your parish? ____________________
- a sports team or club? ____________________

WE BELIEVE

The Church is a community. We are an important part of that community. Being a member of the Church gives us certain responsibilities to one another. We need to take an active role in living as members of the Church.

The fourth law of the Church deals with marriage and the responsibilities of parents. The Church has certain laws regarding marriage that need to be followed. Welcoming and having children is part of the marriage vow between a husband and a wife. They take on the responsibility of teaching their children the faith and helping them to grow in love for God and others.

The fifth and seventh laws deal with helping the Church help others. As Church members we contribute to the support of the Church in many ways. We offer money, time, and our talents. Just as it takes money to feed and take care of our families, it takes money to keep our parish and diocese strong and active. That is one reason that there is a collection at Mass.

Did you know that our parish collection is shared with our diocese? The Church in our diocese helps people with housing, food, medical care, education, and many other needs. The Church also works for justice and peace for all people. We support these good works by giving money or donating our time and talents. We also work to share the good news of Jesus at school, in our neighborhoods, and with all those we meet. This missionary work is our responsibility as members of the Church.

Caring For Our Community
Catholic Diocese of Gary
and
Northwest Indiana Habitat for Humanity

290

Lesson Plan

WE GATHER ___ minutes

✝ **Pray** Pray together the Sign of the Cross and the *We Gather* prayer.

Focus on Life Read aloud the *Chapter Story* and the question that follows. Invite responses. Then have the students read silently the *We Gather* activity and fill in their answers to the questions. Again, invite volunteers to share their responses. Tell the students that in this lesson they will reflect on active participation in the Church community.

WE BELIEVE ___ minutes

Read the Text Have a volunteer read aloud the *We Believe* statement. Then ask the students to read silently the *We Believe* text. Allow time for all to finish. Then review the following:

- The fourth precept of the Church calls married couples to teach their children the faith and to help them grow in love for God and others.
- The fifth and seventh precepts call us to use our money, our time, and our talents to support the Church, and to join in the Church's missionary work.
- The sixth precept calls us to do penance. Doing penance helps us to trust in God, to care for others as Jesus did, and to show we are sorry for our sins.

Do the Activity Read aloud the directions and invite the students to name some of the ways the precepts help us to grow in holiness. Then ask: *Which pre-*

The sixth law deals with the importance of doing penance. Doing penance helps us to focus on God and the things that are important in our lives as Christians. Doing penance helps us to trust in God, to live simply, and to care for others as Jesus did. Doing penance is also a way to show we are sorry for our sins. That is why it is an important part of the sacrament of Reconciliation. Doing penance also has special meaning during the seasons of Advent and Lent.

We may do penance by giving up things we enjoy, like a favorite food or activity. We may go out of our way to practice a work of mercy or to give of our time in a special way. We may devote extra time to daily prayers and worship. And there are days during the Church year when Catholics do penance by fasting from food or not eating meat. Ash Wednesday, Good Friday, and the Fridays of Lent are some of these days.

The precepts of the Church guide our behavior. They help us to grow in holiness as a community of believers. If you could add one more precept, what would it be and why?

____

____

____

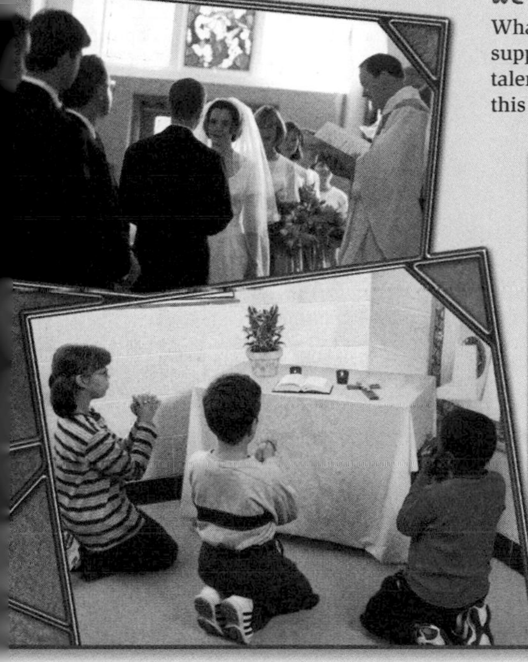

WE RESPOND

What can you and your family do to support the Church? What gifts and talents will you share with your parish this week?

As Catholics...

Each time we gather as a parish to celebrate the Mass we profess our faith by saying the Nicene Creed or the Apostles' Creed. In the Nicene Creed we state, "We believe in one holy catholic and apostolic Church." Our belief in the Church is also a description of it. One, holy, catholic (universal), and apostolic are the four marks of the Church. These marks, or features, identify the Church.

Remember what you believe about the Church as you pray the creed at Mass this week.

291

ACTIVITY BANK

Catholic Social Teaching

Call to Family, Community, and Participation

Activity Materials: large piece of poster board, Catholic magazines or newspapers to cut up for pictures, scissors, glue, colored pens

Remind the students that the fourth precept of the Church calls married couples to instruct their children in the Catholic faith. Then discuss the ways the Church promotes the family as the basic unit of society and calls on governments and other organizations to support and strengthen the family. Invite the students to look through Catholic magazines and newspapers and cut out pictures showing families living out the fourth precept of the Church. Have the students design a collage, and think of a title that best expresses the theme of their collage. Then have the students arrange the pictures on the poster board along with captions explaining the way each picture expresses the theme. Display the finished collage in the classroom or in a hallway.

cept do you think is the most important? Why? After the students have shared their ideas, allow time for everyone to write an answer to the question. Invite volunteers to share their proposals for new precepts and ask, *Why is this precept needed?*

Quick Check

✔ *Why are the fourth and sixth precepts important?* (The fourth precept helps married people raise their families according to God's law; the sixth precept teaches us the importance of doing penance.)

✔ *How are the fifth and seventh precepts connected to one another?* (They both have to do with helping the Church help others.)

WE RESPOND ___ minutes

Connect to Life Ask a volunteer to read aloud the *We Respond* questions. As the students share their answers, write the ideas on the board. Then invite the students to write short notes to their families about sharing gifts and talents with the parish.

Pray Have the students gather in the prayer space. Hand out copies of the Nicene Creed and pray it aloud together.

Plan Ahead for Day 5

Catechist Goal: To review chapter ideas and their relationship to our faith life

Preparation: Make copies of Chapter 25 Test in the Grade 4 Assessment Book (option); have available sentence strips.

Chapter 25 • Day 5

Catechist Goal

- To review chapter ideas and their relationship to their faith life

Our Faith Response

- To apply what has been learned to our lives

Chapter Test

Chapter 25 Test is provided in the Grade 4 Assessment Book.

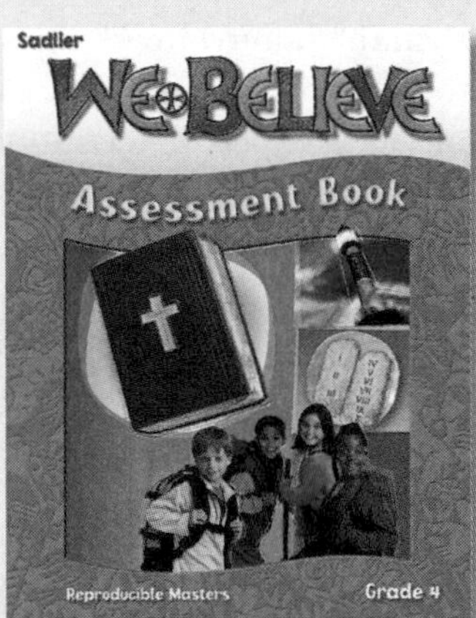

Review

Grade 4 Chapter 25

Write the letter of the phrase that defines each of the following:

1. d parish
2. c precepts of the Church
3. b bishops
4. a pastor

a. the priest who leads the parish in worship, prayer, and teaching

b. the leaders of the Church who continue the work of the apostles

c. the laws to help us know and fulfill our responsibilities as members of the Church

d. a community of believers who worship and work together

Circle the correct answer.

5. Through the _____ the life of Christ in us grows.

precepts (sacraments) responsibilities

6. The _____ precepts of the Church remind us that growing in holiness and serving the Church are important responsibilities.

three (seven) ten

7. _____ is like a door to the rest of the sacraments.

Eucharist (Baptism) Reconciliation

8. Catholics around the world share the same _____ in Jesus and the Church.

(beliefs) customs language

Write a sentence to answer the question.

9–10. What are some things that happen in a parish community?

See pages 284–285.

Interview a classmate to find out what he or she knows about the precepts of the Church. Tape your interview or write a report on it. Share it with the class.

292

Lesson Plan

___ minutes

Chapter Review Remind the students that they are now going to check their understanding of what they have learned. Have them complete questions 1–8. Invite volunteers to read aloud the correct answers. Then ask the students to write their responses to question 9–10 and have volunteers share their answers.

Assessment Activity Invite a student to read aloud the activity directions. Organize the students into pairs for the interviews. In each pair have the first partner interview the second; then, when the interview is finished, have the second student interview the first. During each interview have the student who is asking the questions write down the other student's answers as a reporter would. These notes will form the basis of the students' summary reports. When all have finished, give the students time to write their reports. Then invite the students to share their reports with the class.

___ minutes

Reflect & Pray Gather the students in a circle in the prayer space and ask them to join hands. Read the *Reflect & Pray* text aloud, pausing after each sentence to give the students time to reflect silently.

Key Words Write the *Key Words* on the board. Then ask the students to write a sentence using each word. Invite volunteers to share their sentences.

We Respond in Faith

Reflect & Pray

When you pray for your family, remember your parish family as well. Ask God to bless the Church and all its members. Ask the Holy Spirit to guide the Church so that we may continue Christ's mission in the world.

When you participate at Mass and receive the Eucharist, remember to pray for your brothers and sisters in Christ.

parish (p. 285)
pastor (p. 285)
deacon (p. 285)
diocese (p. 285)
bishops (p. 285)
pope (p. 285)
precepts of the Church (p. 286)

Remember

- The Church is a worldwide community.
- We have responsibilities as members of the Church.
- We celebrate the sacraments.
- We have an active role in the Church community.

Our Catholic Life

Saint Monica and Saint Augustine

Saint Monica was a married woman who lived in northern Africa in the fourth century. She had three children, but she worried most about her son Augustine. He was very intelligent, but his life was going in the wrong direction.

Monica prayed for her son for seventeen years. Finally, Augustine realized that only God could make his life meaningful. After many years, he was baptized. Augustine became a great teacher of our Catholic faith. He was a priest and a bishop. We know him now as Saint Augustine, and his feast day is August 28. His mother Monica is now Saint Monica. She is the patroness of married women. Her feast day is August 27.

Home Connection

Sharing Faith with My Family

Make sure to send home the family page (text page 294).

Encourage the students to read and discuss the story of Saint Josephine Bakhita with their families and to think about someone to nominate to the *Holiness Hall of Fame*.

For additional information and activities, encourage families to visit Sadlier's

www.WEBELIEVEweb.com

Remember Review the *We Believe* statements by having the students use sentence strips to write an example illustrating each of the four statements. Collect the sentence strips and put them in a basket or a hat. Then have the students take turns drawing a strip, reading it aloud, and naming the *We Believe* statement it illustrates.

Our Catholic Life Have volunteers read aloud the text. Then ask: *Why do you think Saint Monica was chosen as a biography subject for this chapter?* (She is the patron saint of married women, and this chapter reminds us of the responsibility Catholic parents have to instruct their children in the faith. Saint Monica devoted her life to this task and prayed for many years for her son Augustine to join the Christian community.)

Chapter 25 Grade 4

SHARING FAITH with My Family

Sharing What I Learned

Discuss the following with your family:

- the Church community
- the precepts of the Church
- the importance of celebrating the sacraments
- our role in the Church.

Our Family of Saints **Saint Josephine Bakhita**

Kidnapped from a wealthy family in Africa and sold into slavery, Josephine later won her freedom. She began to speak out for Catholic missionaries throughout the world.

How can your family help Catholic missionaries?

The Ten Commandments guide us as we try to lead holy lives. With your family, think of someone to nominate to be in a "Holiness Hall of Fame." It should be a person who helps provide for the needs of the Church. In the space, write some reasons why your family chose this person. Then share some ways your family can follow this person's example.

Holiness Hall of Fame

We nominate ______

because ______

As a family, we can ______

Visit Sadlier's www.WEBELIEVEweb.com

Connect to the Catechism
For adult background and reflection, see paragraphs 814, 2041, 2042, and 2043.

294

PUPIL PAGE 294

Chapter 26 We Are Called to Discipleship

Overview

In Chapter 25 the students learned what it means to be a member of the worldwide Catholic Church. In this chapter they will learn about the theological and cardinal virtues and come to see that everyone is called to be a disciple.

Doctrinal Content	For Adult Reading and Reflection *Catechism of the Catholic Church*
The students will learn:	Paragraph
• The virtues of faith, hope, and love bring us closer to God.	1813
• Mary is our model for virtue and discipleship.	967
• The cardinal virtues guide us.	1805
• We are called to live a life of love.	1825

theological virtues (p. 296)

cardinal virtues (p. 300)

Catechist Background

Have you ever been completely dependent on another?

One day the disciples of Jesus approached him and asked why he spoke in parables. He replied, "Because knowledge of the mysteries of the kingdom of heaven has been granted to you, but to them it has not been granted" (Matthew 13:11). Initially, then, Jesus chose a select few with whom to share the "mysteries of the kingdom." Jesus appointed from them "twelve [whom he also called apostles] that they might be with him and he might send them forth to preach" (Mark 3:14). The apostles, in turn, passed on to the Church what they learned from Jesus.

Throughout his public ministry Jesus gave his disciples advice. He told them not to seek out "the righteous but sinners" (Matthew 9:13). He asked them to take up their crosses and follow him (Matthew 10:38). He told them, "Take nothing for the journey, neither walking stick, nor sack, nor food, nor money, and let no one take a second tunic" (Luke 9:3).

Fast forward to the present. Jesus now calls us to be his disciples. Through the apostolic teaching of the Church, he shares with us the mysteries of the kingdom. He commissions us to go out and preach his message by the truth of our words and the power of our example. And the advice he gave his first disciples is still pertinent today. Jesus asks us not simply to "preach to the choir" or convert the converted but to reach out to those in need of his healing and light. He tells us to give ourselves completely to him even in our tragedies and trials. And Jesus warns us about becoming so dependent on the things of this world that we cannot give ourselves to him.

What does it mean to you to depend on Jesus?

Lesson Planning Guide

Lesson Focus	Presentation	Materials
Day 1		
page 295 **We Gather in Prayer** **pages 296–297** *The virtues of faith, hope, and love bring us closer to God.*	• Listen and respond to Scripture in prayer. • Discuss the **We Gather** questions. • Read and discuss the theological virtues in the **We Believe** text.  Do the **We Respond** activity. • Pray together.	For the prayer space: picture of the Last Supper, lists of the theological and cardinal virtues
Day 2		
pages 298–299 *Mary is our model for virtue and discipleship.*	• Discuss the **We Gather** questions. • Read and discuss the **We Believe** text. • Reflect on the **We Respond** statement and question. • Pray to Mary. • Read and discuss peacemaking in the *Blessed are they . . .* text.	• copies of Reproducible Master 26, guide page 295G • colored construction paper, black markers, tape, scissors • grade 4 CD
Day 3		
pages 300–301 *The cardinal virtues guide us.*	• Discuss the **We Gather** question. • Read and discuss the cardinal virtues in the **We Believe** text.  Fill in the chart about the cardinal virtues. • Reflect on the **We Respond** question. • Pray together.	• chart paper, marker
Day 4		
pages 302–303 *We are called to live a life of love.*	• Discuss the **We Gather** questions. • Read and discuss the **We Believe** text. • Reflect on the **We Respond** question. • Read and discuss the pope and young people in the *As Catholics* text.	• slips of paper, basket • brightly colored stationery
Day 5		
page 304 **Review** **pages 305–306** **We Respond in Faith**	• Complete questions 1–10. Work on the *Assessment Activity.* • Complete the *Reflect & Pray* activity. • Review *Remember* and *Key Words.* • Use the *Our Catholic Life* to reflect on the year's study. • Discuss **Sharing Faith with My Family**	• slips of paper, chart paper, a marker • Chapter 26 in the Assessment Book, pp. 51–52 • Chapter 26 Test in Test Generator • Review & Resource Book, pp. 61–63 • Family Book, pp. 74–76

For additional ideas, activities, and opportunities: Visit Sadlier's **www.WEBELIEVEweb.com**

Enrichment Ideas

Chapter Story

Gabrielle had just scored another goal for her soccer team. She ran across the field and gave her friend Rosie a high five. "Way to go, Gaby!" Rosie cheered. After the game Rosie asked Gabrielle if she would like to come over to her house on Sunday morning.

Every Sunday morning Gabrielle went to Mass with her family. She really wanted to go to Rosie's house, but she knew she needed to go to church. Gabrielle looked at the ground and said, "Um, I'm busy on Sunday." Rosie shrugged, "Okay. Maybe next week. You don't have to go to church, do you?"

Gabrielle shook her head no and ran over to her mom, who had watched the game from the sidelines. Gabrielle told her about Rosie's invitation. Gabrielle's mom asked her whether she had invited Rosie to come to Mass with them. Gabrielle mumbled that she hadn't thought of that.

Gabrielle's mom put her arm around her shoulder and said, "You shouldn't be embarrassed to tell your friends that you go to church. Think of everything that God has done for you. Don't you want to share that good news with everyone? Remember that Jesus told us to be witnesses to our faith." That night, before she went to bed, Gabrielle prayed, "Jesus, I'm sorry I was afraid to talk about you to Rosie. Help me to share my faith with her. Amen."

The next day at soccer practice, Gabrielle asked Rosie whether she would like to go to Mass with her on Sunday. "Sure," replied Rosie. "I've never gone to church before." She passed the ball to Gabrielle, and they both laughed.

That Sunday Gabrielle felt a little nervous. What if Rosie didn't like her church? Would she still want to be her friend? But after Mass, Rosie smiled and asked, "Can I come back with you next week?"

▶ *Have you ever been afraid or embarrassed to share our faith?*

FAITH and MEDIA

▶ On day 4, after reading the *As Catholics* text about World Youth Day, invite the students to go online to find pictures and descriptions of recent World Youth Days.

▶ On Day 5 the students will be asked to read the parish bulletin to learn more about the Church and our call to discipleship. Encourage them to visit the parish and diocesan Web sites over the summer to keep up with the news of the local Church.

▶ Mention that students who will be traveling during the summer can use the Internet to find information about Catholic churches and Mass schedules for the places they will be visiting. An online search for "Mass times" will bring up the needed information.

CHAPTER PROJECT: A CALENDAR OF VIRTUE

Explain to the students that this week they will learn about the theological and cardinal virtues. Ask them to list the virtues they try to practice in their daily lives. Then give each student a large piece of construction paper with which to make a *Calendar of Virtue* for the week. Have the students make a header for each day and leave space below it to record their virtuous acts. Have the students decorate their calendars using colored markers and glitter pens. At the end of the week display the calendars in the classroom under the heading *We Are Witnesses to Jesus' Love*. Remind the students that a virtue is a good habit, and that the more we practice the virtues, the easier it becomes for us to be virtuous.

Connections

To Family

Remind the students that their families have been called to discipleship. As the students learn more about the cardinal and theological virtues, take the opportunity to point out some ways to practice these virtues at home. Explain that the practice of these virtues can help a family grow in strength and unity.

To Catholic Social Teaching

Solidarity of the Human Family
The theme of solidarity in Catholic social teaching reminds us that we all belong to one human family. As Catholics we are called to be our brothers' and sisters' keepers. Just as Jesus came to serve, we are called to serve others, regardless of race, class, age, or gender. Ask the students to think of ways they can serve others. Encourage them to reach out to someone they might have ignored, such as a student from a background different from their own.

To Mission

Jesus calls us to be witnesses to our faith. Ask the students to share their faith with others. Encourage them to invite friends to attend Mass with them. Help them to understand that we are called to live in a way that shows others we are followers of Christ. We should joyfully proclaim our faith to others.

Meeting Individual Needs

Students with Auditory Needs

Be aware of any special needs that your students who are deaf or have difficulty hearing may have. Whenever possible, use diagrams or pictures to illustrate the points you make in class. Use overhead transparencies of main points so that the students can readily understand the lesson. If a student has a sign-language interpreter, it is helpful to provide that student with copies of the transparencies ahead of time. This will allow the student to focus on the interpreter and not have to miss the material being shown on the overhead.

ADDITIONAL RESOURCES

Videos *The Gospel with a Smile,* Ikonographics II and Fisher Productions. This video includes *Tape 1: Faith,* the stories of the calming of the sea, the wise and foolish virgins, and doubting Thomas (18 minutes); *Tape 2: Hope,* the stories of Abraham and Sarah, the big catch of fish, and Pentecost (15 minutes); *Tape 3: Charity,* the lost son, the washing of the feet, and the feeding of five thousand (15 minutes).

To find more ideas for books, videos, and other learning material, visit Sadlier's

www.WEBELIEVEweb.com

Developing an Understanding of Vocation

by Sr. Maureen Sullivan, OP, Ph.D.

Sr. Maureen, a Dominican Sister of Hope, is a national religion consultant for William H. Sadlier, Inc. She is currently assistant professor of theology at St. Anselm College in Manchester, New Hampshire. Sr. Maureen received her Ph. D. in theology from Fordham University in New York City.

One of the many topics addressed by the second Vatican Council (1962–65) was that of "vocation." The word itself comes from the Latin word *vocare*, which means "to call."

In Chapter 40 of *Lumen Gentium*, the Dogmatic Constitution on the Church, we read, "The Lord Jesus , the divine Teacher and Model of all perfection, preached holiness of life to each and every one of his disciples, regardless of their situation." (*LG* 40) By virtue of our Baptism, we are all called to holiness. We can be faithful disciples and holy people whatever our particular vocation.

There are those who are invited by God to become holy as lay persons. "By reason of their special vocation it belongs to the laity to seek the kingdom of God by engaging in temporal affairs and directing them according to God's will." (*LG* 31)

Lay people may be called to the married life. They witness to Jesus through their faithful love for each other and through their contributions to society. Married people may be gifted by God with children and become holy even as they form their children in holiness.

Lay people may be called to the single life. They grow in holiness through their loving relationships with family and friends and through their witness to gospel values in their work. God calls some men and women to become holy through living the vowed life in religious communities. "Religious life derives from the mystery of the Church. It is a gift she has received from her Lord, a gift she offers as a stable way of life to the faithful called by God to profess the counsels." (*CCC* 926) Religious who vow a life of poverty, chastity and obedience serve the Church and the world in many ways. These sisters, brothers, and religious priests grow in holiness through a life lived in service and prayer.

God calls some men to the ordained priesthood. "Holy Orders is the sacrament through which the

(continued on next page)

Catechist Development Topics (Topic and Guide Page)

Resources

Lumen Gentium, Dogmatic Constitution on the Church, from the Vatican II Documents.

Lucy Kaylin, *For the Love of God: The Faith and Future of the American Nun.* New York: Harper Collins Publishers, 2000.

Kevin and Marilyn Ryan, ed., *Why I Am Still A Catholic.* New York: Riverhead Books, 1998.

mission entrusted by Christ to his apostles continues to be exercised in the Church until the end of time." (*CCC*, 1536) The priest represents Christ and teaches, governs, and sanctifies in his name. The priest grows in holiness as he cares for the Church, the Body of Christ, and is an example of service and compassion.

God may call us to become holy by any path he chooses. How can we know what God is calling us to be and to do? We can hear God in prayer, certainly through the celebration of the liturgy and the sacraments. We can hear God when we reflect on the gifts and talents he has given us which may point to a certain vocation. We can hear God in the wisdom of people of faith who advise and encourage us.

Whatever way we follow Jesus, we are called to holiness—and a life of love. "Love, in fact, is the vocation which includes all others; it's a universe of its own, comprising all time and space—it's eternal!" (Saint Thérèse of Lisieux, *CCC* 826)

Ways to Implement Developing An Understanding of Vocation

- Have the group read stories about Catholics in different vocations to demonstrate the universal call to holiness. We have many wonderful witnesses to draw from: lay missionaries, saints, etc.
- Invite the priests, sisters, brothers, and lay ecclesial ministers of the parish to share their stories with the group. Have the students prepare and submit questions ahead of time.
- Invite married couples, parents, and single people to share the ways their lives help them to grow in holiness.
- Talk to the students about your own experience of "vocation."

For additional ideas, activities, and opportunities, visit Sadlier's

www.WEBELIEVEweb.com

With thanks to:
Alice Caruso
Curé of Ars
Merrick, New York

Alice encourages her students to explore specific roles within life vocations. Working in groups, the students identify a vocation and role they want to research. (This might be a religious woman in the nursing profession, or a brother who does prison ministry, or a married couple in the Peace Corps.) Each group researches a "A Day in the Life of..." their chosen person, using the Internet, library, personal interviews, etc. The research culminates in a "Views on Vocations" panel. One member of each group is chosen to "become" the person researched and role plays that person's story on a "typical" day. Some students even use costumes and props to convey their message! Alice invites her group to follow up with a bulletin board about the many roles one might have within each life vocation.

Notes

Name ____

Write or draw about one way you have grown in faith this year.

We Are Called to Discipleship

26

Preparing to Pray

In this prayer the students will reflect on the scriptural story of Jesus washing his disciples' feet.

- Select four students to be the readers. Allow time for them to rehearse their parts.
- Tell the students that everyone will read aloud the Scripture passages marked "All."
- Select three students to place items in the prayer space at the appointed time.

The Prayer Space

- Have available a picture of the Last Supper, a list of the theological virtues, and a list of the cardinal virtues.

We Gather in Prayer

Reader: The apostles joined Jesus to share a last supper before he died. While they were getting ready to eat, Jesus got up, took off his outer garment, and prepared to wash their feet. The apostles were shocked. This made no sense to them. Only slaves washed feet! Peter asked a question that was on everyone's mind:

John 13:6–17

All: "Master, are you going to wash my feet?" (John 13:6)

Reader: Jesus told Peter that he would not understand, but he must let Jesus wash his feet. Then Jesus washed the feet of Peter and all the apostles before returning to his place at table with them. Jesus asked the apostles:

All: "Do you realize what I have done for you?" (John 13:12)

Reader: Jesus explained what he had just done. "If I, therefore, the master and teacher, have washed your feet, you ought to wash one another's feet. I have given you a model to follow, so that as I have done for you, you should also do." (John 13:14–15)

All: Jesus, help us understand how to follow your example.

Reader: Jesus gave a powerful example of what he expects from his disciples. If they are to be like him, they must be willing to serve others. At this Last Supper, Jesus had some encouraging words for disciples who follow his example:

All: "If you understand this, blessed are you if you do it." (John 13:17)

295

This Week's Liturgy

Visit **www.webelieveweb.com** for this week's liturgical readings and other seasonal material.

Lesson Plan

We Gather in Prayer ___ minutes

Pray

- Invite the students to gather in a circle in the prayer space with their books open to the opening prayer.
- Pray the Sign of the Cross together. Then signal the first reader to begin.
- After the final reading from Scripture, have the students place the picture of the Last Supper and the lists of virtues in the prayer space.
- Invite the students to share what this story means to them.

Home Connection Update

Invite the students to share their experiences using the Chapter 25 family page. Ask: *Whom did you choose this week for the "Holiness Hall of Fame"?*

Chapter 26 • Day 1

Catechist Goal

- To present the theological virtues of faith, hope, and love

Our Faith Response

- To identify examples of the virtues of faith, hope, and love

theological virtues

Teaching Tip

The Theological Virtue of Hope

Some students—a student who is mourning the loss of a loved one, for example—may find it difficult to feel hope. Encourage these students to understand that even when things might seem hopeless, we can trust that God is with us. Assure the students that even when we are sad, there is a place in our hearts for joy. Be sensitive to these students and keep them in your prayers.

The virtues of faith, hope, and love bring us closer to God.

WE GATHER

✝ *We believe in God—the Father, the Son, and the Holy Spirit.*

Sometimes we get into habits that are not good for us. Have you ever tried to break a habit? What is it like to try to change?

WE BELIEVE

As Catholics we believe that through virtue we can change. A virtue is a good habit that helps us to act according to God's love for us. Virtue helps us to become more like God. Faith, hope, and love are the **theological virtues**. They are called theological virtues because they are gifts from God. The virtues of faith, hope, and love bring us closer to God and help us to want to be with God forever.

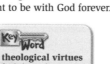

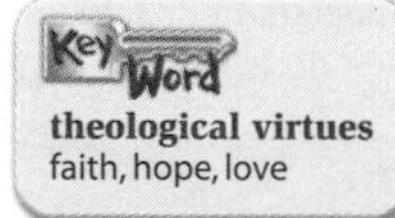
theological virtues
faith, hope, love

The gift of faith enables us to believe in God—the Father, the Son, and the Holy Spirit. Faith helps us to believe and accept all that God has said and done. The gift of faith helps us to believe that God is with us and is acting in our lives.

However, faith is also a choice we make. Because God created us with free will, we choose to believe and to live by what God has made known to us. Within the Church community we respond to his gift of faith. Through prayer, the sacraments, and living out the commandments, our faith grows. The Church guides and strengthens our faith. We remain close to God and God remains with us.

As disciples of Christ we must not only have faith and live by it but we must also show others our belief in God. As Jesus tells us, we are all called to witness to our faith: "Everyone who acknowledges me before others I will acknowledge before my heavenly Father. But whoever denies me before others, I will deny before my heavenly Father" (Matthew 10:32–33).

Lesson Plan

WE GATHER ___ minutes

✝ **Pray** Pray together the Sign of the Cross and the *We Gather* prayer.

Focus on Life Read aloud the *Chapter Story* and the question that follows. Invite responses. Then read aloud the *We Gather* text and invite the students to share their responses to the questions. Tell the students that in this lesson they will learn that the theological virtues of faith, hope, and love are good habits that help us to follow God's will.

WE BELIEVE ___ minutes

Introduce the Meaning Invite one volunteer to read aloud the *We Believe* statement and another to read the first *We Believe* paragraph. Ask why people would want to change. Stress that we are able to change with God's help. God gives us the theological virtues of faith, hope, and love to help us.

Read About the Virtues Have volunteers read aloud the next two paragraphs. Emphasize the following:

- The gift of faith allows us to believe in God.
- Jesus calls us to be witnesses to our faith.

Invite volunteers to read aloud the remaining paragraphs. Then pause to discuss the following:

- The gift of hope allows us to place our trust in Jesus.
- The gift of love allows us to love God and others.
- Love is the fulfillment of everything that God calls us to do and to be.

The gift of hope enables us to trust in Jesus and in God's promise to love us always. We place our trust in Christ's promises. We do not rely only on our own strength, but on the strength of the Holy Spirit. Hope helps us to respond to the happiness that God has placed in our hearts. Hope helps us work to spread the Kingdom of God here on earth, and to look forward to the kingdom in heaven.

As Saint Paul tells us in his letter to the Romans, "Hope does not disappoint, because the love of God has been poured out into our hearts through the holy Spirit that has been given to us" (Romans 5:5).

The gift of love enables us to love God and to love our neighbor. Love is the greatest of all virtues. All the other virtues come from it. Love is the goal of our lives as Christians.

We can love God and one another because God first loves us. God's love for us never ends. He is always there for us. As disciples of Jesus we are called to love and encourage one another. Our parents, guardians, families, and teachers show their love for us by providing for and encouraging us. We can love and encourage others, too. We can be kind to classmates and helpful to people we meet. When we show love for one another, we are truly disciples of Jesus.

Love is the fulfillment of everything that God calls us to do and to be. "So faith, hope, love remain, these three; but the greatest of these is love." (1 Corinthians 13:13)

We Respond

Saint Paul wrote letters to the early Christian communities. Unlike Paul, you may have e-mail and instant messaging.

Write your own letter to a Christian community. Tell the community how faith, hope, and love have made a difference in your life.

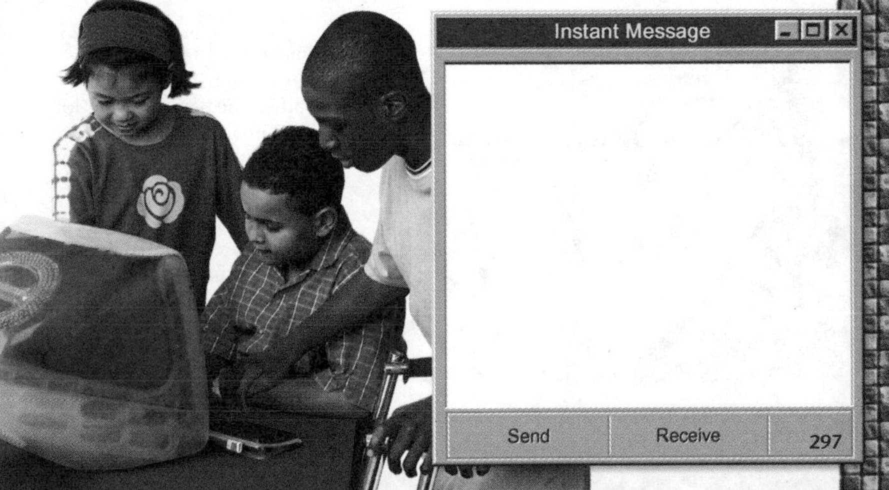

Chapter 26 • Day 1

Activity Bank

Curriculum Connection

Art

Activity Materials: three large sheets of butcher paper, paints and brushes

Invite the students to make a three-panel mural depicting the three theological virtues. The first panel will represent the virtue of faith; the second, the virtue of hope; and the third, the virtue of love. Encourage the students to use their imaginations as they design the panels. They may want to use symbols—the traditional symbols for the theological virtues are a cross (faith), an anchor (hope), and a heart (love)—or they may want to include scenes showing the virtues in action. Display the finished mural in the classroom, a hallway, or another appropriate place.

Think About the Key Word Encourage the students to show their understanding of the theological virtues by listing examples of ways to live the virtues of faith, hope, and love. Allow time for the students to write down their examples; then invite volunteers to share their lists with the class.

Quick Check

✔ *What is a virtue?* (A virtue is a good habit that helps us to act according to God's love for us.)

✔ *What are the theological virtues?* (The theological virtues are faith, hope, and love.)

We Respond ___ minutes

Connect to Life Read aloud the *We Respond* activity directions. Remind the students that readings from the letters Saint Paul wrote to the early Christian communities are proclaimed during the Mass. When all have finished, ask volunteers to share their messages.

Pray Gather together in the prayer space and pray: *God, help us to be strong in faith, steady in hope, and ready to love all in your name. Amen.*

Plan Ahead for Day 2

Catechist Goal: To explain that Mary is our model of virtue and discipleship

Preparation: Make copies of Reproducible Master 26; have available colored construction paper, black markers, tape, and scissors.

Catechist Goal

- To explain that Mary is our model of virtue and discipleship

Our Faith Response

- To follow Mary's example and grow as disciples of Jesus

Lesson Materials

- Grade 4 CD
- copies of Reproducible Master 26
- colored construction paper and black markers
- tape and scissors

Blessed are they...

Blessed are the Peacemakers

After you have completed the lesson, have a volunteer read aloud Blessed are they . . . Invite the students to work in small groups to decide how they can be peacemakers. Call on a representative from each group to report its ideas. Encourage the students to draw themselves (or paste a school picture) and add their names to the banner.

Mary is our model for virtue and discipleship.

WE GATHER

✝ *Mary, pray for us that we may grow in faith, hope, and love.*

When have you had to say yes to your mother, father, or other family members? What made saying yes an easy or difficult decision for you?

WE BELIEVE

Through God's grace, we open our hearts to the influence of the Holy Spirit. We grow in holiness. When we read the gospels, we find an example of holiness in a young Jewish girl named Mary.

Pedro Fresquis (1780–1840), *Our Lady of Sorrows*

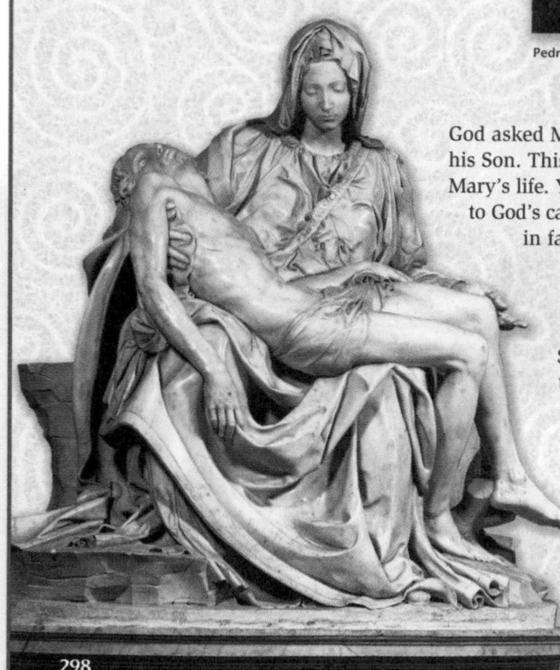

God asked Mary to become the mother of his Son. This would mean a big change in Mary's life. Yet Mary's heart was totally open to God's call. Her yes to God was a response in faith, hope, and love.

Our life as Christians is based on our relationship with God the Father, the Son, and the Holy Spirit. At our Baptism we received the gift of grace. We were given a share of God's very own life.

God wanted all people to live in his love forever. However, humans turned from God. But God promised to be with us always. He loved us so much that he sent his Son to save us.

Michelangelo (1475–1564), *Pietà*

298

Lesson Plan

WE GATHER ___ minutes

✝ **Pray** Pray together the Sign of the Cross and the *We Gather* prayer.

Focus on Life Read aloud the *We Gather* questions and ask the students to share their answers. Encourage those who respond to explain the thoughts and actions that led up to their decisions to say yes. Tell the students that in this lesson they will learn that Mary said yes to God and that we are to follow her example and be disciples of Jesus.

WE BELIEVE ___ minutes

Learn About Mary Ask a volunteer to read aloud the *We Believe* statement. Then invite volunteers to read aloud the *We Believe* paragraphs. Pause to discuss the following:

- Mary responded to God in faith, hope, and love.
- Mary was Jesus' first disciple. She is the perfect model of discipleship.
- Jesus promised his disciples the Holy Spirit would always be with them.
- The Holy Spirit is with us today.

Follow Mary's Example Hand out pieces of colored construction paper. Have the students trace around their feet on the paper and cut out the footprints. On a bulletin board write the sentence *Follow Mary's Example.* Ask the students to use black markers to write on their footprints one way that they could follow Mary's example. (Possible answers include: learn from Jesus; trust in God; love God and others.) Play appropriate music from the Grade 4 CD. Invite the students to sign their footprints and add them to the bulletin board.

Mary was part of God's plan. She was the mother of God's Son. She cared for Jesus. She watched him grow and learn. Mary in turn listened to Jesus and learned from him. As Jesus grew older and began to do his Father's will, Mary "kept all these things in her heart" (Luke 2:51). Her faith, hope, and love of God were strong. She stood by Jesus as he died on the cross and was with his followers after the Resurrection. Mary is the perfect model of the way we should live as disciples of her son, Jesus. She was Jesus' first disciple.

The disciples of Jesus were a community of believers, the Church of Jesus Christ. God gave Jesus' disciples the faith, the hope, and the love to spread the news of Jesus Christ. God promised that the Holy Spirit would always remain with Jesus' disciples. The Holy Spirit would always be with the Church.

Blessed are they...

Write your name in this banner.

The Beatitudes call each of us to find happiness in God. The lives of the saints are examples to us. From them we can learn to trust in God and follow Christ. Christ asks us to have peace in our hearts and to work for peace in our world. How can you be a peacemaker? How can you bring Christ's love to the world?

"Blessed are the peacemakers, for they will be called children of God." (Matthew 5:9)

In the space above, draw yourself as a peacemaker.

The Holy Spirit is with us today. We see the Holy Spirit through the faith, hope, and love of each member of the Church. The presence of the Holy Spirit is felt when these virtues are working in our lives.

Keith Mallett (1948–), *Mother's Hands*

WE RESPOND

Like Mary, we can say yes to God in our lives. Mary's life shows us that all things are possible with God. We can call upon Mary to pray for us that we may grow in faith, hope, and love as disciples of her son Jesus. What can you do this week to grow as a disciple of Jesus?

Holy Mary, Mother of God, pray for us sinners, now and at the hour of our death. Amen.

299

Chapter 26 • Day 2

ACTIVITY BANK

Multicultural Connection

Devotion to Mary Around the World

Activity Materials: Internet and other research resources

Invite the students to learn about the ways Catholics around the world follow Mary's example and express their devotion to her. Organize the students into small groups and assign each group a specific country and devotion to research. For example, one group might research devotion to Our Lady of Guadalupe in Mexico; another group might research the Black Madonna of Czestochowa in Poland; and other groups might research Our Lady of Fatima (Portugal) or Our Lady of Knock (Ireland). Bookmark appropriate Web sites for the students to visit to find information. When all have finished, ask each group to report to the class about its findings.

Complete the Reproducible Master Hand out copies of Reproducible Master 26 and have the students complete the activity. When all have finished, ask volunteers to share their responses.

Quick Check

✔ *How did Mary have the trust and strength to say yes to God?* (Her heart was totally open to God's call.)

✔ *What is God's plan?* (God's plan is that all people live in his love forever.)

WE RESPOND ___ minutes

Connect to Life Read aloud the first *We Respond* paragraph and invite the students to think of times they called upon Mary to help them grow in faith, hope, and love. Then have the students answer the question and share their responses.

Pray Invite the students to gather in the prayer space with their books open to *We Respond*. Draw the students' attention to the pictures of Mary on the pages. Then pray together the prayer to Mary in *We Respond*.

Plan Ahead for Day 3

Catechist Goal: To introduce the four cardinal virtues

Preparation: Have available chart paper and a marker.

Catechist Goal
- To introduce the four cardinal virtues

Our Faith Response
- To choose one way to practice the cardinal virtues on a daily basis

 **cardinal virtues**

Lesson Materials
- chart paper, marker

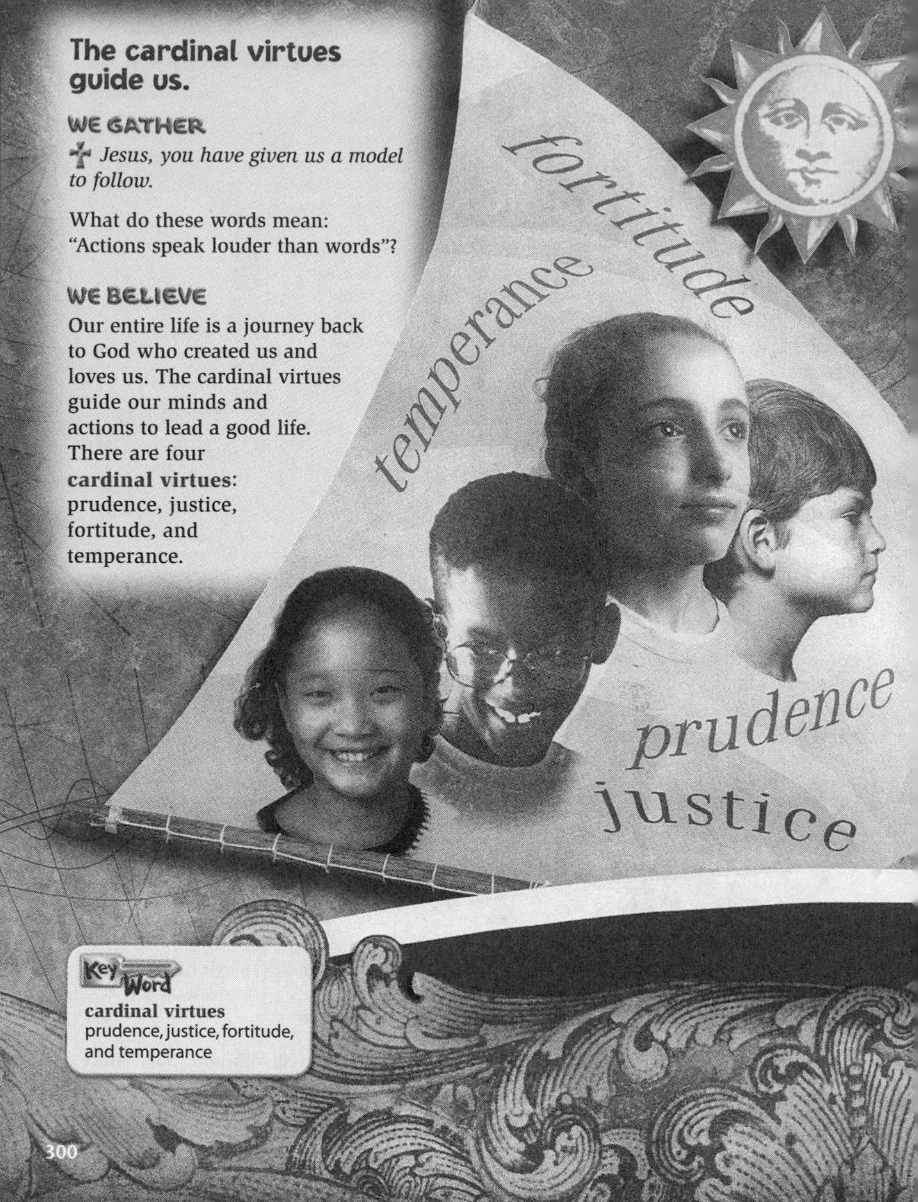

The cardinal virtues guide us.
WE GATHER
Jesus, you have given us a model to follow.
What do these words mean: "Actions speak louder than words"?
WE BELIEVE
Our entire life is a journey back to God who created us and loves us. The cardinal virtues guide our minds and actions to lead a good life. There are four cardinal virtues: prudence, justice, fortitude, and temperance.
fortitude
temperance
prudence
justice
Key Word
cardinal virtues
prudence, justice, fortitude, and temperance
300

Teaching Note
Practicing Prudence

Prudence may be the most difficult of the cardinal virtues for fourth graders to understand and practice. This moral skill is a necessary foundation for the discernment required in making right judgments. Prudence enables us to love wisely and do good in the most effective way. It sees beyond the surface of things and senses the spirit of the law behind the letter.

Lesson Plan

WE GATHER
___ minutes

Pray Pray together the Sign of the Cross and the *We Gather* prayer.

Focus on Life Ask aloud the *We Gather* question and invite the students to respond. You might illustrate the concept of actions speaking louder than words by telling the class in a friendly voice that you enjoy talking to them and then turning away to read something on your desk or stare out the window. After a few moments ask the students how these actions made them feel. Then say: *We must not only say virtuous things but must do them, too.* Tell the students that in this lesson they will learn about the four cardinal virtues.

WE BELIEVE
___ minutes

Learn About the Cardinal Virtues Invite volunteers to read aloud the *We Believe* statement and the first *We Believe* paragraph. Emphasize that practicing the cardinal virtues will help us to lead a good life.

Do the Activity Organize the students into small groups. Ask each group to read the activity directions, discuss quietly the information in the chart, and work together to fill in ways to live out each virtue. Invite a volunteer from each group to share the group's responses. List these on the board under the name of the appropriate virtue.

Reinforce the Key Word Write the names of the cardinal virtues on separate pieces of paper and post them in the four corners of the classroom. Invite the

Read the chart below. The first column names the cardinal virtues. The second column explains how the virtue helps us. In the third column give one example of ways you can use the virtue to guide your actions. Together make a class list of the many ways to practice each of these virtues.

Virtue	The virtue helps us to	How I can live out this virtue
Prudence	make sound judgments and direct our actions toward what is good	
Justice	give to God and our neighbors what is rightfully theirs	
Fortitude	act bravely in the face of troubles and fears	
Temperance	keep our desires under control and balance our use of material goods	

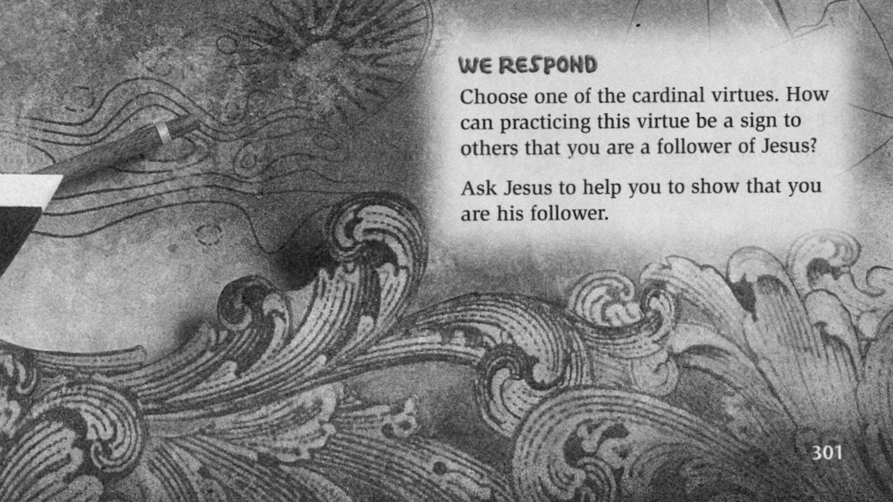

WE RESPOND

Choose one of the cardinal virtues. How can practicing this virtue be a sign to others that you are a follower of Jesus?

Ask Jesus to help you to show that you are his follower.

301

ACTIVITY BANK

Curriculum Connection

Language Arts

Actions speak louder than words. This forceful maxim can provide an ideal springboard for a drama activity centered on the cardinal virtues. Organize the students into small groups and assign each group a cardinal virtue. Ask each group to devise a short skit about living its assigned virtue—a skit that shows in a concrete way that actions do speak louder than words. Have each group act out its skit for the class and invite the other students to name the virtue being portrayed.

students to name ways to follow one of the virtues. As each student gives his or her example, have the student go to the appropriate corner. For example, a student might say *Don't eat too many cookies* and then go to the corner marked *Temperance*. Continue until all the students have given examples, and all the cardinal virtues have been named.

Quick Check

✔ *What are the four cardinal virtues?* (The cardinal virtues are prudence, justice, fortitude, and temperance.)

✔ *What do the cardinal virtues help us to do?* (The cardinal virtues guide our minds and actions and lead us to a good life.)

WE RESPOND

___ minutes

Connect to Life Have a volunteer read aloud the *We Respond* text. Invite the students to reflect silently as they choose a cardinal virtue and write down the way practicing that virtue can show others that they are followers of Jesus.

Pray Invite the students to gather in the prayer space with their books. Then pray again together the *We Gather* prayer.

Plan Ahead for Day 4

Catechist Goal: To teach that we are called to show the love of Christ to others

Preparation: Have available slips of paper, a basket, and brightly colored stationery.

Catechist Goal

- To teach that we are called to show the love of Christ to others

Our Faith Response

- To show the love of Christ to others

Lesson Materials

- slips of paper
- a basket
- brightly colored stationery

We are called to live a life of love.

WE GATHER

✝ *Lord Jesus, help us to put our love into action.*

Think of some situations when you have done something kind for someone. What did you do? Why did you choose to do this?

WE BELIEVE

Love is a very powerful force. Christ loves us so much. He wants us to live in his love forever.

Jesus wants us to love others as he loves us. Do you know where we get the strength to love as Jesus loves? It comes to us from God through the community of the Church. Because we have been baptized, we share in the life and love of God. Each time that we celebrate a sacrament, the life of God grows stronger in us. With God's love strengthening us, we can do all things.

We know that we can count on the Holy Spirit to help us act as loving disciples of Jesus. The Holy Spirit came to us in Baptism and continues to be with us. The Holy Spirit gives us gifts to help us be more like Christ.

God has given us all that we need to show the love of Christ to others. As disciples of Jesus we do not work alone. As members of the Church we:

- share the good news
- pray and work for justice and peace
- visit those who are sick or elderly
- volunteer in shelters for those who are homeless, and in soup kitchens.

We can find many more ways, both simple and difficult, to show the love of Christ in our world.

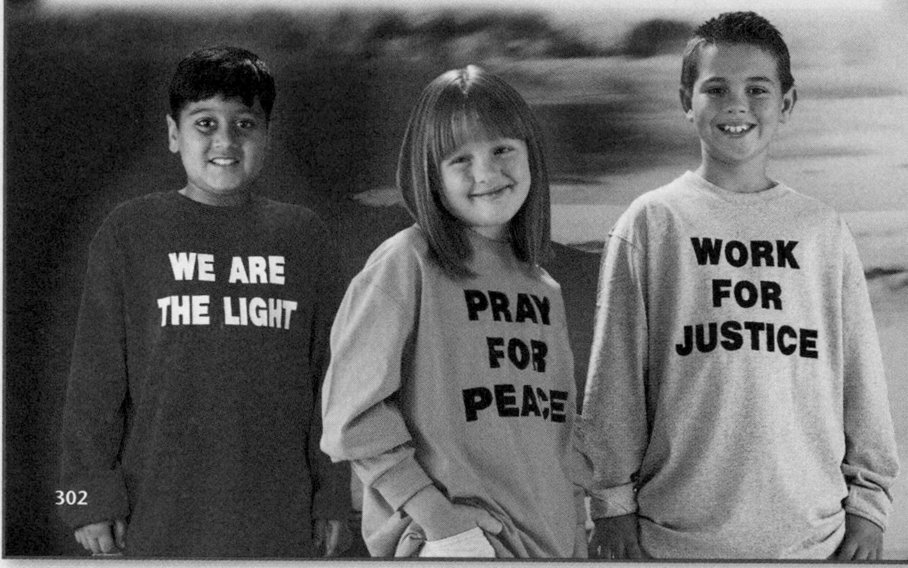

302

As Catholics...

The Pope and Young People

After completing the lesson, read aloud the first two *As Catholics* paragraphs. Emphasize the special dedication of Pope John Paul II to youth. Ask the students to think about this pope's words and discuss the way the pope lives his life as a disciple of Christ. Then read aloud the question. Allow the students time to reflect before inviting volunteers to share their responses.

Lesson Plan

WE GATHER ___ minutes

✝ **Pray** Pray together the Sign of the Cross and the *We Gather* prayer.

Focus on Life Have the students read and reflect on the *We Gather* questions. Hand out slips of paper. Ask the students to use these to write down their reasons for doing something kind and the way it made them feel. Invite the students to share their responses; then gather the slips of paper into a basket and have a volunteer place it in the prayer space. Tell the students that in this lesson they will learn that we are called to live a life of love.

WE BELIEVE ___ minutes

Learn About Love Have a volunteer read aloud the *We Believe* statement. Then ask volunteers to read aloud the *We Believe* text. Pause to emphasize the following:

- Jesus wants us to love others as he loves us.
- The Holy Spirit helps us to act as loving disciples of Jesus.
- Each of us is called to be a light to the world.
- God's love is active and present throughout the world; this love is the Kingdom of God on earth.

Sharing the Good News Have the students work together to write a class newsletter about living a life of love and showing the love of Christ to others. Make copies of the newsletter on brightly colored stationery and distribute them to families, students in other classes, and the parish at large.

Put the Love in Action If possible, organize a class trip to a nearby homeless shelter, soup kitchen, or nurs-

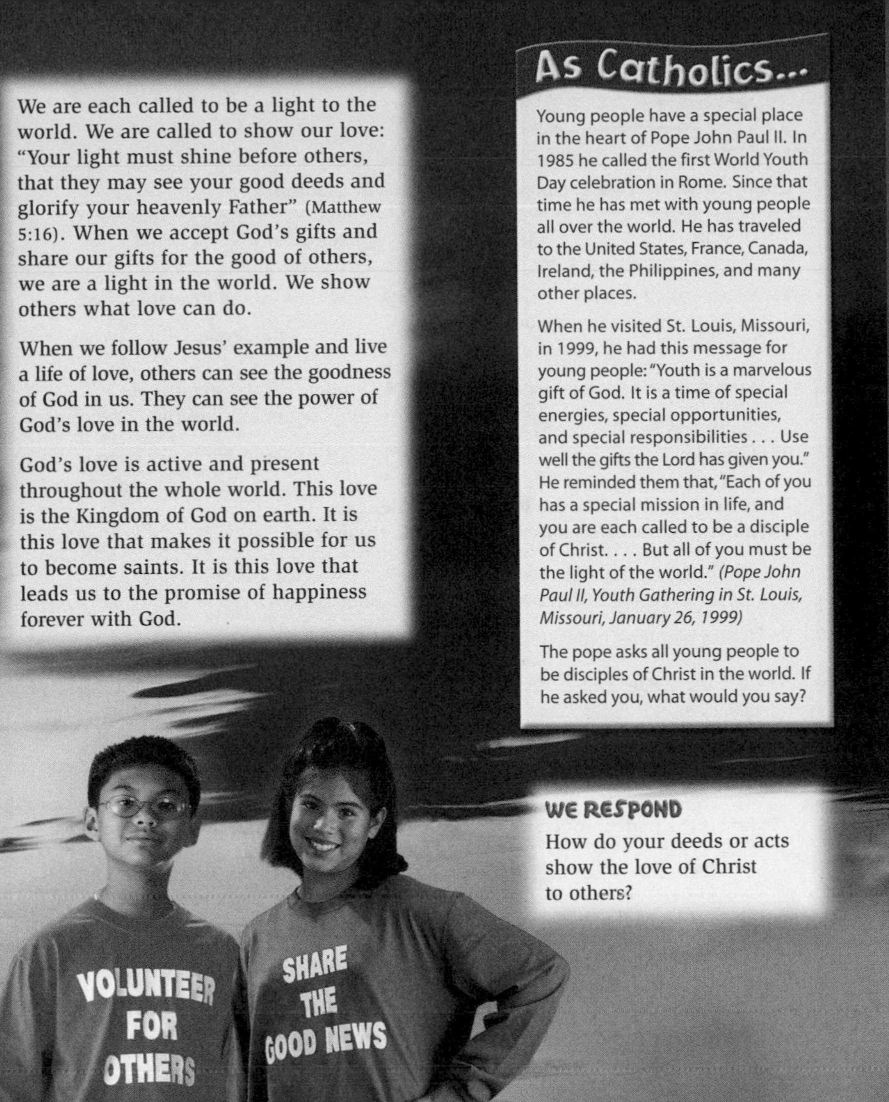

We are each called to be a light to the world. We are called to show our love: "Your light must shine before others, that they may see your good deeds and glorify your heavenly Father" (Matthew 5:16). When we accept God's gifts and share our gifts for the good of others, we are a light in the world. We show others what love can do.

When we follow Jesus' example and live a life of love, others can see the goodness of God in us. They can see the power of God's love in the world.

God's love is active and present throughout the whole world. This love is the Kingdom of God on earth. It is this love that makes it possible for us to become saints. It is this love that leads us to the promise of happiness forever with God.

As Catholics...

Young people have a special place in the heart of Pope John Paul II. In 1985 he called the first World Youth Day celebration in Rome. Since that time he has met with young people all over the world. He has traveled to the United States, France, Canada, Ireland, the Philippines, and many other places.

When he visited St. Louis, Missouri, in 1999, he had this message for young people: "Youth is a marvelous gift of God. It is a time of special energies, special opportunities, and special responsibilities . . . Use well the gifts the Lord has given you." He reminded them that, "Each of you has a special mission in life, and you are each called to be a disciple of Christ. . . . But all of you must be the light of the world." *(Pope John Paul II, Youth Gathering in St. Louis, Missouri, January 26, 1999)*

The pope asks all young people to be disciples of Christ in the world. If he asked you, what would you say?

WE RESPOND

How do your deeds or acts show the love of Christ to others?

303

ACTIVITY BANK

Catholic Social Teaching

Option for the Poor and Vulnerable

The students learned in this lesson that living a life of love means caring for others. Catholic social teaching calls us to care for the poor and vulnerable and to put their needs first. Invite a priest or other parish worker to talk with the class about local Catholic agencies that help the poor. Then work with the students to choose an agency to help, and organize a class fund-raising activity such as a cake sale. Donate the money earned through the fund-raiser to the chosen agency.

ing home to give the students an opportunity to practice discipleship. After the trip invite the students to share their feelings about the volunteer experience. You might also invite them to write about their experiences for the class newsletter. Encourage the students to continue practicing discipleship through volunteer work.

Quick Check

- ✔ *Where do we get the strength to love as Jesus loves?* (This strength comes to us from God through the community of the Church.)
- ✔ *What do we do as members of the Church?* (We share the good news, pray and work for justice and peace, visit the sick and elderly, and do volunteer work.)

WE RESPOND ___ minutes

Connect to Life Read aloud the *We Respond* question. Organize the students into pairs and ask the partners to talk quietly together about their responses to the question.

Pray Invite the students to gather in the prayer space. Have everyone join hands in a circle and think silently for a few moments about living a life of love. Then pray: *Lord, let us share your love with others. Amen.*

Plan Ahead for Day 5

Catechist Goal: To review chapter ideas and their relationship to our faith life

Preparation: Make copies of Chapter 26 Test in the Grade 4 Assessment Book (option). Have available slips of paper, chart paper, and a marker.

Catechist Goal

- To review chapter ideas and their relationship to our faith life

Our Faith Response

- To apply what has been learned to our lives

Chapter Test

Chapter 26 Test is provided in the Grade 4 Assessment Book.

Choose a word from the box to complete each sentence.

cardinal	disciple	theological	light

1. We are called to be a light to the world by showing our love for God and others.
2. Mary is a perfect model for how we should live as a disciple of Jesus.
3. Faith, hope, and love are called the theological virtues.
4. Prudence, justice, fortitude, and temperance are the cardinal virtues.

Write True or False for the following sentences. Then change the false sentences to make them true.

5. False The cardinal virtues help us to want to be with God forever.
The theological virtues help us to want to be with God forever.
6. False There are no role models who show us how to live as disciples of Jesus.
Mary is the perfect model of the way we should live as disciples of Jesus.
7. True We are called to show our love.
8. False The theological virtues guide our minds and actions to lead a good life.
The cardinal virtues guide our minds and actions to lead a good life.

Complete the following:

9–10. As disciples of Jesus we are called to See pages 296–297.

Use the summer months to learn more about the Church. Read your parish bulletins to find how your parish reaches out to those in need. How can you help? Make a plan to follow Jesus and be a light to the world. Share your plan with your family.

304

Lesson Plan

___ minutes

Chapter Review Have the students complete questions 1–8 to check their understanding of what they have learned. Invite volunteers to read aloud the correct answers. Remind the students that as Jesus' disciples we are called to love others. Then ask them to write their responses to question 9–10.

Assessment Activity Read aloud the activity directions and discuss them with the class. Invite the students to write down their thoughts about ways the Church reaches out to those in need and about ways a fourth grader can help in these efforts. Encourage the students, over the summer, to put into action these thoughts about helping others. Urge them to get their family members involved, too. Remind the students that it does not matter how old we are; we can all share the love of Christ with others. Finally, encourage the students to participate in weekly Mass over the summer.

Sharing Faith in Class and at Home At this time you may want to work on pages 317–318 of Chapter 28. Refer to the Lesson Planning Guide on page 313B before you present these pages.

___ minutes

Reflect & Pray Have the students reread the opening prayer and read silently the question. Then invite them to reflect on Jesus' words as they write their prayers of thanksgiving to Jesus for calling us to be his disciples.

Key Words Use a marker to write the *Key Words* as column heads on a piece of chart paper. Invite the students to name the virtues described by each

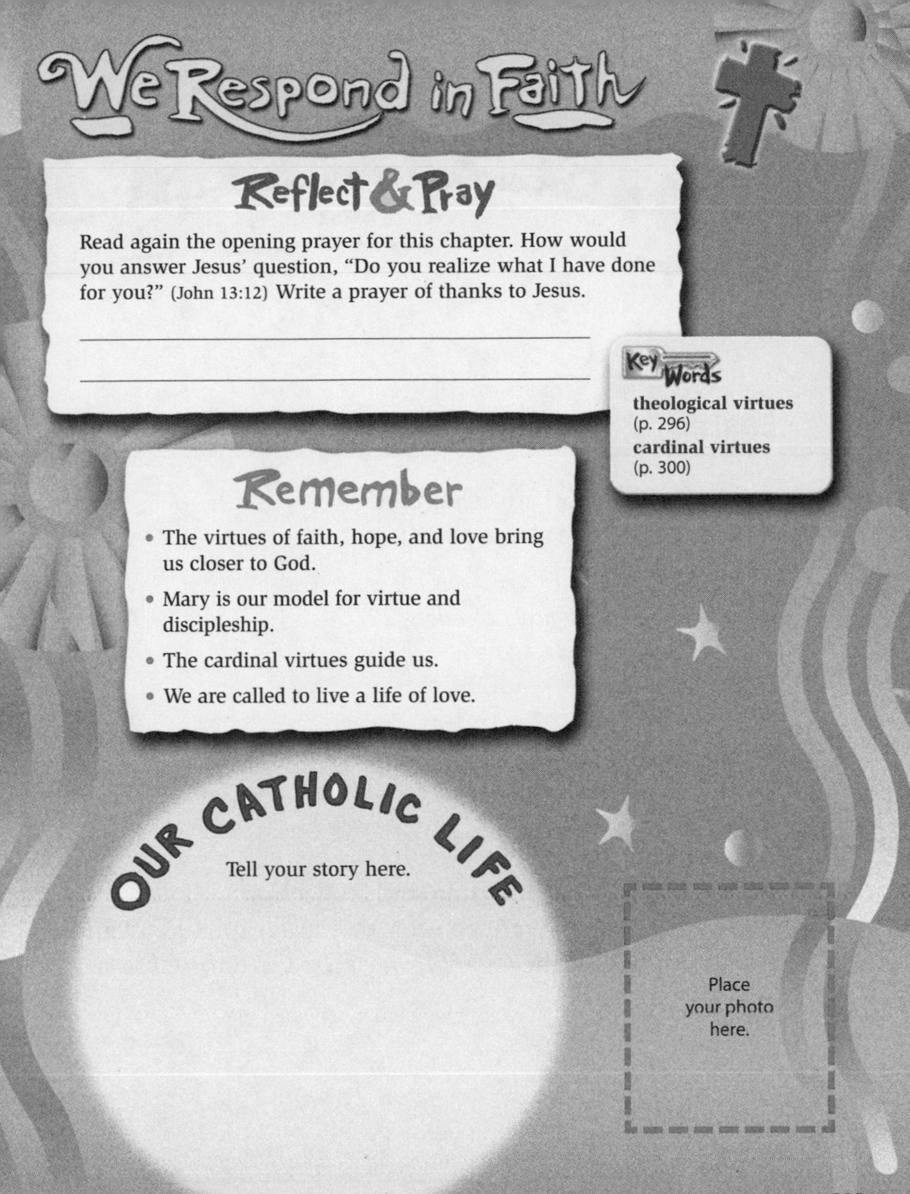

We Respond in Faith
Reflect & Pray
Read again the opening prayer for this chapter. How would you answer Jesus' question, "Do you realize what I have done for you?" (John 13:12) Write a prayer of thanks to Jesus.
Key Words
theological virtues (p. 296)
cardinal virtues (p. 300)
Remember
The virtues of faith, hope, and love bring us closer to God.
Mary is our model for virtue and discipleship.
The cardinal virtues guide us.
We are called to live a life of love.
OUR CATHOLIC LIFE
Tell your story here.
Place your photo here.
305

Chapter 26 • Day 5

HOME CONNECTION

Sharing Faith with My Family

Remember to send home the family page (text page 306).

Encourage the students to read and discuss with their families the text about Saint Francis of Assisi. Remind them, too, to work with their families to nominate another disciple of Jesus for the "Holiness Hall of Fame."

For additional information and activities, encourage families to visit Sadlier's

www.WEBELIEVEweb.com

word. As each is named, write it on the chart under the appropriate head.

Remember Review the four *We Believe* statements by asking the students to find the statements in their books and to write on four separate slips of paper one thing they have learned about each statement. Collect the slips. Then have the students take turns drawing a comment slip, reading it aloud, and naming the *We Believe* statement to which it relates.

Our Catholic Life Allow the students time to discuss and then reflect privately on the ways their faith has grown over this school year. Then encourage them to write down the ways they can continue to grow in faith over the summer and throughout the years to come. Invite the students to place their photo on page 305.

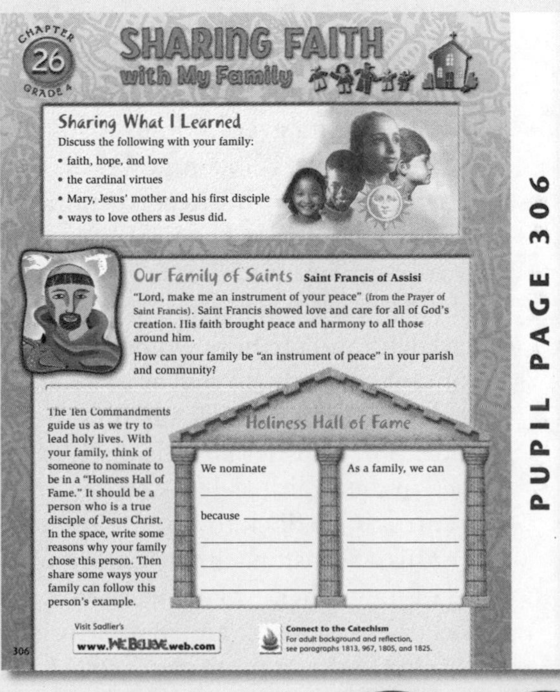

Easter

The fifty days from Easter Sunday to Pentecost are celebrated in joyful exultation as one feast day . . . These above all others are the days for the singing of the Alleluia.

(Norms Governing Liturgical Calendars, 22)

Overview

In this chapter the students will learn that during the season of Easter, we celebrate the Resurrection of Jesus.

For Adult Reading and Reflection
You may want to refer to paragraphs 1169 and 1166 of the *Catechism of the Catholic Church.*

Catechist Background

How have you met the risen Lord?

During the Easter season, the Church celebrates the fulfillment of Jesus' promise: "I lay down my life in order to take it up again. I have power to lay it down, and power to take it up again" (John 10:17–18). In the Easter event, "Jesus is conclusively revealed as 'Son of God in power according to the Spirit of holiness by his Resurrection from the dead'" (CCC 648). Christ's life, works, and teachings are confirmed in his rising.

In his post-Resurrection appearances to Mary Magdalene and the holy women who had come to his anoint his body, as well as to Peter and the other apostles, Christ repeatedly assures them, "Do not be afraid!" The apostles and the disciples are confirmed in their faith as Jesus breaks bread with them and entrusts his flock to Peter.

At his Ascension Christ Jesus returns to the right hand of the Father. At Pentecost, when the seven weeks of Easter are completed, "Christ's Passover is fulfilled in the outpouring of the Holy Spirit" (CCC 731). By the power of the Holy Spirit, the Church is made manifest to the world. And through the sacramental life of the Church, Christ continues his work of salvation.

The Easter season encompasses the fifty days from the Resurrection to Pentecost. As Easter has been called "the Great Sunday," so every Sunday—especially those of the Easter season—is "a little Easter." With every celebration of the Lord's day, Christ's rising is made present once again in the faith community. In our celebration of Eucharist, "the whole community of the faithful encounters the risen Lord who invites them to his banquet" (CCC 1166).

In what ways will you help others to encounter the risen Lord?

Lesson Planning Guide

Lesson Focus	Presentation	Materials
Day 1		
Guide page 307 **Guide and Text page 307** **Introduce the Season**	• Read the *Chapter Story*. • Introduce the Easter season. • Proclaim the words on the banner.	
Day 2		
Guide and Text pages 308–309 **We Gather** **We Believe** *John 21:1–14*	• Discuss the **We Gather** questions. • Read and present the **We Believe** text and the scriptural passage. Express feelings and questions upon seeing the risen Jesus. • Read about the Easter season.	• Simple props: a fish net, many fish cut from poster board, a sheet for a garment, bread, and charcoal in a pan (option)
Day 3		
Guide and Text page 310 **We Respond** *Acts of the Apostles 1:3–12*	Write some ways to share the joy of Jesus' love. • Read about Ascension and Pentecost. • Describe ways the Holy Spirit helps us.	
Day 4		
Guide and Text page 311 **We Respond in Prayer**	• Listen to Scripture. Respond in song.	• the prayer space items: white candle, flowers or plant, "tongues of fire," white tablecloth
Day 5		
Guide pages 312A–312B **We Respond in Faith**	• Explain the individual project. • Explain the group project. • Discuss the **Sharing Faith with My Family** page.	"Send Us Your Spirit," Christopher Walker, #28, Grade 4 CD • copies of Reproducible Master 27, guide page 312A

For additional ideas, activities, and opportunities: Visit Sadlier's **www.WEBELIEVEweb.com**

Focus on Life

Chapter Story

Tom was staring at his favorite picture of him and his dad. They had been shooting hoops when mom snapped the picture. It clearly showed how much fun they were having. And now dad was moving away.

It had been hard for Tom when his parents divorced and dad had moved out. Tom felt sad and even a bit angry, but Tom thought his dad would always live nearby. Now his dad was coming over to explain why he was moving out of state.

"Why do you have to move?" Tom demanded as soon as his dad walked in. "Why can't you stay near us?"

"I'd like to stay closer to you and your mom, but the promotion at work means that I have to move. I hope that you understand," his dad added. "Well, I <u>don't</u> understand," Tom shouted as he ran to his room.

The following Wednesday when Tom came home from school, the phone was ringing. He thought it would be his friend Harrison. Instead, he heard his dad say, "Hi, Tom, how was your day?" Tom told him about his math test and about his friend Harrison. Then Tom added, "I'm sorry I yelled at you dad."

"That's O.K., Tom. I know you are upset and this is hard on you, but we can stay in touch by phone. Plus, you have a long weekend coming up next month. Your mom tells me that you have nothing planned. Would you like to come see my new place?"

"You bet! I can't wait, dad. Thanks!" As Tom hung up the phone, he felt much better.

▶ *How do Tom and his dad show their love for each other?*

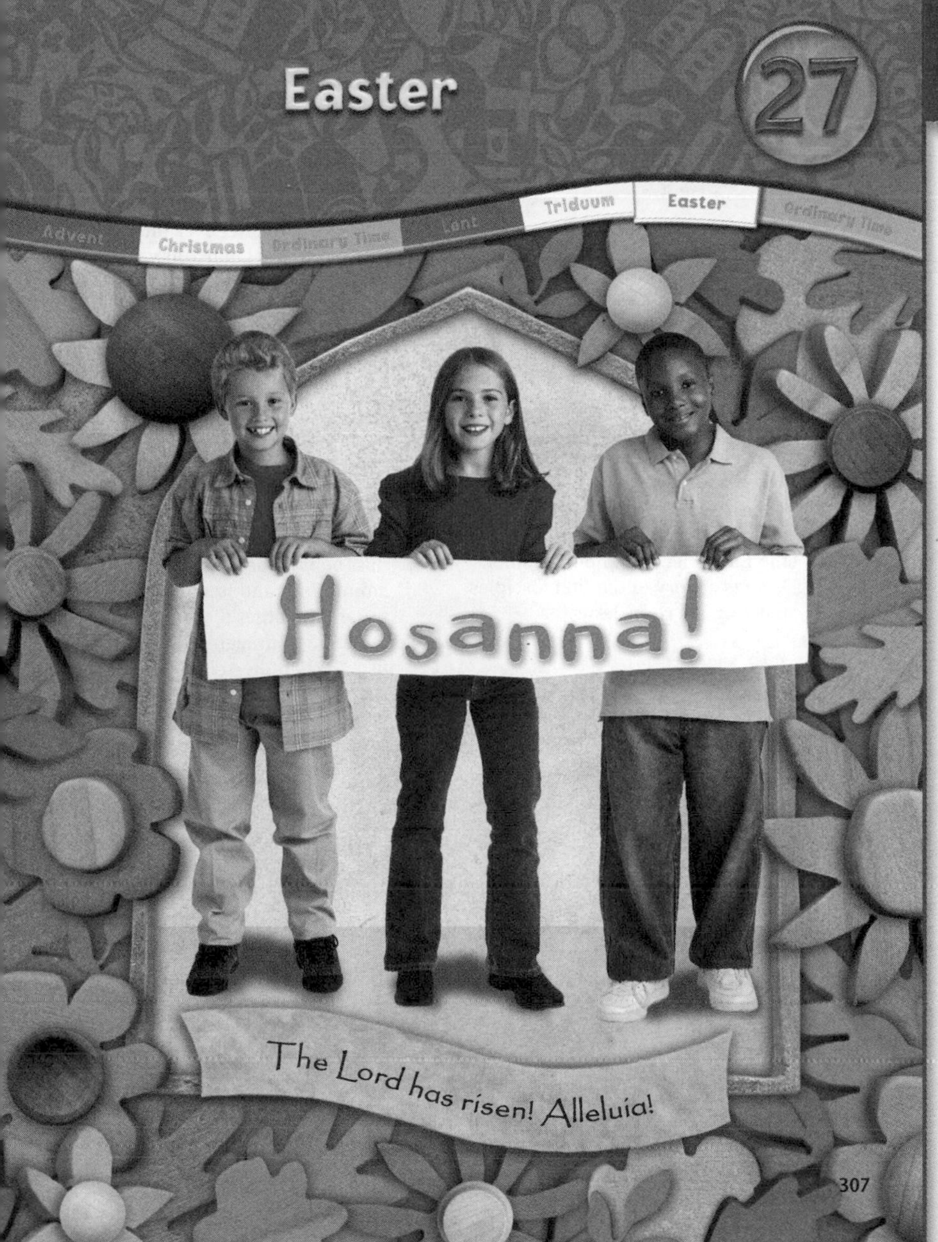

Catechist Goal

- To understand that during the season of Easter, we celebrate the Resurrection of Jesus

Our Faith Response

- To choose a way to continue Jesus' work

ADDITIONAL RESOURCES

Videos *The Magic Boy's Easter,* Gateway Films/Vision Video, 1989. A boy needing surgery meets the healing Christ on his way to the cross and he gets the courage he needs.

He Is Risen, Nest Entertainment, 1998. From the series *Animated Stories of the New Testment*. Sorrow and despair turn to joy and love as the disciples behold their risen Savior. (30 minutes)

To find more ideas for books, videos, and other learning material, visit Sadlier's

www.WEBELIEVEweb.com

Lesson Plan

Introduce the Season ___ minutes

• **Pray** the Sign of the Cross and the words "The Lord has risen! Alleluia!"

• **Read** aloud the *Chapter Story* on guide page 307C. Discuss the closing question to help the students talk about ways loved ones can be present to us even when they are physically absent. (Possible answers include: memories, photos, phone, and e-mail.)

• **Have** a student read aloud the chapter title. Explain: *Easter is a season of celebration and rejoicing in the Church because we have new life in Christ.*

• **Invite** the students to study the photo. Explain: *Notice the sign the students are holding. What does the word mean?* (Hosanna! was the greeting for Jesus on Palm Sunday in Mark 11:9–10. It means "grant salvation" as in Psalm 118:25.)

• **Proclaim** together the words on the banner under the photo.

Lesson Materials

- costumes and props for dramatization (option)
- Grade 4 CD
- copies of Reproducible Master 27

Teaching Note

The Alleluia

The Alleluia or Hallelujah ("Praise Yahweh") is an ancient liturgical invitation to give voice to our praise of God. In songs like Psalm 11, the temple singer begins with a "Hallelujah." In other songs like Psalm 106, the entire choir concludes with the Hallelujah. Throughout the Easter season, the Alleluia is a recurring refrain in the Mass and in the Liturgy of the Hours. To learn or compose various melodies for the Alleluia is a fitting act of seasonal devotion to the risen Lord.

During the season of Easter, we celebrate the Resurrection of Jesus.

WE GATHER

✝ *Risen Jesus, help us to recognize your presence among us.*

Have you ever gone to the bus or train station, or the airport, to meet a friend or a member of your family whom you have not seen for a long time? What was this meeting like?

WE BELIEVE

The season of Easter is a season of meeting. We meet the risen Jesus in the Eucharist and in one another. Here is a story of the first disciples meeting the risen Jesus.

 John 21:1–14

Narrator: Some of the apostles and disciples were together after Jesus' Resurrection. Simon Peter was among them, and he said,

Simon Peter: "I am going fishing."

All: "We also will come with you."

Narrator: "So they went out and got into the boat, but that night they caught nothing. When it was already dawn, Jesus was standing on the shore; but the disciples did not realize that it was Jesus. Jesus said to them,

Jesus: 'Children, have you caught anything to eat?'

All: 'No.'

Jesus: 'Cast the net over the right side of the boat and you will find something.'"

Narrator: The disciples did as he said, and all of a sudden the net began filling with fish! They were not able to pull it into the boat because of the number of fish! So the disciple whom Jesus loved, the apostle John, said to Peter,

John: "It is the Lord."

Narrator: When Simon Peter heard this, he wrapped his garment around him and jumped into the water. The other disciples followed in the boat, dragging the net full of fish. "When they climbed out on shore, they saw a charcoal fire with fish on it and bread. Jesus said to them,

Jesus: 'Bring some of the fish you just caught.'

Narrator: So Simon Peter went over and dragged the net ashore full of one hundred fifty-three large fish. Even though there were so many, the net was not torn. Jesus said to them,

Jesus: 'Come, have breakfast.'"

308

Lesson Plan

WE GATHER ___ minutes

Focus on Life Have students share their responses to the *We Gather* questions. Have volunteers relate their experiences of meeting loved ones they have not seen for a long time. Invite them to identify their feelings before, during, and after each meeting.

WE BELIEVE ___ minutes

- **Read** aloud the *We Believe* statement and the opening *We Believe* paragraph to set the stage for the gospel story.
- **Act** out the story from John 21:1–14. Have students silently read through the story to become familiar with it. Choose students to play the parts of narrator, Simon Peter, John, and Jesus. The rest are "All," the disciples who enact the part of fishermen and partakers in the picnic breakfast on the beach. Distribute the props and present this meeting between the risen Jesus and his followers.

Narrator: The disciples realized that it was the risen Jesus. Jesus "took the bread and gave it to them" and then he gave them some fish, too. This was the third time they had seen Jesus since he was raised from the dead. (John 21:3–5, 6, 7, 9–12, 13)

Imagine you are with the disciples in the boat. What are you feeling when you realize that it is really Jesus? What questions do you want to ask him?

The Easter season is a time of joy and amazement at the risen Jesus among us. It is a time of new life. The Easter season begins on the evening of Easter Sunday and ends fifty days later on Pentecost Sunday, when we celebrate the coming of the Holy Spirit upon the apostles.

At every Mass during the Easter season, the paschal candle is lit to remind us of Jesus' living presence with us. We decorate the church building with flowers as a sign of new and joyful life.

Because Jesus rose on a Sunday, we celebrate every Sunday as a "little Easter." The Sundays of the Easter season are especially important. The early Church called the whole Easter season "one great Sunday," one great day of Resurrection.

Easter is a season of joy and happiness because Jesus rose from the dead. We meet the risen Jesus in the people around us. Jesus even told us that when we care for those in need, we care for him.

EASTER

309

ACTIVITY BANK

Curriculum Connection

Science

Encourage the students to look for and observe signs of new life in nature. Have them notice the growth in flowers such as lilies, crocuses, hyacinths, tulips, daffodils, and narcissus. All these are signs of new life in creation. Have the students observe any butterflies that appear during this time of the year. Other signs of new life occur in the birth of birds and animals during springtime. Encourage the students to visit a local zoo or farm to see the new babies among God's creatures. All these signs of new life reflect the abundance of God's goodness and help Christians to rejoice in their new life in Christ at Easter.

Invite the students to work in small groups for the *We Believe* activity. Have them record their feelings and questions. Call on each group to report its discussion.

• **Have** the students read silently the remaining *We Believe* paragraphs on page 309. Stress the joy of the Easter season. Because Jesus has risen to new life, we have new life in him and his presence with us always. Point out that the Easter season begins on Easter Sunday evening and ends fifty days later on Pentecost Sunday. Emphasize the importance of every Sunday in this joyful season of Easter that has been called "one great Sunday."

Quick Check

✔ *What do we celebrate in the Easter season?* (During the Easter season, we celebrate the Resurrection of Jesus.)

✔ *Why is Easter a season of meeting?* (We meet the risen Jesus in the Eucharist and in one another.)

Connection

To Parish

Weekly Liturgy

Because every Sunday is celebrated as "a little Easter," the Easter season is an appropriate time to deepen the students' appreciation of the Lord's day. Guide them in discovering the ways in which our weekend liturgies remind us of Christ's Resurrection, the most important holy day of obligation in the universal Church. Call their attention to the Nicene Creed, the Memorial Acclamation, and the entire Eucharistic Prayer. Remind them that the Sunday Eucharist is the heart of the Church's life.

What are some ways people can meet Jesus in each of us? What can we do at home and in our neighborhoods to share the joy of Jesus' love?

___

___

During the Easter season the Church celebrates two very important events in the life of the Church.

Ascension

In the United States the Feast of the Ascension is observed around forty days after Easter. Some places observe it on a Sunday and other places observe it on Thursday. When celebrated on Thursday, it is a holy day of obligation. On this feast day we recall the last event of Jesus' public life, his Ascension. We read about Jesus' return to his Father in heaven in the Acts of the Apostles.

Acts of the Apostles 1:3–12

Forty days after his Resurrection, the risen Jesus had gathered with his apostles outside of Jerusalem. He told them that they would receive power when the Holy Spirit came upon them. They would be strengthened to be his witnesses to all the ends of the earth. "When he had said this, as they were looking on, he was lifted up, and a cloud took him from their sight." (Acts of the Apostles 1:9)

Pentecost Sunday

After the Ascension the apostles returned to Jerusalem and awaited the coming of the Holy Spirit.

Pentecost

We celebrate Pentecost fifty days after Easter. It is the last Sunday and final day of the Easter season. On Pentecost Sunday we celebrate the coming of the Holy Spirit to the first disciples. We remember the ways the Holy Spirit helped the apostles as they continued Jesus' work. On Pentecost we celebrate the beginning of the Church, and we rejoice because the Holy Spirit fills our hearts, too!

WE RESPOND

In what ways can the Holy Spirit help you to continue Jesus' work?

Call on the Holy Spirit to be with you.

310

Lesson Plan

WE BELIEVE (continued) ___ minutes

Discuss the questions in the *We Believe* activity. List responses on the board. Invite the students to choose one way of sharing Jesus' love and write it in their books.

• **Ask** a volunteer to read aloud the next two *We Believe* paragraphs. Have the students stand while you read aloud the scriptural passage from the Acts of the Apostles. Pause for a moment. Invite the students to sit down and silently read the concluding *We Believe* paragraphs. Ask the students to underline what we celebrate on Ascension (Jesus' return to his Father) and on Pentecost (the coming of the Holy Spirit to the first disciples and the beginning of the Church).

WE RESPOND ___ minutes

Connect to Life Have the students read the *We Respond* text. Invite the students to consider the ways in which they do the work of Jesus. List these on the board. Have the students compose prayers, calling on the Holy Spirit to be with them and help them do the work of Jesus.

• **Gather** in the prayer space. Invite volunteers to read their prayers aloud.

We Respond in Prayer

Leader: Come, Holy Spirit, fill the hearts of your faithful.

All: And kindle in them the fire of your love.

Leader: Send forth your Spirit and they shall be created.

All: And you will renew the face of the earth.

Reader: A reading from the Acts of the Apostles.

"When the time for Pentecost was fulfilled, they were all in one place together. And suddenly there came from the sky a noise like a strong driving wind, and it filled the entire house in which they were. Then there appeared to them tongues as of fire, which parted and came to rest on each one of them. And they were all filled with the holy Spirit and began to speak in different tongues, as the Spirit enabled them to proclaim."(Acts of the Apostles 2:1–4)

The word of the Lord.

All: Thanks be to God.

Send Us Your Spirit

Refrain: Send us your Spirit, O Lord,
And renew the face of the earth!

May your glory last forever.
May you rejoice in all we do! (Refrain)

311

EASTER

Preparing to Pray

The students will listen to a reading about the coming of the Holy Spirit at Pentecost. They will respond in song.

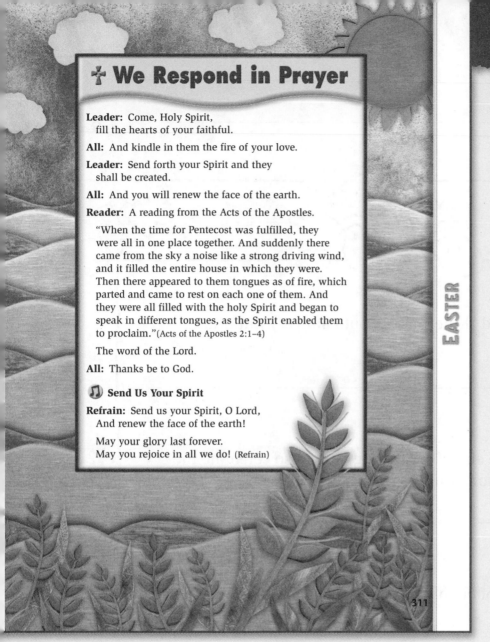

- Assume the role of prayer leader.
- Choose a reader to proclaim the Scripture.
- Practice the song "Send Us Your Spirit."

The Prayer Space

- Gather the following items: large white candle, fresh flowers or a flowering plant, red foil "tongues of fire," white table covering

This Week's Liturgy

Visit **www.webelieveweb.com** for this week's liturgical readings and other seasonal material.

We Respond in Prayer ___ minutes

- **Pray** the Sign of the Cross and the opening prayer.
- **Have** the reader proclaim the scriptural passage from the Acts of the Apostles.
- **Conclude** by singing the song "Send Us Your Spirit," #28, Grade 4 CD.

Name ______________________________

Solve these riddles.

RIDDLE 1

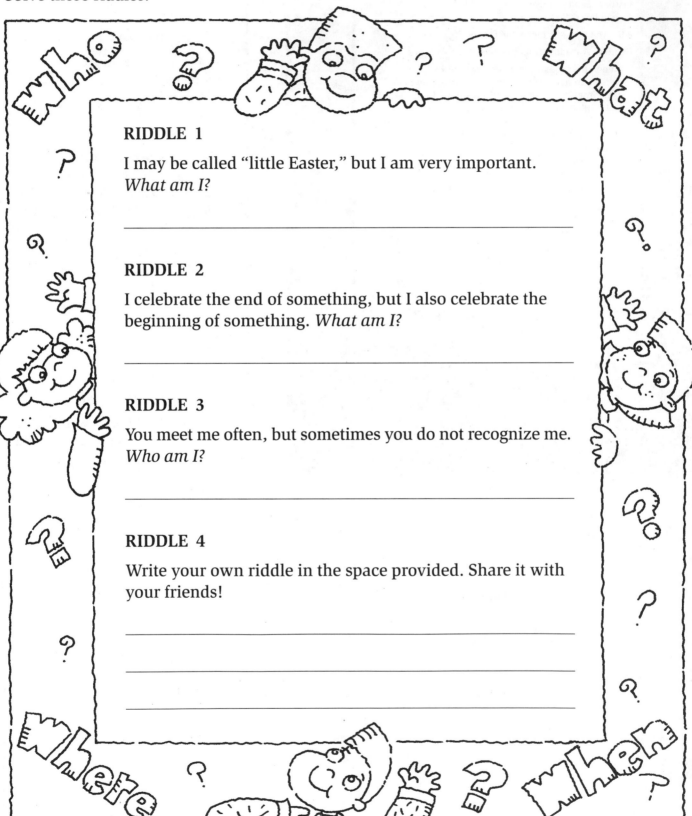

I may be called "little Easter," but I am very important. *What am I?*

____

RIDDLE 2

I celebrate the end of something, but I also celebrate the beginning of something. *What am I?*

____

RIDDLE 3

You meet me often, but sometimes you do not recognize me. *Who am I?*

____

RIDDLE 4

Write your own riddle in the space provided. Share it with your friends!

____

____

____

Individual Project

Distribute the Reproducible Master 27. Point out that the riddles are all based on the chapter. Encourage students to enjoy solving and composing their own riddles to be shared with families and friends. (Answers: 1, every Sunday; 2, Pentecost; 3, the risen Jesus)

Group Project

Pentecost is a glorious celebration of the beginning of the Church and the preaching of the gospel to all nations. It is a fitting time to celebrate all the various ethnic groups represented in the class or the school. Involve the students in planning a Pentecost Fair with their families. Begin by identifying the ethnic heritage groups that are represented in the group. Have students write an invitation to participate in the fair by setting up and/or contributing to cultural exhibits and food booths that reflect the various ethnic identities. Participants might teach songs or dances native to their countries of origin. Celebrate the Holy Spirit as *the* Spirit who joins us together in the universal Church.

Home Connection

Sharing Faith with My Family

Make sure to send home the family page (text page 312).

Call their students' attention to the three discussion themes they will talk about with their families. Invite them to read aloud the "Family Prayer in the Easter Season." Encourage them to serve as the prayer leader when sharing this prayer at home.

For additional information and activities, encourage families to visit Sadlier's

www.WEBELIEVEweb.com

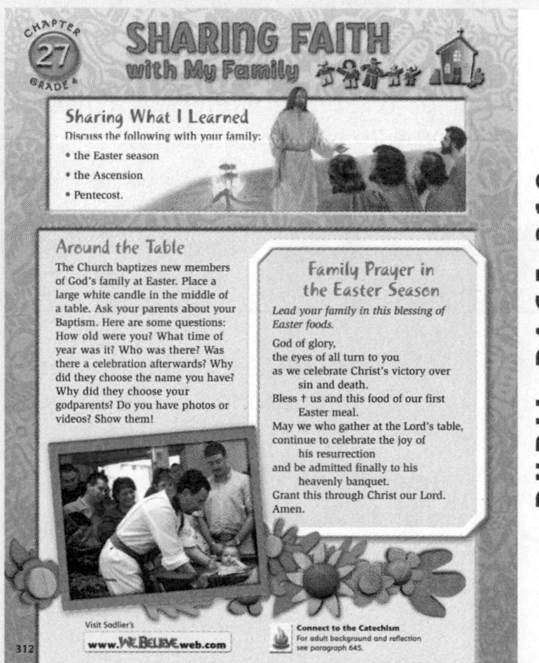

Chapter 27 Grade 4

SHARING FAITH with My Family

Sharing What I Learned

Discuss the following with your family:

- the Easter season
- the Ascension
- Pentecost.

Around the Table

The Church baptizes new members of God's family at Easter. Place a large white candle in the middle of a table. Ask your parents about your Baptism. Here are some questions: How old were you? What time of year was it? Who was there? Was there a celebration afterwards? Why did they choose the name you have? Why did they choose your godparents? Do you have photos or videos? Show them!

Family Prayer in the Easter Season

Lead your family in this blessing of Easter foods.

God of glory,
the eyes of all turn to you
as we celebrate Christ's victory over sin and death.
Bless † us and this food of our first Easter meal.
May we who gather at the Lord's table,
continue to celebrate the joy of his resurrection
and be admitted finally to his heavenly banquet.
Grant this through Christ our Lord.
Amen.

Visit Sadlier's www.WEBELIEVEweb.com

Connect to the Catechism
For adult background and reflection see paragraph 645.

312

PUPIL PAGE 312

Sharing Faith in Class and at Home

Sharing Faith

The Christian family is called to be a model of generosity and charity to those in need, especially to those in need of what the family is, a community of love. . .

(*A Family Perspective in Church and Society,* United States Conference of Catholic Bishops, page 20)

Overview

This chapter will focus on three major concepts of the Grade 4 program: that the Ten Commandments help us put God first in our lives and to treat others with respect; that through prayer we grow closer to God; that we can show our love for others by being kind and understanding.

For Adult Reading and Reflection
You may want to refer to paragraphs 2067, 2072, 2478, and 2638 of the *Catechism of the Catholic Church*.

Catechist Background

What makes it difficult to choose the moral high ground in today's world?

Imagine what it would be like to drive if there were no laws. Without speed limits and police to enforce them, driving would be a sure invitation to calamity. Without signs to provide warnings and directions, drivers would be lost and vulnerable to harm.

Like signposts, the Ten Commandments provide direction, warn us about dangerous behavior, and guide us on our way. They are much more than a list of "thou shalt nots." Rather, they help us place God first in our lives and point the way to loving each other and ourselves more.

Children and young people are bombarded with conflicting messages about what will make them happy. Teaching them to make good choices through solid moral formation is an essential task of catechesis. It is one that starts first in the home. As the complexities of life increase, parents serve as anchors for their children. They ground them by providing a foundation in faith. They encourage them to grow as people of good moral and spiritual character. The Ten Commandments provide direction in this effort by discouraging deceit, envy, and greed, and fostering the practices of respect, love, and holiness. For the Christian disciple, it is the only way to go!

How are you supporting parents in teaching their children to act with justice and love?

Planning Guide

Lesson Focus	Presentation in Class	Presentation At Home
Part 1		
pages 313-314 *The Ten Commandments help us put God first in our lives and to treat others with respect.* **For preview:** before Chapter 8, page 95 **For review:** after Chapter 12, pages 152–153	• Talk about both silly and sensible laws. • Read and discuss *Because We Believe.* • Complete the classroom activities. • Send home the family blessing found on page 318A.	• Talk about why rules are important in a family. • List some family rules that are helpful. • Compose a prayer for the family.
Part 2		
pages 315-316 *Through prayer we grow closer to God.* **For preview:** before Chapter 9, page 107 **For review:** after Chapter 12, pages 152–153	• Read the story and discuss being grateful. • Read and discuss *Because We Believe.* • Prepare a class expression of gratitude. • Explain why giving thanks makes you more aware of what people do for you.	• List some ways your family gives thanks. • As a family agree on one thing for which you are grateful. • Pray together Psalm 103:1-5.
Part 3		
pages 317-318 *We can show our love for others by being kind and understanding.* **For preview:** before Chapter 26, page 295 **For review:** after Chapter 26, pages 304–305	• Read and discuss the story about how to understand others. • Read and discuss *Because We Believe.* • List both helpful and harmful words. • Send home the *We Believe* family survey found on page 313C.	• Talk about ways that Jesus showed love and care for others. • As a family watch and discuss a television show about families. • Pray for someone who needs your family's love and understanding.

For additional ideas, activities, and opportunities: Visit Sadlier's **www.WEBELIEVEweb.com**

We Believe Family SURVEY

Your child brought home three different kinds of family pages this year. Through these pages you shared faith together!

What was your child most enthusiastic about sharing with your family?

____

____

____

What activities sparked spirited family discussion?

____

____

____

What part of these **SHARING FAITH** pages did your family enjoy the most?

____

____

____

What activities did they like most?

____

____

____

Does your family have any special prayers or activities that you would like to share with other *We Believe* families? If so, tell us about them.

____

____

____

Is there anything else you'd like to share?

____

____

____

We'd like to hear from you!

Send us this survey at: *We Believe* Family Survey
c/o Sadlier, 9 Pine Street, New York, NY 10005
or at: www.WEBELIEVEweb.com

Unit Opener Pages
SHARING FAITH as a Family

Chapter Family Pages
SHARING FAITH with My Family

Sharing What I Learned
Discuss the following with your family:
- the fourth commandment
- the domestic church
- our responsibility to our family
- our responsibilities to all people.

Letters from Saint Paul
Saint Paul wrote many letters to the early Christian churches. Here is an excerpt from a letter to the church of Corinth. Read more of Saint Paul's letters in the Bible.

"Encourage one another, agree with one another, live in peace, and the God of love and peace will be with you." (2 Corinthians 13:11)

"You shall love your neighbor as yourself." (Matthew 22:39)

Scripture Pictures
Read this Scripture quote to your family. Ask a family member to use this space to draw a "Scripture Picture" that shows how to live out the quote. Talk about the quote and the picture. Invite other family members to draw their own "Scripture Picture."

Special Family/Class Connection Chapter
SHARING FAITH in Class and at Home

Silly or Sensible? YOU be the Judge!

In Michigan it is illegal to chain an alligator to a fire hydrant.

In Hartford, Connecticut, you cannot cross a street walking on your hands.

SHARING FAITH in Class and at Home

Silly or Sensible? YOU be the Judge!

In Michigan, it is illegal to chain an alligator to a fire hydrant.

In Florida, it's against the law to fall asleep under a hair dryer.

In Minnesota, you can't cross the state line with a duck on your head.

In Hartford, Connecticut, you cannot cross a street walking on your hands.

Why Do We Need Laws?

Laws or rules are everywhere. Sensible laws remind us to behave in ways that will not put others or ourselves in danger. Some laws may seem silly to us. They might need to be changed in order to keep up with the times or with the way a person grows. The best laws help us to become loving and kind.

Because *We Believe*

Laws are really agreements that we live out each day. When we obey a law, we agree to act and think in a certain way.

"LORD, teach me the way of your laws."
Psalm 119:33

In the Bible we read that God made a special agreement with Moses and his people. God promised to be their God if they would be his people. This special agreement is called a *covenant*. God gave Moses and his people the law that he wanted them to follow. The Ten Commandments are God's laws. God's people promised to keep the Ten Commandments as part of their covenant with God.

The Ten Commandments are God's laws for us, too. They help us to put God first in our lives. The Ten Commandments help people and communities treat one another with respect.

How do we show that we believe this?

Laws or rules in our schools and our homes can keep us safe and aware of the need to treat others with respect.

"The Ten Commandments state what is required in the love of God and love of neighbor."

(Catechism of the Catholic Church, 2067)

With Your Class

Think about a school law or rule. Why is it important to follow?

____

If you could write a law or rule for your school, what would it be?

____

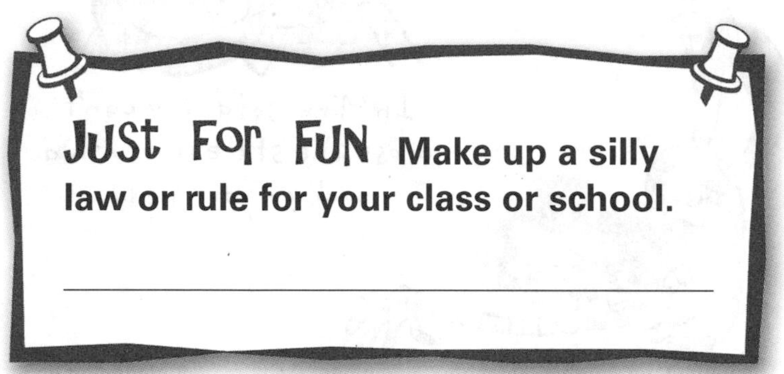

JUST FOR FUN Make up a silly law or rule for your class or school.

____

With Your Family

Read page 313 together. Talk about why rules are important in families.

Name rules that a family might have that help them:

- to be understanding of one another
- to share chores and responsibilities
- to keep peace and harmony in the family
- to help the family respect each person for who he or she is.

What are some rules that you think are helpful for a family?

____

Pray Together

Loving God,
help us to

____

____

____

____

____

____

Bring this page back to school
Keep this page at home

SHARING FAITH

in Class and at Home

When Is It Difficult to Be Thankful?

Amelia felt terrible. Not only did she have a miserable cold, but she also was missing a trip to the zoo. "This is so unfair," she complained to her mother. "I hate being sick."

"I know what you mean," her mother said. "No one likes to be sick, but it can make things worse to keep thinking about how terrible you feel. Try to think of what is good about today!"

Amelia could not think of a single thing, so her mother helped her. There was: the cozy blanket wrapped around her, the movie she watched while lying on the couch, the homemade soup her mother made for lunch. Then she thought about the exciting book she was reading. And she had to admit, even her big brother was being nice to her. Maybe the day had not turned out so badly after all.

Talk About It

- What changed Amelia's mood?
- What can make it hard to remember the good things we have around us?

Because *We Believe*

The first commandment tells us to place God first in our lives. One way we do this is by giving thanks for the many ways God has blessed us. Giving thanks is one of the oldest and most meaningful forms of Christian prayer.

Prayer is listening and talking to God with our minds and hearts. Through prayer we can grow closer to God.

Worship is giving God thanks and praise. We give thanks to God every time we gather together at Mass.

Being thankful means keeping our eyes and ears open to the many ways God's love surrounds us.

How do we show that we believe this?

"In all circumstances give thanks, for this is the will of God for you in Christ Jesus."

1 Thessalonians 5:18

There are many reasons to be thankful each day.

With Your Class

Make a class expression of gratitude for someone who works in your school. This gift of thanks could be a card, a poem, a gift, or a party. Decide how your class will present this gift to the person. Make it a surprise, or schedule a time for the person to visit your classroom.

How does giving thanks make you more aware of what people do for you?

____

With Your Family

Read page 315 together. Talk about ways your family gives thanks. List a few here.

Ways to Give Thanks

1. ______________________________

2. ______________________________

3. ______________________________

4. ______________________________

5. ______________________________

Invite everyone in your family to choose something for which he or she is thankful. Share your responses over a family meal.

Try to agree on one thing for which your entire family is thankful. Write it here:

____

Just For Fun

Name one thing for which you can be thankful today.

____

Make up a riddle or poem about it.

"Every event and need can become an offering of thanksgiving."

(Catechism of the Catholic Church, 2638)

Pray Together

Bless the LORD, my soul;
all my being, bless his holy name!
Bless the LORD, my soul;
do not forget all the gifts of God,
Who pardons all your sins,
heals all your ills, . . .
surrounds you with love
and compassion,
Fills your days with good things.

Psalm 103:1–5

Tough to "Love Your Neighbor"?

Tyler has tried to make friends with Robert, the new boy in his class. He has asked Robert to play soccer with his friends. Robert always makes an excuse. At recess, Robert is always alone. Tyler sat with him during lunch one day, but Robert would not talk to him. Tyler was about to give up. He thought to himself, "Maybe the other kids are right about Robert. Maybe he is just too different."

Here is what Tyler does not know: Robert does not like soccer because he thinks he is too slow to be on a team. He is very shy and is afraid to talk to new people. He thinks they will make fun of him.

What Do You Think?

- How could Tyler try again to become friends with Robert?
- What are some ways you could try to be more understanding of others?

Because *We Believe*

Jesus was a perfect example of love for God and neighbor. Jesus showed his love in many ways. He listened to those who were lonely. He helped people in need. He spoke out for the freedom of all people and for those who were treated unjustly. He treated all people equally and respected the dignity of each person.

When we love as Jesus did, we show love for God and others, too.

The Ten Commandments are more than a list of things to do or not do. They give us ways to love God with our whole heart, soul, mind, and body, and to love our neighbor as we love ourselves.

How do we show that we believe this?

"You shall love your neighbor as yourself."
Matthew 22:39

One way to show our love for others is by choosing words that are kind and understanding.

With Your Class

What words might make someone feel loved and respected?

____

____

Use these words often to show love and respect for others.

What words might make someone feel hurt and unwanted?

____

____

Be careful about using words like these with other people.

With Your Family

Read page 317 together. Talk about the ways that Jesus showed love and care to others.

Choose a television show about families and watch it together. Then discuss these questions:

What was the story about?

____

How did the words used by different characters make things better or worse?

____

"The Ten Commandments are engraved by God in the human heart."

(Catechism of the Catholic Church, 2072)

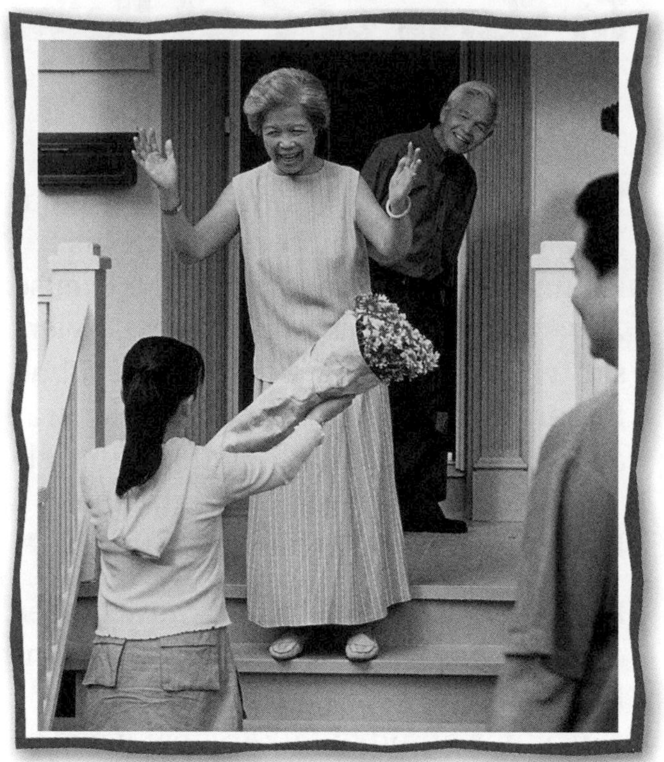

Would you recommend this show to other families? Why or why not?

____

What are some words your family uses to let others know they are loved and valued?

Pray Together

Think of someone who might need your love and understanding. Silently offer a prayer for that person. Ask God for help in being more loving and understanding to all people.

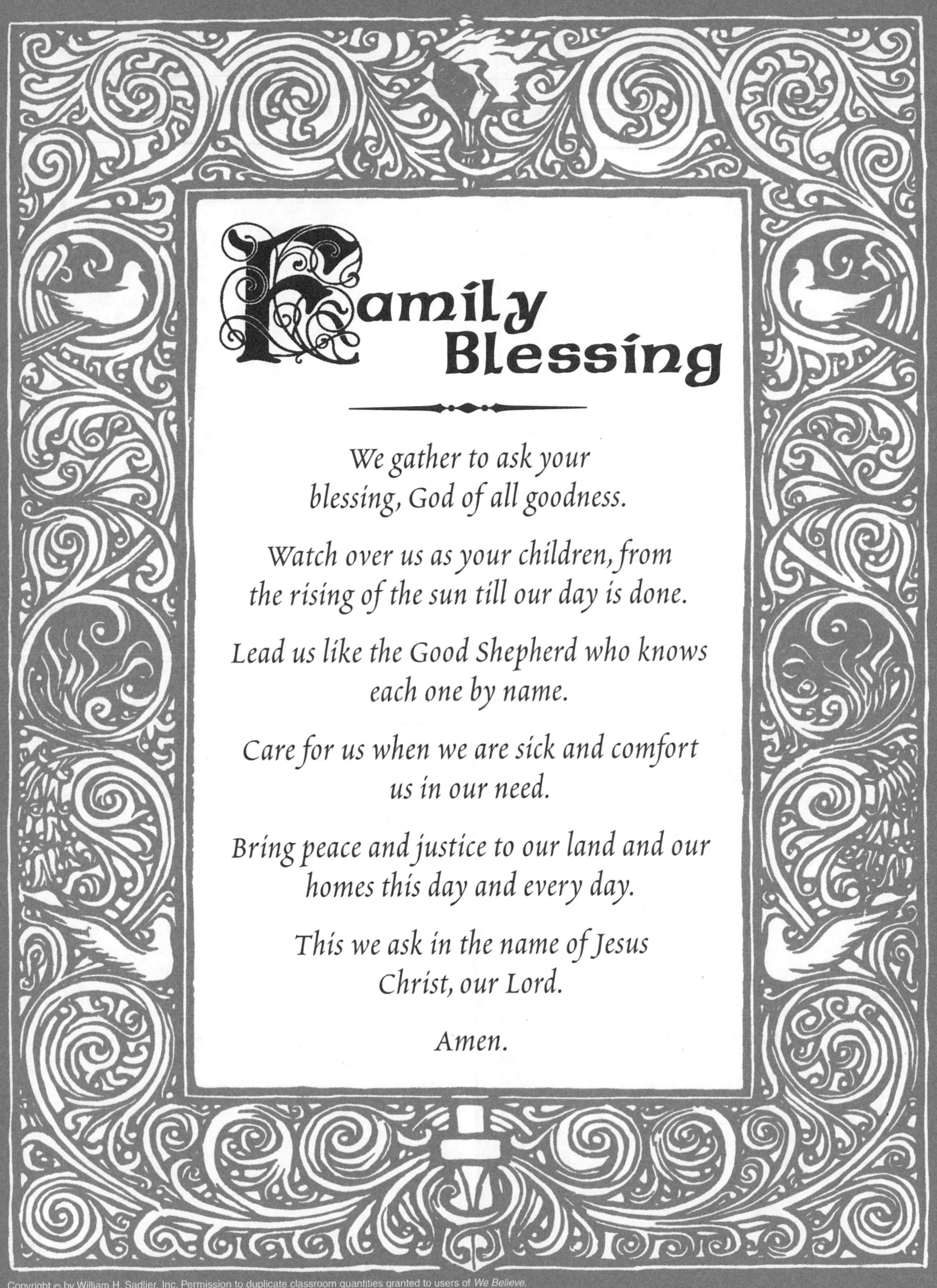

Family Blessing

We gather to ask your blessing, God of all goodness.

Watch over us as your children, from the rising of the sun till our day is done.

Lead us like the Good Shepherd who knows each one by name.

Care for us when we are sick and comfort us in our need.

Bring peace and justice to our land and our homes this day and every day.

This we ask in the name of Jesus Christ, our Lord.

Amen.

ASSESSMENT

In the *We Believe* program each core chapter ends with a review of the content presented, and with activities that encourage the students to reflect and act on their faith. The review is presented in two formats, standard and alternative.

Each unit is also followed by both standard and alternative assessment. The standard test measures basic knowledge and vocabulary assimilation. The alternative assessment allows the students another option—often utilizing another learning style—to express their understanding of the concepts presented.

Using both forms of assessment, perhaps at different times, attends to the various ways students' learning can be measured. You can also see the Grade 4 *We Believe* Assessment Book for:

- standard assessment for each chapter
- alternative assessment for each chapter
- standard assessment for each unit
- alternative assessment for each unit
- a semester assessment which covers material presented in Units 1 and 2
- a final assessment which covers material presented in Units 1, 2, 3, and 4.

For answers to Assessment questions: 17–18, see Chapter 22, pages 252–253; 19–20, see Chapter 23, pages 264–265.

Grade 4
Unit 4

Choose a word or phrase from the box to complete each sentence.

parish	liturgy	Lord's Prayer	ninth	precepts
sacraments	holiness	modesty	tenth	

1. The ___tenth___ commandment calls us to be happy that other people have what they need and want.
2. The ___precepts___ of the Church are laws to help us know and fulfill our responsibilities as members of the Church.
3. ___Holiness___ is sharing in God's goodness and responding to God's love by the way we live.
4. Christ is always present when we celebrate the ___liturgy___, the official public prayer of the Church.
5. ___Modesty___ is the virtue by which we think, speak, act, and dress in ways that show respect for ourselves and others.
6. The ___ninth___ commandment calls us to respect the love between a husband and wife.
7. A ___parish___ is a community of believers who worship and work together.
8. The ___sacraments___ are special signs given to us by Jesus through which we share in God's life.
9. The ___Lord's Prayer___ sums up Jesus' teachings.

319

Write the letter of the sentence that defines each of the following:

10. ___g___ prudence	a. This theological virtue is the source of all other virtues and the goal of our life in Christ.
11. ___a___ love	b. This theological virtue helps us to trust in Jesus and in God's promise to love us always.
12. ___f___ temperance	c. This theological virtue helps us to believe in God and in all he has said and done.
13. ___b___ hope	d. This cardinal virtue helps us to give to God and our neighbors what is rightfully theirs.
14. ___d___ justice	e. This cardinal virtue helps us to act bravely in the face of troubles and fears.
15. ___c___ faith	f. This cardinal virtue helps us to keep our desires under control.
16. ___e___ fortitude	g. This cardinal virtue helps us to make sound judgments.

Answer the questions.

17–18. Mary was pure of heart. She said yes to God because her heart was always open to God's call. How can a fourth grader be pure in heart as Mary was?

19–20. Jesus was poor in spirit. He always placed his trust in his Father, and he asked his disciples to do the same. How can a fourth grader be poor in spirit as Jesus was?

320

Use the clues to unscramble the letters to make words. Write the words in the spaces and circles.

1. God's forgiveness through the priest's words BUIONLASOT

2. work of sharing the good news of Jesus SIMIONS

M I S S I O N

3. community of baptized followers of Jesus RHUCCH

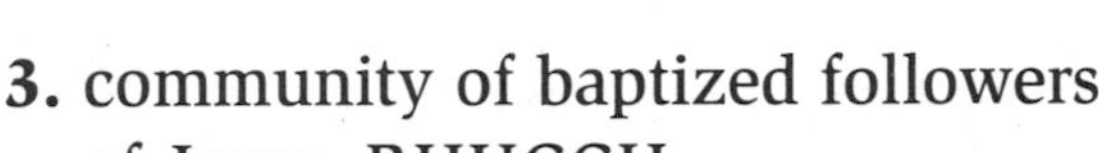

4. attraction to choose sin MAPTOTTEIN

T E M P T A T I O N

5. ability to know good from evil, right from wrong EICOCNCSNE

C O N S C I E N C E

6. those who said yes to Jesus' call PLESSCIDI

D I S C I P L E S

7. person seeking God's forgiveness TENITPEN

P E N I T E N T

8. four books about Jesus' life LESSOPG

G O S P E L S

Write the circled letters here.

Unscramble the circled letters to find the word that finishes this sentence:

We can ask for God's forgiveness in the sacrament of

R E C O N C I L I A T I O N.

Now use each of the eight unscrambled words in a sentence.

The first three commandments help us to show love and respect for God. Write a song or prayer to honor and thank God and to tell him how important he is in our lives.

Design a storyboard illustrating the story of God guiding Moses and his people to freedom.

Read each question below. Write the number of the commandment that would help you to answer it as a follower of Jesus.

__4__ **1.** Should the students listen to the teacher and try to do their best in all their classes?

__5__ **2.** Should someone play rough in a game so that the team can win the city championship?

__7__ **3.** Is it OK for someone to keep a CD found under the seat on the school bus?

__6__ **4.** Should someone watch an R-rated movie over at a friend's house?

__4__ **5.** What can someone do to show respect for family members this week?

__7__ **6.** Is it OK to throw rocks at an empty building?

__7__ **7.** After someone heard classmates talking about a great idea for the fourth grade play, is it right for the person to suggest it in class?

__8__ **8.** When someone hears things that would hurt a neighbor's reputation, should the person tell these things to others?

__8__ **9.** When friends are arguing, should another friend take sides?

__6__ **10.** How can people respect their bodies as special gifts from God?

Across

1. The official public prayer of the Church is called the ______.

3. The theological virtues are ______, hope, and love.

7. Modesty, patience, and kindness are three of the ______ of the Holy Spirit.

8. To ______ something is to desire it unreasonably.

9. A ______ is a community of believers who worship together.

Down

2. Two of the ______ of the Holy Spirit are wisdom and courage.

4. As members of the Church, we are called to grow in ______.

5. The ______ of the Church are laws to help us know and fulfill our responsibilities as Catholics.

6. Prudence, justice, fortitude, and temperance are the cardinal ______.

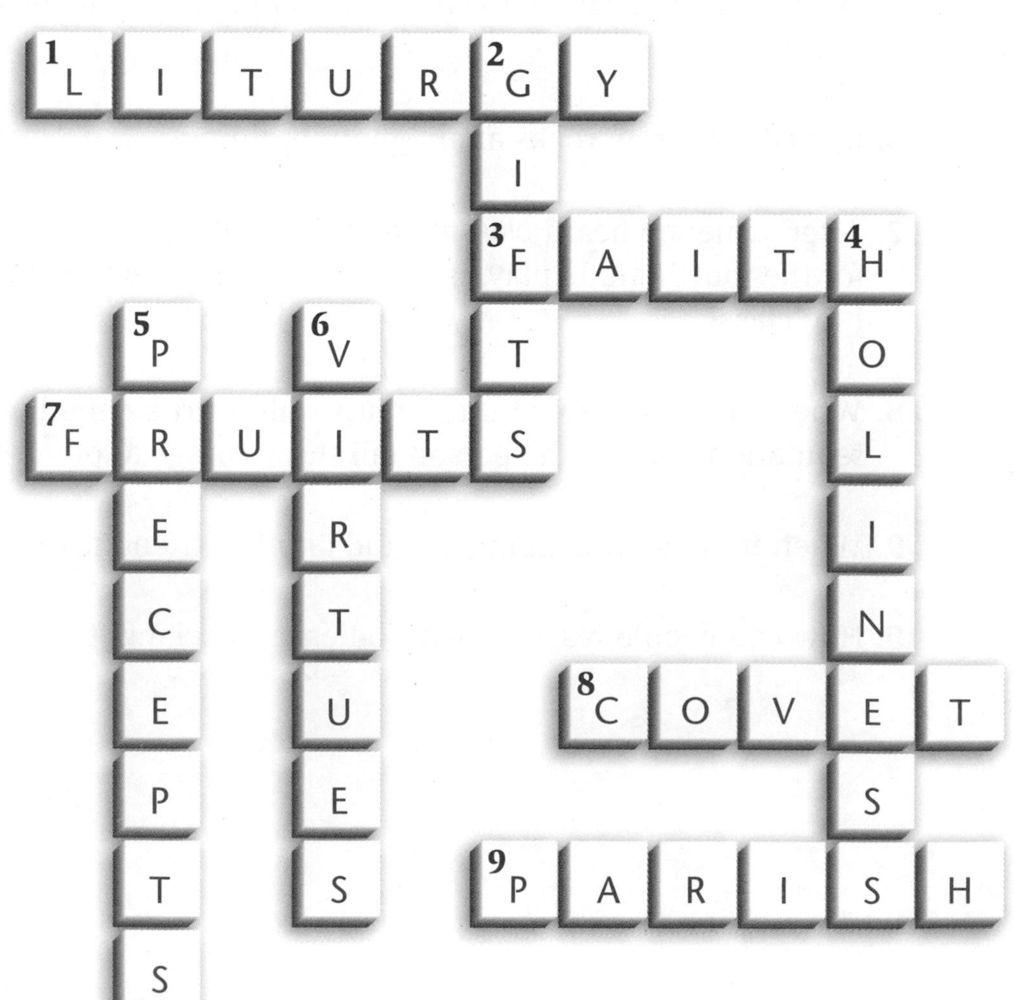

Prayers and Practices

Our Father

Our Father, who art in heaven,
hallowed be thy name;
thy kingdom come;
thy will be done on earth
as it is in heaven.
Give us this day our daily bread;
and forgive us our trespasses
as we forgive those
who trespass against us;
and lead us not into temptation,
but deliver us from evil. Amen.

Glory to the Father

Glory to the Father, and to the Son,
and to the Holy Spirit:
as it was in the beginning,
is now, and will be for ever. Amen.

Act of Contrition

My God,
I am sorry for my sins with all my heart.
In choosing to do wrong
and failing to do good,
I have sinned against you
whom I should love above all things.
I firmly intend, with your help,
to do penance,
to sin no more,
and to avoid whatever leads me to sin.
Our Savior Jesus Christ
suffered and died for us.
In his name, my God, have mercy.

Hail Mary

Hail Mary, full of grace,
the Lord is with you!
Blessed are you among women,
and blessed is the fruit
of your womb, Jesus.
Holy Mary, Mother of God,
pray for us sinners,
now and at the hour of our death.
Amen.

Apostles' Creed

I believe in God, the Father almighty,
creator of heaven and earth.
I believe in Jesus Christ,
his only Son, our Lord.
He was conceived by the power
of the Holy Spirit
and born of the Virgin Mary.
He suffered under Pontius Pilate,
was crucified, died, and was buried.
He descended to the dead.
On the third day he rose again.
He ascended into heaven,
and is seated at the right hand
of the Father.
He will come again to judge
the living and the dead.

I believe in the Holy Spirit,
the holy catholic Church,
the communion of saints,
the forgiveness of sins,
the resurrection of the body,
and the life everlasting. Amen.

Morning Offering

O Jesus, I offer you all my prayers,
works, and sufferings of this day
for all intentions of your most
Sacred Heart. Amen.

Evening Prayer

Dear God, before I sleep
I want to thank you for this day
so full of your kindness and your joy.
I close my eyes to rest
safe in your loving care.

Grace Before Meals

Bless † us, O Lord,
and these your gifts,
which we are about to receive
from your goodness.
Through Christ our Lord. Amen.

Grace After Meals

We give you thanks, almighty God,
for these and all your gifts
which we have received through
Christ our Lord. Amen.

Act of Faith

O God, we believe in all that Jesus has taught us about you. We place all our trust in you because of your great love for us.

Holy, Holy, Holy

Holy, holy, holy Lord,
God of power and might,
heaven and earth are full of your glory.
Hosanna in the highest.
Blessed is he who comes in
the name of the Lord.
Hosanna in the highest.

Prayer to the Holy Spirit

Come, Holy Spirit, fill the hearts of your faithful.
And kindle in them the fire of your love.

Send forth your Spirit and they
shall be created.
And you will renew the face of the earth.

Act of Hope

O God, we never give up on your love. We have hope and will work for your kingdom to come and for a life that lasts forever with you in heaven.

Act of Love

O God, we love you above all things. Help us to love ourselves and one another as Jesus taught us to do.

Prayer Before the Blessed Sacrament

Jesus,
you are God-with-us,
especially in this sacrament
of the Eucharist.
You love me as I am
and help me grow.

Come and be with me
in all my joys and sorrows.
Help me share your peace and love
with everyone I meet.
I ask in your name.
Amen.

Prayer for Vocations

Dear God,
you have a great and loving plan
for our world and for me.
I wish to share in that plan fully,
faithfully, and joyfully.
Help me to understand what it is
you wish me to do with my life.

- Will I be called to the priesthood or religious life?
- Will I be called to live a married life?
- Will I be called to live a single life?

Help me to be attentive to the signs
that you give me about preparing
for the future.

And once I have heard and understood your
call, give me the strength and the grace to
follow it with generosity and love. Amen.

Hail, Holy Queen

Hail, holy Queen, mother of mercy,
hail, our life, our sweetness, and our hope.
To you we cry, the children of Eve;
to you we send up our sighs,
mourning and weeping in this land of exile.
Turn, then, most gracious advocate,
your eyes of mercy toward us;
lead us home at last
and show us the blessed fruit of your womb,
Jesus:
O clement, O loving, O sweet Virgin Mary.

Prayer for Peace

Lord, make me an instrument of your peace:
where there is hatred, let me sow love;
where there is injury, pardon;
where there is doubt, faith;
where there is despair, hope;
where there is darkness, light;
where there is sadness, joy.

O divine Master, grant that I may not so much seek
to be consoled as to console,
to be understood as to understand,
to be loved as to love.
For it is in giving that we receive,
it is in pardoning that we are pardoned,
it is in dying that we are born to eternal life.
Amen.

Saint Francis of Assisi

The Rosary

A rosary is made up of groups of beads arranged in a circle. It begins with a cross followed by one large bead and three small ones. The next large bead (just before the medal) begins the first "decade." Each decade consists of one large bead followed by ten smaller beads.

Begin the rosary with the Sign of the Cross. Recite the Apostles' Creed. Then pray one Our Father, three Hail Marys, and one Glory to the Father.

To pray each decade, say an Our Father on the large bead and a Hail Mary on each of the ten smaller beads. Close each decade by praying the Glory to the Father. Pray the Hail, Holy Queen as the last prayer of the rosary.

The mysteries of the rosary are special events in the lives of Jesus and Mary. As you pray each decade, think of the appropriate Joyful Mystery, Sorrowful Mystery, Glorious Mystery, or Mystery of Light.

The Five Joyful Mysteries

1. The Annunciation
2. The Visitation
3. The Birth of Jesus
4. The Presentation of Jesus in the Temple
5. The Finding of Jesus in the Temple

The Five Sorrowful Mysteries

1. The Agony in the Garden
2. The Scourging at the Pillar
3. The Crowning with Thorns
4. The Carrying of the Cross
5. The Crucifixion and Death of Jesus

The Five Glorious Mysteries

1. The Resurrection
2. The Ascension
3. The Descent of the Holy Spirit upon the Apostles
4. The Assumption of Mary into Heaven
5. The Coronation of Mary as Queen of Heaven

The Five Mysteries of Light

1. Jesus' Baptism in the Jordan
2. The Miracle at the Wedding at Cana
3. Jesus Announces the Kingdom of God
4. The Transfiguration
5. The Institution of the Eucharist

Stations of the Cross

From the earliest days of the Church, Christians remembered Jesus' life and death by visiting and praying at the places where Jesus lived, suffered, died, and rose from the dead.

As the Church spread to other countries, not everyone could travel to the Holy Land. So local churches began inviting people to "follow in the footsteps of Jesus" without leaving home. "Stations," or places to stop and pray, were made so that stay-at-home pilgrims could "walk the way of the cross" in their own parish churches. We do the same today, especially during Lent.

There are fourteen "stations," or stops. At each one, we pause and think about what is happening at the station.

1. Jesus is condemned to die.
2. Jesus takes up his cross.
3. Jesus falls the first time.
4. Jesus meets his mother.
5. Simon helps Jesus carry his cross.
6. Veronica wipes the face of Jesus.
7. Jesus falls the second time.
8. Jesus meets the women of Jerusalem.
9. Jesus falls the third time.
10. Jesus is stripped of his garments.
11. Jesus is nailed to the cross.
12. Jesus dies on the cross.
13. Jesus is taken down from the cross.
14. Jesus is laid in the tomb.

The Seven Sacraments

The Sacraments of Christian Initiation

Baptism

Confirmation

Eucharist

The Sacraments of Healing

Penance and Reconciliation

Anointing of the Sick

The Sacraments at the Service of Communion

Holy Orders

Matrimony

Note:

The parts of the Mass are found on pages 143 to 151.

The parts of the sacrament of Penance and Reconciliation are found on pages 70 to 72.

The Beatitudes are found on pages 34 and 35.

The Corporal and Spiritual Works of Mercy are found on pages 138 and 139.

An Examination of Conscience is found on pages 115, 127, 139, 179, 191, 203, 215, 227, 255, and 265.

Glossary

absolution (p. 71)
God's forgiveness of sins through the words of the priest

assembly (p. 145)
the community of people gathered to worship in the name of Jesus Christ

Beatitudes (p. 34)
teachings of Jesus that describe the way to live as his disciples

bishops (p. 285)
leaders of the Church who continue the work of the apostles

bless (p. 124)
to dedicate someone or something to God or to make holy in God's name

Blessed Trinity (p. 23)
the three Persons in one God: God the Father, God the Son, and God the Holy Spirit

cardinal virtues (p. 300)
prudence, justice, fortitude, and temperance

chastity (p. 199)
the virtue by which we use our human sexuality in a responsible and faithful way

Church (p. 27)
the community of people who are baptized and follow Jesus Christ

conscience (p. 58)
the ability to know the difference between good and evil, right and wrong

consecration (p. 149)
the part of the eucharistic prayer when, by the power of the Holy Spirit and through the words and actions of the priest, the bread and wine become the Body and Blood of Christ

Corporal Works of Mercy (p. 139)
things that we do to care for the physical needs of others

covenant (p. 98)
a special agreement between God and his people

covet (p. 251)
to wrongly desire something that is someone else's

deacon (p. 285)
serves the parish by preaching, baptizing, and assisting the pastor

diocese (p. 285)
a local area of the Church led by a bishop

disciples (p. 23)
those who said yes to Jesus' call to follow him

domestic church (p. 175)
the church in the home, which every Christian family is called to be

envy (p. 260)
a feeling of sadness when someone else has the things we want for ourselves

eucharistic prayer (p. 149)
the Church's greatest prayer of praise and thanksgiving to God

examination of conscience (p. 63)
the act of determining whether the choices we have made showed love for God, ourselves, and others

free will (p. 45)
the freedom to decide when and how to act

fruits of the Holy Spirit (p. 279)
the good things people can see in us when we respond to the gifts of the Holy Spirit

gifts of the Holy Spirit (p. 279)
the seven gifts which help us to follow God's law and live as Jesus did

grace (p. 27)
the gift of God's life in us

greed (p. 263)
an excessive desire to have or own things

holy day of obligation (p. 135)
a day that is set apart to celebrate a special event in the life of Jesus, Mary, or the saints

homily (p. 147)
a talk given by the priest or deacon that helps us to understand the readings and to grow as faithful followers of Jesus

human dignity (p. 185)
the value and worth each person has from being created in God's image

human rights (p. 102)
the basic rights that all people have

idolatry (p. 112)
giving worship to a creature or thing instead of God

Incarnation (p. 20)
the truth that the Son of God became man

justice (p. 36)
respecting the rights of others and giving them what is rightfully theirs

Kingdom of God (p. 36)
the power of God's love active in the world

liturgy (p. 276)
the official public prayer of the Church

Liturgy of the Eucharist (p. 149)
the part of the Mass in which the death and Resurrection of Christ are made present again; our gifts of bread and wine become the Body and Blood of Christ, which we receive in Holy Communion

Liturgy of the Word (p. 147)
the part of the Mass when we listen and respond to God's word

martyrs (p. 223)
people who die rather than give up their belief in the risen Jesus

Mass (p. 145)
the celebration of the Eucharist

mission (p. 38)
the work of sharing the good news of Jesus Christ and spreading the Kingdom of God

modesty (p. 254)
the virtue by which we think, speak, act, and dress in ways that show respect for ourselves and others

mortal sin (p. 47)
very serious sin that breaks a person's friendship with God

original sin (p. 24)
the first sin committed by the first human beings

parish (p. 285)
a community of believers who worship and work together

pastor (p. 285)
the priest who leads the parish in worship, prayer, and teaching

peace (p. 33)
the freedom that comes from loving and trusting God and respecting all people

penitent (p. 71)
the person seeking God's forgiveness in the sacrament of Reconciliation

poor in spirit (p. 264)
those who depend on God completely

pope (p. 285)
the bishop of Rome, who leads the whole Catholic Church

prayer (p. 110)
listening and talking to God with our minds and hearts

precepts of the Church (p. 286)
laws to help us know and fulfill our responsibilities as members of the Church

psalm (p. 120)
a song of praise to honor the Lord

reverence (p. 123)
honor, love, and respect

Sabbath (p. 133)
the day of rest set apart to honor God in a special way

sacrament (p. 276)
a special sign given to us by Jesus through which we share in God's life

sacred (p. 126)
another word for holy

Savior (p. 24)
a title given to Jesus because he died and rose to save us from sin

sin (p. 45)
a thought, word, action, or omission against God's law

Spiritual Works of Mercy (p. 139)
things that we do to care for the minds, hearts, and souls of others

stewards of creation (p. 213)
those who take care of everything God has given them

synagogue (p. 135)
the gathering place where Jewish people pray and learn about God

temptation (p. 45)
an attraction to choose sin

Ten Commandments (p. 98)
the laws of God's covenant given to Moses on Mount Sinai

theological virtues (p. 296)
faith, hope, love

venial sin (p. 47)
less serious sin that hurts a person's friendship with God

virtue (p. 199)
a good habit that helps us to act according to God's love for us

witnesses (p. 223)
people who speak and act based upon what they know and believe about Jesus

worship (p. 110)
giving God thanks and praise

Index

The following is a list of topics that appear in the pupil's text.
Boldface indicates an entire chapter or section.

Acknowledgments

Excerpts from the English translation of the Catechism of the Catholic Church for use in the United States of America, © 1994, United States Catholic Conference, Inc.—Libreria Editrice Vaticana. Used with permission.

Scripture excerpts are taken from the New American Bible with Revised New Testament and Psalms Copyright © 1991, 1986, 1970, Confraternity of Christian Doctrine, Inc., Washington, DC. Used with permission. All rights reserved. No part of the New American Bible may be reproduced by any means without permission in writing from the copyright owner.

Excerpts from the English translation of Lectionary for Mass © 1969, 1981, 1997, International Committee on English in the Liturgy, Inc. (ICEL); excerpts from the English translation of The Roman Missal © 1973, International Committee on English in the Liturgy, Inc. (ICEL); excerpts from the English translation of the Rite of Penance © 1974, International Committee on English in the Liturgy, Inc. (ICEL); excerpts from the English translation of A Book of Prayers © 1982, ICEL. All rights reserved.

Excerpts from Catholic Household Blessings and Prayers Copyright © 1988 United States Catholic Conference, Inc., Washington, DC. Used with permission. All rights reserved.

Excerpt from the prayer "God be in my head" from The Oxford Book of Prayers © 1985, Oxford University Press, Oxford, UK.

English translation of the Our Father, Glory to the Father, Apostles' Creed, Gloria in Excelsis and Sanctus / Benedictus by the International Consultation on English Texts. (ICET)

Amanda Lenhart, Teenage Life Online: the rise of the instant-message generation and the Internet's impact on friendships and family relationships, Pew Internet and American Life Project, June 2001.

Reprinted by permission of the Felice Foundation from D. Leo Buscaglia's book, Born for Love: *Reflections on Loving*. For more information about Dr. Buscaglia's work please contact the Felice Foundation at P.O. Box 265, Palos Verdes Estates, CA 90274. You may also reach us at our Web site: www.buscaglia.com/felice.

Excerpt from the report: *Television in the Home: The 1997 Annenberg Survey of Parents and Children*, from The Annenberg Public Policy Center of the University of Pennsylvania. Reprinted with permission.

"We Believe, We Believe in God," © 1979, North American Liturgy Resources (NALR), 5536 NE Hassalo, Portland, OR 97213. All rights reserved. Used with permission. "Blest Are They," David Haas. Text: The Beatitudes. Text and music: © 1985, G.I.A. Publications, Inc. All rights reserved. Used with permission. "Come, Follow Me," © 1992, Barbara Bridge. Published by OCP Publications, 5536 NE Hassalo, Portland, OR 97213. All rights reserved. Used with permission. "Prayer of St. Francis," dedicated to Mrs. Frances Tracy. © 1967, OCP Publications, 5536 NE Hassalo, Portland, OR 97213. All rights reserved. Used with permission. "We Are His People (Psalm 100)," music © 2000, Mark Friedman. Published by OCP Publications, 5536 NE Hassalo, Portland, OR 97213. All rights reserved. Used with permission. Refrain © 1969, ICEL. Verse © 1970, CCD. All rights reserved. "Glory and Praise to Our God," © 1976, Daniel L. Schutte and New Dawn Music, 5536 NE Hassalo, Portland, OR 97213. All rights reserved. Used with permission. "Lord, I Lift Your Name on High," Rick Founds. © 1989, 1999, MARANATHA PRAISE, INC. (Administered by THE COPYRIGHT COMPANY, Nashville, TN.) All rights reserved. International copyright secured. "The Lord Is Kind (Psalm 103)," music © 2000, Carey Landry. Published by OCP Publications, 5536 NE Hassalo, Portland, OR 97213. All rights reserved. Used with permission. Refrain © 1969, ICEL. Verse © 1970, CCD. All rights reserved. "Open Our Hearts," © 1989, Christopher Walker. Published by OCP Publications, 5536 NE Hassalo, Portland, OR 97213. All rights reserved. Used with permission. "Come to the Feast (Ven al Banquete)," © 1994, Bob Hurd and Pia Moriarty. Published by OCP Publications, 5536 NE Hassalo, Portland, OR 97213. All rights reserved. Used with permission. "Take the Word of God with You," text © 1991, James Harrison. Music © 1991, Christopher Walker. Text and music: Published by OCP Publications, 5536 NE Hassalo, Portland, OR 97213. All rights reserved. Used with permission. "Somos el Cuerpo de Cristo," © 1994, Jaime Cortez. Published by OCP Publications. All rights reserved. Used with permission. "Praise Him with Cymbals," © 1993, Janet Vogt. Published by OCP Publications, 5536 NE Hassalo, Portland, OR 97213. All rights reserved. Used with permission. "We Are the Family," Ray Repp. © 1979, K & R Music Publishing. From the recording Sunrise, In the Dead of Winter. All rights reserved. Used with permission. "You Are Near," © 1971, 1974, Daniel L. Schutte. Administered by New Dawn Music, 5536 NE Hassalo, Portland, OR 97213. All rights reserved. Used with permission. "I Am Special," © 1999, Bernadette Farrell. Published by OCP Publications, 5536 NE Hassalo, Portland, OR 97213. All rights reserved. Used with permission. "Though We Are Many / Make Us a Sign," © 1999, Bernadette Farrell. Published by OCP Publications, 5536 NE Hassalo, Portland, OR 97213. All rights reserved. Used with permission. "New Heart and New Spirit," © 1992, John Schiavone. Published by OCP Publications, 5536 NE Hassalo, Portland, OR 97213. All rights reserved. Used with permission. "We Are Yours, O Lord," © 1996, Janet Vogt. Published by OCP Publications, 5536 NE Hassalo, Portland, OR 97213. All rights reserved. Used with permission. "Lord, You Have Come (Pescador de Hombres)," Spanish text and music © 1979, Cesareo Gabarain. English translation by Robert C. Turpia, © 1987 by OCP Publications, 5536 NE Hassalo, Portland, OR 97213. All rights reserved. Used with permission. "You Call Us to Live," © 1990, Christopher Walker. Published by OCP Publications, 5536 NE Hassalo, Portland, OR 97213. All rights reserved. Used with permission. "Send Us Your Spirit," © 1988, 1989, 1990, Christopher Walker. Published by OCP Publications, 5536 NE Hassalo, Portland, OR 97213. All rights reserved. Used with permission.

Scripture excerpts are taken from the New American Bible with Revised New Testament and Psalms. Copyright © 1991, 1986, 1970 Confraternity of Christian Doctrine, Inc. Washington, DC. Used with permission. All rights reserved. No part of the New American Bible may be reproduced by any means without permission in writing from the copyright owner.

Excerpts from the English translation of The Roman Missal © 1973, International Committee on English in the Liturgy, Inc. (ICEL); excerpts from the English translation of Rite of Baptism for Children © 1969, ICEL; excerpts from the English translation of Rite of Christian Initiation of Adults © 1985, ICEL. All rights reserved.

Excerpts from the English translation of the Catechism of the Catholic Church for use in the United States of America. Copyright © 1994, United States Catholic Conference, Inc.-Libreria Editrice Vaticana.

Excerpts from the General Directory for Catechesis. © 1997, Libreria Editrice Vaticana-United States Catholic Conference, Inc. Used with permission. All rights reserved.

Excerpts from the Sharing the Light of Faith: National Catechetical Directory for Catholics of the United States. © 1979, United States Catholic Conference, Inc., Washington, DC. All rights reserved.

English translation of the canons comes from the Code of Canon Law, Latin English Edition New English Translation. Washington, DC: Canon Law Society of America, 1999.

Excerpts from Sharing Catholic Social Teaching: Challenges and Directions. © 1998, United States Catholic Conference, Inc. (USCC). All rights reserved.

Excerpts from Intelligence Reframed: Multiple Perspectives for the 21st Century by Howard Gardner. Copyright © 1999 by Howard Gardner. Reprinted by permission of Basic Books, a member of Perseus Books, L.L.C.

Catechesi Tradendae, On Catechesis in Our Time, Apostolic Exhortation, Pope John Paul II, October 16, 1979.

Evangelii Nuntiandi, On Evangelization in the Modern World, Apostolic Exhortation, Pope Paul VI, December 8, 1975.

Letter of His Holiness Pope John Paul II to Artist, April 4, 1999.

Redemptoris Missio, On the Permanent Validity of the Church's Missionary Mandate, Encyclical Letter, Pope John Paul II, December 7, 1990.

Ecclesia in America, The Church in America, Post-Synodal Apostolic Exhortation, Pope John Paul II, January 22, 1999.

Lumen Gentium, Dogmatic Constitution on the Church, Pope Paul VI, November 21, 1964.

The Church and Internet, Pontifical Council for Social Communications, February 22, 2002.

Writing/Development Team

Rosemary K. Calicchio
Editorial Director

Lee Hlavacek
Product Developer

Blake Bergen
Grade Level Manager

Joanna Dailey

James P. Emswiler

Maureen Gallo

Janie L. Gustafson, Ph.D.

Kathy Hendricks

Gloria Hutchinson

Mary Ellen Kelly

Catherine Lavin

Joseph Moore

James T. Morgan, Ed.D.

Daniel Sherman

Mary Ann Trevaskiss

Joanne Winne

Sadlier Consulting Team

Patricia Andrews
Director of Religious Education, Our Lady of Lourdes Church, Slidell, LA

Eleanor Ann Brownell, D.Min.
Vice President, Religion

Michaela M. Burke
Director of Consultant Services

Judith A. Devine
National Sales Consultant

Sister Helen Hemmer, IHM
Religion Consultant for Spiritual Formation

William M. Ippolito
Executive Projects Director

Saundra Kennedy, Ed.D.
Consultant Training Specialist

Marie Murphy, Ph.D.
National Religion Consultant

Karen Ryan
Executive Researcher

John M. Stack
National Consultant

Publishing Operations Team

Deborah Jones
Director of Publishing Operations

Vince Gallo
Creative Director

Francesca Moore
Associate Art Director

Jim Saylor
Photo Editor

Design/Photo Staff
Andrea Brown, Kevin Butler, Ana Jouvin, Sasha Khorovsky, Susan Ligertwood, Maria Pia Marrella, Zaniah Renner, David Rosenberg, Bob Schatz, Debrah Wilson

Production Staff
Diane Ali, Monica Bernier, Barbara Brown, Suzan Daley, Tresse DeLorenzo, Arthur Erberber, Joyce Gaskin, Eileen Gewirtzman, Peter Herrmann, Maria Jimenez, Sommer Keller, Miriam Lippman, Vinny McDonough, John Mealy, Yolanda Miley, Maureen Morgan, Julie Murphree, Walter Norfleet, Monica Reece, Martin Smith, Sintora Vanderhorst

---

Photo Credits

Cover Photography: Getty: *wheat & grapes*, Ken Karp: *children*. Eakal Ali: 219 *background*, 286–287 *background*, 302 *background*. AP Photo Archive/Ben Margot: 291, 294 *top right*. Art Resource: 276. Lori Berkowitz: 190 *top*. Jane Bernard: 49, 54 *top right*, 80, 88, 176, 178, 179, 182, 191 *top*, 197, 232, 236 *top left*, 331. Black Sheep/Hideaki Ohmura: 55, 58–59. Orion Press: 74–75 *background*. Bolton Picture Library: 287 *top right*. Karen Callaway: 45 *left*, 54 *top left*, 56, 61, 62, 66 *top left & top right*, 71, 72, 73, 75 *right*, 78 *top center & top right*, 79 *right*, 95, 97, 106 *top right*, 107 *top left*, 112, 118 *top right*, 135, 136 *bottom*, 142 *top center* 144, 145, 146, 147, 148, 149, 154 *top left*, 187, 188–189, 191 *bottom*, 194 *top center & top right*, 196, 200–201, 203 *center*, 206 *top center & top right*, 208, 210, 211, 213, 214, 215, 218 *top left & top right*, 220, 221, 222 *top*, 230 *top left*, 253, 267 *bottom left*, 318, 321, 322, 323 *bottom right & bottom left*, 324, 332, 333. CORBIS/Ronnie Kaufman: *bottom right*; Steve Wilkings: 25; John Welzenbach: 110 *bottom*; Ed Bock: 114, 118 *top center*; Mug Shots: 150 *left*; Paul Barton: 151 *bottom right*; Dan Tardif: 151 *bottom left*; Raymond Gehman: 203 *bottom right*; Rob Lewine: 206 *bottom left*; STOCK MARKET 231; 261 *bottom left*; AFP: 264–265 *top*; Jonathan Blair: 266 *bottom left*; 300, 306 *top left*. CORBIS SYGMA/Pierre Perrin: 202 *center*. Crosiers/Gene Plaisted, OSC: 18, 30, *bottom left*, 42 *bottom left*, 50, 113, 118 *bottom left*, 130 *bottom left*, 185, 194 *bottom left*, 209. Neal Farris: 13 *top*, 14, 19, 31, 43, 45 *right*, 74, 75 *left*, 77, 103, 105, 110 *top*, 117, 130 *top center*, 138, 139, 141, 142 *top right*, 151 *top right*, 155, 156 *center right*, 171, 183, 222 *bottom*, 229, 252 *right*, 258 *top left*, 261 *top right*, 266 *top right*, 270 *top right*, 272, 278, 281, 282 *top right*, 296, 297, 330. Getty: 26–27 *background*, 53, 66 *bottom left*, 85, 106 *bottom left*, 107 *bottom center & bottom right*, 111 *school sign*, 137, 150 *right*, 156 *center left*, 208–209 *grapes*, 219, 230 *bottom left*, 249, 251 *bottom right*, 258 *top center*, 264–265 *bottom*. The Image Works/Bob Daemmrich: 224–225, 230 *top center*. Ken Karp: 10–11, 12 *top*, 16 *top left*, 17, 18 *top right*, 36–37, 38–39, 41, 42 *top left & top right*, 93, 94 *top right*, 119, 126, 127, 129, 130 *top right*, 143, 154 *top left*, 156 *top left*; *bottom left*; *top right*; *bottom right*, 169, 170 *top right*, 172–173, 193, 205, 212, 217, 218 *top center*, 245, 246, 257, 259, 269, 283, 293, 295, 301, 302, 303, 308, 309, 312 *top right*, 316, 323 *top left*. Greg Lord: 15, 27, 29, 30 *top center*, 65, 72–73 *background*, 248 *top*, 314. *The Messenger*/Liz Quirin: 260, 263, 270 *top left*. Natural Selection Stock Photography: 226–227. Panos Pictures/Chris Sattlberger: 203 *top left*; Jan Banning: 203 *center left*; Mark Henley: 267 *top right*. PhotoEdit/Tony Freeman: 79 *center*; 233 *center left*; Richard Hutchings: 233 *background*; 236 *top right*; Michael Newman: 233 *top right*. PictureQuest: 164. Chris Sheridan: 199, 248 *center & bottom*, 254 *top & center*, 255, 258 *top right*. Superstock: 161, 166 *bottom right*, 196–197 *background*, 210–211 *background*, 251 *top left*, 270 *bottom left*, 307, 312 *top left*. TimePix/Jayanta Shaw: 202 *bottom*; Steve Liss: 279, 282 *top center*. W. P. Wittman, Photography: 44, 136–137 *background*, 154 *bottom left*, 177, 182 *bottom left*, 206 *top left*, 218 *bottom left*, 237, 239, 240, 242, 252 *left*, 258 *bottom left*, 294 *bottom left*, 322 *bottom left*, 323 *top right*.

Illustrator Credits

Cover Design: Kevin Ghiglione. Bernard Adnet: 43. Burgandy Beam: 70–71. Teresa Berasi: 214–215. James Bernardin: 20–21, 22–23, 24, 30, 32–33, 46–47, 54, 68, 78, 86–87, 90 *top*, 96, 98–99, 100–101, 106, 108–109, 118, 120–121, 130, 132–133, 134, 142, 174–175, 262–263, 274, 299. Linda Bild: 290–291. Lisa Blackshear: 58, 66. Ken Bowser: 259G, 312A. Janet Broxon: 247, 250–251. Gwen Connelly: 254–255, 259. Margaret Cusack: 195. Jeanne de la Houssaye: 200–201. Florentina: 172, 179. Doreen Gay-Kassel: 184–185. Ed Gazsi: 224, 284–285, 288. Adam Gordon: 43. Peter Gunther: 55G, 195G, 295G. Annie Gusman: 176–177. Lisa Henderling: 276–277. John Hovell: 222–223. Jack Kershner: 219G. W. B. Johnston: 32–33, 108–109, 124–125, 150–151, 174–175, 248–249. Rita Lascaro: 160A, 247G, 271G. Martin Lemelman: 278. Chris Lensch: 56–57, 138–139. Andy Levine: 69, 78. Anthony Lewis: 107. Lori Lohstoeter: 143. Bonnie Matthews: 272–273. Deborah Melmon: 271. Judith Moffatt: 131, 142. Amy Ning: 146–147. Marian Nixon: 19. Lou Pappas: 31G, 67G, 143G. Larry Paulsen: 38–39, *background illustration for* Review, We Respond in Faith, *and* Sharing Faith *pages*. Donna Perrone: 148–149. Ceciliá Pluá: 190–191, 275. Karen Pritchett: 134–135. Jesse Reisch: 183, 186–187. Maria Rendon: 29. Saul Rosenbaum: 63. Rich Rossi: 123. Steve Sanford: 166A. Zina Saunders: 19A, 67G, 183G, 236A, 242A, 283G. Stacey Schuett: 313, 315, 317. Bob Shein: 97, 98–99, 198–199, 202. Neil Slave: 38–39. Suzanne Staud: 34–35, 42. Daryl Stevens: 131G, 171G, 207G. Matt Straub: 260–261. Steve Sullivan: 107G. Susan Swan: 79–83, 85–90, 155–166, 231–241, 307–312. Terry Taylor: 119. Candace Whitman: 67.